ROCK CLIMBS
IN THE
WHITE MOUNTAINS
OF
NEW HAMPSHIRE

THIRD EDITION

(East Volume)

This Book is Dedicated to:

John Turner
Ray Darcy
Will Crowther
Joe Cote
Steve Arsenault
Sam Streibert
Henry Barber
Paul Ross
Jim Dunn
Rick Wilcox
Joe Lentini
Jeff Pheasant
Bryan Delaney
Ajax Greene
Michael Hartrich
Bryan Becker
Kurt Winkler
George Hurley
Susan Patenaude
Doug Madara
Alain Comeau
Steve Larson
John Bouchard
Jim Surette
Maria Hannus
Brad White
Andy Ross
& Chris Gill

Ed Webster leading the second ascent of The Last Unicorn (5.10b) in 1978, on the South Buttress of Whitehorse Ledge, New Hampshire.
Photograph by Jim Boyd.

ROCK CLIMBS
IN THE
WHITE MOUNTAINS
OF
NEW HAMPSHIRE

THIRD EDITION

(East Volume)

by Ed Webster

Published by
MOUNTAIN IMAGERY

© Copyright 1996 by Edward R. Webster.
All rights reserved. ISBN # 0-9653199-0-3

Published and Distributed by:
MOUNTAIN IMAGERY
P.O. Box 210,
Eldorado Springs, Colorado 80025 USA

Additional copies may be ordered from the address above. Retail inquiries are also invited.

Front Cover: Chris Gill on the first free ascent of upper Grand Finale (5.12a / 5.11c R) Cathedral Ledge, New Hampshire in 1988. Photograph by Nick Yardley.

Back Cover: Nick Yardley on Eyeless In Gaza (5.12b) Sundown Ledge - The Main Cliff, New Hampshire in 1988. Photograph by Greg McCausland.

Computer Maps:	Lynn Woodward-Sims / Woodward Designs
Design & Layout **B&W Cliff Photos:**	Ed Webster
5.14d Computer Expert:	Gordon Banks
B&W Printing:	Photo Craft Laboratories
Color Separations:	John Gill, DIGI.COLORado
Scanning:	Advanced Digital Imaging One World Arts
Printing:	Publisher's Press

ACKNOWLEDGMENTS

Writing a climbing guidebook is very much a group effort. This Third Edition, East Volume of the White Mountain rock climbing guide is the culmination of nearly two years of research, fact-checking, climbing, letter-writing, photo-researching, proof-reading, and plain hard work to assemble the descriptions to the 1,245 climbs on the 42 cliffs included herein. Virtually every active White Mountain rock climber, and several no longer quite-so-active White Mountain climbers have contributed their time, energy, and talents to shape and create this guidebook—and I thank you all for your help! Being a guidebook writer, I've finally decided, is a curse, a joy, and ultimately, an honored privilege. The hundreds of hours I've spent sitting in front of my computer have been more than offset by the sunny days on the cliffs researching the routes, having more than a few laughs and beers and climbs with old friends, and by my own satisfaction at having, for the third time in 14 years, set down the history of rock climbing in the White Mountains of New Hampshire, in print and in photographs, for everyone's enjoyment and for posterity. I could never have finished writing this book without the help, support, and encouragement of many, many people: all the local New Hampshire climbers, old and new climbing friends, and my family.

Finishing another climb. Cathedral Ledge, 1974. Photograph by Jeff Burns.

ACKNOWLEDGMENTS

Andy Ross	Gene Ellis	Billy Squier
Bill Lutkus	Jeff Achey	Geoff Tabin
Maria Hannus	Scott Franklin	Steve Ruoss
Brad White	Chris Dubé	Mike Sinclair
Kurt Winkler	Barry Rugo	George Waring
Paul Cormier	Mark Richey	Bruce Normand
Jerry Handren	Rick Wilcox	Dave Kelly
Nick Yardley	Mike Pelchat	Joe & Judy Perez
John Strand	Todd Swain	Harold Consentine
George Hurley	Paul Boissonneault	Hans Bern Bauer
Chris Gill	Susan Patenaude	Stan Hart
Tom Callaghan	Doug Teschner	Ken Sims
Haydie Callaghan	Peter Beal	George Bracksieck
Bill Lowther	Dick Traverse	Sibylle Hechtel
Bob Parrott	Mack Johnson	Michael Kennedy
Steve Larson	Jon Sykes	Bill Boyle
Rob Adair	Tom Dickey	Matt Harris
Jim Ewing	Alain Comeau	Mick Ryan
Larry Hamilton	Peter Lewis	Jay Philbrick
Jim Surette	Jason Laflamme	Chad Lewis
Randy Rackliff	John Climaco	Wanda Allen
Steve Damboise	Dick Peterson	Bud Hikel
Uwe Schneider	Mike Jewell	Jean Hurley
Andy Hannon	Rich Baker	Karen Moffat Winkler
Henry Barber	John Mallery	Janot Mendler Comeau
Joe Lentini	Al Rubin	Patty Wespiser
John Turner	Bob Palais	Chris Martin
Will Crowther	Dennis Goode	Guy & Laura Waterman
Jack Taylor	Bill Bentley	Brooks Dodge
Joe & Karen Cote	Ben Onachila	Chester Dreiman
Paul Ross	Matt Peer	Ben Townsend
Doug Madara	Alec Behr	Peter Hovling
Chris Noonan	Maury McKinney	Tom Armstrong
Jeff Pheasant	Ian Cruickshank	Rick Accomazzo
John Bouchard	Mike Hardert	Christian Beckwith
Michael Hartrich	Jeff Fongemie	George Mallory III
Ken Reville	Jo Ann Fongemie	Romain Vogler
Gerry Lortie	A. J. Jones	Michael Coyne

ACKNOWLEDGMENTS

Andy Ross & Bill Lutkus get the biggest thanks for selflessly donating to me their near masterpiece: *Routes Not Found In That Other Guidebook*, a never completed sport climbing guide and route update to the Mount Washington Valley that they worked on together for several years. Without their gift of this information, the present guidebook would simply not exist, so I am very, very much indebted to them for their help and generosity.

Gordon Banks, climber/kayaking guru, and computer expert, may not have written any of this current guide—but he selflessly passed along his wealth of computer software and publishing knowledge, spending hours huddled in front of my monitor, coaching me, and helping to create this book. Gordon, thank you so very much! I honestly couldn't have done it without you.

Lynn Woodward-Sims, of Woodward Designs, created, refined, and crafted the beautiful maps in this current guide. Lynn endured several go rounds of my tedious, nit-picking revisions with her customary patience and good humor—and didn't mind one bit when I insisted that the first letter in each of the cliff titles All Be Capitalized! Lynn, Thank You For Your Artwork!

Larry Hamilton also deserves a special note of thanks for authoring the entire Crag Y section, taken from his 1989 *Climber's Guide to Crag Y*, which he kindly allowed me to use in this current edition. Thank you very much, Larry!

Several quoted comments in the HISTORY sections of various climbs have been excerpted from Laura & Guy Waterman's excellent history of New England climbing, *Yankee Rock & Ice*, for which permission was granted by the authors, and is greatly appreciated. George Flagg's 1910 illustration of THE OLD ROUTE in Huntington Ravine was also used with the Waterman's permission, and I would also very much like to thank Shirley Foynes Hargraves, Mr. Flagg's granddaughter, for its use in this book.

Another thanks is to Albert Dow who, with great resourcefulness, gave me a copy of his 1980 topo-diagram of Albany Slab which formed the basis for nearly all the current route descriptions. After the passage of 16 years, I found Albert's artistic topo still tucked away in my notes for safe-keeping.

One last thank you is to the author John T. B. Mudge, for his excellent, informative, and highly recommended book, *The White Mountains Names, Places, & Legends*, from which I excerpted several quotations. It's all here: the fascinating, early lore of the White Mountains—the Indian tribes who once resided in these peaceful, green valleys—and the settlers, pioneering adventurers, and scientists who gave these lofty peaks their current names.

A final thanks to my proofreaders: Gene Ellis, Debra Banks, & George Hurley.

ACKNOWLEDGMENTS

The Photographers: The first photographer I wish to thank is Dr. Ralph C. Larrabee, who took the superb picture of his companions climbing the Huntington Ravine headwall in 1912. Kenneth A. Henderson deserves the biggest note of thanks for his astounding array of images of early White Mountain climbing, photographs Ken took with a 14 pound camera that he lugged up the climbs. As Henderson said proudly, "I never dropped it once!" Another dedicated early photographer was Walter Howe, to whom I would also like to give credit. Henderson and Howe's pictures add a priceless historical perspective to the story of New Hampshire climbing that words alone could never duplicate. To the talented, modern photographers listed below, your pictures help "make it real" for the rest of us. Thank you for trusting me with your originals, and for donating your pictures to this book. My very sincere thanks to Nick Yardley, S. Peter Lewis, Paul Ross, Henry Barber, Kurt Winkler, Joe Lentini, Rick Wilcox, Bob Palais, Jeff Achey, Greg McCausland, Cathy Beloeil, Sam Streibert, Jeff Pheasant, Susan Patenaude, Gene Ellis, Haydie Callaghan, Stan Hart, Jane Presser, Dick Peterson, Dave Rose, Jeff Fongemie, Jim Boyd, Dave Watowski, Rich Baker, Alec Behr, Ralph Munn, Albert Dow, Jeff Burns, Anne Rutter, Matt Harris, Charley Bentley, Caolan MacMahon, and Bill Holland; Alan Wedgwood in England for his 1965 Yosemite Valley Camp 4 group portrait, Andy Wiessner for his father's photograph, Brian Underhill for the Underhill family photographs, and William O. Owen, who took the historic, 1929 Henderson-Underhill portrait—with the photo itself being from Ken Henderson's collection.

Additionally, I would like to thank my father, Dr. Edward W. Webster, and mother, Dorothea Webster, and my family, John Webster, Micah Webster, Caleb Webster, Peter Webster, Anne & John Wolfe, Mark Webster, Susan & John MacPhee, Judith & Isham McConnell, and Hina & Laurie McConnell. *Tusen tack* also to Anja Hannus, Martti Hannus, Anne Hannus, and Matti Hannus for their kindness, plus thanks to Julian Freeman-Attwood, Lindsay Griffin, Jordan Campbell, Jan Westby, Paul Teare, Glenn Dunmire, Dale Vrabec, Richard Carpenter, Peggy Carpenter, Valerie Edwards Halpin, Dave Halpin, Jane Henry, Jack Snider, Anna Lowther, Rick Davis, Charlene Davis, Clare Stocker, Susan Mitchell, Dr. Steven Grinspoon, Dr. Brooke Swearingen, Dr. Chester Ridgway, Dr. Cory Sperry, Buddy Thomason, Chris Cline-Cardot, Chip Chace, Candice Boyd, John Gerber, librarian at the AMC Library in Boston, David Emerson at the Conway Public Library, Carrie Gleason at the North Conway Public Library, the entire staff at Photo Craft Laboratories, Kathy Bauer & the staff at Advanced Digital Imaging, John Gill at DIGI.COLORado, and Brent McPhie & Heather Mecham at Publisher's Press.

PREFACE

This guidebook, in its Third Edition since 1982, is the most detailed guidebook and history yet written to technical rock climbs in the White Mountains of northern New Hampshire. The White Mountain region has one of America's longest and most colorful climbing histories, dating back to 1910. As "The Granite State", the state's nickname suggests, the region offers a treasure trove of rock climbs ranging from traditional, multi-pitch classics to the hardest modern sport climbs.

As should be self-evident, this guide is not a reference book for hikers. It is a technical rock climbing guidebook, and nothing more. It should never be used as a learning-to-climb manual, or a substitute for hands-on instruction in the art of rock climbing. A guidebook and the best of modern climbing equipment are poor, unsafe alternatives to comprehensive instruction, safe climbing technique, and good common sense. Rock climbing is a serious craft with a long and demanding apprenticeship. Judgement and experience are paramount to success, and to days of enjoyable climbing out on the crags. Learn to rock climb under the guidance of a knowledgeable friend or peer, an established climbing school, or an organization such as the Appalachian Mountain Club.

I've written this Third Edition, East Volume for several reasons. First, I've fixed several more spelling mistakes, plus relocated INDIAN SUMMER to its correct home on Whitehorse! Most importantly, this guide records for the first time the tremendous wealth of modern sport climbs and first free ascents pioneered in the eastern portion of the White Mountains in the last nine years, a period of unexcelled activity that has elevated New Hampshire rock climbing to a new level of difficulty. Several more never described remote cliffs are also included in this book. I encourage every active climber to send route descriptions of any and all first ascents, info on new areas, and corrections to me at the Mountain Imagery address for inclusion in the next edition of the White Mountain rock guide.

After 25 years of adventures in the White Mountains, starting with my first climb (and rescue from) BEGINNER'S ROUTE on Whitehorse in 1971, I still find the majestic granite ledges, forest-clad mountains, and awe-inspiring beauty of the White Mountain region to be amongst the most beautiful in America. The past year has been a difficult one for me, but this East Volume, Third Edition, with its cataloging of traditional and sport climbs all in one book, new cliffs, brand new photo-diagrams, and an even finer selection of historical photographs, I believe is the best guidebook yet to New Hampshire rock climbing. I have put my life and soul into this guide, and I hope it finds a treasured place on all of your climbing adventures in our beloved White Mountains of New Hampshire.

"I was never really sure this book would actually be finished—but here it is!"

Ed Webster Brownfield, Maine March, 1996 & Boulder, Colorado October, 1996

TABLE OF CONTENTS

INTRODUCTION	1
INTERNATIONAL FREE CLIMBING GRADING CHART	23
SERVICES	35
(PUBLIC TRANSPORTATION, LODGING, CLIMBING SHOPS, CLIMBING SCHOOLS, & INDOOR CLIMBING WALLS)	
REGIONAL MAP of ROCK CLIMBING AREAS **(Page 38 & 39)**	
in THE WHITE MOUNTAINS of NEW HAMPSHIRE	
THE MOUNT WASHINGTON VALLEY...(Map Page 42)	43
Cathedral and Whitehorse Ledges	45
Cathedral Ledge	47
Cathedral Ledge - The Barber Wall	48
Cathedral Ledge - The Lower Left Wall	70
Cathedral Ledge - The Thin Air Face	115
Cathedral Ledge - The Airation Buttress	133
Cathedral Ledge - The Central Section	149
Cathedral Ledge - The Cathedral Roof	169
Cathedral Ledge - The Right Side	175
Cathedral Ledge - The North End	201
Whitehorse Ledge	211
Whitehorse Ledge - The Slabs	214
Whitehorse Ledge - The South Buttress	255
The Guide's Wall	327
Humphrey's Ledge	331
The Pig Pen	350
The Saco Crag	351
The Cemetery Cliff	354
THE CONWAY AREA	357
Band M Ledge	357
Albany Slab	373
THE KANCAMAGUS HIGHWAY AREA..(Map Page 378)	377
Woodchuck Ledge	377
Crag Y	395
By Larry Hamilton.	
Found Ledge	409
Lost Ledge	414
Sundown Ledges **(Map Page 419)**	417
Sundown Ledge - Lost Horizon	422
Sundown Ledge - The Main Cliff	425

Section	Page
Sundown Ledge - The Alcohol Wall	451
Sundown Ledge - Call Of The Wild & Gill's Groove Crag	455 & 456
Sundown Ledge - The Far Cliff	455 & 457
Sundown Ledge - The Outback Cliff	469
The Painted Walls	479
Rainbow Slabs	487
The Crack In The Woods Cliff	501
Table Mountain Slab	502
Bear Mountain Slab	506
Hobbitland	507
Bartlett Haystack	509
Green's Cliff	510
Mt. Hedgehog	512
THE BARTLETT REGION (Map Page 516)	517
Stairs Mountain	517
White's Ledge	525
The IME Crag	532
Mount Stanton	534
The Pick Of The Litter Cliff	535
The Attitash Crag	537
Cave Mountain	538
Hart's Ledge	541
THE JACKSON AREA	544
The Jackson Crag	544
Popple Mountain	545
MT. WASHINGTON & PINKHAM NOTCH (Map Page 516)	547
The Pinnacle Buttress	552
Central Buttress	561
Square Ledge	569
THE NORTHERN AREAS (Map Page 574)	575
The Gorham Slab	575
Mt. Forist	576
Wild River	577
ROUTE INDEX	589
STAR INDEX	599
BIBLIOGRAPHY	605
ADVERTISEMENTS	606
CLIMBING NOTES	621

Leading New Hampshire rock climbers Kenneth A. Henderson & Robert L. M. Underhill, suitably dressed for the occasion, several days after their historic July 22, 1929 first ascent of the East Ridge of the Grand Teton in Wyoming. The picture was taken by William O. Owen, who made the first ascent of the Grand Teton in 1898, in front of his house in Jackson, Wyoming. Henderson & Underhill also made the first ascent of Mt. Owen together, while Underhill pioneered the East Face of Mt. Whitney in the Sierras—plus taught the first Yosemite rock climbers how to belay. Photograph courtesy of Kenneth A. Henderson.

INTRODUCTION

It should come as no surprise that New Hampshire, The Granite State, offers some of the finest rock climbing in the Eastern United States. The ledges, cliffs, and crags of the White Mountains of northern New Hampshire present rock climbers with some of the longest and most varied technical climbs on the East Coast. Cannon Cliff (1,000'), Whitehorse Ledge (800'), and Cathedral Ledge (500') are New Hampshire's three best known cliffs, but they represent only part of a diverse wealth of rock. In addition, there are many excellent outlying cliffs, including Humphrey's Ledge, Band M Ledge, Sundown and Woodchuck Ledges, Rainbow Slabs, plus numerous others. While these cliffs are generally smaller and a bit longer of a hike to reach, they offer equally rewarding climbing in a forested, peaceful atmosphere.

With one or two exceptions, including the remarkable 1910 first ascent of THE OLD ROUTE on the Pinnacle on Mt. Washington, New Hampshire's cliffs were recognized for their rock climbing potential in the late 1920s by members of the Boston-based Appalachian Mountain Club. For that era, the AMC's rock climbing committee comprised one of the most illustrious membership lists of American rock climbing and mountaineering, including Robert L. M. Underhill, Kenneth A. Henderson, brother and sister Lincoln and Miriam O'Brien, and Elizabeth Knowlton, amongst many others. Avid mountaineers and rock climbers, they would return home from summers spent climbing in Chamonix and the Dolomites with, as Underhill phrased it, "chunks" of European hardware and ropes to use upon their forest-covered New England crags and on the region's highest peaks like Mt. Washington in New Hampshire and Mount Katahdin in northern Maine.

After warming up at Boston-area cliffs like Quincy Quarries and Crow Hill, plus Joe English Hill in southern New Hampshire, these pioneering rock climbers ventured farther north, to New Hampshire's White Mountains. Beginning in 1928, each major White Mountain cliff and ledge (a term, it seems, unique to New Hampshire!) was climbed in domino-like succession. First to fall was New Hampshire's tallest rock face, Cannon Cliff in Franconia Notch, whose initial route OLD CANNON, was climbed by Robert L. M. Underhill & Lincoln O'Brien. Mt. Willard at the head of Crawford Notch was next, accomplished by way of its STANDARD ROUTE by Lincoln O'Brien & John Gray in 1929. Close to North Conway, two more STANDARD ROUTES were discovered. Cathedral Ledge was ascended, with difficulty, by Leland W. Pollock, Payson T. Newton, & Robert L. M. Underhill in 1931. And lastly, the friction slabs of Whitehorse Ledge were finally free climbed in their entirety by an AMC team led by Leland W. Pollock in 1932.

Equally notable historical landmarks were the first ascents of two climbs now regarded as New Hampshire's most classic, alpine rock routes. First was THE NORTHEAST RIDGE OF THE PINNACLE in Huntington Ravine on Mount Washington, ascended by William P. Allis, Robert L. M. Underhill, Dana Durand, Kenneth A. Henderson, & Jessie Whitehead in 1928. Next came Cannon Cliff's striking, sharp-edged ridge, climbed by cousins Bradley Gilman & Hassler Whitney on their 1929 first ascent of THE WHITNEY-GILMAN RIDGE. Two more prolific contributors of the early 1930s were Fritz Wiessner and Bill House, who did the first ascent of WIESSNER'S DIKE on Cannon Cliff in 1935. Its crescendo finish up the venerable Old Man Of The Mountains, New Hampshire's state symbol, had of course been climbed previously in 1933 by Wiessner & Underhill. Collectively, these many pioneering rock routes in the White Mountains of New Hampshire were amongst the hardest technical climbs in America for their era.

The early classics of White Mountain rock climbing were all first ascended between 1928 and 1933. The 1929 AMC Bulletin advertised a Pre-season Rock Climbing Dinner and Meeting in Boston, "for addicts, prospective experimentalists, the idly curious, and those who have known all about (climbing) as a matter of course." The 1931 AMC Rock Climbers Meeting maintained, "Its special purpose will be to emphasize the opportunities for first-class climbing that are to be found right here in New England, thus making it worthwhile to take up rock work even if you have no immediate expectations of going out West or to the Alps. To this end, a new collection of slides will be shown, picturing climbing on some of the best courses in the White Mountains, and there will be moving pictures of the new route on Mt. Cannon (Author's note: THE WHITNEY-GILMAN RIDGE), the most difficult climb in New England to date. In addition, Miss Miriam E. O'Brien will give a short illustrated account of a post-graduate rock climb in the Alps." Rock climbing in the White Mountains was here to stay!

THE EAST & WEST VOLUMES OF THIS GUIDEBOOK

This new, two volume guidebook, the Third Edition of *Rock Climbs In The White Mountains of New Hampshire* is a testimony to the long, rich history of north country rock climbing that has filled the intervening years, from 1910 all the way to 1996. The number of climbs has grown so large that for the first time the guidebook has been split roughly in half into two separate volumes, an East Volume and a West Volume, to help keep the books reasonably portable and compact, both in size and weight. This Third Edition, East Volume contains an astounding total of 1,245 routes and variations on 42 separate cliffs.

INTRODUCTION 3

Fritz Wiessner relaxes in Kashmir on the approach to Nanga Parbat on the 1932 German-American Nanga Parbat Expedition. This was Fritz's first Karakoram expedition, one year before the start of his impressive string of first ascents in the White Mountains of New Hampshire — and seven years before Wiessner & Pasang Dawa Lama nearly made the first ascent of K2, the world's second highest peak — without bottled oxygen or radios, turning back at night only 800 feet shy of the summit. Photograph courtesy of Andrew Wiessner.

4 INTRODUCTION

The cliffs and climbs of the eastern part of the White Mountains are described roughly south to north, beginning with Cathedral and Whitehorse Ledges in the Mount Washington Valley near North Conway, dipping south to Band M Ledge, then heading west across the Kancamagus Highway past Woodchuck and Sundown Ledges, Rainbow Slabs and others cliffs before moving north through Bartlett to Stairs Mountain and White's Ledge, up onto Mount Washington and into Huntington Ravine, heading farther north to cliffs near Gorham and Berlin, and finishing with Wild River. The West Volume will include the sport climbs at Rumney, all the cliffs in Franconia Notch—Indian Head, Cannon Cliff, Eagle Cliff, The Eaglet, Echo Crag, Profile Cliff, and Artist's Bluff—plus Owl's Head in Oliverian Notch.

HOW TO USE THE GUIDEBOOK

The individual climbs and cliffs are easily located by route name in either the Alphabetical Route Index or Star Index in the back of the book—or once you've become familiar with the region, you can locate the different areas and cliffs simply by looking at the page headings at the top of each page:

- **The Left Page Heading denotes the Regional Area:**
    (The Mount Washington Valley, The Bartlett Region, etc.)
- **The Right Page Heading identifies the Cliff:**
    (Cathedral Ledge, Sundown Ledge - Main Cliff, etc.)

So no matter where you open up the book, *a quick glance at the upper left or right page headings will tell you, geographically speaking, exactly where you are*. (For example, The Mount Washington Valley, Whitehorse Ledge.) Routes are described across the cliffs from left to right, or from right to left. Remember, also, that *distances and pitch lengths are only approximations*, and all other vital directions, such as "traverse left", or "diagonal up right", *always assume that the climber is facing towards the rock or cliff face*.

MAPS

A map of each major climbing area is found at the start of each regional section (The Mount Washington Valley, The Kancamagus Highway Area, The Bartlett Region, etc.). Use these maps to orient yourself to the local topography, and also to help locate the various parking areas, the start of the approaches to the cliffs, and other nearby hiking trails.

HOW TO USE THE PHOTO-DIAGRAMS

This Third Edition contains many new cliff photos, and photo-diagrams of the routes done in much greater detail than those found in the previous two editions of this guidebook. *Please note that the dotted lines on the photos mark only the general line of each route!* The photo-diagrams are

INTRODUCTION 5

America's finest early woman rock climber and alpinist, Miriam E. O'Brien (later Underhill), top-roping a practice chimney near Boston, probably in 1929. Photograph by Robert L. M. Underhill. Courtesy of Brian Underhill.

Miriam E. O'Brien soloing a climb at the Fells near Boston. Date unknown. Amongst many notable climbs, she made the first all-female ascents of both the Grepon and the Matterhorn. Photograph by Robert L. M. Underhill. Courtesy of Brian Underhill.

Lelland W. Pollock on the crux of Old Cannon (5.6) on Cannon Cliff in 1933. Pollock made the first ascents of both Standard Routes, on Cathedral Ledge in 1931, and the first lead of the Brown Spot crux of Whitehorse Standard in 1932. Photograph: Walter H. Howe Collection.

Herbert C. "Hec" Towle on the summit of Whitehorse Ledge. Hec Towle attempted the first ascent of Whitehorse Ledge in 1928 with Underhill & Holden, and over two decades later, in 1953, he led the first ascent of Beginner's Route on Whitehorse. Photograph by Walter H. Howe.

intended to show you roughly where certain key climbs are located. *Belay stances are also not marked on the photo-diagrams.* Obviously, the route lines should never be relied upon for move-by-move consultation while you are leading a pitch! I feel strongly that written route descriptions used in combination with the photo-diagrams allow each climber to interpret the data and history about an individual rock climb—and help maximize the greatest possible adventure, challenge, and enjoyment from every route included in this guidebook.

The scene: Camp 4, Yosemite Valley, California, 1965. From left to right: Chuck Pratt and Yvon Chouinard, Sam Streibert and Phil Nelson. Streibert has pioneered numerous historic first ascents in the White Mountains for over two decades, including Three Birches, Diagonal, & Intimidation on Cathedral Ledge. Photo by Alan Wedgwood (UK).

GEOLOGY

The majority of White Mountain cliffs are composed of the same igneous rock type: Conway granite. Other regional kinds of rock include Mt. Osceola granite (Frankenstein Cliff), diorite and granodiorite (Band M Ledge), porphyritic quartz syenite (Sundown and Woodchuck Ledges), gray gneiss of the Littleton Formation (parts of Mt. Willard and Mt. Washington), and interbedded quartzite and mica schist (also found on Mt. Washington). While the outward appearances of the cliffs does vary considerably, they are all part of the White Mountain Batholith, which was emplaced approximately 185 million years ago. Differences in structure—perhaps best exemplified by the striking dissimilarity between Cathedral

Joe Cote, author of the first two rock climbing guidebooks to the White Mountains and THE leading local activist on Cathedral Ledge in the late 1960s and early '70s, is seen here on the first ascent of Mines of Moria on Cathedral in 1972. Photo by Paul Ross.

and Whitehorse Ledges—is the result of many unique factors: fracturing of the rock during crystallization, subsequent glacial action (the quarrying of immense, rectangular blocks and layered, exfoliation slabs), and later mechanical and chemical erosion by frost-wedging, wind, and water. Conway granite is not fresh and sparkling like geologically young Yosemite granite, but older and more weathered—a bit like New England itself.

To the climber, the rocks of the White Mountains have a character all their own. The rock surfaces are frequently full of surprises, such as crucial small edges or pockets that appear just when needed most. As a result, climbing techniques on New Hampshire climbs are rarely predictable, as is the case, in my opinion, in most Yosemite cracks or on Shawangunk faces. The moves on Conway granite are refreshingly unique, the granite replete with friction slabs, steep faces, cracks of all widths, unlikely aretes, roofs and overhangs, and frequently, unusual rests and hidden holds.

REGULATIONS

Cathedral Ledge, Whitehorse Ledge, Cannon Cliff, and many other cliffs in the White Mountain region are currently under the management of the New Hampshire Department of Resources and Economic Development, Division of Parks and Recreation. We should consider ourselves very fortunate indeed that the NH Division of Parks at the present time does not regulate the sport of climbing in any way. With the logarithmic increase in the popularity of both traditional rock climbing and sport climbing, it is now vitally important—more than ever before—that all climbers do their very best to preserve and protect the cliffs, hiking trails, and mountain environment that we each enjoy so fully. Be very glad and aware that the White Mountains of New Hampshire remain one of the least regulated major rock climbing areas in the United States—and let's work together to keep it that way, and to preserve the free access to our beautiful cliffs! As an environmentally-conscious, responsible, and concerned climber, show your appreciation of and love for Nature as often as possible. Help to preserve "the Freedom of the Hills" in the White Mountains of New Hampshire by adopting the Access Fund's Honor Code:

1. **Commit yourself to "leaving no trace"**
   Both at the base of the cliff and on the routes. Never leave gymnastic tape on the ground or cigarette butts stuffed into cracks at belay stances. At the end of the day, carry out the litter that others have thoughtlessly left behind, and dispose of trash properly, in a bin at the parking area, or at home.

2. **Hike on existing, developed trails only.**
   Don't trample and injure vegetation.

3. **Respect restrictions that protect natural resources and cultural artifacts.**

4. **Be aware of seasonal cliff closures that protect nesting birds of prey.** *Read the Cliff Closures, and obey them!*

5. **Use discretion when placing bolts and fixed protection.**
   Power drills are illegal in wilderness areas.
   Camouflage all fixed anchors.

6. **Remember: minimum impact guidelines stress leaving the rock in its natural state.**
   Deliberately damaging or altering the rock is illegal on most public lands.

7. **Park in designated parking areas only.**
   Don't park in undeveloped, vegetated areas.

8. Maintain a low profile when climbing.
   No boom boxes, etc.!
9. Dispose properly of human waste.
   Dig a six inch deep hole at least 150 feet from water and bury the waste. Pack out toilet paper in ziplock bags.

Please also read these "words to the wise" from one knowledgeable State Park official (who is also a climber): "If you see some trash on the ground, then go over and pick it up yourself. If you do not agree with how a climber is placing bolts, or think someone else is doing something wrong, then go over and talk to him or her. If that climber is not present, then talk to someone at one of the climbing schools, or to an MRS (Mountain Rescue Service) board of director. They may know the individual, and can help mediate a discussion or solution.

"Basic rules such as camping only in designated areas, the 'carry in-carry out' principle, and observing the peregrine falcon cliff closures are amongst the few regulations that do exist in the White Mountains. The fewer climbing complaints the Division of Parks has to deal with, the longer the New Hampshire climbing community can enjoy their free access to our wonderful cliffs—and self rule while climbing on them."

Although the current government policy in New Hampshire is that rock climbers should regulate themselves, our present freedoms are by no means guaranteed. The few regulations that do exist should be obeyed accordingly—with simple respect. As of this writing (1996), there are no major restrictions prohibiting climbing on any of the White Mountain cliffs listed in this guide. While most of the cliffs are situated on lands held either by the State or National Forest, or are within a State Park, a few cliffs are on private land. As such, climbers should climb at these cliffs only with the clear understanding that they may be held accountable for trespassing, and irresponsible camping or fires on private land near these cliffs may endanger all future climbing at these areas. When climbing on cliffs on private land, please keep as low of a profile as possible, and be polite to the land owners if you meet them. As climbers and responsible citizens, we must be vigilantly aware that our sport is generally viewed with great skepticism by bureaucrats and land owners.

Current Climbing Regulations include:

- No rock climbing in state-protected peregrine falcon nesting areas from April 1st until the end of July each year. Please watch for, and obey, all posted signs in peregrine sensitive areas. Cliff closure lists are posted at local climbing shops at the start of each season.

10 INTRODUCTION

- Signing in (and out!) for rock climbs on Cannon Cliff in Franconia Notch, and in Huntington Ravine on Mt. Washington.
- No illegal camping, either below Cathedral and Whitehorse Ledges, below Cannon Cliff, or on State or National Forest land.

PEREGRINE FALCON NESTING INFORMATION

The New Hampshire Fish & Game Department requests the full cooperation of all climbers in their effort to re-establish one of nature's most elegant birds of prey, the peregrine falcon, back to its natural habitat. Peregrines are a federally listed endangered species, and are being closely monitored by the NH Peregrine Falcon Recovery Group, a coalition of federal and state natural resource agencies and conservation organizations working together to restore a healthy, breeding population of peregrine falcons to the White Mountain region. Cooperating agencies include the Audubon Society of New Hampshire, the US Fish & Wildlife Service, The US Forest Service, the NH Fish & Game Department, and the NH Division of Parks & Recreation.

In the past 10 years, mating pairs of peregrine falcons have once again begun to nest on several White Mountain cliffs. The first peregrines were reintroduced by the NH Fish & Game Department. Since then, other pairs have chosen to return and nest at age old locations on several cliffs. Peregrine falcons, however, choose their own nesting sites each year, and where they lived last year may or may not be where they nest the following season. Hence the importance of reading the cliff closure notices!

> **ALL ROCK CLIMBING SHOULD BE AVOIDED ON ALL OF THE LISTED CLOSED CLIFFS during the peregrine nesting season which extends from APRIL 1ST until the END OF JULY each year, until further notice.**
> ❖ **Thank you for your attention to this important program!** ❖

Some protected peregrine nesting sites in the White Mountains documented since 1981 include Cathedral and Whitehorse Ledges in North Conway, the Painted Walls above the Kancamagus Highway, Frankenstein Cliff, Mt. Willard, and the Webster Cliffs in Crawford Notch, the Eaglet, Eagle Cliff, and Cannon Cliff in Franconia Notch, Rattlesnake Mountain at Rumney, and Owl's Head in Oliverian Notch. "Falcons and their nesting sites, unlike granite cliffs and climbing routes, don't always remain in one specific location," explained Chris Martin, senior biologist with the Audubon Society of New Hampshire. "While falcon pairs often do reuse specific cliffs and ledges year after year, new territories are continually being occupied, while other long occupied sites are occasionally abandoned. Further complicating matters is

Paul Ross during an ascent of the VMC Direct Direct on Cannon Cliff in 1971. A transplanted British climber from the Lake District in England, Paul Ross greatly influenced the White Mountain climbing scene in the 1970s and '80s, pioneered dozens of classic new routes, and authored two guidebooks to the White Mountain region, in 1978 and 1982. He has since returned to live in the Lake District. Photograph courtesy of Paul Ross.

the tendency for falcon territories to encompass several neighboring cliffs—such as the Franconia Notch territory which spans Cannon Cliff, Eagle Cliff, and the Eaglet—with alternate rock faces utilized in other years."

"Recreational rock climbers, however, are among our most frequent sources of information regarding cliffs which have been recently occupied by peregrine falcons," Chris Martin added. "Those of us involved with the falcon restoration project in Hew Hampshire very much appreciate the cooperation and restraint demonstrated by the climbing community, and we look forward to continuing our good working relationship." Indeed, several local climbers, including Paul Cormier, Mike Pelchat, and Jim Shimberg have voluntarily assisted state biologists during their visits to various falcon nesting sites, helped with the banding of the young—and introduced several of the biologists to the thrills of climbing in the process!

Jim Dunn on the first ascent of Zonked Out (5.12b) on Woodchuck Ledge in 1978. This was the first 5.12 free climb to be done in the White Mountains. Note the one bare foot (better for toe jamming in thin cracks!) and the one EB. Photograph by Albert Dow.

CLIMBING NOTES

Once considered a training activity for mountaineering and alpinism, rock climbing has evolved into an independent, fully mature sport. In the past 10 years, the popularity of rock climbing has skyrocketed. Never again will climbing be the secret pursuit of the select few. In fact, perhaps encouraged by the newfound popularity of indoor climbing walls and rock gyms, rock climbing and sport climbing is today (dare I say it?) an accepted and even fashionable pursuit. In America, this is a far cry from 10 to 20 years ago when climbing was considered, at best, a questionable or renegade activity done by people with abnormal mental and social tendencies. Thank God for climbing walls, competitions, and TV coverage... Normal at last!

The purpose of this present guide, besides providing accurate descriptions of the rock routes in New Hampshire's White Mountains, is to preserve the often colorful history of these climbs. Without the rock, as a famous climber/philosopher/surfer once said, there would be no climbing. And without the stories and struggles of the climbers who established these great routes, we'd be left reading a very boring textbook indeed—and climbing is anything but that! Multiple generations of New Hampshire climbers have now blazed the way, establishing classic routes for each era and decade—and it is the next generation of climbers who must learn this tradition and history, and go on to forge their own legacies and landmarks.

The British climber John Turner, justly famous for his ahead of their time first ascents of REPENTENCE and RECOMPENSE on Cathedral in 1958 and 1959, recently observed, somewhat wryly, "It is difficult to imagine that the present climbing generation with its extraordinarily high standards could be interested in the primitive events of the 1950s, but I suppose, in turn, my generation occasionally looked back incredulously at pre-war climbers who had done memorable albeit somewhat easier routes despite hemp rope, knickerbocker breeches, and sometimes nailed boots—but never using any pitons for protection." This looking-back-over-your-shoulder reflection I hope will also be practiced by today's climbing generation, because there is an incalculable merit in the history and traditions of our sport.

Throughout the 1950s and '60s, and as late as the early 1970s, the White Mountain climbing scene was very close-knit, with few participants. Those were the golden days when even on holiday weekends you could still drive out to Cathedral or Whitehorse, or go up on Cannon, and know almost everyone who was out climbing. For better or worse, this is no longer so. Meet up with your friends, but plan on arriving early at the cliff base, or be prepared to wait in line. Or, if it's a little dose of solitude you seek, then hike out to one of the lesser visited White Mountain crags which offer quality climbing in a peaceful, unhurried setting. The sense of adventure on these seldom climbed routes will enliven and enrich you.

While the '70s climbing scene was relatively laid back, rock climbing became cosmopolitan in the 1980s. Grand tours of the western United States, Colorado, Utah, and Yosemite were supplemented by foreign destinations such as England's Peak District, Llanberis Pass in North Wales, and France's Verdon Gorge. In the 1990s, far more exotic climbing spots have become well known: Thailand, Baffin Island, and Norway being just a few of the off-the-beaten track areas American climbers are now turning their attentions to. And sport climbing, in addition to traditional "adventure" free climbing, has become a fully accepted part of modern rock climbing. The achievements of sport climbers has certainly been felt in New Hampshire no less than at other major climbing areas throughout the United States.

Gymnastic diligence, training regiments, new forms of protection, stronger ropes, and sticky-soled climbing shoes have all contributed to the uninterrupted rise in technical, free climbing difficulty—and a plethora of new routes and first free ascents thought to be virtually impossible just a decade ago. In his 1969 guidebook, Joe Cote listed 18 routes on Cathedral Ledge. In Paul Ross & Chris Ellms' 1978 guide, Cathedral had 105 climbs and variations. In 1987, this same cliff boasted 240 routes routes and variations. Now, in this 1996 edition, Cathedral Ledge offers an astounding 380 climbs and variations! Obviously, "Last Great Problems" on any cliff, especially on Cathedral, are transitional at best, and applicable only to a particular generation. Is Cathedral Ledge climbed out? Undoubtedly not! The numbers of routes and variations on Cathedral and Whitehorse, and on all the White Mountain cliffs will continue to rise—and who can honestly predict what new challenges future generations of rock climbers will face?

To quote Andy Ross, "Since the last guidebook came out in 1987, the White Mountains have been booming with new route activity. At first it was just a few diehards thrashing around in the woods, but once the quality of the new climbs became evident, others caught the fever, and the race was on." Really! This 1996 East Volume contains an additional 400 new climbs and variations in the eastern part of the Whites, plus several notable first free ascents, clear testimony of the free climbing surge of the past nine years.

FIXED HARDWARE

On the climbs, please do not place additional pitons, or remove any fixed pitons that others are counting on using. Piton stealing, in my opinion, is one of the most self-degrading acts a climber can stoop to. As much as you may

INTRODUCTION 15

Ed Webster & Henry Barber on the first free ascent of Women In Love (5.12a) on Cathedral Ledge in 1978. "Hot Henry" was one of the world's most influential, breakthrough free climbers in the 1970s and '80s, leaving a legacy of hard new routes and on-sight free solo ascents from Yosemite to Britain, Australia, and Africa. Locally, Barber authored the 1973 Supplement guidebook to the Mt. Washington Valley. Webster also climbed difficult new routes in Colorado and Utah, then in 1988 he was a member of the smallest team (only four climbers) to ascend a new route on Mount Everest, up the Kangshung Face in Tibet, without bottled oxygen, Sherpa assistance, or radios. Photo by Todd Gregory.

not agree with their usage, pitons and bolts provide necessary protection today on hundreds of popular routes, both traditional classics and brave new sport routes. Stealing a piton or chopping a bolt only scars the rock even more, leaving behind a permanent reminder of your own selfishness.

> **PLEASE !!! DO NOT STEAL FIXED PITONS OR CHOP BOLTS !!! THESE PITONS & BOLTS WERE PLACED BY AND AT THE EXPENSE OF THE LOCAL CLIMBING COMMUNITY FOR ALL CLIMBERS TO USE. PLEASE RESPECT THE FIXED GEAR !!! MANY OTHER CLIMBERS BESIDES YOU WILL BE COUNTING ON THIS PROTECTION TO CLIP INTO OR TO BELAY FROM. LET LOCAL CLIMBERS MONITOR AND UPDATE ALL FIXED GEAR.**

A few words of caution about old bolts. In the past decade, Mountain Rescue Service (MRS) volunteer climbers have replaced approximately 500 rusty quarter-inch bolts with new, larger diameter bolts in the White Mountain region. (Using only pre-existing holes is the bolt replacement policy—and this total number includes bolts replaced not just in the Mount Washington Valley, but also on Cannon Cliff and at Rumney.) Unfortunately, other out of the way quarter-inch bolts are getting progressively older and weaker. Personally, I've had three quarter-inch bolts break under hand pressure. All quarter-inch bolts should be treated as potentially suspect. Giving a quick test pull on old, rusty bolts is one safeguard, but just be sure to be holding onto something else at the same time! You should always back up bolts with extra anchors if possible, and equalize fixed, double bolt belay anchors. NEVER trust a single bolt for a belay anchor, especially an old quarter-inch bolt.

NEW BOLTS

As of 1996, standard practice in the White Mountains is to place only ALL stainless steel, large diameter studs, bolt hangers, washers, and nuts on ALL new routes. As the Mountain Rescue Service's rebolting program continues, eventually all bolts in the White Mountains of New Hampshire will be large diameter, stainless steel studs, washers, nuts, and hangers.

THE ROPE

A 45 meter by 11mm kernmantle rope used to be the norm, but nowadays a 50 meter rope, especially on Whitehorse and Cannon, is often helpful to comfortably reach the next belay stance. Some climbers are even starting to use ropes up to 60 meters long. Double 9mm ropes, too, are increasingly popular, both as a safety measure, and for speed and convenience to descend fixed rappel routes. On any of the area's long routes, on Whitehorse, Cathedral, and Cannon, bring a spare rope in case the weather turns bad.

INTRODUCTION 17

Joe Lentini leading Ventilator (5.10b) in 1974. Note the fashions of the day: EBs, white painter's pants, rugby shirt, bandanna—and belaying gloves! In 1972, Ventilator was the first free climb in the White Mountain region to be protected by rappel-placed bolts. Photograph by Ed Webster.

THE RACK

Poorly protected routes, which are generally free climbs, or routes on which you must carry pitons (usually aid climbs) are mentioned in each route description. A standard rack of nuts, from small wired Stoppers and Steel nuts to hand-sized (three inch) nut and/or camming protection will suffice for about 90% of the climbs listed in this guidebook. Such a rack would generally include a variety of nuts: Stoppers, Steel or RP nuts, Hexentrics, Friends, and Tri-cams, with the latter being particularly useful on the Whitehorse slabs. For simplicity's sake, small wired nuts mean Brass, Steel, or RP nuts. Also noted in some descriptions is the definitive Modern Rack. This rack should include a selection of most, or all, of the newest (and typically, the most expensive) types of modern protection available: Friends, Flexible Friends, Camalots, Tri-cams, TCUs, Lowe Balls, and Steel or RP nuts. For your own safety and longevity, it is strongly recommended (and would seem obvious) that you should always carry a modern rack on any climb with a protection rating of R or X.

GRADING SYSTEMS

In America, all of our modern rock climbing grading systems may be traced back to a fundamental outline credited to the great German alpinist Willo Welzenbach. The Class System is a general rating system applicable to all types of mountaineering and rock climbing. Using Welzenbach's system, climbers differentiate between hiking (Classes 1, 2, and 3: a non-technical or non-roped activity) and technical rock climbing (the 4th, 5th, and 6th classes of difficulty) which involves using the climbing rope and a great variety of technical gear: pitons, nuts, carabiners, and slings, etc, for safety.

THE CLASS SYSTEM

Class 1	Walking, an easy stroll.
Class 2	Hiking over rugged terrain.
Class 3	Scrambling, using hand holds for balance.
Class 4	Climbing an easy cliff, but one with sufficient exposure that beginners should be belayed.
Class 5	Free Climbing: belaying, the use of technical climbing gear for safety, and one's hands and feet for progress up the rock.
Class 6	Artificial Climbing: engineering your way up severe sections of rock with pitons, nuts, and a variety of other technical gear for direct assistance.

INTRODUCTION 19

Russ Clune using an unusual racking method during an ascent of Screaming Yellow Zonkers Crack (5.11d) at Woodchuck Ledge in 1985. No clues who his uninhibited belayer was who provided the gear sling! Photograph by S. Peter Lewis.

In addition, there are several even more succinct rating systems rock climbers use: a commitment rating, a free climbing rating, an aid climbing rating, and the star rating which singles out routes of particular merit.

THE COMMITMENT RATING

Placed after the name of a climb (customarily given to a route by the first ascent party) is the Roman numeral commitment rating. This rating is an evaluation of the climb's seriousness, and an estimate of how much time will be required for the ascent: the number of hours (or days) it will take a roped party of two average ability climbers to finish the route under good conditions; i.e., no 3 a.m. party the night before, no thunderstorm en route, etc.

THE COMMITMENT RATING

I	Up to several hours; usually between 1 and 3 pitches.
II	About half a day, up to 5 to 6 pitches. More involved.
III	A full day, up to 7 to 8 hours. Fairly serious.
IV	A substantial undertaking. A very long climb, possibly involving a bivouac.
V	A Big Wall climb lasting 1 1/2 to 2 days. Could be done in a single day by a very strong team.
VI	Multi-day Big Wall climbs taking at least 2 days. Tough.
VII	Extreme multi-week Big Wall ascents in remote alpine or Himalayan situations—the hardest rock climbs on Earth.

FREE CLIMBING

Rock climbing is a sport that can be played in astoundingly different ways. The three primary disciplines in rock climbing are free climbing, aid climbing, and big wall climbing. Of these, free climbing is the simplest and most natural. A free climb at its most basic is the ascent of a cliff face using the rock's natural features for progress: flakes, edges, and cracks in the rock's surface. Fingers grip tenaciously, while sticky, rubber-soled shoes give support. The climber's rope, in addition to other forms of protection such as nuts, pitons, bolts, and natural anchors like flakes, horns, and trees, is only used as a precaution to prevent a serious fall. The climbing rope and the individual pieces of protection are never used for resting or advancement. As soon as a climber does this—uses his equipment for support, to hold his or her weight—they are said to be using aid, and are no longer free climbing. Traditionally, once the protection or rope

INTRODUCTION 21

Jim Surette preparing to install the Space Station belay platform prior to his first free ascent of Liquid Sky (5.13b / 5.11a R) on Cathedral Ledge in 1986—the first 5.13 to be done in the White Mountains. Locally, Surette created a string of daring (and for the most part unrepeated) first free ascents, including Armageddon (5.12b R), Pitch one of Mordor Wall (5.12c), and Police & Thieves, also 5.12c. Photograph by S. Peter Lewis.

is weighted, the leader then lowers off to either the nearest "no-hands" rest, or the ground, rests up, and tries the pitch again.

Sport climbing has altered this "older view" of free climbing to a certain extent. On extreme free climbs (those graded 5.12 and up), climbers often will hang on protection to rest, and work out the next few moves. The goal of sport climbing is to accomplish a redpoint ascent, which (with the exception of pre-placed protection and/or quick draws) is identical to the time honored ideals of traditional free climbing: where the route is climbed from the ground to the top in a single, continuous effort, without weighting the rope, or using any of the protection either for advancement or for a rest.

THE DECIMAL SYSTEM

Free climbing is often referred to as fifth class climbing, which is the basis of the American Decimal rating system (also known as the Yosemite Decimal System). Invented at Tahquitz Rock in southern California in the 1950s, the Decimal system has since been universally adopted across the United States. It is, however, a very subjective rating that realistically denotes the difficulty only of a climb's individual hardest move—about a single five foot section on any given route. The hardest move, or short series of moves, on a climb then gives the route's overall difficulty. The Decimal system is even more subjective because of additional variable factors such as a climber's height, athletic ability, finger strength, etc. Never to be underestimated, either, are temperature and humidity which play a significant role in how difficult (or easy) a climb might feel. And doing a climb for the first time, as climbers like to say, "on-sight", is undoubtedly much harder than it is after you have "wired the moves"! Placed just after the climb's name and the Roman numeral commitment rating, the Decimal rating is the free climbing difficulty of the climb. The American free climbing rating system is categorized as follows:

THE AMERICAN DECIMAL SYSTEM

Beginner	5.0	-	5.4
Intermediate	5.5	-	5.7
Advanced	5.8	-	5.10
Expert	5.11	-	5.12
Sport	5.13	-	5.14

The Decimal system originally divided "the fifth class" of climbing into 10 sub-grades, from 5.0 to 5.9. Over the past 20 years, the system has evolved into an open-ended scale of difficulty with a current high of 5.14. This upward

⌘ INTERNATIONAL FREE CLIMBING RATINGS ⌘

USA DECIMAL	UK	SCANDI-NAVIAN	FRENCH	UIAA	AUSTRA-LIAN
5.14d	E10	—	9a	—	—
5.14c	E9	—	8c+	—	33
5.14b	E9	9+	8c	X+	32
5.14a	E8	9+	8b+	X+	32
5.13d	7a E8	9	8b	X	31
5.13c	7a E7	9	8a+/8b	X-	30
5.13b	7a E7	9-	8a+	IX+	29
5.13a	6c E6	9-	8a	IX+	28
5.12d	6c E6	8+	7c+	IX	28
5.12c	6c E6	8	7c	IX-	27
5.12b	6b E5	8-	7b+	VIII+	26
5.12a	6b E5	8-	7b	VIII+	25
5.11d	6b E5	7+	7a+	VIII	24
5.11c	6a E4	7	7a	VIII-	23
5.11b	6a E4	7-	6c+	VII+	23
5.11a	6a E3-E4	7-	6c+	VII+	22
5.10d	5c XS E3	6+	6c	VII	21
5.10c	5c XS E2	6+	6b+	VII	21
5.10b	5c XS E2	6	6b	VII-	20
5.10a	5b XS E1	6	6a+	VI+	19
5.9	5b MXS E1	6-	6a	VI	18–19
5.8	5a HVS	5+	5c	VI-	16–17
5.7	4c VS	5	5a/b	V+	14–15
5.6	4b VS	5-	4b/c	V	12–13
5.5	4a HS	4+	3c/4a	V-	10–11
5.4	3c S	4	3c	IV+	—
5.3	3b VD	3+	3b	IV	—
5.2	3a D	3	3a	IV-	—
5.1	—	3-	3a	III+	—
5.0	—	—	—	III	—

evolution did not occur at a rapid pace, but gradually over many years, with every newly proposed top grade provoking heated controversy as each younger generation of climbers advanced beyond the existing standards of the old. In the early 1970s, climbers reluctantly extended the Decimal system beyond the old norm of 5.9, the mathematical limit, according to one school of thought. Later, before 5.11 became an accepted grade, the 5.10 level became ridiculously top heavy. More recent advances into the rarefied realms of 5.12, 5.13, and 5.14 have met with some of the same familiar resistance, but not quite to the same extent. Rock climbers, it appears, have become more accepting of change in the past decade, and the inevitable creation of harder and higher free climbing grades.

Two other grading modifications confused the ratings dilemma of the '70s: Jim Bridwell's Yosemite subgrades of a, b, c, & d, which were widely used out West to subdivide the 5.10, 5.11, and 5.12 grades; and the + and - grade modifiers, that were more commonly used in the East. Eventually, the Yosemite system of a, b, c, & d subgrades won the day as this current guidebook reflects. An interesting historical relic, however, one locally peculiar to White Mountain rock climbing, is the belligerent free climbing grade of "Cathedral Ledge" 5.9+, a rating that should always be eyed with the greatest suspicion. Consider yourself forewarned!

ARTIFICIAL CLIMBING

Artificial or direct aid climbing is where technical climbing equipment directly supports the climber's weight and allows improbable sections of rock to be scaled—rock which is either too steep or smooth to be free climbed. As a result, aid climbs tend to be exceptionally spectacular—but also mechanical, laborious, knuckle-bashing—and tedious as hell for the belayer. Its single redeeming factor is that direct aid makes for some of the most outrageous climbs anywhere, whether they are local White Mountain routes like MORDOR WALL, or world-famous ascents such as El Capitan and Half Dome in Yosemite.

Another important point about artificial climbing, again, a consideration unique to New Hampshire: since so many former White Mountain aid routes now are routinely climbed free, there are only a few practice aid routes left. As a result, aid ascents on nuts of the Mount Washington Valley's once popular artificial routes like WOMEN IN LOVE, and THE PROW are still acceptable, *but on nuts only and leaving all fixed protection in place!* These beautiful free climbs must not be scarred by using pitons for aid, which is completely unnecessary and very damaging to the rock. If you can't do these routes aided ONLY on nuts, without hammering in a piton—rappel off.

Aid climbing is the 6th class of Willo Welzenbach's scale, and is rated from AO to A6.

AID CLIMBING RATINGS

AO Use of an anchor for a handhold or a rest during a lead; or a pendulum, tension traverse, or rappel.

A1 Easy aid on secure pitons and/or good nuts.

A2 Awkward aid on tied-off, stacked, or nested pitons often on overhanging rock.

A3 Delicate aid on stacked pitons, rurps, skyhooks, etc.

A4 A series of body-weight aid placements, usually with about a 30 to 40 foot fall potential.

A5 Extreme aid, using all body weight placements, expanding flakes, bashie cracks, skyhooking, etc. The Yosemite definition: at least a 60 to 100 foot fall potential, with a good chance of hitting something and getting severely injured.

A6 Your belay anchor is also so marginal that it too will probably fail if the leader falls. Bring your parachute!

THE STAR (OR QUALITY) RATING

Another system, the star rating, is commonly used to single out routes of particular merit. The number of stars a route receives does not depend on route length, but on overall quality and the popularity of the climb. The use of stars to rate a route's aesthetic qualities was invented by Paul Ross for use in his 1966 rock climbing guide to Borrowdale in England's Lake District. It has since been universally adopted with the three star system proving most popular. While subjective and usually controversial, the star rating helps visiting and local climbers alike to choose the area's best routes.

THE STAR RATING

	No Stars	An average climb. No particular merit.
(*)	**One Star**	A good climb with distinguishing qualities: nice moves, good rock, etc.
(**)	**Two Stars**	An excellent route with fun climbing, exposed moves, etc.
(***)	**Three Stars**	A classic climb of the region, a route with history, great rock, and aesthetic climbing.

THE PROTECTION RATING

The protection on a climb may vary from excellent to nonexistent. Before choosing a climb, it's nice to know not only how technically difficult and long a route is, but also how safe it is. The protection rating accomplishes this. Remember that climbs done since 1980 will have been protected by many new forms of protection: Friends, Tri-cams, Lowe Balls, RP or Steel nuts, and other more recently manufactured, esoteric gear. Any or all of these types of protection could be needed, depending on when the first ascent of the climb was made—and how bold the first ascentionists were. Specific kinds and sizes of protection are generally (but not always) mentioned in the descriptions. The R and X protection ratings were first used by Jim Erickson in his 1980 Colorado guidebook, *Rocky Heights, A Guide to Boulder Free Climbs*, and are simple, concise, and easy to understand.

THE PROTECTION RATING

No Comment If there is no mention of poor protection in the route description then you can generally assume that the protection is good—or at least reasonable.

R Means that protection is poor, or gear is awkward and/or very strenuous to place. Also expect a fairly serious runout or marginal protection that could pull out if you fall.

X A death-wish climb. Hitting a ledge or the ground will be your next stop if you blow it. An X rated climb offers an excellent chance for serious injury.

The protection ratings in this guidebook are quite specific, in fact, they are considerably more exact than protection ratings used at other American climbing areas. With practice, the New Hampshire protection rating system is very easy to understand and use. Protection ratings in the White Mountains are given below in several different formats. For example:

NUTCRACKER I 5.9+
There is no protection rating given for this route, so you can assume that the climb is reasonably protected or well protected.

THE GRIM REAPER I 5.10d R
In this case, the single hardest move or crux section of this climb, rated at 5.10d, has a protection rating of R.

STAGE FRIGHT II 5.12c X
The hardest and most dangerous climb in the White Mountains offers unprotected crux moves of 5.12c with a protection rating of X.

LIQUID SKY III 5.13b (5.11a R)
The crux of this route is rated at 5.13b and is protected, but there is also mandatory unprotected free climbing rated at 5.11a R.

ONE HIT TO THE BODY 5.12b (or 5.11d) (5.10d R / 5.9+ X)
This is the most complicated rating in the entire guide! The climb's original crux is rated 5.12b, but there is also a 5.11d variation around it. Both these sections are well protected, however, because there is no protection rating modifier of R or X after the grade. There is, however, unprotected, mandatory free climbing on the route rated at 5.10d R and 5.9+ X.

Paul Ross aid climbs out the Triangular Roof on Pitch five of The Prow on Cathedral Ledge during the route's historic first ascent in 1972. Photograph by Hugh Thompson.

FIRST ASCENT, FIRST FREE ASCENT, & HISTORY
Placed at the end of each route description is a note about the history of the climb. The first ascent (abbreviated: FA) credits the first climbers to accomplish the route, whether it was done all free or with some artificial aid. The first ascent party also traditionally names and grades the climb, although route grades are sometimes later modified by local consensus

Jim Dunn working out one of the crux moves below the Triangular Roof on the equally notable first free ascent of The Prow (5.11d) in 1977. Dunn, who was born and raised in New Hampshire but later moved to Colorado, is equally well known for his free ascents and new routes out West. His other most famous climbs include, in Colorado, the first free ascent of The Cruise in the Black Canyon and the second free ascent of The Diamond on Long's Peak, the first ascent of the Dunn Route on Moses in Canyonlands, Utah—and the first solo ascent of a Grade VI new route on El Capitan in Yosemite, up The Cosmos which Jim climbed alone in 9 days in 1972. Photograph by Bob Palais.

and/or guidebook authors! The noting of the first free ascent (abbreviated: FFA) acknowledges the first climbers to accomplish a completely free ascent of a climb which previously had at least some artificial moves on it.

The history of many routes, however, is anything but cut and dry. The usual pattern of ascent is one of attempts, failures, repeated attempts (at times, by more than one team), and eventual success. Since the history of a climb is an integral part of any route, I've put a lot of time and effort into researching the histories and evolution of many White Mountain climbs. Hours of research, letters, and phone calls have gone into unraveling the backgrounds of many climbs for the 1982, 1987, and finally, this 1996 Third Edition, East Volume of *Rock Climbs in the White Mountains of New Hampshire*. The expanded sections labeled HISTORY reflect this extra research.

The order in which the climber's names are listed in the first or first free ascent credit is also of importance. Generally, the climber's name listed first is the person who led the hardest sections of the route on the first ascent or first free ascent. Other times the lead is shared equally on a long climb, or one person may be more responsible for finding and conceiving of the climb's possibility. Determining whose name should go first has not always been possible, but I've tried to be as accurate as possible.

ETHICAL CONSIDERATIONS

In their quest for harder free routes, rock climbers have recognized and defined the ethical components of a purely free ascent. In the last 25 years, American climbers have developed an increasingly complex free climbing game that has recently embraced the concepts and new traditions of sport climbing. In its simplest terms, a free climb is a continuous roped ascent of a section of cliff. The climber utilizes only the rock's natural holds for progress and the rope for safety. Ideally, and until only recently, routes were always done "from the ground up"—without previewing or placing protection on rappel, without resting on protection or on the rope, and hopefully, in one try, from the ground to the top, without repeated sieging, yo-yoing, or hangdogging.

On today's hardest free climbs, a perfect ascent—commonly known as a flash (climbing the route on your first try) or a redpoint (a clean ascent after previous attempts)—is still the climber's ultimate goal. The means to achieving a redpoint, such as hangdogging (resting on the rope and/or your protection, and then trying the moves again), or previewing the moves on a top-rope or on rappel, are becoming increasing prevalent as today's generation compete for a limited number of new routes and free ascents. While the meteoric rise in American free climbing standards is in general commendable, the style in which many hard sport routes are accomplished is—in the eyes of older, traditional free climbers—a step backwards. In New Hampshire, there is a devoted group of climbers who wish to preserve traditional, from-the-ground-up ethics, placing all fixed protection on the lead, and drilling all bolts also on the lead, often by hand. What is truly remarkable (and commendable) in the White Mountains is that traditional climbers and sport climbers have maintained an independent, yet harmonious coexistence in the last decade, with each group keenly pursuing their own concepts of how new routes should be established. Please, let's show respect for each group's individual styles, and remember that the ethical dividing lines are these. As long as the rock is not damaged or defaced, fixed protection is not added to or removed, and new routes are not crowded up against older, pre-existing climbs—climbing ethics are an entirely personal matter.

New routes and free ascents in the White Mountains usually involve cleaning the climb on rappel. In New Hampshire, cleaning lichen, moss, and dirt is a necessary and accepted practice. Scrubbing a route on rappel does, however, negate a true on sight lead. Ethically, your partner should clean the climb, then you should lead it, but this is typically above the call of duty—and friendship!

STYLE: FROM THE GROUND UP, OR RAPPEL BOLTED?

Placing bolts or pitons on rappel to protect a new route remains a controversial action, yet its practice in the White Mountains has been virtually (but not quite completely) accepted. Seen with two decades of historical perspective, several extremely popular, now "classic climbs", such as VENTILATOR, STARFIRE, THE ARETE, and CAMBER were all protected by rappel-placed bolts in the 1970s before the practice came under closer scrutiny. In an historic 1979 meeting since dubbed "The Spanish Inquisition", local climbers, however, unanimously decided that placing bolts on rappel represented a backward step and would not be accepted in the White Mountains. (It was directly after this meeting that Paul Ross chopped the bolts on THE ARETE, which was subsequently re-established by Rick Fleming from the ground up, although he placed the crux bolt on aid.) This consensus against rapbolted routes continued through the '80s with relatively few infractions. Several rappel-bolted first ascents saw their bolts removed (even later the very same day, as on ROOM WITH A VIEW) in the early to mid-1980s because certain local climbers had developed a strict code of ethics that on steep slab routes *all* the bolts had to be placed completely free *and* on the lead. At the very same time, other rappel-bolted routes remained curiously intact, such as THE FAUX PAS ARETE, ENDLESS SUMMER, & LONDON CALLING.

INTRODUCTION 31

Steve Damboise holds the first electric drill—right out of its box—to arrive in the Mount Washington Valley, in North Conway in 1988. Photograph by Nick Yardley.

Other notable free routes had all of their bolts drilled on the lead entirely free (and with leader falls, as on BITS & PIECES & CLEAN SWEEP), or while hanging off of skyhooks, a now commonly used practice.

Two distinct schools of thought on bolting new routes have emerged in recent years, yet they share a common strict ideal: that all new bolts placed on White Mountain cliffs should be of large diameter (3/8 inch), and use ALL stainless steel hardware: bolt studs, nuts, washers, and hangers. How these bolts should be placed is where the conflict arises. One group believes that all new or first ascent bolts should be placed on the lead, completely free or as freely as possible, by hand—an admirable goal indeed, especially when drilling fat bolts! Hard-core sport climbers, though, generally don't want to take the time or make the effort. They'd rather be exercising their fingertips making the moves and redpointing the first ascent than straining their forearms and wrists drilling by hand, so the use of power drills and rappel-bolting is widespread— but not by any means fully embraced. In my opinion, the White Mountains are still large enough for both types of climbers "to do their own thing", but in the last several years another extremely serious set of issues has arisen regarding bolts, which is discussed below. It should be evident, however, that by popular consensus, new routes that are established entirely on the lead, and with bolted and fixed protection placed as freely as possible on the lead, earn the greatest and most lasting respect from the climbing community. And the fewer bolts used on any given first ascent, the better.

OVER-BOLTING & ROUTE CROWDING

The new route arena on our cliffs and crags is shrinking. Sad but true, the acreage of unclimbed rock and the potential for quality new routes is slowly dwindling in the White Mountains. This undeniable fact has given rise to several very serious new issues confronting today's climbers:

- New routes that are simply either too close to each other (by less than 15 to 20 feet sometimes), or criss cross almost at random over older, pre-existing climbs.
- New routes where the protection bolts are placed much too close (sometimes within 5 to 15 feet) of existing, traditional climbs so as to interfere with both the aesthetic appreciation of, and the protection (natural or fixed) found on the older climb—which after all, was there first, often by a decade or two.
- "New routes", also typically bolted, which ascend the very same line as an older, pre-existing route—usually a climb that was originally done with little or no fixed protection on the first ascent. Don't assume that a blank slab without any bolts hasn't already been climbed!

- The placement of new protection bolts on old aid routes in order to free climb them. This practice is growing, but is it right?

Read the guidebook before you bolt a "potential" new route. You may be shocked to learn that the climb has already been done. In researching this new edition, I have come across an increasing number of examples of pre-existing climbs that were led (or free-soloed) in bold style on their first ascent often many years ago, only to be recently "bolted" and claimed as "new routes". Over-bolted and retro-bolted climbs, in my opinion, signify a lack of aesthetic awareness of the cliffs, and occasionally, an ignorance of where an older, pre-existing climb went—its exact route up the cliff—of how the original climb was first done, and how it was protected. Learn the history of the cliffs. Over-bolting and route crowding are serious and growing problems that will undoubtedly only get worse as new route possibilities lessen.

ROCK DEFACEMENT

Worst of all, the rock—our most precious resource—is with increasingly frequency being modified: cleaned, chipped, drilled, or glued. Gluing is where epoxy resin or other bonding agents are used to reinforce tenuous hand and foot holds, to keep them from breaking, and to allow a climb to be done. But gluing on completely artificial holds or flakes directly onto the rock, bolting on man-made artificial holds onto the rock, or power-drilling new finger pockets (or enhancing existing pockets) are crimes of a high magnitude, and will simply not be tolerated by climbers in the White Mountains. These latter two practices both occurred at the Main Cliff at Sundown Ledge, prompting a 1991 public forum on these disturbing trends.

The following is quoted from a flyer announcing the 1991 Climber's Town Meeting: "The Climbing Community of the Mount Washington Valley invites all interested parties to participate in an open discussion on: Manufactured Holds on the Boulders & Cliffs in the White Mountains. A Discussion of their Existence, Virtue, & Acceptability." The meeting was held on the evening of December 13, 1991 in the climbing gym at Mt. Cranmore in North Conway. Bill Aughton was the moderator, Chris Gill gave an introduction, and Steve Larson showed slides that documented key incidents. Following a group discussion and a vote by those assembled, all the above-mentioned practices were firmly condemned by the local climbing community. A unanimous decision was reached that night: that there was to be no more gluing of holds, chipping, drilling, or manufacturing of holds in the rock, or the placement of man-made holds on any route in the White Mountain region.

Simply put: if you really need to crank that bad, go to an indoor gym!

34 INTRODUCTION

Kurt Winkler on the first ascent of Adventures In 3D (5.10b / 5.10a R) in 1985 on the THIN AIR Face. All the bolts protecting this route were placed free on the lead by hand. Photograph by Ed Webster.

SERVICES

PUBLIC TRANSPORTATION, INNS & CAMPING, CLIMBING SHOPS, CLIMBING SCHOOLS, CLIMBING WALLS, & RESCUE

BUS SERVICE

Concord Trailways bus service (Phone 800-639-3317 for reservations) runs between Boston and Conway daily Monday through Thursday and twice daily Friday through Sunday. Buses leave from South Station in Boston and arrive on West Main Street in Conway, stopping at First Stop (Phone 603-447-8444) next to the Conway Information Center. Buses stop opposite The Eastern Slope Inn next to IME in North Conway only by prior arrangement. Telephone First Stop in Conway to schedule either a bus pick-up in North Conway or a ride up to Pinkham Notch. Bus service between Conway and the AMC Pinkham Notch Headquarters on Route 16 below Mt. Washington (Phone 603-466-2727 for reservations) is once daily. Confirm by telephone for current schedules.

COUNTRY INNS & CAMPGROUNDS

The following inns and campgrounds are located near many of the White Mountain's major climbing areas.

THE MOUNT WASHINGTON VALLEY

The Nereledge Inn
PO Box 547,
River Road
North Conway, NH 03860
Phone: (603) 356-2831
Fax: (603) 356-7085

The Farm By The River
2555 West Side Road
North Conway, NH 03860
Phone: (603) 356-2694

North Conway Pines Campground
West Side Road
North Conway, NH 03860
Phone: (603) 356-3305

THE KANCAMAGUS HIGHWAY AREA

White Mountain National Forest Campgrounds:

The Covered Bridge Campground   **Phone:** (800) 280-CAMP or
Blackberry Crossing Campground   **Phone:** (603) 447-5448

36 Services

MOUNT WASHINGTON

AMC Pinkham Notch Camp **Reservations:** (603) 466-2727
PO Box 298, **Weather Info:** (603) 466-2725 or
Gorham, NH 03581 (603) 466-2721
To order books and maps, or to make last minute reservations less than
five days in advance: **Phone:** (800) 262-4455

WHITE MOUNTAIN NATIONAL FOREST

For more information, maps, and campsite information, contact:

The Saco Ranger Station (WMNF) **Phone:** (603) 447-5448
RFD #1, Box 94
Conway, NH 03818

> The Conway Ranger Station and Visitor Center is located 100 yards to the west of Route 16, just off the Kancamagus Highway.

White Mountain National Forest **Phone:** (603) 528-8721
PO Box 638,
Laconia, NH 03247

CLIMBING SHOPS

Friendly advice, additional route information, and technical climbing equipment can be found at several local climbing shops.

International Mountain Equipment (IME)
PO Box 494, Main Street **Phone:** (603) 356-6316
North Conway, NH 03860 **Fax:** (603) 356-6492
(Located at the IME Building.) **Mail Order:** (603) 356-7013

Eastern Mountain Sports (EMS)
PO Box 514, Main Street **Phone:** (603) 356-5433 or
North Conway, NH 03860 (603) 356-5434
(Located at the Eastern Slope Inn.)

Ragged Mountain Equipment **Phone:** (603) 356-3042
PO Box 130, **Fax:** (603) 356-8815
Intervale, NH 03845
(Outlet Store at Routes 16 & 302 in Intervale.)

North Country Outfitters **Phone:** (603) 444-6532
99 Main Street **Fax:** (603) 444-5532
Littleton, NH 03561

North Country Outfitters **Phone:** (603) 745-8735
Main Street Linwood Plaza
Lincoln, NH 03251

CLIMBING SCHOOLS

Mountain Guides Alliance Phone: (603) 356-5310
PO Box 266,
North Conway, NH 03860
(Located at Ragged Mountain Equipment in Intervale.)

Eastern Mountain Sports Climbing School
Box 514, Main Street Phone: (603) 356-5433
North Conway, NH 03860 Fax: (603) 356-9469
(Located at the Eastern Slope Inn, behind EMS.)

International Mountain Climbing School
PO Box 1666, Main Street Phone: (603) 356-7064
North Conway, NH 03860 Fax: (603) 356-6492
(Located at the IME Building.)

George Hurley, Independent Guide Phone: (603) 447-3086

Profile Mountaineering Phone: (603) 745-3106
PO Box 607,
Lincoln, NH 03251

A0 Mountain Guides Phone: (603) 726-3030
RR1, Box 1029 Ten Mountain View Road
Campton, NH 03223

The Appalachian Mountain Club Phone: (617) 523-0638
5 Joy Street
Boston, MA 02108

INDOOR CLIMBING WALLS

Mt. Cranmore Climbing Wall North Conway Phone: (603) 356-6301
The Rock Barn (Rumney) Plymouth Phone: (603) 536-2717
White Mountain Rock Gym North Woodstock Phone: (603) 745-2867

MOUNTAIN RESCUE SERVICE (MRS)

The Mountain Rescue Service handles all technical climbing rescues in the White Mountain region. The MRS is fully staffed by local area climbers who volunteer their time and are on call year round. If there has been a climbing accident, please telephone:

1. IME: Office: (603) 356-6316 Weekends / Store: (603) 356-7064
2. NH FISH & GAME DEPT.: (800) 322-5018 or (603) 271-3421
3. NORTH CONWAY FIRE & RESCUE: 911

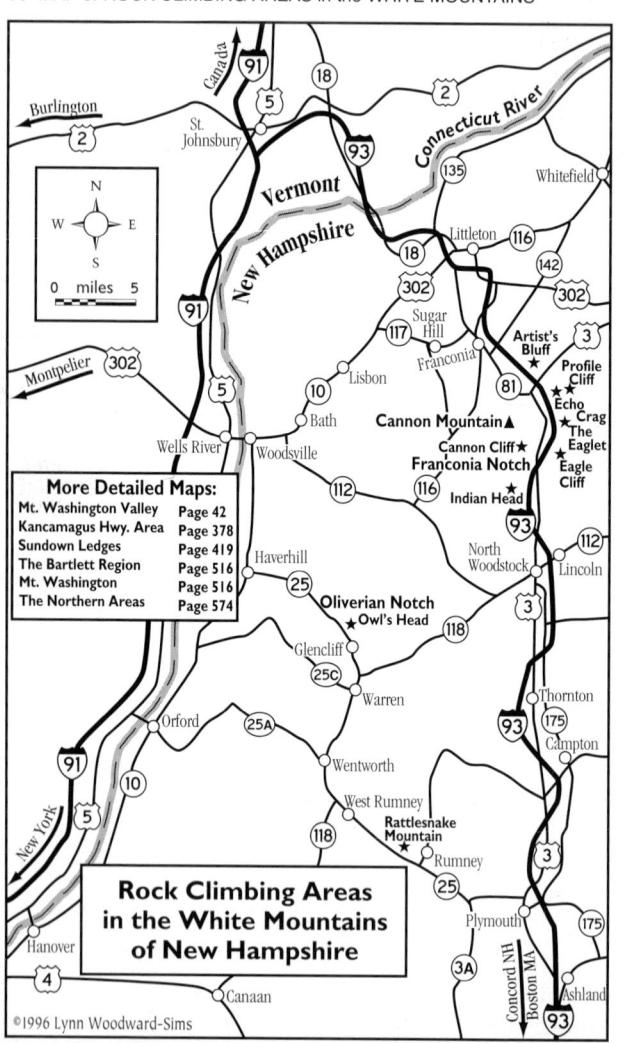

38 MAP of ROCK CLIMBING AREAS in the WHITE MOUNTAINS

More Detailed Maps:

Mt. Washington Valley	Page 42
Kancamagus Hwy. Area	Page 378
Sundown Ledges	Page 419
The Bartlett Region	Page 516
Mt. Washington	Page 516
The Northern Areas	Page 574

Rock Climbing Areas in the White Mountains of New Hampshire

©1996 Lynn Woodward-Sims

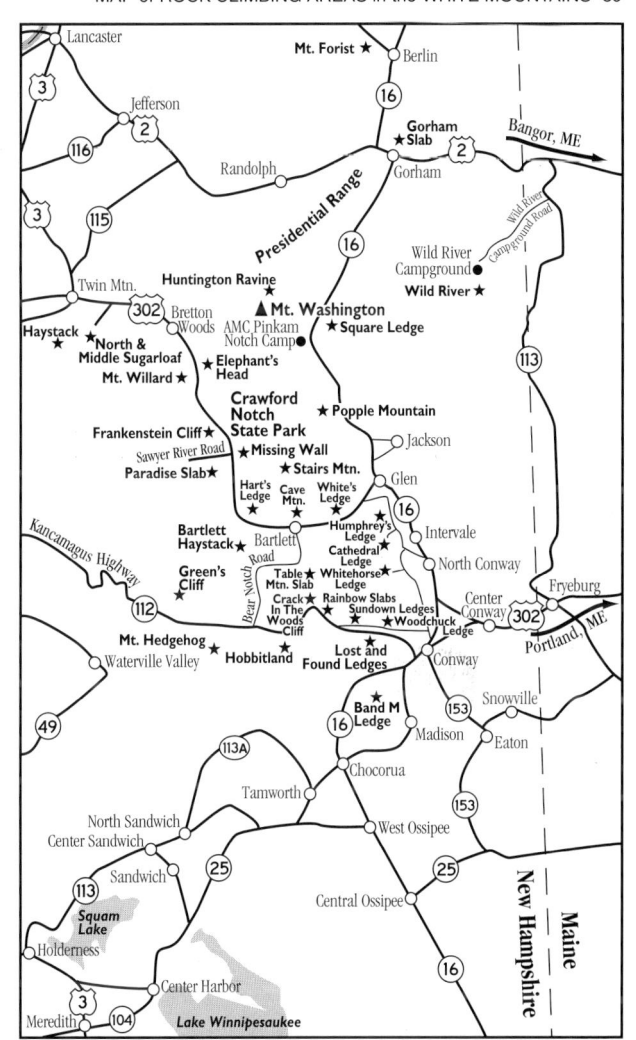

MAP of ROCK CLIMBING AREAS in the WHITE MOUNTAINS 39

"Witness the scene day by day; a boundless scene of hill and dale, mountain and valley, with their sides dressed in gay and bright liveries, not in one somber-suited color, but all the variegated hues which the frosts are capable of putting upon the leaves of the different variety of trees... The pen cannot describe nor the brush of the skillful artists paint so beautiful a picture as nature has spread before us throughout this mountainous country. Man, to realize and appreciate the beauties of this chain of mountains, must first visit them. Neither can he learn them by riding over a railroad at lightning speed, or seated in a pent-up stage coach, catching a glance at their summits now and then, (but only by) seeking their most prominent cliffs and projections, for views (of) the beautiful valleys beneath. Time is also requisite—an hour, nor a day, is not sufficient to study this vast book of nature."

❖ **Lucy Crawford** ❖
History of The White Mountains
(1846)

Whitehorse and Cathedral Ledges seen from the air, with the Moat Mountains in the distance, outside of North Conway. Photograph by Ed Webster.

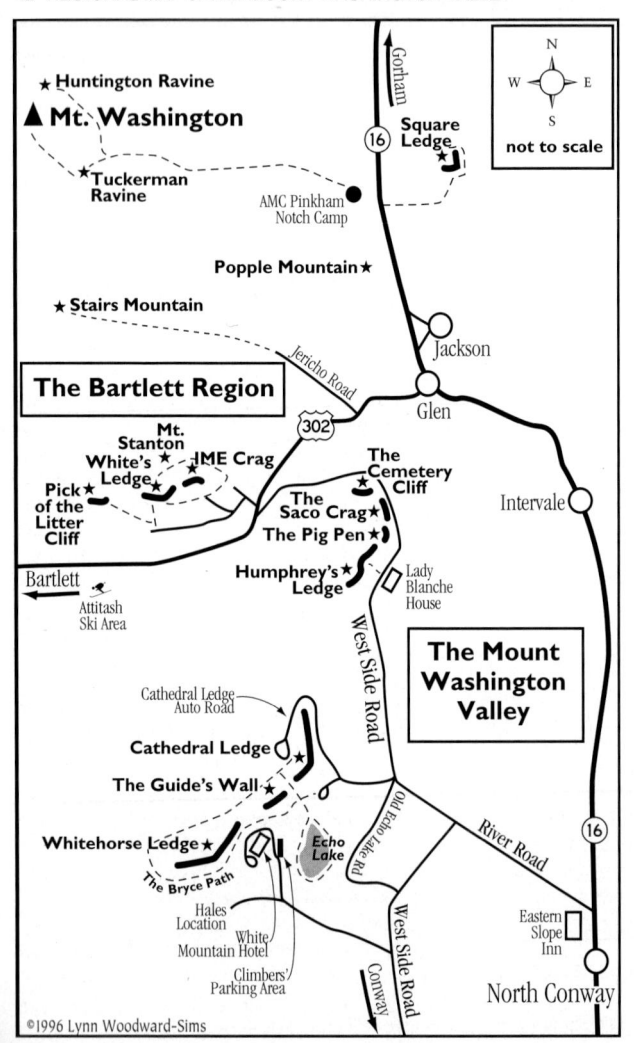

42 REGIONAL MAP of THE MOUNT WASHINGTON VALLEY

THE MOUNT WASHINGTON VALLEY

Home to Cathedral and Whitehorse Ledges, the Mount Washington Valley is one of the most popular rock climbing centers in the eastern United States. Short approaches to nearly all the climbs, solid granite, good nut and fixed protection, and a variety of classic climbs all serve to ensure the region's continued reputation. In addition to Cathedral and Whitehorse Ledges, there are several excellent smaller cliffs in the valley, including the Guide's Wall, Humphrey's Ledge, the Pig Pen, and the Saco Crag. Cathedral and Whitehorse are described first since they offer the bulk of the routes: as of this Third Edition, 520 separate climbs and variations!

The fertile Saco River valley from Conway up to Bartlett was once the home of the Pequawket Indians, who inhabited the region prior to the arrival of the first white settlers in 1764. The Indian name for the region, Pequawket, meant "Clear Valley Lands Bordered by a Crooked River", an obvious reference to the meandering Saco River, Saco being the Abenaki word for "flowing out". The town of Conway was named after an Englishman, Henry Seymour Conway. The Mount Washington Valley itself has long been recognized for its scenic beauty, its pleasing intervales or meadows, and the lofty embrace of the surrounding ledges and mountains. "North Conway almost owes its existence," a 19th century guidebook said, "to artists who find here the most lovely scenery to transfer to canvas." One could say North Conway thrives today because of vacationing, outlet shops, hiking, skiing—and rock and ice climbing—probably in that order.

Benjamin Champney (1817-1907), co-founder of North Conway's first artist colony in 1850, and one of the White Mountain School of painting's premiere landscape painters, wrote of the area's natural beauty in vibrant tones in his 1899 autobiography, *Sixty Years of Art and Artists*. "North Conway is one of the most charming places in the world to me. I have seen valleys both in this country and in Europe, but I do not recall one where more beauty is centered. The valley is broad, the mountains high, but not too high or near to block out the sunlight. The meadows or intervales are bright and fresh, broken with fields of grain and corn, giving an air of fruitfulness and abundance. Elms and maples are scattered here and there in picturesque groups, breaking the monotony of broad spaces.

"The Saco River winds through all these pleasant scenes, adding the charm of its silvery ripples to the picture. The Saco Valley is beautiful... but nowhere in its course is there so much to admire as from just above Intervale down through North Conway. If one was a poet, no more charming scene could be found to inspire a pastoral. Echo Lake beyond the river is a gem set in exquisite surroundings, reflecting Cathedral and Whitehorse Ledges like a mirror. And when the day is calm, the cliffs repeat the voice or horn many times with added softness and melody.

"These ledges are very grand and noble objects, too. Their height is overpowering as one stands at their base gazing upward. Moat Mountain beyond these grand cliffs is a marked feature in the general view. One learns to love its outlines and changing light and shade as the scene moves on, or when it is partly shadowed by the clouds; or again, when the clouds pass over it in heavy masses, leaving some points visible, and others lost in charming mystery. In truth, Moat Mountain is... quite as interesting as Mt. Washington and its lofty brothers which are seen at a greater distance."

Pastoral scene with Whitehorse & Cathedral Ledges. Photo by Ed Webster.

The cliffs stay wet until mid April (watch for falling ice blocks!), but spring climbing is pleasant until the black flies and mosquitoes come out in mid May and June. Although summers are hot and humid, the days are long, and mornings and evenings stay cool and pleasant for climbing. September and October are the best months for rock climbing. Autumn's invigorating temperatures and nature's tapestry of foliage colors make the autumn the finest season for climbing on any of the crags, except up on Mt. Washington where winter's snow and ice are just a month away.

CATHEDRAL & WHITEHORSE LEDGES

Cathedral and Whitehorse Ledges, New Hampshire's two most popular cliffs, have been climbed upon ever since 1928 when Robert L. M. Underhill, Herbert C. Towle, and A. J. Holden, Jr., made their first attempt on STANDARD ROUTE on Whitehorse Ledge. Cathedral Ledge was climbed by its own STANDARD ROUTE in 1931 by Leland W. Pollock, Payson T. Newton, & Robert L. M. Underhill. Whitehorse STANDARD was finally free climbed in its entirety in 1932 by an AMC team led by Pollock, while a year later, William P. Allis freed Cathedral Ledge's STANDARD ROUTE when he added the difficult DIRECT START.

Fortunately for posterity—and for rock climbers—the environmental movement began early in North Conway, and Cathedral and Whitehorse Ledges stand today much as they have stood for all millenniums past. In 1899, afraid that the owner of Cathedral Ledge, Richard H. Davis, might quarry some of the cliff (a small amount of quarrying was done below Mordor Wall), twenty-two summer visitors and residents from Center Conway on up to Jackson raised $1,000 and bought the land the cliff is on. A year later, a similar fund-gathering effort collected enough money to purchase Whitehorse Ledge from John H. Smith. Both cliffs were then deeded to a Dr. Merriman, who in turn "conveyed the ledges to the state by deed" on April 10, 1901—and saved these beautiful, glacially-sculpted, granite cliffs for future generations to marvel at, enjoy, and climb upon.

Today, both Cathedral and Whitehorse Ledges lie within the boundaries and jurisdiction of Echo Lake State Park, approximately three miles to the west of the town of North Conway. Two important Echo Lake State Park regulations concern climbers. The Cathedral Ledge auto road leading to the summit of the cliff technically closes at 6 PM (although particularly on long summer evenings, the gate does stay open until dusk), so be wary of leaving your car parked at the turnaround on top of the cliff while you're off doing a quick evening climb, or you might get locked in. Secondly, no fires or camping is allowed below either Cathedral or Whitehorse Ledges. Please camp at a private or in a State Forest Service campground.

PEREGRINE FALCON ALERT

The New Hampshire Fish & Game Department requests the full cooperation of all rock climbers in their effort to re-establish one of nature's most elegant birds of prey, the peregrine falcon, back to its natural habitat. Peregrine falcons are a federally listed endangered species and are being closely monitored by the NH Peregrine Falcon Recovery Group who is working to restore a healthy, breeding population of peregrine falcons to the White Mountain region. In the past 10 years, mating pairs of peregrines have once again begun to nest on several White Mountain cliffs. Peregrine falcons, however, choose their own nesting sites each year, and where they lived last year may or may not be where they nest the following season. In recent years, peregrine falcons have nested at both Cathedral and Whitehorse Ledges—hence the importance of reading the seasonal cliff closure notices!

> **ALL ROCK CLIMBING SHOULD BE AVOIDED ON ALL OF THE LISTED CLOSED CLIFFS** during the peregrine nesting season which extends from **APRIL 1ST UNTIL THE END OF JULY** each year, until further notice.
> ❖ Thank you for your attention to this important program! ❖

THE BRYCE PATH

HIKING TO THE TOP OF THE LEDGES: The summits of Cathedral and Whitehorse are conveniently reached, or descended from, by way of the Bryce Path. This well-used trail was laid out in 1907 by James Bryce (later Viscount Bryce), British ambassador to America and an early president of the Alpine Club in England. To hike up to the top of either Cathedral or Whitehorse Ledge, start on either of the following two trails:

- From The White Mountain Hotel parking lot, hike north (right) through the woods below the Whitehorse Slabs along a trail for several minutes to a clearing, or:
- You may also reach this clearing from the dirt road that forks left before the base of Cathedral Ledge. Park, then continue walking along the dirt road through the woods to the clearing.
- From the right side of the clearing, the Bryce Path now leads to the west up a steep hill to the forested saddle between the two ledges where well-blazed trails lead to either summit. Turn left to hike to the top of the Guide's Wall and Whitehorse Ledge, or go right to hike up to the summit of Cathedral Ledge, the tourist lookout, and the auto road turnaround.

CATHEDRAL LEDGE

Formerly known as Hart's Ledge or Hart's Looking Glass as the cliff was easily seen from Hart's Tavern just across the road, Cathedral Ledge has long been one of North Conway's most majestic and often visited landmarks. *The White Mountains: A Guidebook For Travelers*, published in 1876, offers this poetic description of the formation that eventually gave the cliff its name: "An easy climb carries one to a singular cavity in this ledge, which visitors have named 'The Cathedral'. And truly the waters, frosts, and storms that scooped and grooved its curves and niches seemed to have combined in frolic mimicry of Gothic art. The cave is 40 feet in depth and about 60 feet in height, and the outermost rock of the roofing spans the entrance with an arch, which, half of the way, is as symmetrical as if an architect had planned it... The front of the recess is shaded with trees, which kindly stand apart just enough to frame off Mt. Kiarsage (sic) in lovely symmetry—so that a more romantic resting place for an hour or two on a warm afternoon can hardly be imagined." Indeed, legend has it that a marriage took place under the Cathedral Roof in about 1880.

Cathedral Ledge offers a wide variety of rock climbs, everything from moderate free routes to 5.13 desperates, plus several spectacular aid climbs. The Conway granite forming the ledge was dramatically quarried during the last glacial period, the Wisconsin Glaciation, which reached its climax 18,000 to 20,000 years ago. The subsequent weathering of the cliff surface makes for wonderfully diverse climbing, running the gamut from thin face routes to all widths of jam cracks. The climbs are now described from left to right, beginning with the Barber Wall (Upper Left Wall) situated above the REFUSE tree ledge on the cliff's left-hand side.

Climbers should be aware of bottles, cans, and rocks that tourists are prone to toss off the top of Cathedral Ledge from the fenced overlook on the summit. Be particularly alert when climbing between REFUSE and THE PROW, and on the THIN AIR Face.

DRIVING TO CATHEDRAL LEDGE: When driving north on Route 16 through North Conway, turn left at the stoplight just after (north of) the Eastern Slope Inn onto the River Road. Follow this to the T junction with the West Side Road, and continue straight ahead through open fields, then turn left (sign) into the chalet development beneath Cathedral Ledge. Climbers customarily park along either side of the road beneath the cliff, near the Cote Boulder (on your left, hidden in the woods), or farther along the road, on both sides, or below the Practice Slab for routes on Cathedral's North End. Just beyond the pullouts for the Practice Slab is the steel gate at the base of the Cathedral Ledge auto road.

THE APPROACH & DESCENT: The approaches to climbs on Cathedral are typically short and leisurely. You may also want to park at the turnaround at the top of the auto road, then hike right and down (facing out) for climbs on the Barber Wall (Upper Left Wall), or around to your left (facing out) to circle around the right-hand side of the AIRATION Buttress. To descend from the top of Cathedral Ledge, hitch-hike or walk down the auto road, or hike down the trail circling around the cliff's right-hand (northern) end.

THE BARBER WALL

Cathedral Ledge's Upper Left Wall, by popular usage, has been renamed in honor of Henry Barber—who did so much to advance the standards of worldwide free climbing, and who made several of his first important free ascents here on this renowned wall. To approach the Barber Wall from the top of the cliff, drive to the top of the auto road, park at the turnaround, and walk out towards the fenced, tourist overlook. Hike to your right (facing out) through the woods staying a ways back from the cliff edge, then look for a fairly obvious trail that descends to your right down a dirt gully and circles around the far, left end of the Barber Wall and onto a large tree ledge. The first major route, NUTCRACKER, is the farthest left vertical crack of the Barber Wall's many prominent crack systems.

ALPHA AREA I 5.9 R
One of Cathedral's most obscure climbs. Finding it is probably the crux. Locate a broken bulge at the extreme left end of the Barber Wall, about 100 feet left of NUTCRACKER.
1. Surmount the bulge and climb up a slab to the top. 40', 5.9 R
HISTORY: Ajax Greene & Rob Taylor made the first ascent on September 30, 1973. Due to poor protection, dirt, and moss, the leader used a top-rope for the last move.

FAULT LINE I 5.11b
Start from a small terrace at the very left-hand end of the Barber Wall. Look for a single bolt protecting a 20 foot face beneath a small ledge with a tree.
1. Face climb up a narrow, white streak in brown rock (bolt; 5.11b) to a small ledge with a pine tree on the left. Finish straight up a short face past one more bolt to the top. 40', 5.11b
FA: Gerry Lortie & Bill Lowther October 15, 1994

ALPHA CORNER I 5.9+
A worthwhile climb, the right-facing corner 50 feet left of NUTCRACKER, the most easily identifiable vertical crack on the Barber Wall's left side.
1. Climb the awkward corner, step right, and layback up a flake to reach the pine tree growing at the top of the cliff. 60', 5.9+

Henry Barber starting the first pitch of Women In Love (5.11d) in 1978 on the route's first free ascent. Photograph by Ed Webster.

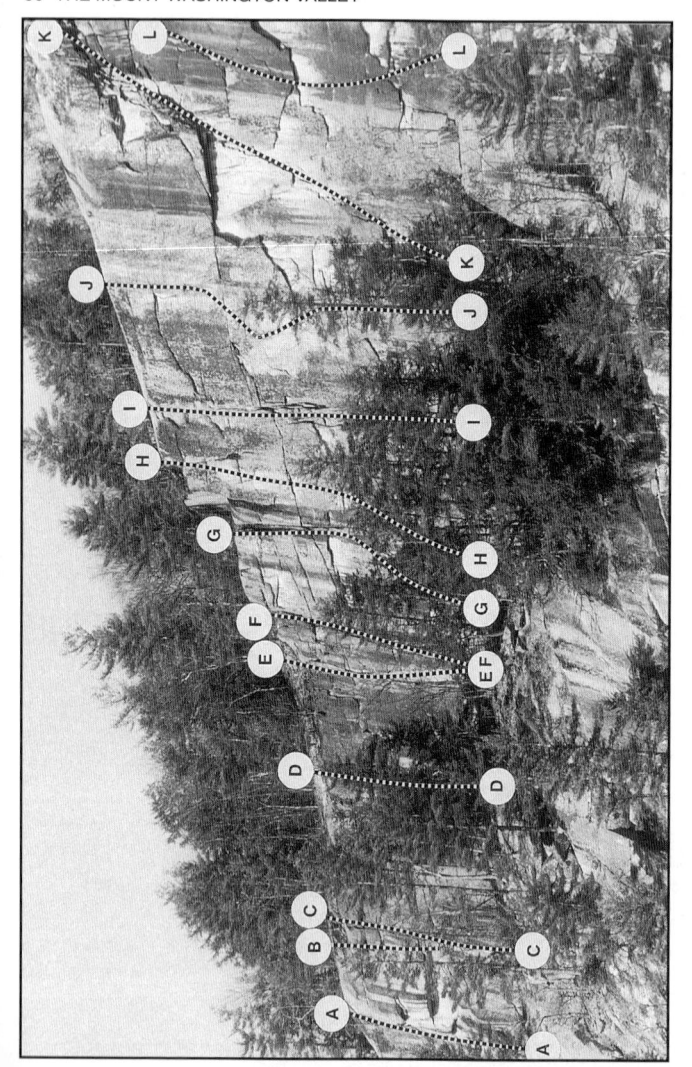

50 THE MOUNT WASHINGTON VALLEY

CATHEDRAL LEDGE – THE BARBER WALL

A.		ALPHA CORNER I 5.9+	Page	48
B.	*	DRESDEN I 5.10d	Page	53
C.	***	NUTCRACKER I 5.9+	Page	53
D.	*	DOUBLE VEE I 5.9+	Page	56
E.	**	CHICKEN DELIGHT I 5.9	Page	56
F.	*	LAYTON'S ASCENT I 5.9	Page	56
G.	**	NOMAD CRACK I 5.10b	Page	56
H.	***	GRAVEROBBER I 5.11d	Page	58
I.	*	THE GRIM REAPER I 5.10d R	Page	58
J.	**	HOMICIDAL MANIAC I 5.11d	Page	59
K.		ASYLUM I 5.11a	Page	59
L.		QUESTION OF ETHICS I 5.10d	Page	59

HISTORY: The Alpha Club is an English Lake District rock climbing club that Paul Ross temporarily reactivated in New Hampshire. Two American members, Henry Barber & John Bragg, did the first ascent on March 24, 1973.

VARIATION: **BETA WAY** I 5.9

Better get some extra beta for this route!

1a. On ALPHA CORNER, don't step off to the right, but continue straight up the corner to a mantleshelf move and a quartz dike. 60', 5.9

FA: Kurt Winkler & Barry Moore July, 1978

Henry Barber leading Alpha Corner (5.9+) in 1976. Photo by Paul Ross.

TREMORS I 5.11d or 5.12b (*)

Begin just to the right of ALPHA CORNER, and left of NUTCRACKER. If you exit left at the top, avoiding the route's final crux, the grade is 5.11d.

1. Climb up a slab to reach several, steep flakes (piton) at the left end of an overlap. Face climb past two bolts (5.11d) to a stance, then escape up and left, or finish up and right over a bulge (bolt; 5.12b) to a double bolt anchor on top. 60', 5.11d or 5.12b

HISTORY: Bill Lowther & Jon Sykes did the first ascent with one aid point on the top bulge on October 10, 1994. After top-roping the route, Gerry Lortie & Tim Kemple made the first free ascent on November 20, 1994.

CATHEDRAL LEDGE - THE BARBER WALL (NUTCRACKER) 53

DRESDEN I 5.10d (5.7 R) (*)
Strenuous. The original line climbed the unprotected slab (5.7 R) below and to the left of the upper finger crack, however most parties now prefer to climb the first half of NUTCRACKER, step left at the horizontal break, and finish up the DRESDEN finger crack. Normal rack.
1. Jam up the short, testing, vertical finger crack (5.10d) just to the left of the top section of NUTCRACKER. 75', 5.10d

HISTORY: Ed Webster & Jim Dunn made the first ascent of the climb on July 18, 1976—with Dunn following in bare feet, the traditional climbing technique used in Dresden, Germany.

Jim Dunn on Dresden's first ascent (5.10d) in 1976. Photo: Ed Webster collection.

VARIATION: **DRESDEN DIRECT** I 5.11a R or X
The Real Dresden! Although usually top-roped, this very serious face climb has been led. Dubious wired nuts protect the crux, so beware!
1a. Climb up the face just to the left of NUTCRACKER, moving up and left (5.11a R or X) onto the slab leading up to the horizontal break, then step back right into the upper DRESDEN finger crack. 35', 5.11a R or X
FA: Henry Barber, Rob DeConto, & Polly DeConto Autumn, 1985

NUTCRACKER I 5.9+ (***)
One of Cathedral Ledge's best climbs, the striking finger and hand crack at the left end of the Barber Wall. Well protected and popular.
1. Climb the superb, vertical crack system (5.9+) to a horizontal break, then hand jam straight up to the top. 75', 5.9+

HISTORY: Joe Cote, Dick Arey, & Ward Freeman aid climbed the first ascent in May, 1969. Henry Barber & Bob Anderson accomplished the route's first free ascent on September 22, 1972. "Bob and I were both climbing pretty seriously back then," remembered Henry Barber. "We'd never aided any of the climbs on the wall, we just walked up there, and thought: 'These'll go free.' And then we free climbed them."

ONE STEP BEYOND I 5.12a (5.11a R or X)
Deception? Start 20 feet to the right of NUTCRACKER, and just to the left of a large pine tree. To lead the route, poor protection demands top-rope rehearsal, a modern rack, and double ropes. A popular testpiece—but only when securely belayed from above!

1. Start up the left-hand of two thin, vertical seams (RP nuts; but still 5.11a R or X), then step up and left to a horizontal break and your first real protection. Continue face climbing up to and past a small flake (bolt; 5.12a), making several mantle moves to the top. 75', 5.12a (5.11a R or X) If you choose to top-rope the route, a considerably safer option, you can start the route more easily up the appealing, black face just to the right of NUTCRACKER.

HISTORY: After previously top-roping the route, Andy Ross & Chris Gill made the first ascent in August, 1988, using "Gunks-style tactics": namely by protecting the initial seam with RP nuts using one rope, plus running a second rope anchored high up in the nearby pine tree. "After getting grief for placing a bolt on the sacred Barber Wall, I wanted to add another bolt at the start of the route, but I also didn't need the hassle," admitted Ross.

LAWN DARTS I 5.11c (5.9 X)
You're gonna bounce on the lawn if you fall off this route. Start 25 feet to the left of DOUBLE VEE. The route is very seldom climbed due to extremely poor protection, lichen, and moss. At the start, however, you can also begin up JOLT to make the climb somewhat safer. Prior top-roping recommended!

1. Begin at a pocket and head up the steep, blank face past an invisible fixed piton to the top of the cliff—and safety. 65', 5.11c (5.9 X)

FA: Chris Gill & Andy Ross August, 1988

JOLT I 5.12a (*)
Rev up on a few espressos before trying this one! Start 10 feet to the left of DOUBLE VEE. A popular route, with great protection—and a fingery crux.

1. Face climb up a black streak using good horizontal edges, finishing past three bolts with some very thin, technical face moves (5.12a) up to a good ledge. Move left along the ledge, and up to the top. 65', 5.12a

HISTORY: After placing the three protection bolts on rappel, Joe Lentini & Dennis Goode made the first ascent on June 7, 1992.

CATHEDRAL LEDGE - THE BARBER WALL (JOLT) 55

Joe Lentini at the crux of Jolt (5.12a) in 1995, belayed by Dennis Goode. Photograph by Ed Webster.

DOUBLE VEE I 5.9+ (*)
Locate two, short flaring corners stacked one atop the other, to the right of NUTCRACKER. Small wired nuts and cams are very helpful.
1. The crux is gaining the first V groove, but the top flare is also tricky. 75', 5.9+
FA: Sam Streibert, John Reppy, & Harold May   September, 1963
FFA: Bob Anderson & Henry Barber   September 22, 1972

OFF THE HOOK I 5.11c (*)
The improbable wall 10 feet to the right of DOUBLE VEE. Stick clip the first bolt, and bring small wired nuts for the final, thin crack.
1. Face climb past a narrow overlap to a good hold (bolt), then past two more bolts (5.11c crux at second bolt) to a ledge. Finish up a vertical seam. 75', 5.11c
FA: Tom Callaghan & Steve Wooding   August, 1988

CHICKEN DELIGHT I 5.9 (**)
Ascends the left-hand of two diverging sister cracks which form a perfect V on the wall 100 feet to the right of NUTCRACKER.
1. After a strenuous start finger jamming up a sustained crack to a rest, a bolt protects a long reach to a handhold which has delighted many. 75', 5.9
FA: Joe Cote & Dick Arey   April, 1969
FFA: Henry Barber & Bob Anderson   September 22, 1972

VARIATION: FOR CHICKENS ONLY I 5.9
1a. Climb the crux of CHICKEN DELIGHT to the rest, step left, and climb the left-hand parallel crack system to the top. 35', 5.9
FA: Mack Johnson & Brian Dutton   June 22, 1986

LAYTON'S ASCENT I 5.9 (*)
The sister climb of CHICKEN DELIGHT, the right-hand crack.
1. Layback and jam up the steep, strenuous crack system. 80', 5.9
HISTORY: Joe Cote & John Merrill made the climb's first ascent in June, 1969, and named the route for Cote's newborn son, Layton. Henry Barber & Bob Anderson free climbed the route on September 23, 1972.

BIG DEAL ROCK CLIMB I 5.12a (*)
Begin five feet to the right of LAYTON'S ASCENT below a thin, right-slanting seam. Modern rack. Strenuous—and seldom repeated.
1. Above a flake, climb up the seam (bolt), then up the steep, sustained face above (5.12a) past several more bolts and two horizontal cracks. 90', 5.12a
FA: Chris Gill   July, 1990

NOMAD CRACK I 5.10b (**)
Begin 20 feet right of LAYTON'S ASCENT. Awkward and strenuous!
1. Undercling up a thin, challenging, right-diagonalling crack (5.10b). After the crack widens, climb more easily up to the finish. 90', 5.10b

CATHEDRAL LEDGE - THE BARBER WALL (NOMAD CRACK) 57

Dave Rose finishing off the crux of Nomad Crack (5.10b) in 1983.
Photograph by S. Peter Lewis.

FA: Joe Cote & Larry Poorman March, 1970
FFA: Henry Barber & Bob Anderson September 23, 1972

GRAVEROBBER I 5.11d (★★★)
Start 15 feet right of NOMAD CRACK at the bottom of the WANDERER finger crack. Extremely sustained moves at the bolts. Bring a normal rack with extra medium sized Friends.

1. Climb the WANDERER finger crack (5.10d), then face climb up the cleaned streak of rock above past several bolts, over a bulge (5.11d), and up another finger crack. Move right, and finish up a short, vertical hand crack that parallels NOMAD CRACK on the right up to a big pine tree. 110', 5.11d

HISTORY: In the Summer of 1977, Ed Webster & Peter Williams climbed WANDERER as a variation start to NOMAD CRACK. Andy Ross & Chris Gill made the first complete ascent of the route in July, 1990.

Steve Wunsch on the first free ascent of The Grim Reaper (5.10d R) in 1974. Photograph by Paul Ross.

THE GRIM REAPER I 5.10d R (★)
The route's fearsome reputation has barely diminished, although camming units do offer significantly better protection that a rack of Hexes! The scythe is sharpest at the top. Modern rack. Begin near the middle of the prominent traverse ledge 35 feet to the right of NOMAD CRACK.

1. Climb round-edged vertical cracks up the center of a relentlessly steep wall. Save your strength for the final insecure moves (5.10d R) which are the technical and psychological crux. 130', 5.10d R

HISTORY: After cleaning the route on rappel, Henry Barber & Bob Anderson made the first ascent on September 27, 1972. Fortunately, they left their rappel rope in place. Inches from success, Barber fell and grabbed the rope, fearing a groundfall. In 1974, John Bragg & Steve Wunsch made the second and first free ascent, also taking several falls prior to success.

CATHEDRAL LEDGE - THE BARBER WALL (LICHEN DELIGHT)

HOMICIDAL MANIAC I 5.11d (**)
Bring a bulletproof vest. Start 30 feet right of GRIM REAPER. Modern rack!
1. Face climb past a bolt, climb up cracks until they end (bolt), then move left across a cleaned face to a belay in the horizontal crack above. 90', 5.11d
2. Traverse right and climb the outside edge of a small, left-facing corner past two bolts to "dicey gear" and the top. 60', 5.11c
FA: Chris Gill & Greg McCausland   October 5, 1987

ASYLUM I 5.11a
Appeals to the lunatic fringe. The climb ascends the left-hand of two, right-diagonalling dikes to the right of THE GRIM REAPER and HOMICIDAL MANIAC. Intimidating, but surprisingly well protected. Modern rack.
1. After a deceptively easy start, struggle up a shallow, very awkward, right-facing corner (5.11a), and belay at any of several stances in the upper dike. 150', 5.11a If you have a 165 foot rope, run it out to the top of the cliff.
FA: John Bragg & Jeff Pheasant   September 17, 1973

QUESTION OF ETHICS I 5.10d
The right-hand dike offers an intricate, boulder problem crux.
1. Climb up a series of ledges just to the left of LICHEN DELIGHT to an overlap (5.8). Face climb past two bolts (5.10d) into the upper dike, which is climbed with poor protection to the finish. 130', 5.10d
HISTORY: Bolts drilled on rappel to protect this and other new climbs in the area prompted the infamous 1979 "Spanish Inquisition" when local climbers re-evaluated—and at that meeting rejected—protecting routes with rappel placed bolts. Steve Larson & Jim Dunn made the first ascent in June, 1979.

LICHEN DELIGHT I 5.11a (***)
A classic and historic free climb, this was New Hampshire's first 5.11. Start below a left-facing dihedral capped by a roof to the right of ASYLUM and QUESTION OF ETHICS. Well protected. Bring a normal rack.
1. Hand jam up the corner to an alcove below the roof. Step right into strenuous, thin finger cracks (5.11a), and jam straight up to a good ledge. 110', 5.11a
2. Finish up the left of two grooves, same as QUESTION OF ETHICS. 50'
FA: Dave Cilley & Sibylle Hechtel   July 22, 1971
FFA: Henry Barber with Al Rubin   October 21, 1972

VARIATION #1: LICHEN IT A LOT I 5.10d (**)
This very popular, slightly easier variation avoids the route's regular crux.
1a. Above the first alcove, undercling left out the roof into the narrow, left-facing corner rising above. Finish up this dihedral. 100', 5.10d
HISTORY: Bryan Delaney & Jeff Pheasant climbed the first ascent of this securely protected, well-travelled variation in the Summer of 1976.

60 THE MOUNT WASHINGTON VALLEY

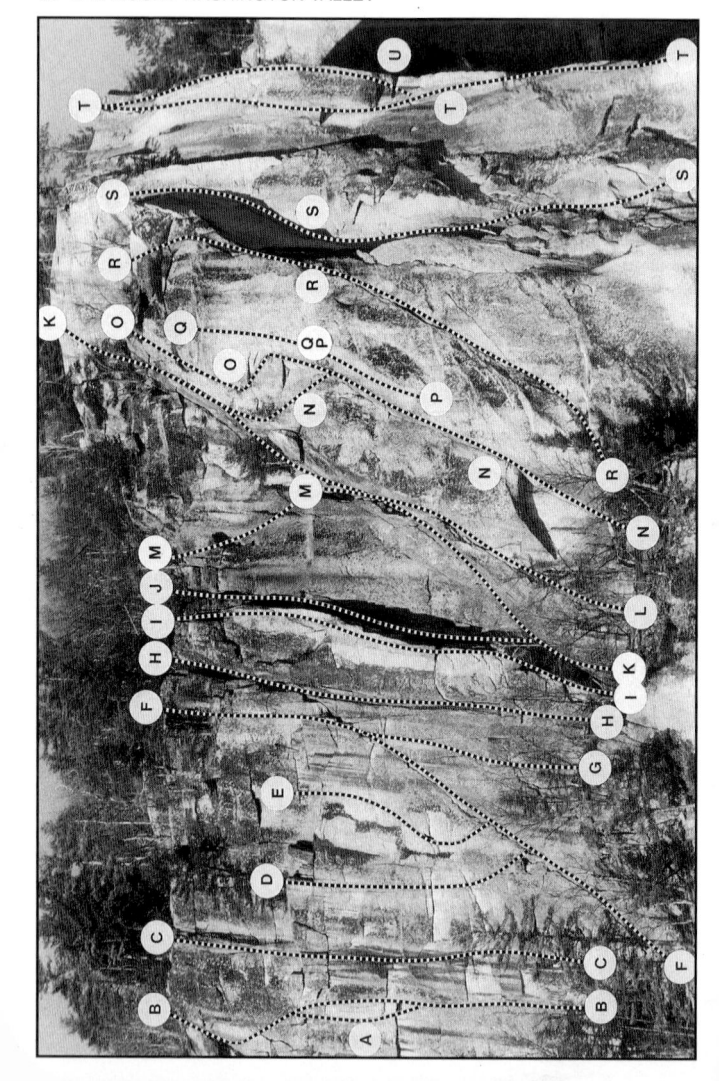

CATHEDRAL LEDGE
(LICHEN DELIGHT to EDGE OF THE WORLD)

A. **	LICHEN IT A LOT I 5.10d	Page 59		K. ***	UPPER REFUSE I 5.5	Page 66
B. ***	LICHEN DELIGHT I 5.11a	Page 59		L. ***	BLACK LUNG I 5.8	Page 67
C. *	RECONCILIATION II 5.11d (5.11a R)	Page 62		M. *	FINAL GESTURE I 5.7+	Page 67
D.	MEDUSA II 5.12b	Page 62		N. ***	THE BOOK OF SOLEMNITY II 5.9+	Page 68
E. *	HATFUL OF HOLLOW I 5.12a	Page 62		O. *	WEBSTER'S UNABRIDGED I 5.11a	Page 68
F. ***	RETALIATION II 5.9	Page 62		P. *	FOOL'S GOLD I 5.10d	Page 68
G. *	YOUTH CHALLENGE II 5.10d	Page 64		Q. **	BAD DOGS I 5.12d	Page 70
H. ***	CHOCKLINE II 5.10d	Page 64		R. ***	WOMEN IN LOVE II 5.12a (or Clean A2)	Page 90
I. **	THE ARETE I 5.11b R	Page 65		S. ***	RECOMPENSE III 5.9	Page 96
J.	BLACK CRACK I 5.10b R	Page 66		T. ***	THE PROW III 5.11d (or 5.7, Clean A2)	Page 103
				U. ***	EDGE OF THE WORLD I 5.13c	Page 106

VARIATION #2: **THE DIRECT FINISH** I 5.10b
2a. Above the belay, climb a finger crack over a bulge. 5.10b
FA: Doug Madara & Kim Smith late 1970s

RECONCILIATION II 5.11d (5.11a R) (*)
A serious free climb embodying both difficulty and danger. Ascends the crack system immediately to the right of LICHEN DELIGHT. Modern rack. Carry many small wired nuts for the crux and a #4 Friend for Pitch two. The more effort you spend placing protection, the safer the climb is.
1. Climb up a detached block. From its top, finger traverse left with poor protection (5.11a R) and gain a vertical finger/hand crack (5.11d). Clip a bolt, then climb up an easier V groove to a good belay ledge. 120', 5.11d (5.11a R)
2. Follow the strenuous 5.10d finger crack above to the top. 40', 5.10d
HISTORY: Dave Cilley & Tom Beranger did the first ascent on April 18, 1970. Ed Webster cleaned the route on rappel and attempted it free in 1976. On October 9, 1983, Dave Rose & Tom Nonis freed Pitch two. Neil Cannon with Peter Lewis made the first free ascent on October 20, 1983.

MEDUSA II 5.12b
Sooner or later they all go free! Begin on the small, tree-covered ledge up and to the right of RETALIATION, the prominent, right-diagonalling crack.
1. Climb up and left across RETALIATION to a stance (bolt). Continue straight up a steep wall by side-by-side bolts, then past a seam to a poorly-placed bolt. Move left into a hand crack, climb it to a ledge, then jam a 5.10 crack on the left to reach a tree ledge. 130', 5.12b
2. Finish up a wide crack (5.8) on the right past a birch tree. 50', 5.8
HISTORY: Ed Webster & Dave Linden did the first ascent on July 17, 1976, using three bolts from an old attempt. After two afternoons of effort, Jim Surette with Steve Larson made the first free ascent in September, 1986.

HATFUL OF HOLLOW I 5.12a (*)
Ascends the steep, cleaned-off stripe of rock between MEDUSA and RETALIATION. More extreme face moves! Normal rack.
1. Climb the first pitch of RETALIATION, and belay at a stance. 60', 5.6
2. Face climb up and left past three bolts (5.11d) to a horizontal ledge (bolt), mantleshelf, then move right. Sustained face climbing leads past three more bolts (5.12a) to a ledge with a pine. Rap off the tree with two ropes. 75', 5.12a
HISTORY: After cleaning and bolting the climb on rappel, Andy Ross made the first ascent in July, 1990, doing the route in one long lead.

RETALIATION II 5.9 (***)
The long, right-diagonalling crack system 100 feet to the left of UPPER REFUSE provides a good introduction to 5.9. Awkward, but very enjoyable jamming. The route is quite popular, and protects well with a normal rack.

1. Layback and jam up the slanting crack to a belay ledge on the right. 60', 5.6
2. Follow the right-leaning crack past a bulge (5.9) and into a niche. Rest, continue up right, then step left onto a lovely belay ledge. 100', 5.9
3. A moderate crack and a short corner lead to the top of the cliff.

FA: Dave Cilley & Dean Cilley   May 2, 1970
FFA: Joe Cote & Eric Radack   October 17, 1971

Bill Bentley on Hatful Of Hollow (5.12a) in 1991. Photo by Charley Bentley.

GERIATRIC CHALLENGE I 5.10b R

Start six feet to the left of YOUTH CHALLENGE. Normal rack.

1. Climb the shallow, right-facing corner (5.10b R), with a blind wired nut placement to protect the crux move, up to a ledge with a bolt. 45', 5.10b R

2. Head up the right-hand crack (5.10a), the same crack YOUTH CHALLENGE traverses into from the left (for a grand total of 10 feet of new climbing!) to merge with YOUTH CHALLENGE, and above, RETALIATION. 80', 5.10a

3. Finish up the easy top pitch of RETALIATION.

FA: Mack Johnson & John Godfrey   July 19, 1987

YOUTH CHALLENGE II 5.10d (*)

A popular, hard 5.10 testpiece, offering intricate, well protected climbing.

1. Off the center of a small tree ledge 50 feet left of UPPER REFUSE, jam up a short, vertical finger crack (5.10d) to a good stance with a bolt. 40', 5.10d

2. Climb the left of two finger cracks, step right into its companion (5.9+), and join RETALIATION at the niche. Escape out left up to the regular RETALIATION belay. 100', 5.9+

3. Finish up the moderate final pitch of RETALIATION to the top.

HISTORY: Jim Dunn, Jane Wilson, & Ed Webster made the first ascent of the climb on September 20, 1976. A trivia question: what inspired the route's name? The slogan painted on the side of Dunn's secondhand VW bus that he'd recently bought from a Christian youth camp: "Youth Challenge Outreach. One Way, One Job."

Jim Dunn in the Youth Challenge bus in 1977. Photos by Paul Ross.

CHOCKLINE II 5.10d

A former shock line, now well protected with modern gear. Carry Friends up to a #4, plus small wired nuts. Begin just to the left of the base of THE ARETE and UPPER REFUSE. Not terribly popular.

1. Climb a hard, mossy crack (5.9) to a belay ledge. 40', 5.9

2. Make strenuous moves from an arch into a vertical crack system (5.10d) which gradually widens from fingers to fist to offwidth. Duck under a chockstone at the top, and finish up a gully. 120', 5.10d

FA: Dean Cilley & Dave Cilley   October 25, 1969
FFA: Henry Barber & John Bragg   August 19, 1973

CATHEDRAL LEDGE (THE ARETE) 65

Ed Webster leading the first ascent of The Arete (then rated 5.11b) in 1978.

THE ARETE I 5.11b R (**)
A controversial climb and now a very committing lead up the spectacular, knife sharp arete just to the left of BLACK CRACK and UPPER REFUGE. Carry a modern rack. Meditation won't hurt your chances either.

1. Stay as true to the edge of the arete as you can at first, laybacking several fragile flakes up to a peg. Make a hard move (5.10c) to a small, obvious roof, then follow thin cracks to a bolt and a stance. Face climb straight up (5.11b R) to a ledge, then follow incipient cracks (5.9 R) to the top. 165', 5.11b R

HISTORY: Paul Ross cleaned and bolted the route on rappel before Ross, Mike Heintz, & Ed Webster top-roped the climb. Webster & Ross then made the historic first ascent on September 3, 1978. In 1979, after the climb had become a famous and very frequently climbed testpiece, Paul Ross chopped all of the protection bolts following the 1979 "Spanish Inquisition" bolting debate held in North Conway. Rick Fleming & Joe Lentini subsequently replaced the crux bolt on the lead, but with aid, in 1980, pulled their rope, then did the climb from the ground up in one push. Given the current R rating, the route has never regained its former popularity, is very rarely led—and in the opinion of the author, since the crux bolt was replaced using aid, the entire climb should have all of its bolts replaced and be restored to its original condition.

BLACK CRACK I 5.10b R
The closest version of a Yosemite-style offwidth on the East Coast.
1. Jam the painfully obvious offwidth crack in the back of a large, right-facing corner above the base of the ramp on UPPER REFUSE. A peg and a bolt on the right-hand wall of the dihedral offer some hope of protection. 150', 5.10b R
HISTORY: The first ascent was made by Mike Stultz, George Eypper, & Joe Cote in July, 1970. A six inch bong was placed for protection. While not specifically used for aid, it was impossible for Stultz to completely avoid coming into contact with it. As his weight came onto the bong, it moved, and Stultz completed the lead with the sinking feeling that if he fell it might not hold. After a bolt was placed (probably on rappel) by an unknown party, Henry Barber & Dave Masury made the first free ascent in September, 1971.

REFUSAL I 5.11c
The old aid variation to BLACK CRACK goes free, but is seldom climbed.
1. Jam up the vertical finger crack (5.11c) eight feet to the right of BLACK CRACK, finishing up that route's final 5.6 chimney. 150', 5.11c
FA: Sam Streibert, John Reppy, & Harold May   September, 1963
FFA: Neil Cannon, Alison Osius, & Rob Walker   August 23, 1983

UPPER REFUSE I 5.5 (***)
This is the easiest escape route off the REFUSE tree ledge that splits the left side of Cathedral Ledge into upper and lower walls. The long ramp rising above the ledge's right end gives two or three pitches of moderate, enjoyable, and well protected face climbing. Extremely popular—and usually crowded.
1. Face climb up the right-diagonalling ramp (5.3; many variations possible) to a cozy belay stance on the right with two fixed pitons. 90', 5.3
2. Climb a V groove for 30 feet (old peg), then continue more easily to a small tree ledge. Belay here, or finish up either the corner/crack on the left (5.6), or the exposed arete and finger crack (5.5) on the right. Both finishes reach a good ledge with a two piton anchor. 100', 5.5 or 5.6
3. Walk off left, or climb any of several additional, short pitches to reach the tourist lookout on top of the cliff. The most popular finish takes an easy line up a flake and a short slab up the final outcrop to the tourist lookout. 45', 5.4
HISTORY: Yale University climbers R. S. G. Hall, Walter Spofford, & Merrill apparently made the first ascent of this popular route in 1935.

VARIATION: **HAPPILY EVER AFTER** I 5.6
This variation ascends the obvious, shallow corner/crack on the left side of the UPPER REFUSE ramp. A useful bypass—with a happy ending, hopefully!
1. Climb a little ways up the ramp on UPPER REFUSE, step just left to the corner and crack, follow it over a steep section (5.6), then continue up to the

pine tree belay near the top of UPPER REFUSE. 125', 5.6
FA: Unknown.

BLACK LUNG I 5.8 (***)
One of Cathedral's best intermediate free climbs, with a strenuous, but well protected crux—if you can just hang on. Immediately to the right of UPPER REFUSE is a prominent, right-diagonalling jam crack. Bring a normal rack.
1. Climb the crack. The hardest moves are up a short, awkward headwall near the top. Belay halfway up UPPER REFUSE at the two piton anchor. 90', 5.8
FA: Henry Barber, Dave Cilley, & Frank Dean October 1, 1972

FINAL GESTURE I 5.7+ (*)
Normally used as a finish to BLACK LUNG. Semi-popular. Large gear.
1. From the middle belay stance on UPPER REFUSE, continue up the ramp for about 40 feet, then step left (peg) and climb an awkward, overhanging crack up the right side of a large block. Belay on top of the block (large nuts needed), or higher up, in the woods. 60', 5.7+
FA: Paul Ross & Ajax Greene April 27, 1974

END OF STORY I 5.11c
Located between FINAL GESTURE and LAST GASP. RP nuts and other small wired nuts give surprisingly good protection. Normal rack.
1. Begin as for FINAL GESTURE, then continue up a very thin crack past a bolt (5.11c), over an overhang, to the top. 60', 5.11c
FA: Andy Ross, Terry Young, & Jerry Handren July, 1989

LAST GASP I 5.10d R
Thirty feet above FINAL GESTURE is a short, left-leaning groove.
1. Make awkward moves with tricky protection up the groove past two fixed pitons to the top. 35', 5.10d R
HISTORY: The pitons were placed in the late 1970s by Bryan Delaney, who never finished the route. Tom Callaghan & Peter Lewis made the first ascent of the climb on August 30, 1983.

THE SCENIC ROUTE I 5.8 (5.7 R)
A useful climb, especially during rush hour on UPPER REFUSE.
1. Climb just right of BLACK LUNG around the left-hand edge of the roof on THE JOKE BOOK up good holds past a tiny ledge to a larger one. Follow a thin crack up right, then merge with BLACK LUNG to the belay stance and two piton anchor on UPPER REFUSE. 90', 5.8
2. Staying to the right of UPPER REFUSE, face climb up the low-angled arete on the right past a wide crack at the top of THE BOOK, keeping as close to the edge as possible, to the top. 100', 5.8
FA: Mack Johnson & Chris Noonan May 22, 1979

THE BOOK OF SOLEMNITY II 5.9+ (***)

A great line and an all-time New Hampshire classic, with a famous first pitch, a spacious belay ledge, and the superb upper dihedral. With sticky rubber, the route is "only" 5.9+, the traditional grade for this route! Immediately to the right of UPPER REFUSE is a beautiful open book that starts above the right-hand end of the REFUSE tree ledge.

1. Make increasingly difficult moves up the dihedral to the first roof, face climbing past three pitons (5.9+) around the roof's right edge to a large and comfortable belay ledge on the right with a double bolt anchor. 65', 5.9+

2. Climb the upper dihedral. When it ends (peg), make a tricky traverse left (5.9+), low or high, to better holds. Finish easily up REFUSE. 110', 5.9+

HISTORY: Broken glass, dirt, and lichen made the first ascent of this route, all climbed and cleaned on the lead, quite difficult. On August 22, 1971, Joe Cote, Sibylle Hechtel (who later made the first all-female ascent of El Cap), & Steve Arsenault succeeded on Pitch one. According to Hechtel, Cote had cleaned a peace sign in the lichen in one spot, and the original working title for the route was "Joe's Peace Sign Climb." On a later effort, Cote & Bob Anderson still couldn't figure out the crux traverse left on the second pitch. Not to be denied, Joe Cote & Steve Arsenault returned the next weekend, on October 30, 1971, and finally completed the first ascent of this great favorite.

VARIATION #1: THE JOKE BOOK I 5.12a

A ridiculous pitch—but no laughing matter! Bring many wired nuts.

1a. Climb the well protected, right-curving arch/roof starting by BLACK LUNG, and finishing at the crux of the first pitch of THE BOOK. 40', 5.12a

FA: Rob Adair, rope-solo   June 20, 1986
FFA: Bob Parrott with Polly DeConto   July 6, 1986

VARIATION #2: WEBSTER'S UNABRIDGED I 5.11a (*)

This difficult direct finish makes THE BOOK completely independent of REFUSE. Even with a modern rack, protection is still tricky.

2a. When THE BOOK's upper dihedral ends, step up to a small, horizontal overlap, protect, then undercling left (5.11a) into a shallow corner/flake that leads straight up to a ledge with a double ring bolt anchor. 60', 5.11a

FA: Ed Webster & Mack Johnson August, 1977

FOOL'S GOLD I 5.10d (*)

Don't be deceived by any old shiny piece of stone! Traverse right from UPPER REFUSE to reach the route's start, or begin up THE BOOK OF SOLEMNITY for a more sustained climb.

1. From the belay ledge at the top of Pitch one of THE BOOK, layback up an obvious flake to a blank wall protected by two bolts (5.10d). Belay on a small ledge with a two bolt anchor at the start of BAD DOGS. 50', 5.10d

CATHEDRAL LEDGE (THE BOOK OF SOLEMNITY) 69

Moving up to the crux 5.9+ roof on the classic first pitch dihedral of The Book Of Solemnity (5.9+) in 1986. Photograph by Ed Webster.

2. Traverse left into THE BOOK OF SOLEMNITY, which is followed farther left (5.9+) over onto REFUSE, and on up to the top. 65', 5.9+
FA: Gene Vallee, Kim Smith, & Alain Comeau June 10, 1978

BAD DOGS I 5.12d (**)
The higher you go, the harder it gets! One of Cathedral's thinnest and most difficult face climbs. Climb up to, or rappel down, to reach the belay ledge and double bolt anchor directly above FOOL'S GOLD.
1. From the belay, move left to a bulge, then follow a plumb line straight up a steep, blank face on micro holds past four bolts (5.12d). The last clip is from a difficult stance. Double ring bolt anchor on top. 50', 5.12d
FA: Bill Lutkus August 20, 1991

THE GOLDEN BOOK OF BAD DOGS I 5.10d (*)
With a name like this, what a great combination!
1. Cruise up the first pitch of THE BOOK. 65', 5.9+
2. Up FOOL'S GOLD (5.10d) to the BAD DOGS two bolt anchor. 50', 5.10d
3. Face climb past the first bolt on BAD DOGS (5.10c), then traverse off to the left, finishing up the top of THE BOOK. 65', 5.10c

THE 5.10 COMBINATION II 5.10b (*)
Another wandering and intriguing mix-up of pitches.
1. Climb VENTILATOR (5.10b) to the REFUSE tree ledge. 90', 5.10b
2. Head up the first dihedral (5.9+) on THE BOOK. 65', 5.9+
3. Start up Pitch two of WOMEN IN LOVE, but step right into the BEAST Flake, and belay on the right on RECOMPENSE. 60', 5.9
4. After the crux layback on RECOMPENSE (5.9), traverse right into GYPSY, and finish up THE PROW's top 5.10a finger crack. 100', 5.10a

THE LOWER LEFT WALL & VENTILATOR SLAB

The following routes are described from left to right across Cathedral's Lower Left Wall. Several of the cliff's best intermediate climbs such as FUNHOUSE and BOMBARDMENT are found here, in addition to a host of extremely thin (and typically very committing) face climbs that ascend the VENTILATOR Slab—the unrelenting slab between BOMBARDMENT and THREE BIRCHES. Approach from the Cathedral Ledge auto road up a good hiking trail that leads directly up to the base of THREE BIRCHES, the prominent, right-curving arch located near the center of the Lower Left Wall.

GARDEN STATE THRUWAY I 5.5
Walk horizontally left from the base of PLEASANT STREET around a small buttress to a grassy ledge at the base of a friction slab. Obscure at best.
1. Head up the cleaned-off slab to a pine tree. 5.4

2. Climb a dike diagonally right to the woods. 5.5
FA: John Bouchard & Richard Estock June, 1981

PAPILLON I 5.7+
Terra Incognita? Next to the previous climb, on the slab's left-hand side, is a 40 foot high corner capped by a six foot roof. Normal rack.
1. Climb up the corner, move right under the roof, and up to a belay. 5.7+
FA: Paul Kallows & Paul Murphy July 22, 1978

HAPPY TRAILS I 5.8 R
A good companion to its neighbors, but with longer runouts. Start at the extreme left side of the lower wall at a right-facing corner with a wide crack just left of PLEASANT STREET and BOMBARDMENT.
1. Climb the corner crack past a chockstone, step right onto a ripply dike, and follow this up the slab to a tree ledge. 70'
2. Continue up the same dike to a junction with the PLEASANT STREET arch. Pull over the arch on small holds at first (5.8) to better holds and a dike (fixed peg). Belay at a tree at the top of BOMBARDMENT. 100', 5.8 R
3. Exit easily right, or finish left (5.5) up a narrow dike. 5.5
FA: Kurt Winkler, Karen Moffat, & Polly DeConto July 17, 1981

CHICKEN LITTLE I 5.10b
Just left of PLEASANT STREET & BOMBARDMENT is a short, steep wall.
1. Face climb up the slightly overhanging wall past a piton and a bolt (5.10b) to a thin crack, then mantleshelf. Tree belay. 35', 5.10b
FA: Bill Lowther with Anna Lowther April 7, 1995

PLEASANT STREET I 5.7 (5.6 R) (*)
Very popular. Begin on a small ledge with a birch 20 feet uphill from a long horizontal ceiling and 200 feet left of THREE BIRCHES, the 30 foot arch.
1. From a horizontal crack, step right, then face climb up a narrow, faint dike (with no more protection) to an oak tree belay and ledge on the left. 50', 5.6 R
2. Layback and jam up the prominent, left-curving arch to its top, swing over it, and head up to the large, REFUSE tree-covered ledge. 100', 5.7
HISTORY: The first pitch was climbed by Joe Cote & A. J. LaFleur in August, 1972 during their first ascent of VENTILATOR. Wayne Wyman, Ned Bergman & Leo Belanger climbed the main arch on October 14, 1972.

VARIATION: **ONE WAY STREET** I 5.6
Another obscure expedition destined to lead nowhere—or up to REFUSE.
1. Above the PLEASANT STREET arch, diagonal left to a belay at blocks.
2. Climb cracks and chimney to ledges. From their left end, climb a slab left to a flaring chimney. Cracks and a gully lead to the REFUSE tree ledge.
FA: Dave Cilley, Wayne Wyman, & Gordon Bailey October 15, 1972

72 THE MOUNT WASHINGTON VALLEY

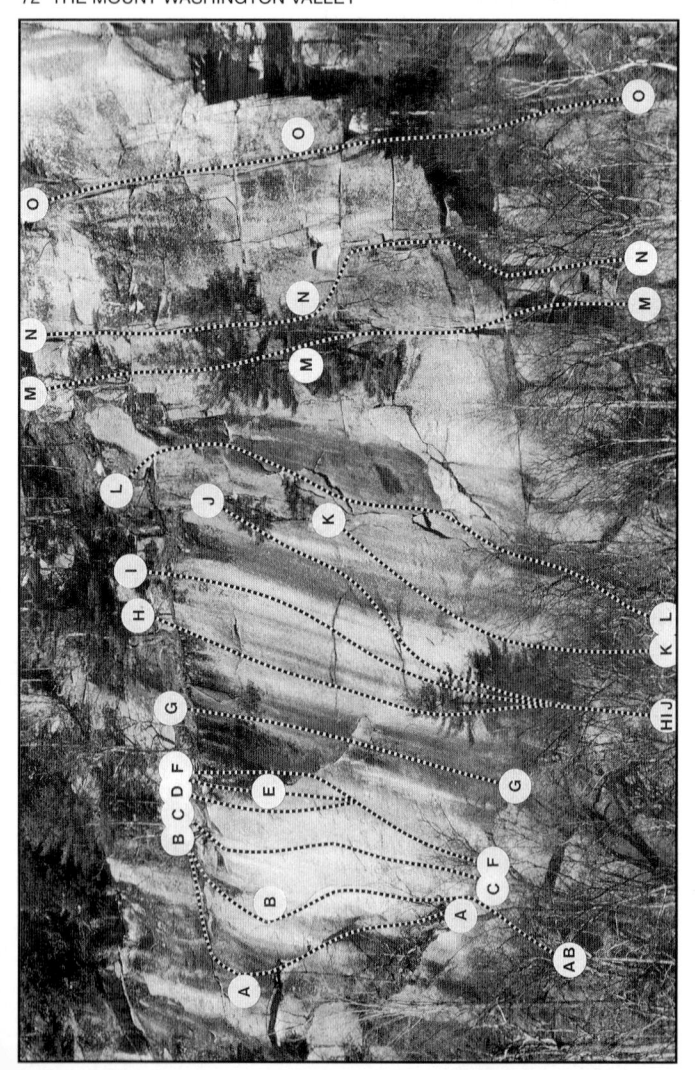

CATHEDRAL LEDGE – LOWER LEFT WALL
(The VENTILATOR Slab)

A.	*	**PLEASANT STREET** I 5.7 (5.6 R)	Page	71
B.	**	**BOMBARDMENT** I 5.8 (5.6 R)	Page	75
C.	**	**WESTERN LADY** I 5.11b	Page	75
		with **CALIFORNIA GIRLS** I 5.11d R		
D.	*	**THE POINT** I 5.10d R	Page	76
E.	*	**BARBER DIRECT** I 5.10c R	Page	76
F.	***	**VENTILATOR** I 5.10b (5.6 R)	Page	75
		HYPERVENTILATOR I 5.11d (5.10d R)	Page	76
G.		**REPO-MAN** I 5.11d	Page	77
H.	*	**EGO TRIP** I 5.11c (or 5.11b)	Page	77
I.	**	**STARFIRE** I 5.11b	Page	78
J.	*	**ONCE UPON A CLIMB** I 5.11c	Page	78
K.	*	**THREE BIRCHES** II 5.8+	Page	79
L.	**	**FUNHOUSE** I 5.7	Page	80
M.	***	**POOH** I 5.7	Page	81
N.	**	**ORC** II 5.8	Page	81

74 THE MOUNT WASHINGTON VALLEY

Jo Ann Brisson concentrating on the crux moves at the start of Ventilator (5.10b / 5.6 R) in 1990. Photograph by Jeff Fongemie.

BOMBARDMENT I 5.8 (5.6 R) (***)
Very popular, one of Cathedral's best 5.8s. A fine route for its grade with well protected, fun crack climbing, and several exciting moves. What was the "bombardier" on the first ascent? An irate squirrel! Normal rack.
1. Do the first pitch of PLEASANT STREET, the thin slab. 50', 5.6 R
2. Climb a vertical, finger and hand crack which splits the slab just to the right of and above the PLEASANT STREET arch. After the crack curves left and ends, face climb along a faint dike up to the trees. 100', 5.8
FA: Dave Cilley, rope-solo October 6, 1972

WESTERN LADY I 5.11b (**)
A thin face climb with solid runouts—and a testpiece for its grade. Ascends the smooth slab between BOMBARDMENT and VENTILATOR. Start below the left end of the long horizontal overlap.
1. Surmount the left end of the initial ceiling. 40', 5.8
2. Climb a thin finger crack just to the right of BOMBARDMENT to a very narrow overlap or eyebrow. Face climb up to the first bolt, angle a bit left to reach the second bolt, then traverse right along an incipient fracture to the easy tree ramp at the top of VENTILATOR. 90', 5.11b
HISTORY: After cleaning the route, top-roping it, and placing two bolts on rappel, Rick Fleming & Mark Frisch did the first ascent on October 24, 1977.

DIRECT FINISH: **CALIFORNIA GIRLS** I 5.11d R (*)
Not often led, for very obvious reasons! There is no protection at all.
1a. For added difficulty and danger, climb up and slightly left after WESTERN LADY's second bolt, making a long runout (5.11d R) to the trees. 45', 5.11d R
HISTORY: John Strand made the variation's first ascent on April 29, 1985, without falls—mainly due to extreme fear.

VENTILATOR I 5.10b (5.6 R) (***)
The grade of this climb has fluctuated ever since the first ascent, starting with a low of 5.9 and rising gradually to the currently accepted grade of 5.10b! Equally amazing, this challenging face climb has been led barefoot as well as in mountain boots. Except on hot humid days (when the route should definitely be avoided), this is an all-time classic slab pitch whose every move will require your undivided attention. From the base of THREE BIRCHES, walk uphill and left to reach the common starting ledge for PLEASANT STREET, BOMBARDMENT, and VENTILATOR. It's better to lead the route in one long pitch since the white birch tree at the start of the crux slab is dying.
1. Above a horizontal crack, climb the initial slab on PLEASANT STREET (5.6 R) to a narrow ledge with a white birch. Step right, then make thin, committing face moves for 12 feet (5.10b) to a hard clip into a ring bolt. Continue over a tiny eyebrow to the second bolt, then move past the third bolt, clip a

fourth bolt on the left, if desired (on THE POINT), step down slightly, then move right into a short finger crack leading to the lower, right end of a small tree ledge. 90', 5.10b Scramble up a groove or ramp to the REFUSE tree ledge.
HISTORY: Setting a precedent for other new and difficult face climbs in the White Mountains, Joe Cote & A. J. LaFleur top-roped the route, placed three bolts on rappel to protect it, and made the historic first ascent in August, 1972.

DIRECT FINISH #1: **BARBER DIRECT** I 5.10c R (*)
Both Direct Finishes to VENTILATOR involve very long runouts.
1a. From VENTILATOR's top, third bolt, face climb straight up (5.10c R), avoiding the normal finger crack finish, until finally reaching a good hold. Join the easy ramp/groove on the right. 5.10c R
FA: Henry Barber & Budge Gierke April 24, 1973

DIRECT FINISH #2: **THE POINT** I 5.10d R (*)
Risk the consequences! Makes VENTILATOR longer, more sustained, and more runout. The route avoids VENTILATOR's normal ramp finish by climbing the upper, blank slab just to the left of the BARBER DIRECT. There are two bolts: one at the variation's start, and one on the top bulge.
1b. Climb VENTILATOR to its third and last bolt, face climb left to a fourth bolt, then head straight up (5.10d R) to a thin horizontal crack on WESTERN LADY before making easier moves to the top bulge (bolt; 5.10d). 135', 5.10d R
HISTORY: John Bouchard & John Burke made the first ascent in 1984, after cleaning the route, and placing the first bolt free on the lead. Bouchard led the route first try without a top-rope ascent. In April, 1995, Bill Lowther & Gerry Lortie climbed the final bulge, and placed the top bolt also on the lead.

CUFF LINK I 5.11d R (*)
A unique combination link-up of several of the VENTILATOR slab's hardest routes. An extremely sustained pitch: go for broke!
1. Start up VENTILATOR (5.10b), then traverse left along a seam to join WESTERN LADY at its first bolt. Continue up LADY (5.11b), step left, and finish up CALIFORNIA GIRLS (5.11d R), the crux. 145', 5.11d R
HISTORY: Attempting to complete the first link-up, Tom Callaghan fell from the final hard move, plunging at least 50 feet. Fortunately, he landed on his chalkbag which saved him from serious injury. John Strand led the route for the first time in April, 1988.

HYPERVENTILATOR I 5.11d (5.10d R)
Yet another frightening face climb with long fall potential. Putting a paper bag over your head won't help one bit! The crux moves are protected, but most of the rest is not. Begin just to the right of VENTILATOR.
1. Climb past a bolt (5.10d R) to a bad peg sticking out of a flake on the

right. Belay at a small tree on the top ramp on VENTILATOR. 90', 5.10d R
2. Face climb up the steep, smooth slab to the right of the easy, upper groove on VENTILATOR with the crux after the second bolt (5.11d). Continue with fall potential (5.10d R) to a third bolt and the top. 50', 5.11d (5.10d R)
HISTORY: After John Bouchard placed the first bolt, Jim Surette & Jim Ewing climbed Pitch one in September, 1985. The full route was completed by John Bouchard, Joe Lentini, & Jim Surette later that same month.

REPO-MAN I 5.11d (*)
Gravity may repossess you at any moment. Still one of the hardest, most sustained, and runout routes on the VENTILATOR Slab. All the bolts were placed on the lead. Begin below the right-hand end of the long, horizontal overlap uphill and to the left of THREE BIRCHES. Very sustained.
1. Climb a thin crack above the right end of the large, bottom overlap to a belay at the large STARFIRE pine tree below the crux slab. 45', 5.9
2. Starting at the STARFIRE pine, face climb up into a shallow, left-slanting depression (long runout to first bolt; 5.11d crux at third bolt), heading straight up the slab past four more bolts to the top. 140', 5.11d R
HISTORY: Kurt Winkler & Karen Moffat first attempted the route in May, 1979, climbing the first pitch and placing two bolts on Pitch two. After Chris Gill added one more bolt in 1985, John Bouchard finished the climb on his second day of effort, placing the last four bolts in September, 1985, with Mike Hannon & Ruthann Brown. An historical note: after Andy Ross led the climb's third ascent, he admitted himself to Memorial Hospital in North Conway with cardiac distress.

EGO TRIP I 5.11c (or 5.11b) (**)
If the grade is a little over your head... at least so is the protection! The route ascends the unrelentingly steep slab just to the left of STARFIRE's crux pitch. Hard climbing and heaps of bolts have made this a popular, head-swelling outing. Begin 35 feet to the left of THREE BIRCHES, or five feet to the right of the right-hand end of the large, horizontal overlap 40 feet up. Bring along a dozen quick draws.
1. Face climb straight up a smooth, steep slab (just left of Pitch one of STARFIRE) past three bolts to the big pine tree. 60', 5.10d
2. Continue straight up a white streak in the slab above past the center bulge (5.11c; the line of the first ascent) past twelve bolts to the top. 130', 5.11c (You can also move slightly left, then back right, avoiding the crux bulge at 5.11b.)
HISTORY: The route's crux pitch had been top-roped previously. All of the bolts on this climb were drilled on rappel. Pitch one was first climbed by Brad White, Ian Cruickshank & Mike Hardert in October, 1990. The crux second pitch was added later that same month by Ian Cruickshank & Brad White.

STARFIRE I 5.11b (*)
In much the same genre as the previous routes, STARFIRE offers delicate and sustained face climbing with bolt protection, but finishes up a thin finger crack. Begin 30 feet to the left of THREE BIRCHES.

1. Follow a series of holds and a shallow, left-facing flake (two old pegs) up to a big pine tree, a key landmark on the VENTILATOR Slab and the Lower Left Wall. 60', 5.8 (Be careful of getting pine sap from the tree on your rope!)

2. Run it out to the first bolt, face climb right of the second bolt, and continue up an improbable slab past three more bolts (5.11b) into a welcome finger crack which slants up and right, joining THREE BIRCHES. 120', 5.11b

HISTORY: The climb was first top-roped by Michael Macklin, then bolt protected on rappel. After unsuccessful attempts were made to lead the route, Michael Hartrich was eventually recruited, and Hartrich & Joe Cote made the first ascent on September 27, 1975. A trivia question: what is the climb's "other" traditional name? (Yo-Yo.)

ONCE UPON A CLIMB I 5.11c (*)
This excellent slab route begins 25 feet to the left of THREE BIRCHES.

1. Climb cleaned flakes up and right past three pitons and a bolt (5.9) to a double bolt belay 10 feet to the right of the STARFIRE pine. 40', 5.9

2. Climb up, then trend diagonally right across a black streak on a headwall past seven bolts (5.11c crux after the third bolt), finally joining THREE BIRCHES at a large pine tree. 80', 5.11c. Or, for a longer, more sustained pitch, from the last bolt continue face climbing straight up to join with STARFIRE's top finger crack. 120', 5.11c

HISTORY: The crux pitch had been top-roped previously. Bill Lowther & Mark Lynch made the first ascent of Pitch one in December, 1992. Bill Lowther, Ozzie Blumit, & Mark Lynch made the route's first complete free ascent in April, 1993. All the bolts except one were placed free on the lead.

TRUE TEMPER I 5.11d (5.10d R)
Start halfway between ONCE UPON A CLIMB and SON OF A BIRCH.

1. Head up a steep wall past a bolt & two pins to a stance in solution pockets. Climb the steep slab above on small crystals (5.11d; bolt) to easier climbing up and right, joining SON OF A BIRCH at a stance at its last bolt, then move up to small trees on the right on THREE BIRCHES. 75', 5.11d (5.10d R)

HISTORY: After first top-roping the route, Gerry Lortie, Bill Lowther, & Jon Sykes made the first ascent on April 18, 1994. All the bolts and pitons were placed free on the lead. While Sykes was placing the first bolt (on the lead), his True Temper hammer head flew off the shaft and hit him in the head—but somehow he didn't fall off!

CATHEDRAL LEDGE (THREE BIRCHES) 79

SON OF A BIRCH I 5.11d (5.10d R) (*)
A controversial climb involving top-rope ascents and an aid-placed bolt.
1. Starting just left of THREE BIRCHES, undercling up and slightly right to a stance with side-by-side bolts. Face climb a steep wall (5.11d), then make a scary runout (5.10d R) to lower angled rock and another bolt on a bulge. Belay at small trees on the right on THREE BIRCHES. 75', 5.11d (5.10d R)
HISTORY: John Strand top-roped the route on October 22, 1983. In the Spring of 1984, John Bouchard & Yves Laforest (Canada), placed two bolts side-by-side during attempts to lead the route. After a top-rope ascent of his own, Paul Niland returned to the route with John Strand. Strand added another bolt on aid on the lead before Niland finally completed the pitch, placing one final bolt, on September 23, 1984. Two days later, John Bouchard made the second ascent, ignored the aid-placed bolt on the crux, and took several long leader falls prior to success. Bouchard removed the offending aid-placed bolt soon thereafter, making this an extremely serious and hard lead.

DEAD BIRCHES I 5.12c (Top-rope) (*)
One of the hardest face climbs on the VENTILATOR Slab.
1. Climb 25 feet up THREE BIRCHES to a jug on the left side of the arch. Swing left onto a stance, then face climb straight up a steep slab (5.12c) to the belay stance on THREE BIRCHES. 75', 5.12c
FA: Paul Niland, top-rope September 23, 1984

THREE BIRCHES II 5.8+ (**)
A very popular, yet a hard 5.8, and one to be avoided during any humid or wet weather. The 30 foot tall, right-facing arch at the start is a key landmark for finding all other nearby climbs. Protection is good, but carry some larger nuts.
1. The slippery arch at the start (5.8+) is the route's crux. Above, climb an easier crack to a detached block and small maple trees. 75', 5.8+
2. To the right of a large pine tree, layback a large flake system up and right to an awkward mantleshelf move (5.8) leading over a final, steep headwall or bulge up to the REFUSE tree ledge. 100', 5.8
HISTORY: Sam Streibert, John Reppy, & Harold May made the first ascent in September, 1963. This was Streibert and Reppy's second time climbing together, and following Sam's recent climbing trip to Britain and Europe, the first ascent was made mostly with nuts.

VARIATION #1: **THE EASY FINISH** I 5.6
2a. Head straight up easy, but dirty cracks above the large pine.

BIRCH HOUSE I 5.8 R
Variations never cease! An obscure combination. Begin 20 feet to the right of the bottom arch on THREE BIRCHES.

80 THE MOUNT WASHINGTON VALLEY

1. Starting on a block, face climb up (5.8 R) the right side of the slight rib on ONE HIT TO THE BODY to some trees. 50', 5.8 R
2. Follow a flake system right to the FUNHOUSE tree ledge. 40', 5.4
3. Finish up a corner just to the left of the FUNHOUSE bulge. 5.7
FA: Todd Swain & Brad White Summer, 1982

ONE HIT TO THE BODY II 5.12b (or 5.11d) (5.10d R / 5.9+ X) (*)

Although something of an eliminate line, the route has very unique climbing. Some parties choose to avoid the original 5.12b crux on the left at 5.11d. Begin 15 feet to the right of the THREE BIRCHES arch. Bring modern small gear to supplement mostly fixed protection.

1. Face climb up a slight rib on reasonable holds, but with no protection (5.9+ X), clip a piton high in the THREE BIRCHES arch, then traverse right to a large log and belay. 50', 5.9+ X
2. Step up to a fixed pin on the left before making a 5.11 traverse right on unique pockets to a bolt. The FA party stepped right to surmount a difficult bulge (5.12b) to a second bolt, while later ascents have climbed the bulge on the left (5.11d). An easier runout (5.11a) gains a good belay ledge with small Friend anchors. 45', 5.12b or 5.11d
3. After a hard mantle onto good holds at the start, clip a bolt, then face climb past shaky RPs up a seam to a tree on the FUNHOUSE ledge. 40', 5.10d R
4. Usually avoided: go left on easy bulges to a black streak just below the trees, then diagonal right to a large tree. 50', 5.8+ Dirty

HISTORY: After Tom Callaghan & John Strand climbed the crux pitch on May 27, 1986, John Strand & Scott Stevenson completed the route on May 30, 1986. Only the crux bolt was placed with aid, from a skyhook. All other protection was placed free on the lead.

FUNHOUSE I 5.7 (***)

With its variety of fun, stimulating, and well protected climbing, this is one of Cathedral's best intermediate routes. It is often combined with UPPER REFUSE (5.5), or BLACK LUNG (5.8) and FINAL GESTURE (5.7+) on the upper wall. Start about 75 feet to the right of THREE BIRCHES on a small tree ledge above an obvious V groove, and below twin inside corners.

1. Stem and layback up the right-hand dihedral (5.7; piton) to a ledge, then climb straight up a crack to a long, narrow belay ledge. Belay below an obvious, vertical crack (which is the second pitch of POOH). 75', 5.7
2. Overcome a tricky bulge (5.6) just to the left of POOH, squeeze by a pine tree, and climb an enjoyable clean face on angular holds to reach the REFUSE tree ledge. 100', 5.6

HISTORY: Joe Cote & Larry Poorman made the notable first ascent of this classic route in the Summer of 1969.

CATHEDRAL LEDGE (FUNHOUSE & POOH) 81

VARIATION #1: THE LEFT-HAND CORNER I 5.8 (*)
1a. At the start, layback up the strenuous, left-hand dihedral. 30', 5.8
FA: Unknown.

VARIATION #2: INCIPIENT ARETE I 5.10b R
Seldom climbed, with tricky wired nut protection. Modern rack.
2a. Climb the arete to the left of THE LEFT-HAND CORNER, with the crux moves getting off the ground. 40', 5.10b R
FA: Rich Baker, rope-solo July, 1985

POOH I 5.7 (**)
The jammed block in the overhang just to the right of FUNHOUSE marks the route. An excellent and popular climb with several quite befuddling combinations, especially getting to and past the jammed block! Make sure to use several long slings to avoid extreme rope drag on the first pitch.
1. Climb up a vertical jam crack, then traverse right to the jammed block. Swing awkwardly out onto it (5.6), climb a short chimney, and walk left across a long, narrow ledge to an obvious, vertical jam crack. Belay at a tree on this comfortable ledge. 80', 5.6
2. Jam straight up the delightful upper crack (5.7), a great pitch, to easier slabs and the large REFUSE tree ledge. 110', 5.7
FA: Larry Poorman, Joe Cote, & Gil Offenhartz Summer, 1969

ROLLIN' & TUMBLIN' II 5.10b (5.9 R)
Even with its outrageous horizontal stomach traverse, this is still not a very well-travelled route for some reason... Carry a modern rack.
1. The short, dirty, left-facing corner just right of POOH to a ledge. 5.9
2. Stomach traverse left on a large jammed flake, then climb a thin vertical crack with one 5.10b move over a bulge. Good belay ledge above. 5.10b
3. Tough to start: jam up a hand crack to another big ledge. 40', 5.8+
4. To the right of POOH, make tricky 5.9 moves into a dike, step back right on chicken heads, and surmount a bulge on the right to a slab. 5.9 R
HISTORY: Ed Webster, Joe Lentini, & Ajax Greene made the first ascent in August, 1976, trundling off a huge block en route, hence the name.

ORC II 5.8
Should you be walking over the BRIDGE OF KHAZAD-DUM on your way to MORDOR, stay clear of the ORCS. An awkward and strenuous climb, yet still appealing in its own unique way. Most parties avoid Pitch one by traversing right from the jammed block on POOH, climbing up SCIMITAR, or traversing left from the base of REFUSE below SOLSTICE.
1. Climb the very dirty, right-facing corner about 45 feet to the right of FUNHOUSE. Belay on the second ledge.

82 THE MOUNT WASHINGTON VALLEY

CATHEDRAL LEDGE – LOWER LEFT WALL
(The FUNHOUSE Area)

A.	*	**PLEASANT STREET** I 5.7 (5.6 R)	Page	71
B.	**	**BOMBARDMENT** I 5.8 (5.6 R)	Page	75
C.	***	**VENTILATOR** I 5.10b (5.6 R)	Page	75
D.	**	**EGO TRIP** I 5.11c (or 5.11b)	Page	77
E.	**	**THREE BIRCHES** II 5.8+	Page	79
F.	*	**ONE HIT TO THE BODY** II 5.12b (or 5.11d) (5.10d R / 5.9+ X)	Page	80
G.	***	**FUNHOUSE** I 5.7	Page	80
H.	**	**POOH** I 5.7	Page	81
I.		**ROLLIN' & TUMBLIN'** II 5.10b (5.9 R)	Page	81
J.		**ORC** II 5.8	Page	81
K.	*	**ENERGY CRISIS** II 5.11b (5.11a R)	Page	84

2. Struggle through an awkward, bomb bay chimney above (5.8) to easy cracks and the Ballroom, a huge belay ledge. 60', 5.8
3. Climb a short, steep headwall (5.8) into the final vertical groove. 5.8
FA: Larry Poorman & John Merrill   April 12, 1970
FFA: Bob Anderson, Mark Haymond, & Eric Radack   October, 1971

VARIATION: **SCIMITAR** I 5.8
To the right of ORC's first pitch is a right-facing, slanting corner.
1a. Layback the extremely dirty corner to a tree ledge. 60', 5.8
FA: Ed Webster & Joe Lentini 1974

THE 5.8 COMBINATION II 5.8+ (**))
A superior link-up of pitches up the full height of Cathedral's left-hand side. A worthwhile, varied adventure for intermediate climbers.
1. Layback up the LEFT-HAND CORNER start of FUNHOUSE. 75', 5.8
2. Climb Pitch three of ROLLIN' & TUMBLIN', the hand crack above the narrow ledge, leading up to the spacious platform, the Ballroom. 40', 5.8+
3. Do ORC's upper pitch, the headwall and upper groove. 80', 5.8
4. Then BLACK LUNG, the crack right of UPPER REFUSE. 90', 5.8
5. And finish up FINAL GESTURE (5.7+), the awkward, overhanging crack behind the detached block to the left of UPPER REFUSE. 60', 5.7+

ENERGY CRISIS II 5.11b (5.11a R) (*)
A high octane free climb with intriguing moves and a dicey start that's tricky to protect. Fuel up, then conserve as you go. Modern rack. Begin on the ground roughly 100 feet to the right of FUNHOUSE, or 75 feet left of A. P. TREAT at a 25 foot high headwall with incipient vertical cracks.
1. Decipher the headwall (5.11a R), then diagonal right (5.7 R) up a friction arete to a tree ledge. Belay on the left beneath roofs. 5.11a R
2. Handtraverse left under a roof to a hand crack splitting the roof (5.9). Good cracks lead up the sharp arete to the Ballroom. 50', 5.9
3. Off the right-hand end of the Ballroom, climb past two pegs (5.11b) and gain a hand crack splitting a bulge. Easier moves lead right across a slab to a thin crack and a sloping belay stance. 45', 5.11b
4. Climb the clean, finger crack (top pitch of SOLSTICE) to the finish. 5.8
HISTORY: After some cleaning on rappel, Jeff Butterfield & Doug Madara climbed the first two leads in the Spring of 1981. Ed Webster & Doug Madara made the first complete ascent on October 13, 1981.

SLINGS & ARROWS I 5.9+ R
Another thin face route, just to the left of STICKS & STONES.
1. Face climb straight up (bolt; 5.9+ R) past moss to the trees. 45', 5.9+ R
FA: Unknown.

CATHEDRAL LEDGE - STICKS & STONES SLAB 85

Tom Callaghan about to fall off of Sticks & Stones (5.11b R) in 1984, belayed by the attentive Chris Gill below. Photograph by S. Peter Lewis.

STICKS & STONES I 5.11b R (5.10a X)
Will break my bones, but names will never hurt me. Right of FUNHOUSE by 150 feet, and below and to the left of the start of REFUSE, is the STICKS & STONES Slab, a short, cleaned-off slab with several very thin face climbs. STICKS & STONES ascends the middle of the cleaned, steep face 25 feet to the left of A. P. TREAT. This is a short, dangerous face climb with groundfall potential, so rig a top-rope—or bring an alert belayer with running shoes!
1. Hard face climbing leads past an RP placement to a minimal stance (bolt), then move up and left (5.11b R) to easier moves (5.10a X) in the death zone. Run to the trees! 45', 5.11b R (5.10a X)

HISTORY: Chris Gill, Peter Lewis, & Tom Callaghan made the first ascent September 10, 1984. Earlier, Callaghan injured his ankle and nearly hit ck after falling off the crux.

86 THE MOUNT WASHINGTON VALLEY

BROKEN BONES I 5.10c (5.9+ R) (*)
Start halfway between STICKS & STONES and A. P. TREAT. This right-hand face route is somewhat better protected than STICKS & STONES.
1. Climb past a bolt (5.10c) & cruise (5.9+ R) to the trees. 45', 5.10c (5.9+ R)
FA: Unknown.

A. P. TREAT I 5.8 (*)
Well protected & popular, this is the clean, rounded arete up the right side of the STICKS & STONES slab. Try not to slobber with excitement on the crux!
1. Climb the right-hand shoulder of the STICKS & STONES Slab (peg) to a hard move (bolt; 5.8) over a bulge to the tree ledge above. 50', 5.8
FA: John Bouchard & Richard Estock   May, 1981

SOLSTICE II 5.12d (5.11a R)
A very technical and psychologically demanding route, now free. Ascends the thin crack out the center of the daunting, blocky roofs between ORC and TRAVESTY. Begin just around the corner to the left of the base of REFUSE. Modern rack, double ropes, titanium finger strength, and supreme mental control are all mandatory.
1. Start below the right-hand end of a white overlap, below blocky, orange roofs. Pull past two pitons, moving up and left to gain a ledge (Friends) above the first roofs. Rest, drop back down, traverse up and left to a stance (scary), then crank past the lip of the main roof at a thin vertical crack (pitons) using a series of bouldery moves (5.12d). Above the lip, face climb up the slab above (5.11a R) to a 5.8 finger crack & the REFUSE tree ledge. 130', 5.12d (5.11a R)
FA: Jeff Pheasant, rope-solo   June 21, 1974
FFA: Jim Surette   May 27, 1987

TRAVESTY II 5.8, Clean A2
A practice aid climb, one of the last few remaining. Awkward moves. The first ascent was climbed all-nuts. Start at jumbled blocks below a bolt, just to the left of the start of REFUSE. Bring a couple of skyhooks, too.
1. Aid to the bolt, then switch to the left-hand crack. After a second bolt, a hook move gains the belay ledge. 100', Clean A2
2. Climb 5.8 flakes right of a dirty corner to the REFUSE tree ledge. 40', 5.8
FA: Ed Webster & Jeff Butterfield   Summer, 1976

BROWN'S FIST I 5.9+ (*)
Strenuous. If you cheat by stepping right onto REFUSE, it's only 5.8.
1. The perfect hand crack out the roof left of REFUSE's first pitch. 75', 5.9+
HISTORY: Henry Barber made the first ascent on October 1, 1972. The route was named in honor of English rock climber Joe Brown, inventor of the hand jam, whom Henry climbed with in England and North Wales

REFUSE I 5.9 (******)
Less exposed than THIN AIR, REFUSE was one of the best introductions to climbing on Cathedral until the REFUSE tree was cut down in 1991. Pitch one is still somewhat popular, but now leads to an awkward, unpleasant 5.9 layback/squeeze chimney. UPPER REFUSE, the right-slanting ramp, offers superb 5.5 climbing, but is normally approached either up FUNHOUSE or POOH, both 5.7. Locating the start of REFUSE helps considerably in finding the base of other routes on this part of the cliff. From the center of the small talus slope 100 feet above the Cathedral Ledge auto road, hike straight up an eroded trail towards the base of THE PROW Buttress. At the cliff base, hike left to another worn trail heading steeply uphill (and left) towards a large, left-facing corner. This is BROWN'S FIST. REFUSE is hidden around an outside corner 20 feet to the right on a small, but good ledge with two trees. You should now be at the base of a left-facing corner with broken, vertical cracks.

1. Climb the cracks in the corner for 40 feet, using a combination of jamming and chimneying. After a rest, conquer the twin cracks above, the 5.6 crux. An easier method traverses left around the corner 30 feet to an easy crack. Belay on a large comfortable ledge. 60', 5.5 or 5.6.

2. The famous REFUSE tree (a hemlock) died and was cut down in 1991. The new alternative is to struggle up the awkward 5.9 chimney/corner behind the tree stump to the right end of the large, tree ledge halfway up the climb. 50', 5.9

3. UPPER REFUSE ascends the prominent, right-diagonalling ramp 100 feet left of the tree ledge's right-hand end. Face climb up the moderate ramp (many variations possible) to a cozy stance with a two piton anchor. 90', 5.3

4. Follow a groove for 30 feet (old peg) and continue to a small tree ledge. Belay here, or finish up the corner/crack on the left (5.6) or the exposed arete (5.5) on the right. Both finishes reach a good ledge with a piton anchor. 100', 5.5 or 5.6

5. Any of several additional, short pitches may be done to reach the tourist lookout on top of the cliff. The most popular route takes an easy line up the short outcrop overhead. More difficult and exposed are THE COMEAU FINISH (5.6) or COMMANDO RUN (5.8) farther right. Coming over the top in this way can usually get you a cold drink on a hot summer's day — or at the very least, a quick ride down the auto road!

HISTORY: A Yale University team, R. S. G. Hall, Walter Spofford, & Merrill apparently made the first ascent of this ever popular, historic route in 1935. John Turner (UK) & Richard Wilmott (Canada) climbed and named the route on May 23, 1960, finding old pitons on Pitch one. They also climbed the famous REFUSE tree, now of course gone. "About nomenclature: most of our (route) names were thought up in bars after hard days when we were scarcely at our intellectual peaks," John Turner recalled. "Repentence originated in the

American Legion in Berlin, NH (at the time, an otherwise dry town)... After that name, it seemed appropriate to continue with vaguely ecclesiastical names, which seemed accidentally to begin with 'Re'. Plainly we were running out of ideas by the time we got to Refuse."—named for its beer bottles and cans.

VARIATION: **OUTCAST** I 5.10b (Top-rope)
1a. The sharp arete just to the left of Pitch one of REFUSE. 75', 5.10b
HISTORY: Peter Beal top-roped the arete in April, 1990.

THE CULPRITS I 5.9+ (*)
A useful variation now that the REFUSE tree is gone. The well protected, thrilling crux is a better alternative (although harder) than the awkward 5.9 corner on REFUSE's now normal second pitch. Keep moving; don't stop!
1. Climb the first pitch corner and cracks on REFUSE. 60', 5.6
2. From the REFUSE tree stump, make a wild finger traverse left across an overhanging wall, underneath a small roof (bolt; 5.9+) to the small, but secure belay ledge on TRAVESTY (piton anchor). 35', 5.9+
3. Climb Pitch two of TRAVESTY, laybacking up clean flakes (5.8) just to the right of a dirty corner to reach the REFUSE tree ledge above. 40', 5.8
HISTORY: Uwe Schneider & Peter Hovling did the first ascent in September, 1993, three years after they cut down the famous REFUSE tree which had been dead for several years and was becoming increasingly hazardous. After the first day's sawing, the tree was cut most of the way through—but not all. The very next day, Jim Ewing was descending the cliff after free-soloing up a nearby route, and decided to solo back down the REFUSE tree. "When I arrived at the top of the tree, I noticed that the slings that had been tying it to another tree were gone. I pushed on the tree a little, though, and determined it was safe to climb down. When I got to the bottom, I found a HUGE chunk cut out of it," Ewing vividly recalled. Fortunately for Uwe and Peter, Jim did not meet up with them down on the road. Ewing also denies ever making the statement, "I did think the tree was swaying back and forth a little more than usual." Several days later, Schneider & Hovling finished sawing down the famous tree that had assisted rock climbers up—and sometimes down—REFUSE since 1935.

MYSTERY MAN I 5.12a
A covert operation above the first pitch of REFUSE.
1. Climb BROWN'S FIST (5.8) to the REFUSE belay ledge. 75', 5.8
2. Face climb up the steep wall above past two bolts. 50', 5.12a
3. Right of the first pitch of WOMEN IN LOVE, friction with difficulty diagonally right up a steep, clean slab past three bolts (5.11d) until you can join with RECOMPENSE farther right. 5.11d
FA: John Bouchard Summer, 1985

CATHEDRAL LEDGE (WOMEN IN LOVE) 89

Bryan Delaney free climbing Pitch one of Women In Love (5.11d) for the first time in 1975, on the first ascent of the Women In Love / Book Of Solemnity Link-Up. Photograph by Ed Webster.

WOMEN IN LOVE III 5.12a (or Clean A2) (***)
One of the Northeast's most elegant free climbs, ascending the long, right-slanting crack system to the right of THE BOOK OF SOLEMNITY. Superb situations and climbing, particularly on the last pitch. Normal rack. If you aid the climb, please use only nuts, and leave all fixed protection in place. Begin by walking across a ledge 30 feet to the right of THE BOOK.
1. Climb a perfect diagonal finger crack with increasing difficulty (5.11d) to a good belay ledge with a fixed anchor. 70', 5.11d
2. Continue up the right-slanting crack system past several fixed pitons (5.11b), staying to the left of the BEAST Flake, and belay on a foothold stance at a no-hands rest (bolt). 80', 5.11b
3. Surmount a small, notched roof, then follow the thin crack to two bolts on a smooth face. Clip in, down climb slightly, then conquer the blank wall on the left (5.12a) to a rest. With complete exposure, layback up a short, right-slanting corner past two pitons to the top. 60', 5.12a

HISTORY: Joe Cote & John Porter made the first ascent of this historic climb in September, 1971. The route was named in honor of Cote's wife Karen & Porter's girlfriend. After Cote's last drill bit broke on the final pitch, the women drove into town to EMS, bought several more drills, drove back to the top of Cathedral, and lowered them to the stranded climbers, enabling them to complete the route! By 1975, only the last pitch had not been climbed free. Henry Barber & Ed Webster made the equally notable first free ascent of the climb on September 16, 1978. Several tries were required on the crux top pitch. In a moment of high drama, after finally succeeding on the 5.12a crux, Barber dislocated his shoulder on the last move of the climb, but completed the lead. Webster followed successfully, and 15 minutes later, in extremely hot pursuit, Mark Hudon & Max Jones repeated the last pitch free! Only a few days earlier, Webster (who had recently inspected the final pitch on rappel) solemnly assured Hudon that: "There's no way that last pitch will ever go free. It's just completely blank up there."

WOMEN IN LOVE/BOOK OF SOLEMNITY LINK-UP II 5.11d (***)
Historically this was a major free climbing breakthrough. It is still a popular combination, being easier than a complete free ascent of WOMEN IN LOVE.
1. Free climb the first pitch of WOMEN IN LOVE. 70', 5.11d
2. Climb partway up WOMEN IN LOVE's second lead, then, after a difficult layback (5.11b), traverse left across a narrow ledge into the top of THE BOOK OF SOLEMNITY, which is followed left up to the top. 5.11b

HISTORY: Bryan Delaney & Ed Webster made the first ascent of the link-up on June 28, 1975. Their climb was also the first free ascent of the first pitch of WOMEN IN LOVE.

CATHEDRAL LEDGE (WOMEN IN LOVE) 91

Ed Webster on the Pitch three crux moves of Women In Love (5.12a) in 1978 on the route's first free ascent. Photograph by Todd Gregory.

92 THE MOUNT WASHINGTON VALLEY

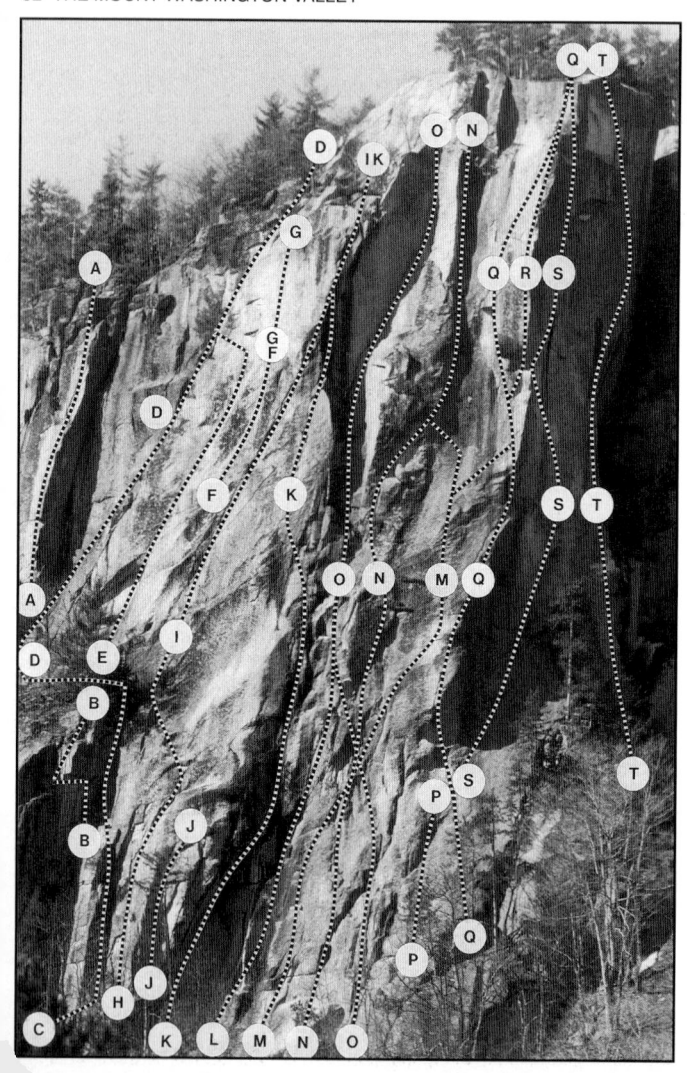

CATHEDRAL LEDGE
(THE ARETE to CRAZY WISDOM)

A.	**	**THE ARETE** I 5.11b R	Page	65
B.	*	**THE CULPRITS** I 5.9+	Page	88
C.	**	**REFUSE** I 5.9	Page	87
D.	***	**UPPER REFUSE** I 5.5	Page	66
E.	***	**THE BOOK OF SOLEMNITY** II 5.9+	Page	68
F.	*	**FOOL'S GOLD** I 5.10d	Page	68
G.	**	**BAD DOGS** I 5.12d	Page	70
H.	***	**WILD WOMEN** III 5.12a (5.10b R)	Page	94
I.	***	**WOMEN IN LOVE** III 5.12a (or Clean A2)	Page	90
J.	*	**WILDEBEAST** I 5.11d	Page	94
K.	***	**THE BEAST 666** III 5.12a	Page	94
L.		**IN THE BELLY OF THE BEAST** I 5.10d	Page	96
M.	**	**WILD KINGDOM** III 5.11c or 5.11d	Page	102
N.		**GYPSY** III 5.9+	Page	99
O.	***	**RECOMPENSE** III 5.9	Page	96
P.	**	**ANOTHER PRETTY FACE** I 5.10a	Page	104
Q.	***	**THE PROW** III 5.11d (or 5.7, Clean A2)	Page	103
R.	***	**EDGE OF THE WORLD** I 5.13c	Page	106
S.	***	**LIQUID SKY** III 5.13b (5.11a R)	Page	106
T.	*	**CRAZY WISDOM** III 5.11b, A1 (12 Points of Aid)	Page	110

94 THE MOUNT WASHINGTON VALLEY

WILD WOMEN III 5.12a (5.10b R) (***)
One of the White Mountains' most sustained free climbs. The route evolved over the years with the effort of several climbers. Pitch one, known as WILD, climbs the finger crack up the steep wall just to the right of Pitch one of REFUSE. Carry a modern rack, for use on WILD.

1. WILD I 5.11b (*) With new gear, protection is now adequate. Climb the finger crack directly. When it ends, step right to gain a horizontal crack and a rest. With awkward protection, gain a ledge (5.11b) on the right. Belay on a higher ledge with a bolt. 120', 5.11b

2. The Bashie Groove: Climb the short, testing groove (bolt). Dicey runout (5.10b R). 35', 5.10b R (The bashie used for pro on the first ascent is long gone!)

3. Climb the first pitch (5.11d) of WOMEN IN LOVE. 70', 5.11d

4. Do the second pitch (5.11b) of WOMEN IN LOVE. 80', 5.11b

5. Finish up the last pitch (5.12a) of WOMEN IN LOVE. 60', 5.12a

HISTORY: WILD was first climbed with aid by Jeff Pheasant, rope-solo, in the Summer of 1974. Ed Webster, Ajax Greene, & Jim Dunn freed WILD in one try in the Summer of 1976. Webster & Dunn did the Bashie Groove a month later, while Barber & Webster made the first free ascent of WOMEN IN LOVE on September 16, 1978. The complete climb was finally strung together in one push by Ed Webster & Jeff Achey in August, 1979.

VARIATION #1: VALLEY GIRL I 5.6+
Gag me with a spoon!

2a. The dirty finger crack (5.6+) just to left of the Bashie Groove. 35', 5.6+

FA: Brooks Bicknell & Chris Gill September, 1982

WILDEBEAST I 5.11d (*)
The strenuous corner/crack hidden between WILD and THE BEAST 666. Bring double ropes and a modern rack if you plan to finish up WILD.

1. Ascend the corner (5.11d), continuing straight up to a difficult move and a hanging belay at a two bolt belay/rappel anchor. 60', 5.11d Just before the corner narrows, you can also step left around the outside corner onto a foot ledge, and finish up the crux of WILD (5.11b) to a bolt anchor. 120', 5.11d

HISTORY: John Burke rope-soloed the first ascent on aid to the double bolt anchor in the Autumn of 1983. Neil Cannon, Dave Rose, & Jim Surette free climbed the complete pitch in the Summer of 1984.

THE BEAST 666   III   5.12a   (***)
THE CERBERUS   III   5.12d   (***)
A difficult free route with two lines of ascent at the start. The original aid line, renamed THE CERBERUS (5.12d), goes free using the original aid pitons for protection, making it one of the area's most serious, hard free routes. Double ropes are mandatory on this gymnastic testpiece. DUNN'S OFFWIDTH at

5.11c, while awkward and insecure, is considerably easier. Begin 40 feet right of REFUSE on a comfortable, flat tree ledge in a small, Cathedral-like alcove. The initial 5.10 cracks stay dry on rainy days and are popular to run laps on.

1. In the back of the alcove, climb a right-diagonalling finger crack (5.10b) to a prominent V groove—or climb the shallow groove on the right (5.9) past a piton. Above, stem up the technical V (5.11c) to a rest.

THE CERBERUS I 5.12d (***)

1. Place protection, down climb slightly, then make a series of wild dynamic moves (5.12b) across the overhanging wall on the left to gain the start of a thin, vertical finger crack (5.12d; the original aid line) that is climbed to the belay stance. (The fixed pitons probably need replacing.) 5.12d

Jim Surette on the first free ascent of The Cerberus (5.12d) in 1985. Photograph by Ed Webster.

DUNN'S OFFWIDTH I 5.11c (The complete route is 5.12a) (***)

1a. From the rest, the 1977 free ascent continued directly up the offwidth/squeeze chimney above (5.11b), which is definitely easier, and considerably more popular than THE CERBERUS! The hard stemming moves up the V groove at the start of the pitch, however, are still 5.11c.

2. Climb a short easy pitch to the base of the BEAST Flake, a spectacular, detached flake just to the left of RECOMPENSE.
3. Layback and jam up the BEAST Flake's left side. Belay on top. 125', 5.9
4. Climb an exposed, layback crack on the right to a junction with the last 50 feet of WOMEN IN LOVE. 70', 5.12a

HISTORY: Paul Ross & George Meyers made the first ascent on July 5, 1972. After many attempts, Jim Dunn freed most of the first pitch, finishing up the obvious offwidth crack, in May, 1977. Jim Surette accomplished the first free ascent of the original first pitch aid line, which he renamed THE CERBERUS, after five afternoons' worth of attempts, on October 24, 1985.

VARIATION #1: TALCUM POWER I 5.10b X
Ascends the right-hand wall of THE BEAST alcove.
1a. Layback up a shallow, right-facing corner (peg), then face climb right (5.10b X) up to a ledge. 45', 5.10b X Finish up any of several routes.
FA: Mark Sonnenfeld & Jeff Achey August, 1977

VARIATION #2: IN THE BELLY OF THE BEAST I 5.10d
A free climb up the grooves above TALCUM POWER.
1b. Start up TALCUM POWER (5.10b X), or climb the bottom of the grooves on the right (easier). Angle up and left past two pitons into the first corner, then climb the dirty, overhanging V groove above. 5.10d Finish as desired
FA: Alison Osius, Peter Lewis, & Joe Lentini September, 1984

RECOMPENSE III 5.9 (***)
A natural, aesthetic, and well protected line up one of the tallest sections of Cathedral Ledge—and for 1959, a series of plucky leads by John Turner. One of the finest rock climbs in America. The final pitch ascends the celebrated, curving layback corner just left of the top of THE PROW and directly below the tourist lookout. Carry a normal rack. Route finding, however, is complicated at the start. Hike up to the base of THE PROW Buttress (the massive buttress to the left of the THIN AIR Face), looking for a clearing and a ledge about 30 feet up. Scramble onto this ledge and belay. You should now have the tree ledge of the THE BEAST alcove on your left, see RECOMPENSE directly overhead, and THE PROW on the right skyline.
1. There are two starts. Climb straight up into a crack system, or solo up an easy crack on the right past two trees to a higher belay ledge. Climb another short crack, step left around the corner, and continue partway up another crack. Belay on any of several stances to avoid rope drag on the next lead. 5.5
2. Follow old pitons up a finger crack on the left, then, above a stance, reach left and layback up a strenuous crack (5.7) to another ledge. Mantleshelf, then climb easier rock to a good belay ledge with a double bolt anchor. 130', 5.7

CATHEDRAL LEDGE (RECOMPENSE) 97

Bryan Becker on the 5.9 layback moves on the last pitch of Recompense in 1975. John Turner's original wooden wedge is just below Becker's left foot.

Mark Sonnenfeld leading the Beast Flake on Recombeast (5.9) in 1978. Photographs by Ed Webster.

3. Pass by birch trees to their right to enter a prominent chimney system and crack line. At the chimney's top, swing into a layback (5.8+), & climb to a good stance at a tree stump below the final, impressive, curving dihedral. 100', 5.8+

4. Layback up the strenuous, sustained corner (5.9) to a narrow rest ledge at half height. More thought-provoking moves, stemming and finger jamming, lead up the top dihedral (also 5.9) to an exposed and dramatic finish. 110', 5.9

HISTORY: On May 17, 1959, John Turner (UK) & Dr. Michael Ward (UK also; Ward was the doctor on the 1953 British Everest expedition and also made the first ascent of Ama Dablam in Nepal) made "an exploration which took us far enough up Pitch three to realize that we had no pitons big enough to protect Pitch four; whereupon we abseiled off to collect at least a psychological belay (one of Ben Poisson's wooden wedges) to use on the next attempt," recalled John Turner. "But by then it was too late to go back up again, and too early for the bar in North Conway, so we did my now eponymous flake (TURNER'S FLAKE), then called "The Direct Start to Thin Air". I led Dick Morden; Mike Ward led the second rope with Claude Lavallée as his second. At the very top of the pitch, both of Mike's feet slipped, leaving him dangling momentarily on poor handholds, horrifying his newly-married, non-climbing wife, Jane, who was sitting underneath. The following morning, May 18, 1959, I was assembling my rudimentary rack for the final push on RECOMPENSE, and Mike said he had been given a choice: either he could join me on a memorable first ascent, or he could stay married. He had chosen the latter. Fortunately, Richard Wilmott was around to take his place. After Mike returned to England, we totally lost touch, and I have never discovered how the marriage worked out." After climbing the first ascent of all but the last 40 feet of this popular and historic route, Turner & Wilmott traversed right and finished up the parallel, right-hand corner, now GYPSY. The finish up the top dihedral was added all free by John Reppy & Harold May on July 5, 1963. Just for the record: Bryan Delaney pulled out Ben Poisson's wooden wedge with his fingers in 1975 — that years earlier had protected the crux 5.9 layback on the final corner.

RECOMBEAST III 5.9 (***)

The addition of the BEAST Flake makes for an even more exhilarating climb, and is a very popular combination. Remember to carry some large protection for the flake itself. Great jamming and situations; highly recommended.

1 & 2. Climb the first two leads of RECOMPENSE. 5.5 & 5.7

3a. Before entering the chimney line on RECOMPENSE, climb out left into the BEAST Flake. The 5.9 layback entry move is best protected high on the right. A wild and exposed pitch! Hand and fist jam plus layback up the left edge of the exposed, sharp-edged flake to a small stance atop the flake. 125', 5.9

4a. Down climb to your right a little awkwardly (5.9) back into the RECOMPENSE corner, then jam and layback up the top section of RECOMPENSE Pitch three to reach the belay stance at the base of the final dihedral. 40', 5.9

5. Undercling and layback up the strikingly beautiful, curving corner (5.9 at the start and top) on RECOMPENSE to the finish. 110', 5.9

HISTORY: Paul Ross & George Meyers made the first ascent of THE BEAST (including the BEAST Flake) on July 5, 1972. Also in 1972, during the first ascent of KING CRAB, Cathedral's left to right girdle traverse, Paul Ross & Dave Cilley traversed from WOMEN IN LOVE over to the top of the BEAST Flake, and then into RECOMPENSE. In July, 1977, Mike Heintz & Bob Palais made the first recorded ascent of RECOMBEAST, climbing the link-up as it is popularly done today.

VARIATION #1: **RECONSIDER** I 5.10d (*)
A new and challenging pitch between RECOMPENSE and GYPSY.

3a. From the double bolt belay on RECOMPENSE, step right to a bolt in a shallow, flaring corner (5.10c). Climb straight up a slab (or step left) to a left-facing corner above a small birch. Continue up the corner for 20 feet, step left, then back right to a pin and a tricky nut placement (5.10d) to blocks. Undercling up and left to a belay at the stump on RECOMPENSE. 150', 5.10d

FA: Brad White & Ian Cruickshank October, 1994

VARIATION #2: **THE ROTATION** I 5.12c (**)
Climbs out the exposed, overhanging left wall of the top, curving dihedral on RECOMPENSE. You couldn't ask for a much more dramatic or wilder pitch! Use double ropes to safely make the clips, and bring six quick draws.

1. From the belay stance for THE FAUX PAS ARETE near the top of the final RECOMPENSE corner, face climb left across an unlikely, bulging wall past four bolts (5.12c) to a stance (and a rest) on the corner's left-hand arete (piton). Step back right onto the face, and finish on good holds to the top. 60', 5.12c

HISTORY: After a massive cleaning effort on rappel opened up the exposed, overhanging left wall of the RECOMPENSE dihedral, the route was protected by bolts, and Bill Lutkus made the first ascent on August 25, 1989.

GYPSY III 5.9+
As the route has gotten cleaner over the years, GYPSY has become a slightly more popular venture. Start at the base of RECOMPENSE.

1. Climb a shallow, 40 foot corner to a small stance. Pine tree belay.

2. Continue up a right-facing corner and step left to easier ground. Belay on a ledge just below the mantleshelf move on Pitch two of RECOMPENSE. There are several fixed pegs on this pitch.

3. A right-facing corner (peg) is climbed to a ledge, then diagonal left across a slab, and belay near the RECOMPENSE chimney.

Bill Lutkus leading the first ascent of The Rotation (5.12c) in 1989, belayed by Uwe Schneider. Photograph by S. Peter Lewis.

CATHEDRAL LEDGE (REFUSE VARIATION FINISHES) 101

4. Up a small crack to a pointed block, and traverse right (5.9+) into the base of a big, right-facing corner, the route's main feature. Tree belay. 5.9+
5. Continue up the corner (Turner's RECOMPENSE finish) to a pine.
6. Finish up the final, right-facing dihedral of COMMANDO RUN. 30', 5.8
HISTORY: John Bragg & Ajax Greene did the route's first ascent in August, 1973. Pitch five, Turner's Finish, was first climbed by John Turner (UK) & Richard Wilmott on the first ascent of RECOMPENSE on May 18, 1959. Ed Webster & Kurt Winkler added COMMANDO RUN on October 15, 1985.

VARIATION FINISHES above REFUSE & RECOMPENSE

All the previous climbs end on the same ledge system, 40 feet below the summit of Cathedral Ledge and the tourist lookout. Above this ledge rises a short headwall with the following routes. All are excellent finishes, or just separate climbs in their own right. They are now described from left to right across the small tree ledge at the top of REFUSE and RECOMPENSE.

REFUSE FINISHES I 5.3–5.4
Any of several possible finishes up the final wall's left side.

LITTLE BRUCE I 5.11d X
To the right of the REFUSE finishes are two slight arches.
1. Boulder up the left-hand weakness. No pro. 25', 5.11d X
FA: John Bouchard, free-solo September, 1985

LITTLE STALKING I 5.11d R
Ascends the right-hand weakness above a short, blank face between LITTLE BRUCE and THE LOOKOUT CRACK.
1. This serious piece of climbing has only one nut for protection. Bring a microscope to look for holds and a very attentive spotter. 25', 5.11d R
HISTORY: Previously top-roped by Michael Hartrich. Kurt Winkler, Doug Madara, & Steve Larson made the first ascent on May 9, 1981.

THE LOOKOUT CRACK I 5.8+ (*)
Well worth looking for, this sinker crack is a good intro to harder jamming.
1. Climb the vertical, finger crack to the left of LITTLE FEAT. 30', 5.8+
FA: Unknown.

LITTLE FEAT I 5.9- (*)
These jams are so good, you won't need your feet at all. Very popular.
1. Starting directly above RECOMPENSE, climb a short finger crack on locker finger jams to the tourist lookout. Congratulations! 35', 5.9-
FA: Chris Noonan & Jim Dunn August, 1977

COMMANDO RUN I 5.8 (*)
Make a dash for the hidden corner to the right of LITTLE FEAT and directly above GYPSY. Well protected, strenuous, and exposed.

1. Layback quickly up the short, right-facing corner. 35', 5.8

HISTORY: After an extremely determined cleaning effort, Ed Webster & Kurt Winkler made the route's first ascent on October 15, 1985.

DON'T FLY OVER RUSSIA I 5.11a R (*)
Evasive action may be required on the crux of this short pitch. The usual approach is via a short traverse right from the top of RECOMPENSE.

1. Stem up the right-facing dihedral (5.11a R) just to the left of THE PROW's 5.10 FINISH. Tricky wired nut protection. 40', 5.11a R

HISTORY: Neil Cannon, Peter Lewis, Dave Rose, & Chris Plant (UK) made the first ascent on September 10, 1983—the same day the Soviet Union shot down Korean Airlines Flight #007 over the South China Sea.

THE COMEAU FINISH I 5.6 (*)
For a 5.6, what an outrageously exposed situation!

1. From the ledge at the top of RECOMPENSE, traverse horizontally right onto the final 30 feet of THE PROW (5.6).

FA: Alain Comeau & partner 1984

WILD KINGDOM III 5.11c or 5.11d (** or ***)
King of the jungle? This difficult face climb threads its way between GYPSY and THE PROW. There are two finishes: an independent line on the left, THE FAUX PAS ARETE (5.11c), located just to the right of the last pitch of RECOMPENSE; or heading out right, and finishing up THE PROW (5.11d). Start in a capped, right-facing corner 30 feet to the right of TALCUM POWER.

1. Climb up the crack (pins), cross right over RECOMPENSE, and belay at a stance (more pitons) at the base of a corner 10 feet to the right of the usual RECOMPENSE belay. 5.10b

2. Face climb out right past three bolts (5.11b), then continue up to the good horizontal crack on THE PROW, and arrange a semi-hanging belay. 5.11b

3. A beautiful pitch. Face climb straight up, making a 5.10b move after the second bolt, then climb left on unusual pockets and knobs to a double bolt belay anchor. 5.10b The route now has two separate finishes:

4. Angle left (across GYPSY), climbing through an overhang and up the right side of a giant flake to join RECOMPENSE. Belay at the rest stance halfway up the final pitch of RECOMPENSE.

THE FAUX PAS ARETE I 5.11c (***)
5. Face climb up the exposed, white arete to the right of RECOMPENSE's top corner. The moves are very sustained (5.11c) and bolt-protected. 60', 5.11c

THE PROW FINISH II 5.11d (**)
3a. Face climb up and right to bolts on the steep wall just left of the finger crack at the start of THE PROW's fourth pitch, continuing up the 5.11b finger crack on THE PROW to the Space Station belay and a double ring bolt anchor. 5.11b

Jerry Handren on the Faux Pas Arete (5.11c) in 1988. Photo by Nick Yardley.

4a. Continue up into THE PROW's crux, left-facing dihedral (5.11d), then crank out the Triangular Roof (also 5.11d) to a small belay ledge. 70', 5.11d

5a. Climb THE PROW's 5.10 FINISH finger crack to the top. 85', 5.10a

HISTORY: John Bouchard, Mark Richey, & Chris Hassig climbed the first two pitches in July, 1981. John Burke had cleaned, top-roped, and rappel-bolted the final arete before John Bouchard made the first ascent of THE FAUX PAS ARETE in the Spring of 1984. John Bouchard & Steve Larson completed WILD KINGDOM via THE PROW FINISH later that summer.

THE PROW III 5.11d (or 5.7, Clean A2) (***)

Formidable and spectacular, THE PROW is one of the longest, most sustained free climbs in the eastern United States. Done as a purely free ascent, the climb is one of the White Mountain's hardest and most elusive challenges. The route has also remained an extremely popular aid climbing extravaganza, but fewer fixed pitons are in place these days, so plan on carrying a larger rack of nuts. Three of the belays are hanging. From the start of RECOMPENSE at the base of THE PROW Buttress, solo up an easy 15 foot crack past two trees to a ledge. There are three equally popular starts to the route: the 5.7 and 5.10 starts begin here, while the original 5.9 "bolted slab" begins 20 feet down and right at a large pine tree on a good ledge, with a smooth slab rising above. The various separate starts of THE PROW are now described from left to right:

THE 5.7 START I 5.7 (***)

1. This is the easiest start, recommended for parties aid climbing the route as the original aid dowels up THE 5.9 SLAB are long gone. From the ledge, follow a prominent groove system up and right (5.7) to a small belay ledge at the base of an overhanging bulge—which is Pitch two. 65', 5.7

THE 5.9 SLAB I 5.9 (***)

1a. The original start, the "bolted slab." Begin on the lower ledge at a pine tree. Face climb up the center of the slab (5.9) past several bolts. 60', 5.9

ANOTHER PRETTY FACE I 5.10a (**)

1b. Begin 10 feet right of THE 5.7 START below a smooth face. Face climb up the slab past three bolts (5.10a) up to the regular belay ledge. 60', 5.10a

2. Two bolts connect with a crack splitting the prominent bulge overhead. Handtraverse in from right to left to gain the crack (or climb directly up to the crack; 5.11d), climb this awkward, bulging crack (5.11c), then face climb past several bolts (5.10b) to a hanging belay at a good horizontal crack. 50', 5.11c or 5.11d (or Clean A2)

3. Move right around the corner into a secure flake. At a bolt, step back left into another flake. Follow this flake up and right to another hanging belay, this time at a double ring bolt anchor. 50', 5.10a (or Clean A1)

4. Decipher a very technical bulge (5.11d), either directly (harder) or on the left (bolt; 5.11c) to gain a long, vertical finger crack. Jam up this strenuous crack (5.11b) to a small stance known as the Space Station belay which also has a double ring bolt anchor. 60', 5.11d (or Clean A1)

5. Step left, layback up a narrow flake, then make extreme moves (5.11d) into the left-facing corner leading up to the Triangular Roof, one of the route's most obvious features. Undercling out the roof (also 5.11d) to a small, exposed belay stance just above the lip. 70', 5.11d (or Clean A2)

6. Climb a nice 5.9 finger crack up a steep slab, then move right to the final 5.6 jam crack on the skyline. 85', 5.9 (or 5.6, Clean A1)

THE MARCH OF IDES I 5.8

6a. Ascend the very exposed arete on the right, up a straight-in crack. 85', 5.8

THE 5.10 FINISH I 5.10a (*)

6b. Climb straight up a final, thin crack over the top bulge (5.10a), instead of angling off to the right to the regular 5.6 jam crack. 85', 5.10a

Louise Shepherd (Australia) on the crux of the fourth pitch of The Prow (5.11d) in 1985, belayed by Alison Osius. Photograph by S. Peter Lewis.

HISTORY: The first ascent of this historic climb was made by Paul Ross & Hugh Thompson in April, 1972. Interestingly, this was also Ross's first new route on Cathedral. In 1973, to prevent crack destruction, the entire route was fixed with pitons. Also in 1973, Michael Hartrich, Jeff Pheasant, Rick Mulhern, & John Bragg free climbed the first 5.9 slab. In April, 1976, Rick Fleming & Mark Bon Signor freed the last pitch. In May, 1976, John Bragg & Joe Lentini spearheaded efforts to free climb the entire route, freeing the second and third pitches, with Bragg climbing the start of Pitch two directly. Finally, after some cleaning on rappel, rearranging the location of a few fixed pitons, and over a year of attempts, Jim Dunn with Jay Wilson made the route's first continuous free ascent on July 14, 1977.

VARIATION #1: ANOTHER PRETTY FACE I 5.10a (**)
FA: Matt Peer & Elaine Stockbridge Peer August 26, 1982

VARIATION #2: THE BLANK BULGE I 5.11c
4a. Avoids the regular 5.11d bulge at the start of Pitch four. Face climb left (bolt) around the bulge (5.11c), then back right into the upper finger crack. 35', 5.11c
HISTORY: In September, 1978, Max Jones & Mark Hudon climbed the variation's first ascent without using any protection bolts. These were placed later, on the first ascent of WILD KINGDOM.

VARIATION #3: THE MARCH OF IDES I 5.8
FA: Chris Gill & Camilla Girgus August 28, 1982

VARIATION #4: THE 5.10 FINISH I 5.10a (*)
FA: Unknown.

EDGE OF THE WORLD I 5.13c (***)
One of New Hampshire's hardest free pitches ascends the outrageously exposed sharp arete to the right of THE PROW's fifth pitch. Begin at the double ring bolt, hanging Space Station belay on THE PROW.
1. Face climb up and around to the right-hand side of the arete (bolt) before making an extreme crank (5.13c) up onto the sharp arete, to a slight rest. Continue up the arete past two more bolts (5.12d), and a nut placement (#6 Rock) to easier ground (5.10d) and the edge's top. Arrange a hanging belay at a three bolt fixed belay station located six feet right of the arete and level with THE PROW's belay stance above the Triangular Roof. This anchor is very convenient for top-roping the route, plus has the added advantage that you can look down and see your partner following the pitch. 60', 5.13c
2. Move left, joining the last pitch of THE PROW to the top.
HISTORY: Jim Surette cleaned, rappel-bolted, and attempted the route in May, 1987, but shoulder surgery in September ended his efforts. Scott Franklin made the impressive first ascent after two days of effort in October, 1987.

LIQUID SKY III 5.13b (5.11a R) (***)
The first 5.13 in New Hampshire, this is still one of the most difficult free climbs in the White Mountains. An exposed, gymnastic free climb up Cathedral's Yellow Wall. There is a substantial amount of fixed protection, plus two hanging belays. Start at the base of THE PROW.
1. Climb THE PROW's 5.9 bolted slab, angle right to a bolt, and free climb diagonally right past more bolts on a slab below the steep upper wall (5.10d R) to the base of the YELLOW BRICK ROAD bolt ladder. 175', 5.10d R
2. Free climb the bolt ladder to a no-hands rest (5.11), traverse up and left past a bolt (5.12a), do a difficult mantle, then climb left (5.11) following a series of flakes and grooves past another bolt to the double ring bolt hanging belay at the

CATHEDRAL LEDGE (EDGE OF THE WORLD) 107

Scott Franklin on the first ascent of Edge Of The World (5.13c) in 1987. Photographs by Cathy Beloeil.

108 THE MOUNT WASHINGTON VALLEY

top of THE PROW's fourth pitch. 110', 5.12a (Space Station belay on the FFA).
3. Traverse right around the corner onto the Yellow Wall, across a thin crack (pegs) into a marginal, vertical crack. The 5.13b crux is between this marginal crack and the sinker finger crack above. Continue with difficulty to a no-hands ledge, then climb a short, vertical crack above a bashie (5.11a R) until you can step left onto THE PROW and finish. 150', 5.13b (5.11a R)

Jim Surette on the first free ascent of Liquid Sky (5.13b / 5.11a R) in 1986, belayed by Ruthann Brown & Randy Rackliff on the Space Station platform. Photograph by S. Peter Lewis.

HISTORY: Jeff Pheasant & Paul Ross aid climbed across the traverse at the start of Pitch five, to first link THE PROW with YELLOW BRICK ROAD, in 1976. John Bouchard & Titoune Bouchard made the first ascent of the first pitch, diagonalling up right from THE PROW in the Autumn of 1983. The bolt ladder at the start of Pitch two was then free climbed by John Bouchard & Yves Laforest (Canada) the next Spring. Hugh Herr & John Bouchard added the traverse out left to join up with THE PROW, finishing Pitch two in August, 1984. Jim Surette, with Randy Rackliff (and several other extremely patient belayers), made the first free ascent of this historic route in September, 1986, after a week's worth of attempts. Three pitons were placed on rappel to protect the crux pitch.

YELLOW BRICK ROAD III 5.13b (5.11a R), A3 (*)

The original route up the Yellow Wall is now outdated as an aid climb since the entire route (except for about 50 feet) has been free climbed. The final two pitches are the shared finish with LIQUID SKY (5.13b), one of the White Mountain's hardest free climbs. The climb makes a direct line up the Yellow Wall—the smooth, sheer face just to the right of THE PROW.

1. Begin at the base of THE BIG FLUSH, the horrible gully that splits Cathedral Ledge into two halves. After a 5.8 mantleshelf, climb up a cleaned slab to a right-diagonalling ledge system. You can also scramble up to this same system of ledges from the base of the 5.9 bolted slab on THE PROW.

2. The John Bouchard Memorial Bolt Ladder. Climb the bolt ladder via extremely sustained face climbing (5.13) plus some easy A1 aid. The initial section of the ladder goes free up to a ledge where LIQUID SKY angles off left to the Space Station belay on THE PROW. After 50 more feet of A1 aid on bolts, arrange a spectacular hanging belay below a prominent overlap. 5.13, A1

3. After a skyhook move to the left (A3), climb an exposed and difficult crack system (The same as LIQUID SKY; 5.13b) to a small belay ledge. Please do not add or remove any pitons on this pitch. A3 & 5.13b

4. Free climb up a short, vertical crack above a bashie (5.11a R), step to the left, and finish up THE PROW. 5.11a R

HISTORY: John Bouchard installed the bolt ladder on Pitch two in November, 1975, attempting to create the so-called "easiest route up Cathedral Ledge". Unfortunately, he suffered a hernia before he could complete this noble effort, leaving the rest of the climb to be finished by Jeff Pheasant & Paul Ross in May, 1976. John Bouchard & Yves Laforest (Canada) then free climbed the first part of the Pitch two bolt ladder in the Spring of 1984, and Jim Surette with Randy Rackliff made the first free ascent of the route's top two pitches as the finish to LIQUID SKY in September, 1986.

THE WORM DRIVE BUTTRESS

This is the small—and now considerably cleaner—buttress between the base of THE PROW and THE BIG FLUSH, directly below the Yellow Wall.

THE BRAIN POLICE I 5.11c
Start 15 feet to the left of TRUE LIES, or 30 feet left of WORM DRIVE.
1. Face climb up a short, overhanging wall, angling left past three bolts. Lower off the top bolt. 30', 5.11c
HISTORY: Bill Lowther rope-soloed the first ascent, placing the bolts on the lead on aid in August, 1995. Bill Lowther & Chris Small made the first free ascent later that same month.

TRUE LIES I 5.12b
Sustained! Start 15 feet to the left of WORM DRIVE.
1. Face climb past a piton and three bolts (5.12b crux after the second bolt) up to a double ring bolt anchor. 55', 5.12b
HISTORY: After first top-roping the route, Gerry Lortie, Tim Kemple, & Dan Pacheco made the first ascent on September 23, 1995. All the bolts were drilled on the lead by hand. The second bolt, placed off a hook, required four hours of drilling and several leader falls!

WORM DRIVE I 5.10c
The original route on the buttress climbs the longest cleaned-off stripe. Begin beside a big maple 50 feet right of the 5.9 slab starting ledge on THE PROW.
1. Worm drive straight up a cleaned face past three bolts (5.10c getting to the second bolt) to a double bolt anchor on a nice belay ledge. 40', 5.10c
2. Step right and worm drive (5.6) past three more bolts up a cleaned slab to a large pine tree growing at the top. 65', 5.6 Rappel off the tree to descend.
HISTORY: After extensive cleaning on rappel, Uwe Schneider & Craig Taylor made the first ascent in August, 1993. The first two bolts were placed free on the lead from natural stances; the third bolt was added later on rappel.

CRAZY WISDOM III 5.11b, A1 (12 Points of Aid) (*)
Ascends the steep, right-hand side of the Yellow Wall, finishing at the tourist lookout. Start below THE BIG FLUSH. Bring a full rack with a #4 Camalot.
1. Scramble (Class 4) up into the throat of THE BIG FLUSH gully to a right-facing corner on the left with a double bolt belay on a good ledge.
2. Stem and layback up the right-facing corner past three bolts (5.10c past the first bolt), then step left at the top. Continue up and right to a belay stance with a two bolt anchor below a steep, clean friction slab. 60', 5.10c
3. Step left from the belay, friction on excellent granite up to the first bolt, climb (5.8) to a short crack and a good hold above (bolt), then step left and friction straight up (5.9-) to a nice ledge with a double bolt anchor. 70', 5.9-

CATHEDRAL LEDGE (CRAZY WISDOM & PEANUT GALLERY)

4. Head up towards the right edge of the Yellow Wall. Jam and layback up a gently overhanging finger crack (5.9) on the Yellow Wall side of the arete to a hidden bolt and a stance around the corner on the right. Clip the next bolt, and undercling (5.10b) into a shallow, left-facing corner (5.11b; bolt), then continue straight up to a great ledge with a triple bolt anchor. 70', 5.11b

5. Aid (A1) a ladder of 12 bolts up and right across an overhanging wall to a hanging belay at a triple bolt anchor at the base of a crack system. 50', A1 (You do not need aiders to climb the bolt ladder.)

6. Layback and jam up a finger crack (5.8) for 40 feet (care needed; some loose rock) to a good ledge. Climb up the wide, 5.9 layback crack on ROYAL ARCHES REMINISCENCE to an exposed traverse ledge, and finish the route by exiting left along this ledge to the tourist lookout on top. 120', 5.9

HISTORY: After previous efforts on the route, and with help from Andrew Brosnan, Carolyn Hemstedt, and Carla Mason, Uwe Schneider & Craig Taylor made the climb's first continuous ascent on July 26, 1994.

VARIATION: BEER CAN BYPASS I 5.7

2a. From the double bolt belay at the start of the route, step out left to a bolt, and climb up a shallow, left-facing corner (bolt), finishing up and right to the double bolt belay at the top of Pitch two. 80', 5.7

FA: Craig Taylor & Uwe Schneider July 22, 1994

ROYAL ARCHES REMINISCENCE II 5.10b (5.9 R)

A well hidden, seldom climbed route. A broken tree branch has caused the route to be upgraded. From the start of the 5.9 bolted slab at the base of THE PROW, diagonal up right following a ledge system through trees to the bottom of a cleaned slab just to the left of THE BIG FLUSH.

1. Climb the initial cleaned slab (5.9 R) past one bolt in the lichen on the right until you can traverse right to a conspicuous pine tree. 5.9 R

2. From the branch of this tree (hence the climb's name, in honor of its Yosemite counterpart), step left (5.10b) onto the face and ascend the right side of a large, detached flake (5.9; #4 Friend) to the tourist lookout. Part of the upper flake also recently detached, making the final moves harder. 5.10b

HISTORY: Frank Zahar & Jeff Lea made the first ascent on October 23, 1971. Ajax Greene, Jeff Pheasant, & Joe Cote climbed the route's first free ascent on September 1, 1973. The original bolts on Pitch one, unfortunately, were chopped, but one has apparently been replaced.

THE PEANUT GALLERY FLAKE I 5.11b

The grim offwidth crack/flake at the top of the Yellow Wall, just left of THE BIG FLUSH. Painful on a top-rope, horrifying on the lead. It is normally top-roped from the tourist fence. On the lead, carry large cams and Big Bro's.

1. From the top of the pine tree on ROYAL ARCHES REMINISCENCE, make a barn-door layback move left to enter the crack, then groan, struggle, and thrash back up it to the top. Have fun! 60', 5.11b

HISTORY: Henry Barber made the first ascent of this notorious top-rope problem in 1973. In 1976, under the cover of darkness, several well known local climbers failed to pry off the flake using a ten-ton car jack. After Jim Dunn made unsuccessful attempts to lead the climb, Ken Sims & Mack Johnson made the route's first continuous ascent in July, 1979, protecting the pitch with large Hexentrics and Tube Chocks. Sims was so gripped towards the top of the pitch that he failed to notice he had inadvertently clipped his unbelayed haul rope—not his lead rope—into his last few pieces of protection! "I just sort of went for it, for a little bit," Sims remembered.

AWAY THE WEE MAN I 5.11a (Top-rope) (*)
A spectacular top-rope problem up the sharp arete just to the right of THE PEANUT GALLERY FLAKE. Use the tourist fence as the anchor.
1. Lower down 35 feet to the top of the pine tree, swing the tree back and forth until you can grab the first bucket, then face climb up the arete on sharp square-cuts, moving slightly right back to the top. 35', 5.11a
HISTORY: Jerry Handren, Andy Ross, & Chris Gill made the first ascent in June, 1988. Swinging the tree back and forth was the key to success.

DRY ROASTED I 5.13a (**)
Bring extra water. The route ascends the unrelentingly steep outside face of THE PEANUT GALLERY FLAKE. Approach by rappelling off the summit of the cliff to a bolt anchor. As evidenced by the many obviously snapped off small flakes, the route was "judiciously cleaned" (to use another local activist's polite wording) prior to the first ascent. Several moves are height dependent.
1. Face climb past a nut placement and four bolts on small, square-cut edges (5.13a) up the outside face of THE PEANUT GALLERY FLAKE. 50', 5.13a
HISTORY: Duncan McCallum (Scotland) made the first ascent of the route with Nicki Young (Scotland) on May 4, 1988, on his second day of effort.

THE BIG FLUSH II 5.6 Not Recommended.
This is the large, vertical, tree-filled gully which splits Cathedral Ledge in half. Rotten rock, lichen, moss, and extensive archaeological deposits of old beer cans and broken glass make this a climb to stay well away from.
FA: Bob Mitchell & Andy Turcotte 1967

DEVIL'S DISCIPLE I 5.9
The following two routes, actually worth doing, ascend the small buttress on the upper, right-hand side of THE BIG FLUSH. To reach their common start, rappel 140 feet off two trees north of the tourist lookout to a tree ledge.
1. Ascend the dirty dihedral (5.9) to the left of DEVIL'S ADVOCATE. 5.9
FA: Joe Cote & Michael Hartrich 1975

CATHEDRAL LEDGE (DRY ROASTED) 113

DEVIL'S ADVOCATE I 5.10b
The right-diagonalling crack system to the right of DEVIL'S DISCIPLE.
1. Climb a finger crack to an overhang, move over this, and finish up a V groove inside corner to the top. 5.10b

FA: Joe Cote, Ed Sklar, & Dick Arey   September 22, 1974
FFA: Jim Dunn, Jane Wilson, & Joe Cote   September, 1976

Duncan McCallum (Scotland) on the first ascent of Dry Roasted (5.13a) in 1988. Photograph by Nick Yardley.

George Hurley takes a rest after the 5.8 R runout on Windfall (5.10a / 5.8 R), one of the most popular hard routes up the THIN AIR Face, in 1995. Photograph by Ed Webster.

THE THIN AIR FACE

The following climbs ascend the THIN AIR Face, the steep, open, horizontally striated face located to the right of the prominent, tree-filled gully known as THE BIG FLUSH. The routes offer superb face climbing on plentiful, sharp-edged holds, but protection can often be lacking or hard to arrange. Small Tri-cams, TCUs, Flexible Friends, and wired nuts are frequently helpful. To reach the next climbs, hike up to the base of the STANDARD ROUTE, the prominent, tree-filled chimney system near the center of Cathedral Ledge. The main section of the THIN AIR Face is 150 feet uphill and to the left of STANDARD. The first climb, ROSE MADDER, ascends the upper, left-hand side of the THIN AIR Face, just to the right of THE BIG FLUSH.

ROSE MADDER I 5.9
The farthest left-hand route on the THIN AIR Face. The crux is the same as for DMZ. Rose Madder is an oil color used in painting.
1. Face climb past the first two bolts on DMZ (5.9), then branch left up a brown water streak past three more bolts (5.7), over a small roof, and up to a ledge (pin). Finish up a final headwall to a low-angled, stepped slab leading to the double bolt anchor in the GOOFER'S DELIGHT cave. 160', 5.9
FA: Bill Lowther & Dan Pacheco September 13, 1995

DMZ I 5.9 (*)
The route ascends the right side of the brown water streak on the far, left side of the face which, in winter, is the ice climb GOOFER'S DIRECT.
1. Face climb past two closely spaced bolts (5.9), then head straight up past one more bolt to a double bolt ring anchor. 140', 5.9 Most parties rappel off.
FA: Mike Cody & Todd Swain June 12, 1982

DAWN PATROL I 5.8 R
Begin in the same spot as DMZ, at the bottom of a right-leaning crack, and just left of a major lichen streak. Modern rack, with small nuts and Friends.
1. Follow the crack until it ends, step left, then face climb with poor protection (5.8 R) straight up the face past a peg to a belay anchor. 130', 5.8
FA: Todd Swain & Mike Cody June 12, 1982

BEHIND ENEMY LINES I 5.5 R
Although this is the easiest multi-pitch route up Cathedral Ledge, it is very dirty, not well protected, and has seldom, if ever, been repeated.
1. From the base of DAWN PATROL, work right 15 feet, then climb up past ledges to a finish just to the right of DAWN PATROL. 140', 5.5 R
2. Finish up NO MAN'S LAND, or escape easily up and right to reach the AIRATION traverse ledge below the AIRATION Buttress.
FA: Todd Swain, solo July 25, 1982

116 THE MOUNT WASHINGTON VALLEY

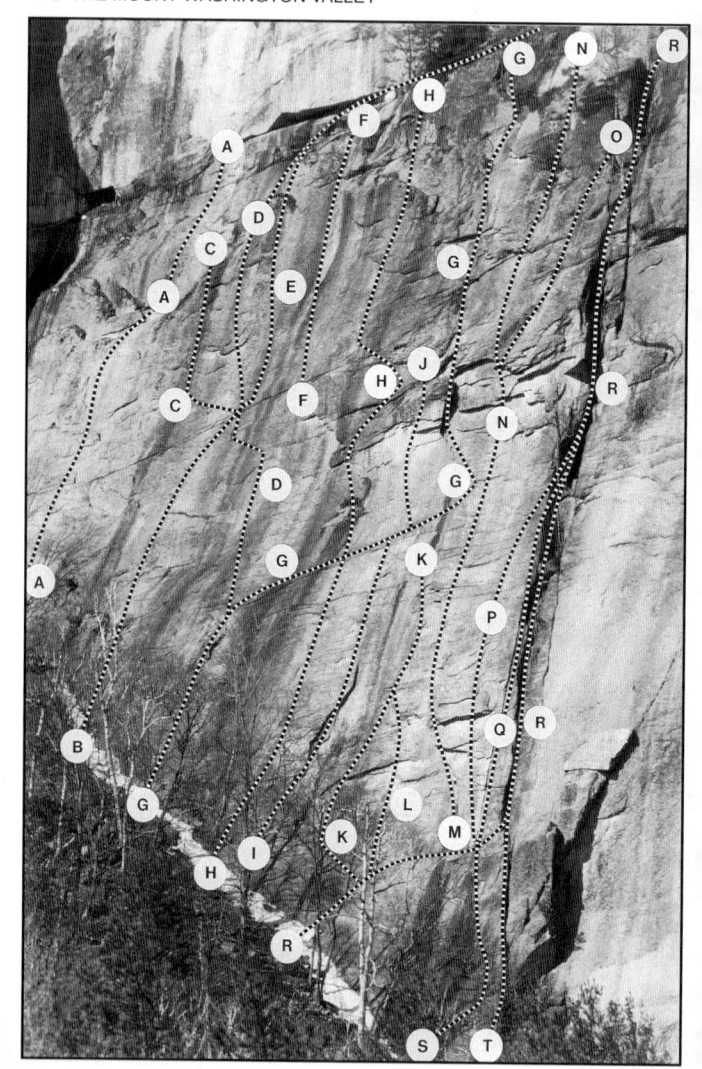

CATHEDRAL LEDGE
(The THIN AIR Face)

A.	***	**STILL IN SAIGON** I 5.8	Page	118
B.	*	**NO MAN'S LAND** II 5.6 R	Page	119
C.		**THE DARCY ROUTE** II 5.6 X	Page	118
D.	***	**RAPID TRANSIT** II 5.10a or 5.10b	Page	120
E.	*	**SPACE WALK** II 5.9+ R	Page	122
F.	***	**ONION HEAD** II 5.11c	Page	122
G.	***	**THIN AIR** II 5.6	Page	125
H.	*	**ADVENTURES IN 3D** II 5.10b (5.10a R)	Page	123
I.	*	**THINNER** I 5.8 R	Page	126
J.	*	**OZONE BYPASS** I 5.11c	Page	126
K.	***	**WINDFALL** I 5.10a (5.8 R)	Page	127
L.	***	**FREEDOM** I 5.10a	Page	127
M.	***	**TURNER'S FLAKE** I 5.8	Page	128
N.	**	**THE MISSING LINK** III 5.10a (5.7 R)	Page	128
O.	*	**LANCELOT LINK / SECRET CHIMP** I 5.10b	Page	129
P.	*	**PRO CHOICE** I 5.10c	Page	129
Q.	***	**THE TOE CRACK** I 5.7	Page	131
R.	**	**STANDARD ROUTE** II 5.6 R	Page	130
S.	*	**THE TOE CRACK DIRECT START** I 5.8	Page	132
T.	*	**THE DIRECT START to STANDARD** I 5.7+	Page	131

STILL IN SAIGON I 5.8 (***)

Now clean, this is one of Cathedral's best 5.8 routes. Popular, with reasonable protection and fun, challenging moves. Find a large tree with exposed roots growing at the upper, left end of the THIN AIR Face, and climb the clean stripe of rock above the tree. Bring a normal rack with several extra slings.

1. Make nice 5.8 face moves (bolt) up a slab at the start, then face climb straight up past several pitons to a block. Mantleshelf (5.8) up to another bolt, climb a flake system to a hidden piton, then angle up and right to a large, sloping belay ledge with a chained, double bolt anchor. 155', 5.8

HISTORY: John Strand & Mike Cody did the first ascent on June 19, 1982. Brad White & Ian Cruickshank scrubbed it & added a direct start in May, 1994.

DIRECT FINISH: **MISS SAIGON** I 5.8

2. From the chained anchor, step two feet right, then head straight up onto a shelf. Continue straight up smaller ledges to a clean face, climbed to a horizontal crack. Move above the crack with increasing difficulty (5.8) past a bulge to reach the far, left end of the AIRATION traverse ledge and a two bolt anchor located at the common start of TOURIST TREAT and CAMBER. 75', 5.8

FA: Tom Callaghan & Haydie Callaghan   October, 1994

THE DARCY ROUTE II 5.6 X

In ironic twists of both history and fate, this was the original line of THIN AIR, led and so named by Ray Darcy in 1956—one of Cathedral Ledge's oldest climbs. While the "other" THIN AIR route has gone on to attain cult status in Northeastern rock climbing, this steep and very unprotected face climb has rarely been repeated. Carry ring pitons and a metal-stepped etrier (see photo), or preferably, plenty of nerve and a modern rack. It's right-hand neighbor, DARCY'S TRAVERSE (5.6) is an easier and safer, though still challenging choice for those wishing to tackle this left-hand section of the THIN AIR Face.

1. Climb to the right of the two small ledges just above the ground that are 100 feet uphill and left from THIN AIR. Face climb more or less straight up (several pegs at healthy intervals) to the prominent crack system that angles across the face. Gain this crack and belay 15 feet higher on a small ledge with a multiple bolt anchor. 5.5 R

2. Climb straight up (peg) to a small overlap (shared by RAPID TRANSIT), then undercling left, pull over the ceiling, move left, and face climb straight up a prominent, brown water streak on the left without any protection for roughly 40 feet until you can escape left (5.6 X; don't fall!) onto the finishing ledge just to the left of the double bolt chained anchor on RAPID TRANSIT. 90', 5.6 X   At the start of the pitch, you can also face climb diagonally left.

HISTORY: Ray Darcy, Stan Hart, & Rittner Walling did the first ascent of this very bold climb in July, 1956. "The route was Ray's idea, and he led the whole thing. Ray was wiry and just incredibly focused when he was climbing," Stan Hart recalled. "There was plenty of thin air around on that straight-up face, it was a clean, airy climb, and the name Thin Air, also Ray's choice, I thought was just the perfect route name. It summed up everything about the climb in two words." John Turner added, "Ray was a colorful and eccentric person. For one thing, while we were all students at MIT he drove a used hearse, which was a great climbing car because it had plenty of extra room to stow gear. But the hearse was all banged up. Whenever Ray got into a traffic accident, he would collect the insurance money and not bother fixing up the hearse. That's how he paid for his climbing trips, I think." As Jack Taylor elaborated: "Used hearses were popular, cheap, and roomy. You could sleep four people in the back."

Ray Darcy penciled the following note on the back of this photograph: "Expansion bolt Darcy surveying the upper part of the Thin Air route on Cathedral." This picture and Darcy's caption prove that THE DARCY ROUTE was the original line of THIN AIR. Look carefully, and you'll notice that Darcy's etrier is clipped to a bolt—which has long since disappeared. Photo by Stan Hart.

NO MAN'S LAND II 5.6 R (*)

A nice face climb with, unfortunately, a poorly protected crux. Not for 5.6 leaders. Walk uphill 100 feet left of THIN AIR to a clean, stepped section of rock below a small pine tree growing on a ledge 20 feet above the ground. Bring a modern rack with Tri-cams and small wired nuts. Semi-popular.

1. Climb up to the small pine 20 feet up, then make a short traverse right into a narrow, left-slanting dike. Climb this (5.5 R) to a good horizontal crack and belay. 75', 5.5 R (May also be combined with Pitch two.)

120 THE MOUNT WASHINGTON VALLEY

2. Continue up the dike past a narrow flake (5.6 R) to a good ledge with fixed anchors and a chain. 5.6 R Most parties rappel off with two ropes.
3. To continue, take the line of least resistance up to the cave on GOOFER'S DELIGHT, and escape right across the AIRATION traverse ledge. 5.5
HISTORY: David Tibbetts & Howard Peterson, in all likelihood, did the first ascent in August, 1970. Todd Swain later climbed and named the route in 1980.

DARCY'S TRAVERSE II 5.6 (*)
The original line up the THIN AIR Face. A safer, although wandering line up the steep face to the left of THIN AIR. Good situations, but care must be taken to protect the second on the long, horizontal traverse on Pitch two.
1. Climb Pitch one of THE DARCY ROUTE. Climb to the right of the two small ledges just above the ground, 100 feet uphill and to the left from THIN AIR. Face climb more or less straight up (several pitons at healthy intervals) to the prominent crack system that angles across the face. Gain this crack, and belay 15 feet higher on a small ledge with a multiple bolt anchor. 90', 5.5
2. Traverse right across the upper THIN AIR Face along a quite prominent, horizontal crack line to a good ledge (pitons) just left of THIN AIR. 60', 5.4
3. Continue right, merging with the top pitch of THIN AIR. 5.6
HISTORY: According to the original write-up in the December, 1958 issue of Appalachia, Ray Darcy & Fran Coffin in all likelihood made the first ascent of this climb—and not today's normal THIN AIR route—in July, 1955, making this the initial route up the THIN AIR Face. "At one point there is a very long traverse across the face where two expansion bolts had to be placed because of the absence of piton cracks," goes the account. When John Turner (UK) & Craig Merrihue unknowingly made the first recorded ascent of the present day THIN AIR route in August, 1956, they did not find a single bolt on the climb.

RAPID TRANSIT II 5.10a or 5.10b (***)
A heavily travelled classic climbed for the sheer beauty of the moves or as a convenient way to access routes on the left side of the AIRATION Buttress. The crux offers well protected, impeccable face climbing that is definitely not 5.9-!
1. Climb the first pitch of THIN AIR to a fixed piton anchor. 50', 5.2
2. Face climb straight up to a stance (bolt), then head slightly left to reach the right-hand end of a long, narrow ledge about 75 feet off the ground (piton). Now make delicate face moves up a steeper, nearly blank headwall. If you climb just to the right of the crux bolt, the moves go at a surprising 5.10a, while the mantleshelf move to the left of the crux bolt is 5.10b. Clip the second bolt (with relief), balance traverse left, and climb up to THE DARCY ROUTE belay ledge which has a multiple bolt anchor. 125', 5.10a or 5.10b
3. From the belay, face climb straight up (ring piton) over a small overlap, then up a steep headwall (bolt; 5.9) past a fixed piton and two more bolts to

CATHEDRAL LEDGE - THE THIN AIR FACE (RAPID TRANSIT) 121

Ed Webster on the first ascent of Rapid Transit (5.10a or 5.10b), clipping in on Pitch three (5.9) in 1985. Compare this picture with the preceding photo of Ray Darcy. The narrow overlap is the same one. Photograph by Kurt Winkler.

the final 5.9 bulge. Belay at the double bolt, chained anchor on the stance above. 90', 5.9 You can rappel off from here back to the ground with two 50 meter ropes, or instead, climb up and right to the AIRATION traverse ledge.

HISTORY: The start of the second pitch and a short section on DARCY'S TRAVERSE had been climbed earlier. After cleaning, Ed Webster & Kurt Winkler did the first ascent of the route on October 31, 1985. The first ascent party also added an extra bolt on Pitch three plus the chained anchor in 1995

SPACE WALK II 5.9+ R (*)
Still a serious and rarely climbed route up the highest section of the THIN AIR Face. Plenty of raw courage, small wired nuts, and an anti-gravity pack will boost your chances. Begin just right of THIN AIR at a water-streaked groove.
1. Climb up the shallow groove (5.7 R) and belay on THIN AIR. 5.7 R
2. Face climb to a bolt above, then angle left to a long, narrow ledge where the climb intersects with THE DARCY ROUTE. (At this point, climbing the smooth slab on RAPID TRANSIT makes for a much more sustained pitch.) Belay at the multiple bolt anchor on THE DARCY ROUTE. 5.7 (or, if combined with Pitch two of RAPID TRANSIT, either 5.10a or 5.10b).
3. Twenty feet to the right of the top pitch of RAPID TRANSIT, face climb up to a bolt, step back down, then left, and move up to a second bolt. Now head straight up (5.9+ R) to the right-hand end of a small blueberry ledge. Small wired nuts below your feet on the crux. 5.9+ R

HISTORY: Doug Madara, Paul Ross, & Andrew Ross made the first ascent on August 27, 1977 — when Andy Ross was only 12 years old.

ONION HEAD II 5.11c (***)
A sustained, bolt-protected face climb up the center of the SPACE WALK Headwall. An exposed position and great moves make this a soon-to-be classic.
1. Climb Pitch one of THIN AIR to a fixed piton anchor. 50', 5.2
2. Head up RAPID TRANSIT, climbing its crux past two bolts (5.10a or 5.10b), then step right onto the traverse ledge on DARCY'S TRAVERSE to reach a double bolt anchor on a good stance that is 20 feet to the right of the RAPID TRANSIT / DARCY ROUTE multiple bolt belay. 100', 5.10a or 5.10b
3. Face climb straight up past five bolts (5.11c crux after the second bolt) to a good stance. Continue up black rock past two final bolts, still on 5.11 moves, until easier climbing gains the top. 160', 5.11c

HISTORY: Tom Callaghan top-roped the pitch in September, 1990. Bill Lowther & Ozzie Blumet did the first ascent over three days in June, 1993. They placed all the bolts free on the lead, except the last one, then freed the pitch.

007 II 5.9+ (*)
A well protected mission, however, the crux underclinging moves on Pitch two require a cool, calculated approach. "Shaken, but not stirred!"

CATHEDRAL LEDGE - THE THIN AIR FACE (ADVENTURES IN 3D)

1. Climb the first pitch of THIN AIR to a fixed piton anchor. 50', 5.2
2. Face climb to a bolt up and left, then aim for a block and a prominent undercling crack on the left side on the THIN AIR Buttress. Undercling the crack up and left, then pull over. Belay on a good ledge on the right with a fixed piton anchor on DARCY'S TRAVERSE. 100', 5.9+
3. Follow the ramp to the right, then follow weaknesses up and left to a bushy ledge. 80', 5.7 Finish as desired.
FA: Doug Madara & Paul Ross September 1, 1977

ADVENTURES IN 3D II 5.10b (5.10a R) (*)

A full length route incorporating parts of several obscure climbs. Varied moves, with a crescendo finish up the smooth face immediately left of the top of THIN AIR. Begin at the groove at the start of SPACE WALK.
1. Just right of the brown water groove, face climb straight up (5.8 R) a gray face (peg) to the traverse ledge on THIN AIR. 75', 5.8 R.
2. Ascend a prominent water streak to a clump of bushes (bolt). Above a block, undercling cracks back to the right (5.10b) across the left-hand front side of the THIN AIR Buttress. After a hard face move (bolt; 5.9), climb a short headwall to a good ledge (piton anchor) on DARCY'S TRAVERSE. 80', 5.10b
3. This beautiful pitch climbs the upper, right side of the SPACE WALK Headwall. Step left and make delicate face moves up a white nose of rock to a bolt 20 feet up. Head left up thin grooves (5.10a R) to a stance and a second bolt. Angle right to a steep headwall (bolt) and the bushy ledge above. 90', 5.10a R
4. A short corner/crack gains the AIRATION traverse ledge.
HISTORY: Pitch one, climbed previously, was an obscure variation to THIN AIR. The crux on Pitch two was an old aid variation to THIN AIR called VICE CRISPIES, done in 1971 by John Porter & Phil Ostrowski. The upper part of Pitch two, part of GATE CRASHER, was climbed in August, 1978 by Mike Heintz, Paul Ross, & Andrew Ross without the bolt. Ed Webster & Kurt Winkler free climbed Pitch two on October 31, 1985, then returned the next day to make the route's first complete ascent.

VARIATION: **START ME UP** I 5.7 R

A useful alternate start with any of the previous climbs.
1a. Just left of THIN AIR, climb easy steps that go up 25 feet and end. Take a straight line to a steep bulge 60 feet up and climb over its right side (5.7 R) to the right end of a narrow, grassy ledge. 5.7 R Finish as desired.
FA: Kurt Winkler & David Stone September 15, 1981

GATE CRASHER II 5.9

An obscure combination that pre-dates ADVENTURES IN 3D.
1. Climb directly up the inside of the THINNER corner with some fixed protection to the THIN AIR traverse ledge. 120', 5.8

124 THE MOUNT WASHINGTON VALLEY

Mike Jewel & partner on the third pitch (5.5), of Thin Air (5.6) in 1986. Photograph by Ed Webster.

CATHEDRAL LEDGE - THE THIN AIR FACE (THIN AIR) 125

2. Face climb left across the water streak to bushes and the block on 007. Undercling left on 007, then traverse straight right (5.9) taking a line 15 feet higher than the 5.10b ADVENTURES IN 3D undercling, and belay on a small stance. Friends helpful. 5.9

3. Climb the short headwall (5.9; bolt), the same as ADVENTURES IN 3D, to the belay ledge (fixed pitons) on DARCY'S TRAVERSE. 30', 5.9

4. Follow 007 up and right to the top. 5.7

HISTORY: Mike Heintz, Paul Ross, & Andrew Ross did the first ascent in August, 1978. The Pitch 3 bolt was added in 1985 on ADVENTURES IN 3D.

THIN AIR II 5.6 (***)

Exceptionally popular—and deservedly so. One of New Hampshire's great rock climbs, whose true history has finally come to light after 40 years! This beautiful climb ascends the center of the improbable, exposed face to the left of STANDARD ROUTE. With its many positive holds, the climb is similar in character to a steep, Shawangunk face climb. Protection is generally adequate, although care must be taken by the leader to safely protect the second on the long traverse on Pitch two. Begin 150 feet left and uphill from STANDARD at a broken, stepped section of rock. Bring a normal rack with extra slings.

1. Start on the left up a series of steps (5.3; the easiest way), or face climb straight up on sharp holds (5.5; not as much protection) up to a small, but comfortable belay stance with a fixed piton anchor. 50', 5.3 to 5.5

2. Traverse right, staying high (a little harder); or low, stepping down off of the belay stance (slightly easier), traversing past fixed pitons until you can gain an obvious, long, foot ledge (protected by two bolts) which leads horizontally to the right across the exposed face to a good belay stance with a double bolt anchor on the right. 50', 5.6

3. Face climb up and right (peg), then back left (piton), finally up into an obvious, right-facing corner. Belay at the top of the corner on a comfortable, exposed ledge with another double bolt anchor. 60', 5.5

4. Follow a crack system straight up to a stance at a horizontal break (fixed natural thread) below a small overlap. Step left to a shallow, right-facing corner, climb the corner, then surmount the overlap (5.6), exposed but on better holds, before moving up and slightly right, finally reaching a good belay ledge with a large pine tree. 120', 5.6

5. Scamper up a dirty groove on the left up to the large, tree-covered ledge below the AIRATION Buttress. Walk off easily to the right through the woods.

HISTORY: "I was also a student at MIT in 1955 and '56, so I knew Ray Darcy," explained John Turner. "I was very envious when he told me he'd just done a new route up Cathedral called Thin Air. He suggested I should do the second ascent and told me where the climb went. Two weeks later, in August of 1956, my favorite partner at the time, Craig Merrihue, a student at Harvard, and I repeated Darcy's climb"—or so Turner and everyone else thought for the next 40 years. Darcy's verbal description of his route (or routes; he had done two separate lines up the face at this point) to Turner had mentioned "a high traverse", but instead, according to John: "We traversed low along a narrow, easy ledge with very little protection that ended near the top of the flake I climbed several years later." They found no bolts anywhere on the route, nor did they place any bolts themselves. (Turner himself never carried a bolt kit.) On the top pitch, finding two fixed pitons (probably placed by Darcy on the FA of DARCY'S TRAVERSE in 1955), they made the reasonable assumption that they had indeed repeated Darcy's new route. In fact, they had made the first recorded ascent—unknown to them—of a route that would become one of New England's most popular rock climbs. Tragically, on March 14, 1965, Craig Merrihue and Dan Doody (a member of the 1963 American Everest Expedition) were killed in a fall while climbing Pinnacle Gully in Huntington Ravine on Mount Washington. This fine climb stands in Merrihue's memory.

VARIATION #1: **THINNER** I 5.8 R (*)
This popular variation ascends the face just to the left of the shallow, right-facing corner to the left of TURNER'S FLAKE and below the long traverse on THIN AIR's second pitch. Good moves, but a bit runout. Modern rack.
1a. Start below the corner at a bulging slab (the original line), or traverse easily right across ledges to broken rock just left of the corner. Climb the face up to a break angling out left, before thin moves lead back right to the top of the corner (original line). Most ascents now stay closer to the arete on the right. From the corner's top, climb short, steeper sections (5.8 R) to the two bolt belay at the end of THIN AIR's Pitch two traverse. 125', 5.8 R
FA: Mark Lawrence & Kurt Winkler Spring, 1971

VARIATION #2: **THINNER STILL** I 5.10a (Top-rope)
1b. Face climb directly up to the THINNER corner. 25', 5.10a
FA: Unknown.

VARIATION #3: **OZONE BYPASS** I 5.11c (*)
Between THIN AIR and SPACE WALK, what do you have? The OZONE BYPASS... Start at the double bolt belay at the end of the long traverse ledge on THIN AIR. Bring four quick draws, plus some extra gear. Popular.
2a. Climb up and left to the first bolt, then crank straight up the bulging overhang past one more bolt and two bolts (5.11c) to the block belay ledge on THIN AIR and a double bolt anchor. 60', 5.11c
FA: Brad White & Ian Cruickshank May, 1993

VARIATION #4: **THE 5.8 CORNER** I 5.8
An obscure variation to the last pitch of THIN AIR.

CATHEDRAL LEDGE - THE THIN AIR FACE (WINDFALL)

4a. Right of the final, dirty groove, climb up a short slab to a 15 foot corner (5.8), which is ascended to the large, tree-covered AIRATION ledge. 5.8
FA: Unknown.

WINDFALL I 5.10a (5.8 R) (***)

An unexpected find, very popular, with high quality face climbing. The route follows an independent line up the beautiful, steep open face between THINNER and TURNER'S FLAKE. Begin at the regular, left-hand start of STANDARD ROUTE. Carry a good selection of small cams and wired nuts, plus plenty of slings.

1. Climb the initial flake on STANDARD, then traverse up and straight left across narrow ledges (5.7 R) to two pitons. Now face climb up and slightly right over a long, narrow overlap (5.10a). Once established on the upper face, step up and right 10 feet to a peg, then continue face climbing straight up to an awkward mantleshelf move at a good flake (5.8 R; bolt once you've stood up). Continue slightly right, then back left past two more fixed pitons to a double bolt anchor (the WINDFALL belay) on a good stance above the THINNER dihedral, and just below the right end of the Pitch two traverse on THIN AIR. 130', 5.10a (5.8 R) Continue as desired, or rappel off with two ropes. If you rappel off with one rope, tension traverse off to the left near the bottom to reach some ledges—or you'll end up short.

HISTORY: Andy Ross & Jerry Handren first top-roped the route carrying a plastic milk bottle filled with beer with them, for the extra challenge, in 1985. Tom Callaghan & Haydie Callaghan then made the first ascent of this classic face route, placing all the fixed protection free on the lead, on April 21, 1987.

DIRECT START: CAPITOL GAINS I 5.11d X

No pro, but it can also be easily top-roped off the WINDFALL pitons.
1a. Face climb directly up a black water streak (5.11d X) to the small ledge where WINDFALL's first, side by side fixed pitons are located. 30', 5.11d X
FA: John Strand, free-solo June, 1988

VARIATION: FREEDOM I 5.10a (***)

Well protected, thin face moves lead up to and over the overlap 15 feet to the right of WINDFALL. Locate two bolts on a smooth, white face directly above the start of STANDARD ROUTE. The route merges with WINDFALL at its bolt—and is actually better protected and more direct than its neighbor. Bring a modern rack with wired nuts, assorted small cams, and several extra slings.
1a. Head up the easy flake on STANDARD, then face climb straight up white rock past two bolts (5.10a) to the right side of the WINDFALL overlap. Swing over at a jug (5.9), then face climb up and right to a small flake before angling up left to the bolt on WINDFALL. Finish up WINDFALL to its fixed, double bolt belay at the good belay stance above. 130', 5.10a

HISTORY: The route had been previously top-roped by numerous climbers. After also top-roping the climb a week earlier, Ed Webster & Harold Consentine made the first ascent on August 20, 1995. The two bolts were placed on the lead, the first free, and the second on aid.

TURNER'S FLAKE I 5.8 (***)

This committing, strenuous lead ascends the prominent, left-curving layback flake just to the left of STANDARD ROUTE. Carry several large Friends and Camalots for protection—but bear in mind that the crack was originally led in 1958 by John Turner and Dr. Michael Ward without any protection at all!

1. Start at the base of STANDARD. Jam and layback up the large flake system (5.8) to a stance on the right at a bolt. Continue up a narrow, left-facing corner (also 5.8), and belay on the left at the WINDFALL double bolt belay and stance. 135', 5.8 Continue as desired up any of several different routes.

HISTORY: After John Turner & Dr. Michael Ward (both UK) retreated from their initial foray up onto RECOMPENSE on May 17, 1959, it was "too early for the bar in North Conway, so we climbed my now eponymous flake (then called "The Direct Start to Thin Air"). I led the first rope with Dick Morden (our primitive pitons did not fit anywhere, so it was done without protection), while Mike Ward led the second rope, accompanied by Claude Lavallée from Canada," remembered Turner about their notoriously serious lead. (See RECOMPENSE for the rest of the story!) In Appalachia, Turner wrote: "The pitch is less difficult than it appears, but the complete absence of protection is a little discouraging... The standard was thought to be easy fifth class throughout."

THE MISSING LINK III 5.10a (5.7 R) (**)

Simian ancestry? Similar to a Gunks overhang, the crux moves out the band of yellow roofs between the mid sections of THIN AIR and STANDARD ROUTE are popularly done on their own, usually with an escape left onto THIN AIR. The full route is a combination of new and old pitches, with a very long runout on Pitch three that has seldom been repeated.

1. Climb up TURNER'S FLAKE to a stance on the right (bolt). 110', 5.8
2. Ascend the sharp arete to the cave on STANDARD. 45', 5.7
3. Traverse out left to a thin, vertical crack leading up to a band of yellow roofs. After the troublesome first roof, step left, and pull the lip (5.10a) onto the face above. Run out the rope straight up, eventually stepping right (5.7 R) to a belay at a large horizontal crack. Beware of rope drag. 125', 5.10a (5.7 R)
4. Climb the cleaned stripe of rock above, then finish up a tricky, 15 foot inside corner (5.8) to the AIRATION walk-off ledge. 5.8
5. Follow PINE TREE ELIMINATE to the top. 120', 5.8+

HISTORY: TURNER'S FLAKE was done by John Turner (UK), Dick Morden (Canada), Dr. Michael Ward (UK), & Claude Lavallée (Canada), on

May 17, 1959. Michael Hartrich & Rick Ruppel did PINE TREE ELIMINATE in 1973. The route was linked up by Ed Webster & Paul Ross in July, 1976.

VARIATION #1: **THE DIRECT START** I 5.8 R
Begin between the normal start and DIRECT START to STANDARD.
1a. Climb a very thin, vertical fracture (5.8 R) up the smooth slab. 60', 5.8 R
FA: Mike Heintz & Paul Ross   August, 1978

VARIATION #2: **LANCELOT LINK / SECRET CHIMP** I 5.10b (*)
Climbs through the roofs just to the right of THE MISSING LINK. Normal rack. Begin from the WINDFALL double bolt belay stance.
2a. Start up THE MISSING LINK, do the crux of THE LINK, then move right at a bolt (5.10b) on hidden holds past the next overlap to a second bolt, and up the face to the top, either heading left, or escaping up and right (much more popular) onto STANDARD ROUTE. 150', 5.10b
FA: Steve Wooding & Dave McDermott   August, 1989

PRO CHOICE I 5.10c (*)
A beautiful climb up the steep, inviting face between TURNER'S FLAKE and THE TOE CRACK. Bring a modern rack with extra slings. Popular.
1. Climb the initial traverse flake (5.5) on STANDARD ROUTE to a belay on a good stance at the base of THE TOE CRACK. 60', 5.5
2. Step left onto the face, then continue straight up (bolt; 5.9) to the crux overlap (bolt). Make a very awkward step up (5.10c) past the overlap to reach the third bolt, then face climb straight up, finishing up the arete above THE TOE CRACK to the Cave on STANDARD ROUTE. 100', 5.10c (These two pitches may be combined if desired. 165', 5.10c)
HISTORY: Uwe Schneider & Jennifer Putscher made the first ascent in August, 1989. After cleaning and inspecting the route on rappel, the bolts were placed free on the lead from stances. Putscher had just returned from attending a pro choice rally in Washington DC.

REPULSION II 5.8 or 5.9
Another long combination climb taking a direct line up the left edge of the STANDARD ROUTE chimney. The 5.9 crux can be easily avoided on the right.
1. Climb the first pitch (5.5) of STANDARD ROUTE, or the TOE CRACK DIRECT START (5.8). 70', 5.5 or 5.8
2. Jam up THE TOE CRACK (5.7), then trace the beautiful arete up the chimney's left-hand edge. Belay in the cave on STANDARD. 5.7
3. Skirt the cave on the left, climbing up a steep face split by a thin crack to a piton at the second overlap. Belay on a good ledge above. 5.8
4. Either climb a few hard moves (5.9) up the left-hand wall of the chimney (peg & bolt), or escape easily up STANDARD ROUTE to the top. 5.9

130 THE MOUNT WASHINGTON VALLEY

HISTORY: In July, 1956, Stan Hart, partnered by Gardiner Perry, attempted to bypass the Cave on STANDARD to the left—but took a dramatic 60 foot leader fall on Pitch three, pulled out several pitons, and bruised his ribs. Todd Swain & Brad White linked up the whole route on November 1, 1980.

STANDARD ROUTE II 5.6 R (**)

One of the oldest climbs in the region, STANDARD was the first rock climb up Cathedral Ledge, and is a much finer route than it might at first appear. The renowned crux, the less than well protected Cave Wall (5.6 R) is still quite testing by modern standards. The vertical, tree-filled, chimney crack several hundred feet to the right of THE BIG FLUSH, and just to the right of the THIN AIR Face, marks the line. Occasional loose stones and gravel should be handled carefully, especially when there are other climbers below you. The original start, up a slender, white flake or narrow corner, is 60 feet uphill and to the left of the very base of the chimney system. Carry a normal rack.

Arthur Murray starting up the Cave Wall crux of the Standard Route (5.6 R) in 1936.
Photograph by Kenneth A. Henderson.

1. Climb an easy, 20 foot high, left-facing corner/flake, then traverse horizontally to your right across a series of small holds and flakes (piton) to a tricky step (5.5) down

CATHEDRAL LEDGE (STANDARD ROUTE & THE TOE CRACK)

and right onto a small ledge. Belay in the main chimney on a ledge. 70', 5.5
2. Head straight up the chimney, pulling over an awkward chockstone (5.5). Belay in the comfortable, cool, and spacious Cave at a large tree. 120', 5.5
3. Climb the famous Cave Wall on the right with no protection (5.6 R) until you can clip a sling high on the left. Stay in the chimney, pass by a troublesome overhang, and belay at another tree on a ledge in the upper chimney. 125', 5.6 R
4. Finish up a dirty gully, exiting right up a short, steep step. 5.4

HISTORY: Leland W. Pollock, Payson T. Newton, & Robert L. M. Underhill made the first ascent of this extremely historic route in June, 1931—and went to a lot of trouble before doing so. After being defeated by both of the direct starts to the chimney itself, they rappelled down the upper part of the route, and with Leland Pollock leading, climbed back to the top of the cliff. Later, with the help of a weighted string, they managed to rig a climbing rope around a tree (now gone) partway up the regular first pitch, and then tension traversed right into the chimney. Underhill wrote, "This is not the first instance in which the 'rope traverse' of modern European rock climbing has been found necessary in the White Mountains."

VARIATION #1: **THE DIRECT START** I 5.7+ (*)
Start just uphill from the chimney's base. Fritz Wiessner later wrote with some understatement: "This climb is good practice for the climber who wants to improve his crack and chimney technique." An impressive lead for 1933!
1a. Climb an easy, stepped dike (bolt) up into a notoriously awkward offwidth chimney/crack (5.7+). Halfway up the crack, look for a very helpful fixed piton on the face to the left. 90', 5.7+ Join STANDARD.

HISTORY: William P. Allis did the first ascent of this strenuous crack in the Summer of 1933, and as a result, made the first completely free ascent of STANDARD ROUTE, as the first ascent party had gained the chimney by tension traversing right from a convenient tree. When Fritz Wiessner led the second ascent of Allis's DIRECT START that same summer, Robert Underhill declined to follow, so Fritz politely asked if the next few pitches continued up the same crack to the top. After Underhill assured him that they did, Fritz untied, threw down the climbing rope, and free-soloed up the remainder of the route—including the notorious Cave Wall.

VARIATION #2: **THE TOE CRACK** I 5.7 (***)
This ever popular, enjoyable, well protected, all time classic crack ascends the long toe and hand width crack just to the left of the main chimney on STANDARD ROUTE's second pitch. Great protection with a normal rack.
2a. Climb the long, vertical crack (5.7) with superb jamming, just to the left of the normal route. When the crack finally ends, step left (bolt), and follow an enjoyable, airy arete (also 5.7) to the Cave belay on STANDARD. 110', 5.7

3a. A popular continuation from the Cave traverses straight left across the face (5.4, but totally unprotected) to join with THIN AIR, however, you may also finish up STANDARD ROUTE, starting with the Cave Wall (5.6 R).
FA: Unknown.

VARIATION #3: **THE TOE CRACK DIRECT START** I 5.8 (*)
A worthwhile addition to THE TOE CRACK, with good protection.
1b. Climb up the easy dike of STANDARD's DIRECT START to a bolt, then step left and climb a thin vertical crack (5.8) to a piton on the right. Step left again into a flake/crack system leading up to THE TOE CRACK. 60', 5.8
FA: Unknown.

VARIATION #4: **SAFETY IN NUMBERS** I 5.9 R
This climb ascends the exposed arete just downhill and to the right of the easy, staircase dike on THE DIRECT START to STANDARD ROUTE.
1c. Face climb up the arete (5.9 R), with nice moves but very little protection, eventually merging with the top of the dike. 50', 5.9 R
HISTORY: Tom Callaghan, Haydie Callaghan, John Strand, & Steve Angelini made the variation's first ascent in August, 1989.

VARIATION #5: **THE DIRECT FINISH** I 5.7+
4a. At the top, struggle up the final, obvious offwidth crack. 40', 5.7+
HISTORY: This pitch was first climbed by Leland W. Pollock & Robert L. M. Underhill on the second ascent of STANDARD ROUTE on October 12, 1931.

VARIATION #6: **GILL'S CRACK** I 5.11b (Top-rope)
Just to the left of STANDARD ROUTE's DIRECT FINISH are two thin, vertical finger cracks.
4b. The left-hand crack has only been top-roped. 35', 5.11b
HISTORY: Chris Gill top-roped this variation in September, 1985.

VARIATION #7: **MADARA'S CRACK** I 5.10b
4c. Jam up the somewhat easier right-hand finger crack. 35', 5.10b
FA: Doug Madara 1978

THE AIRATION BUTTRESS

This is the large, white buttress sitting above the THIN AIR Face, and just to the right of THE BIG FLUSH. It offers a close-knit collection of some of Cathedral's hardest free climbs: TOURIST TREAT, THE CREATION, STAGE FRIGHT, and HEATHER—all 5.12s. Other popular climbs here include CAMBER, REVERSE CAMBER, AIRATION, and PINE TREE ELIMINATE. To reach the start of any of the next climbs, do a route up the THIN AIR Face (THIN AIR, RAPID TRANSIT, etc.) to gain the access ledge that runs along the base of the AIRATION Buttress; or, drive up the Cathedral Ledge auto road, park at the turnaround, and hike along a path down and around the right side of the AIRATION Buttress (left side when facing out) until you walk straight left through the woods on the path to the large ledge at the base of PINE TREE ELIMINATE and AIRATION. Farther left, the sloping AIRATION Buttress traverse ledge (5.4 at its left-hand end) leads to the starts of CAMBER, TOURIST TREAT, and eventually, GOOFER'S DELIGHT. The routes are now described from left to right across the buttress, beginning with CLEAN SWEEP which ascends the blank slab to the left of the GOOFER'S DELIGHT crack system.

CLEAN SWEEP I 5.11b (**)

A committing face climb on excellent rock up the gray face to the left of GOOFER'S DELIGHT. Rappel about 100 feet from on top of the AIRATION Buttress down to a small belay stance with a two bolt anchor.

1. Face climb up and right surmounting a bulge at a small corner (scary) and continue past two bolts. Angle back left past two more bolts to the crux (5.11b) gaining a long, narrow ledge. One hard face move gains the top. 100', 5.11b

HISTORY: Tom Callaghan & John Strand made the first ascent on August 15, 1985. Three days were required to clean the route (some of it was done tandem on the same rappel rope, using wire push brooms!) then it took two more days to establish the climb. In an impressive effort, all the protection bolts were placed free on the lead.

VARIATION: AUTOCLAVE I 5.12c R (*)

You might want to top-rope this route first, unless you are a highly skilled doctor of face climbing—with a fully paid life insurance policy.

1. Climb CLEAN SWEEP to the third bolt, then move up and right on extremely thin moves (5.12c R) to a tiny ledge and the top. 90', 5.12c R

HISTORY: After Tom Callaghan & John Strand top-roped the pitch in July, 1988, John Strand led the first ascent in November, 1988.

GOOFER'S DELIGHT II 5.9+

A sustained and strenuous crack climb, especially if combined with TABU, which makes for anything but a goofy outing. Start in the left-hand of two,

134 THE MOUNT WASHINGTON VALLEY

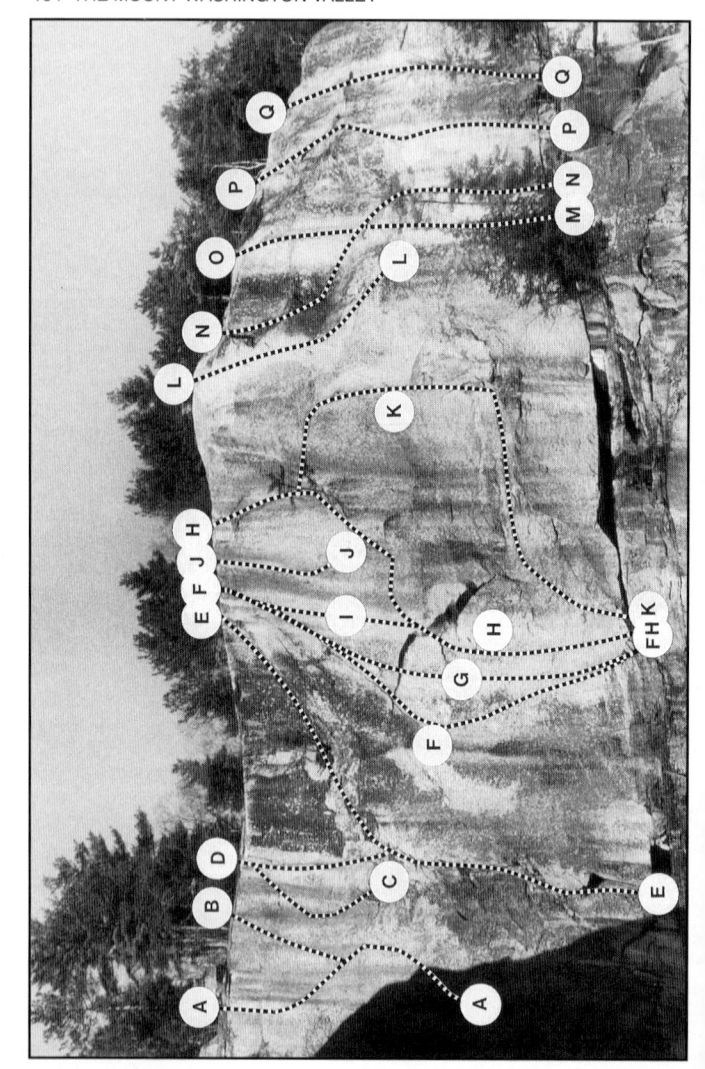

CATHEDRAL LEDGE – THE AIRATION BUTTRESS

A.	**	**CLEAN SWEEP** I 5.11b	Page 133	J.	*	**ROOM WITH A VIEW** I 5.12a (5.10d R)	Page 140
B.	*	**AUTOCLAVE** I 5.12c R	Page 133	K.	*	**THE CREATION** II 5.12b (5.10 R)	Page 140
C.	*	**HIPPODROME** I 5.10c	Page 136	L.	**	**REACH THE SKY** I 5.11c	Page 142
D.	***	**TABU** I 5.9 R	Page 137	M.	***	**STAGE FRIGHT** II 5.12c X	Page 142
E.		**GOOFER'S DELIGHT** II 5.9+	Page 133	N.	***	**AIRATION** I 5.11b	Page 142
F.	***	**TOURIST TREAT** II 5.12c	Page 137	O.		**KILL YOUR TELEVISION** I 5.11 R	Page 142
G.	*	**ENDLESS SUMMER** II 5.12b (5.9 R)	Page 137	P.	***	**HEATHER** I 5.12b	Page 145
H.	***	**CAMBER** II 5.11b	Page 137	Q.	***	**PINE TREE ELIMINATE** I 5.8+	Page 146
I.	***	**REVERSE CAMBER** I 5.10b	Page 138				

136 THE MOUNT WASHINGTON VALLEY

Tom Callaghan leading the first ascent of Clean Sweep (5.11b) in 1985. Photograph by Haydie Callaghan.

rectangular caves located at the left end of the AIRATION Buttress traverse ledge. The route's first five feet, jamming out the lip of the cave, is the crux! The initial belay is at a double bolt anchor inside the left cave.

1. Thrash over the lip of the cave (5.9+), jam a crack up and around a second overhang, then continue up a nice hand crack to a good belay stance at a two bolt anchor next to a white birch tree. 100', 5.9+

2. Follow a dirty, right-diagonalling crack (5.6) through the lichen to the top, or (a better choice), finish up TABU (5.9 R). 5.6 or 5.9 R

FA: Henry Barber & Bill O'Connell   Summer, 1970
FFA: Henry Barber & Bob Anderson   October, 1972

VARIATION #1: **HIPPODROME** I 5.10c (*)

Ascends the face between AUTOCLAVE and TABU. From the top of the AIRATION Buttress, rappel down to the TABU belay on a small ledge with a white birch tree and a double bolt anchor. Tricky protection; modern rack.

2a. Climb a left-leaning, steepening groove until it ends. Thin moves (5.10c)

lead up & right to a bolt, then escape right into the TABU finger crack. 70', 5.10c
HISTORY: After cleaning the route, Uwe Schneider & Ben Onachila made the first ascent on August 7, 1992, placing the bolt free on the lead.

VARIATION #2: **TABU** I 5.9 R (***)
A magnificent piece of face climbing. Too bad it isn't longer! A bit necky on the lead. The route is frequently top-roped, however, dries quickly after a rain, and is usually approached from above on rappel.
2b. From a two bolt anchor beside a white birch tree, climb up an aesthetic, clean, white slab past a bolt into a short finger crack. 50', 5.9 R
FA: John Bragg & Henry Barber August 19, 1973

TOURIST TREAT II 5.12c (***)
One of many transitional "Last Great Problems" on Cathedral Ledge, TOURIST TREAT ascends the prominent, cleaned crack system on the left side of the AIRATION Buttress. Begin 60 feet to the right of GOOFER'S DELIGHT at the base of the crack. Double bolt anchor for the belay.
1. After an incipient vertical crack (5.10b), face climb past several bolts to a rest on a stance. (This start is also commonly used to begin CAMBER.) The bulge above, split by a thin finger crack, is the 5.12c crux. Some of the protection is fixed. Belay in the upper crack. 5.12c
2. Progressively easier crack climbing gains the top.
HISTORY: Jeff Pheasant did the first ascent of the climb, rope-solo, in November, 1975. In August, 1979, Ed Webster cleaned the route on rappel and free climbed the start up to the crux bulge. Several talented climbers then attempted the route free before Lynn Hill & Russ Raffa made the notable first free ascent of the climb in August, 1984.

ENDLESS SUMMER II 5.12b (5.9 R) (*)
Ascends the unlikely steep wall between TOURIST TREAT and CAMBER. Look for three bolts. Thin edges lead to a boulder problem crux. The first section of the route is the same as TOURIST TREAT.
1. From the rest stance on TOURIST TREAT, face climb straight up past three bolts, making thin moves over a bulge (5.12c crux after third bolt) to gain a vertical dike which is followed up to and over the main overlap. Scary moves lead up or left (5.9 R) to reach TOURIST TREAT. 120', 5.12b (5.9 R)
2. Finish easily up the TOURIST TREAT crack system to the top.
HISTORY: After cleaning the route, top-roping it, and placing the bolts on rappel, Peter Beal & Kris Hansen made the first ascent on August 22, 1986.

CAMBER II 5.11b (***)
An excellent and exceptionally popular route, with well protected, varied climbing, and a singularly spectacular setting. The route ascends the appealing, smooth face and prominent overlap just to the right of TOURIST TREAT.

1. Climb the start of TOURIST TREAT (5.10b), or the face on the right past a bolt (easier, but watch for rope drag). Face climb with increasing difficulty up to the main overlap (bolt & peg), which is the 5.11b crux. Arrange a hanging belay just above the lip on a sloping stance with a two bolt anchor. 90', 5.11b

2. Face climb right to a bolt, drop down, then traverse up and right (5.10d) onto a narrow ledge with a pine tree. Follow a shallow groove straight up, and when it ends, make a thin escape (5.10b) right to the top. 80', 5.10d

HISTORY: At the time of the first ascent, this was quite a controversial route involving cleaning on rappel and aid placed protection. After Jeff Pheasant placed the first bolt on the lead, and fell off, Jim Dunn completed the crux pitch. None of the bolts were placed on rappel. Jim Dunn, Jeff Pheasant, & Ed Sklar made the first ascent in November, 1978. Camber, the slight arch found in skis, was also Jim Dunn and Martha Morris's dog.

DIRECT FINISH: **REVERSE CAMBER** I 5.10b (***)

An incredibly exposed, equally popular pitch up the beautiful white face directly above the hanging belay at the top of CAMBER's first pitch. It is probably one of Cathedral's most frequently top-roped pitches, and dries quickly after a rain. The route is also well protected on the lead.

2a. From the CAMBER double bolt hanging belay, face climb straight up past two drilled pitons (5.10b), then stay right (more 5.10) past two bolts, finally stepping left to join the last few feet of GOOFER'S DELIGHT. You may escape left sooner if you want, after the second bolt, into the final, easy dike. 90', 5.10b The final headwall has also been top-roped (5.11b).

HISTORY: Jim Dunn first top-roped the pitch and the 5.11b headwall in August, 1980. Ed Webster & Roger "Strappo" Hughes (UK) then made the first ascent using the harder, right-hand finish, placing all the bolts on the lead (the first two on aid) on August 25, 1980. What made their ascent more memorable occurred when Susan Patenaude tried to drive up the auto road just before it got dark to pick them up. Hence the following conversation, shouted between an anonymous climber below on the Cathedral Ledge auto road, and Webster standing on top of the AIRATION Buttress:

"Ed! Uh, Sue didn't make it up there to pick you up... She's been arrested!"
   Pause. "What!!???"

"A park ranger just arrested her for trying to drive around the gate, which was closed... She's been driven to the police station in North Conway."

   Another pause. "WHAT!!!???" Fortunately, the story had a happy ending: the overzealous Echo Lake State Park ranger stopped Sue 30 feet before she drove onto State Park property, and the judge threw out the case. The metal gate that closes the auto road has long since been moved to a better location just beyond the parking for Cathedral's North End or Practice Slab.

CATHEDRAL LEDGE (CAMBER & REVERSE CAMBER) 139

Alison Osius on the crux roof of Camber (5.11b) in 1984.
Photograph by S. Peter Lewis.

REVERSE CAMBER / ROOM WITH A VIEW LINK-UP I 5.12a (*)
Superb, sustained face climbing in a tremendous position!
2a. Starting from the hanging belay on CAMBER, face climb up REVERSE CAMBER (5.10b) to its third bolt, move right (5.11d), and finish up ROOM WITH A VIEW, with the crux being the very last move (5.12a). 80', 5.12a
FA: John Strand & Karl Mallman September, 1988

ROOM WITH A VIEW I 5.12a (5.10d R) (*)
A controversial bolt-protected face climb up the steep, clean slab just to the left of CAMBER's second pitch finish. Very sustained moves, and quite scary at the start. Popular only on a top-rope!
1 & 2. Climb the first two pitches of CAMBER, and belay at the pine tree on the curving ledge halfway up the top pitch. 5.11b & 5.10d
3. Off the left-hand end of the curving pine tree ledge on CAMBER, face climb straight up the face (5.10d R to the first bolt) continuing past three more bolts to the top, with the last move being the 5.12a crux. 70', 5.12a (5.10d R)
HISTORY: After previewing the climb on a top-rope, Peter Beal placed five bolts on rappel, and made the first ascent with Tom Nonis & Steve Angelini on June 14, 1986. (Beal's first bolt protected the initial, but now 5.10d R moves off the ledge.) All of his bolts, however, were removed later the same day in a fit of ethical Puritanism by several local climbers. Steve Larson replaced one bolt on the lead, took several sizable leader falls, and failed to complete the route. During a later top-rope attempt, Larson's bolt broke under hand pressure. Had it broken on Steve, he would have fallen at least 80 feet! John Bouchard seized the moment, placed four more bolts on the lead, but also eventually failed. Returning after a summer climbing trip to Europe, Jim Surette finally led the pitch in August, 1986.

THE CREATION II 5.12b (5.10 R) (*)
At last, THE CREATION has occurred! A supremely thin face climb between CAMBER and STAGE FRIGHT, starting at the base of CAMBER. If you survive Pitch one, protection on the crux is good.
1. Climb straight up to a bolt, then diagonal right onto a large sloping ledge. Off the right end of this ledge, climb up flakes to a difficult mantleshelf and a hanging belay at a bolt anchor. 5.10 R
2. Face climb left past a bolt (5.12b), then head up past bolts and fixed bashies. Move up and left, then step down to the large pine for a rest. Finish up CAMBER directly up the wall above past flakes (5.10b) to a mantleshelf move, and the top. 90', 5.12b
HISTORY: Jim Dunn discovered the line in the late 1970s, cleaned and protected the route on rappel, but never finished it. Jim Surette & John Burke made the first ascent on their second day of effort, on May 14, 1985.

CATHEDRAL LEDGE - THE AIRATION BUTTRESS 141

Jeff Achey (belaying) and Ed Webster on Pitch two of Camber (5.11b) in 1979.
Photograph by Jane Presser.

REACH THE SKY I 5.11c (**)

One of the best 5.11s on the buttress. The crux, however, is definitely height dependent. From the GOOFER'S DELIGHT hand crack at the highest point on top of the AIRATION Buttress, rappel to a belay ledge with a triple bolt anchor that is 25 feet up and left of the AIRATION pine tree. For a 3 star route, climb up AIRATION to reach this belay ledge.

1. Move left to a bulge (bolt), make a long, hard reach (5.11c) to a peg, then climb a steep, sustained slab past four bolts and a piton to the top. 80', 5.11c

HISTORY: Tom Callaghan, Haydie Callaghan, & John Strand did the first ascent on August 2, 1988, drilling the route on the lead—with a Bosch.

STAGE FRIGHT II 5.12c X (***)

This well-named climb, one of the East's most serious and difficult leads, is the discontinuous, vertical finger crack immediately left of AIRATION. Carry a modern rack, but beware that if your protection rips after a fall from the crux, groundfall is likely. A bold statement of excellence by Hugh Herr.

1. With increasing difficulty, climb the thin finger crack to the crux bulge where the crack all but disappears. Face climb straight up the incipient vertical crack (5.12c X) to its end. Join AIRATION above. 75', 5.12c X

HISTORY: Sam Sargent & Todd Eastman did the first ascent in August, 1975. After extensive previewing and an estimated 20 days of attempts with some gear left in place, Hugh Herr made the historic first free ascent in July, 1985.

AIRATION I 5.11b (***)

THE 5.11 finger crack on Cathedral Ledge. Extremely popular. Partway across the AIRATION Buttress, and directly above the tree ledge at the top of THIN AIR, rises a short, but testing finger crack. Carry many wired nuts.

1. Climb the classic, but somewhat painful finger crack to a pine tree, with the crux 5.11b moves at two thirds height. 70', 5.11b

2. Continue up and left to a ramp and the final 5.7 corner.

FA: Sam Streibert & Joe Cote May, 1969
FFA: Henry Barber, John Bragg, & Bob Anderson August 23, 1973

VARIATION #1: PETTY LARSONY I 5.12a (Top-rope)

2a. Saved for future generations! Top-rope the vertical, orange wall (5.12a) just to the left of KILL YOUR TELEVISION. 45', 5.12a

FA: Peter Beal, top-rope July, 1986

VARIATION #2: KILL YOUR TELEVISION I 5.11 R

2b. Climb the thin crack between PETTY LARSONY and JESSIE to face moves up right to a flake and the top. 5.11 R

HISTORY: Peter Beal & Kris Hansen made the first ascent of this variation finish on July 18, 1986.

CATHEDRAL LEDGE (STAGE FRIGHT & AIRATION) 143

Hugh Herr on Stage Fright (5.12c X) in 1985. Photograph by S. Peter Lewis.

Peter Mayfield leading Airation in 1979. Photograph by Jeff Achey.

VARIATION #3: **JESSIE** I 5.10d
Man—and woman's—best friend. Jim & Martha's dog after Camber.
2c. Ascend the corner's right-hand wall past a bolt. 5.10d
FA: Jim Dunn & Martha Morris August, 1977

HEATHER I 5.12b (***)
One of the first 5.12 crack climbs to be accomplished in the region, this viciously painful finger crack is located on the very steep wall between AIRATION and PINE TREE ELIMINATE. A small pine tree (treat it carefully) grows at the base of the crack system, which is offset to the left at half height. Well protected.

1. Use the tree to gain the crack (or avoid the tree; harder), jam up the crack, then step left into the upper crack. (There is a possible rest on AIRATION on the left.) Now move back right, and struggle past a desperate bulge, the crux. 130', 5.12b

HISTORY: Ed Webster & Sam Sargent aided the first ascent in June, 1976. After many tries, Rick Fleming made the first free ascent on October 10, 1980. In the Spring of 1985, Jim Surette & Hugh Herr upped the ante —by free climbing the start without using the tree.

John Bouchard on Heather (5.12b) in 1985. Photograph by S. Peter Lewis.

146 THE MOUNT WASHINGTON VALLEY

PINE TREE ELIMINATE I 5.8+ (***)
An extremely popular crack climb, but a route certainly not to be underestimated! Sustained and notoriously strenuous for a 5.8. Above the right end of the AIRATION tree ledge, a beautiful hand-width crack slices straight up the wall with a small niche 20 feet up.

1. Jam and layback up the crack to the niche, rest, then follow the crack over two more bulges to the finish. 120', 5.8+

Ann Yardley on Pine Tree Eliminate (5.8+). Photograph by Nick Yardley.

HISTORY: Michael Hartrich & Rick Ruppel made the first ascent of the climb in 1973 when the tree was still standing. After the route had been repeated once or twice, the tree (actually a hemlock) was chopped down.

PLAY MISTY I 5.11d
Short, but right to the point. Ascends the thin, vertical crack just to the right of PINE TREE ELIMINATE. Well protected.
1. Layback over a strenuous bulge (5.11d) past a peg onto a ledge. Easier jamming leads to the top. 110', 5.11d
FA: Ed Webster & Bill Kane   June, 1976
FFA: Nigel Shepherd (UK), Bill Wayman (UK), Kim Smith,
    & Doug Madara   June 14, 1978

PLAYMATE I 5.11b (Top-rope)
Easier than PLAY MISTY!
1. Climb the arete (5.11b) immediately right of PLAY MISTY. 100', 5.11b
FA: Peter Beal, top-rope August, 1986

THE PRACTICE CHIMNEY I 5.7
1. The moderate chimney crack to the right of PLAY MISTY. 5.7
FA: Unknown.

PRACTICE MAKES PERFECT I 5.8
1. The finger crack just to the right of THE PRACTICE CHIMNEY. 5.8
FA: Unknown.

THE SPANKING I 5.11c (*)
For naughty boys and girls. THE SPANKING ascends the thin, vertical crack 20 feet to the right of THE PRACTICE CHIMNEY. Well protected.
1. Climb the thin crack past intricate moves (peg) to the top. 5.11c
HISTORY: An obscure aid climb, John Bouchard & John Burke made the first free ascent in the Summer of 1983.

ERASER HEAD I 5.12a
Right of THE SPANKING is a left-diagonalling ramp and a short face.
1. Gain the ramp and make extreme face moves (bolt; 5.12a) to the woods. 5.12a
FA: John Bouchard September, 1985

BOOK 'EM DANO I 5.7
The shallow, open book 20 feet to the right of ERASER HEAD.
1. Climb the corner past a small tree, avoiding the block on the right. 25', 5.7
FA: Unknown.

THE WORKOUT CRACKS I 5.9 & 5.10
Pump out! Above the far, right-hand end of the THIN AIR walk-off ledge are several short, practice jam cracks of varying widths.
HISTORY: Jim Dunn trained on these cracks in the late 1970s.

148 THE MOUNT WASHINGTON VALLEY

Jim Surette hanging around on The Mordor Roof (5.11d) in 1985.
Photograph by S. Peter Lewis.

THE CENTRAL SECTION

The middle part of Cathedral Ledge is one of the most majestic, sweeping granite walls in New Hampshire. All the climbs on this part of the cliff are major undertakings, requiring either sustained amounts of direct aid or very difficult free climbing. At present, ten Grade IV climbs grace the wall.

APOCALYPSE III 5.11d (**)

Takes an impressive line just to the right of STANDARD ROUTE up the smooth, beautiful face left of ARMAGEDDON. Carry a normal rack to a #3 Friend, plus the absolute stickiest shoes you can find! Start at the base of the easy dike on THE DIRECT START to STANDARD ROUTE.

1. Climb the staircase on THE DIRECT START, cross to the right over the STANDARD ROUTE chimney, then step down and right to a good belay stance below a steep, right-facing dihedral under the DIAGONAL Block. 75', 5.4

2. Layback and stem up the overhanging corner/dike beneath the DIAGONAL Block past two bolts (5.10d) to a rest, then struggle up a wide crack to a deluxe belay on top of DIAGONAL's big block at a two bolt anchor. 75', 5.10d

3. Climb 10 feet up the DIAGONAL dike, and step left to a fixed piton. Face climb straight up the beautiful, open face past several bolts on 5.8 slab moves, then continue with increasing difficulty past more bolts, making a slippery, leftwards traverse across a smooth slab underneath an eyebrow past two bolts (5.11d) to a hanging belay at a two bolt anchor next to STANDARD. 90', 5.11d

4. Hard moves off the hanging belay lead past the first bolt, then step left (5.10c), and head up the face just to the right of STANDARD ROUTE's Cave Wall past an obvious horizontal crack to reach a large and comfortable belay ledge with a double bolt anchor. 60', 5.10c

5. Step right, then face climb (5.7) straight up to loose flakes under an awkward overhang (bolt). Pull past this (5.9+), continue up easy ground to a second bolt, then run it out past one last bolt to the top. 160', 5.9+

HISTORY: Uwe Schneider & George Gipson made the first ascent of this often looked at route on May 20, 1990. The route was first inspected and cleaned on rappel, and the majority of the bolts were placed on the lead, three on aid. The first ascent party later added one extra protection bolt, and two of the double bolt anchors on rappel.

ARMAGEDDON III 5.12b R (*)

The day of reckoning finally came! This phenomenal route was the first to tackle the unlikely, smooth face between STANDARD and DIAGONAL. Once an unrepeated problem in skyhooking, Jim Surette free climbed the route in a brilliant effort, leaving a testament in stone for future generations to aspire to. One of the area's most thrilling leads. You don't even want to think about falling off the last move on the headwall!

1. Climb the first pitch of DIAGONAL to the block belay and a two bolt anchor at the start of the upper DIAGONAL dike. 100', 5.5

2. Head past two bolts up the dike, then face climb out left (5.9+) past more bolts to a rest. Above a piton and a small flake, make a series of extreme face moves (5.12b R) up the crux headwall, finally mantling onto a good ledge. 5.12b R

3. Continue straight up into a diagonal groove. At its top, face climb out right, then up the edge of several narrow grooves to the woods.

HISTORY: Doug Madara & Paul Ross did the first ascent of this landmark climb on July 5, 1975, using several skyhook moves on the crux headwall. The route was attempted free by several parties before Jim Surette & John Bouchard made the second, and more importantly, the historic first free ascent on May 23, 1985. Several tries and long leader falls were required prior to success.

ROPE DRAG III 5.12b (5.7 R), A0 (3 Points of Aid)
A challenging route between ARMAGEDDON and GRAND FINALE.

1. Climb the chimney on THE DIRECT START to STANDARD ROUTE (5.7+), then branch right to reach the comfortable double bolt belay on top of the DIAGONAL Block. 100', 5.7+

2. Continue up DIAGONAL for 40 feet to a belay on a ledge with another two bolt anchor just to the left of the dike. 40', 5.5

3. Face climb straight up (5.7 R) to an old bolt on ARMAGEDDON. Face climb straight up, then angle up and right past five bolts (5.12b crux after the third bolt), climbing a blank slab to a two bolt hanging belay just to the left of the DIAGONAL dike. 125', 5.12b

4. Climb the slab right of the belay past a bolt and a pin. Mantle onto a stance, aid up three bolts (A0), then pendulum left 15 feet to a hold by a small overlap. Gain a stance (5.11d) at the base of a groove, climb the groove (5.10 R) for 15 feet to a bolt. Finally, move up and left to a good belay ledge with a two bolt anchor. 100' 5.11d (5.10 R), A0

5. Fifteen feet left of the belay, head up clean black rock, move back right past three pitons, and climb flakes and cracks, joining GRAND FINALE. 140', 5.9

HISTORY: The first ascent was made in August, 1992, by Bill Lowther, Ozzie Blumet, Gerry Lortie, & Kelly Coleman. The route required eight days of effort and was climbed from the ground up every day, without fixed ropes. Six bolts were placed on aid off hooks, the rest free on the lead, then the route was led free, except for the three aid points and the short pendulum on Pitch four.

DIAGONAL II 5.9+ R (*)
This striking line is the prominent, right-diagonalling dike running up the left margin of the smooth, black-streaked Mordor Wall. Although it is the easiest free climb up Cathedral's central section, it has a notorious, poorly protected, strenuous, and insecure crux. Retreat down the diagonalling dike is also very

CATHEDRAL LEDGE (DIAGONAL & FREE FINALE)

awkward. Don't be deceived by the easy climbing at the start. Modern rack.

1. Climb either the normal start of STANDARD, or THE DIRECT START to STANDARD, up the 5.7+ chimney, and angle out to the right to a double bolt anchor on top of an immense, detached block. 100', 5.5 or 5.7+

2. Face climb up the deceptively easy dike (5.6) past a flake on the left to the pronounced final bulge, the climb's crux. Belay on the right on a small stance at a multiple bolt anchor shared with GRAND FINALE. 120', 5.6

3. Climb the spectacular, bulging dike on awkward, slanting holds with tricky nut protection (5.9+ R) to easy terrain above. Wade through poison ivy, or climb the unprotected slab on the left, to another two bolt belay. 150', 5.9+ R

4. Scramble easily up to the woods a short ways above.

HISTORY: John Turner (UK) & Brian Rothery made the first attempt on the dike in 1959. "There was no indication of anyone having been up there before," said Turner, "and I was able to insert only one dubious piton about 30 feet up the second pitch before reaching the stance subsequently bolted by Art Gran. With no prospect of getting anything in before the bulge, and a probable 100 foot fall before pulling the piton out if the bulge turned out to be 5.10, I chickened out. Art went up there independently later the same year, I think immediately after he had led the second ascent of REPENTENCE, got up to the bulge, placed a couple of belay bolts, and also backed off." Mike Stultz & Sam Streibert made the first ascent in August, 1970.

FREE FINALE III 5.12a (5.11c R) (***)

Superb rock, an exposed position in the center of the Mordor Wall, and hard, rewarding climbing make this a modern free climbing classic. FREE FINALE free climbs the upper two pitches of GRAND FINALE. Bring a modern rack. The route starts at the DIAGONAL Block.

1. Climb THE DIRECT START to STANDARD (5.7+), and continue up and right to a double bolt belay on top of the DIAGONAL block. 100', 5.7+

2. Face climb down and right with a very awkward sequence (5.12a) around the corner, then continue up a small, right-facing corner or arch past bolts to the double bolt anchor on Freak Out Ledge. 45', 5.12a

3. Sustained moves lead up a thin, vertical crack (5.11c), then face climb up a steep slab just right of the original rivet ladder past four bolts (also 5.11c) to a belay stance with a multiple bolt anchor on DIAGONAL. 100', 5.11c

4. Cross left over DIAGONAL, continuing up a very exposed bulge (5.11c R) past several fixed bashies, a bolt, and pitons to easier 5.8 climbing and a secure belay beside a flake and a bush (bolt). 80', 5.11c R

5. Slab climb left to a finish up several inside corners. 75', 5.7

HISTORY: After several days of effort, Chris Gill & Greg McCausland made the first free ascent of the top pitches of GRAND FINALE in August, 1988.

152 THE MOUNT WASHINGTON VALLEY

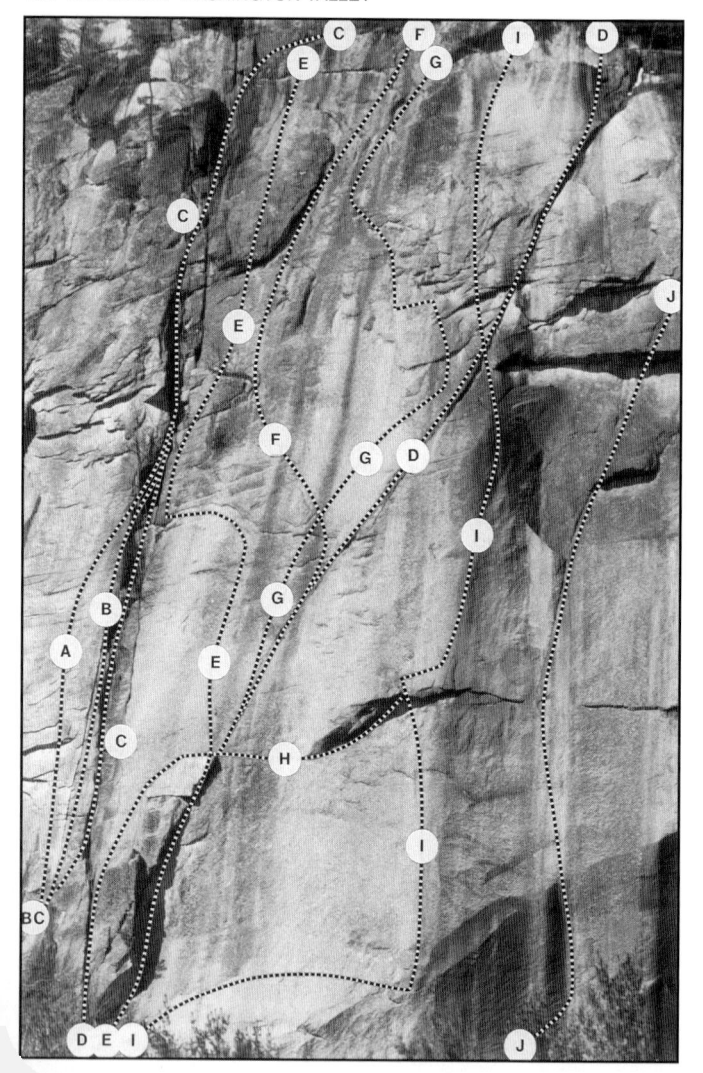

CATHEDRAL LEDGE – CENTER
(PRO CHOICE to MORDOR WALL)

A.	*	**PRO CHOICE** I 5.10c	Page	129
B.	***	**THE TOE CRACK** I 5.7	Page	131
C.	**	**STANDARD ROUTE** II 5.6 R	Page	130
D.	*	**DIAGONAL** II 5.9+ R	Page	150
E.	**	**APOCALYPSE** III 5.11d	Page	149
F.	*	**ARMAGEDDON** III 5.12b R	Page	149
G.		**ROPE DRAG** III 5.12b (5.7 R), A0 (3 Points of Aid)	Page	150
H.	***	**FREE FINALE** III 5.12a (5.11c R)	Page	151
I.	***	**GRAND FINALE** IV 5.12b (5.11c R), Clean A2 or 5.8, Clean A3	Page	154
J.	***	**MORDOR WALL** IV 5.7 (or 5.12c), A3	Page	155

Chris Gill on the first free ascent of Free Finale (5.12a / 5.11c R), on the thin crack at the start of Pitch three (5.11c), in 1988. Photograph by Nick Yardley.

GRAND FINALE IV 5.12b (5.11c R), Clean A2 or 5.8, Clean A3 (***)
This high quality Big Wall climb similar to its neighbor, MORDOR WALL, has now mostly been free climbed. If you do aid the route, use only nuts and skyhooks. Very spectacular climbing in an exposed and beautiful setting. Start 30 feet to the left (uphill) of MORDOR WALL.
1. Hook moves lead past two bolts up a slightly overhanging, blank wall to twin, A1 cracks. Free climb to a tree belay. 60' 5.6, Clean A2
2. Make a wild traverse to the right (5.10d R) across an exposed traverse flake to a small belay stance with a four bolt anchor. Equally scary for the leader and the second. 50', 5.10d R (or Clean A2)
3. Face climb straight up, following a bolt and dowel ladder to aid moves over an obvious ceiling to "Freak Out Ledge", and a two bolt anchor. (This pitch has now been led free except for two points of aid.) 80' 5.12b, A1 (or Clean A2)
4. Free climb (5.11c) or aid (A2; nuts only) up a tricky, thin crack system to a rivet ladder (A1), or face climb up the steep slab just to the right of the rivets past four bolts (5.11c), to a small belay stance with a multiple bolt anchor just to the right of DIAGONAL. 100', 5.11c (or Clean A2)
5. Move left over DIAGONAL up an overhanging wall (5.11c R) via difficult and committing free climbing past fixed bashies, a bolt, and pitons (or A3; leave the fixed bashies in place) until the angle lessens, then free climb (5.8) to a secure belay beside a bush with a bolt anchor. 80', 5.11c R (or 5.8, Clean A3)
6. Slab climb left to a finish up several inside corners. 75', 5.7

HISTORY: Paul Ross & Mike Heintz made the first ascent of the climb over several days in August, 1977. Tom Callaghan & John Strand free climbed the second pitch on August 2, 1983. In 1984, John Strand & Tom Callaghan freed Pitch three except for two aid points. Pitches four & five were free climbed by Chris Gill & Greg McCausland in August, 1988, using a short variation to the right of the original rivet ladder on Pitch four.

MORDOR WALL IV 5.7 (or 5.12c), A3 (***)
Still regarded as one of the classic Big Wall climbs on the East Coast, much of MORDOR WALL has now been free climbed, including the outrageous first pitch. Originally rated A4, the blank, black-streaked wall in the center of Cathedral Ledge offers climbing similar to a Yosemite Big Wall, and remains a very popular aid climb. An A3 rack should be carried, including several bashies and pointed skyhooks for Pitch two. To free climb Pitch one, carry a modern rack. At the base of the wall is a right-curving, expanding flake leading up into a narrow, left-facing dihedral. DO NOT aid Pitch one with pitons.
1. Climb across the flake and up into the corner (bolt) to a hanging belay at a triple bolt anchor. As a free lead, the flake is expanding, hard to protect, extremely technical, and double ropes are mandatory. There is still one point of aid at the top of the corner, getting to the anchor. 90', 5.12c, A0 (or Clean A2)
2. Traverse horizontally right across the sheer wall on bat hooks and bolts to an incipient, vertical crack (A3; fixed bashies usually in place). At the base of the upper slab, arranging another hanging belay at a two bolt anchor. 120', A3.
3. Nine bolts (These used to be bat hooks also; A1) lead to a beautiful, vertical A1 crack. Aid the crack, and belay on the left-hand end of a scenic, comfortable ledge called the Sidewalk at a multiple, fixed piton anchor. 130', Clean A1
4. The MORDOR Roof: the rest of the route goes free. If aided, please leave all fixed protection in place. Climb a thin crack (bolt at its top) to the six foot overlap just left of the PENDULUM Roof, then undercling and swing over the center of the MORDOR Roof (peg) using a wild, upside down heel-hook (5.11d) to reach a hanging belay on PENDULUM. 75', 5.11d (or Clean A2)
5. Climb the vertical crack system (5.9) on the right to the top. 150', 5.9
HISTORY: Joe Cote & John Merrill aided the first pitch in 1967 with no intention of going any higher. In the Summer of 1970, Joe Cote & Steve Arsenault climbed the route to the Sidewalk on PENDULUM, and rappelled off just before dark. The MORDOR Roof was added later that same summer by Steve Arsenault & Scott Brim, who approached the pitch from above. Arsenault's 1970 bat hook lead of the second pitch (then known as "the Terror Traverse") was originally done without any protection bolts. Arsenault finally placed a bolt at the end of the traverse after friends watching from below convinced him he was risking a groundfall. (Sadly, over the years, several extra bolts have

156 THE MOUNT WASHINGTON VALLEY

been added to the Pitch two traverse.) In August, 1979, on his third attempt (all starting from the ground), Ed Webster free climbed the MORDOR Roof with Choe Brooks (UK). After first top-roping the pitch, Jim Surette led MORDOR WALL's first pitch free in September, 1985, after two days of effort.

Jim Surette free climbing the first pitch of Mordor Wall (5.12c, A0) in 1986. Photograph by Ed Webster.

CATHEDRAL LEDGE - THE CENTRAL SECTION (MINES OF MORIA)

VARIATION: **THE FRENCH CONNECTION** I A3
This short variation links the top of the first pitch of MORDOR WALL to the belay stance at the end of the second pitch of GRAND FINALE.

1a. Aid climb up to a small roof on bolts and skyhooks (A3). Angle off to the left to reach the four bolt anchor at the end of the second pitch of GRAND FINALE. A3 Continue up GRAND FINALE.

HISTORY: Alain Comeau rope-soloed the first ascent on May 5, 1979.

BONGO FLAKE VARIATION IV 5.9 (or 5.11d), A3
This direct two pitch variation connects with PENDULUM ROUTE after climbing the blank, overhanging wall between MORDOR WALL and MINES OF MORIA. Start just to the right of a large boulder sitting on the ground 80 feet to the right of the MORDOR WALL. Bring the usual A3 assortment of gear, including many KBs and blades.

1. Nail the left side of a large, black flake system, up a right-leaning corner to a belay stance with a double bolt anchor. 70', A3

2. Aid a thin, right-leaning crack system (more A3) up the overhanging wall. After the angle lessens, belay on a ledge on the left. A3

3. Finish up PENDULUM ROUTE. Climb the long, vertical 5.8 crack to the Sidewalk belay ledge on the left and a double bolt anchor. 100', 5.8

4. Climb the PENDULUM Roof. 45', 5.11d (or Clean A2)

5. Finish up the final jam crack on PENDULUM ROUTE. 150', 5.9

FA: Joe Cote & Steve Arsenault Summer, 1970

CRACK BETWEEN WORLDS II 5.11d R (*)
Probably the hardest squeeze chimney on the East Coast, CRACK BETWEEN WORLDS ascends the overhanging, bomb bay chimney on the right side of BONGO FLAKE. A serious and very strenuous lead.

1. Undercling a flake to gain the crack. Next either struggle up the chimney (harder, but more secure), or undercling and layback up the outer edge (easier, but minimal protection) to the ledge on top of BONGO FLAKE. 70', 5.11d R

HISTORY: After six days of attempts spread over a month, Kurt Winkler & Barry Moore made the first ascent on their 18th try, on July 13, 1980. The ropes were pulled down after each attempt.

MINES OF MORIA IV 5.6 (or 5.11d), A2 (**)
Next to THE PROW, this is Cathedral's second most popular aid climb—but don't tumble into the abyss. The notorious fourth pitch, THE BRIDGE, is exceptionally strenuous, either free or on aid. To do the full aid route, a good selection of pitons and nuts is needed, including many large cams and/or Tri-cams and Hexentrics for THE BRIDGE. Begin the climb 35 feet to the left of the large tree growing at the base of PENDULUM ROUTE, and below a sloping ledge just above the ground.

1. Above the ledge, climb an A1 bolt ladder to a spacious, sloping terrace. Traverse right past a large, detached flake to trees. Clean A1

2. Step left, aid the hollow flake, then follow a long bolt ladder (A1) up the overhanging wall to a narrow flake. Nail this (A2) to a stance just over the crest. A2

3. Aid 20 feet up the dihedral above, then make a short pendulum left into a parallel corner system. Follow this to a ledge at the base of THE BRIDGE. A2

4. Free climb (5.11d) or aid (Clean A2) THE BRIDGE OF KHAZAD-DUM, the large, right-facing corner capped by a huge roof. A very unique pitch! There are two free cruxes: the first flare—and at the lip! 5.11d or Clean A2

5. Above a tree ledge, a right-diagonalling dike leads to the top.

HISTORY: Joe Cote, John Porter, & Paul Ross made the climb's historic first ascent on May 8, 1972. THE BRIDGE was first led free in July, 1976 by Bryan Delaney with Joe Lentini, who approached the pitch on rappel from above.

VARIATION #1: **THE DIRECT START** I A4

The small arch 15 feet to the right of the normal start.

1a. Aid the arch on bashies and thin blades. Belay at a tree. A4

FA: John Burke, rope-solo 1985

VARIATION #2: **SOFT IRON ROUTE** II A3+ (**)

This spectacular variation bypasses the Pitch two bolt ladder on MINES OF MORIA's second pitch, giving much more interesting climbing. A safely overhanging, good introduction to A3+. Carry KBs, bashies, hooks, & brass offsets.

1. Follow MINES OF MORIA aiding up a short bolt ladder to a small stance on the left with a fixed piton anchor. 45', A1

2a. Head up and left (old pin) into an orange groove system in the gently overhanging wall (A3+ plus three well spaced bolts). Aid over an overhang (bolt) to an A1 crack which splits the upper headwall (bolt). Move right over the lip to a low-angled crack and belay on the right at a stance. 155', A3+ Rappel off, or finish up MINES OF MORIA to the top.

FA: Jason Laflamme, rope-solo April, 1995

TOPLESS TELLERS I A4 (**)

Once all is revealed, sometimes you'll discover there wasn't much there to begin with—especially on this thin aid lead. Hard A4 completely bypasses the long bolt ladder on MINES' second pitch. Carry bashies, rurps, etc., the usual A4 bag of trinkets. Some trickery was also used on the first ascent, so beware! Right of the Pitch two bolt ladder on MINES are two dihedrals: the right corner is SEVENTH SOJOURN, the left is TOPLESS TELLERS.

1. Aid up the left-hand corner (A3), step left to gain a right-slanting seam (A4) with several thin moves, and finish left across a blank wall to the right-facing flake/crack (A2) above the end of the MINES bolt ladder. Sustained A4.

FA: Chris Rowins & Tiger Burns July, 1983

CATHEDRAL LEDGE (PENDULUM ROUTE)

Ajax Greene at the lip of the Pendulum Roof during the first free ascent of Pendulum Route (5.11d) in 1976. Photograph by Ed Webster.

PENDULUM ROUTE IV 5.11d (***)
This was the first climb to ascend the central section of Cathedral Ledge, and one of the first routes in the eastern United States to make use of Yosemite aid climbing techniques. As a free climb, PENDULUM was also the first "free way" up the middle of the cliff. The protection is generally good. Carry Friends and small wired nuts. A huge tree at the base of the cliff, uphill and right of the large clearing at the base of the MORDOR WALL marks the start.

1. Chimney against the PENDULUM tree (5.8), gain the cliff, step right to an overhanging dihedral, and climb it (also 5.8) to a tree ledge. 90', 5.8

2. Undercling across a tricky, hard to protect overlap to the right (5.10b) to another small, tree-covered ledge with a piton anchor. 40', 5.10b

3. Climb cracks and corners in the back of the main groove. At a bolt, step left into a thin, vertical crack (old pegs). Jam over a small roof (5.9+), and belay on the higher of two ledges at a double bolt anchor. 140', 5.9+

4. Drop down off the ledge (piton), then make a thin 5.10b traverse left across the face to another good ledge with a multiple bolt anchor. 40', 5.10b

5. At this point, the original route made an immense pendulum to the left into the vertical 5.8 crack that leads up to the PENDULUM Roof, the route's final obstacle. The free version uses a two pitch variation to bypass the pendulum. Climb the shallow groove on the left (5.10b), part of MINES OF MORIA, up to the good belay ledge at the bottom of THE BRIDGE OF KHAZAD-DUM corner and roof. 60', 5.10b

160 THE MOUNT WASHINGTON VALLEY

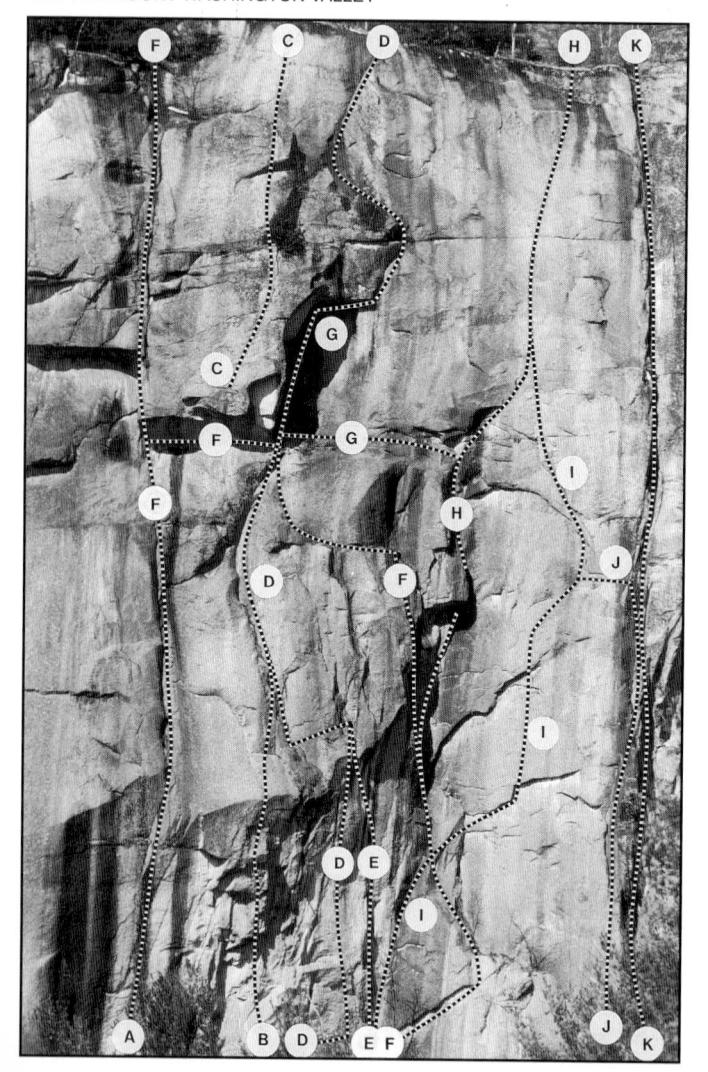

CATHEDRAL LEDGE – CENTER
(BONGO FLAKE to CATHEDRAL DIRECT)

A.		**BONGO FLAKE VARIATION** IV 5.9 (or 5.11d), A3	Page	157
B.	**	**SOFT IRON ROUTE** II A3+	Page	158
C.	**	**DIVISION OF LABOR** II 5.10d	Page	162
D.	**	**MINES OF MORIA** IV 5.6 (or 5.11d), A2	Page	157
E.	**	**TOPLESS TELLERS** I A4	Page	158
F.	***	**PENDULUM ROUTE** IV 5.11d	Page	159
G.	***	**THE BRIDGE OF KHAZAD-DUM** IV 5.11d	Page	163
H.	***	**LIGHTS IN THE FOREST** IV 5.11c	Page	163
I.	***	**SEVENTH SOJOURN** IV 5.12b (5.9 R)	Page	167
J.		**OPTION 9A** III 5.11a	Page	168
K.		**CATHEDRAL DIRECT** III 5.7 (or 5.12a), Clean A2	Page	173

6. Head left under the PENDULUM Roof, and down climb a 5.9 slab (top-rope protection) to the Sidewalk, a great ledge with a two bolt anchor. 60', 5.9
7. Next, climb back up to, then lunge out the spectacular, six foot horizontal PENDULUM roof, with your protection in a thin finger crack above a small tree (5.11d). The moves are very awkward and dynamic, but well protected. Belay on a small stance just over the lip. 40', 5.11d
8. Climb a long, vertical crack past bushes to the top. 150', 5.9

HISTORY: Steve Arsenault & Paul Doyle made the historic first ascent on September 2, 1967. Pitch three was free climbed by Henry Barber & Paul Ross during their first ascent of THE BIG PLUM in October, 1972. Pitch two was freed by John Bragg & Ajax Greene in 1973. The first free ascent was made by Ed Webster & Ajax Greene in August, 1976. The crux roof took several tries.

DIVISION OF LABOR II 5.10d (**)
This unusual, highly exposed route is located to the right of Pitch eight of PENDULUM. Approach by rappelling 162 feet to a two bolt anchor on a good belay ledge (just a bit exposed!) right above the lip of the PENDULUM Roof.
1. Face climb right past two bolts (5.10d) into a widening finger crack which is climbed to a tree belay. 60', 5.10d
2. Climb over a bulge past two bolts (5.10d), then slab climb to a small roof, surmount the roof at a finger crack, and belay above at shrubs. 70', 5.10d
3. Finish up MOE. Layback a nice, thin flake to a stance next to some quartz crystals, then finish over a hard bulge (bolt; 5.10c) to the trees. 40', 5.10c
FA: Steve Weeks & John Strand July 25, 1987

THE MORDOR ROOF IV 5.11d (***)
Another combination climb, something akin to a magical mystery tour of the central section of Cathedral. The crux out the MORDOR Roof is a wild, body length roof and heel hook that is fortunately well protected.
1. The PENDULUM tree and V groove on PENDULUM. 90', 5.8
2. Pitch two (5.10b) of PENDULUM, the tricky overlap. 40', 5.10b
3. The long 5.9 chimney pitch of LIGHTS IN THE FOREST. 140', 5.9
4. Pitch four of THE BRIDGE, the hand crack and traverse left. 5.8
5. Traverse left beneath the PENDULUM Roof, down climb a 5.9 slab, then walk left on the Sidewalk to MORDOR WALL. Multiple piton anchor. 5.9
6. Free climb Pitch four of MORDOR WALL, jamming up a fun finger crack (bolt at its top) to the MORDOR Roof. Undercling (peg) to the lip, turn upside down, and heel-hook over (5.11d). Arrange a hanging belay after merging with the PENDULUM ROUTE. 75', 5.11d
7. Climb the PENDULUM crack system to the woods. 100', 5.9

HISTORY: After prior attempts with George Hurley & John Bouchard, Ed Webster made the first free ascent with Choe Brooks (UK) in August, 1979.

CATHEDRAL LEDGE (MORDOR ROOF & THE BRIDGE)

DIRECT FINISH: **PEER PRESSURE** I 5.11a R
Avoids the top pitch of PENDULUM. Carry small wired nuts.
7a. Above the MORDOR Roof, avoid PENDULUM by stepping left into a left-facing flake. Climb the flake, then follow a dike to the top. 100', 5.11a R
FA: Bob Parrott & Jim Surette July, 1985

THE BRIDGE OF KHAZAD-DUM IV 5.11d (***)
A wild combination climb incorporating several of the best free pitches in the center of Cathedral, climaxing with a spectacular and famous crux: THE BRIDGE. Carry a large selection of Camalots and Friends for protection on THE BRIDGE on Pitch five. You'll need them all!
1. Up the PENDULUM tree, then a V groove on the left. 90', 5.8
2. Tackle Pitch two of PENDULUM, the 5.10b overlap. 40', 5.10b
3. The third lead of LIGHTS IN THE FOREST, the nose. 140', 5.9
4. Head up the 5.8 hand crack, then traverse horizontally left (5.7) with sparse protection to a good belay ledge at the base of THE BRIDGE. 5.8
5. Free climb THE BRIDGE OF KHAZAD-DUM (5.11d), the large roof and right-facing corner. Struggle around an incredibly awkward bulge (5.11d), then jam and undercling right (bolt) under the huge roof, finally laybacking around the lip. A real arm destroyer! Belay above on a tree ledge. 5.11d
6. Scramble easily left, or up a right-diagonalling dike to the woods.
HISTORY: Many people take credit for the first three leads. Rappelling down to reach the pitch from above, Bryan Delaney with Joe Lentini made the first free ascent of THE BRIDGE in July, 1976, after several efforts. Jim Dunn & Bryan Becker did the climb's first continuous free ascent in September, 1976.

VARIATION: **HEAT WAVE** I 5.12a (*)
Ascends the steep, exposed friction slab to the right of THE BRIDGE OF KHAZAD-DUM. Great situation and moves, but pick a cool day. Start on the belay ledge at the base of THE BRIDGE. Carry a normal rack.
1. Face climb up and right past bolts (5.12a) to a belay stance with a double bolt anchor at the prominent horizontal break. 100', 5.12a
2. Make a hard move (5.10c) off of the belay, then trend right, finishing up LIGHTS IN THE FOREST (5.9 runout) to the top. 150', 5.10c
FA: John Mallery & Dave Jacobson July, 1988

LIGHTS IN THE FOREST IV 5.11c (***)
This superb free climb offers an enjoyable variety of well protected pitches up Cathedral's exposed center. A popular adventure. On Pitch five, the free ascent climbs a 5.11b slab to the left of the original A3 aid line. Normal rack.
1. Climb Pitch one of either PENDULUM, or THE BRIDGE OF KHAZAD-DUM to the comfortable tree ledge on PENDULUM ROUTE. 90', 5.8

2. Pitch two of PENDULUM. Undercling right across a tricky, hard to protect overlap (5.10b) to another small tree ledge with a piton anchor. 40', 5.10b

3. Climb PENDULUM's third pitch to the bolt, then layback the 5.9 corner on the right to gain a moderate chimney behind a large nose of rock. Head up the spectacular, but easy chimney to a good belay stance above. 140', 5.9

4. Climb a 5.8 hand crack straight up to a curving overlap, the route's crux. Move right around the overlap (5.11c; bolt), and belay at a small stance with fixed anchors at the base of the large, upper slab. 100', 5.11c

5. Surmount a bolt-protected 5.9 bulge. (The original line continues straight up above a small ledge, with one A3 move to gain a prominent horizontal crack.) The free variation angles left to a steep swell in the slab with another bolt. Climb the slab (bolt; 5.11b), then traverse right onto another small but comfortable stance with a double bolt anchor. 75', 5.11b

6. Face climb past a bolt (5.9) which protects a runout to easier, but memorably unprotected climbing up the exposed, final slab to the trees. 125', 5.9

HISTORY: Ed Webster & Paul Ross made the first ascent of this beautiful climb on July 18, 1976. Webster led all the pitches. After the pair were benighted on the last pitch, Ross followed the final 5.9 slab by putting his feet on the chalk marks glowing in the dark! In keeping with tradition, Neil Cannon & Jim Surette free climbed the fourth pitch (also getting benighted!), then returned on August 12, 1984, and added the new, free fifth pitch, rappelling down to it from above. Jim Surette & Scott Stevenson then made the first continuous free ascent of the entire route in the Autumn of 1984.

THE THREE STOOGES SLAB

Directly above THE BRIDGE is the Three Stooges Slab. Walk in from the auto road as if heading for the AIRATION Buttress, but instead, walk straight out to the cliff edge and the top of the Stooges Slab. Rappel with two ropes to a ledge at the base of the next three climbs, now described from left to right:

LARRY I 5.10a R

1. A short finger crack leads to a stance and a short bulge (5.10a R). Above the bulge, run it out to the top. 40', 5.10a R

HISTORY: After Paul Boissonneault top-roped the first ascent in July, 1982, John Strand led the climb in October, 1983.

MOE I 5.10c (*)

The best route on the STOOGES Slab.

1. Layback up a thin flake to a stance by quartz crystals and a bolt, then climb over a bulge (5.10c) to the woods. 40', 5.10c

HISTORY: After top-roping it first, John Strand returned with Steve Weeks to lead the route on July 26, 1982.

CATHEDRAL LEDGE (LIGHTS IN THE FOREST & STOOGES SLAB) 165

CURLY I 5.11a (Top-rope)
Fifteen feet down & right of MOE is a stance at the base of a shallow scoop.
1. Climb the scoop, trending slightly left, over the top bulge. 50', 5.11a
FA: Al Rubin, top-rope July, 1982

Jim Surette & Neil Cannon free climbing the fifth Pitch (5.11b) of Lights In The Forest (5.11c) in 1984. Photograph by S. Peter Lewis.

Chris Gill, belayed by Greg McCausland, free climbing the Pitch two dihedral (5.12b) on Seventh Sojourn (5.12b / 5.9 R) in 1988. Photo by S. Peter Lewis.

SEVENTH SOJOURN IV 5.12b (5.9 R) (***)

One of New Hampshire's finest, long, hard traditional free climbs ascends the center of the singularly imposing wall immediately to the right of LIGHTS IN THE FOREST. The route has two 5.12b cruxes. Bring a good sized modern rack, plus double ropes. Start at the PENDULUM tree.

1. Climb Pitch one of PENDULUM ROUTE. Chimney up against the tree (5.8), gain the cliff, step right to an overhanging dihedral, and climb it (5.8) to a comfortable tree ledge. 90', 5.8

2. Above the left end of the PENDULUM belay ledge, intense stemming leads up a blind V groove past a bolt to tricky protection (5.12b) and finally to a peg where you can step right to a belay stance. 60', 5.12b

3. Undercling right underneath a large, horizontal overlap, pull over it at a vertical break (5.11d), then face climb (5.9 R) straight up to and then over a second overlap (5.11d; large Friends) before moving right across the face to a double bolt anchor at a good stance. 130', 5.11d (5.9 R)

4. Climb past a bolt, head up a left-facing arch (5.10b), then traverse right 10 feet to an extremely difficult mantleshelf move (5.12b). Above, continue up a challenging slab (5.11d), finally angling up and left to another good belay stance on LIGHTS IN THE FOREST. 90', 5.12b

5. Finish up LIGHTS IN THE FOREST. Surmount a bolt-protected 5.9 bulge, then angle left to a steep swell in the slab (bolt). Climb the slab (5.11b), and traverse right to a narrow, belay ledge with a double bolt anchor. 75', 5.11b

6. Face climb straight up past a bolt (5.9) that protects a pretty exciting runout to easier climbing up the exposed, final slab leading to the woods. 125', 5.9

6a. Do the first 5.9 moves on the last pitch, then friction straight up (5.11b X), going for it up the top slab to the trees. 125', 5.11b X

HISTORY: Ed Webster made the first ascent of the climb, rope-solo, over two days in September, 1979, inspired by his recent 7th ascent of the Pacific Ocean Wall (then A5) on El Capitan in Yosemite Valley. The first half of SEVENTH SOJOURN, which originally included two A4 pitches, was left fixed before the successful ascent the next day. The entire route eventually went free only after considerable effort and attempts by several talented climbers. Jim Surette & Chris Gill first free climbed the exposed third pitch, and the arch at the start of Pitch four in October, 1985. After placing a protection bolt on the former A4 groove, Greg McCausland & Chris Gill free climbed the second pitch in June, 1988, before Gill returned to free climb all of the technically demanding fourth pitch that September with Mark Pelletier. Gill also led the first ascent of the unprotected sixth pitch variation finish. Chris Gill & Andy Ross finally teamed up to make the historic first free ascent of the complete route in one push in October of 1988.

FOREST OF FANGORN IV 5.7, A3

A lengthy and intricate aid route, yet remarkably unpopular. Maybe because you can't see the forest through the lichen. Bring a large assortment of pitons and a wire brush. Begin 30 feet to the right of the PENDULUM tree.

1. Nail a thin, right-slanting crack past several bolts (that protects the sport route LUCIFER IN CHAINS, which shares the same crack) to a horizontal crack (A3), aid across this, then continue to a hanging belay by a roof. A3

2. Continue diagonally left in the same crack across the overhanging wall to the tree ledge on PENDULUM. 70', A3

3. Aid climb thin, disjointed cracks straight above the right end of the tree ledge. Join the chimney on CATHEDRAL DIRECT, then pendulum right to BONFIRE LEDGE. A3

4. Off the left end of BONFIRE, climb a chimney to a right-leaning crack, then move up into another chimney system. 5.7, A3

5. From a bolt belay, use two bolts to reach a horizontal crack which goes left around the corner into a vertical groove. Up this, jog left again, and belay next to a small tree at a vertical crack. A3

6. Follow the crack up a steep, licheny face to the top. A2

FA: Dave Linden & Joe Cote Summer, 1976

OPTION 9A III 5.11a

A free-er version of FOREST OF FANGORN. No traffic jams on this bypass!

1. Climb Pitch one of PENDULUM, up the tree and corner. 90', 5.8

2. Undercling across the overlap (5.10b), Pitch two of PENDULUM. From the PENDULUM belay ledge, traverse easily down and right to a bolt & piton belay at the base of FOREST OF FANGORN's third pitch. 70', 5.10b

3. Climb cracks and face past fixed pitons (5.10) to a stance. Follow nice cracks past more pitons. When progress begins to look unlikely, move right to an arete, which is climbed by using a secret hand hold (5.10c) in the CATHEDRAL DIRECT chimney (pitons). Belay at three pitons on a stance at Cote's Pendulum point on FOREST OF FANGORN. 145', 5.10c

4. Instead of penduluming to Bonfire Ledge (as for FANGORN), traverse left (5.10) to a face, which is climbed to a stance (bolt). Continue past two bolts (5.11a) to the belay at the top of Pitch three on SEVENTH SOJOURN and LIGHTS IN THE FOREST. 40', 5.11a Rappel off from here, or...

5 & 6. Finish up LIGHTS IN THE FOREST. 5.11b & 5.9

HISTORY: After Bill Lowther & Jon Eagleson had earlier free climbed Pitch three, on May 29, 1994, Bill Lowther, Ozzie Blumit, & Gerry Lortie linked-up the climb, plus made the first free ascent of Pitch four.

THE CATHEDRAL ROOF

The dramatically overhang walls of the Cathedral Roof offer several of the ledge's hardest and most technical sport climbs. All are bolt protected, all are strenuous, all are intensely fingery. The following set of sport routes are located between PENDULUM ROUTE and WHITE EYE:

POWER CHILD I 5.13c (*)
You'll need Popeye's arm strength for this one. Start at the PENDULUM tree. Six bolts lead to the anchor.
1. Stem up the tree, then move right at a shallow, right-slanting finger crack just to the right of the tree. At a horizontal crack 15 feet up, make powerful undercling moves up and right to a double bolt anchor. 35', 5.13c
FA: Steve Damboise   September, 1992

LUCIFER IN CHAINS I 5.13a
This is the hellishly thin, right-slanting crack 35 feet right of the PENDULUM tree, and 40 feet left of BALLHOG. There are three bolts and no fixed anchor. This is also Pitch one of the aid route, FOREST OF FANGORN.
1. Starting 15 feet right of the crack, boulder traverse up and left on rounded holds to reach the first bolt. Continue up the crack past two bolts over bulges to reach the far, right-hand end of the PENDULUM tree ledge. 50', 5.13a
FA: Jerry Handren   June, 1992

THE BALLHOG II A3
A strenuous alternate to FANGORN's first pitch. Start at an overhanging, thin, vertical groove 40 feet right of LUCIFER IN CHAINS in front of a boulder on the left side of the Cathedral Roof. A large aid rack is required.
1a. Nail the crack to a roof, climb it on two bolts, thrash over the lip, and merge at FANGORN's hanging belay at the top of its first pitch. 80', A3
FA: Todd Swain & Rich Couchon, with Curt Robinson   July 3, 1979

PINSNATCHER I A4
This time consuming aid lead climbs the vertical crack line 15 feet right of THE BALLHOG, & just left of DAY OF THE MAILMAN. Bring an A4 rack.
1. Aid straight up the thin, vertical A4 seam/crack just left of MAILMAN, joining that route briefly before continuing out an overhanging crack system over several bulges to join CATHEDRAL DIRECT above the roof. 75', A4
FA: Chris Rowins & Tiger Burns   Summer, 1978

DAY OF THE MAILMAN I 5.13a
A classic and striking line! Practice your daily routine first. Start 20 feet to the right of BALLHOG at a short right-facing corner leading up to the main roofs. Stick clip the first bolt—and the anchors if you want to! Five bolts lead to a double ring bolt anchor.
1. Slime up the start (often wet) to a sloping stance. At the second bolt, swing

170 THE MOUNT WASHINGTON VALLEY

left around the corner on pockets, then lunge (the crux) to the top. 35', 5.13a

HISTORY: Andy Hannon & Jerry Handren made the route's first ascent on November 5, 1994. Hannon named the climb for his Uncle Bob, a mailman.

SANCTUARY I 5.13b (***)

One of Cathedral's best sport routes, featuring impressively dynamic moves out an incredibly sustained overhanging prow. This visionary climb is the left-hand of three routes which ascend part, or all, of the eroded dike at the back of the Cathedral Roof. Eight bolts lead to the anchor.

1. Starting at the left-hand base of the dike, face climb up and left following an overhanging face/corner up to the bulging prow at the lip. The sequential crux at the third bolt, on small crimpers, involves moving powerfully out the roof to a good horizontal flake. The awkward layback/undercling moves out and around the final prow to the left provide a fittingly strenuous finish to reach the top stance which has a double bolt anchor. 50', 5.13b

HISTORY: Jerry Handren bolted the route and made the first ascent of this futuristic and historic sport route in May, 1992.

Andy Hannon on the crux moves of Sanctuary (5.13b) in 1995.

CATHEDRAL LEDGE - THE CATHEDRAL ROOF (SANCTUARY)

Steve Damboise on The Mercy (5.13d) in 1995. Photographs by Ed Webster.

WHAT WAS, WAS OVER I 5.13c (**)
1. The Future Is Here! Link the crux roof of SANCTUARY (5.13b) with the final several bolts on THE MERCY to reach the chained anchor at the lip for a phenomenal feat of finger strength and endurance. 45', 5.13c
FA: Andy Hannon August 16, 1996

THE MERCY I 5.13d (**)

Even more powerful, even more sequential. The most difficult free climb on Cathedral Ledge ascends the main section of the eroded dike at the back of the Cathedral Roof. Pray that no more of the hand holds break off. Eight bolts lead to the chained anchor near the lip of the roof.

1. Starting at the back right-hand side of the dike on THE DEVIL MADE ME DOG IT, face climb and lunge strenuously up and slightly left out the overhang past eight bolts (5.13d) to the chained, two bolt anchor. 45', 5.13d

HISTORY: Steve Damboise first bolted the climb in 1991. Some of the holds were chipped and glued. Following numerous attempts by other talented climbers, Andy Hannon made the first ascent of the route on July 12, 1996, after 10 days of determined effort spread over several months.

THE DEVIL MADE ME DOG IT I 5.12a (*)

The aid route SPACE CASE has metamorphosed into a popular, short sport route, often used as a warm-up. Begin 10 feet to the right of SANCTUARY.

1. Climb up and right out the overhang protected by four bolts to the fixed piton anchor at the block belay on CATHEDRAL DIRECT. 35', 5.12a

HISTORY: Stoney Middleton & Chris Rowins aid climbed the first ascent (at A4) in August, 1976. Jerry Handren made the first free ascent in May, 1992. In a timely return to traditional ethics, Handren bolted this and the next three routes on the lead—from a ladder.

BOIL MY BONES I 5.12c (*)

Start on THE DEVIL MADE ME DOG IT. Four bolts lead to the anchor.

1. Wickedly strenuous moves lead out right, across a horizontal break from left to right, to a final lunge to a sloper at the lip just right of the block belay on CATHEDRAL DIRECT. Fixed piton anchor. 35', 5.12c

FA: Jerry Handren May, 1995

GENERATION WHY I 5.13b (**)

Nearly the same as BOIL MY BONES, only in reverse and much harder.

1. Start up GRANDMOTHER'S CHALLENGE, then finger traverse and heel-hook left to the final desperate lunge for the top. Five bolts. 35', 5.13b

FA: Andy Hannon September 12, 1996

GRANDMOTHER'S CHALLENGE I 5.12b (*)

Now upgraded, and bolted for leading. Begin 15 feet to the left of the start of the handtraverse on MOLSON'S MADNESS. Stick clip the first bolt. Three bolts and one peg lead to the fixed anchor.

1. Climb up and left out the overhang, using an unusual knee lock, lunge your way out to the lip, and finish left, handtraversing along MOLSON'S MADNESS to a fixed piton anchor at the block belay. 35', 5.12b

CATHEDRAL LEDGE (MOLSON'S MADNESS & CATHEDRAL DIRECT)

HISTORY: In an inspired effort, Jim Dunn top-roped the climb's first ascent in 1978, and graded the route 5.11+. Jerry Handren bolted and first led the climb in May, 1995.

MOLSON'S MADNESS I 5.12a (***)
The favorite beer and exercise of frustrated, rainy day free climbers is the notoriously strenuous free version of CATHEDRAL DIRECT's first pitch. Six bolts and one piton at the end of the traverse flake now protect the lead. Start on the right side of the Cathedral Roof. Very popular.
1. Hand and finger traverse left (5.12a) along the outrageous, horizontal crack/edge to a piton anchor at the block belay under the main roof. 40', 5.12a

HISTORY: After pre-placing several pitons on aid, Jim Dunn made the first free ascent of the pitch in August, 1977. John Bouchard eventually bolted the route because aid climbers kept stealing the fixed pegs.

CATHEDRAL DIRECT III 5.7 (or 5.12a), Clean A2
The Cathedral Roof is the immense overhang in the cliff's center that gives Cathedral Ledge its name. The overhang is a popular place for climbers to congregate on rainy days, especially now that it is home to several extreme sport routes that remain completely dry even during the summer monsoon. This spectacular aid climb takes a wild path through the center of the main overhang before ascending a long, vertical chimney system to the top.
1. Starting at the right side of the Roof, aid climb left across a line of bolts (awkward A2), or free climb (5.12a) along the horizontal crack/flake to reach a belay perch in the overhang's center. The free version of this pitch is called MOLSON'S MADNESS. 35', Clean A2 or 5.12a
2. Continue aiding out the center of the roofs (strenuous A2; fixed) to reach a fixed anchor at the lip. Rappel off from here, or use two bolts to reach a rotten gully on the left. 75', Clean A2
3. Follow the gully to a jam crack on the right. Climb this to another gully, then step down and right onto Bonfire Ledge, the large, tree-covered ledge directly above the Cathedral Roof. 5.5
4. Above a platform, climb a corner, and step left under a large block. Surmount it, then move left across a chimney to jam cracks in the face to the left. Climb these cracks and another chimney to a good ledge (bolt). 140', 5.6
5. Climb straight up the chimney to a tree belay. 80', 5.4
6. Easy scrambling takes you to the finish and the top.

HISTORY: Joe Cote, Richard Arey, & Jeffrey Jacobs made the first ascent on November 31, 1968, placing only one bolt, at the belay at the end of Pitch four. Because of the extremely cold weather, the trio built a fire on Bonfire Ledge to stay warm, hence the ledge's unusual name.

174 THE MOUNT WASHINGTON VALLEY

Mark Hudon leading the first free ascent of White Eye (5.12b) in 1978. This was the second 5.12 done in the White Mountains—and the first route of that grade to be climbed on Cathedral Ledge. Photograph by Ed Webster.

WHITE EYE III 5.12b, A0 (*)
The first 5.12 on Cathedral Ledge, and one of the first in New England. After the technical crux, the expanding flake above calls for quick thinking. The route is named for the large, white, right-facing corner above Bonfire Ledge, a feature that is actually part of FORTITUDE. Begin below an obvious, vertical flake system just to the right of the Cathedral Roof. Carry small wired nuts and TCUs. Few if any parties ever finish the entire route.
1. Climb up 20 feet onto a good ledge, then undercling a thin, arching flake up and right (5.12b) to where the flake cuts back horizontally to the left. Now make continuously difficult moves up the remainder of the expanding flake (5.11c), and belay at a stance on the left with fixed anchors. 70', 5.12b
2. A short pitch leads up to Bonfire Ledge. 40'
3. From a large pine on the left, climb a short wall and traverse right to a short inside corner leading up to the WHITE EYE. 5.10b
4. Climb a short corner on the left, then tension traverse left (A0) into a huge chimney system that leads to the finish.
HISTORY: Steve Arsenault & Sam Streibert made the first ascent of the climb on April 20, 1968. After Jim Dunn had earlier tried to free climb the crux (which involves a very long reach) by wearing a double boot over one EB for extra height, Mark Hudon & Max Jones made the notable first free ascent of Pitch one on September 18, 1978.

VARIATION: **THE DIRECT START** I 5.11a
1a. Start at the base of MOLSON'S MADNESS. Climb up and right past a thin arch (small wired nuts) to reach the WHITE EYE starting ledge. 25', 5.11a
FA: Unknown.

FORTITUDE III 5.12b X
This seldom done climb boasts an extremely dangerous start. Double ropes are mandatory on the first pitch, and small wired nut protection must be weighted in place, or it'll be levered out! While Pitch one has groundfall potential, the upper 5.12a pitch up the WHITE EYE is well protected, and can be accessed from INTIMIDATION. Eighty feet to the right of the Cathedral Roof are three short pinnacles.
1. From the top of the left-hand pinnacle, follow a left-curving arch (5.12b X) onto a sloping ledge (bolt). A bizarre flake leads to Bonfire Ledge. 5.12b X
2. From Bonfire Ledge, climb a dihedral to a pine tree, then layback up a narrow corner (5.10b) to the base of the WHITE EYE. 5.10b
3. Layback and stem up the back of the WHITE EYE (5.12a) to the roof. Traverse right below it (only 5.8!), and swing over an overlap to a stance. 5.12a
4. Climb a perfect dihedral to a large pine tree. Finish up and left on rotten rock, or rappel from the pine with two ropes.

HISTORY: Joe Cote & Gene Ellis made the first ascent of the route on July 2, 1972. Ed Webster with Mike Heintz freed the upper section of the route up the WHITE EYE (Pitch three) on June 25, 1978. In August, 1984, Hugh Herr & Neil Cannon made the first free ascent of the entire route. Cannon decided to stay silent as he watched most of Herr's protection fall out behind him on Pitch one. Fortunately, Hugh didn't realize he'd die if he fell—and the climb went free.

BLD (BONFIRE LEDGE DIRECT) II 5.6, A4

A short and obscure aid route. More groundfall potential. Bring mostly thin pins, KBs, and bashies. Seldom repeated.

1. Jam up a nice crack (5.6) to the top of the right-hand pinnacle. 5.6
2. After some easy aid, hairy A4 hook moves gain a bolt ladder that leads up to Bonfire Ledge. A4

FA: Donn Stahlman & Don Stevens May 10, 1970

EXASPERATION I 5.11d (*)

A good, steep climb, quite sustained and strenuous. The route ascends the vertical, rounded groove just to the left of Pitch one of INTIMIDATION. Bring a few small cams along to supplement a sport rack.

1. Follow a crack with a small tree growing in it to a stance. Climb the groove past several fixed pitons and five bolts (crux at the third bolt) to the belay stance (two pitons & a bolt) atop Pitch one of INTIMIDATION. 85', 5.11d

HISTORY: All protection was placed on the lead, some on aid, before Tom Callaghan & Haydie Callaghan made the first ascent of the climb in September, 1992, after several days of effort.

SOLITUDE CRACK III 5.10b, A1 (3 Points of Aid on bolts)

This classic-looking line ascends the left-hand of a pair of vertical, sister cracks located to the right of the WHITE EYE when the cliff is viewed from a distance. The route needs more traffic to clean it up.

1 & 2. Climb the first two leads of INTIMIDATION (5.10b & 5.8), and belay on the right-hand end of Bonfire Ledge. 5.10b
3. Face climb up and then right to a mantleshelf. Step back left into a thin crack which is followed to a belay just beneath a prominent bulge. Dicey protection with small wired nuts.
4. Overcome the bulge using three points of aid on bolts (A1). Belay on a ledge on the right. A1
5. Jam the long, vertical crack system (dirty) to a pine tree.
6. An easy chimney leads to the finish.

FA: Steve Arsenault & Bruce Beck   June 23, 1968
FFA: Jim Dunn & Mark Whitton   Summer, 1977

CATHEDRAL LEDGE - RIGHT (SOLITUDE CRACK) 177

George Hurley leading Pitch two (5.8) of Intimidation (5.10b) in 1985, belayed by Ian Turnbull. Photograph by S. Peter Lewis.

178 THE MOUNT WASHINGTON VALLEY

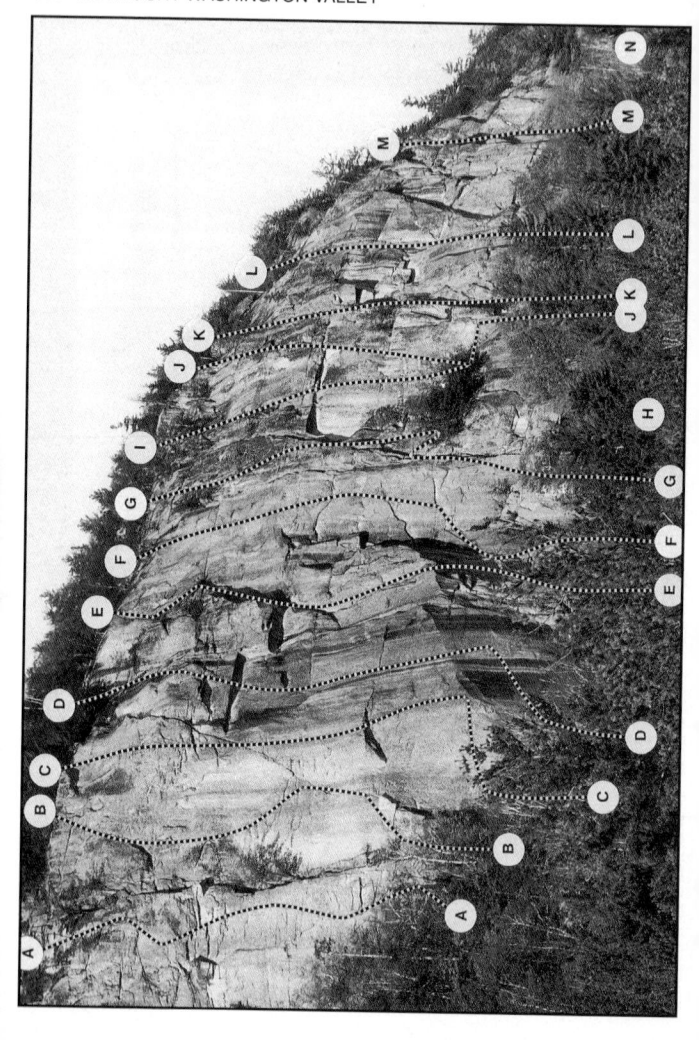

CATHEDRAL LEDGE – CENTER & RIGHT SIDE

A.	**	THE MISSING LINK III 5.10a (5.7 R)	Page	128
B.	*	ARMAGEDDON III 5.12b R	Page	149
C.	***	GRAND FINALE IV 5.12b (5.11c R), Clean A2 or 5.8, Clean A3	Page	154
D.	***	MORDOR WALL IV 5.7 (or 5.12c), A3	Page	155
E.	**	MINES OF MORIA IV 5.6 (or 5.11d), A2	Page	157
F.	***	SEVENTH SOJOURN IV 5.12b (5.9 R)	Page	167
G.		FOREST OF FANGORN IV 5.7, A3	Page	168
H.		The Cathedral Roof	Page	169
I.		SOLITUDE CRACK III 5.10b, A1 (3 points of aid on bolts)	Page	176
J.	***	INTIMIDATION III 5.10b	Page	180
K.	*	REPENTENCE II 5.10a R	Page	184
L.	*	REMISSION II 5.8 R	Page	187
M.	***	DIEDRE II 5.9+	Page	191
N.		The Practice Slab or North End	Page	201

180 THE MOUNT WASHINGTON VALLEY

INTIMIDATION III 5.10b (***)
One of Cathedral's most popular 5.10 climbs, INTIMIDATION ascends the right-hand of the two sister cracks on the right side of the cliff, just to the right of WHITE EYE. Clean and aesthetic crack climbing are the route's well known trademarks. Begin below the left of two, parallel, right-facing corners halfway between CATHEDRAL DIRECT and REPENTENCE. With two wired nuts threaded together for extra reach, the 5.10b crux on Pitch one is safe.
1. Make an awkward move to gain entry into the left-hand corner (5.10b), then layback up the dihedral to a stance (bolt). Make a puzzling step back across the left wall of the corner, and belay on a good ledge with a double piton & bolt fixed anchor. 90', 5.10b
2. Climb the short, flaring dihedral above. When it ends, make an unprotected traverse straight left (5.8) onto Bonfire Ledge. 5.8 (Pitches one and two may be combined if desired. 155', 5.10b)
3. A thin flake leads up right to the base of a finger crack. Follow the finger crack (5.9) to a belay on a sloping ledge on the left, or make it a long pitch by jamming up a steep hand crack to a good ledge on the right. 150', 5.9
4. Jam and layback up a rounded 5.9 crack that diagonals right. Above some bushes, climb a short corner, then make a long runout up a moderate dike in a slab, stepping left at one point, to the top. Exit right to the woods. 145', 5.9
FA: Steve Arsenault & Bruce Beck   June, 1968
FFA: Sam Streibert & Dennis Merritt   June, 1971

VARIATION: **SLEEPING SWAN** I 5.10d
Quiet elegance. At the start of the hand crack two thirds of the way up Pitch three of INTIMIDATION, traverse right onto the ANTLINE Ledge and belay.
4a. Above the ledge's left side, jam a finger crack (5.10d) that parallels INTIMIDATION. When it ends, traverse right, and swing up onto a ledge. 35', 5.10d
FA: Ed Webster & Jane Wilson October, 1976

THE BICYCLE ROUTE III 5.11b (5.10b R) (**)
Long and intricate, the route has become reasonably popular. Protection, except for Pitch six, is adequate. An integral line criss-crossing over INTIMIDATION, offering a variety of good, sustained free climbing—and a notable history. Modern rack helpful.
1. Climb the first pitch of INTIMIDATION. 90', 5.10b
2. At the top of the first little corner, face climb past a bolt, then layback up a narrow flake (5.11b) to a belay ledge on the right. 60', 5.11b
3. Jam up the painfully obvious, vertical 5.9 hand crack with a white birch growing out of it to reach the tree-covered ANTLINE Ledge. 70', 5.9
4. Climb a short 5.9 jam crack (just to the right of SLEEPING SWAN) to a belay ledge on INTIMIDATION. 30', 5.9

CATHEDRAL LEDGE - RIGHT (INTIMIDATION & BICYCLE ROUTE) 181

5. Follow the right-diagonalling 5.9 crack on INTIMIDATION to a long, horizontal overlap. Traverse straight left under the ceiling, then pull over it strenuously (5.11b) past fixed pegs to gain the upper face. Good belay ledge on left (piton anchor). 90', 5.11b
6. Face climb up a shallow groove to a stance (bolt; maybe missing), then make a long runout (5.10b R), angling right to merge with INTIMIDATION. 5.10b R
7. Climb the final easy dike on INTIMIDATION to the woods.

Susan Patenaude on Pitch two (5.11b) of The Bicycle Route (5.11b / 5.10b R) during the first ascent in 1980. Photograph by Ed Webster.

HISTORY: The climb has one of the most colorful histories of any route in the area. To ensure that the facts are recorded with some degree of accuracy, the story will be told in full. While cleaning the route on rappel in 1976, Ed Webster placed a bolt on the final slab, then was unable to even climb up to it. Everyone got a good chuckle out of this, but the best was yet to come.

Several years later, just for fun, Alain Comeau and several conspirators "borrowed" Webster's ten speed bicycle, rappelled down, and hung it off the offensive bolt, no doubt as a warning against any future ethical slippages! Paul Ross even went so far as to sneak Webster's camera along to photograph the event for posterity. But—as fate would have it—John Bragg & Jay Wilson were climbing INTIMIDATION later that very same day. One can only imagine their incredulity upon noticing a ten speed bicycle suspended out in the middle of a blank wall, and the subsequent argument over who saw it first! The bicycle was speedily rescued, albeit on a top-rope.

When the conspirators discovered the premature rescue of the bicycle, it was seized from Bragg and Wilson, and returned to its ignominious perch for the second time in the same day! There it remained for about two weeks until Webster finally rescued it—and alas, the poor bicycle was never quite the same again. On September 23, 1980, Ed Webster & Susan Patenaude made the route's first ascent, but found an easier way around the famous bicycle bolt—which was finally incorporated into the next variation:

DIRECT FINISH: **TRAINING WHEELS** I 5.11b R (*)
Carry a modern rack with many small wired nuts.
6a. After the first bolt, trend up and left via a series of incipient, flaring cracks (5.11b R) to the final, improbable swell in the steep slab. Climb over the bulge (5.11b) past the famous bicycle bolt onto easier ground leading to the top of the cliff. 5.11b R

HISTORY: The tale of TRAINING WHEELS is almost as amusing as that of THE BICYCLE ROUTE. In 1983, thinking that he was on the normal route, Steve Larson climbed all the way up to the bicycle bolt. Falling off the crux, fortunately Steve was held by the bicycle bolt, but the preceding bolt broke! Unnerved, Larson wisely retreated. In the Spring of 1984, Jim Surette & Alison Osius climbed the Direct Finish only to discover that Neil Cannon & Jay Dautcher had climbed it a week earlier (also under the mistaken impression that they were on the regular 5.10b finish), but as Cannon admitted: "It did seem a little too hard!"

ANTLINE III 5.10b
This seldom done route has better climbing than might be guessed, with some good jam cracks plus a very unusual chimney. Normal rack.
1. Climb the first pitch of INTIMIDATION. 90', 5.10b
2. Continue up the shallow corner on INTIMIDATION, then branch right up a series of rounded cracks to a ledge. Next, squirm up a very bizarre, subterranean-like chimney (5.5) behind a giant flake to the ANTLINE ledge.
3. Climb enjoyable hand cracks off the right side of the ledge (5.9), then hand-traverse left to an awkward mantle (also 5.9). Belay at trees on a ledge. 5.9

CATHEDRAL LEDGE - RIGHT (ABRAKADABRA)

4. Climb a flake to an inside corner, join INTIMIDATION, and climb the last, easy dike up a slab to the finish.
FA: Bob Proudman & Garvin Morris August 18, 1968
FFA: Bob Anderson & Mike Sogard September, 1971

HOCUS POCUS II 5.11d (*)

A spellbinding combination. Carry a normal rack to a #4 Friend—and your magic dust. If you only want to climb the upper three pitches, rappel straight down to the yellow corner double bolt belay, in two long rappels, starting from a double bolt anchor at the finish of INTIMIDATION.

1. Climb Pitch one of INTIMIDATION (5.10b) to the stance (bolt), then gain a slab directly above (5.10a). Traverse right across a long, sloping ledge, and belay at the base of a slanting crack on ABRAKADABRA. 120', 5.10b
2. Jam up the right-slanting crack, move left, then face climb straight up ABRAKADABRA's difficult (and very thin) bolted slab (5.11c) to a double bolt anchor on a good belay ledge. 90', 5.11c
3. Climb up a shallow yellow corner past two bolts (5.11d) to a piton, then continue past two more bolts (5.9) to a traverse left past a flake. Belay on the ANTLINE Ledge. 110', 5.11d
4. Jam the ANTLINE cracks (5.9) to a stance with a two bolt anchor. 40', 5.9
5. Face climb straight up past two bolts (5.10b at the first bolt) up a steep slab to a nice finger crack leading to a flat ledge and the large pine tree growing at the finish of INTIMIDATION. 140', 5.10b

HISTORY: Bill Lowther, Jon Sykes, & Gerry Lortie conjured up the first two and a half pitches on June 3, 1995. After rappelling down to the start of Pitch three, Bill Lowther & Gerry Lortie finished the top section on June 17, 1995.

ABRAKADABRA III 5.11b (*)

Upgraded from 5.10d since the crux flake broke in 1995. Just wishing won't get you up this route! Superb, hard stemming. The climb ascends the right-hand, parallel dihedral 25 feet to the right of INTIMIDATION. Normal rack.
1. Climb a 5.7 blocky, right-facing dihedral, then mantle left onto a ledge at the base of the crux corner. Make increasingly difficult layback moves (5.10bc) up the strenuous corner past two pitons to a bolt. Powerful stemming (5.11b) gains the corner's top, exited with an awkward mantleshelf. Belay on a ledge at a double welded cold shut anchor on the right. 80', 5.11b
2. Climb a slanting corner for a couple of moves, then step left to a tiny stance. Layback a fragile flake (5.9) to the bolted slab (the line of the first ascent; now 5.11c). Instead, make a "not very obvious step" left into a right-facing corner, and jam a pretty, arching finger crack into a bizarre niche. Chimney straight left and belay on the ANTLINE Ledge. 100', 5.9
3 & 4. Follow the upper pitches of ANTLINE to the top. 5.9

HISTORY: Paul Ross & George Meyers made the first ascent on July 7, 1972. The first pitch was free climbed by Ed Webster & Bryan Delaney on June 22, 1975. Ed Webster returned with Michael Macklin and made a free ascent of the entire climb on August 19, 1975. The bolted slab was then free climbed by Steve Larson & Andy Tuthill on the first ascent of PASSING THOUGHTS in September, 1982. The crux flake cracked in August, 1995, giving John Bouchard (leading the pitch) a near heart attack. After Bouchard cleaned off the flake, Brad White & Jay Philbrick added a bolt to the new crux, and made the re-first free ascent of Pitch one on September 23, 1996.

PASSING THOUGHTS III 5.11c (**)
No day dreaming here! Begin 10 feet left of REPENTENCE. Pitch six is the highlight of the route, with excellent, spectacular, and sustained jamming.
1. Climb a dirty groove to the REPENTENCE belay. Bolt anchor. 70', 5.8
2. Traverse down and left, then climb up a corner to a sloping ledge with a tree (on ABRAKADABRA). 40', 5.9
3. Climb the right crack, step left just before REPENTENCE, and climb flakes to a belay stance below a bolt ladder. 50', 5.8
4. Free climb the bolted slab (5.11c) on ABRAKADABRA. 30', 5.11c
5. Traverse right into the REPENTENCE chimney, and climb it for 60 feet to a belay ledge on the left.
6. Move down, then right, onto a slab. Follow a corner past two overhangs, then climb a spectacular finger and hand crack (5.11c) up the exposed, right-hand wall of the REPENTENCE chimney. 90', 5.11c
7. Finish up slabs to the woods.
FA: Steve Larson & Andy Tuthill September, 1982

REPENTENCE II 5.10a R (*)
In the late 1950s, this route represented an important advance in American free climbing standards. One can only marvel at John Turner's 1958 lead of the crux offwidth, which at the time was one of the country's hardest free pitches. Although a bit mossy and dirty, the climb is well worth doing, and ascends the left-hand of the two, vertical chimney cracks to the right of the Cathedral Roof.
1. Climb up a shallow, mossy chimney (5.8) past an old peg to a good belay ledge on the left with a double bolt belay anchor. 70', 5.8
2. Offwidth up a notorious squeeze chimney (5.10a R) past a six inch bong (not used by the first ascent party). Most people face left (with their right side in the crack), but the crux may be climbed facing either direction. Considerably easier chimneying leads to a belay stance above. 70', 5.10a R
3. Up the chimney to flakes on the left wall and a good ledge. 125', 5.8
4. Step back right into the chimney, and follow it to a huge chockstone. Stem over it (5.6) to reach the top. 130', 5.6

Mike Stultz leading the first free ascent of Repentence (5.10a R) in 1970. Note the bolt providing him protection—not used by Turner & Gran in 1958—and the selection of pitons, a bong, and the primitive tube chock on his rack! Photograph by Sam Streibert.

HISTORY: John Turner (UK) & Art Gran made the first ascent of this very historic climb on June 29, 1958, using one piton as a foot hold below the crux offwidth, a nearly negligible form of direct aid. REPENTENCE may well have been the first 5.10 climbed in America as it pre-dated Chuck Pratt's lead of The Crack Of Doom in Yosemite Valley by two years. As John Turner recalled, "The route was Art's idea. He stood on the piton for a time (placed by a prior team, below the crux), came down to reflect, and suggested I should take a look. I still remember feeling that I had passed the point of no return after stepping off the piton, and wondering what I had gotten myself into: but happily it all worked out! The route name reflected both my feelings at the crux, and the biblical associations of a Cathedral.

"Although we did both step on the piton below the crux, there was certainly no bolt in place on the first ascent. In fact, whenever I came across a bolt on a climb, I studiously avoided clipping into it. To me, bolts represented the end of climbing. My own arbitrary and antiquated ethical considerations precluded the use of bolts under any circumstances. This prejudice was respected by Art Gran, who with unwonted tactfulness did not even carry bolts when we climbed together," Turner explained.

The offending bolt—which later disappeared just as mysteriously—may, however, have have been placed by Art Gran himself prior to his successful second ascent of the route in the Summer of 1959 (but, according to Turner, Gran still stepped on the piton). The climb's first free ascent was made by Mike Stultz & Sam Streibert in a light drizzle in 1970. According to Streibert, Stultz climbed up the crux offwidth left side in, stepped on the bolt to pause and look around, descended for a rest, then led the crux free, facing right side in. It should be mentioned that neither the bolt used for protection by Stultz & Streibert on their free ascent, nor the bong (placed later by Joe Cote) which protects the crux today were in place when Turner & Gran made the first ascent of the route in 1958.

REALITY CHECK III 5.8, A4+ (**)

One of the East's most serious aid routes. Save yourself the expense: get psychological counseling first. Begin on a ledge 20 feet above the ground, five feet to the right of REPENTENCE, and just to the left of ANGEL'S HIGHWAY. Bring a modern aid rack: all sizes and types of skyhooks, bashies (many), rurps, and assorted pitons.

1. Move up and right into a blank corner which leads up to a curving flake. After a bolt at 30 feet up, more bashies lead to a second bolt and a small ledge. Aid up and right (bolt) to a two bolt belay on ANGEL'S HIGHWAY. 100', A4
2. Move right to ANGEL'S HIGHWAY and climb the 5.8 slab. Continue up a corner, aid up three bolts, then step left on two bolts into a shallow seam

(A4+; 50 foot fall potential) which is climbed past one marginal rivet to a horizontal crack under a roof. Traverse right along the crack to a tree ledge on the right. 100' 5.8, A4+ Most parties will choose to rappel off from here as the top two pitches are very dirty.

HISTORY: Paul Cormier & Brad White made the first ascent in November, 1993, incorporating Todd Swain's PEARLY GATES variation to ANGEL'S HIGHWAY on Pitch two which Swain climbed rope-solo in January, 1981.

ANGEL'S HIGHWAY III 5.8, A2

After an incredibly contrived, heavily bolted first pitch, the upper section offers fun aid climbing up steep granite. The route takes an uncompromisingly direct line up the blank wall between the parallel chimney systems of REPENTENCE and REMISSION. Carry mostly wired nuts and thin pitons.
1. Above a ledge, several dowels connect with a short-lived crack. A long ladder of poorly placed bolts (several lacking hangers) leads over a bulge to a small belay stance with a double bolt anchor. 100', A2
2. Friction right across a slab (5.8), climb to a horizontal crack, and use three bolts to reach a shallow, right-facing dihedral (A2) that leads up to a tree-covered ledge. 90' 5.8, A2
3. Off the left end of the ledge, climb a corner to a second corner with a pine tree. A 5.8 slab takes you to the woods.
FA: Paul Ross & Rosie Andrews June 6, 1972

REMISSION II 5.8 R (*)

Traditional Cathedral 5.8! Although this is the easiest, full length climb up Cathedral's right-hand side, some dubious rock and occasionally poor protection make this is a route for experienced teams only. REMISSION ascends the intimidating chimney system 100 feet to the right of REPENTENCE. Start behind a large oak tree growing at the base of the cliff.
1. Climb the dihedral behind the tree, then step right into a vertical crack system leading up to a good belay ledge. 120', 5.8
2. Head up the corner on the right, then climb diagonally left 30 feet around an outside corner. Face climb up the face on the right (horn) to a sloping belay ledge below the impressive, upper chimney. Flake anchor. 100', 5.8 R
3. With difficulty (5.8), enter the dark recesses of the upper chimney and climb it. Belay in the chimney at a tree. 130', 5.8 Scramble easily to the top.
HISTORY: Richard Wilmott (Canada) & John Turner (UK) did the first ascent of this demanding route on July 1, 1960. In his account in Appalachia, Turner described the ascent as "an interesting climb of medium 5th class."

WARLOCK III 5.12c (5.10b R)

Watch out you don't fall under the spell. This long route initially used aid on every pitch, including A4 sections on Pitches three and four, which offer excellent, sustained climbing, whereas the remainder of the route often gets ugly. If you want to only climb the good stuff, approach via BURNING BRIDGE or REMISSION, then rappel off after Pitch four. Modern rack.

1. Start as for BURNING BRIDGE, in an overhanging rotten groove a few yards right of REMISSION. Continue up this groove past twigs and dirt to an awkward exit (5.10b R) over a bulge at its top. Easier and cleaner rock leads to the large ledge at the end of REMISSION's first pitch. 120', 5.10b R

2. Traverse right under a ceiling until it is possible to step up and mantleshelf (5.10b) onto a lower angled face. Continue up this face to a good ledge, also on BURNING BRIDGE. 70', 5.10b

3. Climb the right-angling corner above past 3 old bolts (5.11d) to a sloping ledge with a bolt/pin anchor. 70', 5.11d Same as Pitch 3, BURNING BRIDGE.

4. Ascend the clean, open corner up above, stemming past two bolts (5.12c), continuing strenuously several fixed pitons (5.11d), and finally exit left at the top onto a large, sloping terrace with a fixed piton & bolt anchor. 70', 5.12c

5. From the terrace's left end, unpleasant climbing (needs cleaning) leads up a crack/corner (5.10b R) past two old bolts, joining REMISSION. 100', 5.10b R

6. Scramble up the REMISSION chimney to the top. 5.4

Paul Ross enjoying a beer during the first ascent of The Warlock in 1972. Photograph courtesy of Paul Ross.

CATHEDRAL LEDGE - RIGHT (BURNING BRIDGE)

HISTORY: Paul Ross, George Meyers, & Bill Aughton climbed the first ascent on July 6, 1972, grading the route A4. Jim Ewing & Larry Hamilton made a number of attempts, and added two new protection bolts on Pitch four, before completing WARLOCK's first free ascent on October 2, 1988. "I opted to place a couple of bolts on the fourth pitch in order to preserve the thin seam that would be crucial to free climbing. It took me several trips up there to work out the moves, and a few more times to finally get it," Jim Ewing remembered. "It was Larry's insistence that we keep going back until we finally freed it. After a truly spectacular trundle of large, loose blocks on Pitch two, the route went free."

BURNING BRIDGE III 5.11d (5.9 R)

The route was named for the climb's first 20 feet, the right-facing, crumbly flake which involves some of the worst rock on Cathedral. The first ascent party broke off so many holds they thought this section might become unclimbable. After the start, however, the climbing definitely improves! Start the same as for REMISSION, on a vegetated platform. Modern rack.

1. A few yards right of REMISSION is a small rotten corner. Climb past the first overhang in this corner to two fixed pitons, then traverse right to the base of an obvious arch on clean rock. Layback the arch and surmount the bulge at its top (bolt; 5.11c) to reach a good stance. Run out the slab above (5.9 R) until you reach a large belay ledge on REMISSION. 130', 5.11c (5.9 R)

2. Climb 20 feet up the REMISSION corner, then traverse right past an undercling (5.8) to a good belay ledge on WARLOCK. 50', 5.8

3. Ascend the obvious, right-diagonalling corner above (with difficulty) past three old bolts (5.11d at the top), and belay on a sloping ledge with a bolt and fixed piton anchor. 70', 5.11d (This pitch was originally part of the crux A4 aid pitch on WARLOCK.)

4. Drop down off the right end of the sloping belay ledge to a traverse line that continues right past an old bolt (5.8) into a large, broken corner. 70', 5.8

5. At this point the route joins THE BRITISH ARE COMING and DON'T FIRE for their final pitch. Climb the top corner (5.9) and slab to the trees. 5.9

HISTORY: Jim Ewing, Larry Hamilton, & Rich Baker free climbed Pitch one on August 16, 1987—one of the hottest days of that summer. Jim Ewing & Larry Hamilton did the first complete free ascent of the route in July, 1988.

THE BRITISH ARE COMING III 5.9, A3 (*)

More intricate aid. The upper 5.9 corners were freed later, and are usually accessed up THE LAST TEMPTATION and DON'T FIRE. Start 80 feet to the right of REMISSION at two large blocks that form a short chimney. Carry an A3 rack, including rurps.

1. Atop the right-hand block, aid up three bolts, then nail a horizontal crack to the right (A3) to several more bolts and a grassy belay ledge. A3

2. Nail cracks connected by more bolts to a bolt ladder, then tension right to holds from the top bolt, and belay on a small ledge below an obvious roof.
3. Skirt the left side of the overhang, move right into the exposed, upper dihedral (5.9), and climb up to a good ledge. 5.9
4. Layback the final corner (5.9) to a friction slab and the top. 5.9

HISTORY: This route was the scene of an infamous "first ascent race" between '70s arch rivals, Joe Cote and Paul Ross who, as legend has it, shared beers at the belays. The date was May 21, 1972, and Paul Ross, Rosie Andrews, & Hal Wilkins won—beating Joe Cote & Dick Arey on DON'T FIRE UNTIL YOU SEE THE WHITES OF THEIR EYES to the top. On August 27, 1977, Ed Webster & Jim Dunn free climbed pitches three & four.

GOLDEN III 5.10b

Serious climbing—and a seldom climbed route. You won't be "golden" until the last move is over. After the climb crosses DON'T FIRE, it finishes up a parallel dihedral system farther to the right.

1 & 2. Climb the triple ledges of DIEDRE (5.8), and Pitch two of THE LAST TEMPTATION, the 5.9+ handtraverse. 5.8 & 5.9+
3. From the belay, move 10 feet left to the base of a vertical water groove, and climb it directly (5.10b) past fixed pitons to a belay on the right (peg). 5.10b
4. Follow the hand crack and corner above, then head right up onto a slab (old peg). Angle left into another corner, and belay higher on a ledge (peg).
5. Climb up 15 feet, then traverse right with difficulty for 20 feet to reach the base of a parallel, right-facing corner. Layback up the dihedral to the route's fitting climax: 5.10b jamming over a roof. 5.10b

FA: Doug Madara & Paul Ross September, 1980

DON'T FIRE UNTIL YOU SEE
THE WHITES OF THEIR EYES III 5.11c R (*)

With Pitch one free, the entire original route has now been free climbed. Start 75 feet right of the double blocks on the ground at the base of THE BRITISH ARE COMING. Look for a short, overhanging orange wall. Sustained free climbing, with small wired nuts on the crux. Modern rack.

1. Above a mossy ledge 15 feet up, climb up a shallow, slightly left-leaning crack (just left of the orange wall) with increasing difficulty past two old bolts to a bulge (5.11c R). Belay on THE LAST TEMPTATION ledge. 80', 5.11c R
2. Directly above, climb over a bulge (5.10c) past several bolts to a thin finger crack, and a large belay ledge higher up. 5.10c
3. Jam a 5.9 hand crack up a black dihedral, then exit left on angular holds. Climb another corner to a ledge and belay. 5.9
4. This excellent pitch laybacks up the large, prominent corner above (5.9) to the upper slabs and the forest. 5.9

CATHEDRAL LEDGE - RIGHT (LAST TEMPTATION & DIEDRE)

HISTORY: Joe Cote & Dick Arey made the route's first ascent on May 21, 1972, joining Paul Ross, Hal Wilkins, & Rosie Andrews on the final Pitch four dihedral. On August 27, 1977, Ed Webster & Jim Dunn free climbed Pitch two, approaching up THE LAST TEMPTATION. Doug Madara freed the crux first pitch, after two days of effort, with Bill Supple in August, 1988.

THE LAST TEMPTATION II 5.10d (*)

If you've managed Pitch two, try not to revert to any sinful ways on the crux up above—by grabbing one of the bolts! Still a challenging free climb whose puzzling crux baffles many a would-be suitor. Protection is good.

1. Climb DIEDRE's triple ledges to a large ledge. 80', 5.8
2. Take a deep breath, then launch across a long and notoriously strenuous handtraverse left (5.9+) to a good belay ledge. 40', 5.9+
3. The crux follows a diagonal groove up and right before laybacking a tricky groove to a blank face (5.10d) well protected by several bolts. 65', 5.10d
4. Most rappel off from here, or finish up DON'T FIRE on the left. Otherwise, from the second ledge, jam a hand crack up right to a large pine tree. 5.9+
5. An overhanging four inch crack leads to easier ground. 5.6.

HISTORY: Joe Cote & Larry Poorman made the first ascent of the climb in August, 1970. The aid was subsequently eliminated to just a single point by Bob Anderson & Joe Cote before Henry Barber & Steve Hendricks made the route's first free ascent in May, 1972.

THE WEZ II 5.12b (*)

A technical pitch, ascending the flaring dihedral directly above the triple ledges on DIEDRE. Adequate protection, with effort. Modern rack.

1. Climb the triple ledges on DIEDRE to a big ledge. 80', 5.8
2. Head straight up the obvious corner, past a protection bolt at the start. Very technical moves (5.12b) lead up the flaring, inside corner with tricky wired nut protection until you can join LAST TEMPTATION on the left. 75', 5.12b

HISTORY: Ed Webster cleaned the climb & placed the bolt on aid in 1980 before "Road Warriors" Neil Cannon & Russ Clune did the first ascent on July 22, 1984. The name was inspired by John Bouchard's current video obsession.

DIEDRE II 5.9+ (***)

A required climb for those new to the area, especially if you're keen on unexcelled, perfect hand jamming. Spacious belays and good protection add to the attraction. Locate a series of dihedrals about 100 hundred yards left (south) of Cathedral's North End or Practice Slab. The Pitch three corner, which you can see between the tree branches overhead from the trail along the cliff base, has a white birch tree growing in it. Carry a normal rack.

1. Climb a series of three ledges, the so-called triple ledges, up a chimney to a large, comfortable ledge. 80', 5.8

192 THE MOUNT WASHINGTON VALLEY

> Bob Palais makes the crux clip on the second pitch of Diedre (5.9+).
> Photograph by Jeff Achey.

2. Move up the corner above, make an awkward step right, and escape right from under a roof (5.9+; peg) onto another big ledge with a piton anchor. 50', 5.9+
3. Ascend the aesthetic, open book with excellent jamming past a large, white birch tree to a third good belay ledge with more birches. 85', 5.8
4. Balance up and right along an easy flake to a blueberry terrace on the right.
5. The prominent chimney/hand crack above the center of the ledge leads to the top. There are two enjoyable sections of 5.9 jamming, including the last few moves—which may be avoided on the right at 5.8. 100', 5.9

HISTORY: The first ascent of this extremely popular climb was made by Joe Cote & Dick Arey on July 20, 1968. In 1970, the route was done free, but in several stages. The second pitch was first free climbed by Sam Streibert and Mike Stultz in August, 1970. Pitch three was freed soon afterwards by Dennis Merritt & Bob Mitchell. After starting up KAREN'S VARIATION, George Eypper & Larry Winship free climbed the last pitch of DIEDRE, also in August, 1970. Finally, on August 7, 1971, Joe Cote & Ben Read made the first continuous free ascent of the entire original route.

CATHEDRAL LEDGE - RIGHT (DIEDRE & BUDAPEST) 193

Dave Rose leading Budapest (5.11d) in 1986. Photograph by S. Peter Lewis.

> DIEDRE's three variation finishes are now described from left to right:

VARIATION #1: **BUDAPEST** I 5.11d (***)
This exposed, unrelenting, straight-in finger and hand crack has become a very popular testpiece. Strenuous jamming, with the hardest moves saved for last! Well protected with a normal rack.

1–3. Climb the first three leads of DIEDRE: 5.8, 5.9+, & 5.8
4a. Follow the same vertical crack system straight to the top of the cliff. The crux is the final move! 120', 5.11d

HISTORY: Ed Webster & Jim Dunn made the first ascent in July, 1979. Webster (who found and spent hours cleaning the route on rappel) fell on the crux on his first attempt, then lowered off to rest. With Dunn eagerly awaiting (demanding?) his own turn, Webster shook out, and fortunately fired off the crux on his next try. Dunn followed as cooly as could be, took out all the nuts, breezed through the crux moves—then down climbed them, and calmly reclimbed the crux a second time. His comment: "That was nice."

VARIATION #2: **DIEDRE DIRECT** II 5.9+
Right of BUDAPEST are two more prominent parallel cracks, both much wider.
4b. Climb up the left-hand of these two vertical cracks. 5.9+
FA: Sam Streibert & Dennis Merritt August, 1970

VARIATION #3: **PISS EASY** II 5.10c
Hardly! Carry large protection, Camalots, Friends, Big Bro's, etc.
4c. Climb the strenuous, right-hand, fist/offwidth crack. 5.10c
HISTORY: After attempts by others had failed, Henry Barber & Bob Anderson made the first ascent on October 27, 1972.

KINESIS II 5.11d (**)
An extremely complicated crux makes for a refined vertical dance.
1. Climb up the triple ledges of DIEDRE. 80', 5.8
2. On the right, jam a short, diagonal crack up a steep wall to a ledge. 35', 5.9
3. Follow a finger crack up an exposed, intricate arete on the right to several very unlikely face moves at the top (bolt; 5.10d). A short corner takes you up to the large, blueberry terrace on DIEDRE. 100', 5.10d
4. The large, open corner to the right of DIEDRE is the last pitch of DELIGHTMAKER. The final lead of KINESIS climbs the right-hand wall of the DELIGHTMAKER corner up a series of three flakes to a stance. A bolt protects the intricate 5.11d crux, gaining the top finger crack. 90', 5.11d
HISTORY: After the climb was cleaned on rappel in July, 1978, Ed Webster & Ken Sims climbed all but the crux moves on Pitch four. Ed Webster & Bruce Dicks finished the route in one push on August 19, 1978.

Ken Sims following Pitch three of Kinesis (5.11d) on the first attempt in 1978. Photograph by Ed Webster.

DELIGHTMAKER II 5.11d (*)

This seldom repeated climb, deserving of more attention, offers a variety of pleasing, hard climbing. Locate a small tree growing on a ledge 30 feet above the ground, and 25 feet to the left of KAREN'S VARIATION.

1. Step off the tree onto a stance. Thin, sustained face climbing (5.11d) leads up a blank face and bolt ladder into a flaring groove. Mantle onto a slab (also 5.11) and belay on the ledge above. 80', 5.11d

2. Climb a 5.9 right-leaning crack onto KAREN'S VARIATION. 5.9
3. Above the blueberry terrace, climb the sustained, overhanging dihedral (5.11c) between the upper pitches of DIEDRE and KINESIS. (Same as the last pitch of REMIRRETH.) 100', 5.11c

HISTORY: The first two pitches, with a finish up DIEDRE, were done by Joe Cote & Jeff Fraser in the Autumn of 1974. The final corner was climbed by Joe Cote & Ed Sklar as the finish of REMIRRETH on September, 20, 1974. Ed Webster with Mack Johnson free climbed the entire route except for one point of aid (a bolt on Pitch one) on June 15, 1978. The final corner took several tries. After a previous attempt, the remaining aid point was eliminated by Jim Surette & Alison Osius in June, 1985, with several falls. The entire route has probably never had a continuous free ascent.

KAREN'S VARIATION II 5.8 (5.9 with a finish up DIEDRE)
To the right of DIEDRE is a mossy chimney. It is not a popular route.
1 & 2. Follow the crack system for two pitches to the terrace on DIEDRE. 5.8
3. Finish up the last pitch of DIEDRE, the 5.9 chimney. 100', 5.9

HISTORY: Joe Cote & Dick Arey made the first ascent on August 31, 1968, and named the route for Joe's wife, Karen.

REMIRRETH II 5.11c
Originally an obscure aid climb, the entire route has now been free climbed. HUNTING HUMANS makes for a better (and cleaner) start.
1. Follow the mossy, dirty, vertical crack system five feet right of KAREN'S VARIATION to a large ledge on the right. 5.6
2. Climb the left-most corner above the ledge to a difficult crux (5.11b) at its top. (Same as HUNTING HUMANS.) 5.11b
3. Above the blueberry terrace, climb the large, right-slanting dihedral to the top (same as Pitch three of DELIGHTMAKER). 5.11c

HISTORY: Originally an aid climb put up by Joe Cote & Ed Sklar on September 20, 1974, the entire route now goes free. On June 15, 1978, Ed Webster with Mack Johnson free climbed the final corner as part of DELIGHTMAKER. In the Autumn of 1984, John Bouchard & Mark Strueli freed Pitch two during the first ascent of HUNTING HUMANS.

HUNTING HUMANS II 5.11b (*)
A better link-up of pitches, more sustained, and considerably cleaner. Begin at the base of LADY LARA. Modern rack, definitely.
1. Climb to the first bolt on LADY LARA, then step down and left onto a steep slab. Face climb to a flake and a difficult mantleshelf move (5.10d), then finish up corners to a good belay ledge. 5.10d
2. Above the ledge, free climb the left-most dihedral (wired nut protection) to the crux moves (5.11b) at the corner's top. 5.11b

CATHEDRAL LEDGE (JACK THE RIPPER)

3. Finish up DIEDRE, DELIGHTMAKER, or KINESIS. 5.9, 5.11c, or 5.11d
FA: John Bouchard & Mark Strueli Autumn, 1984

VARIATION: **THE HUMAN BOOK** I 5.12b
2a. Begin up HUNTING HUMANS, but move left over to and then up a very blank dihedral (5.12b), protected by two bolts. 40', 5.12b
FA: Jerry Handren Summer, 1987

LADY LARA II 5.11d R (*)
This very serious free climb ascends the thin, right-diagonalling crack system approximately 40 feet to the right of KAREN'S VARIATION. Very seldom repeated. Bring a modern rack, with many small wired nuts.
1. Climb up to two bad bolts (easily backed up) at a small pedestal. Follow the thin, diagonal crack/corner for 35 feet. When the crack gets too narrow for fingers, pull strenuously around the left arete, and move up to a stance. 5.11d R
2. Ascend the central dihedral off the ledge, up a finger crack past a bolt (5.10d). Belay on the good ledge just above. 5.10d
3. Head up an obvious crack system past a small roof (5.8) onto slabs to the right of the top pitch of KINESIS. 5.8
HISTORY: Joe Cote & Dick Arey made the first ascent in the Summer of 1972, naming the route for Joe's daughter, Lara. Steve Larson & Neil Cannon free climbed Pitch one on August 5, 1984. Steve Larson & Jim Surette accomplished the first continuous free ascent a month later.

VARIATION: **A FISTFUL OF DOLLARS** I 5.11d
Start 40 feet right of Pitch two of LADY LARA. Tape highly recommended!
2a. Right of the sloping belay ledge, climb a short fist crack to a mantle ledge, then jam up a thin crack to the belay. 5.11d
HISTORY: After an earlier try with Steve Larson (and cleaning on rappel), Neil Cannon & Jim Surette made the first ascent on October 14, 1984.

JACK THE RIPPER II 5.12a (*) or 5.11c (**)
Try not to choke on the crux. At Cathedral's North End, uphill to the left of the Practice Slab, are two parallel, vertical cracks. JACK THE RIPPER ascends the left-hand crack, which begins as a hairline seam and eventually widens to perfect hand width. THE POSSESSED is the right-hand crack.
1. Face climb up a steep, mossy slab with an incipient, vertical crack (5.12a) past two bolts to a good belay ledge with a fixed piton anchor. 35', 5.12a
1a. An easier start, Pitch one of DAGGER, avoids the original A3 rurp crack. Climb 20 feet up THE POSSESSED to a bolt, step back down and left to an insecure 5.9+ groove, and climb this to a good ledge on the left. 40', 5.9+
2. Finger jam past a troublesome bulge (5.11c), then dash up the widening hand crack to a large belay ledge on the right. 75', 5.11c Most parties will rappel off here, from a double bolt anchor, with two ropes.

198 THE MOUNT WASHINGTON VALLEY

2a. Pitch two of DAGGER climbs a crack up right, then traverses left along a horizontal crack back onto the regular pitch.

3. Climb a flake on the right, and finish up a corner and crack.

HISTORY: Joe Cote & John Merrill aided the first ascent in April, 1970. (Trivia question: what was the climb's original name? "Jack The Rurper.") Later, Joe Cote & Milt Camille added DAGGER up the short groove and horizontal crack, and finished JACK THE RIPPER using just two points of aid. Ed Webster, Greg Newth, & Jim Dunn free climbed Pitch two in September, 1976, after starting up Pitch one of DAGGER. Jim Damon & Bill Lutkus made the first free ascent of the original A3 start in July, 1988.

THE POSSESSED II 5.11d (***)

One of the most popular and strenuous of all the traditional testpieces, THE POSSESSED climbs the striking, overhanging crack system up the steep wall 30 feet to the right of JACK THE RIPPER, uphill and to the left of the Practice Slab. A small rock pedestal marks the start. Normal rack.

1. Above the pedestal, a bolt protects moves to a ledge below the main portion of the crack. Layback the wide crack (peg) to a good hold on the right, then surge up several extreme moves (5.11d) to a good belay ledge above. which has a double bolt belay/rappel anchor. 100', 5.11d

2. A second pitch (extremely overgrown) was climbed, but most parties will prefer to rappel off with two ropes rather than continuing to the top.

Doug Madara using early hangdogging technique trying to free The Possessed (5.11d) in 1975. Photographs by Ed Webster.

CATHEDRAL LEDGE - RIGHT (THE POSSESSED & BLACK MAGIC) 199

HISTORY: One of the few new routes to be completed on Cathedral Ledge in winter, Ed Webster, Ken Nichols, & John Dowd aid climbed the first ascent on February 17 & 18, 1974. After Ed Webster & Doug Madara freed all but the crux moves in the Summer of 1975, Jim Dunn made the historic first free ascent of the climb in October, 1975, after several days of effort.

Jim Dunn on his first attempt to climb Black Magic (5.11c) in 1976.

BLACK MAGIC II 5.11c

An unpopular, even evil route, that should probably be cleaned between each ascent! Climbs the dirty, vile-looking crack system out the left side of THE ROOF, 20 feet right of THE POSSESSED. Carry large Friends.

1. Jam and layback up the crack (5.10c) to a rest under the roof. Make awkward moves around the roof (5.11c), and escape right through bushes. 110', 5.11c

HISTORY: After cleaning the climb on rappel and on aid, Jim Dunn, Ajax Greene, & Ed Webster did the first ascent in July, 1976. Dunn led it barefoot.

THE ROOF I 5.9

A rarely climbed route which suffers from the same excesses of dirt and overgrowth as BLACK MAGIC. Start at the left side of the Practice Slab.

1. Climb up to and around the right side of THE ROOF. 90', 5.9

FA: Joe Cote and partner   Summer, 1972
FFA: Henry Barber & Budge Gierke   October 22, 1972

Henry Barber leading the first free ascent of They Died Laughing (5.9) in 1972. Photograph courtesy of Henry Barber.

THE PRACTICE SLAB or NORTH END

The Practice Slab is located at the North End of Cathedral Ledge. It is a fine place to round out the day or just do a couple of fun, short climbs. Routes on the Practice Slab, however, are predominantly crack climbs between 75 feet and 90 feet long, and protect well with nuts. To descend, rappel off the two bolt anchor at the top of THEY DIED LAUGHING (two ropes) or from the trees growing at the top of CHILD'S PLAY and KIDDY CRACK (with one rope) on the right-hand side of the slab. The descent trail runs through the woods well to the right of the slab. To hike up and set up a top-rope, from KIDDY CRACK walk right along the cliff base to the lower, right corner of an often wet 45 degree slab. Angle sharply left along a natural weakness, staying very low on the wet slab, until you reach a faint climber's trail which passes left directly below the THRESHER Slab to a large, flat ledge at the top of the Practice Slab. The routes are now described from left to right:

BE SHARP OR BE FLAT I 5.10a X
A serious venture with groundfall potential on the crux. Stick to top-roping the route—or be extremely sharp!
1. Just to the left of THE SLOT, boulder over a short bulge/arete to a ledge with a hidden peg. Face climb straight up a steep, committing wall aiming for a poor piton, and don't blow it. 90', 5.10a X
FA: Tom Callaghan, Jeff Brewer, & Dave Rose August, 1985

THE SLOT I 5.10b (**)
Easily identified by its small pea pod, this thin finger crack slices up the Practice Slab's left side, just to the left of THEY DIED LAUGHING. A real finger burner. Carry many wired nuts.
1. Jam up the thin, sustained crack, step right at its top, and finish up THEY DIED LAUGHING for the last 20 feet. Double bolt anchor on top. 85', 5.10b
FA: Joe Cote & Dick Arey   May 10, 1970
FFA: Bob Anderson & Henry Barber   July 31, 1973

VARIATION: **THE DIRECT FINISH** I 5.10b
Very tricky moves. Need a sandbag? Carry a modern rack with RP nuts.
1a. Climb THE SLOT finger crack until it jogs hard right. Protect, then step up and left (5.10b) on slopers into a faint groove, laying away up the groove past RP nuts to the top. 20', 5.10b
FA: Chris Gill & Chris Noonan August, 1990

MERRILL'S VARIATION I 5.9+
Another ten finger work out, ascending the flake and extremely thin finger crack immediately to the left of THEY DIED LAUGHING. Normal rack.

1. A series of very tricky crack and face moves (5.9+) gain THEY DIED LAUGHING, which is followed more easily to the top. 90', 5.9+
HISTORY: John Merrill led the first ascent on aid in the Autumn of 1969. Jeff Pheasant & Ajax Greene did the first free ascent on September 3, 1973.

THEY DIED LAUGHING I 5.9 (***)
One of the cliff's single most popular crack climbs, and a good introduction to 5.9 moves. Protection couldn't be a whole lot better! Normal rack.
1. Climb the continuous, vertical crack system just to the left of the slab's center. There are several attention-getting sections, including a tricky bulge halfway up (5.9) and the very last move. Double bolt anchor on top. 80', 5.9
2. This pitch is best ignored. Walk to the ledge's far left end, then climb a short, dirty inside corner, followed by an obvious crack to the top. 5.5
HISTORY: Kevin Bein, Cherry Merritt, & Bill Waterman aided the first ascent on May 25, 1969. After Henry Barber freed the first pitch in 1972, Joe Cote convinced him he hadn't really done "the first free ascent" because he hadn't free climbed the second pitch, too. Of course, only Cote knew where the upper pitch went (and that it was already free, at 5.5!) So, Henry Barber & Joe Cote made the first free ascent, of the entire climb, on September 24, 1972.

FAILSAFE I 5.11d R
A hard, dangerous free climb up the incipient crack just left of BIRD'S NEST.
1. Climb the crack. When it ends, make a one foot mantle onto a bucket, then face climb to the top, past a wired nut and a skyhook. 90', 5.11d R
HISTORY: Joe Cote & Larry Poorman made the route's first ascent in the Autumn of 1969, naming the climb CAMC. John Bouchard, Jim Surette, & John Burke accomplished the first free ascent in September, 1984.

BOSWELL'S BIG BREAK I 5.11b (Top-rope)
This "neat top-rope problem" combines several previously climbed sections.
1. Start up BIRD'S NEST to a ledge, move left standing on a horizontal break, then face climb "and drift left" on thin moves to the base of a corner, which is laybacked to a ledge just right of THEY DIED, and the top. 80', 5.11b
FA: Andy Ross & Nick Yardley, top-rope May 12, 1987

BIRD'S NEST I 5.9- (***)
Another perennial favorite, but beware of overcrowding during seasonal migrations from the south. Sinker finger jams—and protection!
1. Just left of RECLUSE, climb a vertical finger crack to wedged blocks. Two finger cracks converge into the final hand crack. Two bolt anchor. 90', 5.9-
HISTORY: Dave Cilley & Sue Durgin made the climb's first ascent in the Autumn of 1969, and found a bird's nest en route. Henry Barber led the first free ascent on September 28, 1972.

CATHEDRAL LEDGE - NORTH END (THEY DIED LAUGHING & RECLUSE) 203

RECLUSE I 5.10d (***)
A very popular testpiece (with a traditional grading) that still repulses many. Ascending the first vertical crack system to the left of CHILD'S PLAY, the route offers an overhanging, challenging start right off the ground.

1. Make very hard boulder problem-type moves (5.10d) up thin finger jams into the upper crack, which yields more easily to the top. 90', 5.10d

HISTORY: Joe Cote & Dick Arey aided the first ascent on November 4, 1968. In September, 1971, Bob Seymour made a risky bet with Henry Barber—for a six pack of beer—that the route couldn't be free climbed. Bob lost.

Henry Barber succeeds on the first free ascent of RECLUSE in 1971. Note the piton hammer and etriers he is carrying! Photograph: Henry Barber collection.

CHILD'S PLAY I 5.6 (***)

As the easiest short climb on Cathedral Ledge, this route has probably been climbed more times than any other pitch in New Hampshire! CHILD'S PLAY protects easily with nuts, and can be done in either one or two pitches. On the right-hand side of the Practice Slab is a moderate, vertical crack system with a comfortable ledge on the right at half height.

1. The hardest moves are off the ground (5.6), standing up in a small alcove, and just below the top (5.5) of the crack. Tree anchors above. 70', 5.6

HISTORY: The original line of ascent did the first half and finished up FLAKE LEFT. Jeff Pheasant & Ed Webster made the first complete ascent of the route on April 18, 1973. A large bush used to grow in the upper crack.

Ed Webster on the first ascent of Child's Play (5.6) in 1973. Photo: Jeff Pheasant.

VARIATION #1: FLAKE LEFT I 5.6

An old and obscure climb, complete with several rusting relics.

1a. From the ledge at half height, move left to a layback flake (5.6) which is followed to the top. There are a couple of old pitons. 50', 5.6

FA: Unknown.

VARIATION #2: **LISA** I 5.7 R

Lost love? A seldom climbed, poorly protected variation to CHILD'S PLAY.
1b. From the middle ledge, traverse straight left across a horizontal crack, then climb directly up an unprotected face (5.7 R) to reach the layback flake on FLAKE LEFT which is followed to the top. 50', 5.7 R
FA: Ed Webster & Kurt Blichen July 18, 1973

THE MANTLESHELF PROBLEM I 5.7+ (*)

This frustrating and awkward mantleshelf move rebuffs many. Make sure that your climbing shoes are absolutely dry before you give it a try!
1. Just to the right of CHILD'S PLAY, mantleshelf with difficulty (5.7+) up onto an obvious hold, and face climb to the middle ledge. 20', 5.7+
HISTORY: Ed Webster cleaned the ferns off the hand holds and free-soloed the problem on June 3, 1973.

VARIATION: **GENERATION X** I 5.10b (Top-rope) (*)

Takes a challenging and enjoyable line up the cracks and blank face between the upper sections of CHILD'S PLAY and KIDDY CRACK.
1a. Above the middle ledge, climb the incipient, vertical crack just to the left of KIDDY CRACK, step left onto a sloping stance, then move up past a right-slanting finger crack. Finish straight up a smooth face, the crux, (5.10b) to the trees above. 40', 5.10b
FA: Unknown.

KIDDY CRACK I 5.7 (***)

A mature climbing technique will get you far—well, at least 60 feet!
1. Layback the slippery, vertical finger crack (5.7) 40 feet to the right of CHILD'S PLAY for 30 feet to the center ledge. A second, higher thin crack (also 5.7) leads to the trees above. 60', 5.7
HISTORY: Bob Anderson free-soloed the initial crack on October 27, 1972. The 5.7 finish was added later, after cleaning.

There are also two, short girdle traverses of the Practice Slab.

SLAP HAPPY I 5.10b

The right to left girdle traverse of the slab.
1. The crux was a 5.10b handtraverse across the upper horizontal fracture leading from CHILD'S PLAY over to RECLUSE. 5.10b
FA: Jeff Pheasant & Michael Hartrich late 1970s

SUSPENDED ANIMATION I 5.8

The left to right girdle of the Practice Slab.
1. Takes the lower traverse crack between RECLUSE and CHILD'S PLAY. 5.8
FA: Matt Peer & Dana Seavey April 27, 1981

SKELETONS IN THE CLOSET II 5.9
An obscure route, reclaimed by Mother Nature since the first ascent.
1. Do any number of routes to the top of the Practice Slab.
2. Above the finish of THEY DIED LAUGHING, climb a narrow ramp or corner which diagonals right past bushes.
3. The pair of parallel finger cracks (5.9) high up on the wall to the right. 5.9
FA: Jeff Butterfield & Mike Niedoroda September 1, 1978

THE THRESHER SLAB

This is the steep, clean slab up above and 100 yards to the right of the Practice Slab. The routes are described from left to right.

EXILES IN BABYLON I 5.9+
Begin 30 feet to the left of THE THRESHER.
1. Reach for a horizontal finger crack below a bolt. Balancey climbing leads past the bolt to a stance with a hidden piton. Finish up a small open book (RP nuts helpful here) to the top. 60', 5.9+
FA: Claude Muff, Blair Folts, & Louis Dandurand Autumn, 1986

THE THRESHER I 5.10b R (*)
This short, bolt-protected face is well worth looking for. A good lead.
1. Face climb up the steep, clean slab (5.10b R) past several well spaced bolts—all drilled on the lead. The crux is at the top. 60', 5.10b R
FA: Jeff Butterfield & Mike Niedoroda August 26, 1978

KNIGHT IN WHITE SATIN I 5.10d (*)
Steep, thin face moves similar to VENTILATOR. The crux is between the second and third bolts. Start 15 feet to the right of THE THRESHER.
1. Face climb up and left past four bolts up a steep slab. 60', 5.10d
FA: Brad White & Barbara Knight July, 1989

> These two large boulders are located in the woods below Cathedral.

THE NOSTRIL BLOCK

This is the large granite block tucked away in the woods below the THIN AIR Face. Below MORDOR WALL, hike up to the base of the STANDARD ROUTE chimney, then horizontally left a short ways. The routes are described left to right, heading downhill and left from a large, jammed chockstone.

PICKING WINNERS I 5.11b (*)
Have you picked any good winners lately? Begin 20 feet left of the chockstone.
1. Strenuous climbing leads up a seam (5.10d) past two fixed pitons, then move left to a ring bolt (5.11b) on a bulge. 60', 5.11b
FA: Tom Callaghan, John Mallery, & John Strand July 18, 1988

CATHEDRAL LEDGE - THRESHER SLAB & NOSTRIL BLOCK

ROUGH TRADE I 5.11d
Start 15 feet to the left of PICKING WINNERS. Carry many RP nuts.
1. Climb a thin, right-slanting crack/seam, protected by many small wired nuts. When the seam ends, step left, and finish (bolt) up a short, shallow, right-facing corner. 60', 5.11d
FA: Rich Baker, Jim Ewing, & Chris Misavage August, 1989

WHERE GERBILS DARE I 5.9-
The overgrown crack system eight feet right of NOSTRIL. This climb is undoubtedly destined for the obscurity it so richly deserves!
1. Jam thin cracks up into a bushy, right-facing corner. 50', 5.9-
HISTORY: After cleaning the route on rappel, Dave McDermott & Mack Johnson (who followed the climb with a broken leg) made the first ascent on July 29, 1985.

NOSTRIL I 5.9+ (*)
This very obscure, yet classic jam crack starts as an offwidth and narrows progressively to fingertips. Hike downhill and left of PICKING WINNERS to the base of the crack. Carry Friends and wired nuts.
1. Jam up the strenuous, offwidth/fist crack until it narrows, then finish up a shallow, right-facing corner. 60', 5.9+
HISTORY: Eben Damp & partner made the first ascent in 1978.

NO TICKET TO GLORY I 5.7+
Yet another incredibly popular, must-do classic!
1. Climb the short 5.7+ crack on the crag's left side. 35', 5.7+
FA: Unknown.

THE COTE BOULDER
The big boulder in the woods below MORDOR WALL has good bouldering.

CATHEDRAL LEDGE GIRDLE TRAVERSES

THE BIG PLUM V 5.10d, A0 (Several rappels & pendulums) (**)
A unique and demanding climb with difficulties that never seem to end. The right to left girdle traverse of Cathedral is one of the hardest girdle traverses in the United States. Leader and second must be equally capable, since on many occasions the second will palpably begin to feel the sharpness of his end of the rope! Carry two ropes and a normal rack.
1. Climb RECLUSE (5.10d), the crux of the entire climb, to the top of the Practice Slab. A fine example of British humor. 90', 5.10d
2. Walk across a ledge to the top, left-hand end of the Practice Slab.
3. Head left, up a crack to a ledge and go to its left end. 80'
4. Make a 5.9+ handtraverse left to KAREN'S VARIATION. 50', 5.9+

5. Head left along the terrace, down DIEDRE to birches. 120', 5.4
6. Climb up BUDAPEST to yet another hard handtraverse to the left (5.9) to a piton, then pendulum down and left to a belay ledge. 5.9, A0
7. Rappel 60 feet to the top of the crux on LAST TEMPTATION.
8. Climb ledges left to top of Pitch two, THE BRITISH ARE COMING.
9. Rappel to a ledge 80 feet below. Belay on it's left end.
10. Angle left to a belay, top Pitch one, REMISSION. 85', 5.7+
11. Climb both the second & third pitches of REMISSION to a long belay ledge on the left. 150', 5.8
12. Walk to the ledge's left end, top Pitch two, ANGEL'S HIGHWAY.
13. Rappel 135' off a small tree into the REPENTENCE chimney.
14. Up the chimney 30 feet, then left up cracks on ABRAKADABRA, through a horizontal chimney to the ANTLINE ledge. 120', 5.7
15. Walk to the left end of the ANTLINE Ledge.
16. Rappel 90 feet and tension left over to Bonfire Ledge.
17. Walk to left end of Bonfire Ledge, to CATHEDRAL DIRECT.
18. Rappel then traverse ledges left onto PENDULUM ROUTE. Most ascents reach here in one day. On the first ascent, Paul Ross & Henry Barber left a rope fixed here, and made an urban bivouac.
19. Climb the superb third pitch of PENDULUM ROUTE. 140', 5.9+
20. Climb Pitch four of PENDULUM, down and left to a ledge. 40', 5.10b
21. Make a 120 foot pendulum left on PENDULUM into the 5.8 crack system. Belay on the Sidewalk ledge at the top of crack. 5.8, A0
22. From the ledge's left end, make a difficult pendulum/tension traverse left off a bolt to the well-named Freak Out Ledge. Double bolt anchor. 5.9, A0
23. Rappel 150 feet, and swing left into STANDARD ROUTE.
24. Climb the next pitch of STANDARD ROUTE to the Cave. 120', 5.5
24a. Or climb up TURNER'S FLAKE instead. 120', 5.8
25. Traverse left a full pitch left to the top of Pitch one of THIN AIR.
26. Continue horizontally left into THE BIG FLUSH gully.
27. Climb a 5.9 tree left of BIG FLUSH, then down left to THE PROW.
28. Head up the first pitch of RECOMPENSE. 5.5
29. Climb Pitch two of RECOMPENSE to a small ledge (bolt). 130', 5.7
30. Layback the superb BEAST Flake to its top. 125', 5.9
31. Rappel and tension left to the tree-covered ledge and REFUSE.
32. Walk to the left-hand end of the REFUSE tree ledge.
33. Climb NUTCRACKER (5.9+) and shake hands with your partner!
HISTORY: Henry Barber & Paul Ross made the first ascent of this historic climb on October 19 & 20, 1972. Along the way they also dispatched with the first free ascent of PENDULUM ROUTE's third pitch.

CATHEDRAL LEDGE - GIRDLE TRAVERSES (THE BIG PLUM & KING CRAB)

KING CRAB V 5.9+, A0 (Several rappels)
Cathedral's reverse girdle takes a completely different line from left to right.
1. Climb the first pitch of PLEASANT STREET. 50', 5.6 R
2. Pitch two of PLEASANT STREET leads to the REFUSE tree ledge. 5.7
3. Walk right to the base of the ramp on UPPER REFUSE.
4. Climb the first pitch up the ramp on UPPER REFUSE. 90', 5.3
5. Head right across THE BOOK to a belay on WOMEN IN LOVE.
6. Move up and right over to the BEAST Flake. Belay on top.
7. Make an awkward traverse right into upper RECOMPENSE. 40', 5.9
8. Climb the crux of RECOMPENSE (5.9), then traverse right into the GYPSY Corner. Belay above the Triangular Roof on THE PROW. 5.9
9. Make a 150' rappel (very spectacular) into THE BIG FLUSH.
10. Traverse horizontally right to the top of Pitch one, THIN AIR.
11. Do the classic face traverse right to the Cave on STANDARD. 5.5
12. Down climb Pitch two of STANDARD ROUTE. 120', 5.5
13. Climb the DIAGONAL dike to the bolt belay below the crux. 120', 5.6
14. Rappel and tension right to the Sidewalk belay on PENDULUM.
15. Up to PENDULUM Roof, then right to base of THE BRIDGE.
16. Traverse right to a peg, then rappel 40 feet to a ledge.
17. Rappel 150 feet to the top of Pitch two, PENDULUM ROUTE.
18. Make an easy traverse right to CATHEDRAL DIRECT & Bonfire.
19. Right, then climb INTIMIDATION to the ANTLINE ledge. 5.9
20. Rappel with difficulty down onto ABRAKADABRA.
21. Climb the next pitch of REPENTENCE to a belay ledge on left. 5.8
22. Climb REPENTENCE over the final chockstone, & right on slabs. 5.6
23. Rappel off the belay tree to a tree ledge on ANGEL'S HIGHWAY.
24. Up REMISSION to a poor tree; rappel right to WARLOCK. 5.8, A0
25. At the right end of a sloping ledge, rappel and tension off to the right from a bolt to ledges on THE BRITISH ARE COMING.
26. Move right and up the 5.9 thin crack on LAST TEMPTATION. 5.9
27. Make a strenuous (5.9+) handtraverse right onto DIEDRE. 5.9+
28. Walk to the right end of the blueberry terrace by KINESIS.
29. Make another difficult handtraverse right (5.9+) to a ledge. 5.9+
30. Traverse right on slabs and ledges to a corner.
31. Ascend the corner, up last pitch of JACK THE RIPPER, to the top.

HISTORY: In 1972, Paul Ross & Dave Cilley climbed the traverse over to STANDARD ROUTE. Doug Madara & Paul Ross completed the line of the girdle traverse on July 21, 1975, starting at STANDARD ROUTE.

Karen T'Kint running it out on Pitch three of Sliding Board (5.7 / 5.4 R) on the granite slabs of Whitehorse Ledge in 1995. Photograph by Ed Webster.

WHITEHORSE LEDGE

Whitehorse Ledge, situated half a mile to the south of Cathedral Ledge, is noted for some of the finest granite slab climbing on the East Coast. Like its steeper neighbor, Whitehorse is also part of Echo Lake State Park. The cliff has two distinct halves, each offering remarkably different kinds of climbing for being so close to one another. The Slabs offer smooth, glaciated friction routes up to 800 feet high, while the South Buttress is 650 feet tall, with a predominance of steep, sustained face climbs. Climbing on the open friction slabs or the steep face of the South Buttress is a truly delightful experience on a crisp spring day, in midsummer when Echo Lake sparkling below, or in the autumn when the trees are at the height of nature's colorful tapestry.

This poetically named ledge got its unusual name from "a light colored spot far up on its rocky sides that resembles a white horse dashing up the cliff at a mad gallop. When the light is just right, this resemblance is very striking and may be seen from quite a distance." Another source, the tourist pamphlet, *North Conway & Vicinity* (1896) states that, "On one of the ledges, the white horse stands out plain and full, and can be plainly seen from the streets of North Conway." The outline of the white horse (located on the South Buttress in the ceilings to the right of the final roofs on CHILDREN'S CRUSADE) is indeed still visible, if you know exactly where to look (see photograph).

For climbers unfamiliar with friction climbing, a day on the slabs of Whitehorse can be, at the very least, educational, and at the worst, harrowing. As Robert Underhill summed it up in 1929, "The interest of White Horse Ledge lies in the peculiar type of climbing that must be employed. The slabs are literally holdless throughout much of their extent, and the ascent is possible only by relying upon the friction of the soles and hands (on the rock), together with a well-considered distribution of weight." Friction climbing does indeed require poise, balance, fluidity, and perhaps most of all, a cool head when you're out on the sharp end of the rope. Protection is frequently poor, and runouts can be very long indeed. Wearing sticky soled climbing shoes and maintaining your upward momentum will greatly improve your chances. A selection of small to medium Tri-cams is also invaluable to use in the small solution pockets (or "miarolitic cavities") that punctuate the slab's surface. Beginning leaders and climbers new to Whitehorse are advised to choose the STANDARD ROUTE over BEGINNER'S ROUTE since STANDARD is much better protected. Pitons and bolts are frequently the only protection on many of the climbs. Fortunately, the Mountain Rescue Service (MRS) and local climbers have rebolted many of the most frequently used protection bolts and double bolt anchors in recent years. Old bolts and pitons, however, should always be used with caution, equalized, and backed up whenever possible.

Since the opening of the White Mountain Hotel in 1990, the granite friction slabs of Whitehorse Ledge have never been quite the same. What had until then been a semi-wilderness experience became a new, overnight sensation: sport friction climbing, with the hotel and the climber's parking area only minutes away from the base of the Slabs! Some will resent the intrusion of this man-made structure into the once enchanted, forested wilderness joining Echo Lake and the cliff, but what is done is done. Excellent views of Whitehorse may be had from anywhere on the Hales Location golf course, and the approach from the hotel to the cliff now takes all of several strenuous minutes.

DIRECTIONS TO WHITEHORSE LEDGE: To drive to Whitehorse from North Conway and Route 16, turn left at the stop light just to the north of IME and EMS, and drive out the Bridge Road past the popular Saco River swimming area. Continue straight ahead to reach the parking below Cathedral Ledge. To park at The White Mountain Hotel directly below the Slabs, turn left at a T junction onto the West Side Road, drive nine tenths of a mile, and turn right into the hotel entrance. From Conway, drive north on West Side Road for 5.2 miles, then turn left. At the golf course, turn right, and drive towards the hotel.

PARKING FOR WHITEHORSE LEDGE: There are two choices of where to park for climbing on Whitehorse:

- First is the climber's parking area at The White Mountain Hotel. PLEASE DO NOT PARK in The White Mountain Hotel's main parking lot—or your car might get towed. Park in the climber's parking area (look for the sign) that is just below the hotel, on the right, on the dirt shoulders on either side of the maintenance shed road. Please maintain friendly, cordial relations with the hotel and staff, and don't park in their main lot—which during the summer months often gets completely full. From the climber's parking area, you can stroll over to the cliff base in all of about five minutes.

- Park on the Cathedral Ledge auto road below Cathedral, or the short, dirt side road on the left at a sandy turnaround, and hike in along the Bryce Path.

THE APPROACH TO WHITEHORSE LEDGE: From The White Mountain Hotel parking lot's right side, to approach the Slabs, hike along a quick trail through the woods to reach the base of the massive, friction slabs. Traditionalists may still enjoy parking on the Cathedral Ledge auto road or side dirt road on the left below Cathedral, and hiking in along the Bryce Path, a delightful 15 minute wooded approach. From the base of the Slabs, hike 10 minutes farther left, and you'll reach the first steeper climbs up the South Buttress of Whitehorse. Please refer to the South Buttress chapter for more specific approach and route information.

WHITEHORSE LEDGE - DIRECTIONS, PARKING, & THE APPROACH 213

This 1907 postcard of White Horse Ledge (as the cliff was originally called) above Echo Lake clearly shows the location of the white horse which gave the cliff its name. These postcards were very popular in the early 1900s.
Postcard courtesy of the North Conway Public Library.

Dean Peabody looking towards the slabs of Whitehorse Ledge in 1930 from the parking area below Cathedral Ledge. Photograph by Kenneth A. Henderson.

WHITEHORSE DESCENT OPTIONS: To descend from the top of the Slabs, hike north on a climber's footpath towards Cathedral Ledge. (Be very careful NOT to hike to the west over the summit of Whitehorse Ledge onto the Red Ridge Link trail which heads towards the Moat Mountains!) The climber's footpath soon joins the more heavily travelled Bryce Path, which leads you quickly down (north) to the wooded saddle between Cathedral and Whitehorse Ledges. At the col, turn right at a boulder, then follow the trail down a steep hill to a clearing. Turn right to return to the climber's parking lot at The White Mountain Hotel, left for the base of Cathedral. To descend from climbs on Whitehorse's South Buttress, rappel back down your route of ascent (CHILDREN'S CRUSADE, SCIENCE FRICTION WALL, and LOST SOULS / CEMETERY GATES each have double bolt rappel routes down them); or hike north over the summit of Whitehorse (towards Cathedral Ledge) to reach the Bryce Path; or circle back to the southwest then east through the woods along the Bryce Path, down and around back to The White Mountain Hotel. This latter descent is harder to follow, as well as much longer. More specific descent options are given in the South Buttress section.

BOLTED DESCENT ROUTES: Since the Slabs become nearly unclimbable after a rain, carry a second rope if the weather is at all threatening when you begin. A smart move is to keep rappel anchors in mind as you ascend. If you do get caught out in the rain, or decide to retreat before reaching the top, helpfully there are now convenient double bolt rappel routes down the following climbs: BEGINNER'S ROUTE, THE SLABS DIRECT, WAVELENGTH, STANDARD ROUTE / THE QUARTZ POCKET, WEDGE / INTERLOPER, SEA OF HOLES, and DIKE ROUTE. If the weather breaks and the worse comes to worst, use the trick every British climber knows by heart: put your socks over your climbing shoes, forget about the rain, and go for it!

The routes on Whitehorse are now described from right to left in the usual direction that one walks below the various climbs, beginning with the right side of the Slabs, and concluding with the far, upper left side of the South Buttress. The tree-filled, corner system of MISTAKEN IDENTITY conveniently marks the dividing line where the Slabs end, and the South Buttress begins.

THE SLABS

BEGINNER'S EASY VARIATION II 5.3 (*)
The easiest multi-pitch climb on the friction slabs ascends the very right-hand margin of the cliff. After Pitch one, the route is independent of BEGINNER'S ROUTE, has reasonable protection for Whitehorse, plus offers the added bonus of an easy escape right into the woods from nearly anywhere on the climb. There is some loose rock, however. Normal rack.

WHITEHORSE LEDGE - THE SLABS (BEGINNER'S ROUTE)

1. Climb the bottom slab to the big pine tree on BEGINNER'S. 120', 5.2
2. Traverse 20 feet right into a slightly crumbly gully, and climb up the gully to a belay above, in the trees. 130', 5.2
3. A short easy pitch leads up through trees and over some loose rock to the base of the next clean slab. 75', 5.1
4. Above, climb the slab for 20 feet, then step right into a delightful, low angle, double hand crack splitting a beautiful slab. 90', 5.3
5 & 6. Choosing the easiest possible line, climb up and around the right side of the final overlaps into the woods above. Finish up easy dikes, but with poor protection, up the summit slabs to the top.
FA: Unknown.

BEGINNER'S ROUTE II 5.5 (5.4 R) (***)

Although this is a much finer climb than the name might suggest, due to route's unprotected nature, beginners are strongly advised to choose either the BEGINNER'S EASY VARIATION (further to the right, towards the woods), or STANDARD ROUTE, the prominent arch in the center of the Slabs, which is a much better protected and only slightly harder climb. At the far, right-hand side of the Whitehorse friction slabs, look for a big pine tree growing 120 feet above the slab's base.

1. Scamper up the easy, lower slab to the pine tree. Several variations. There is a double ring bolt anchor on a stance just to the left of the pine. 120', 5.2
2. To the left of the pine tree, follow a vertical crack over the left side of a horizontal overlap, then face climb up a narrow, vertical dike (an eroded staircase of basalt intruded into the granite) up a steeper slab past two bolts (5.4) to a small belay stance on the left with a double bolt anchor. 140', 5.4
2a. From the pine, you may also climb a crack (5.4 R) straight up through a tiny overlap. When the crack ends, traverse 30 feet left to reach the same double bolt belay. Good moves, but protection is widely spaced. 140', 5.4 R
3. Continue up an obvious, easy, low-angled groove (5.1) to a small belay stance on the right with another double bolt anchor. 110', 5.1
4. Layback and friction up an easy, prominent, right-slanting arch. Belay beside a good flake from two bolts at the top of the arch. 90', 5.2
5. Step up onto a blank, 10 foot headwall (5.5), then friction quickly to your left (5.4 R) across an unprotected slab to hidden pockets (and protection) before climbing more easily straight up to the cozy Smile Belay Ledge which has a double ring bolt anchor. 140', 5.5 (5.4 R)
6. Continue up into a left-facing groove with a white layback flake. Climb this flake for 50 feet, then step up and right to a 20 foot, steeper headwall (5.4) with old pitons. Belay on the good ledge just above the headwall, below the last big overlap. 100', 5.4

216 THE MOUNT WASHINGTON VALLEY

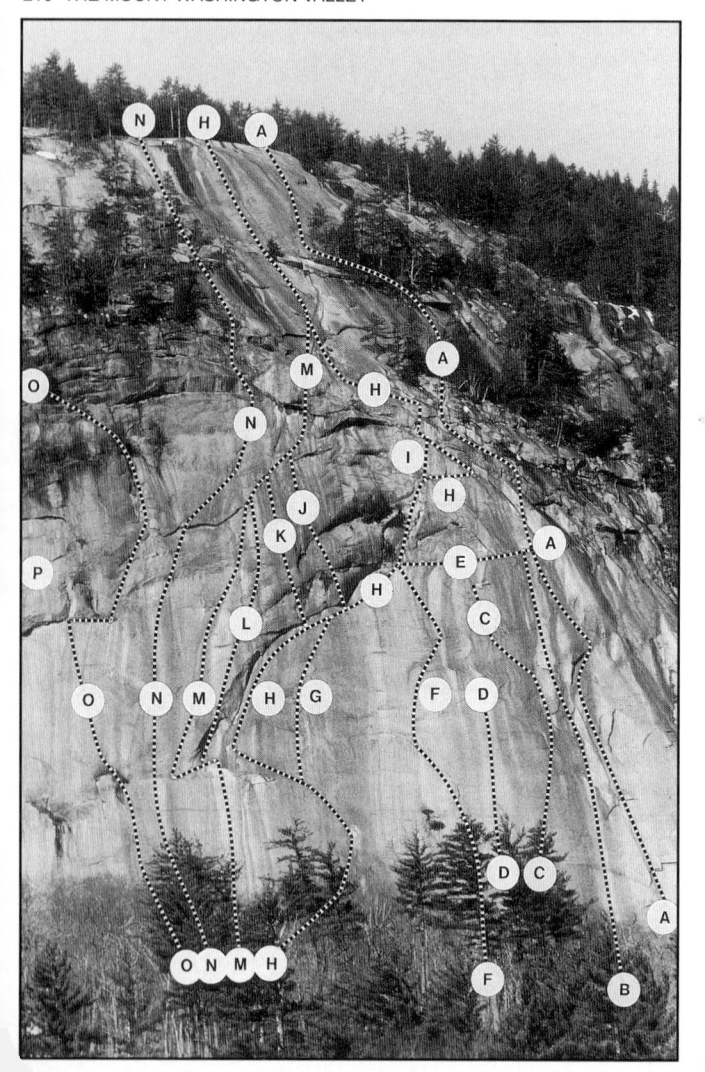

WHITEHORSE LEDGE – THE SLABS
(Right Side)

A.	***	**BEGINNER'S ROUTE** II 5.5 (5.4 R)	Page	215
B.		**WHITE WILDERNESS** II 5.7 X	Page	218
C.	**	**THE NINTH WAVE** II 5.9+ R	Page	219
D.		**STOP IF YOU DARE** I 5.8 X	Page	220
E.	**	**EASY DOES IT** II 5.4 (5.2 R)	Page	226
F.	**	**THE SLABS DIRECT** II 5.7 R (5.4 X)	Page	221
G.	***	**THE QUARTZ POCKET** I 5.3	Page	225
H.	***	**STANDARD ROUTE** II 5.5 (5.2 R)	Page	221
I.	***	**THE DIRECT FINISH** I 5.7	Page	226
J.	***	**WAVELENGTH** II 5.8	Page	228
	*	**THE DIRECT START** II 5.7+		
K.	**	**BLACK JADE** II 5.10b (or 5.10a R)	Page	228
L.		**TIDAL WAVE** II 5.10b (5.8 R)	Page	229
M.	***	**SLIDING BOARD** II 5.7 (5.4 R)	Page	229
N.	***	**INTERLOPER** II 5.10b (5.8 R)	Page	230
O.	***	**WEDGE** II 5.6 (5.5 R)	Page	237
P.		The Wedge Buttress	Page	239

7. Traverse left around the outside of a detached block onto a ramp that diagonals left (bolt) beneath the upper trees. To finish, break right up a short, steep dike onto a large tree ledge (or continue heading left to join up with STANDARD ROUTE). 100', 5.3

8–10. Above the tree-covered ledge, scramble up an easy dike system up and right on moderate slabs to the summit of Whitehorse.

HISTORY: A large AMC climbing party led by Herbert C. Towle, with Edith MacDonald, Philida Willis, Neilan Labarre, & Anne Brooks made the first ascent of this historic route on July 4, 1953. (A comment was later made that if a certain member of the team had done the climb, then it definitely was "a beginner's route"! Obviously all the climbers were climbing pretty well that day, however, because BEGINNER'S ROUTE is not really for beginners.) Another bit of trivia: what was the route's original name? (Route #3.) In days of old, STANDARD ROUTE was called Route #1, and DIKE ROUTE, the second route up Whitehorse, was known as Route #2.

VARIATION #1: **THE RIGHT-HAND FINISH** II 5.4 R

5a. Angle right into a shallow groove. Belay below the final overlaps at a white birch tree. 5.4 R

6a. Climb up and left along a left-slanting ramp beneath the overlaps to join the regular route on the good belay ledge at the end of Pitch six.

7–10. Follow BEGINNER'S ROUTE to the top. 5.3

FA: Unknown.

VARIATION #2: **BEGINNER'S DIRECT** II 5.7 R

A harder and more direct line. Climb the first three leads of BEGINNER'S, and belay on the right at a double bolt anchor on a small stance.

4b. Partway up the large, right-slanting arch, traverse left onto a steep slab, step over a bulge (5.7 R), then run the rope out straight up to the Smile Belay Ledge (which has a double ring bolt anchor) on the regular BEGINNER'S ROUTE. 150', 5.7 R

5b. Just right of the belay, climb the left-facing groove that merges with STANDARD ROUTE just to the right of the Brown Spot crux. Continue left up the ramp on STANDARD, up the short, right-facing, layback corner, and belay at a small stance to the left. 130', 5.5

6–9. Finish on STANDARD ROUTE up the summit dikes and slabs. 5.2 R

FA: Unknown.

WHITE WILDERNESS II 5.7 X

This generally very unprotected friction route ascends the prominent white streaks immediately left of BEGINNER'S ROUTE, following a direct line up to the Brown Spot on STANDARD. Bring a modern rack, including Tri-cams, plus Friends to a #3.5. Start at the slab's base, just to the left of BEGINNER'S.

WHITEHORSE LEDGE - THE SLABS (THE NINTH WAVE) 219

1. Friction up a steepening swell in the slab to the easier angled rock above. Belay at solution pocket using a natural thread anchor. 70', 5.3

2. Friction up & right to the next belay, at a small horizontal overlap. 110', 5.2

3. Step back left onto the long, vertical, white streak located between WAVE BYE BYE and BEGINNER'S ROUTE. Place protection, then friction straight up the completely unprotected white streak (5.7 X) to a belay at crystal pockets a little higher, which are 20 feet to the left of the double bolt belay at the top of Pitch two of BEGINNER'S. 165', 5.7 X

4. Climb up to a shallow, right-facing corner with a fixed piton belay. 90', 5.2 (Junction with THE NINTH WAVE continuation.)

5. Above the belay, angle left up a beautiful ramp onto the next white streak. Protect, then climb directly over a small, horizontal overlap on a steep, white bulge (5.7 R) onto the upper streak above. Belay 30 feet higher at a solution pocket on the left. 145', 5.7 R (Similar to BEGINNER'S DIRECT.)

6. Up the white streak to the Smile Belay ledge and a two bolt anchor. 80', 5.4

7. Step left and friction up steepening, dark-colored rock to a bolt that protects a 5.6 bulge located below and to the right of the Brown Spot. Merge with STANDARD ROUTE, and belay at fixed pitons at the base of the left-slanting ramp just after the Boilerplate. 80', 5.6

8–11. Finish up STANDARD ROUTE to the top. 5.5 & 5.2 R

HISTORY: Several sections of the route had been done previously. Kurt Winkler & Bunny Goodspeed first explored and ascended the lower white streak on May 26 & 27, 1989. Kurt Winkler, James Roshind, & Leon Fairbanks made the first complete ascent of the climb, joining STANDARD ROUTE, on September 29, 1990.

VARIATION: **THE DIRECT FINISH** I 5.9

8a. After joining the STANDARD ROUTE ramp above the Boilerplate, climb up the ramp for 20 feet (piton), then make hard moves (5.9) up and right gaining the final ramp on BEGINNER'S ROUTE. Finish straight up a second headwall above (5.8) to the trees. 60', 5.9

FA: Alain Comeau & Kurt Winkler Autumn, 1993

THE NINTH WAVE II 5.9+ R (**)

Even with sticky rubber this is still a very slippery lead. The route ascends the center of the steep, smooth swell in the slab between BEGINNER'S ROUTE and STANDARD ROUTE. Scramble 200 feet up the lower, easy slabs to reach the base of the Wave and several belay bolts.

1. Above a small, sickle-shaped rib, friction up the unrelenting slab (5.9+ R) making a long runout until the angle eases. Belay at a double bolt anchor above. 100', 5.9+ R Most parties rappel off from here, or finish up THE SLABS DIRECT (5.7) on the left. However, you may also:

2. Friction up and slightly right with no protection to a belay at a shallow, right-facing flake (piton) next to BEGINNER'S. 100', 5.3
3. Continue up a beautiful ramp onto the white streak (of BEGINNER'S DIRECT). Just below the steeper wall above, traverse left 10 feet to pockets in a shorter bulge. Move over the bulge and belay on a good stance above at a crystal pocket with a natural thread anchor. 145', 5.4
4. Friction straight up the open slab to a horizontal flake (piton), and belay higher at the base of an obvious layback crack. 100', 5.4
5. Climb up the layback flake past rusty fixed pitons (THE OLD VARIATION) to an old bolt (5.6), and merge with STANDARD ROUTE just to the right of the Brown Spot. 90', 5.6
HISTORY: Michael Hartrich, Jeff Pheasant, & Bill Findieson made the first ascent in May, 1974. Where they climbed on the upper pitches is conjecture, but was probably similar to the route described. According to sailing lore, the ninth consecutive wave on the open seas is always the biggest one of all!

WAVE BYE-BYE I 5.9+ R
Twenty feet right of THE NINTH WAVE is a belay bolt at the wave's base.
1. Friction up the even more unlikely looking slab to the right of THE NINTH WAVE to the double bolt anchor. 100', 5.9+ R
HISTORY: Chris Ellms & Howard Peterson made the first ascent in the Summer of 1976. After finishing the route and rappelling back to the base of the Wave, the pair were caught in a torrential downpour. To escape, they glissaded out of control down the water slide of the lower slabs, with Peterson literally removing the seat of his pants in the process!

SOUTH BUTTRESS OF WANKERS WALL I 5.8+ R
THE NINTH WAVE's easiest route, but that's not saying much!
1. From the two bolt belay at the base of the Wave, angle left to two small, sloping ledges, then head back up right onto easier ground, up to the double bolt anchor on THE NINTH WAVE. 100', 5.8+ R
FA: Jeff Pheasant & Michael Hartrich May, 1974

STOP IF YOU DARE I 5.8 X
Ascends the completely unprotected smooth slab between WANKERS WALL and THE SLABS DIRECT. Get up a good head of speed first!
1. Fifteen feet right of the initial, thin flake on SLABS DIRECT, slab climb straight up a slight groove (5.8 X) to the wave's top, then traverse left to the two bolt anchor at the top of Pitch three of SLABS DIRECT. 140', 5.8 X
HISTORY: Michael Hartrich free-soloed the first ascent in 1974, but never named the route. The climb was finally briefly mentioned in the 1987 NH guidebook. STOP IF YOU DARE was written up and named in the IME new route book in 1992 by a later ascent party, who also did the climb without bolts.

WHITEHORSE LEDGE - THE SLABS (SLABS DIRECT & STANDARD) 221

THE SLABS DIRECT II 5.7 R (5.4 X) (**)
Long runouts, but superb friction climbing if you're up to it! Ascends a direct line up the smooth central slab to the right of the STANDARD ROUTE arch. The crux is definitely not well protected.

1. From the base, friction straight up the slabs (5.1) towards the thin, vertical flake that breaks through the left side of THE NINTH WAVE. Belay on a small stance at a double ring bolt anchor. 165', 5.1

2. Continue easily up a line of small potholes (5.2) to a belay pocket and sloping stance at a chained, two bolt anchor below a thin, vertical flake 40 feet to the left of THE NINTH WAVE. 120', 5.2

3. Layback up the flake (piton), then friction straight up (5.7 R; crux going over the bulge) to a better flake and protection where the angle finally relents. Continue up and slightly left on easier terrain to a sloping stance with a chained, double bolt anchor. 135', 5.7 R

4. Surmount the bulge above (bolt), then friction straight up (5.6) onto a ramp. Continue easily up and right, but with no protection for the rest of the pitch (5.4 X) to the next double bolt chained anchor out in the middle of the open slab below the STANDARD ROUTE arch. 140', 5.6 (5.4 X)

4a. A variation climbs straight up past the first bolt (5.6), then steps left from the easy ramp, and climbs directly up a white streak (5.5 R) and over an overlap (pockets above) to the natural thread belay in the STANDARD ROUTE arch. Go this way if you are heading up WAVELENGTH. 130', 5.6 (5.5 R)

5-7. Join STANDARD (5.5) by heading straight up to the arch, or for a high quality finish of the same grade, climb WAVELENGTH (5.7+ or 5.8).

HISTORY: Paul Ross, Ben Wintringham & Marion Wintringham (all UK) made the first recorded ascent of the climb on June 15, 1973.

STANDARD ROUTE II 5.5 (5.2 R) (***)
The single most popular rock climb in the White Mountains ascends the prominent, right-curving arch in the center of the Whitehorse Slabs. After several enjoyable, moderate pitches of friction climbing, the final series of overlaps are the crux. Although this is by far the best protected route on the Slabs, careful route finding is still necessary, especially on the crux pitch, the Brown Spot and the Boilerplate, to ensure a successful ascent. Hike through the woods until you are below the middle of the slabs and the large, central arch. Scramble 150 feet up an easy depression or trough to a comfortable, flat platform known as the Starting Ledge. There are a multitude of variations possible throughout the climb. Carry a normal rack with extra slings.

- **DESCENT OPTIONS:** If you are caught out in the rain, the easiest retreat down STANDARD ROUTE (depending on where you are) is either to rappel down THE QUARTZ POCKET Variation just to the right of the main arch down to the Toilet Bowl, and then back to the Starting Ledge; or, from the top of the main arch or from the double ring bolt anchor on Lunch Ledge, rappel down the chained, double bolt anchors on THE SLABS DIRECT. If the weather is at all threatening when you start the climb, or if you are unsure of your abilities, then definitely bring two 50 meter ropes along in case you have to retreat.

1. From the right end of the Starting Ledge (piton), friction up and right to a large pothole nicknamed the Toilet Bowl, which has a two bolt anchor. 80', 5.3

2. Friction up and left past a flake to good ledges at the base of the main STANDARD ROUTE arch, and a double ring bolt anchor. 90', 5.2

3. Layback up the back of the arch (5.4) to an awkward, semi-hanging belay (piton), or traverse right (5.3) to THE QUARTZ POCKET belay stance which has a double bolt anchor. 145', 5.3 or 5.4

4. Angle up and right along the arch up friction slabs to a sloping belay stance at fixed slings around a natural thread anchor. 100', 5.3

5. An easy slab leads up and right to the top of the main arch. A short, steep section up a dike gains the famed Lunch Ledge which has a double ring bolt anchor below the route's hardest section, the final overlaps—and the famed Brown Spot and Boilerplate. 140', 5.3

6. The crux pitch is next. The Brown Spot is the easiest finish, but since there are also several harder finishes, careful route finding is necessary. For the Brown Spot (5.5): climb up 15 feet from the right end of Lunch Ledge, make one thin friction move right to a bolt, then down climb a ramp for 10 feet. Step right onto a narrow, brownish foothold (the Brown Spot) to another bolt, then climb a delicate slab (the Boilerplate; 5.5) onto a left-diagonalling ramp with several old pitons. Either belay at the base of the ramp at fixed pitons (rope drag can be a problem above), or follow the ramp up and left to a short, layback corner (which is also 5.5). Most parties belay on a small stance just above this short corner, and slightly to the left. (Nut anchor.) 150', 5.5 (Above the 5.5 layback corner, you can also escape up and right, with even more rope drag, to the trees at the top of BEGINNER'S ROUTE.)

7. Friction 40 feet left, traversing across an easy slab using a handrail-like flake beneath an overlap to reach an easy dike, and belay on the comfortable ledge above (with a good nut anchor) at the base of the upper slabs. 80', 5.2

8. Follow the easy, stepped dike straight up to another overlap and a small pine tree. Bypass them on the left (or climb directly over the overlap at a double crack; one 5.5 move) to a tree ledge. 140', 5.2 R (or 5.5)

9. Finish by climbing up either of the two, upper dikes in the summit slabs. The easier of the two finishes is up the left-hand dike, although the right-hand dike is also fairly straightforward. 250', 5.2 R

WHITEHORSE LEDGE - THE SLABS (STANDARD ROUTE) 223

Bill Burling, John C. Hurd, & Dean Peabody climbing Standard Route (5.5) on Whitehorse Ledge on May 30, 1930. Ken Henderson took this marvelous photo from the base of the Standard Route arch looking north towards Cathedral. Peabody is actually standing "on" the Toilet Bowl! Photograph by Kenneth A. Henderson.

A 1950s leader climbing the infamous Brown Spot crux of Standard Route (5.5) in the traditional style of the era. Note the sneakers, the rope tied around his waist—and the lack of any bolts for protection. Photograph by Walter H. Howe.

WHITEHORSE LEDGE - THE SLABS (THE QUARTZ POCKET)

HISTORY: In the Spring of 1928, Robert L. M. Underhill, Herbert C. Towle, & John Holden, Jr. climbed to the top of the arch, but were thwarted by a sudden cloudburst. With only one rope for the three of them, the descent down the wet slabs proved memorable. Underhill lowered his partners the full rope length to the only ledge in sight, wrapped his end of the rope around a small tree, carefully lowered himself to the halfway point— and let go of the other end of the rope! He had hoped the friction of the rope sliding around the tree would slow him down. It didn't! As he began to accelerate out of control, the well-muscled Holden fortunately "reached out and tackled me onto the ledge. It was then that I realized how helpful it was to have brought a football player along," Underhill recalled. In October, 1929, Robert Underhill & Kenneth Henderson descended the summit slabs, tied a rope onto a convenient pine, rappelled down, then navigated through the final overlaps above the Brown Spot. Their rope, however, was left in place, allowing subsequent parties to hand-over-hand up it, and finish the climb through the troublesome overlaps. Henderson and Underhill realized they had not made a "legitimate" ascent, and advocated that "a few fixed pitons, judiciously placed where they could be lassoed from below would make possible this 30 or 40 feet." The Brown Spot, today's 5.5 crux, "thought unclimbable a short time ago," admitted Underhill, was finally free climbed by Leland W. Pollock, leading an AMC party, on July 2, 1932.

VARIATION #1: THE DIRECT START TO THE ARCH I 5.3 R (*)
This direct route bypasses the Toilet Bowl well to its left.
1a. Above the Starting Ledge, climb directly up the smooth slab to the base of the main arch. Peg in a pocket halfway up. 175', 5.3 R
FA: Unknown.

VARIATION #2: THE QUARTZ POCKET I 5.3 (***)
These are two, classic, well-worn pitches! Very Popular.
2a. Climb the layback flake just up and left of the Toilet Bowl straight up to a quartz-filled pocket and belay ledge (with a double bolt anchor) located 40 feet to the right of the STANDARD ROUTE arch. 150', 5.3
3a. Continue directly over a short bulge (5.3), then follow finger pockets (Tri-cams useful) up a fun slab to rejoin the main arch on STANDARD at the natural thread anchor at the top of Pitch four. 125', 5.3
FA: Unknown.

VARIATION #3: THE OLD VARIATION I 5.6
This obscure variation completely avoids Lunch Ledge by staying low (below Lunch Ledge), moving slightly right, and climbing directly up to the Brown Spot crux of the regular route.
5a. Belay at the top of the main arch at the base of the vertical dike leading up

to Lunch Ledge. Just to your right, climb up a short crack to a right-leaning arch with a small bush. Head right into a groove, step right over a slab to another groove (piton), then make thin moves (old bolt; 5.6), joining the ramp to the right of the Brown Spot. Finish up STANDARD ROUTE. 150', 5.6
FA: Unknown.

VARIATION #4: **THE DIRECT FINISH** I 5.7 (***)
This more difficult, but enjoyable direct finish above Lunch Ledge is also a useful way to bypass parties traumatized by the Brown Spot.
6a. Off the right end of Lunch Ledge, climb up into a left-facing dihedral to a fixed piton. Step right, up onto a smooth face, clip a bolt, then make delicate moves right (5.7) across a smooth slab or face to gain the upper ramp on STANDARD ROUTE just below the upper, 5.5 layback corner. 80', 5.7
HISTORY: Craig Merrihue & John Turner (UK) made the first recorded ascent of "the super-smooth slab" of THE DIRECT FINISH in the Spring of 1956. "Merrihue had led the pitch once before... It was already an established variation, and of course, there were no bolts then," recalled Turner.

VARIATION #5: **THE BOLT LADDER** I 5.9 (*)
The most challenging finish above Lunch Ledge. Thin moves!
6b. Climb up THE DIRECT FINISH to the bolt, then face climb straight up the center of the smooth slab (bolt) over a thin bulge (5.9), instead of angling more easily (5.7) off to the right. 75', 5.9
HISTORY: Rick Wilcox & Marty Bowin installed a short bolt ladder (since removed) up this slab during their winter ascent of STANDARD ROUTE in 1968. John Bragg & Rick Wilcox returned and made the first free ascent of the pitch in 1974.

VARIATION #6: **LEFT-OUT** I 5.7 R
An obscure, but enjoyable finish, if you're into that sort of thing.
6c. Climb to the top of the left-facing corner on THE DIRECT FINISH above the right end of Lunch Ledge. Move left, then climb over a short bulge (5.7 R). A short corner just to the left of the regular, final 5.5 layback corner leads to easier ground. 75', 5.7 R
HISTORY: Herbert C. Towle first top-roped the initial, inside corner—shared with THE DIRECT FINISH—but the date, and how he finished, is unknown.

EASY DOES IT II 5.4 (5.2 R) (**)
Although this is a real wandering albatross of a route, it is in fact the simplest way to climb the center of the Whitehorse slabs. The route ascends the first five pitches of STANDARD ROUTE using THE QUARTZ POCKET Variation before traversing horizontally right (just below Lunch Ledge) to join with the final several leads of BEGINNER'S ROUTE. Careful route finding is necessary to avoid harder climbing. Start below the middle of the slabs and

the large, central arch of STANDARD ROUTE. Scramble 150 feet up an easy depression or trough to a comfortable platform called the Starting Ledge.

1. From the right end of the ledge (piton), friction up and right to a large pothole nicknamed the Toilet Bowl, which has a double bolt anchor. 80', 5.3
2. Climb up and left up the slab to a vertical, layback flake (5.3) leading to a quartz-filled pocket and a belay stance (with a double bolt anchor) 40 feet to the right of the STANDARD arch. 150', 5.3
3. Continue straight over a short bulge (5.3), then follow finger pockets (Tricams useful) up a fun slab to rejoin the main arch on STANDARD ROUTE at the natural thread belay anchor at the top of its fourth pitch. 125', 5.3
4. An easy slab leads up and right to the top of the STANDARD arch. Belay at the base of the staircase-like dike leading up to the famed Lunch Ledge. 80', 5.3 (DO NOT climb up to Lunch Ledge.)
5. Now friction horizontally right, down a bit, and straight right to reach the Smile Belay Ledge (which has a two bolt anchor) on BEGINNER'S. 75', 5.3
6. Finish on BEGINNER'S ROUTE. Continue up into a left-facing groove with a white layback flake. Climb this for 50 feet, then step up and right to a 20 foot headwall (5.4) with old pitons. Belay on a good ledge below the last big overlap before the trees. 100', 5.4
7. Traverse left around the outside of a detached block onto a ramp which diagonals left (bolt) beneath the trees. To finish, break right up a short, steep dike onto a large tree ledge (or continue left to join STANDARD). 100', 5.3
8–11. Climb up long, easy dikes to reach the summit. 400', 5.2 R
FA: Unknown.

BODY SURFING II 5.11a R or X
A new wave friction climb with almost no protection. Luckily the moves do get easier as the protection gets farther and farther away! The scariest, hard slab route on Whitehorse to date. The crux ascends the featureless slab to the right of the WAVELENGTH dike. If you think you might want to take the plunge, wear more than a bathing suit. Carry several large Friends.
1–4. Climb the first four pitches of STANDARD ROUTE.
5. Partway up Pitch five of STANDARD, climb straight above a peg past two horizontal cracks, one quite wide (large cams needed), and the second thin. Belay at the big overlap just to the right of WAVELENGTH. 5.11a
6. Down climb slightly left, gain the steep slab just right of the 5.8 crux of WAVELENGTH (5.10d R) and run out the rope (5.11a X), trending up and right to reach a shallow gully. Belay at a stance above Lunch Ledge. 5.11a X
HISTORY: After climbing Pitch five on August 1, 1985, Jim Ewing returned the next day with Rich Baker to make the first complete ascent of this rarely repeated route.

228 THE MOUNT WASHINGTON VALLEY

WAVELENGTH II 5.8 (***)
with THE DIRECT START II 5.7+ (*)
A well-travelled, deservedly popular route with excellent climbing. The original 5.8 crux is more frequently climbed than the 5.7+ DIRECT START to the top dike. The original 5.8 route is described first. Normal rack.

1–4. Climb the first four pitches of THE SLABS DIRECT, trending left on the fourth pitch (5.5 R) to reach either: a belay stance (piton) in the arch on STANDARD ROUTE for THE DIRECT START (5.7+); or the sloping stance at STANDARD's natural thread anchor higher up the arch (at the top of STANDARD's fourth pitch) for original WAVELENGTH. 165', 5.5 R

5. From the natural thread, original WAVELENGTH (5.8) climbs straight over a steep, brown bulge in the STANDARD arch (Tri-cam; 5.8) to another bulge above (bolt). Now angle left, making a long reach (5.8) to a pocket, and swing left into the WAVELENGTH dike. Face climb up the exposed dike past two more bolts (5.7) to a double ring bolt anchor at a small stance. 120', 5.8

5a. For THE DIRECT START (5.7+), belay at a piton in the STANDARD arch (top of its fourth pitch). Step left from the belay onto a short slab leading to a flake about 30 feet to the left of original WAVELENGTH. Layback up the flake, step over it to the left, and face climb straight up the WAVELENGTH dike—the narrow dike on the steep, bulging wall to the right of SLIDING BOARD. Tricky face moves with nut protection lead up the dike (5.7+) past several bolts (5.7) to the normal double ring bolt anchor and stance. 130', 5.7+

6. Traverse right on a slab to a shallow, right-leaning corner which leads to a steep, open dihedral higher. Continue up this, then diagonal right to a ramp that heads back left. 5.6 Alternatively, finish up the short, vertical SLIDING BOARD dike (5.5; double ring bolt anchor at its base) directly above. 5.5

7. At the left end of the ramp, climb up a short, steep, right-facing corner, and belay on the good ledge above. 5.7

8 & 9. Finish on the easy, upper dikes on STANDARD ROUTE. 250', 5.2R

HISTORY: Alain Comeau & Janot Mendler Comeau climbed the first ascent of this classic route in July, 1981. On October 18, 1985, Alain Comeau & Herb Hollingsworth, plus Ed Webster & Kristina Kearney, made the combined first ascent of the 5.7+ Direct Start.

BLACK JADE II 5.10b (or 5.10a R) (**)
A gem of a pitch up the unlikely, blank black slab between TIDAL WAVE and WAVELENGTH. Protection is remarkably good, but carry along both a #3 Friend & a short piece of 5mm perlon! Start at the base of WAVELENGTH.

1–4. Climb the first four pitches of STANDARD ROUTE.

5. Approximately 40 feet to the left of original WAVELENGTH, step over the STANDARD arch, and move up 30 feet to another arch. Fifteen feet

WHITEHORSE LEDGE - THE SLABS (WAVELENGTH & SLIDING BOARD)

right of TIDAL WAVE, slab climb past a bolt (5.10b), or traverse right then step back left (5.10a R), to a thin flake (peg). Now forge up the center of the improbable, black slab above (5.9; bolt) past small pockets to belay stances on either INTERLOPER or WAVELENGTH. 150', 5.10b (or 5.10a R)

HISTORY: Ed Webster & Alain Comeau made the first ascent on October 19, 1985. All the protection was placed free on the lead.

TIDAL WAVE II 5.10b (5.8 R)

Don't get swept away by the thrill of how far you are above your last piece of protection. TIDAL WAVE surfs an intricate and challenging line between SLIDING BOARD and STANDARD ROUTE. Hang 10! Modern rack.

1. Climb up to the base of the STANDARD arch. 175', 5.3 R

2. Layback a short way up the arch, then climb left at the first possibility onto a beautiful white streak (bolt), then friction up and right (5.8 R) to a small overlap. Belay in a pocket on the right with a bolt anchor. 5.8 R

3. Climb to another bolt that protects hard moves (5.10b) into a thin, curving flake. Climb the flake, protect, then dash straight up the white streak above for as long as you dare. 5.10b Step left onto SLIDING BOARD to finish.

FA: Alain Comeau & Kim Smith July, 1978

SLIDING BOARD II 5.7 (5.4 R) (***)

Enchanting slab climbing with a short crux of delicate face climbing makes this one of the best rock climbs on the East Coast. There are, however, some typically long, Whitehorse-sized runouts. This superb route ascends the smooth, undulating slabs just to the left of STANDARD ROUTE up to, and over, the final overlaps. Exceptionally popular. Begin at the Starting Ledge at the bottom of STANDARD. Bring a normal rack with several Tri-cams.

1. Climb to the base of the arch on STANDARD ROUTE. Belay here at a two bolt anchor, or 30 feet to the left at the INTERLOPER double ring bolt anchor at the base of a steep slab. 175', 5.3 R

2. The crux pitch (5.7) climbs a shallow depression up and right through the steep, granite wave just to the left of the STANDARD ROUTE arch. Clip the first bolt, then make thought-provokingly thin friction moves (5.7), keeping your momentum going, up to a second bolt. Belay above on a stance at a short, vertical crack on the right (old peg), or head diagonally left to another sloping stance at two ring bolts on INTERLOPER. 80', 5.7

3. This long, classic friction pitch with almost no protection climbs slightly up and left, then straight up a smooth slab (5.4 R) past one lonely bolt to a small, comfortable ledge with a double ring bolt anchor. 130', 5.4 R

4. Step right, and layback up a beautiful, white flake with a good crack. When it ends, face climb on secure pockets straight up to a cozy belay stance (nut anchor) at the top of a small, right-slanting arch. 110', 5.6

5. A very faint dike, easy but with no protection, leads diagonally right across a lower angled slab. Now follow the dike straight up (5.5 R) to a small birch tree, then right; or preferably, climb up the right-hand dike (5.6) which has better protection. Belay on a tiny stance below the final, steep overlap and dike at a double ring bolt anchor. 125', 5.5 R or 5.6

6. Make several tricky face moves up the dike over the final, steep headwall (5.5) to gain a good ledge on your right at the base of the final slabs. 75', 5.5

7 & 8. Finish up STANDARD ROUTE in two, long easy pitches up dikes and slabs to the top of the cliff. 250', 5.2 R

HISTORY: Will Crowther & Bob Gilmore made the first ascent of this well-loved, historic climb in either 1959 or 1960. "There were a lot of blanks on the maps in those days. We were lucky," Crowther remembered, adding, "I liked the slabs, and it didn't bother me too much being 100 feet out from my protection." Footwear, by this time, had been upgraded from sneakers to vibram-soled klettershoes. On the climb's first ascent, Crowther placed only one bolt, the bolt protecting the crux 5.7 slab moves at the start. On a subsequent ascent, he added a second bolt, the one just above the 5.7 crux. By the mid-1960s, the route's completely unprotected third pitch was nearly as infamous as the lower technical crux. The bolt in the middle of Pitch three (probably first added in the mid 1960s) has greatly reduced the seriousness of what was Bob Gilmore's original, and equally daring, lead.

INTERLOPER II 5.10b (5.8 R) (***)

The most popular, hard route on the slabs, INTERLOPER ascends the long, thin, white stripe between SLIDING BOARD and WEDGE. Top quality slab climbing, adequate protection—and an unusually strenuous & baffling crux.

1. From the Starting Ledge on STANDARD, friction up to the base of the crux of SLIDING BOARD, and belay, semi-hanging, at a double ring bolt anchor at the base of a smooth, steep wave just left of SLIDING BOARD. 185', 5.3

2. Face climb past a single bolt (5.10a) straight over the bulge (taking a line 15 feet left of SLIDING BOARD) to a sloping stance at two ring bolts. 80', 5.10a

3. The white stripe. Follow it straight up (5.8 R) past one bolt to another double ring bolt anchor at a small belay stance beneath a short, vertical headwall—which is the route's crux. 120', 5.8 R

4. Traverse right beneath the bulging wall to a bolt. A surprisingly difficult undercling and layback move (5.10b) gains a thin finger crack/flake in the center of the bulge. Belay at the small overlap above, at a notch. 70', 5.10b

5. Friction diagonally right with poor protection (5.5 R) to a small flake and belay stance (peg) below a short swell. 80', 5.5 R

6. Climb up into the final overlaps following a ramp system back to the left. Near the top, break right onto the final slabs. 150', 5.8

WHITEHORSE LEDGE - THE SLABS (SLIDING BOARD & INTERLOPER) 231

Chris Bonington (UK) on Sliding Board in 1982. Photograph by Paul Ross.

HISTORY: Complicated! After a long traverse right from near the top of DIKE ROUTE in 1965, Bill Brace & Guillermo Herrera did most of Pitch six, continuing left up a ramp system to a large, flat ledge. Paul Ledoux & John Yates then climbed Pitch five on July 6, 1974. Starting from the bush clump on WEDGE, Paul Ross & Mike Heintz made the first ascent of Pitches three & four, linked the climb together, and named the route on July 11, 1977. Mike Heintz & Alain Comeau added the Direct Start (Pitch two) in June, 1978.

DIRECT FINISH #1: **TOP SECRET** I 5.8+

6a. Make a 5.8 move over a swell above the belay. Climb up the ramp system left for 15 feet to a lipped groove angling out right to a stance. Make a long reach to a jug, climb up to a tree, then step right around a corner. 5.8+
FA: Kurt Winkler, Alain Comeau, & Joe Lentini May 16, 1983

DIRECT FINISH #2: **CATLIN-INGLE FINISH** I 5.10b R

Makes INTERLOPER sustained for its entire length.

6b. Climb up to the base of the left-leaning ramp, traverse five feet right until you can make a 5.9 step over the overlap onto steep friction (5.10b R). Step right to a crack, then slab climb straight over a bulge (5.10b). 5.10b R
FA: Alex Catlin & Dean Ingle June 17, 1986

THE LAST WAVE

This steep slab offers a good direct finish for any of the harder routes in the center of the Whitehorse Slabs. THE LAST WAVE is located above the higher of two tree ledges left of the top dikes on STANDARD ROUTE. The slab may also be approached from WEDGE and DIKE by diagonalling up and right towards the top of the cliff. There are seven separate routes on the slab, which are now described from right to left.

THE RIGHT DIKE I 5.6 R

Obviously, the right-slanting dike up the right side of the slab.
1. Climb the dike. 100', 5.6 R
FA: Joe Lentini, free-solo May, 1984

WAVY GRAVY I 5.7 R

The unprotected center of the wave.
1. The crux is at the start. 100', 5.7 R
FA: Joe Lentini, free-solo May, 1984

THE LAST WAVE I 5.8 or 5.9+ (*)

The best route on the Wave.
1. Climb up to an overlap and a bolt, then step right and friction up a water groove (5.8). A more direct and harder route climbs straight up a beautiful white streak (5.9+) to a second bolt, which the 5.8 route also uses. Finish up easier slabs to a tree ledge. 100', 5.8 or 5.9+

WHITEHORSE LEDGE - THE SLABS (THE LAST WAVE) 233

Albert Dow leading the Direct Start to Interloper (5.10b / 5.8 R).
Photograph by Joe Lentini.

234 THE MOUNT WASHINGTON VALLEY

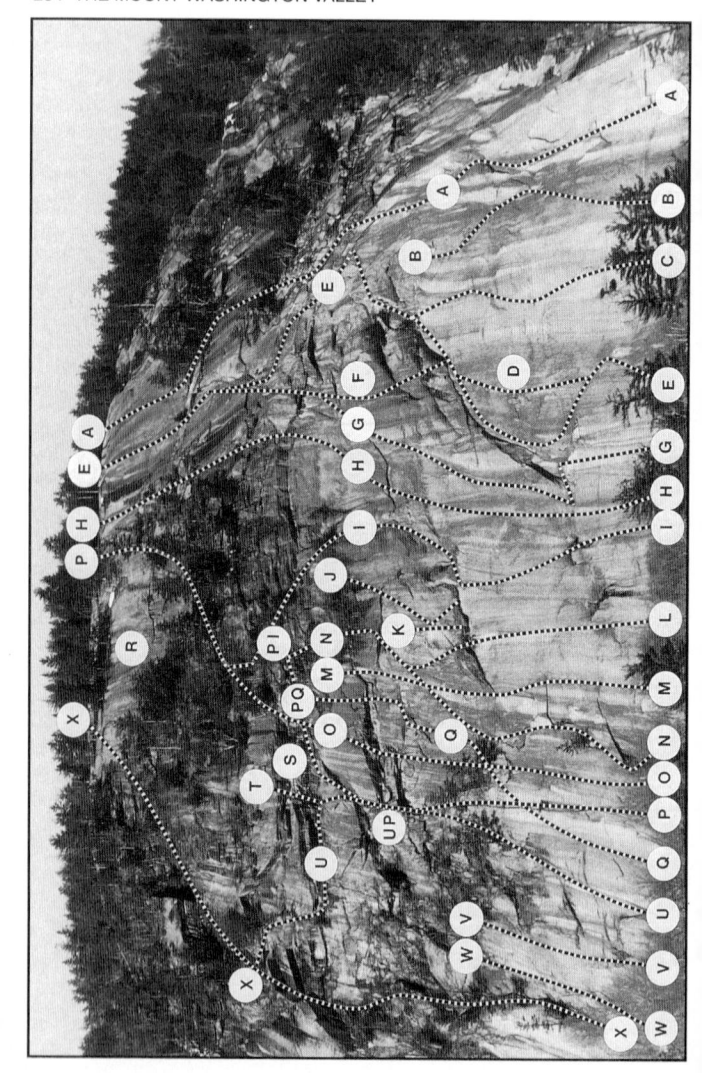

WHITEHORSE LEDGE – THE SLABS

A. ***	BEGINNER'S ROUTE II 5.5 (5.4 R)	Page 215	
B. **	THE NINTH WAVE II 5.9+ R	Page 219	
C. **	THE SLABS DIRECT II 5.7 R (5.4 X)	Page 221	
D. ***	THE QUARTZ POCKET I 5.3	Page 225	
E. ***	STANDARD ROUTE II 5.5 (5.2 R)	Page 221	
F. ***	WAVELENGTH II 5.8 DIRECT START II 5.7+	Page 228	
G. ***	SLIDING BOARD II 5.7 (5.4 R)	Page 229	
H. ***	INTERLOPER II 5.10b (5.8 R)	Page 230	
I. ***	WEDGE II 5.6 (5.5 R)	Page 237	
J. *	NEEDFUL THINGS I 5.11b (5.8 R)	Page 240	
K. *	FINGERTIP TRIP I 5.10a	Page 240	
L.	SLIPSHOD II 5.6 R	Page 241	
M. ***	SEA OF HOLES II 5.7	Page 242	
	***	SEA OF HOLES with THE DIRECT FINISH II 5.8	Page 244
N.	STADTMÜLLER–GRIFFIN ROUTE II 5.6	Page 244	
O. *	OLD TIMES II 5.8 R	Page 246	
P. *	DIKE ROUTE II 5.6	Page 248	
Q. **	PATHFINDER II 5.9	Page 248	
R.	The Last Wave	Page 232	
S.	The Dike Roof		
T. **	THE WHITE ZONE II 5.12a	Page 250	
U.	THE MINER-JOSEPH-KING ROUTE II 5.6 R	Page 252	
V.	CRAZY HORSE I 5.9 R	Page 252	
W. *	WAITING FOR COMEAU I 5.9	Page 253	
X.	MISTAKEN IDENTITY II 5.6	Page 253	

WHITEHORSE LEDGE - THE SLABS 235

Joe Cote leading the fourth pitch of Wedge (5.6 / 5.5 R) in 1972. Note the piton hammer and RR (Royal Robbins) climbing shoes. Photograph by Gene Ellis.

WHITEHORSE LEDGE - THE SLABS (WEDGE) 237

HISTORY: Joe Lentini, Chris Gill, & Mike Jewel made the first ascent via the 5.8 water groove in May, 1984, without placing any bolts. Several days later, unaware of the previous ascent, Dick Peterson & Brad White made the first ascent of the harder, more direct route, placing two bolts on the lead.

SURFING PRIMITIVES I 5.8 R
The faint dike located 10 feet to the left of THE LAST WAVE.
1. Protect at the overlap, then run it out up the dike to the trees. 100', 5.8 R
FA: Kurt Winkler & Doug Bowen August 11, 1989

STUDENT DAZE I 5.7+ R
Start 20 feet to the left of THE LAST WAVE.
1. Undercling a flake left into a corner, go right to another flake, and finish up a slab. 100', 5.7+ R
FA: Chris Gill & students Summer, 1984

ROCKFISH I 5.8+ R or X
Climbs through the overlap/bulge about 45 feet to the left of THE LAST WAVE. There is no protection above the overlap.
1. Head up towards a break in a troublesome bulge, continue to a large pocket in the slab above, and run it out to the top. 110', 5.8+ R or X
FA: Uwe Schneider & Bob Fish June, 1992

BUBBLE OF ENLIGHTENMENT I 5.5 R
Begin 25 feet to the left of STUDENT DAZE atop a flat stone next to a tree, 15 feet above the tree-covered slope below.
1. Traverse 20 feet horizontally left past two pine trees growing close to the wall above until you can step left over an overhang. Follow cracks, some hollow, thin flakes, and pockets to a lower angled slab, then angle right to a large pine tree and belay. 120', 5.5 R
FA: Kurt Winkler & Bob Garrison October 14, 1987

WEDGE II 5.6 (5.5 R) (***)
This long, enjoyable climb ascends the broad, open slab and higher inside corners to the left of STANDARD ROUTE and SLIDING BOARD. Begin from the Starting Ledge on STANDARD, and locate two, small bush clumps to the left of the base of the STANDARD ROUTE arch. Five pitches of superb climbing are followed by several leads of lesser quality. Be mentally prepared for a couple of "typical" (read: very long) Whitehorse runouts up the central slab. Carry a normal rack with extra slings.
1. Diagonal left up an easy slab past a bolt to the right-hand of two, obvious clumps of bushes. Belay at the double ring bolt anchor just above the bush clump. A long pitch; climb together, or belay at the bush clump. 210', 5.3
2. Make a long, exciting lead up the center of the open slab above (5.5 R)

frictioning past a single bolt to a small belay stance directly above with another double ring bolt anchor. 165', 5.5 R

3. Climb straight up to a bolt protecting a very smooth slab, the 5.6 crux. Gain the major horizontal fracture at the base of the steeper buttress above (the WEDGE Buttress), then traverse horizontally right along the crack to a secure, flat belay ledge. 60', 5.6

4. Climb a slab to layback moves up a short, right-leaning corner. From a stance above (bolt), make delicate face moves (5.6) up and right (hidden piton) to easier moves leading to another comfortable ledge on the right with a double ring bolt anchor. 80', 5.6

5. Head straight up enjoyable, well protected grooves, climbing up a flake to a small pine tree (sling anchor) on a tree ledge. 130', 5.5 (There is a well used rappel descent from here, using two ropes, down a series of double ring bolt anchors on WEDGE and INTERLOPER.)

6. Original WEDGE steps back right and climbs the final overlap by underclinging right (5.7) across a horizontal crack to easier overlaps . 5.7 Or:

6a. To maintain the climb at a 5.6 grade, walk left along the slab to a short, little corner that breaks through the next overlap. Climb this (5.6) past old pitons and a bolt (same as DIKE ROUTE) to the trees. 5.6

7 & 8. Finish easily up and right through trees and across slabs. 350'

HISTORY: Will Crowther and three friends from the MIT Outing Club made the first ascent in 1958 or 1959, without placing a single bolt, one year before the first ascent of SLIDING BOARD. Crowther first led the second and third pitches in a most unusual manner. Finding himself most of the way up the crux 5.6 slab, completely out of rope, and with no protection in sight, his belayer tied a second rope on. Will kept going, eventually placed a piton in the horizontal crack at the base of the WEDGE Buttress, and completed the pitch. His three friends were then obligated to follow the crux slab by simul-climbing "in wedge formation" (hence the name of the route), all belayed on the same rope! Later, Crowther added three bolts to the climb: the two belay bolts at the top of Pitch two, and the crux bolt at the start of Pitch three. "We wanted to make the route a good climb—and you had to belay somewhere!" Crowther explained. And what was Will Crowther's footwear on WEDGE's first ascent? In the late 1950s, he wasn't wearing klettershoes, or even EBs. Will was wearing ordinary tennis shoes.

VARIATION #1: **THE RIGHT-HAND VARIATION** I 5.6 R
This zig zagging right-hand variation up the crux slab has even less protection than the more direct, original line. Start at the top of WEDGE's first pitch.

2a. Climb up and right to two bolts and a stance. 70', 5.4

3a. Diagonal up right, back left to a bolt, then slab climb straight up (5.6 R)

to the same good belay ledge at the base of the upper corners. 5.6 R At the first bolt, you can also angle back left to the smooth slab on the original route.
FA: Unknown.

VARIATION # 2: **THE DIRECT FINISH** I 5.9
6b. To the right of WEDGE's original 5.7 finish, a vertical dike ascends a steep bulge with very hard moves (5.9) past a bolt. 40', 5.9
HISTORY: The bolt was placed on aid by the MIT Outing Club. In 1969, Sigma Alpha—a fraternity?—made the first free ascent.

MU II 5.9+
If your friction coefficient is too low, this route won't be very a–musing. This is an intriguing link-up, completing a route first begun back in 1974.
1. Friction easily up to the first bolt on Pitch one of WEDGE.
2. Climb past WEDGE's right-hand bush clump to the two bolt belay at the top of the first pitch of WEDGE's RIGHT-HAND VARIATION. 5.4
3. Slab climb straight up (bolt; 5.6 R) to the excellent, flat belay ledge at the end of Pitch three of WEDGE. 5.6 R
4. The overlap on INTERLOPER curves down to the left to form a corner. Traverse right then up, gaining the upper of two, small stances on the corner, and move up a slab to intersect WEDGE halfway up its fourth pitch. Traverse left across a steep wall along a thin, horizontal dike (bolt), onto a slightly lower angle slab. Step left again, then up past marginal pitons, or from above the second piton, head slightly right to potholes (Friend). Eventually gain the tree-covered ledge on STADTMÜLLER–GRIFFIN ROUTE. 5.9+
5. Off the right-hand end of the tree ledge, climb up a crack for one move, then angle left and up to a belay ledge on WEDGE.
6 & 7. Climb THE DIRECT FINISH to WEDGE (5.9) to the top. 40', 5.9
HISTORY: Paul Ledoux & John Yates climbed the bottom pitches intersecting with WEDGE on July 6, 1974. Paul Ledoux & Doug Haller finished the route via the potholes on September 8, 1985 before John Yates & Paul Ledoux climbed the first completely direct ascent on September 21, 1985.

THE WEDGE BUTTRESS
This is the steep, compact buttress in the center of the Whitehorse Slabs between WEDGE and SEA OF HOLES. Climb either the first two pitches of WEDGE or up SLIPSHOD to reach the base of the buttress, which has a long, prominent, horizontal crack at its base.

THE BOOKLET I 5.9 (*)
Left of the fourth pitch of WEDGE is an attractive, 20 foot open book.
3. Above the crux slab on WEDGE, climb up the dihedral past a bolt (5.9) to a stance with a piton on the right. Surmount a bulge onto the upper slab, and

face climb past two more bolts and an overlap. Belay above on the large, tree-covered ledge on STADTMÜLLER–GRIFFIN ROUTE. 150', 5.9

HISTORY: Paul Ledoux & Bill Gooch reached the stance up and right of the open book, and climbed the upper slab on July 22, 1978. Alain Comeau & Janot Mendler Comeau made the first direct ascent of this pleasantly challenging variation in the Summer of 1981.

NEEDFUL THINGS I 5.11b (5.8 R) (*)
The hardest free climb up the Slabs ascends the smooth, bulging face in the very center of the WEDGE Buttress to the left of THE BOOKLET. What you might really need is a just a good handhold!

1 & 2. Climb the first two pitches of SLIPSHOD to the double bolt belay stance at the top of the white streak, 40 feet below the buttress. 5.6 R

3. Climb the slab up to the horizontal break at the base of the WEDGE Buttress. Left of THE BOOKLET, head left up a narrow ramp past two bolts, then mantle (5.11b) onto a stance with a third bolt. Continue up and left to a good stance, clip the top bolt on FINGERTIP TRIP, then climb up and right (5.8 R) to a final bolt, finishing straight up to a double bolt belay anchor just right of STADTMÜLLER–GRIFFIN ROUTE. 140', 5.11b (5.8 R)

4. Head straight up clean rock over two small roofs to the trees. 5.8

HISTORY: Bill Lowther & Ozzie Blumet made the first ascent on July 13, 1992. All the bolts were placed free on the lead, except for the second one.

FINGERTIP TRIP I 5.10a (*)
This relatively unknown route should become popular. You don't have to be frostbitten to enjoy the climb! Reasonable protection and nice moves.

1. Climb the first pitch of WEDGE to the double bolt belay above the right-hand bush clump. A long pitch. 200', 5.3

2. Continue up the second lead of WEDGE, traversing left under the WEDGE Buttress (5.6), and belay on top of the detached block on the left, on SLIPSHOD. 150', 5.6 (You can also climb SLIPSHOD to get here.)

3. Underclip up past a bolt at a small flake (5.10a crux at second bolt), then face climb out right onto the upper slab. Finish past one more bolt (5.8), frictioning straight up the slab to a double bolt anchor on the ledge above, on STADTMÜLLER–GRIFFIN ROUTE. 65', 5.10a

HISTORY: Ed Webster & Kurt Winkler made the first ascent on April 14, 1991. What made their climb somewhat unusual was that Webster, missing eight fingertips from frostbite he suffered climbing a new route up the Kangshung Face of Mt. Everest in 1988, led the route free, placing the three bolts on the lead—and Winkler, newly frostbitten after a forced bivouac at the top of the ice climb Slipstream in the Canadian Rockies—followed the pitch with still-bandaged, frostbitten fingers.

Kurt Winkler on the first ascent of Fingertip Trip (5.10a) in 1991. Photograph by Ed Webster.

SLIPSHOD II 5.6 R

A better climb than many have thought, taking a direct line up the slabs to the left of WEDGE, and joining STADTMÜLLER–GRIFFIN ROUTE higher up. There is a very long runout on Pitch two.

1. Aiming towards the left-hand bush clump on WEDGE, scramble up 4th class friction slabs for about 200 feet, belaying at a white, layback flake immediately to the left of the left tree clump on WEDGE. 200', 4th class

2. Above the flake, head straight up a smooth slab following the left side of a prominent white streak to a two bolt anchor above a small pocket. 140', 5.6 R

3. Slab climb up to a short, steep wall. Surmount it just left of a large, jammed block (or harder still, farther left) with an awkward move onto a good ledge (possible belay). Moving slightly left, climb up a slab following a dike with unusual finger pockets. Merge with STADTMÜLLER–GRIFFIN, then head up right to a ledge below a notched overhang with a two bolt anchor. 135', 5.6

4. Follow STADTMÜLLER–GRIFFIN until above the notched overhang, then climb straight up past a right-diagonalling flake to finger pockets up a cleaned streak in a dirty wall. Belay on the large, tree ledge above. 80', 5.5
5. From the ledge's left end, diagonal left to an arch, follow it down left, then step over it as soon as possible onto a slab (bolt). Continue up a right-facing corner, turn it at the top, and belay on the long traverse on DIKE ROUTE.
6. Using a sharp-edged flake, gain a sloping ledge in the roofs above, and traverse right to a belay on DIKE. Finish up slabs & ledges heading right.
HISTORY: Paul Ledoux with an assortment of partners including Bill Reenstra, Don Rolph, Greg Meyers, & Jim Fiasconaro pieced together the first ascent of the climb between May 29 & June 12, 1971.

VARIATION #1: **THE 5.7 FLAKE** I 5.7
3a. Head left up a smooth slab to a sloping belay at the left end of the large horizontal overlap on WEDGE. 5.4
4a. Surmount the overlap, angle up right across a narrow ledge with old pitons, and continue right to a fairly prominent, steep, left-facing layback flake. Layback up the flake and over a tricky 5.7 bulge. Belay on the good ledge with a double bolt anchor below the notched overhang on the STADTMÜLLER–GRIFFIN ROUTE above. 5.7
HISTORY: Tradition has it that this pitch was climbed in the 1960s. A large flake has also fallen off, making the pitch harder than before.

VARIATION #2: **THE CRYSTALLINE DIKE** I 5.8 R
This is the dike 20 feet left of the white, arching flake on THE 5.7 FLAKE.
3a. Climb the right-hand of two dikes with little protection (5.8 R) to the ledge and double bolt anchor on STADTMÜLLER–GRIFFIN ROUTE. 65', 5.8 R
HISTORY: Paul Ledoux top-roped the dike in 1971. Ed Webster & Alain Comeau climbed the pitch on the lead in October, 1985.

SEA OF HOLES II 5.7 (***)
with THE DIRECT FINISH II 5.8 (***)
An excellent and popular route with smooth slab climbing and one or two tricky bulges, depending on whether you include THE DIRECT FINISH. SEA OF HOLES takes a perfectly straight line up the white streak between SLIPSHOD and STADTMÜLLER–GRIFFIN. THE DIRECT FINISH adds one more perplexing overlap and a short slab to a higher, double bolt anchor. Start directly below the white streak, halfway between SLIPSHOD and the bottom exfoliation flakes on STADTMÜLLER–GRIFFIN ROUTE. Bring a normal rack including several small to medium size Tri-cams. Nearly everyone rappels the route from the top of the fourth pitch, making four easy rappels with two ropes from double ring bolt anchors back to the ground.

Alain Comeau leading the first ascent of Sea Of Holes (5.7) in 1985.
Photograph by Ed Webster.

1. Friction straight up the relatively easy slab (5.2) for a full rope length to a small belay ledge with a double ring bolt anchor. 160', 5.2

2. Friction straight up a clean slab (piton) to the right end of a narrow overlap (natural thread). Step over this, then climb the center of the slab past a fragile flake to the right-hand end of the next ceiling. Belay on a sloping stance with another double ring bolt anchor. 125', 5.5

3. Move left to a thin, hidden flake, then friction straight up a shallow groove to the left end of the large WEDGE Buttress above. Step over the obvious arch at holes, then climb either the white streak on the left (with less protection), or the brown slab straight up (more holes and protection) to a small ledge and white flake with a double ring bolt anchor. 120', 5.5

4. Step left, layback a pretty white flake/corner (5.5), then face climb straight up holds and a slab to a shallow, left-facing corner (piton) and the final, crux bulge. Surmount the bulge (thought-provoking 5.7; bolt) and move up into the DARCY-CROWTHER arch. Climb up the arch, then undercling horizontally right onto a tree ledge. Friction back left up and across cleaned off holds in a mossy slab to a large pine tree (with a sling anchor), and belay. 150', 5.7

THE DIRECT FINISH I 5.8 (***)

4a. Climb over the crux bulge (5.7) on the normal fourth pitch to reach the DARCY-CROWTHER arch. Above, step awkwardly out left onto the upper slab, making a tricky move (5.8) to a hidden finger pocket, then friction up to a double ring bolt anchor. 150', 5.8 Descend the route by making four long rappels back to the ground using the ring bolt anchors.

5. Or, if desired, friction straight up, finishing up DIKE ROUTE up the right-facing, shallow corner with old pegs and a bolt (5.6) to a large pine tree. 5.6

6 & 7. Fourth class up and right across short slabs and tree ledges to reach the top of the ledge near STANDARD ROUTE. 5.2

HISTORY: Sections of the climb had been done previously. Ed Webster & Alain Comeau made the first ascent of this extremely popular route on October 21, 1985. Alain Comeau & Mike Hardert added THE DIRECT FINISH over the final bulge up to the top ring bolt anchor in May, 1994.

STADTMÜLLER–GRIFFIN ROUTE II 5.6

While not as well-travelled as other climbs on the slabs, the route offers a stimulating variety of moves. Protection, for once, is also reasonably good. Begin 200 feet left of WEDGE below a fairly obvious overlap or exfoliation flake that curves up to the right, with several trees growing above it. Belay on several, small ledges beneath the route's initial overlap/ceiling.

1. Protect in the arch, then slab climb around the left side of the overlap, unprotected, before moving back up right to some trees. Layback a flake, undercling right, and belay at a good tree. 150', 5.5

2. Step over a large overlap (5.4), then head up left on easy flakes to the right-hand end of the large tree ledge on DIKE ROUTE. 150', 5.4

3. Head right (easy, but sparse protection) across a friction slab (old pin) to a multiple bolt anchor on a good but small stance at the base of a white, layback flake. Belay here (on SEA OF HOLES), or continue up Pitch four. 90', 5.4

4. Layback a short flake on the right, then face climb up and right to a secure, but exposed ledge with a two bolt anchor below a notched overhang. 60', 5.6

5. Make a low traverse to the right around the overlap, and climb an incipient, vertical crack up a slab covered with dried moss (bolt; 5.6) to finish up a sequence of pockets in a dirty wall to a large, tree-covered ledge. 90', 5.6

5a. You can also surmount the notched ceiling just right of the belay with a tricky move (5.6). Above the lip, traverse right (bolt), then finish up the series of pockets in the dirty wall to the good tree ledge. 80', 5.6

6. Above the tree ledge is a dike running up a slab. Finish up DIKE ROUTE by gaining the dike directly (with help from a tree), or by making a rising traverse to it from the left end of the ledge. Above another ledge (possible belay), finish up a shallow, 20 foot right-facing corner (also part of DIKE ROUTE) with several old pitons and a bolt (5.6) to a large pine and easier ground. 110', 5.6 (The first ascent party climbed a left-slanting crack past a birch tree, 75 feet to the right of the 5.6 DIKE corner.)

7 & 8. Fourth class up and right across short slabs and tree ledges to reach the top of the cliff near STANDARD ROUTE. 5.2

HISTORY: After first attempting the climb in 1956, Jack Taylor returned in 1957 or 1958 with Bert Hirtle, and made the route's first ascent. "We didn't use much protection on the climb," Jack Taylor remembered. "When I first saw a guidebook many years later, I was shocked to see the claim made by Stadtmüller and Porter that they had done the first ascent." Several years later, in May, 1963, Hugo Stadtmüller and John Porter also climbed the route and added the notched ceiling on Pitch five, which Taylor and Hirtle had traversed around to the right. Stadtmüller, one of the most gifted climbers of his day, was tragically killed with John Griffin in an avalanche in Huntington Ravine on Mt. Washington on April 4, 1964—and this fine route was named in their memory by John Porter.

THE DARCY-CROWTHER VARIATION II 5.6 (*)

A worthwhile, yet seldom climbed route with adequate protection. The main features are the twin blocks split by a hand crack (also used by PATHFINDER) and the obvious, right-curving arch just to the left of the crux pitch of SEA OF HOLES. A good option to choose if other routes on the Slabs are crowded.

1 & 2. Climb the first two leads of either STADTMÜLLER–GRIFFIN ROUTE (5.5) or DIKE ROUTE (5.2) to the large tree ledge on DIKE.

3. Friction up and right to a small overlap, then face climb up to the first of three sharp, horizontal flakes (pin). Continue straight up to an overlap below two, large white blocks or flakes split by a vertical hand crack. Climb the crack to a nice ledge (with two fixed pitons) on top of the blocks. 125', 5.6
4. Traverse right past a bush along a narrow ledge underneath a prominent overlap until below an obvious break. Layback over the notch in the overlap (piton; 5.6), then continue up a prominent, right-curving arch to a large tree ledge on the right. 100', 5.6
5. From the left end of the tree ledge, make a rising traverse up and left to reach another ledge (possible belay) and a finish on DIKE ROUTE. Climb a shallow, right-facing corner with old pegs and a bolt (5.6) to the trees. 5.6
6 & 7. Fourth class up and right across short slabs and tree ledges to the top. 5.2
FA: Ray Darcy & Will Crowther 1956

OLD TIMES II 5.8 R (*)

A fine combination of pitches, some with very poor protection, between DIKE ROUTE and DARCY-CROWTHER, with a finish up CORBETT'S CRACK. An additional bolt protects what had previously been an extremely serious runout on the crux slab. The route's major feature is the right-slanting, narrow gangway through the overlap about 60 feet right of the arch on DIKE ROUTE. Several hundred yards to the left of STANDARD ROUTE, scramble up easy slabs to the base of the easy dike on DIKE ROUTE. Twenty feet farther right is a smooth, open slab with a small, curving overlap 80 feet up.

1. Friction up the slab's center (5.6 R; no protection) to the small, curving arch. Belay here from Friends placed in the overlap. 80', 5.6 R
2. Climb the unprotected slab (5.7 R) to the DIKE tree ledge. 85', 5.7 R
3. From the right side of the DIKE tree ledge, head up right on a smooth slab to a thin, layback flake (5.4). Continue (5.5; old peg) to a good ledge on the left (another pin) below the main overlap. 90', 5.5
4. Pull onto the narrow gangway splitting the large overlap above, undercling right (5.7), and exit onto a fine friction slab. Head straight up the exposed, upper slab (bolt; 5.8 R crux) to the double ring bolt anchor on PATHFINDER under the right end of DIKE ROUTE's massive overhangs, below CORBETT'S CRACK. 100', 5.8 R
5. Climb the strenuous, overhanging CORBETT'S CRACK (5.8), formed by a huge detached flake, through the ceilings to a nice slab on the left. Belay at its top at trees. 70', 5.8
6. Easy scrambling or a pleasant, steep slab gains the top. 70', 5.8 R
HISTORY: Several sections of the route including CORBETT'S CRACK, climbed by Barry Corbett in 1956, had been done earlier. Neil Cannon, Paul Ross, & Alan Roberts made the first complete ascent on October 11, 1983.

WHITEHORSE LEDGE - THE SLABS (OLD TIMES & PATHFINDER) 247

Maria Hannus just above the crux overlap on the first ascent of Pathfinder (5.9) in 1995. Photograph by Ed Webster.

PATHFINDER II 5.9 (**)

This new line up the left-hand side of the Slabs offers a nice variety of climbing—well protected friction, intricate face moves, even a short overhang, the crux. Only one move, getting past the overhang, is 5.9. The rest of the climb is 5.7 and 5.8, or easier. Immediately left of the easy, bottom dike on DIKE ROUTE is a prominent white stripe. Solo up to the starting ledge on DIKE, and belay at a bolt just to the left of the white streak. Bring along a normal rack up to a #3 Friend, including small Tri-cams.

1. Friction up the white stripe to a bolt 50 feet up, then make harder moves above a piton in a flake (5.7) to a second bolt. At pockets (small Tri-cams), traverse to your right back onto the white streak, to easier moves up to the third bolt. Belay on DIKE ROUTE at a double ring bolt anchor. 165', 5.7

2. Continue up the easy dike for 20 feet, clip a bolt on the right, and belay at the right-hand end of the large tree ledge on DIKE. 75', 5.5

3. Friction up and right to a small overlap, then face climb up to the first of three sharp, horizontal flakes (pin). Continue straight up to an overlap below two, large white blocks or flakes split by a vertical, hand crack. Climb the crack to a nice ledge (with two fixed pegs) on top of the two blocks. 125', 5.6

4. Step right on a narrow ledge behind a bush, then face climb straight up past three pitons up an incipient vertical crack (5.8) and thin exfoliation flake to reach the main overlap above. Step right, clip a bolt, then make a 5.9 move up and over the overlap before stepping left to an exposed, double bolt belay stance. (The 5.9 crux overlap and step-up is 10 feet to the left of the DARCY-CROWTHER overlap/arch, and 30 feet left of SEA OF HOLES.) 75', 5.9

5. Layback a small arch up and right, step up onto a slab (bolt) just left of the final, double ring bolt belay on SEA OF HOLES, and friction (5.6) up to the next overlap (peg) and a stance. Clip one final bolt, finish up the prow above (5.7), then step left to the final double ring bolt belay beneath the DIKE Roof. 70', 5.7 Finish up DIKE ROUTE, on the right, or rappel four times down SEA OF HOLES to return to the ground.

HISTORY: Ray Darcy & Will Crowther first climbed Pitch three in 1956. In June, 1994, Bill Lowther rope-soloed the first ascent of the Pitch four crux overlap (but started the pitch much farther left), plus climbed the narrow arch at the start of Pitch five. On their third try, Ed Webster & Maria Hannus (Sweden) made the route's first complete ascent, linking the various sections together while being attacked by hordes of black flies, on June 6, 1995. The Pitch one bolts were placed on rappel; the rest were drilled on the lead.

DIKE ROUTE II 5.6 (*)

The second route up Whitehorse, DIKE ROUTE climbs the right-hand of two parallel dikes on the far, left-hand side of the Slabs. (Resembling a staircase,

WHITEHORSE LEDGE - THE SLABS (PATHFINDER & DIKE ROUTE)

dikes are formed by an intrusion of basalt into the granite.) Several variations are possible on this climb, with the easiest route described below. While the dike does begin on the ground, most parties rope up on the large, sloping ledge about 100 feet up. Two parallel dikes rise above this ledge: THE MINER-JOSEPH-KING ROUTE ascends the harder, poorly protected, left-hand dike (double bolt anchor at its base), while DIKE ROUTE takes the easier, lower angled, right-hand staircase. There is a fixed piton anchor at the start.

1. Climb the easy, but somewhat poorly protected right-hand dike (old piton) to a cozy belay pocket with a two bolt anchor. 125', 5.2

2. Follow the easy dike past a double ring bolt anchor (top of Pitch one, PATHFINDER) to a large tree ledge. Scramble left to the highest point. 150', 5.2

3. Continue to the base of a narrow, right-slanting arch (DIKE ROUTE's crux) that breaks through the left side of a large, horizontal overlap.

4. Layback halfway up the arch, then step left (5.6) over the arch onto an exposed slab. Continue to a small stance under the huge, upper roofs. 135', 5.6

5. Traverse horizontally right below the large overhangs to a double ring bolt anchor on a small ledge. 80', 5.5 (This is PATHFINDER's top anchor. To descend, rappel four times with two ropes down SEA OF HOLES.)

6. Continue right around the corner, and climb the final overlap by way of a shallow, right-facing corner past old pins and a bolt (5.6) to a big pine. 65', 5.6

7 & 8. Fourth class up and right across short slabs and tree ledges to reach the top of the ledge near STANDARD ROUTE. 5.2

HISTORY: Fritz Wiessner climbed the first ascent of the route in the Summer of 1933, probably with Robert Underhill, his companion on all his other significant first ascents achieved during that productive summer. "Fritz was a magician on rock," Underhill said admiringly. "He was very, very good. But he wouldn't go climbing unless I promised he could lead! Fritz loved to do first ascents—a new climb was always better than an old one." Underhill wrote up the climb in Appalachia in 1933, but from his description, they don't seem to have climbed the entire traditional route: "A second route was made up White Horse Ledge, starting 200 feet to the left of the usual course. This route, which starts for 250 feet up an easy crack and then traverses left up through a band of trees, really gives good climbing only at its top, where it finishes up a chimney requiring a bold exit." The exact location of the final chimney and bold exit have not been determined.

VARIATION: **CORBETT'S CRACK** I 5.8

6a. Partway across DIKE ROUTE's long traverse on Pitch five, a fierce looking crack is formed by a huge, detached flake wedged in the DIKE ROUTE overhangs. Jam the crack strenuously to easy slabs above. 40', 5.8

HISTORY: Legend has it Barry Corbett did the climb in 1956.

250 THE MOUNT WASHINGTON VALLEY

ANCIENT JOURNEYS I 5.11a+ (*)
An obscure, old aid line, now free. The route ascends the thin, overhanging crack system out the DIKE Roof, 30 feet right of CORBETT'S CRACK.

1–5. Climb either SEA OF HOLES with THE DIRECT FINISH (5.8) or PATHFINDER (5.9) to reach the double ring bolt anchor just to the right of the base of CORBETT'S CRACK under the DIKE Roof. 5.8 or 5.9

6. Climb the initial headwall on the right (bolt) onto a small ledge, swing past a pointed flake, and jam up the overhanging crack above (peg) which starts at hands and narrows to fingers. The crux is getting over the lip. 60', 5.11a+

HISTORY: The first ascent party is unknown, but left behind old ring pitons as evidence of their passage. Steve Larson & John Bouchard made the first free ascent in October, 1995.

THE WHITE ZONE II 5.12a (**)
More than just rock climbing, it's a way of life! Great setting, too. This route takes the prize for being the steepest free pitch on the Whitehorse Slabs. Overhanging face climbing leads up the center of the imposing DIKE Roof up a large, white wall. Start by climbing any of several routes (SEA OF HOLES, PATHFINDER, DIKE, etc.) which will take you up to a double bolt anchor below THE WHITE ZONE in the center of the DIKE Roof.

1. From the belay, climb up and left on a sharp flake to a difficult mantleshelf move (5.10b) up onto a shelf (bolt), then traverse right (bolt) into THE WHITE ZONE to a rest at the third bolt. Face climb straight up the steepening wall on large holds past three more bolts to the top, finishing with a desperate mantleshelf (5.12a) over the lip. Belay at the two bolt anchor above. 70', 5.12a

HISTORY: Uwe Schneider, Rob Adair, Dennis Goode, Bill Lutkus, & Craig Taylor created and climbed the route in July, 1993.

DARK HORSE I 5.8 R (*)
A somewhat overlooked slab climb, with one very committing runout—and a real long shot if you're new to the joys of unprotected friction climbing! Solo up to the starting ledge on DIKE ROUTE, and belay at the double bolt anchor at the base of the MINER-JOSEPH-KING ROUTE.

1. Between the two dikes of MINER-JOSEPH-KING and DIKE ROUTE (and just left of PATHFINDER's white streak) is a narrow, horizontal overlap. Start up the left-hand dike, move right to the overlap and protection, step past the ceiling, then friction up and right (5.8 R) to a second overlap. Belay on a tiny stance just above at a two bolt anchor. 90', 5.8 R

2. Make another long runout up the slabs above to the tree ledge on DIKE ROUTE. 130', 5.7 R Or, angle up and right (5.6) to reach the double ring bolt anchor on PATHFINDER, and continue as desired.

FA: Mike Heintz, Kim Smith, & Jim Boyd August 22, 1978

WHITEHORSE LEDGE - THE SLABS (WHITE ZONE & DARK HORSE) 251

Alex Drummond in The White Zone (5.12a) in 1995. Photograph by Rich Baker.

THE MINER-JOSEPH-KING ROUTE II 5.6 R

One of the least popular routes on the slabs, the first two leads ascend the less obvious, harder, poorly protected, left-hand dike of DIKE ROUTE's two starts. Bring a compass to navigate your way up the entire climb, which eventually skirts around the left-hand side of the DIKE Roofs. At the left end of the Whitehorse slabs, scramble up about 100 feet to reach a large, sloping ledge where both starts of DIKE ROUTE commence. MINER-JOSEPH-KING begins at the two bolt anchor at the left end of this comfortable ledge.

1. The left-hand dike has much harder friction and face moves and much less protection than the regular, right-hand dike. Tiny stance. 150', 5.6 R
2. Continue more easily (5.3) up the dike to the DIKE ROUTE tree ledge. 5.3
3. Scramble up towards the large, right-slanting arch on DIKE.
4. The crux pitch of DIKE ROUTE: layback halfway up the arch, step over it (5.6) to the left, and face climb to a stance under the DIKE Roofs. 135', 5.6
5. Traverse left, then down, to old pitons and a bolt. 90'
6. Step down again, then move left until it's possible to climb up to a large overhang. Traverse farther left around the corner, and follow two dihedrals through the roofs above into the trees. 150', 5.6
7. Traverse down and left under overlaps to a detached flake, then squeeze behind it to reach trees on the right below a big slab. 110'
8. Friction up slabs and head towards easy ground on the right. Scramble up overgrown slabs between overlaps to the top.

FA: Larry Miner, David Joseph, & Harry King September 5, 1955

ALTERNATE FINISH: **THE NANDOR VARIATION** II 5.8+
An obscure conclusion to the upper section of MINER-JOSEPH-KING.
1–4. Climb the first four pitches of THE MINER-JOSEPH-KING ROUTE to the horizontal traverse below the large band of roofs on DIKE.
5. Go left to trees under a small overlap, use a tree to make a long reach to higher holds, and face climb to a larger overlap. Undercling left to bushes. 130', 5.6
6. Climb MINER-JOSEPH-KING through two corners in the overlaps to another overhanging dihedral (5.8), which is ascended to the trees. 150', 5.8
7. Dirty ramps are followed towards a corner in a vertical wall, then finish up a dog-leg crack to the woods. 150', 5.8+

FA: Lonnie Smith & Rob Pratt June 15, 1980

CRAZY HORSE I 5.9 R

This poorly protected route climbs the smooth slabs just left of the MINER-JOSEPH-KING dike. Begin on the ground on the left side of the Slab's toe, 75 feet right of the large, tree-filled corner, the line of MISTAKEN IDENTITY.
1. Climb a smooth slab (5.9 R) past several very thin flakes or wrinkles (small wired nuts helpful). Belay from a bush at the left end of an overlap

WHITEHORSE LEDGE - THE SLABS (WAITING FOR COMEAU)

near the start of THE MINER-JOSEPH-KING ROUTE. 5.9 R

2. Follow a line of potholes (Tri-cams) up a slab, making a long runout to the tree ledge on DIKE ROUTE. Rappel off, or follow DIKE.

HISTORY: Alan Chase & John Mallery did the first ascent in the Spring of 1980. Sadly, that July, Chase disappeared with three partners on Denali in Alaska, apparently avalanched in "the Valley of Death" on the Northeast Fork of the Kahiltna Glacier during their approach to climb the Cassin Ridge.

MAN-O-WAR I 5.9+ (5.7 R) (*)

Begin 20 feet to the right of WAITING FOR COMEAU.

1. Climb the slab with poor protection (5.7 R) to a block and a hanging belay off of large Friends. 5.7 R

2. Follow a crack until it ends, then at pockets, traverse up and left on nice brown rock to the two bolt belay on WAITING FOR COMEAU. 5.9+

3. Finish up and right (bolt) to a scoop and the trees.

FA: Paul Boissonneault, John Strand, & Tom Callaghan   June, 1981

WAITING FOR COMEAU I 5.9 (*)

The obvious flake system up the wall just right of MISTAKEN IDENTITY.

1. Underclinging across an overlap (often wet), and climb to where the flake ends. Make a hard 5.9 move left into a diagonalling crack/groove, and belay above from two bolts. 5.9

2. Slab climb straight up past another bolt to the tree ledge above.

HISTORY: Once Alain Comeau showed up in the Summer of 1979, he quickly polished off the first ascent with Albert Dow & David Stone.

DIRECT START: **CASH FLOW** I 5.10b R or X

1a. Friction straight up to the end of the underclinging flake on WAITING FOR COMEAU, and finish on that route. 5.10b R or X

HISTORY: Alain Comeau drilled several bolts here in "EB days", then removed them. John Strand free-soloed the first ascent in April, 1989, hoping the snowbank at the base would catch him if he fell, which luckily, he didn't.

MISTAKEN IDENTITY II 5.6

There will never be a problem mistaking this line: the large, tree-filled corner at the far, left end of the Slabs. It is the cliff's dirtiest and least aesthetic route, and was the scene of the only climbing fatality on Whitehorse. MISTAKEN IDENTITY does, however, conveniently mark the dividing line between the Whitehorse Slabs and the South Buttress of Whitehorse. For obvious reasons, the climb is not recommended and no more information is known.

HISTORY: The first ascent went unrecorded, but it was probably climbed in the 1930s. The route was named in August, 1971, following an ascent by Frank Dean, Mike Lee, Al Dushane, & Larry McGee.

Susan Patenaude on the first ascent of Webster's Finish (5.11a) to Science Friction Wall in 1980. Photograph by Ed Webster.

THE SOUTH BUTTRESS

Historically, the South Buttress of Whitehorse was completely neglected for several decades during which time the Mount Washington Valley's other more accessible cliffs were explored in depth. For years, the Dike Traverse (now part of ERADICATE) was the only climb on the entire 650 foot South Buttress—and it didn't even go the top of the cliff! Until the early 1970s, climbers seemed to believe there was virtually no worthwhile climbing to the left of the Whitehorse Slabs. The myth slowly began to fade in the mid '70s, and today the South Buttress is a popular destination offering many unusual and difficult free climbs in an exposed and tranquil setting.

The South Buttress is split into several distinct sections: the ETHEREAL CRACK Buttress and the CHILDREN'S CRUSADE area, the renowned Wonder Wall, and the far, left side which hosts the TRANQUILITY Slab, the INFERNO Wall (above the INFERNO tree ledge), and several smaller crags and cliffs, such as the Cosmic Crag, the Steak Sauce Crag, the Where In The Blazes Cliff, and the Gargoyle Buttress. The approach for any of the routes on the South Buttress's left-hand side, for climbs up the WONDER WALL, routes farther to the left in the vicinity of INFERNO, or up the TRANQUILITY Slab, is somewhat complicated and should be followed exactly.

THE INFERNO & WONDER WALL APPROACH: Thirty feet to the left of THE JAWS OF DOOM (a large, wet corner several hundred feet to the left of ETHEREAL CRACK), make several bouldering moves off the ground (5.6) to small ledges leading up to a 20 foot wide traverse or access ledge running straight left across the lower part of the face. (This 5.6 start is identical to the first pitch of THE ELIMINATE.) Now walk left beneath a smooth vertical wall (below the bolted sport climb LONDON CALLING, and the crux second pitch of WONDER WALL) along the ledge to a bushy slope. This same spot may also be reached by bouldering up an unpleasant, dirty, and often wet slime gully (5.4) formed by the left side of the cliff base and a broken buttress on the left (the Gargoyle Buttress). Approaching up the 5.6 access ledge start on THE ELIMINATE, then heading left across the traverse ledge over to the base of INFERNO is much easier, safer, faster—and drier.

Now scramble up the slope until you can see a large, right-slanting dihedral above: this is the INFERNO Corner. The TRANQUILITY Slab is located just to the left of this corner. To reach climbs on the WONDER WALL, the next section is 4th class, and although very exposed, can be soloed if desired. Scramble up below the INFERNO Corner, climb a 15 foot, V groove on the right, then traverse along a series of narrow ledges 300 feet to the right into a tree-filled gully. This gully leads up and right to the comfortable WONDER WALL tree ledge below the sweeping expanse of the upper Wonder Wall.

Russ Clune on the first free ascent of Wonder Wall (5.12a / 5.8 X) in 1981. Photograph by Ed Webster.

WHITEHORSE LEDGE - SOUTH BUTTRESS (SHORT ORDER) 257

BOLTED RAPPEL DESCENTS: Many parties now prefer to utilize any of several double bolt rappel routes to descend South Buttress climbs, a faster and exhilarating, but potentially more dangerous option. The following routes all have double bolt rappel descents, allowing you to rappel down to your pack at the base: SHORT ORDER, SLEEPING BEAUTY, CHILDREN'S CRUSADE and THE DIRECT FINISH to CHILDREN'S CRUSADE, TOTAL RECALL, THE ELIMINATE, THE LAST UNICORN, SCIENCE FRICTION WALL, and LOST SOULS / CEMETERY GATES.

SOUTH BUTTRESS DESCENT OPTIONS: Descent from the top of the South Buttress is also less than straightforward. The fastest route down is to walk due north through the woods on vague trails to the open, granite summit of Whitehorse Ledge. Hike north along the Bryce Path towards Cathedral, down to the saddle just north of the Guide's Wall, and back to either parking area: at The White Mountain Hotel, or at the base of Cathedral. Be careful NOT to take the left-hand (or western branch) of the Bryce Path which forks just below the summit—unless you want to hike the long way back to The White Mountain Hotel all the way around the South Buttress's far, left side.

The first climbs on the Buttress are just left of the tree-filled corner of MISTAKEN IDENTITY. Walk to the left side of the Slabs until below that climb. The many enjoyable South Buttress routes are now described from right to left.

TOUTE SUITE I 5.11b (or straight up; 5.12a) (*)
Be quick, or lose your chance! The steep slab just left of MISTAKEN IDENTITY. Start 30 feet right of the AVENGER finger crack. Short and popular.
1. Step left on several small holds to clip the first bolt, then face climb straight up to the second bolt. Step left to a bulge with a hidden hold (5.11b), then crank up to easier ground. If you climb straight up above the second bolt, it's go-for-it 5.12a. 45', 5.11b or 5.12a
HISTORY: A. J. Jones & Peter Lewis had top-roped the climb in 1989, before Ian Cruickshank & Brad White made the first ascent on May 22, 1992.

SHORT ORDER I 5.9 (***)
Quick service, but only if you're over five foot eight inches tall. You'll understand after you've done the climb. The route ascends the clean, white, rounded arete just to the left of MISTAKEN IDENTITY. Begin on the ground below a short slab, just to the left of AVENGER's initial finger crack. A well protected classic, with challenging yet enjoyable climbing.
1. Above a horizontal crack, a 5.7 move (bolt) gains a shoulder. Friction past a tree, then move right onto a sloping ledge. Belay at a peg in a pocket. 50', 5.7
2. Move straight up over a troublesome bulge to gain a slab. Face climb out right to a bolt, then make a long reach left (TCU; 5.9) to a thank god hold.

258 THE MOUNT WASHINGTON VALLEY

WHITEHORSE LEDGE – THE SOUTH BUTTRESS (RIGHT SIDE)

A.		CASH FLOW I 5.10b R or X	Page 253	K.	CIRCLE OF LIFE I 5.9	Page 261
B.	*	WAITING FOR COMEAU I 5.9	Page 253	L.	The Echo Roof	
C.		MISTAKEN IDENTITY II 5.6	Page 253	M.	The Ethereal Crack Buttress	Page 265
D.		AVENGER I 5.9 R	Page 260	N.	*** CHILDREN'S CRUSADE II 5.9	Page 276
E.	***	SHORT ORDER I 5.9	Page 257	O.	*** THE DIRECT FINISH to CHILDREN'S CRUSADE III 5.11a	Page 276
F.	**	SLEEPING BEAUTY I 5.10d	Page 260	P.	*** SOUTH BUTTRESS DIRECT III 5.11b R, A1 (5 Points of Aid)	Page 286
G.	**	WIZARD OF OZ I 5.12c	Page 260	Q.	*** ATLANTIS II 5.10b (or 5.9)	Page 309
H.		1-800-CLIMB-IT I 5.12b	Page 261	R.	The Tranquility Slab	Page 312
I.	*	CAROLINA DREAM'IN I 5.11c (5.10b R)	Page 261	S.	The Inferno Wall	Page 317
J.	**	MAN'S BEST FRIEND I 5.8	Page 261			

Above two more bolts, a hollow, white flake (piton) is laybacked up to a pine tree (with a bolt back-up). 100', 5.9 Rappel the route easily with two ropes.
HISTORY: Ed Webster, Bryan Rossin, & Richard Rossin did the first ascent on July 7, 1980. Webster cleaned the lichen and placed the bolts on the lead.

AVENGER I 5.9 R
Begin at the base of a short finger crack between SHORT ORDER and TOUTE SUITE. The crux moves are a bit unprotected. Modern rack.
1. Climb the short, vertical finger crack (5.7) up to the same slabby belay ledge and piton anchor as for SHORT ORDER. 45', 5.7
2. Diagonal left up the face past several solution pockets to a bolt and a 5.9 runout. A prominent finger crack and flake is laybacked to the top. 5.9 R
FA: Alain Comeau & Janot Mendler May, 1980

VIGILANTE I 5.10b R or X
Scramble up to the trees below SLEEPING BEAUTY and start at a very slight groove on the right. Bring along a skyhook!
1. Make hard stemming moves up the groove, then reach right to a pocket, and move up and right to finish up AVENGER. 5.10b R or X
HISTORY: After top-roping the route in July, 1982, John Strand returned to lead the climb in October, 1983.

SLEEPING BEAUTY I 5.10d (**)
The most obvious route up the steep wall to the right of the ECHO Ceiling, SLEEPING BEAUTY is the thin, left-diagonalling finger crack. Bring many small wired nuts for the crux, which is strenuous to protect. Left of SHORT ORDER, scramble to the highest trees on a ledge below a left-facing V corner.
1. Climb the corner (large nut) to cracks leading to a sloping belay stance with a two piton anchor at the base of a pretty, left-leaning finger crack. 5.9
2. Jam the fingertip crack (5.10b) to a two bolt anchor. Rappel with two ropes.
HISTORY: After John Rilley had cleaned the climb on rappel, Alain Comeau, Franck Vernoy, & Matt Stein made the first ascent in October, 1976. A week later, Alain Comeau & Bryan Becker did the first free ascent.

> The next three sport routes climb the steep face left of SLEEPING BEAUTY.

WIZARD OF OZ I 5.12c (**)
The best bolted sport route here. Start 15 feet left of SLEEPING BEAUTY.
1. Climb up a shallow groove to a stance, face climb past two bolts (5.11c crux after the first bolt) up to a pocket and a piton in a corner/roof, then head up past a flake to a large stance. Continue up and left past three bolts (also 5.11c) to a double bolt anchor on the traverse ledge above. 80', 5.11c
2. Move up and left to an extremely smooth, black face with three bolts, finishing up the face (5.12c) just to the right of the final two bolts. 45', 5.12c

HISTORY: Bill Lowther & Ozzie Blumet made the first ascent from the ground up in June, 1992. After five days of effort, they placed all the bolts on the lead, only three of them using aid, and finally free climbed the pitch.

CAROLINA DREAM'IN I 5.11c (5.10b R) (*)
An unlikely looking, now popular face climb up the chocolate brown water streaks just to the right of the large ECHO ceiling. This was the original route up this steep face. The start is the same as for SLEEPING BEAUTY.

1. After a bolt, slab climb left to a flake that allows access to the steep, smooth wall to the right of the immense roof. Face climb up the blank wall (5.11c) past two bolts to a sloping belay ledge. 90', 5.11c

2. A shallow corner leads up and left (5.10b R) to the top. 40', 5.10b R The original finish traversed right & up SLEEPING BEAUTY to a two bolt anchor.

HISTORY: Bob Rotert & Peter Beal made the first ascent of the route in October, 1980, finishing up SLEEPING BEAUTY. The 5.10b R finish was climbed by Doug Madara & Chris Gill in the Spring of 1984.

1-800-CLIMB-IT I 5.12b
Begin just to the right of MAN'S BEST FRIEND. The route criss crosses over WIZARD OF OZ from left to right. There are two obvious flakes on the steep, brown wall to the right of the ECHO Roof. CAROLINA DREAM'IN ascends the left-hand flake, CLIMB-IT takes the right-hand flake.

1. Climb up a beautiful layback flake (5.7), and mantle onto a stance (piton). Climb straight up the slab (bolt) to the right-hand layback flake. Layback the flake (piton) then face climb up the slab above past three bolts (5.12b crux after the first bolt) to the double bolt anchor on WIZARD OF OZ. 100', 5.12b

HISTORY: Bill Lowther rope-soloed the first ascent in October, 1992, placing the bolts from skyhooks. Bill Lowther & Ozzie Blumet made the first free ascent of the climb in April, 1993, after several days of effort and attempts.

MAN'S BEST FRIEND I 5.8 (**)
A faithful, friendly pitch of slab climbing below the ECHO Roof. Start 20 feet to the left of CAROLINA DREAM'IN. Quite popular.

1. From the trees, move left to a bolt on a black bulge (5.8). Climb smooth slabs above (bolt) to a two bolt belay. 100', 5.8 Rappel off 80 feet down and right.

FA: John Strand, rope-solo June, 1988

CIRCLE OF LIFE I 5.9
Begin 40 feet to the left of MAN'S BEST FRIEND. Bring Tri-cams.

1. Climb up a gray stripe in the slab past two bolts (5.9), joining a flake on the right (bolt). Follow the flake as it trends left. When it ends, slab climb left past a pocket to a fixed anchor on ECHO at a bolt and two pitons. 120', 5.9

FA: Bill Lowther, rope-solo July 24, 1995

ECHO II 5.5 (*)

This old and wandering route offers a couple of good pitches. Start below the center of the large ceiling beside a rock resembling an iron sloping into the ground. Pitch one all by itself is a very enjoyable lead. Normal rack.

1. Jam a short hand crack on the iron's left side, climb a slab to a small overlap, step right, and mantle onto a ledge. Step right again and climb a shallow groove (bolt) to a small belay stance with a fixed piton anchor. 90', 5.5
2. Traverse diagonally left beneath the roof (5.4), past two narrow ledges, and belay near the roof's left-hand end. 75', 5.4
3. Follow a slanting crack and corner farther left to a large, tree ledge. 80', 5.4
4. Off the ledge's right, layback a short chimney (bolt) to a cave (peg). 75', 5.5
5–7. Head up right to a clean slab above a ceiling. Finish up and right to the top.
FA: Earle Whipple & Bob Jahn July 3, 1960.

BULLETPROOF I 5.9

Begin at the left end of the ECHO Roof, just right of CEILING.

1. From the right, boulder up to a tree growing 25 feet up. Step right to a small corner, then move up a slab past shallow potholes to a thin crack/ramp (old piton). Friction to the left end of a white flake, joining ECHO. 5.9
FA: John Strand & Lonnie Smith July 6, 1982

CEILING I 5.6

The direct start to ECHO. On the far left side of the large, smooth slab below the ECHO Ceiling is a 20 foot, vertical layback flake.

1. Layback up the flake (bolt), and belay at a tree on the right.
2. Climb out right, then wander up the slab above, taking the path of least resistance (old pins) to a belay at a protruding block on a ledge. 5.6 Join ECHO.

HISTORY: Walter Herrmann & Tom Mitchell made the first recorded ascent on July 4, 1962, and mentioned finding a few old pitons.

LADIES & GENTLEMEN II 5.9

Some good climbing, but the route is uneven both in difficulty and quality. Start at the initial layback flake on CEILING.

1. Layback the flake, then stay left up a shallow groove to a rounded arete (poor bolt). Mantle (5.8) onto the open white slab, and friction straight up to a tree on the roof's left side. 140', 5.8
2. Angle 30 feet left, traverse right below a small band of roofs, then climb up and over to a tree belay higher. 75', 5.6
3. Friction straight up a slab above the belay. 75', 5.6
4. Climb straight up corners, a crack, and then a wall to a big belay tree growing above in a corner or alcove. 80', 5.7
5. On the left, climb thin cracks (5.9) in a small corner to a stance. 45', 5.9
6. Gain a chimney slot, and finish left up easier ground. 100'

WHITEHORSE LEDGE - SOUTH BUTTRESS (FUTURE SHOCK)

HISTORY: "Guys & Dolls" Ed Webster, Susan Patenaude, Doug Madara, Paul Ross, & Suzanne Ross did Pitch one on September 4, 1980. Paul Ross returned two days later with Hugo & Isabella Tosco to make the route's first complete ascent—and changed the route name to honor his more "proper" companions.

THE LAST TANGO I 5.11c (*)

No waltzing here! This is the right-hand of several very thin, bolt-protected face climbs on the impressive slab between CEILING and ETHEREAL CRACK.

1. Just left of the flake on CEILING, face climb up an increasingly difficult slab past several bolts to the final bulge—the 5.11c crux. Tree belay. 100', 5.11c

HISTORY: After first being attempted by Bryan Delaney & Bruce Kumph in 1975, Paul Ross chopped their bolts in a fit of ethical pique. The route was then re-established and finished with two points of aid in June, 1981 by Alain Comeau & Janot Mendler Comeau. Russ Clune & Rosie Andrews climbed the first free ascent in August, 1982.

VARIATION: LAST DANCE I 5.11d (Top-rope)

1a. From the first bolt on FUTURE SHOCK, diagonal up and right across the face (5.11d) to join the crux (5.11c) of THE LAST TANGO. 5.11d

FA: John Strand, top-rope, February, 1987.

FUTURE SHOCK II 5.11c, A1 (3 Points of Aid) (**)

The future is, well, almost here. Only the last few moves on Pitch two above the belay pocket have yet to be freed. A bold and elegant line, FUTURE SHOCK ascends the narrow, left-slanting, bolt-protected dike up the center of the imposing, steep slab to the left of THE LAST TANGO.

Chris Gill leading Pitch one of Future Shock (5.11c) in 1984. Photograph by S. Peter Lewis.

1. Delicate and occasionally spicy face climbing leads diagonally left up the dike past several bolts (5.11c) to a small stance with a two bolt anchor. 50', 5.11c

2. Rappel off, or traverse left from the belay, gaining a solution pocket (5.11b), then aid up a smooth wall on three bolts (A1) to a small ledge, mantleshelf, and traverse right to a slab and a tree belay. 60' 5.11b, A1

HISTORY: Alain Comeau & Janot Mendler Comeau made the first ascent of this often looked at route in June, 1981. That same month, Steve Larson & Alain Comeau freed the first pitch, and the start of the second.

John Strand on the first ascent of Unwanted Guests (5.12b) in 1988. Photograph by Karl Mallman.

UNWANTED GUESTS I 5.12b (******)
Excellent climbing up the improbable slab 20 feet left of FUTURE SHOCK.
1. Face climb up past three bolts (5.11d), then traverse right past a fourth bolt (5.12b) to join FUTURE SHOCK. Belay at its bolt anchor. 85', 5.12b

HISTORY: The route was drilled free on the lead in one day, with the first ascent completed by Karl Mallman, John Strand, & Elaine Aliberti in September, 1988. On his first attempt, Strand climbed all the way to the dike on FUTURE SHOCK, but fell, taking a 45 foot swing. Mallmen then drilled the final fourth bolt and finished the lead.

VARIATION: SHOCK THERAPY I 5.12d (Top-rope)
1a. Face climb straight up (5.12d) from the third bolt on UNWANTED GUESTS straight up to the FUTURE SHOCK double bolt anchor. 5.12d
FA: Gerry Lortie & Tim Kemple October 29, 1994

ANSWERED PRAYERS I 5.12c (******)
The unlikely steep slab just right of AIWASS's second pitch. Better be religious!
1. Climb partway up Pitch one of AIWASS to a small roof on the right. Undercling and mantleshelf (bolt) onto a stance, then face climb past two bolts (5.12c) to the base of an exfoliation flake/crack. Climb the flake, head over a bulge to a stance, and finish past two more bolts to a tree. 140', 5.12c

HISTORY: Bill Lowther, Ozzie Blumet, & Mark Lynch did the first ascent on October 14, 1992. All bolts were placed free on the lead, but they were unable to free all the moves. A week later, Bill Lowther & Mark Lynch made the first free ascent, taking several falls. Along with UNWANTED GUESTS, this is one of the area's hardest slab routes where all the bolts were placed free on the lead.

AIWASS III 5.11d or 5.12a (*)

Now entirely free, this was one of the first full length climbs on the South Buttress. To the left of FUTURE SHOCK is the 50 foot high ETHEREAL CRACK Buttress, home to several very popular climbs. AIWASS climbs the right side of this same buttress, then follows an intricate line to the ledge's top.

1. Climb the easy right side of the buttress to a tree beside a flake.

2. Make extreme face and smearing moves to the right past two bolts (5.12a) to reach the AIWASS flake (5.8) which is climbed to a tree ledge. 80', 5.12a

2a. Starting farther right, face climb past a bolt to a hidden pocket (5.11d), and merge with the AIWASS flake above. 5.11d

3–4. Two pitches (5.5 & 5.6) climb easy slabs and the 30 foot ECHO corner to a large, tree-covered ledge below a bulge. 5.5 & 5.6

5. The original line climbs a 5.8 blocky bulge and inside corner on the left. A better way is to climb the short, 5.8+ corner/groove on the right (small wired nuts helpful) onto a huge, sloping ledge. 75', 5.8 or 5.8+

6. Bold moves up a steep overlap (5.10d; bolt) lead to a hidden hold. Overcome another bulge (5.10a) to a belay (pin) on the left. 5.10d

7. Finish up and right, or make three long, two rope rappels back to the ground.

HISTORY: Paul Ross, Rosie Andrews, & John Porter did the first ascent on June 21, 1972. After repeated tries, Jim Dunn freed Pitch two in 1979, using the 5.11d right-hand variation. In July, 1983, in a landmark event in local friction climbing, John Strand freed the original Pitch two aid line. Tom Callaghan & John Strand made the entire route's first free ascent on August 3, 1983.

VARIATION: **THE AFTERMATH** II 5.10b

If you get lost, just keep going! An obscure variation up corners right of the last pitches of AIWASS. At the top of Pitch five, traverse right on easy ledges through oak trees for about 45 feet to a right-facing, zebra-striped corner.

6a. Climb the corner and move right around a block to a horizontal crack. 5.7

7a. Layback up a small, narrow corner (5.10b) on the left. 40', 5.10b

8a. Walk off right to a dirty finish, or rappel off with two ropes.

FA: Lonnie Smith & Peter Beal September 2, 1980

THE ETHEREAL CRACK BUTTRESS

The following collection of one pitch climbs is located on the 50 foot high, detached flake between the starts of AIWASS and BEELZEBUB. These routes are extremely popular, both on the lead and as top-rope problems. They are now described from right to left:

WEBSTER'S WORKOUT I 5.11b (Top-rope)
1. Just to the right of SEVENTH SEAL, climb up the smooth face (5.11b) and brown water streak to a short, vertical crack. 40', 5.11b
FA: Ed Webster, top-rope Summer, 1980

SEVENTH SEAL I 5.10a (***)
An old favorite, the low-angled, thin finger crack located just to the right of ETHEREAL CRACK. Carry a variety of wired nuts and small cams.
1. Climb the vertical, right-hand finger crack. 50', 5.10a
HISTORY: Alain Comeau, Gene Vallee, Ed Sklar, Al Rubin, Jeff Butterfield, Paul Niland, & John Rilley teamed up to make the first ascent of this popular classic in June, 1976.

DUNN'S DIVERSION I 5.11b X
The very blank face between ETHEREAL CRACK and SEVENTH SEAL.
1. Up the smooth face, trending right, joining SEVENTH SEAL. 50', 5.11b X
HISTORY: Most people will be content with a well anchored top-rope on this route, as was Jim Dunn who made the climb's first ascent in the Spring of 1980. Pushing the limits of the leadable, John Bouchard made the first "sharp end" ascent in the Autumn of 1983, using pointed skyhooks and air voyagers for protection.

ETHEREAL CRACK I 5.10d (or 5.11a) (***)
A short classic of the area, ETHEREAL CRACK is the left-hand and harder of the two finger cracks on the buttress. Carry many wired nuts.
1. Traverse left across a narrow ledge to reach the crack. After a hard move to start (5.10d), finger jam up the thin crack to a horizontal break, and escape right. At the top of the crack, you can also finish left (5.11a), utilizing a tiny solution pocket. 50', 5.10d (or 5.11a)
HISTORY: After previous attempts that same day by Joe Lentini & Bryan Delaney who discovered the climb (and a memorable leaderfall by Lentini), Ed Webster & Bryan Becker made the first ascent on June 22, 1975, using the harder, left-hand finish. On the second ascent, Michael Hartrich exited right.

UP ROPE I 5.11d (*)
Climbs the entire height of the steep wall just to the left of ETHEREAL CRACK. Begin at the base of the bottom headwall, 15 feet right of PERSONA. Double ropes recommended. Care is needed when clipping the second bolt.
1. Face climb past three bolts (5.11d crux after first bolt) up to a flake that gains the base of the upper, lower angled slab. Continue past two more bolts (5.10d) to the top of the buttress. 65', 5.11d
HISTORY: Bill Lowther & Ozzie Blumet made the first ascent in December, 1992, placing all the bolts (except the second one) free on the lead.

WHITEHORSE LEDGE - SOUTH BUTTRESS (ETHEREAL CRACK) 267

Joe Lentini climbing the crux of Ethereal Crack (5.10d) in 1975.
Photograph by Ed Webster.

268 THE MOUNT WASHINGTON VALLEY

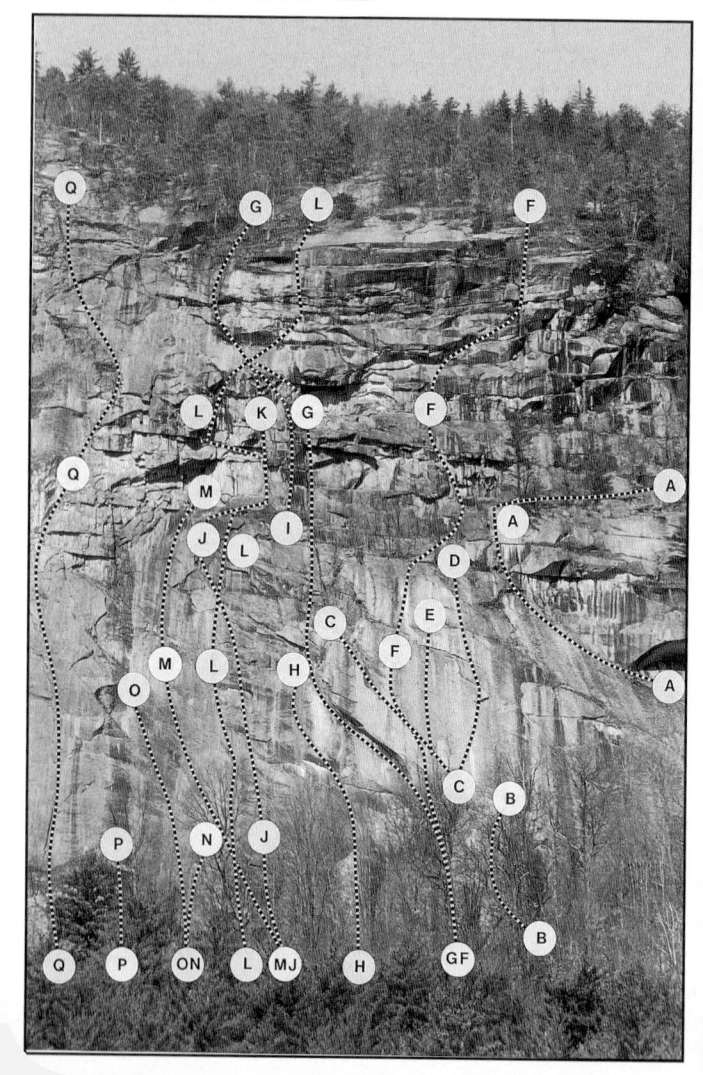

WHITEHORSE LEDGE – SOUTH BUTTRESS
(ETHEREAL CRACK to THE ELIMINATE)

A.	*	**ECHO** II 5.5	Page	262
B.	***	**ETHEREAL CRACK**	Page	266
		I 5.10d or 5.11a		
C.	***	**LOOSE LIPS** I 5.10a	Page	271
D.	**	**BITS & PIECES** I 5.11b R	Page	271
E.	**	**SWINGING HIPS** I 5.10d	Page	272
F.	*	**THE ANTICHRIST** III 5.12a	Page	272
G.		**BEELZEBUB** III 5.10c	Page	273
H.	**	**REVOLT OF THE DIKE**	Page	273
		BRIGADE II 5.11a (5.9+ R)		
I.	*	**CINNEREA** II 5.11a	Page	273
J.	***	**CHILDREN'S CRUSADE**	Page	276
		II 5.9		
K.	***	**THE DIRECT FINISH**	Page	276
		to **CHILDREN'S CRUSADE**		
		III 5.11a		
L.	***	**TOTAL RECALL** III 5.11b	Page	278
M.	*	**PROBLEM CHILD** II 5.10d R	Page	279
N.	*	**CRUSADE OF THE LIGHT**	Page	279
		BRIGADE I 5.11b		
O.	*	**OBJECTS ARE CLOSER**	Page	279
		(THAN THEY APPEAR)		

270 THE MOUNT WASHINGTON VALLEY

Dennis Goode on Loose Lips (5.10a) in 1995. Photograph by Joe Lentini.

FROG HAIRS I 5.10d R
This seldom if ever repeated, seriously unprotected face climb starts on the ground between UP ROPE and PERSONA. Protection at the seam, hopefully.
1. Climb up the steep, blank face (5.10d R) to a thin, vertical seam. 50', 5.10d R
FA: Lonnie Smith & partner 1981

PERSONA I 5.9+ (*)
Just to the right of THE BEELZEBUB CORNER is a nice arete.
1. Climb the face 10 feet to the right of the corner to gain the bottom of a thin, vertical finger crack leading up the arete. Climb the arete to the tree ledge above. 60', 5.9+ (If you use the tree, the route's only about 5.8.)
FA: Mack Johnson & Kurt Winkler June 3, 1979

THE BEELZEBUB CORNER I 5.4 (**)
One of the area's better one pitch 5.4s. Safe, fun, and quite popular.
1. The left-facing dihedral up the left side of the ETHEREAL Buttress. 60', 5.4
FA: Unknown.

LOOSE LIPS I 5.10a (***)
Sink ships—or is it just new routes? This unusually scenic pitch is often linked with one of the lower cracks on the ETHEREAL CRACK Buttress for a longer adventure. Above the bolt-protected crux, wired nuts protect the upper flake. The climb has several strange (but fun) moves on it, especially getting started!
1. Climb any of the previous routes to the top of the buttress. 60'
2. Stem across the top of the large flake, then face climb past three bolts (5.10a) onto a narrow ledge. Balance traverse left across the ledge to a thin, spectacular, and exposed flake system which is laybacked and jammed to a stance on the left with a double bolt belay/rappel anchor. 90', 5.10a Rappel off.
HISTORY: In August, 1979, an "accidentally overheard" conversation encouraged Jim Dunn, Martha Morris, & Ken Sims to race up the first ascent of this route, only to be caught red-handed stealing the climb—and joined just in time—by Alain Comeau who'd originally spotted the line.

BITS & PIECES I 5.11b R (**)
If you fall, that'll be all that's left. Actually, the falls are long and clean. Both BITS & PIECES and SWINGING HIPS ascend the superb, steep face to the right of LOOSE LIPS. Carry several Friends.
1. Climb to the top of the ETHEREAL CRACK Buttress. 60'
2. Warm up on the crux of LOOSE LIPS (5.10a) to a stance, then step right past a bolt onto the steep upper slab. Sustained face moves (5.11b R) lead to a minimal stance and a second bolt. Move over a small roof to a belay stance with a double bolt anchor below a steep wall. 80', 5.11b R
3. Easier climbing leads straight up (piton; 5.9) to the tree ledge above. 70', 5.9

HISTORY: Tom Callaghan & John Strand made the first ascent in epic fashion on September 9, 1984. All the bolts were placed on the lead in excellent style—with three hours of continuous drilling and three broken drill bits required to get in the second bolt!

SWINGING HIPS I 5.10d (**)
A little bit easier and safer than its neighbor. Dance up the nearly invisible dike to the left of BITS & PIECES.
1. Climb any route to the top of the ETHEREAL CRACK Buttress. 60'
2. After the crux of LOOSE LIPS (5.10a), traverse left 25 feet, then face climb with difficulty (5.10d) up a very faint, left-leaning dike past three bolts. 5.10d

FA: Jim Ewing & Larry Hamilton   July 14, 1985

THE ANTICHRIST III 5.12a (5.9 R) (*)
A new, difficult, full length route up the South Buttress. Although the climb does indeed cross over LOOSE LIPS, none of its bolts interfere with that route.
1. Climb THE BEELZEBUB CORNER to the tree ledge. 60', 5.4
2. Move up the slab left of BEELZEBUB's second pitch (bolt), then step up to a stance on the right (bolt). Traverse right on narrow ledges to reach the overhanging edge (5.12a) which is surmounted to gain the face above (bolt). Join the LOOSE LIPS crack for 30 feet to a good stance (possible belay to reduce rope drag), then face climb straight up past two bolts to a shallow, left-facing corner (piton), finishing up and right to a two bolt belay/rappel station. 150', 5.12a
3. Slab climb up a white streak (bolt) to trees. 80', 5.6 R
4. Scramble up to the ECHO corner. Climb the slab just left of the corner to a left-leaning, black overlap/flake with two bolts. Follow cracks to the left (pin), then make an awkward step onto a ledge, clipping a bolt above. Face climb past a bolt and two pitons, move up and left, and belay at a bolt and Friends. 130', 5.11d (You can escape right here, if desired, onto a large traverse ledge.)
5. Up sharp holds just right of the belay onto a ledge, and move left past two bolts to an awkward mantle (5.11d). Continue past a poor bolt (5.12a) to a roof traverse, underclinging right to a belay on AIWASS at a pin & horn. 80', 5.12a
6. Move left to a block and ledge, then with a piton at your feet, climb over an unprotected 5.9 bulge up and right to an easy wide crack and the top. 100', 5.9 R

HISTORY: In October, 1991, Bill Lowther rope-soloed the first ascent of the first four pitches, using some aid, and placing most of the bolts free on the lead. Bill Lowther & Ozzie Blumet made the route's first complete ascent in May, 1992. Only the third bolt on Pitch two was placed on rappel. As Lowther explained, "I couldn't believe that local climbers were trying to destroy a traditionally climbed, ground-up route, so I transgressed on that one bolt." On April 30, 1994, Gerry Lortie with Bill Lowther made the first free ascent of the entire route, free climbing the one aid point originally used on Pitch five.

BEELZEBUB III 5.10c

A difficult full length route, seldom if ever repeated. Unfortunately, the large, left-leaning arch on the second pitch is often wet.

1. Climb the enjoyable BEELZEBUB CORNER (5.4) up the left side of the ETHEREAL CRACK Buttress to a comfortable tree ledge on top. 60', 5.4
2. Layback and jam your way up the large, left-curving arch (5.9+) above to the double bolt belay on LOOSE LIPS. 100', 5.9+
3. Bypass a large flake on the left and climb easily to the large, tree-covered ledge beneath the massive, final overhangs.
4. Ascend the large, right-facing corner (the dihedral right of CHILDREN'S CRUSADE DIRECT FINISH), and belay on a ledge 60 feet up beneath a roof.
5. Very exposed. First move up 20 feet, head down a bit, traverse left 10 feet, and reach a sloping ledge with a two bolt anchor (shared with THE DIRECT FINISH to CHILDREN'S CRUSADE) beneath the upper slabs. 5.10b
6. Make a hard 5.10c face move up to a stance, traverse easily left, then follow a dike to a large flake, and belay here. 5.10c
7. Climb cracks up to a tree, and aim for the top.

HISTORY: One of the oldest South Buttress routes, Paul Ross, Hugh Thompson, & Rick Wilcox did the first ascent on June 13, 1972. Henry Barber, Bob Anderson, John Bragg, & Al Rubin made the first free ascent on August 24, 1973. Barber dislocated his shoulder while leading Pitch five through the upper ceilings, making for an epic, painful finish.

VARIATION #1: BOY'S BRIGADE I 5.9

1. Climb the shallow flake just left of THE BEELZEBUB CORNER. 60', 5.9
FA: Doug Madara, David Stone, & Alain Comeau   October, 1981

VARIATION #2: CINNEREA II 5.11a (*)

Climbs the overhangs between BEELZEBUB and CHILDREN'S CRUSADE DIRECT FINISH. Start on the traverse ledge at slings right of the latter route.

1. Climb up a series of ledges past a hidden piton and two bolts (5.10b). Continue straight up cracks to a slanting ledge, move left past two more bolts in white rock, and climb through an overhang (5.11a) to the CHILDREN'S CRUSADE DIRECT FINISH double bolt belay above the lip. 140', 5.11a

HISTORY: Bill Lowther & John Pollard made the first ascent on September 15, 1991, placing all the bolts free on the lead. Cinnerea, a flower, was the name of Bill's daughter Carey's cat.

REVOLT OF THE DIKE BRIGADE II 5.11a (5.9+ R) (**)

Improbable face climbing of high quality. Just to the left of BEELZEBUB are several flakes on a short, vertical wall. Carry a modern rack.

1. Difficult face climbing (5.9+ R) up flakes (two original pitons are missing) leads past two bolts to a small belay stance by a tree (peg). 50', 5.9+ R

274 THE MOUNT WASHINGTON VALLEY

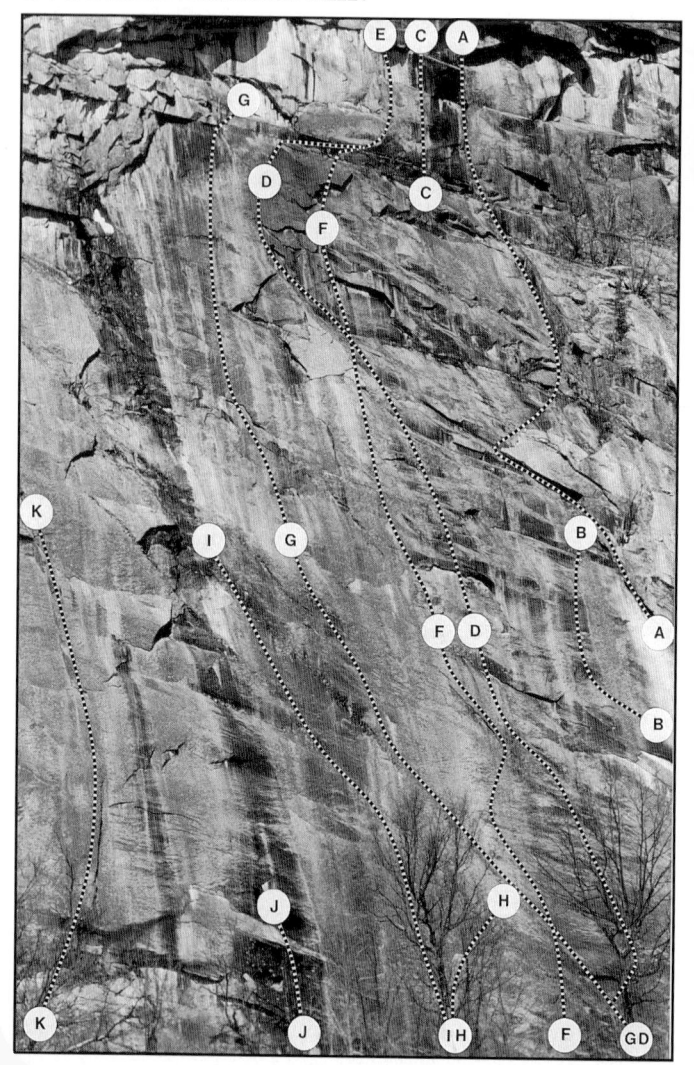

WHITEHORSE LEDGE – SOUTH BUTTRESS (CHILDREN'S CRUSADE Area)

A.		**BEELZEBUB** III 5.10c	Page	273
B.	**	**REVOLT OF THE DIKE BRIGADE** II 5.11a (5.9+ R)	Page	273
C.	*	**CINNEREA** II 5.11a	Page	273
D.	***	**CHILDREN'S CRUSADE** II 5.9	Page	276
E.	***	**THE DIRECT FINISH to CHILDREN'S CRUSADE** III 5.11a	Page	276
F.	***	**TOTAL RECALL** III 5.11b	Page	278
G.	*	**PROBLEM CHILD** II 5.10d R	Page	279
H.	*	**CRUSADE OF THE LIGHT BRIGADE** I 5.11b	Page	279
I.	*	**OBJECTS ARE CLOSER (THAN THEY APPEAR)** I 5.12b	Page	279
J.	*	**DRESS RIGHT** I 5.11b	Page	280
K.	***	**THE ELIMINATE** IV 5.11c (5.8 R)	Page	280

2. Ascend a rising dike past two pitons to an unlikely looking, large overlap on the right. Undercling and mantleshelf (5.10d), then two bolts protect the crux traverse left (5.11a) on thin friction to face climbing up and right past two more bolts to join BEELZEBUB. 5.11a Descend from the LOOSE LIPS double bolt rappel station with two ropes.

HISTORY: Ed Webster & Susan Patenaude made the first ascent on July 10 & 11, 1980. All fixed protection was placed free on the lead.

VARIATION: **NOBLE INTENTIONS** I 5.10b R or X

The short, steep bolted face just to the left to Pitch one of DIKE BRIGADE.

1. Face climb past two bolts to a poor cam (5.10b R or X; groundfall potential), and finish past one more bolt to the DIKE BRIGADE belay. 50', 5.10b R or X

FA: Chris Gill & Chris Noonan   October, 1991

CHILDREN'S CRUSADE   II   5.9   (***)
with THE DIRECT FINISH   III 5.11a (***)

One of the most elegant and popular South Buttress routes, this was the climb that removed the psychological barrier from many similar, high angle, bolt-protected, face climbs in the area. A tremendous adventure. The route ascends the faint, vertical dike up the center of the steep wall to the left of the ETHEREAL CRACK Buttress. THE DIRECT FINISH to CHILDREN'S CRUSADE breaks through the final overhangs up a vertical dihedral in an outlandish position. Superb rock, climbing, and protection.

1. Scramble up a left-trending dike (ERADICATE) to a small overlap (piton in a hole). Traverse right (5.9) to gain the main dike which is climbed (bolts; memorable 5.9) to a stance on the left with a double bolt anchor. 130', 5.9

2. A bolt protects a 5.9 move to an overlap, which is climbed on the left. Easier moves lead past a peg, over small ceilings on sharp holds, then continue straight up to a sloping belay ledge with a two bolt anchor. 100', 5.9

3. Climb a crack on the left to 5.8 face moves up a slab to gain a long traverse ledge and a convenient, double bolt anchor. The left-facing corner system in the overlaps to your right is the line of THE DIRECT FINISH (5.11a). If you choose to rappel off, traverse right across the ledge to a big tree ledge, and make two rappels with two ropes to reach the ground. The first rappel is off a tree, the second is from the LOOSE LIPS double bolt rappel station.

THE DIRECT FINISH to CHILDREN'S CRUSADE III 5.11a (***)

4. From the middle of the traverse ledge under the final overhangs, climb up a shallow, left-facing corner to a small overhang, then step right to a rest. Stem and layback up the strenuous dihedral above (5.11a) past some fixed protection to the crest of the overhangs, and an exit left (very exposed) onto a sloping belay ledge with a double bolt belay/rappel anchor. 90'. 5.11a

5. After a thin 5.10c move, wander through the easier, final overlaps. 5.10c

WHITEHORSE LEDGE - SOUTH BUTTRESS (CHILDREN'S CRUSADE) 277

Ed Webster climbing Pitch one of Children's Crusade (5.9) in 1981. Photograph by Anne Rutter.

HISTORY: Alain Comeau & Mike Heintz made the historic first ascent of the first three pitches of CHILDREN'S CRUSADE in November, 1978, drilling the bolts on the lead. Ed Webster & Susan Patenaude added THE DIRECT FINISH on July 24, 1980. A bolt and a piton were placed on aid on the crux.

VARIATION: SIDEWINDER I 5.10d
For an even more sustained route, climb the steep, difficult face to the left of Pitch two of CHILDREN'S CRUSADE.
2a. Diagonal left to a flake, then continue across the steep, unprotected face to a rest ledge (bolt). Go straight up, then angle right to a steep wall (5.10d) with another bolt. Merge back right onto CHILDREN'S CRUSADE. 5.10d
FA: Alain Comeau & Mike Heintz   November, 1978

TOTAL RECALL III 5.11b (***)
Taking a futuristic line up the invisible vertical dike immediately to the left of CHILDREN'S CRUSADE, this challenging route then wanders through the dramatic, upper ceilings—the ERADICATE roofs. Highly recommended, with superb rock, incredible positions, and good protection.
1. Start as for CHILDREN'S CRUSADE and walk left across a sidewalk to a flake with two pitons (5.10d). Face climb up and right across the ERADICATE Dike, then follow a faint, left-slanting dike with very sustained climbing on small, square-cut edges past five bolts (5.11b at the fourth bolt), eventually moving right to the CHILDREN'S CRUSADE double bolt belay. 100', 5.11b
2. Step left past two bolts on SIDEWINDER (5.10a at the second bolt), then head straight up to a slab, trending left to a bulge (5.9; bolt). Finish straight up, rejoining CHILDREN'S CRUSADE at the next two bolt anchor. 100', 5.10a
3. Climb straight up above the left-hand belay bolt to a right-curving arch, and pull over the small overlap at a thin, vertical finger crack (5.10b). Belay at the foot of THE DIRECT FINISH to CHILDREN'S CRUSADE. 60', 5.10b
4. Do the first 40 feet of CHILDREN'S CRUSADE DIRECT FINISH. At the roof (pin), traverse left, underclinging past a bolt to a hanging belay (KB & bolt) at the end of a 30 foot traverse. 70', 5.10b (Belay before the next overlap.)
5. Pull past an overlap above the belay onto a slab, then move up past a hanging block (The Dong; bolt) and through an overhang (5.11a; fixed nut & piton). Continue up a huge, right-facing corner, up and right to a big ledge. 60', 5.11a
6. Climb to your right up a slab (bolt), move farther to the right crossing over THE DIRECT FINISH to CHILDREN'S CRUSADE (pin), and carry on right, finally climbing past a right-facing corner/overlap onto a large terrace. Finish up a vertical dike, cranking out a wild overlap (5.10a; bolt). 140', 5.10a You can rappel the entire route with two ropes, starting from the large pine at the top of Pitch six by making four long rappels down CHILDREN'S CRUSADE.
HISTORY: Brad White & Ian Cruickshank made the first ascent of the route, after five previous attempts, in October, 1990.

ERADICATE III 5.7 R, A3
The route finishes the South Buttress's oldest route, originally called DIKE TRAVERSE, which for many years was the only climb on the entire buttress!

WHITEHORSE LEDGE - SOUTH BUTTRESS (TOTAL RECALL)

Spectacular nailing through the upper roofs. Carry KBs, blades, and pegs to two inches. Seldom repeated.

1 & 2. Face climb up the prominent, left-leaning dike (5.7 R) to the left of BEELZEBUB for two leads to a big tree on the left. 5.7 R

3. Ascend a right-facing corner to a sloping belay ledge. 80'

4. Aid the obvious dihedral on the right, then nail (A3) through the wild upper roofs past bolts. Fixed anchors. 150', A3

5. Climb a slab straight up to a dike, over a steep wall, to the trees.

HISTORY: The climb's first two pitches, described in Joe Cote's 1969 guidebook as DIKE TRAVERSE, are quite old. Jeff Pheasant completed the climb, rope-solo, in April, 1976.

PROBLEM CHILD II 5.10d R (*)

Similar to CHILDREN'S CRUSADE, on good holds, but a bit more runout. Bring a modern rack and double ropes. A peg is missing on the crux.

1. Climb the ERADICATE Dike to a belay at a bolt. 130', 5.7

2. A hidden pin protects face climbing over a bulge (bolt). Make thin moves left to a good ledge with three bolts. 80', 5.9-

3. Climb up and left (peg), then follow a series of flakes straight up to the base of a prominent slab (bolt). A peg on the left (needs to be replaced) protects a runout up a slight rib in the slab's center (5.10d R). Another pin and an overlap (care needed of loose blocks) mark the finish. Exit right to trees. 110', 5.10d R Rappel the route with two ropes, to the three bolt belay and to the ground.

FA: Tom Callaghan, John Strand, & Steve Angelini September 24, 1986

DIRECT START: CRUSADE OF THE LIGHT BRIGADE I 5.11b (*)

Start 30 feet to the left of the ERADICATE Dike.

1. Climb a short slab to a bolt on a bulge. A hard dynamic move (5.11b) leads to a poor piton. Handtraverse right (scary) to a bolt, then face climb straight up (5.11a) to a piton belay just below ERADICATE. 70', 5.11b

HISTORY: Ed Webster & Kurt Winkler did the 5.11 lunge in May, 1982. Steve Angelini, Tom Callaghan, & John Strand finished the route in July, 1984.

OBJECTS ARE CLOSER (THAN THEY APPEAR) I 5.12b (*)

Watch your Rear View! A sustained face pitch with many hard moves in a row. Start up CRUSADE OF THE LIGHT BRIGADE. Trick move on the crux.

1. Climb the first section of LIGHT BRIGADE past the 5.11b lunge to reach a shallow, right-facing corner with a knifeblade. Continue up and left to a hidden pocket (Tri-cam placement), mantleshelf, step left, then face climb straight up past bolt protection (5.12b) on very sustained moves to a double bolt anchor on the ERADICATE Dike. 140', 5.12b

HISTORY: After placing the protection bolts on the lead, on aid, Chris Gill & Nick Yardley made the first ascent in June, 1989.

DRESS RIGHT I 5.11b (*)
A good short route. Carry small wired nuts. Start 30 feet to the right of THE JAWS OF DOOM below an obvious black water streak.

1. Climb a right-facing flake to an improbable overlap move (bolt; 5.11b). Gain a detached flake, step right, climb a corner, then mantle onto a ledge. Belay at a double bolt anchor. 40', 5.11b Rappel off.

FA: Tom Callaghan & Haydie Callaghan September, 1990

THE JAWS OF DOOM I 5.7
To the left of CHILDREN'S CRUSADE and ERADICATE is a large and often wet, right-facing corner: THE JAWS OF DOOM.

1. Climb up and right, finishing up a bomb bay chimney. 5.7

HISTORY: Paul Boissonneault & Steve Larson did the first ascent on January 3, 1979 on their first winter ascent of THE ELIMINATE, and rated the route 5.7, A2. George Hurley & Chris Gill freed it (at 5.7!) on September 21, 1984.

THE ELIMINATE IV 5.11c (5.8 R) (***)
The first complete route up the South Buttress is currently one of the hardest long free routes on Whitehorse. Double ropes are helpful and bring a modern rack. There are three possible finishes, with FIRING ALL EIGHT being the most direct, best protected, and on secure rock. Starting just to the left of THE JAWS OF DOOM chimney, the first pitch ascends the 5.6 ledges which form the access route for all routes on the WONDER WALL and farther left.

1. Make tricky moves off the ground (5.6) up a 10 foot corner to easy ledges on the left. Scramble up right to a tree belay at a steep, right-facing corner. 60', 5.6

2. Stem off a tree, then two bolts protect moves up into a narrow, right-facing corner. Stem up the corner, layback up the left arete (5.11c), then step back right into the dihedral. When the corner fades, face climb over a bulge (bolt) to a ledge and traverse left 20 feet to a scary mantle (5.8 R) onto a narrow shelf. Walk 20 feet back right to a ledge with a fixed piton anchor. 80', 5.11c (5.8 R)

3. Jam up a prominent, left-facing corner (5.10d) to bushy ledges below the upper headwall. From the corner's top, move right 40 feet on a ledge (bushes) to a double bolt anchor 10 feet left of the 3 CYLINDERS corner. 140', 5.10d

FIRING ALL EIGHT I 5.10d (Complete Route: IV 5.11c / 5.8 R) (***)
Very straight, direct—and always dry—this finish makes THE ELIMINATE a truly classic free climb. Well protected with a modern rack. Blast away!

4. Step left to a large overhang (piton), make hard undercling moves (5.10d) to bucket flakes over the lip—and pull the overhang, moving left again to an obvious crack left of a large flake. Climb the flake (5.10b) to a peg on the left, step up and right, then balance traverse back left under a small roof. Step left again, and make difficult layback moves up a very shallow, right-facing corner to a double ring bolt anchor at a stance. 60', 5.10d

WHITEHORSE LEDGE - SOUTH BUTTRESS (THE ELIMINATE) 281

5. Start with difficulty (peg; 5.10c) up to a ledge, then traverse right (bolt; 5.10d), making exciting moves above the void at the lip of a large overlap into a large, left-facing corner (5.9), protected by four fixed pins. At the corner's top, step 15 feet right, and pull past an overlap to another double ring bolt anchor on a large ledge. 140', 5.10d Rappel off with two 50 meter ropes, or...

6. Finish up a lower angled face, moving up and left over a short headwall up a right-facing, corner/crack (5.8) to reach the woods and the top. 150', 5.8

HISTORY: Paul Ross, Frank Dean, & Marty Bowin made the first ascent of this long, difficult route on September 19, 1971. In May, 1978, Doug Madara & Mark Richey free climbed Pitches two and three. Paul Boissonneault & Felix Modugno added the 3 CYLINDERS Dihedral Variation in October, 1982. Later that month, Doug Madara & Mark Richey freed the original aid line using just three points of aid. After getting benighted on a prior attempt, Neil Cannon free climbed the entire route (but not via the complete, original Pitch four aid line)—up CANNON FIRE—with Jerry Handren in the Autumn of 1984. Brad White & Ian Cruickshank added FIRING ALL EIGHT, the now standard finish, on September 6, 1996.

FINISH #1: 3 CYLINDERS I 5.9+ (Complete Route: IV 5.11c / 5.8 R) (******)
A two pitch variation finish up a dihedral, but unfortunately, the corner is often wet. Start at the double bolt anchor at the beginning of FIRING ALL EIGHT.

4a. Step right, then climb up a short, left-facing corner. After eight feet, the corner switches direction to become a more prominent right-facing dihedral. Belay 50 feet higher on a stance with a two bolt anchor. 60', 5.9

5a. Make an exciting, exposed balance traverse left (5.9+) across a foot ledge to the two ring bolts at the top of THE ELIMINATE's fourth pitch. 40', 5.9+

FINISH #2: CANNON FIRE I 512a (5.10b R)
Poor protection, old gear, and extreme moves—an attractive combination!

4. Belay at an old ring peg at blocks below the steep upper headwall. Climb blocky rock 25 feet to a prominent roof. Protect here, step down, then move left (5.10b R), making a hard mantleshelf onto a sloping ledge. Continue up a right-facing arch past two fixed pins, face climbing (5.12a) to another mantle onto a stance with a double ring bolt anchor. 90', 5.12a (5.10b R)

> There are several one pitch climbs along the base of the next section of the cliff. ELIMINATE DIRECT is the first of this short, yet very challenging genre.

ELIMINATE DIRECT I 5.10d (*)
This short direct start, frequently climbed as a route in itself, ascends the shallow, right-facing corner between THE JAWS OF DOOM and the 5.6 access ledges normal start of THE ELIMINATE.

1. Climb up the corner. When it ends at a small overhang, make tricky moves (5.10d) up onto THE ELIMINATE access ledge. 40', 5.10d
FA: Jeff Butterfield & Gene Vallee July 8, 1979

CAUSE FOR CONCERN I 5.12a
Especially if the peg comes out... Start at the base of the arete just to the left of ELIMINATE DIRECT. Carry a modern rack.
1. Climb the arete, move out left onto the face past horizontal breaks, and crank past a fixed pin (5.12a) up to the traverse ledge. Tree belay. 40', 5.12a
FA: Peter Beal with Kris Hansen April, 1990

HEAD CEMENT I 5.10d R (*)
Very popular, especially if you're into fly fishing. Scamper up onto the access ledge (5.6) at the base of THE ELIMINATE, or climb ELIMINATE DIRECT for a harder start. HEAD CEMENT begins 30 feet to the left of THE ELIMINATE's second pitch. Normal rack—plus a skyhook!
1. After a hard move off the ledge (protectable with a hook), climb up and right, then back left to a stance (bolt). Climb up to weird, nut/piton protection, mantleshelf to reach a second bolt, use a crack on the left to reach a third bolt, and then mantle again, finally onto a good ledge. A final bolt protects a traverse left to a tree belay on SOUTH BUTTRESS DIRECT. 45', 5.10d R
HISTORY: Chris Gill & Kurt Winkler made the first ascent on May 19, 1984. Protection was put in on the lead, with the second and third bolts placed with tension from a hook and a knifeblade. The ropes were pulled after every attempt.

WHIP FINISH I 5.11b (**)
An excellent and popular route that starts 20 feet to the left of HEAD CEMENT. There are two cruxes: at the first bolt—and mantling up onto the sloping ledge at the top!
1. Face climb straight up, then move up and right past bolt protection (5.11b), finally mantling onto a sloping ledge on the left, which has a double bolt belay/rappel anchor. 45', 5.11b
FA: Chris Gill & Patty Wespiser September, 1990

VARIATION: **PORTLAND CEMENT** I 5.10d (*)
The concrete finish to HEAD CEMENT and the best way to complete that route. Beware of bafflingly hard face moves!
2a. Climb HEAD CEMENT to the top ledge and a bolt. Place nuts in a flake, then make a hard mantle move onto the ledge above. Clip another bolt, do a frustratingly hard face move (5.10d) on tiny edges to reach better holds, and mantle up to THE ELIMINATE belay. 25', 5.10d
FA: Rob Adair & Dan Hutchens November 1, 1987

WHITEHORSE LEDGE - SOUTH BUTTRESS (LONDON CALLING) 283

LONDON CALLING I 5.12b (**))
Walk left along THE ELIMINATE traverse ledge to reach this popular, although very awkward, sport route. Start 30 feet to the left of Pitch two of SOUTH BUTTRESS DIRECT below a steep, vertical wall.
1. Face climb up a left-angling series of holds past a total of five bolts (5.12b) and a narrow overlap to a ledge with a double bolt anchor. 80', 5.12b
HISTORY: After cleaning and placing the bolts on rappel, Jim Surette made the first ascent after two days of effort on March 23, 1986.

Jim Surette on the first ascent of London Calling (5.12b) in 1986.
Photograph by S. Peter Lewis.

CURE FOR THE BLUES I 5.10d (*)
Judging from the severity of the moves, more like the cause for the blues! Just left of ELIMINATE DIRECT, a semi-circular flake appears glued to the wall.
1. Undercling the flake up to more holds, handtraverse right, then make a hard technical move (5.10d) over the top to a ledge. 5.10d
FA: Doug Madara & Kurt Winkler September 28, 1980

TREACH CRACK I 5.10b (To-Reach-The-Crack?)
1. Above the access ledges at the start of THE ELIMINATE is a short, vertical finger crack. After hard moves (5.10b) to gain the crack, climb it. 5.10b
HISTORY: Doug Madara & Kurt Winkler did the first ascent on September 28, 1980, naming the climb Birch Tree Crack. The tree later disappeared. TREACH CRACK was Winkler's original route name.

BEGINNER'S BLESSING I 5.4 (*)
A good introductory lead, fun, and well protected.
1. Climb the first crack to the left of Pitch one of THE ELIMINATE. There is a birch just off the ground, and another tree higher. 80', 5.4 Rappel from trees.
FA: Unknown.

THE GUNSLINGER II 5.12a (*)
The crux of this challenging route ascends the beautiful white streak up the steep face immediately right of Pitch three of SOUTH BUTTRESS DIRECT.
1. Start up BEGINNER'S BLESSING. 80', 5.4
2. Climb the 5.10a flake on SOUTH BUTTRESS DIRECT (piton) to a good stance, traverse along the ledge (which narrows considerably) to the right, then climb the top section of WHIP FINISH (5.11c) traversing right past several bolts up to a ledge. Traverse easily back left along the ledge, and belay on SOUTH BUTTRESS DIRECT at a double bolt anchor. 85', 5.11c
3. Gain the smooth slab on the left, then face climb past five bolts (5.11c) to a large stance. Next move right past a bolt (5.12a) to a pocket and a small stance (bolt), then continue up past a small roof and corner (piton), moving left onto the LAST UNICORN traverse ledge. Belay at a piton & bolt anchor 25 feet to the right of the start of THE LAST UNICORN. 150', 5.12a
4. Climb up past bushes and broken rock onto a ledge. A 5.9 flake on the left (piton) gains a higher ledge. Now traverse right and climb a steep, unusual, gently overhanging wall (5.12a) on hidden pockets past seven bolts. The pitch (and the climb) ends at a hanging belay at a double bolt anchor. 60', 5.12a
HISTORY: Bill Lowther rope-soloed the first ascent of Pitch four, with aid, in August, 1993. Bill Lowther & Gerry Lortie added the third pitch on April 23, 1994, placing the bolts on the lead, two free, three on aid. After several attempts, Lowther & Lortie free climbed the route on May 22, 1994.

WHITEHORSE LEDGE - THE SOUTH BUTTRESS (THREE SAINTS)

WAITING FOR WEBSTER I 5.9 X

To the left of BEGINNER'S BLESSING is a steep face sprinkled with a few sharp holds—but virtually no protection. Webster never did show up!
1. Solo up the face (5.9 X) to a ledge, then climb a nice finger crack up the slab on the left to a tree ledge. 100', 5.9 X
FA: Doug Madara & Peter Long (UK)   July, 1980

ARNO'S CORNER I 5.10b (*)

The left-facing corner just right of the long, vertical crack of THREE SAINTS.
1. Climb up the left-facing corner to a peg. On the left, move past an overhang to easier ground. Above, a narrow dihedral protected by three pitons (5.10b) gets you to THE ELIMINATE traverse ledge. 100', 5.10b (Arno was their dog.)
FA: Bill DeMallie & Lorraine DeMallie   July 28, 1980

THREE SAINTS I 5.9 (*)

Or is it Three Snakes? Good, solid 5.9 jamming gets you to the traverse ledge.
1. The obvious, vertical crack in black rock with a small roof at the top. 100', 5.9
HISTORY: Ed Webster, Bryan Becker, & Jim Dunn made the first ascent on August 30, 1976. Webster was left tied off below the top roof for half an hour while Dunn & Becker chased a piliated woodpecker through the woods!

MEATLOAF IN MOTION I 5.12a (5.9 R)

Start this awkward pitch 15 feet to the left of THREE SAINTS.
1. Climb up the face past several horizontal cracks to a bolt and a piton that protect an overlap or bulge (5.12a), then move left near the top (5.9 R) past another overlap, and up to the traverse ledge. 100', 5.12a (5.9 R)
FA: Mack Johnson & Andy Ward   September 6, 1986
FFA: Chris Gill & Mark Wilson   August 9, 1987

THE LAST STRAND I 5.11c (*)

It looks easy; it's not! Start 20 feet to the right of HOLLOW MEN.
1. Climb to a small overlap (bolt). Underclinging/mantleshelf onto a sloping hold (5.11c), then face climb up and slightly right up a dirty face following a thin seam/crack past pitons (5.8) to THE ELIMINATE traverse ledge. 100', 5.11c
HISTORY: John Strand & Steve Weeks did the first ascent in the Summer of 1985, intending to go higher—but never did. The bolt was added later.

HOLLOW MEN I 5.11c (*)

Begin 10 feet right of the first pitch of HALLOWED EVE. Normal rack.
1. Climb up to a shallow, right-facing corner (pin), crossing left over HALLOWED EVE at a horizontal crack to a bolt. Move left again, underclinging over a bulge (5.11c). Continue left past flakes (peg) to a bolt on the final bulge which gains the sidewalk belay (piton) above. 80', 5.11c
FA: Brad White & Ian Cruickshank   September 18, 1991

THE WONDER WALL

The Wonder Wall, described next, offers several of the most spectacular and unusual rock climbs in New Hampshire. Bob Anderson, who established the first route up the wall, AIRY AERIE, in 1972, called it "The Diamond of the Northeast", after the famous Diamond on Long's Peak in Colorado. But where the Diamond is almost entirely crack climbing, the Wonder Wall has very steep face climbs on small, sharp edges. There are no easy routes on the wall, long runouts can test even the boldest at heart, and much of the existing protection is frequently from pitons and bolts. Carry a modern rack on all Wonder Wall routes.

WONDER WALL DESCENT OPTIONS: While some climbers will prefer to hike down the Bryce Path (described in the Whitehorse introduction), many climbers have begun to rappel the entire height of the Wonder Wall. The most commonly used rappel station is located at the top of SCIENCE FRICTION WALL, just left of the finishes of SOUTH BUTTRESS DIRECT and THE LAST UNICORN. With two 165 foot (50 meter) ropes, rappel directly (and barely) to a two bolt anchor on the 5.4 traverse ledge (on SKY STREAK) left of the start of THE LAST UNICORN. If you only have a 150 foot (45 meter) rope, rappel to the bolt anchor at the top of THE LAST UNICORN's first pitch, then to the large, white pine below, next on down to THE ELIMINATE traverse or access ledge, and finally to the ground.

SOUTH BUTTRESS DIRECT III 5.11b R, A1 (5 Points of aid) (***)
An impressive solo first ascent in winter, now a lengthy and increasingly popular free climb. Small wired nuts needed on the crux.
1. Climb Pitch one of THE ELIMINATE onto the access ledges. 5.6
2. Above the tree ledge, 60 feet left of THE ELIMINATE, climb up a flake (5.10a) to a ledge, then aid climb up three bolts and two rivets (A1) up a blank wall to a belay ledge. 70' 5.10a, A1
3. Climb a long, vertical corner (5.7) on the left. A bit dirty. 5.7
4. Continue past blocks and up through trees to a prominent spruce tree.
5. The Road Cut pitch is the climb's crux. Climb up blocky, angular rock to a 15 foot headwall split by a thin crack (5.11b R). Mantle onto a ledge, then face climb past a couple of bolts to a ledge with a two bolt anchor. 5.11b R
6. To the right of the top pitches of THE LAST UNICORN, face climb straight up the steep, wide open face (5.10b) following a long bolt ladder to an overlap. Step right onto the "surreal arete", and climb this to a pine tree on a ledge. 130', 5.10b Traverse left across a good ledge to the SCIENCE FRICTION WALL double ring bolt belay/rappel anchor and rap off, or...
7. An easy pitch up a crack through some trees gains the summit.

WHITEHORSE LEDGE - SOUTH BUTTRESS (THE WONDER WALL)

HISTORY: Jeff Pheasant made the notable first ascent of the climb, rope-solo, over two days in February, 1976. His effort remains one of the only major first ascents in the White Mountains to have been soloed in the winter. On June 27, 1978, Ed Webster & Jeff Pheasant made the route's first free ascent using the free variant on Pitch five. The Road Cut Pitch, the original fifth pitch, was free climbed in June, 1979, by Ed Webster & Peter Mayfield.

Jeff Pheasant on Pitch six (5.10b) of South Buttress Direct (5.11b R, A1) during the first free ascent in 1978. Photograph by .Ed Webster.

VARIATION: **ORIGINAL FREE VARIANT** I 5.9 R

5a. Bypass the awkward Road Cut Pitch by climbing diagonally up to the right on fractured, angular rock until a poor bolt protects a 5.9 move back to the left onto the original route. An obscure variation at best! 5.9 R

FA: Ed Webster & Jeff Pheasant June 27, 1978

288 THE MOUNT WASHINGTON VALLEY

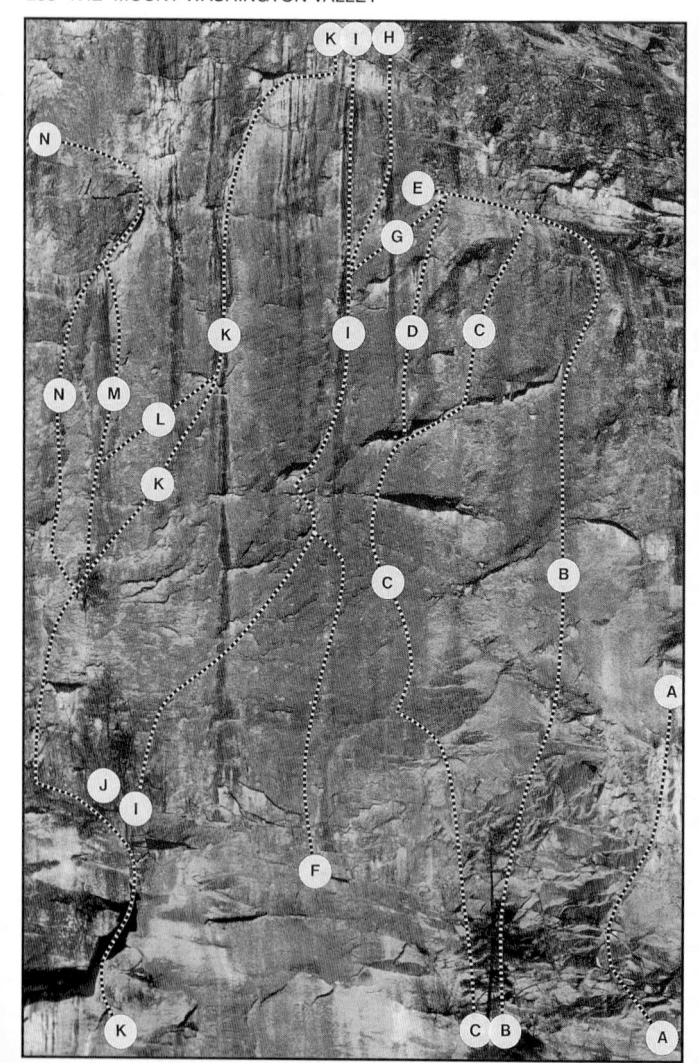

WHITEHORSE LEDGE – SOUTH BUTTRESS
(Wonder Wall Close-up)

A.	*	**THE GUNSLINGER** II 5.12a	Page	284
B.	***	**SOUTH BUTTRESS DIRECT** III 5.11b R, A1 (5 Points of Aid)	Page	286
C.	***	**THE LAST UNICORN** III 5.10b	Page	290
D.	**	**THE CENTAUR** I 5.11a	Page	290
E.		Science Friction Wall rappel station	Page	257 & 286
F.	**	**SKY STREAK** I 5.10b	Page	294
G.	**	**WEBSTER'S FINISH** I 5.11a	Page	292
H.		**BRAT TRACK** I 5.11c R	Page	292
I.	**	**SCIENCE FRICTION WALL** III 5.12b (5.8 R)	Page	292
J.		The Wonder Wall tree ledge	Page	255
K.	***	**WONDER WALL** III 5.12a (5.8 X)	Page	294
L.	**	**LADYSLIPPER to WONDER WALL** I 5.9+	Page	296
M.	***	**LADYSLIPPER** II 5.9+ (5.7 R)	Page	296
N.		**HARVEST** II 5.9 R	Page	296

THE LAST UNICORN III 5.10b (***)

Three pitches of well protected 5.10b face climbing have made this the most frequented route on the Wonder Wall. An East Coast classic, with great rock, good protection, and a beautiful and exposed situation. There is also one very memorable hanging belay. The climb begins from the prominent spruce tree halfway up the cliff, which is mentioned in the SOUTH BUTTRESS DIRECT description. As a result, the approach to reach the start of THE LAST UNICORN is a bit complicated. Follow the description given in detail at the beginning of the South Buttress section to approach the WONDER WALL. Solo up THE ELIMINATE access ledges (5.6) just left of THE JAWS OF DOOM, hike up and left until below the INFERNO Corner, then traverse up and right to the 4th class ledge traverse, heading straight right to gain the comfortable tree ledge at the base of the WONDER WALL. To reach the start of THE LAST UNICORN, down climb 15 feet off the right-hand end of the WONDER WALL tree ledge, then traverse horizontally right for nearly a full pitch (5.4) to reach the large spruce tree. Normal rack.

1. Left of the spruce, climb a sequence of angular holds (5.8) past two pitons to a stance. At shallow, parallel corners, make a very puzzling 5.10b move past a bolt, and belay on the ledge above at a two bolt anchor. 65', 5.10b

2. Face climb slightly left past two bolts (5.9) up to a vertical flake. Climb a fingery headwall (5.10b) past three bolts to a prominent overlap, and undercling right to a very exposed hanging belay at a two bolt anchor. 100', 5.10b

3. Difficult moves lead up the final open groove (5.10b) past four bolts and one piton, laybacking with great exposure to the top. 80', 5.10b To rappel off, walk 30 feet to your left to the double ring rappel station at the top of SCIENCE FRICTION WALL, and use two 50 meter ropes to descend the wall.

HISTORY: High school climbing partners Ed Webster & Jeff Pheasant reunited to make the first ascent of this historic route on August 10 & 11, 1978. A rope was left fixed overnight on the first two pitches. Webster placed the three headwall bolts on Pitch two on aid, while Pheasant placed all the bolts on Pitch three also on aid while wearing his sneakers! Afterwards, the rope was pulled, and each section was led free. The rest of the fixed protection was placed free on the lead.

DIRECT FINISH: THE CENTAUR I 5.11a (**)

You couldn't dream up a much wilder situation than this...! Recommended.

2a. Above the crux 5.10b bolted headwall on the second pitch of THE LAST UNICORN, make dramatic moves straight out the final overlap past a peg and two bolts up a steep face to reach a good ledge at the SCIENCE FRICTION WALL double ring bolt belay/rappel anchor. 140', 5.11a

FA: Chris Dubé & Larry Sodano July 23, 1989

WHITEHORSE LEDGE - SOUTH BUTTRESS (THE LAST UNICORN) 291

Kurt Winkler & Alain Comeau on the second pitch of The Last Unicorn (5.10b) in 1986. Photograph by Ed Webster.

292 THE MOUNT WASHINGTON VALLEY

SCIENCE FRICTION WALL III 5.12b (5.8 R), or 5.11a (5.8 R) (**)
Until 1991, it was all Science Fiction until the entire original line was finally free climbed in a very determined effort. The route's main feature is a long, spectacular, black water streak running up the right margin of the WONDER WALL, just to the left of THE LAST UNICORN. This crux pitch now has excellent protection as all of the original dowels have been replaced with large diameter bolts. To reach the climb's start, locate Pitch two of HALLOWED EVE, the left-leaning corner just to the left of WONDER WALL's 5.12a crux on its second pitch. Begin SCIENCE FRICTION WALL about 100 feet uphill and left of the left-slanting HALLOWED EVE corner, aiming for the large overlap/ceiling on your right. Bring a modern rack with 14 quick draws!
1. Traverse moderate rock out to the right, staying on the slab below the huge ceiling, and belay near its right-hand side.
2. Struggle up a short, awkward 5.9 offwidth (large nut needed), then climb more easily up to the right side of the WONDER WALL tree ledge. 5.9
3. A serious pitch. Step out right, then make a long runout straight up (5.8 R) to a bolt and peg. Go right, up to another pin, then face climb (5.9) past a bolt to a stance below a small roof on the left with a two bolt anchor. 5.9 (5.8 R)
4. Face climb straight up the prominent black water streak past many bolts to a rest where progress begins to look unlikely, then conquer a short bulge on the right (5.11a). There are now three separate finishes of increasing difficulty:

WEBSTER'S FINISH I 5.10b (The complete lead is 5.11a) (**)
4a. Above the 5.11a bulge, traverse straight right across an exposed face past two bolts (5.10b) to gain a good belay ledge on the right with a double ring bolt belay/rappel anchor, the SCIENCE FRICTION rappel station, which is used by several different routes. 75', 5.10b

BRAT TRACK I 5.11c R
The R rating mostly relates to the hollow flake your last protection is behind!
4b. Above WEBSTER'S FINISH, continue face climbing higher up the bolt ladder until the angle steepens, then move right (5.11c) to a hollow flake (Friends), and face climb straight up (5.11c R) into a short, right-facing corner that leads to the top. 110', 5.11c R

THE ORIGINAL ROUTE I 5.12b (**)
4c. Increasingly difficult face climbing leads up the prominent, black water streak, protected by a long string of bolts (5.12b). The crux moves are at the top of the water streak. 110', 5.12b

HISTORY: John Bragg & Paul Ross climbed the first two pitches in the mid-1970s. Pitch three was first climbed by Doug Madara & Alain Comeau, who left a rope fixed. A week later, on July 11, 1978, Paul Ross & Kim Smith jumared the rope and bolted up the final water streak to the top. On

WHITEHORSE LEDGE - SOUTH BUTTRESS (SCIENCE FRICTION WALL) 293

September 4, 1980, Ed Webster & Susan Patenaude made a partial free ascent of the route, creating WEBSTER'S FINISH to the right, after adding two bolts on aid from skyhooks. Jim Surette, Steve Larson, & Harrison Dekker made the first ascent of BRAT TRACK in September, 1985. After several previous days of effort by Steve Larson, Chris Gill, & Chris Noonan earlier in the Autumn of 1991, Steve Larson & Scott Stevenson made the historic first free ascent of the route's original line in December, 1991.

Doug Madara leading the first ascent of Pitch three (5.9 / 5.8 R) of Science Friction Wall (the entire route is now 5.12b) in 1978. Photograph by Paul Ross.

DIRECT START: **SKY STREAK** I 5.10b (**))

This much better protected start to SCIENCE FRICTION WALL has become the Voie Normal for that route. As opposed to the regular third pitch, rated at 5.9 (5.8 R), which has a notorious runout, SKY STREAK is more consistent in difficulty, protection, and quality with SCIENCE FRICTION WALL's upper face. Start at the SCIENCE FRICTION WALL two bolt rappel station partway across the 5.4 traverse ledge between the WONDER WALL tree ledge and the large spruce tree at the base of THE LAST UNICORN.

1. From the belay, step left a few feet and face climb straight up a short, steep headwall past two bolts (5.10b) to easier climbing, a ledge (bolt), and a rest at the base of the upper wall. Continue face climbing past two more bolts (5.9) before traversing left after placing a nut in a hidden flake. Join the regular first pitch, and climb past its second bolt to reach the double bolt anchor above, at a stance under a small roof. 100', 5.10b

HISTORY: Uwe Schneider & Chris Stevens made the first ascent on April 29, 1991, placing all the bolts on the lead, the first two from skyhooks, and the rest from stances.

WONDER WALL III 5.12a (5.8 X) (***)

This long and involved route has its technical crux down low, and a dramatic, exposed conclusion. The upper wall is unique to the East Coast. A phenomenal expedition if you do the entire climb, but either section of the route, done separately, is also highly recommended. One hundred feet left of THREE SAINTS is a dirty, often wet gully, bordered by a friction slab on the right. This slab is the start of WONDER WALL. Carry a modern rack.

1. Up the slab (5.7 R), then right near the top. Walk left on a big ledge to a two bolt anchor below a thin, left-facing flake with several bolts above. 75', 5.7 R
2. The crux pitch face climbs past a peg (5.10a) into the flake system, then heads up a faint groove past three bolts (5.12a) to a small ledge. 50', 5.12a
3. Continue straight up a bulging headwall (5.10b) past several more bolts to easier climbing, right then left. Finish up an offwidth crack (one 5.9 move; large nut needed) to the WONDER WALL tree ledge. 5.10b
4. From the center of the WONDER WALL tree ledge, layback up the left side of a flake to a small pine tree. 50', 5.6
5. Face climb diagonally right past a loose flake to a bolt, then make a long runout straight up (5.8 X) to a mantle move and (thank god), another bolt. After a third bolt, belay on a small, exposed stance with a fixed anchor at the base of the final, right-facing crack/dihedral. 90', 5.8 X
6. Step right, jam and layback up a prominent, right-facing, yellow corner/crack (5.9) to a roof, then handtraverse right (5.10a) to the end (the normal finish), or climb directly over the final roof (5.10c). 130', 5.10a or 5.10c

WHITEHORSE LEDGE - THE SOUTH BUTTRESS (WONDER WALL)

HISTORY: Jeff Pheasant & Paul Ross made the first ascent of this historic climb on May 4, 1976. Upper WONDER WALL was free climbed several weeks later by John Bragg & Al Rubin, who finished straight over the final roof. After top-roping part of the crux the previous day, and rearranging one protection bolt on aid, Ed Webster & Russ Clune made the first continuous free ascent of the entire route on October 1, 1981.

Jeff Pheasant on the first ascent of Wonder Wall in 1976. Photo by Paul Ross.

VARIATION #1: **VENI-VIDI-WIMPI** I 5.11a R
"I came, I saw, I wimped out." Start 30 feet left of Pitch two of WONDER WALL. Be extremely careful of the expanding, loose flake. Modern rack.
1a. Mantleshelf (5.11a) up to the first bolt, then climb past an undercling to a thin, dangerous flake. "Belay somewhere, and finish as desired." 80', 5.11a R
HISTORY: The route was named in honor of a famous quotation by Julius Caesar: "I came, I saw, I conquered." Chris Gill, Big Wall Greg McCausland, "and a Brit named Mike" made the first ascent in October, 1987.

VARIATION #2: **TICKET TO RIDE** I 5.9 R
This might be a one way ticket! More scary flakes.
3a. From the belay, traverse ledges horizontally right, then forge up a steep wall on several loose, scary flakes. 5.9 R
HISTORY: In August of 1977, on an early attempt to free climb WONDER WALL, Ed Webster & Bob Palais found this gripping variation.

VARIATION #3: **RAIN DANCE** I 5.9
Bizarre and awkward climbing that stays dry, if it happens to start raining...! This unusual route traverses from left to right underneath the large overlap/roof whose right side is also climbed on Pitch four of WONDER WALL. Start at the base of the approach gully leading to the WONDER WALL tree ledge. Bring a normal rack including several large cams.
1. Up the gully (5.7 at start) until level with the big overhang. Tree belay. 80', 5.7
2. Traverse directly right, with very awkward moves, scrunched up underneath the huge roof (5.9) to a belay halfway across. 50', 5.9
3. Join WONDER WALL's fourth pitch, making one 5.9 move up an offwidth crack, and head up to the right end of the WONDER WALL tree ledge. 75', 5.9
FA: Kurt Winkler & Nathan Richer October 10, 1988

VARIATION #4: **LADYSLIPPER to WONDER WALL** I 5.9+ (**)
A much safer, popular alternative to WONDER WALL's fifth pitch.
5a. Face climb up LADYSLIPPER (5.9+; bolt protection), then traverse right to the WONDER WALL belay near the base of the final, crack/corner. 5.9+
FA: Unknown.

LADYSLIPPER II 5.9+ (5.7 R) (***)
Captivating, delicate, and exposed face climbing with bolt protection has made this one of the Wonder Wall's most popular routes. While really only a direct start to HARVEST, it has better protection and much finer climbing.
1. Layback up the left side of the flake above the center of the WONDER WALL tree ledge. 50', 5.6 (This short pitch is common to, from right to left: WONDER WALL, LADYSLIPPER, HARVEST, and AIRY AERIE.)
2. Face climb straight up past two bolts directly up the middle of the face between HARVEST and WONDER WALL. From flakes, step right and make a series of 5.9 face moves past three more bolts to the large ear of rock on the left. Climb the wild, partially detached flake (5.9; same as HARVEST) up to a two bolt anchor and a belay stance at a large pine tree. 5.9+
3. Finish up HARVEST: move left 30 feet, then head up the steep wall above (5.7 R) on big holds to easy ramps and the woods. 100', 5.7 R
HISTORY: Ed Webster & Susan Patenaude made the route's first ascent on September 1, 1979. All the bolts were placed free on the lead except one.

HARVEST II 5.9 R
The next prominent line located to the left of Upper WONDER WALL and LADYSLIPPER ascends a narrow, right-facing corner system capped by a partially detached ear of rock. Carry a modern rack. Protection is behind an expanding flake, so care is needed. Start on the WONDER WALL tree ledge.
1. Layback the left side of the small, central flake. 50', 5.6
2. Move left into a shallow dihedral. When it ends, step right, then back left

WHITEHORSE LEDGE - SOUTH BUTTRESS (LADYSLIPPER) 297

Ed Webster climbing Ladyslipper (5.9+ / 5.7 R) in 1981.
Photograph by Susan Patenaude.

298 THE MOUNT WASHINGTON VALLEY

WHITEHORSE LEDGE – SOUTH BUTTRESS
(Wonder Wall Overview)

A.	***	**THE ELIMINATE** IV 5.11c (5.8 R)	Page	280
B.	*	**THE GUNSLINGER** II 5.12a	Page	284
C.	***	**SOUTH BUTTRESS DIRECT** III 5.11b R, A1 (5 Points of Aid)	Page	286
D.	**	**LONDON CALLING** I 5.12b	Page	283
E.		The Eliminate traverse (or access) ledge	Page 255 &	280
F.	***	**THE LAST UNICORN** III 5.10b	Page	290
G.		Science Friction Wall rappel station	Page 257 &	286
H.	**	**SKY STREAK** I 5.10b	Page	294
I.	**	**SCIENCE FRICTION WALL** III 5.12b or 5.11a (5.8 R)	Page	292
J.	***	**WONDER WALL** III 5.12a (5.8 X)	Page	294
K.	***	**LADYSLIPPER** II 5.9+ (5.7 R)	Page	296
L.	**	**WONDERS NEVER CEASE** II 5.10c (5.9 R)	Page	301
M.	**	**HALLOWED EVE** III 5.9+ R	Page	301
N.	***	**LOST SOULS** III 5.10a	Page	302
O.	**	**CREOLE LOVE CALL** III 5.10b R	Page	304
P.	***	**INFERNO** II 5.8	Page	310
Q.	***	**ATLANTIS** II 5.10b (or 5.9)	Page	309

(unprotected), and layback a hollow flake up to a ledge (bolt). Jam and layback up the huge, detached flake or ear (5.9) on the right to a double bolt anchor beside a large pine tree. 120', 5.9 R

3. Move left 30 feet, then launch up a steep wall (5.7 R) on big, angular holds to easy ramps and the forest. 100', 5.7 R

FA: Ed Webster & Hank Armantrout August, 1979

AIRY AERIE II 5.9 R

The first route up the WONDER WALL. Offering an attractive combination of poorly protected face climbing plus difficult route finding, this obscure climb has seldom, if ever, been repeated. Begin on the WONDER WALL tree ledge.

1. Layback the initial 5.6 flake, as for the preceding routes. 50', 5.6

2. Move left into a shallow dihedral (also on HARVEST), but continue farther left to grassy cracks and a belay stance. There are small trees en route.

3. Angle left to a bulge, move over it, then head up and left to the next belay.

4. Fourth class to the top of the cliff.

FA: Bob Anderson & Dennis Merritt August, 1972

Mack Johnson on Pitch one (5.9+) of Wonders Never Cease (5.10c / 5.9 R) during the first ascent in 1987. Photograph by Ed Webster.

WHITEHORSE LEDGE - SOUTH BUTTRESS (HALLOWED EVE)

WONDERS NEVER CEASE II 5.10c (5.9 R) (**)
Ascends the black water streak between the crux pitch of HALLOWED EVE and HARVEST above the center of the WONDER WALL tree ledge. Sustained, exposed, and wondrous face climbing. Bring a modern rack.
1. Face climb up a brown pillar (peg) over the steep, initial headwall, then follow the water streak (5.9+) past a bolt and a piton to a double bolt anchor on a good stance on AIRY AERIE. 110', 5.9+
2. Move right, then face climb up a steep wall just to the left of HARVEST past several bolts (5.10c) up to a ledge. The original finish angles left across a flake (5.9 R) to easier ground. The Direct Finish (5.9) ascends a thin flake straight up. 140', 5.10c (5.9 R), or 5.10c

HISTORY: *Ed Webster & Mack Johnson climbed the first ascent of the route on August 5 & 6, 1987. All the fixed pitons and bolts were placed on the lead, but on Pitch two, Webster broke a drill bit, and got really gripped finishing drilling the hole while hanging off a couple of A3 hooks! On the afternoon of August 11, 1987, after doing the first ascent of CREOLE LOVE CALL, Ed Webster & Kurt Winkler repeated the climb and added the Direct Finish.*

HALLOWED EVE III 5.9+ R (**)
A lengthy, spectacular, and sustained free climb. The fourth pitch, the crux, ascends the beautiful, rust-colored face to the left of AIRY AERIE. Typical of most of the WONDER WALL routes, protection is difficult on several leads. With modern gear, the climbing is considerably safer than it was in 1976! Begin at the base of the South Buttress between the starts of THREE SAINTS and WONDER WALL at a 20 foot, right-facing, hooking corner.
1. Climb partway up the initial corner, then make 5.9 R moves right to a stance (bolt). Another hard move gains the traverse ledge. Walk 100 feet left, past WONDER WALL's crux pitch, to an obvious, left-leaning dihedral. 5.9 R
2. Ascend the left-slanting corner and hand crack (5.9). At its top, step right to a good belay stance with a small pine tree. 75', 5.9
3. Climb up a steep wall on good holds, then move left to a blank slab. A few tricky 5.9 moves up an incipient fracture past a tiny overlap gain another tree belay. 5.9 Solo up the 4th class tree gully to the WONDER WALL tree ledge.
4. Above the tree ledge's left-hand side, face climb straight up the rust-colored face (piton) to a rest at half height at another peg. Step right, face climb up (5.9+ R) and then back left, to an obvious, white birch tree, and belay at the bottom of a right-diagonalling tree ramp. 150', 5.9+ R
5. Climb up the ramp quite easily past trees to a large pine, and belay.
6. Follow an easy crack and corner on the left to the woods and the top.

HISTORY: *Ed Webster & Bill Aughton did the first ascent on two consecutive afternoons (and evenings) in September, 1976. Each time they were benighted,* prompting the name. On the successful ascent, they were so late getting back that the IME rescue squad was even called out, and met them on the descent!

VARIATION FINISH: **SEPTEMBER MORN** I 5.10a R (*)

This alternate finish face climbs slightly to the left of the normal fourth pitch. Start at the left side of the WONDER WALL tree ledge. Modern rack.

4a. Climb a short arete split by a thin, vertical crack (5.9) onto the upper face. Trend left until near SOUTHERN BELLE, then face climb straight up a clean, white face (5.10a R) to the white birch on HALLOWED EVE. 150', 5.10a R

FA: Rob Adair & Kim Peters   September 28, 1986

SOUTHERN BELLE II 5.7+ X

Although this is the easiest route up the WONDER WALL, route finding is extremely difficult, and protection is essentially nonexistent. A 5.7 route for 5.10 leaders. Start from the very left side of the WONDER WALL tree ledge. Small wired nut protection. Carry a modern rack.

1. Climb over a short headwall to a piton 30 feet up, then begin a long traverse diagonally left with wired nuts behind thin flakes for protection. Aim for the right-hand side of a horizontal overlap on your left. Skirt its right end to a small belay stance in a vertical flake system. 140', 5.7+ X

2. Step left, climb straight up for 20 feet, then make an awkward 5.7 traverse back right to reach the base of the easy, right-diagonalling tree ramp mentioned in the HALLOWED EVE route description. Belay at a pine tree. 5.7

3. On the left, climb cracks to a groove and a final dike.

HISTORY: Ed Webster & Paul Ross made the first ascent of this gripping route (with a rack of Stoppers and Hexentrics!) on August 3, 1976 when Ross introduced Webster to the Wonder Wall for the first time. A trivia note: what was the climb's original name? (Moonraker.)

LOST SOULS III 5.10a (***)

You might lose your soul to the ecstasy on this full length route. One of the most popular newer climbs on the South Buttress. Locate the massive oak tree below INFERNO. After ascending the center of a large slab up to the INFERNO to WONDER WALL fourth class traverse ledge, the route breaks through the center of the overhangs to the right of CREOLE LOVE CALL, and left of SOUTHERN BELLE. From the cliff base below the INFERNO Corner, scramble up and right to a clump of trees 40 feet up and belay. Carry a normal rack with extra slings.

1. Step right on a foot ledge, then climb up a short slab (5.9; bolt) to an overlap or headwall. Protect, climb steeply up and left on a black flake, then face climb up and left to a piton on a gray slab. Continue face climbing straight up a stepped slab past two pitons in pockets to a double bolt belay halfway across the INFERNO to WONDER WALL traverse ledges. 125', 5.9

Bill Aughton following the crux fourth pitch of Hallowed Eve (5.9+ R) on the first ascent in 1976. Photograph by Ed Webster.

2. The crux pitch climbs up to a bolt, mantles onto a ledge (pin), and traverses right to a weakness in the overhangs above. Climb through this on jugs past two bolts, move right delicately (5.10a) onto the steep, upper face, and face climb straight up past three more bolts (sustained), past the flake belay stance on SOUTHERN BELLE. Continue trending up and left, following this flake system to a two piton & bolt belay on a good ledge on the left. 150', 5.10a

3. Traverse left across the ledge, clip a bolt, then launch up a difficult (5.9+) exposed, rounded arete, continuing past one more bolt (5.9) to an excellent ledge with a double bolt anchor. 45', 5.9+

4. Climb steeply up the shallow, flaring corner above (wired nuts and small cams) on square-cut holds (piton) over a bulge (5.10a) to a small tree. Join PURGATORY, finishing up a dike to the top. 150', 5.10a Or, to make a quick descent, rappel twice with two ropes, very steeply, off a double bolt anchor beside the pine tree on the left, down to the double bolt anchor and a small stance on CEMETERY GATES, and then to the ground.

HISTORY: Bill Lowther rope-soloed the first pitch, returned with Ozzie Blumit & Jon Eagleson to climb Pitch two, and finally completed the route with Jon Sykes in October, 1993.

CREOLE LOVE CALL III 5.10b R (**)

An intimidating face climb up the center of the steep, smooth wall between LOST SOULS and PARADISE LOST. Modern rack needed.

1. Climb up the black arete up the left-hand side of the lowest slab (5.8), 25 feet to the left of Pitch one of LOST SOULS, to reach a belay stance on the left side of the INFERNO to WONDER WALL traverse ledges. 125', 5.8

2. Just to the right of the start of Pitch two of CEMETERY GATES, traverse right across a flake or overlap until you can pull over onto the steep face above. Face climb up (piton) into a prominent black water streak (bolt) that leads to the center of a long, narrow, horizontal overlap. Layback a flake out the overlap, then face climb up and right (bolt) to the fixed two piton & bolt belay anchor and belay ledge shared with LOST SOULS. 150', 5.10b

3. Face climb right, then up (5.10b R) across a difficult face, finally joining the easy, right-slanting tree ramp on SOUTHERN BELLE. 5.10b R

4. Climb flakes and cracks up and left, finishing up the dike on PURGATORY.

HISTORY: Seeking to correct Webster's mistake of locating INDIAN SUMMER in the 1987 guide as ascending this same stretch of rock (which it certainly doesn't!), Kurt Winkler & Ed Webster made the first ascent of this route, placing all fixed protection free on the lead, on August 11, 1987.

CEMETERY GATES I 5.10d (*)

The crux pitch, located just to the left of CREOLE LOVE CALL, offers very good free climbing up to a double bolt anchor on a small belay/rappel stance.

Michael Hartrich on the top pitch of Lost Souls (5.10a) in 1995.
Photograph by Ed Webster.

306 THE MOUNT WASHINGTON VALLEY

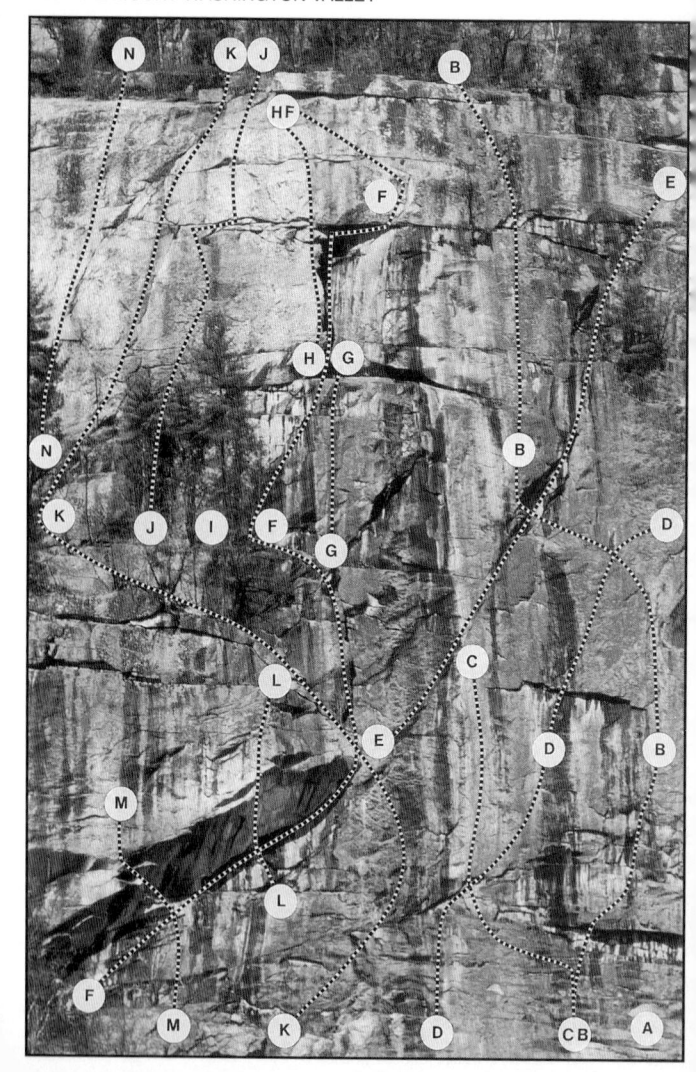

WHITEHORSE LEDGE – SOUTH BUTTRESS
(The INFERNO Corner Area)

A.		**INFERNO to WONDER WALL tree ledge traverse ledges**	Page	255
B.	***	**LOST SOULS** III 5.10a	Page	302
C.	*	**CEMETERY GATES** I 5.10d	Page	304
D.	**	**CREOLE LOVE CALL** III 5.10b R	Page	304
E.		**PARADISE LOST** II 5.10d R	Page	309
F.	***	**ATLANTIS** II 5.10b (or 5.9)	Page	309
G.	*	**COFFIN NAIL** I 5.9+	Page	309
H.		**WORKSHOP ORGY** I 5.12a	Page	310
I.		The Inferno tree ledge		
J.	*	**IN YOUR FACE** II 5.10d	Page	310
K.	***	**INFERNO** II 5.8	Page	310
L.	**	**INDIAN SUMMER** II 5.12b	Page	312
M.	*	**WAKE UP CALL** I 5.9+	Page	312
N.	**	**TRANQUILITY** II 5.10b	Page	312

1. Climb Pitch one of LOST SOULS up the center of the lower slab (5.9) to reach the INFERNO to WONDER WALL traverse ledges. 120', 5.9

2. Move up and left to a piton at a small, notched roof. Climb past this onto a smooth headwall, face climbing past five bolts (5.10d) to a small belay stance with a double bolt anchor—a useful rappel station. 90', 5.10d

HISTORY: Bill Lowther rope-soloed the first ascent of the climb, placing all the bolts free on the lead except two, in October, 1992. Bill Lowther, Ozzie Blumet, & Gerry Lortie free climbed the route in August, 1993.

Kurt Winkler on the first ascent of Creole Love Call (5.10b R) in 1987. Photograph by Ed Webster.

WHITEHORSE LEDGE - SOUTH BUTTRESS (ATLANTIS) 309

PARADISE LOST II 5.10d R

An obscure, yet difficult ascent, seldom repeated. The climb ascends the right-diagonalling dike up the steep wall to the right of the INFERNO Corner. Protection is definitely better with a modern rack!

1. Climb the first pitch of INFERNO up the face to the right of the huge, right-facing corner to a niche and belay. 130', 5.7

2. Down climb 15 feet, then step right into the dike. Above a bolt, make dicey 5.10d R moves to a second bolt, then step back left into the upper dike which is climbed to a good belay ledge. 90', 5.10d R

3. Chimney up behind a large flake, climb out left (5.8) onto a ledge, and finish up and right to the woods. 130', 5.8

HISTORY: Henry Barber placed the first bolt in the early '70s. Ed Webster, Jane Wilson, & Michael Kennedy made the first ascent in September, 1976.

PURGATORY II 5.8

A seldom climbed route, easier than hell to find. Good luck!

1. Climb the first pitch of INFERNO to the niche. 130', 5.7

2. Continue up a moderate, right-facing corner (5.4) to a tree ledge. You should now be below the huge ATLANTIS dihedral and roof. 40', 5.4

3. Traverse horizontally right 15 feet, then climb up the face to cracks and a large ledge. Belay at a pine tree on the right. 5.8

4. Climb a straightforward crack and face to the top.

FA: Bob Anderson & Wayne Christian August 12, 1972

ATLANTIS II 5.10b (or 5.9) (***)

This unusual route ascends the large, right-facing corner and roof above the INFERNO Corner. For such a wild climb, it is remarkably safe and well protected. The top 5.10b finger crack can be avoided to make the entire route a 5.9.

1. Climb directly up the entire height of the INFERNO Corner, jamming and underclinging all the way up the crack/corner (5.9) to the niche belay. 140', 5.9

2. The 5.4 corner (as for PURGATORY) straight up to the INFERNO ledge.

3. Layback the thin flake system above (5.9; similar to WHEAT THIN in Yosemite) to a good belay ledge at the base of the upper dihedral/roof. 40', 5.9

4. Chimney up a wide crack in the back of the immense corner. At the roof, make an exciting 5.9 handtraverse right to the base of the final, finger crack (5.10b). Beware of rope drag (which can be fierce!) while climbing the finger crack. The 5.10b finger crack may be easily avoided by continuing to traverse off right to a pine tree and a double bolt rappel station. 150', 5.10b (or 5.9)

HISTORY: Ed Webster & Doug Madara climbed the route's first ascent in September, 1976, finishing with the 5.10b finger crack.

VARIATION #1: **COFFIN NAIL** I 5.9+ (*)

This is the steep, bolted face just to the right of the Wheat Thin flake on Pitch three of ATLANTIS. Some very good moves.

3a. Climb up a slightly overhanging dike (5.9+) past five bolts. 50', 5.9+

HISTORY: Bill Lowther, Gerry Lortie, & Barry Marchesault made the first ascent on August 14, 1993. All the bolts were placed on the lead, the first and last free, and the middle bolts on aid.

VARIATION #2: **WORKSHOP ORGY** I 5.12a

The sharp, exposed arete on the left side of the ATLANTIS Corner.

1 & 2. Do the first two pitches of ATLANTIS or INFERNO.

3. Climb the Pitch three layback flake on ATLANTIS. 40', 5.9

4a. From the belay at the base of the ATLANTIS Corner, face climb up the left wall of the dihedral (bolt) until you can gain the sharp arete on the left. Face climb straight up the outside face of the arete (5.9+) past several bolts to a large horizontal break, then over a bulge (5.12a) to the top. 125', 5.12a

HISTORY: Steve Larson & Chris Noonan made two attempts on the route from the ground up in October, 1989, and reached the horizontal break. Steve Wooding, Dave McDermott, S. Comstock, Jon Paulding, & Rich Petersen placed several extra bolts on rappel, and made the first ascent in July, 1990.

IN YOUR FACE II 5.10d (*)

The route ascends the wall to the right of the upper 5.8 crack system on INFERNO. Approach via HOTTER THAN HELL. Well protected. Start from the left end of the highest small tree ledge.

1. Climb straight up past horizontal cracks (and protection) to a left-facing ear of rock. Mantle onto the ear (bolt), then make a difficult high step (5.10a), up and right. Continue up the face past two horizontal cracks. Above the second crack, more hard moves lead past a second bolt (5.10d) until you can traverse left to the tree belay on INFERNO. 100', 5.10d

2. Step out right, and climb up past a piton and a bolt (5.10a) to a mantleshelf. At a second bolt above, face climb straight up (5.10d), or step right onto easier ground (5.8). 70', 5.10a

HISTORY: Uwe Schneider, Chris Stevens, & Brian Tessier made the first ascent in May, 1992, after placing the bolts on rappel.

INFERNO II 5.8 (***)

A route to be savored, even on a hot day. This well designed climb is one of the most popular adventures on the entire South Buttress. The upper finger and hand cracks are legendary. To reach the start, climb up and across THE ELIMINATE access (or traverse) ledges just to the left of THE JAWS OF DOOM, then scramble uphill to the left until you can see a prominent, right-facing dihedral: the INFERNO Corner. This corner is the most prominent landmark for finding any of the climbs on the left side of the South Buttress. Scramble up ledges to a large oak tree and belay.

WHITEHORSE LEDGE - SOUTH BUTTRESS (INFERNO) 311

1. Climb an easy V groove on the right, then head directly up the face past two pitons following the path of least resistance until you meet the right-slanting main corner on the left. Jam and layback up to a small stance just left of a niche. 130', 5.7 (The INFERNO tree ledge can be reached in one pitch of 165 feet.)
2. Gain the tree-covered ledge on the left. Walk about 80 feet left, and belay beneath an aesthetic, vertical finger and hand crack. 40', 5.4
3. Scramble up a short, bushy groove to the crack. Great finger and hand jamming (5.8) leads to a comfortable, scenic ledge with a tree anchor. 5.8
4. Step left, and climb another nice crack diagonally right to the top. 5.8
HISTORY: One of the first full routes up the South Buttress, Bob Anderson & Wayne Christian climbed the first ascent of this classic in August, 1972.

DIRECT START: **HADES** I 5.6 R
1a. Start at an oak 40 feet left of the INFERNO walk up. Above a ledge 15 feet up, climb the right edge of the left-hand, black water streak to a ledge. 40', 5.6 R
HISTORY: Todd Swain made the first recorded ascent in 1978.

Dennis Goode & partner on Inferno (5.8) in 1987. Photograph by Ed Webster.

INDIAN SUMMER II 5.12b (**)

Sunny days are here again now that this route has been relocated to its correct home! Climbs the overhanging left wall of the INFERNO Corner. Although incredibly steep and strenuous, the holds are good. Approach up and right via easy ledges to a ledge below the INFERNO Corner. Small Friends needed.

1. Right of the belay, climb moderate slabs up to a belay niche. 40', 5.7

2. Step right to a flake system running up and out the overhanging wall. Strenuous laybacking past fixed pins leads to a difficult lip encounter (5.12b). Continue up steep slabs and a groove to the INFERNO tree ledge. 90', 5.12b

HISTORY: The route was first cleaned, protected, and attempted by Tom Callaghan & John Ray in November, 1984. John Mallery, Tom Callaghan & John Strand made the first ascent on October 29, 1986.

WAKE UP CALL I 5.9+ (*)

Breaks through the slanting roof left of INDIAN SUMMER at a much easier grade. From the start of INFERNO, solo 15 feet to a ledge with a tree clump.

1. Climb a short V groove on the right, then face climb left to jammed blocks under the roof. Gain a stance on the blocks (bolt), then traverse left (exciting) past a piton to a ledge. Climb past the lip on buckets (bolt; 5.9+) straight up to a double bolt anchor on a sloping stance just above. 60', 5.9+

FA: Bill Lowther & Dan Pacheco October 24, 1995

THE TRANQUILITY SLAB

The steep, open slab to the left of the INFERNO Corner, and below the large, INFERNO tree ledge on the left side of the South Buttress is known as the TRANQUILITY Slab. Giving a variety of slab and face climbs, the slab is home to the ever popular HOTTER THAN HELL (often combined with Upper INFERNO) plus several other harder, multi-pitch routes such as BACKDRAFT and UNFORGETTABLE FIRE which ascend both the TRANQUILITY Slab and the INFERNO Wall above the central tree ledge.

TRANQUILITY II 5.10b (**)

The slab's original route is an appropriately named climb, well worth the long, peaceful approach. Just to the left of the oak tree at the bottom of INFERNO is a large block sitting on the ledge at the base of the TRANQUILITY Slab.

1. Layback the right side of the block or flake to reach a thin, left-slanting crack. Follow the crack (5.7) to a bush and a small stance in the slab's center. 5.7

2. Continue up the crack system, up and right over a small overhang, to the large, INFERNO tree-covered ledge in the middle of the cliff.

3. About 20 feet left of INFERNO's upper pitches, jam a thin finger crack (5.10b) that widens to hands. Finish over an unlikely blank bulge (5.10b) on the left above a small pine—or escape right up INFERNO (5.8). 5.10b

HISTORY: Michael Hartrich & Jeff Pheasant climbed the first two pitches in the mid-1970s. Ed Webster & Matt Stein linked the climb together in August, 1976, and finished with the 5.10b "blank bulge" on Pitch three.

TRUE STORIES I 5.11c (5.11a R / 5.10a X) (**)

Which you might get to tell—if you survive. Yet another excellent, scary runout route up the TRANQUILITY Slab. Don't let the awful truth (of how far out you are from your last pro) break your concentration. Modern rack.

1. Twenty feet to the right of HOTTER THAN HELL are two old bolts. Clip these, then go left past a bolt on a bulge (5.11c), running the rope out to join the crux (5.10a X) on Pitch one of BURNING DOWN THE HOUSE. Belay on the INFERNO tree ledge. 150', 5.11c (5.10a X)

2. Climb the bold, unprotected 5.11a R direct start to Pitch two of BURNING, step left to a bolt on UNFORGETTABLE FIRE (5.11b), and finish up that route to the top (5.11b). 140', 5.11b (5.11a R)

HISTORY: Todd Swain & Dick Peterson placed the first two bolts on Pitch one in the early 1980s, attempting to climb the arete on the right. John Strand & Brian Jones (UK) made the first ascent in September, 1988.

HOTTER THAN HELL I 5.9 (***)

Don't be deviled by the crux of this scorchingly popular route. Fun and well protected face climbing combined with the upper, finger/hand cracks on INFERNO makes for an excellent, varied climb. From below INFERNO, walk 80 feet left on a ledge until below the 70 degree TRANQUILITY Slab.

1. Climb up to a bolt visible from below. Traverse right past another bolt into the 5.7 left-diagonalling crack on TRANQUILITY. Continue face climbing up the steep slab on the right past two more bolts to a thin 5.9 move by the last bolt. Belay under an overhang split by a crack. 5.9

2. Climb the crack (as for TRANQUILITY) to the INFERNO tree ledge. 5.7

HISTORY: Matt Peer & Craig Stemley made the first ascent on May 29, 1980, placing all of the bolts on the lead. Thinking he'd probably fall off the crux move if he stopped to place another bolt, Matt went for it, successfully. The local consensus was that the unprotected crux runout should stay, as that was how the route was first led, but eventually Peer decided to add the crux bolt on rappel—"much to the dismay of the resident hardmen"—but to the greater benefit of most climbers!

BACKDRAFT I 5.11c (5.8 R) (**)

You'll definitely feel the heat on this difficult, steep face climb. The first pitch could fade into obscurity, but the upper lead is extraordinary! Bring a modern rack—need it be said? Start between HOTTER THAN HELL and BURNING DOWN THE HOUSE at a small break in the bottom overlap.

1. Climb straight up the face, crossing HOTTER THAN HELL, aiming (5.8 R)

314 THE MOUNT WASHINGTON VALLEY

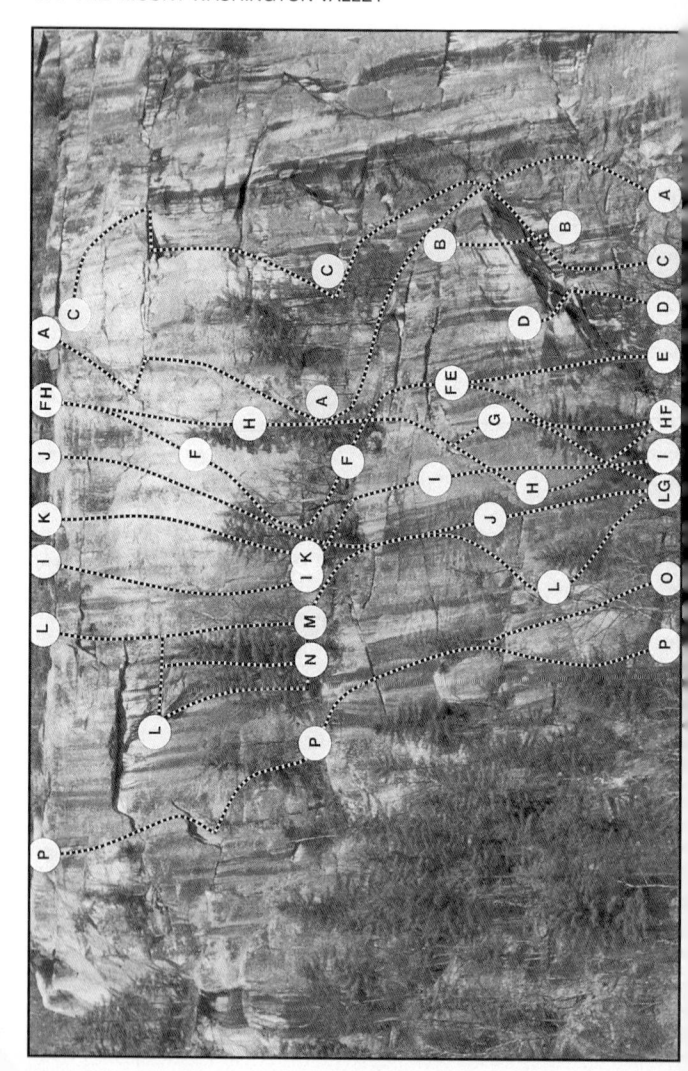

WHITEHORSE LEDGE – SOUTH BUTTRESS
(The INFERNO Wall & TRANQUILITY Slab)

A. ***	INFERNO II 5.8	Page 310	
B. **	INDIAN SUMMER II 5.12b	Page 312	
C. ***	ATLANTIS II 5.10b (or 5.9)	Page 309	
D. *	WAKE UP CALL I 5.9+	Page 312	
E. **	TRUE STORIES I 5.11c (5.11a R / 5.10a X)	Page 313	
F. *	BURNING DOWN THE HOUSE II 5.11a R (5.10a X)	Page 316	
G. ***	HOTTER THAN HELL I 5.9	Page 313	
H. **	TRANQUILITY II 5.10b	Page 312	
I. **	BACKDRAFT I 5.11c (5.8 R)	Page 313	
J. **	UNFORGETTABLE FIRE II 5.11b (5.9 R)	Page 316	
K.	BULLET THE BLUE SKY I 5.11c	Page 317	
L.	SURREAL II 5.10c (5.9 R)	Page 317	
M. *	THE TAINT I 5.11d	Page 317	
N.	BROWN STAR I 5.10b R	Page 317	
O. *	FOOTSY-QUENCE II 5.9 R	Page 318	
P.	THE GRAND ILLUSION II 5.10b (5.9 R)	Page 318	

for an orange piton. Continue up the clean face to a good horizontal crack, then climb a thin face past two bolts (5.10c) to reach a huge pine tree on the middle INFERNO tree ledge. 150', 5.10c (5.8 R)

2. Just to the right of THE TAINT (and to the left of BULLET THE BLUE SKY), climb up a very steep face past five bolts (5.11c crux after the third bolt) and two pitons to a tree belay at the top of the cliff. 120', 5.11c

HISTORY: Tom Callaghan, Haydie Callaghan, & Bill Boyle climbed the first pitch in September, 1990. In November, 1990, Tom Callaghan & Haydie Callaghan added the crux second pitch.

BURNING DOWN THE HOUSE II 5.11a R (5.10a X) (*)

An excellent and stimulating climb on fine rock, yet very poorly protected in several places. Think before you dash back in. Start a few feet to the right of HOTTER THAN HELL at a fallen slab. Modern rack recommended.

1. Climb directly to the second bolt of HOTTER THAN HELL, move up to a stance, then angle right to a bolt in dark rock. Face climb to another small stance and the final bolt. Step right into a shallow groove with no protection to easier climbing, safety, and the INFERNO tree ledge. 150', 5.10a X

2. Just to the left of TRANQUILITY's top crack is a diagonal finger crack that's hard to see from below. Just left of a pine, boulder up the face to a stance below a hanging block (5.10c). Face climb right beneath the block to the base of the finger crack (piton). Continue up the finger crack (5.10d) to a rest above a bulge, then climb thin cracks and grooves with difficult protection to an obvious traverse right to the tree belay on INFERNO. 5.11a

2a. An alternate start boulders directly up the face right of the hanging block (bold; 5.11a R) to the fixed piton at the base of the finger crack. 5.11a R

3. Finish diagonally right up the last crack on INFERNO (5.8), or for a final thrill, over the "unlikely blank bulge" (5.10b) on TRANQUILITY.

HISTORY: Tom Callaghan, John Strand, & Haydie Donahue made the first ascent in August, 1984, after several attempts. The right-hand start on Pitch two was added by Callaghan & Strand the following summer.

UNFORGETTABLE FIRE II 5.11b (5.9 R) (**)

U2 will love this route. Fantastic climbing on super rock, although there are typically unprotected easier sections. Both pitches may be split. Start the same as for HOTTER THAN HELL. Modern rack and plenty of nerve required. The start of Pitch two is the same as BURNING DOWN THE HOUSE.

1. Climb to the first bolt on HOTTER THAN HELL, then face climb straight up aiming for a prominent, black water streak. Moderate, poorly protected climbing (5.9 R) leads to a good ledge at the base of the streak. After interesting climbing up to a lonely bolt (on SURREAL), make thin moves (5.10c) over a bulge to the INFERNO tree ledge. 150', 5.10c (5.9 R)

WHITEHORSE LEDGE - SOUTH BUTTRESS (INFERNO WALL)

2. The start of Pitch two of both BURNING DOWN THE HOUSE and UNFORGETTABLE FIRE are the same. Straight above is a small pine tree. Boulder up (5.10c) to an obvious undercling and protection (at the same "hanging block" as BURNING DOWN THE HOUSE). Climb onto a ledge, then a short flake leads to a bolt. Overcome this (5.11b) and follow slanting, finger cracks to a final, difficult headwall (also 5.11b) with a piton and a bolt. 120', 5.11b (For variety, the finishes of TRANQUILITY, BURNING DOWN THE HOUSE, and UNFORGETTABLE FIRE are all interchangeable.)

HISTORY: Tom Callaghan & John Strand made the first ascent on October 8, 1986, after several prior attempts and with help from Karl Mallman.

> The following three routes ascend the center of the INFERNO Wall above the INFERNO tree ledge. They are described from right to left.

BULLET THE BLUE SKY I 5.11c
This little known, but very difficult route ascends the steep face between the top pitches of UNFORGETTABLE FIRE and BACKDRAFT.
1. Climb past 2 bolts (5.11c) to easier (5.10d) moves up a steep wall. 120', 5.11c
FA: Ted Hammond & Tom Armstrong April, 1986

THE TAINT I 5.11d (*)
Start on the INFERNO tree ledge just to the right of BROWN STAR, below a small overlap with a bolt 20 feet up.
1. Climb straight up past the bolt and fixed pitons to 5.11d moves past RP protection to gain the base of the bolt ladder that finishes THE GIRDLE TRAVERSE. Climb the bolt ladder directly (also 5.11). 120', 5.11d

HISTORY: After cleaning the route on rappel and top-roping it, Bob Parrott & Rob Adair made the first ascent in April, 1986.

BROWN STAR I 5.10b R
Begin at the base of the final corner on SURREAL.
1. Move right around the arete of the dihedral to a small, right-facing corner (piton). Continue up a brown streak (poor bolt) to a ledge. 60', 5.10b R
FA: Bob Parrott & Rob Adair April, 1986

SURREAL II 5.10c (5.9 R)
The steep slab left of TRANQUILITY. Start as for HOTTER THAN HELL.
1. Use that route's first bolt to protect a traverse to the left into a left-facing dihedral. Layback to its top, then face climb to a clump of birches. 5.8
2. Head right into no-man's-land, face climbing up a black streak (5.9 R) to "the lonely bolt". Hard face moves (5.10c) gain the INFERNO ledge. 5.10c (5.9 R)
3. Finish as for THE GIRDLE TRAVERSE. Climb up a prominent, left-facing dihedral, step right, and face climb a few feet to the right of a short bolt ladder with three bolts (5.10b) to the top. 5.10b

318 THE MOUNT WASHINGTON VALLEY

HISTORY: Doug Madara & Paul Ross did the first ascent on June 30, 1978 also doing the first free ascent of the last pitch of THE GIRDLE TRAVERSE

FOOTSY-QUENCE II 5.9 R (*)
Begin 40 feet left of HOTTER THAN HELL at a 15 foot pillar. More of a variation start to GRAND ILLUSION as they share the same second pitch.
1. Climb the front face of the pillar or block, then step left into a crack (peg). When the finger crack ends, step right across a slab to a stance (5.9-; bolt). Climb a flake on the left to a tree. 85', 5.9-
2. Same as GRAND ILLUSION. Continue up a vague, left-facing flake (peg), to ramps and horizontal cracks leading to the INFERNO ledge. 100', 5.9 R
FA: Tom Callaghan, Steve Callaghan, John Strand, & John Mallery July 3, 1981

THE GRAND ILLUSION II 5.10b (5.9 R)
An obscure, full length climb that eludes many, taking a line up the TRANQUILITY slab's left side, then on up to the top of the ledge. Begin 40 feet to the left of SURREAL where an overhang fades to reveal a corner and notch.
1. Climb up roughly 25 feet, then layback through the notched overhang before angling up and left (5.9) to a small ledge. Step across a slab, and head up a right-facing corner above a tree ledge. 100'. 5.9
2. Right of the belay, climb a groove slanting back left. Go straight up thin cracks past a prominent horizontal crack. Above, face climb (less protection) to the trees. 100', 5.9 R
3. Walk slightly left to a break in the steep wall with a peg 10 feet up. Above the piton, exit left on a flake to a small oak tree at 30 feet. Step left over a slab to a yellow corner. 50', 5.10b
4. Climb the slab to the right of the corner past a thin flake to a roof. Layback around the roof (5.8+), then climb shallow grooves left to a ledge. 60', 5.8+
5. Climb the slabby wall left to the summit. No protection. 5.6 R
FA: Doug Madara & Paul Ross July 1, 1978

FALL LINE I 5.9+
Start 150 feet to the left of BROWN STAR at a black prow of rock.
1. Climb up a 10 foot high flake on the right (peg) to horizontal cracks, and handtraverse left to a ledge. Continue over steep flakes and past small ledges (hidden pins). Move left onto a black face with a horn, then up past two bolts (5.9+) to easier climbing and the trees. 140', 5.9+
HISTORY: Bill Lowther made the first ascent, rope-solo, on September 23, 1993 — and took a leaderfall when a hold broke!

FREE FALL I 5.9+ The sister climb to FALL LINE.
1. Start up that route, but climb left onto a ledge (or climb directly up over a bulge, no protection, harder). From the ledge, move right, and face climb steeply past three bolts to the top. 140', 5.9+

WHITEHORSE LEDGE - SOUTH BUTTRESS (CATHONIAN SLAB) 319

HISTORY: After an earlier attempt with Jon Sykes, Bill Lowther & Gerry Lortie made the first ascent on July 31, 1994.

THE CATHONIAN SLAB

Several routes on the 40 foot slab below the TRANQUILITY Slab offer alternative starts to those routes. From right to left, they are:

UNDERWORLD I 5.6 X
1. Climb the obvious white streak in the center of the slab. 40', 5.6 X
FA: Uwe Schneider & students Summer, 1987

CRISS CROSS I 5.7+
Look for two cracks in the slab that cross over each other.
1. Climb up the cracks (5.7+), with natural gear. 40', 5.7
FA: Uwe Schneider, Chris Stevens, & Brian Tessier April, 1992

CROSSWALK I 5.7
Start 20 feet to the left of CRISS CROSS.
1. Diagonal up and right to clip a piton on the left. Step left (5.7) over a bulge, then climb straight up past horizontal cracks and a bolt to the top. 40', 5.7
FA: Uwe Schneider, Chris Stevens, & Brian Tessier April, 1992

BRIMSTONE I 5.5
The left-hand route up the slab.
1. Friction and face climb past two bolts (5.5) directly up to the start of HOTTER THAN HELL. 40', 5.5
FA: Uwe Schneider, Chris Stevens, & Brian Tessier April, 1992

GENERATION GAP I 5.5
An obscure route located on broken cliffs directly below THE COSMIC CRAG and well to the left of GRAND ILLUSION.
1. Up an obvious crack, then right to a ledge with an oak. 50', 5.5
2. Ascend a low-angled, open groove, then move right to a large ledge with several cracks in a corner. 50', 5.5
3. Layback the longest crack above (5.5), finishing up a slab. 70', 5.5
FA: Andrew Ross & Paul Ross August 29, 1978

> There are several short cliffs hidden in the woods at the far, left end of the South Buttress of Whitehorse: the Gargoyle Buttress, the Steak Sauce Crag, the Where In The Blazes Cliff, and the Cosmic Crag.

THE GARGOYLE BUTTRESS

This is the 50 foot high, blocky buttress just to the left of the slime gully, the usually wet drainage corner to the left of ARNO'S CORNER, THREE SAINTS, and HOLLOW MEN. The routes are described from right to left.

WILKINSON SWORD I 5.10a
Ascends the overhanging arete on the right side of the Gargoyle Buttress, just to the left of the slime gully. Use your razor sharp wit—and a normal rack.
1. Climb the arete (5.10a), grab the Gargoyle, stand on it, and finish. 50', 5.10a
HISTORY: On June 6, 1996, Fossil Club members Steve Larson, Joe Klemotovitch, Chris Noonan, Dennis Goode, & Rob Adair did the first ascent.

ECONOMY OF FORCE I 5.12a (**)
Powerful moves! Start just to the left of WILKINSON SWORD and the wet approach gully to the left of THREE SAINTS. Be forewarned: the route overhangs 20 feet in 50 feet! Six bolts lead to the anchor. A popular pump.
1. Face climb up an extremely overhanging orange wall past six bolts. 50', 5.12a Rappel off the convenient pine tree at the top.
FA: Brad White November 7, 1995

BRAINDEAD I 5.11b
Begin just to the left of ECONOMY OF FORCE.
1. Start on a large block. Gain a shallow, left-leaning ramp at a bolt. Climb up past a bolt and pin, then struggle over the lip (5.11b) onto a large ledge with a bolt and a bashie. Traverse right to a piton & bolt anchor. 50', 5.11b
2. Climb the overhanging wall above on jugs past three bolts. 30', 5.10b
HISTORY: Bill Lowther rope-soloed the first ascent in August, 1993, placing the crux bolt, and the bolts on Pitch two, on aid. Bill Lowther & George Hurley made the first free ascent on September 2, 1993.

THE STEAK SAUCE CRAG

The next several climbs are located on a small, but enjoyable outcrop below the left side of the South Buttress. From THREE SAINTS, traverse down and straight left, skirting the bottom of the scraggly Gargoyle Buttress for a few minutes until you reach the cliff. A popular one pitch crag. The routes are listed from right to left.

DROID WHERE PROHIBITED I 5.10d
Start to the right of HORSE OF A DIFFERENT COLOR.
1. Face climb past two bolts (5.10d) to the top. 5.10d
HISTORY: Ward Smith, Jon Regini, & Chris Smith made the first ascent in October, 1985. Ward's drill bit broke on the lead, and he was forced to go for it! The second bolt was later added on rappel.

COLOR MY WORLD I 5.8+
Start a few feet to the right of HORSE OF A DIFFERENT COLOR.
1. Face climb up a dark streak to a short dihedral and the top. 5.8+
FA: John Strand, free-solo October, 1983

WHITEHORSE LEDGE - SOUTH BUTTRESS (STEAK SAUCE & BLAZES)

HORSE OF A DIFFERENT COLOR I 5.10b (*)
This is the obvious, thin crack system running up the cliff's upper, right-hand side, approximately 100 feet to the right of STEAK SAUCE.
1. Climb up the thin crack, step left to a pine tree, and make easy moves past a bolt to reach the top. 5.10b
FA: Todd Swain & Kim Speckman   March 29, 1980
FFA: Doug Madara & Harold Consentine   July 29, 1980

WOODEN NICHOLS I 5.11a
The face to the left of HORSE OF A DIFFERENT COLOR.
1. Face climb past a horizontal crack, potholes, and a bolt. 5.11a
HISTORY: After some cleaning on rappel, Peter Lataille & Ward Smith made the first ascent on May 30, 1986, placing the bolt on the lead.

STEAK SAUCE I 5.12c (**)
You will probably want to train on a diet of raw meat before devouring this short testpiece. The obvious, painfully desperate, finger crack on the cliff's left side. The crux is undoubtedly the start!
1. Climb up an extremely fingery, thin crack over a 15 foot bulge (5.12c) onto considerably easier climbing above. 50', 5.12c
HISTORY: Todd Swain & Rick Couchon made the first ascent in June, 1979. Many climbers then attempted the route free without success. After several days of attempts, Jim Surette with John Burke made the first free ascent on May 13, 1985.

POWDERFINGER I 5.10d (*)
This climb really is short but sweet! And surprisingly strenuous.
1. Climb a left-arching finger crack on the crag's left-hand side. 35', 5.10d
FA: Jeff Butterfield & Gene Popier   April, 1981

THE WHERE IN THE BLAZES CLIFF

At the far, left side of the South Buttress, on the southwest facing summit slabs looking towards the Moat Mountains, is yet another small cliff. From the open summit of the South Buttress, walk roughly northwest along the yellow-blazed Bryce Path that circles back around and down to Echo Lake. Hike down and left a short distance until you can see the cliff. You can also approach by struggling way to the left from the INFERNO tree ledge.

HORIZONTAL CHIMNEY I 5.7+
A unique, but exceedingly awkward bomb bay chimney.
1. Struggle up the chimney, and exit right at the top. 100', 5.7+
FA: Roger Martin & Paul Ross   May 29, 1976

CRACK DETECTIVES I 5.8+
To the right of the previous climb, a crack splits a three foot roof.
1. Climb past some loose-looking blocks to the crack, and jam over the roof to a belay tree above. 100', 5.8
FA: Kurt Winkler, Sandy Robinson, & Dennis McKinnon October 6, 1983

CRACK COLLECTION I 5.7
Sixty feet to the right of CRACK DETECTIVES is a finger crack.
1. After the initial crack, step right, climb another corner crack, and then two more cracks to the finish. 5.7
FA: Roger Martin & Paul Ross May 29, 1976

THE COSMIC CRAG

Hot climbs in a cosmic setting! You can approach this popular, 50 to 75 foot cliff most easily from the top of INFERNO, or by hiking up the Bryce Path around the left side of the South Buttress (about 30 minutes from Hales Location) until near the top of Whitehorse, and then bushwhack horizontally to your right. The Cosmic Crag is also located uphill to the right of The Where In The Blazes Cliff. The routes are described from left to right.

LAST EXIT I 5.9
The farthest, left-hand route on the cliff, the sharp groove.
1. Climb the shallow, left-facing corner (5.9) to a low-angled crack. 50', 5.9
FA: Andrew Ross & Paul Ross August 24, 1978

GRAVITATIONAL MASS I 5.10d (*)
Float up the overhanging wall to the left of HERE COME THE JUGS.
1. Face climb past three bolts on good holds (crux between the second and third bolts) up the overhanging wall to a double bolt anchor. 50', 5.10d
HISTORY: Uwe Schneider & "Curious" George Gipson did the first ascent in May, 1990, after cleaning and bolting the route on rappel.

HERE COME THE JUGS I 5.7 (*)
Discovered at last! Thirty feet to the right of LAST EXIT is a beautiful, right-facing corner. Moderate climbing, fun, and well protected.
1. Climb up the short dihedral (5.7) past several small trees. 75', 5.7
FA: Henry Barber & Dave Cilley October 2, 1972

BABY FACE I 5.10c (*)
Begin 10 feet to the right of HERE COME THE JUGS.
1. After tricky moves off the ground, face climb past two bolts (5.10c) to a horizontal crack (poor wired nuts), then step right (harder and unprotected), or go left (easier), finishing up HERE COME THE JUGS. 75', 5.10c
FA: Joe Desimone & Kris Hansen June, 1987

SIDEREAL MOTION I 5.11b

The motion with which Time is calculated. The route takes a rising traverse line between COSMIC AMAZEMENT and BABY FACE. There are five bolts.

1. Start up COSMIC AMAZEMENT and step left (5.9), or boulder straight up (5.11b), to reach the first bolt. Traverse left past four more bolts, then climb straight up to the top. 80', 5.11b

HISTORY: Uwe Schneider, Peter Hovling, Chris Stevens, Craig Taylor, plus George Hurley who came walking by, made the first ascent in May, 1991. In his youth, Uwe Schneider attended Maine Maritime Academy. "Sir! I am greatly embarrassed and deeply humiliated that due to unforeseen circumstances beyond my control, the inner workings and hidden mechanisms of my chronometer are in such inaccord with the Great Sidereal Motion with which Time is generally reckoned that I cannot with any degree of accuracy state the correct time, Sir!"

COSMIC AMAZEMENT I 5.9 (**)

Forty feet to the right of HERE COME THE JUGS is a rather amazing layback crack in a left-facing corner.

1. Layback up the strenuous, left-leaning crack and flake. 75', 5.9

FA: Paul Ross & Andrew Ross   August 29, 1978

THE UNCERTAINTY PRINCIPLE I 5.10d (*)

The route climbs the flaring groove 15 feet right of COSMIC AMAZEMENT, the same V groove as SPLIT DECISION, which was climbed previously.

1. A difficult boulder problem (5.10d) enters the groove, clip the first bolt, stem up the groove (bolt), then undercling left (bolt; 5.10a) to the top. 60', 5.10d

FA: Uwe Schneider & Chris Stevens   May, 1991

SPLIT DECISION I 5.10d

This climb ascends the same V groove as THE UNCERTAINTY PRINCIPLE, but instead finishes up and right. It was originally climbed without any bolts.

1. Make a 5.10d move into the groove, clip the first bolt, climb halfway up the groove (bolt), and escape right up square-cut holds (5.8) to the top. 60', 5.10d

FA: Kurt Winkler & James St. Jean   July 5, 1990

COSMIC BOOKS I 5.7

Forty feet to the right of COSMIC AMAZEMENT are twin dihedrals.

1. Climb the left-hand of two, right-facing corners. 60', 5.7

FA: Kurt Winkler & James St. Jean   August 1, 1984

BIFOCAL UKULELE I 5.8

The crag's farthest right-hand route ascends the steep face off to the right of COSMIC BOOKS. Normal rack.

1. Climb straight up a brown wall on unusual triangular holds to the first bolt,

make an awkward move (5.8) to a good hold, and climb past a second bolt to a belay at the trees. 50', 5.8
HISTORY: Chris Stevens & Uwe Schneider made the first ascent in May, 1991, after cleaning the route and bolting it on rappel.

THE CITADEL BOULDER

This fun, practice rock is a 22 foot, Matterhorn-shaped boulder just off the Bryce Path, only about 300 yards from the White Mountain Hotel. From the hotel, turn left on the Bryce Path, and walk left for several minutes. To set up a top-rope, solo up the STANDARD ROUTE to clip the bolt anchor on top.

STANDARD ROUTE I 5.3
The easy groove on the boulder's East side.

THE NORTH FACE I 5.10d
Climb straight up the boulder's steep North Face.

THE NORTHEAST RIDGE I 5.9+
Make a rising traverse from right to left to the top.

THE SOUTH FACE I 5.5
A good beginner top-rope, up a moderate slab.

THE GIRDLE TRAVERSES OF WHITEHORSE LEDGE

THE GIRDLE TRAVERSE OF WHITEHORSE (***)
III 5.8 (5.7 R), A1 (3 points of aid on bolts), or 5.10b (5.7 R)
A grand adventure, a long and unique climb, and the first girdle traverse done in the White Mountains. The route begins on the right margin of the Slabs and traverses left across the entire width of Whitehorse, ending on the far, left-hand side of the South Buttress. The route is highly recommended, and the three aid points on the last pitch, on bolts, may be easily climbed just with slings. Leader and second should, however, be of equal ability, since protection on several leads is somewhat sparse. Carry a spare, 50 meter 9mm rope for a rappel.
1–3. Climb the first three pitches of BEGINNER'S ROUTE. 5.4
4. Continue up BEGINNER'S DIRECT (5.7 R), angling left over the arch to a two bolt belay near STANDARD ROUTE. 5.7 R
5. Traverse left to STANDARD ROUTE. The first ascent party climbed a very awkward "forearm traverse" (5.8) along a prominent, horizontal crack at the arch's top. Avoid this by down climbing the arch for 60 feet to a fixed anchor.
6. Down climb a bit more, then bear left on ramps and cracks just above the STANDARD arch to a stance on SLIDING BOARD at a two bolt anchor.

WHITEHORSE LEDGE - THE GIRDLE TRAVERSES 325

7. Straight left (5.6 R) across a slab to a ledge on WEDGE. 5.6 R
8. Follow the obvious, horizontal crack (at the base of the WEDGE Buttress) left past pitons to a nut belay.
9. Continue left to the large, tree ledge on DIKE ROUTE.
10 & 11. Scramble left, up a bit on tree ledges past MISTAKEN IDENTITY and above CEILING. Do not traverse the highest tree ledge above CEILING.
12. Down climb a chimney crack (5.5; old bolt) on ECHO to trees. 5.5
13. Walk left across a narrow sidewalk beneath overhangs past THE DIRECT FINISH to CHILDREN'S CRUSADE to a double bolt anchor.
14. From the two bolt anchor, rappel with two ropes 100 feet down a steep slab to a tree and ledge on the left on ERADICATE. A0
15. A moderate, enjoyable traverse leads left to a fir tree. 5.3
16. Continue traversing straight left past a couple of fixed anchors (and past THE LAST UNICORN) to the large, WONDER WALL tree ledge. 5.4
17. Step down off the ledge, then make a long, easy traverse left under a steep band (past LOST SOULS and CEMETERY GATES) across sloping ledges to a belay on a small ledge below the INFERNO Corner.
18. Climb Pitch one of INFERNO, up the face (5.7) and corner. 5.7
19. Walk left across the INFERNO tree ledge to a left-facing corner.
20. Layback the dihedral, step right, and belay on a ledge.
21. Aid from slings off three bolts (A1), or free climb the face just to the right (5.10b), to a final crack. A1 or 5.10b. Shake hands and go out for a pint!
HISTORY: Paul Ross & Hugh Thompson made the historic first ascent of this climb on May 25, 1972. The last pitch was freed by Doug Madara & Paul Ross on June 30, 1978, during their first ascent of SURREAL.

THE NEW WAVE TRAVERSE III 5.9 (5.7 R)
The reverse girdle of Whitehorse, with novel climbing, takes a completely different line across the cliff!

1 & 2. Climb the first two leads of TRANQUILITY (5.7) to the tree-covered ledge on INFERNO. Walk to its right end. 5.7
3. Down climb the INFERNO Corner (5.7), then solo across the access ledges (past LOST SOULS) to the WONDER WALL tree ledge. 5.7
4. Step down off the ledge's right end, and traverse straight right (5.4) to the large spruce tree at the start of THE LAST UNICORN. 5.4
5. Continue horizontally right to a small tree and ledge. 5.3
6. Down climb the ERADICATE Dike (5.7 R) to a ledge and old pegs about 50 feet above the ground. 5.7 R
7. Move down a bit, then step right onto CHILDREN'S CRUSADE, and climb its first pitch (5.9) to a double bolt belay. 5.9
8 & 9. Climb the next two leads of CHILDREN'S CRUSADE. 5.9 & 5.8

10. Traverse right across a tree ledge, then climb up the chimney crack (5.5; old bolt) on ECHO. 5.5

11 & 12. Walk across ledges to the DIKE tree ledge's right end.

13. Climb up THE DARCY-CROWTHER VARIATION (5.6), up slabs towards an overlap. Two piton anchor above double, white blocks.

14. Pull over the overlap, and follow the arch up and right (5.5) to a tree ledge. Walk right to a junction with WEDGE. 5.5

15. Down climb Pitch five of WEDGE, down grooves (pegs).

16. Traverse right below the overlaps past INTERLOPER, and belay over on SLIDING BOARD.

17. Climb the fifth pitch of SLIDING BOARD (5.5 or 5.6) to below the final headwall, belaying just to the left of an obvious arch. 5.5 or 5.6

18. Traverse under the arch to a junction with STANDARD.

19 & 20. Finish on STANDARD ROUTE, up the final dikes. 250', 5.2 R

FA: Mack Johnson & Paul Ross July, 1979

THE GUIDE'S WALL

This is the small cliff between Cathedral and Whitehorse Ledges, easily seen from the clearing along the Bryce Path on the approach to Whitehorse. Historically, Tom Lyman climbed here in the early 1970s, but his routes went unrecorded. More recently, the cliff has been cleaned and offers over a dozen climbs. There are three approaches: bushwhack from the clearing up to the cliff, hike up the Bryce Path to the crag's top, or do a route on Whitehorse and round out the day by hiking down the Bryce Path to the top of the Guide's Wall, then down around the cliff's left side (right side, facing out) to reach the start of the climbs. There is also a double bolt rappel anchor (two ropes needed) at the top left end of the Guide's Wall (right side, looking out).

FLYING DUTCHMAN I 5.8

The crag's farthest left route, up a shallow, left-facing corner starting 40 feet up.
1. Climb up and right on angular holds to the corner and large pine on top. 5.8
FA: Ed Webster, Peter van der Toorn Vrythoff, & Jeanne Smits (Holland) October 5, 1981

DUTY CALLS I 5.8

The cleaned-off slab located just downhill from the previous route.
1. Climb up the slab to cracks, some protection, and the top. 5.8
FA: John Bouchard & Steve Arsenault November, 1980

HAPPY FACE I 5.5 R

This route ascends an open face to the right of DUTY CALLS. From the Bryce Path, traverse south along a ledge just below the top of the cliff until you reach a triple tree rappel anchor, two pines and an oak.
1. Follow the rappel line back up the face (5.5 R) to the trees. 85', 5.5 R
FA: George Hurley & Jeff Carter May 2, 1990

ZIGGURAUT I 5.9 (*)

Begin just to the right of mossy corners, 100 feet left of PYRAMID.
1. Undercling an obvious flake to an arete and follow a flake to the top. 70', 5.9
FA: Todd Swain & Ned Getchell April 23, 1983

PYRAMID I 5.8

Walk down to the right past a tree-filled groove to an outside corner with a finger crack on its face. Well protected.
1. Climb the crack (5.8) to the top. 5.8
FA: John Bouchard & Richard Estock June, 1981

THE VISITORS I 5.9

Begin just to the left of A STITCH IN TIME below a small overhang.
1. Climb past the overhang on its right side up to a flake (piton), then make a traverse left (5.9) to a pine tree belay. 5.9

2. Go up and slightly right for 60 feet, angle left to a flake directly above the belay, and layback up this to the finish.
FA: Kurt Winkler & Jim Hancock April 10, 1981

A STITCH IN TIME I 5.9 (**)
Saves nine? The best climb on the cliff, complete with enjoyable moves, unusual finger pockets, and copious amounts of fixed protection. The route ascends the prominent cleaned-off stripe just left of the center of the cliff.
1. Climb easily at first, then make fingery moves (5.9) on small pockets up a 20 foot headwall past fixed pitons. Traverse a bit right, then step back left to a 5.9 face move (bolt). Belay on a small ledge (nuts), or continue. 140', 5.9
FA: John Bouchard & Steve Arsenault November, 1980

FOLLOW YOUR OWN ROAD I 5.10d (5.8+ R)
1. Start up STITCH IN TIME, then step right at a piton. Two bolts protect face climbing leading up to a committing mantleshelf move (5.8+ R) onto a ledge. Above, another bolt protects a thin face move (5.10d) until you can wander up the face above (5.8) to the top. 150', 5.10d
HISTORY: Uwe Schneider & Kris Pastoriza did the first ascent on June 21, 1989. After cleaning, the bolts were placed on the lead, the second bolt on aid.

LAUNCH THE KITTY I 5.11b (*)
Either you like cats—or you don't! The hardest climb on the cliff. Begin 30 feet downhill and right of STITCH IN TIME below an obvious roof.
1. Climb up a face past two bolts to a break in the roof (bolt), then pull past the roof (5.11b) up to a double bolt anchor. 60', 5.11b
HISTORY: Bill Lutkus, Dave Karl, & Uwe Schneider made the first ascent on July 18, 1989, after cleaning and bolting the route on rappel.

THE CAGE I 5.7
Right of the former route is an amphitheater with a raven's nest. Where the cliff descends farther is this two pitch route.
1. Climb directly up a cleaned slab to a tree belay.
2. Head straight to the top (5.7) past a pin on the crux overlap. 5.7
FA: John Bouchard & Stan Grodsky Autumn, 1980

CLIENTS ARE PEOPLE TOO! I 5.7
Sixty feet to the right of THE CAGE, a tree grows against the cliff.
1. Climb the tree and a rounded arete to a cleaned, left-facing corner. Belay on tree ledges on the left. 80', 5.6
2. From the highest ledge, climb a steep face using sharp holds up a thin, vertical crack. A short, right-facing corner leads to the top. 100', 5.7
FA: Todd Swain & Ned Getchell April 23, 1983

ACE'S PLACE I 5.7
The right-hand side of the Guide's Wall is formed by a large, low-angled slab with a short, vertical wall at its base.
1. Climb either of two finger cracks (5.7) on the left side of the first wall. 5.7
2. Slab climb straight up past a bolt to a tree belay.
3. A slab leads to a corner and a small overhang. 5.7
FA: John Bouchard & friend August, 1980

VARIATION #1: KIMBERLLY'S FOLLY I 5.8
1a. Just to the right, climb up a jam crack past two pegs. 5.8
FA: John Bouchard & Michael Hannon May, 1981

VARIATION #2: CLING-ON I 5.9
1b. Farther to the right, climb up to a narrow overlap (piton), making a hard undercling move (5.9) to get past it. 5.9
FA: John Bouchard 1981

FEAR FACTOR I 5.9
To the right of a short wall is a gully and a steep buttress.
1. Climb a thin crack up the face of the buttress past two pins. 5.9
FA: John Bouchard Spring, 1981

DONDONGO I 5.8
An obscure route right of ACE'S PLACE. Find a large pine below a crack.
1. Climb up the crack, followed by a slab above. 160', 5.8
FA: Kit Dover & Tom Bowker July 3, 1988

THE HORIZONTAL BOP II 5.9
The left to right girdle traverse of the Guide's Wall.
1. Climb PYRAMID's start to a huge pine tree. 75', 5.6
2. Step down onto a foot ledge on the right. When it ends, make crux moves (5.9) across STITCH IN TIME (peg). Climb up a flake and across easier rock to a hanging belay. 130', 5.9
3. Head straight right climbing parallel cracks to a broken corner, then diagonal up right past a rotten log to the top. 120', 5.4
FA: Todd Swain & Mark Wallace April 14, 1983

330 THE MOUNT WASHINGTON VALLEY

Jim Dunn on the crux second pitch of Robinson Crusoe (5.10b R) in 1985. Photograph by Ed Webster.

HUMPHREY'S LEDGE

This 300 foot, south-facing cliff is located a couple of miles north of Cathedral Ledge along the West Side Road in a quiet part of the Mount Washington Valley. The cliff's reputation for crumbly rock is not entirely justified, although there are several routes where both the climbing and protection does require extra care. Popular climbs on Humphrey's include the historic, central chimney crack of the WIESSNER ROUTE, as well as modern climbs like STICKY WICKET, ROBINSON CRUSOE, THE GREAT ESCAPE, and the sport route, PROCESSION. Protection on Humphrey's is generally adequate given a bit of imagination and a varied, modern rack. Route finding, however, can be quite a challenge on some of the face climbs.

To reach the cliff, drive north from Cathedral Ledge along the West Side Road for 1.7 miles to the Lady Blanche House on your right, a local historic site. Please park across the street from the house on the sandy shoulder, and obey all posted no-parking signs. A climber's trail opposite the Lady Blanche House leads steeply uphill from a collection of popular boulders to reach the cliff base at the WIESSNER ROUTE, the obvious, vertical chimney crack. The climbs on Humphrey's Ledge are described first to the left, and then to the right of this prominent landmark. The quickest descent from the top of Humphrey's is to rappel back down your route with two ropes (look for anchors on the way up), or rappel down the double ring bolt anchors on ROBINSON CRUSOE. Otherwise circle around which ever side of the cliff you happen to be closest to—a horrendous bushwhack either way!

WIESSNER ROUTE II 5.8 R (**)

The impressive, narrow chimney system in the center of the cliff. For its era, a daring lead by Fritz Wiessner, and an even more outrageous free-solo. Bring a normal rack with a selection of large cams.

1. Jam the awkward 5.8 crack on the chimney's right wall to a stance. 45', 5.8
2. Enter the chimney proper and squeeze up it with little protection (and a lot of effort) to a good ledge with a piton anchor. 5.8 R
3. Strenuous moves gain the upper chimney which is followed more easily to the top of the cliff. 5.8 R Rappel back down the route with two ropes.

HISTORY: "We were driving along the West Side Road one day," Robert Underhill recalled, "and I said to Fritz, 'There's an obvious climb.' So we did it." Fritz Wiessner & Robert Underhill made the first ascent, however, of only the last pitch of the climb in the Summer of 1933. They scrambled up a system of broken ledges (THE OLD ROUTE) to the top of the pillar on THE GUIDE'S ROUTE, rappelled and tensioned left into the upper chimney, and used a shoulderstand to start today's third pitch. Bothered that they had avoided the climb's main challenge, Fritz Wiessner & Roger Whitney

(Hassler Whitney's brother) returned to make the climb's first complete ascent in 1935. As Fritz remembered it: "The first chimney is a little bit of hard work, but then it's not too bad above..." Given his penchant for crack climbing, Fritz enjoyed the route so much that he later free-soloed it.

THE GREAT ESCAPE II 5.11d (**)
Sleight of hand? Levitate up the blank, vertical wall left of the WIESSNER ROUTE. Assorted wired nuts, zero gravity, and a #1 Friend are useful.
1. Scramble up a short slab immediately left of WIESSNER's to a stance. Make a 5.10b move past a bolt to better holds and a small spike of rock. Two bolts protect extremely thin face moves (5.11d) to a rest at the base of a faint groove. Climb this (5.8), running it out to the belay on WIESSNER's. 5.11d
2. Traverse flakes to the left to a tree, then swing right onto an exposed arete. Above a juniper tree (possible belay), ascend an obvious 5.9 dihedral to the top, and another good tree. 5.9 Rappel back down the route using two ropes.
HISTORY: Ed Webster & Kurt Winkler made the first ascent on September 21, 1981. The two crux bolts were placed on the lead on aid.

THE HURLEY WARNING WALL II 5.10d R (*)
A committing climb up the fierce face to the left of THE GREAT ESCAPE. Start on a slab 20 feet to the left of WIESSNER ROUTE. Modern rack.
1. Climb the slab to the left end of a ledge (piton & bolt). Face climb past a knifeblade to a bolt just right of a black water streak, then move left to a third bolt and a stance. Step left, then face climb straight up (5.10d R) with poor wired nut protection before moving up and right to better holds. Finish straight up to a stance (piton on left). 100', 5.10d R
2. Go diagonally right 30 feet, then left under small roofs to a grass ledge. Climb a blocky corner to a ledge on the right with a juniper. 70', 5.9
3. Angle up a slab to the left-hand of two corners and the top. 45', 5.9
HISTORY: Doug Madara, David Stone, & George Hurley made the first ascent on November 10, 1982. Hurley had made several prior attempts on the route, in one instance falling and injuring his foot.

HERE COMES THE SUN II 5.8 R
Start 75 feet to the left of the WIESSNER ROUTE. Not an overly popular climb, as it has some loose rock.
1. Diagonal across an easy slab from right to left onto a small tree ledge. Move up a rotten dike (5.8 R) to a yew tree and belay. 5.8 R
2. Traverse out left to more trees, then up a steep dihedral to face climbing, and a comfortable tree ledge.
3. Climb the narrow groove on the face directly above, the 7, to moderate slabs and the top. 150', 5.7
FA: Michael Hartrich & Paul Ross April 20, 1973

HUMPHREY'S LEDGE (STRAIGHT UP) 333

JAGEN DIE SIEBEN II 5.9+

A varied route. Pitch three, the 7, is superb. Start below the same tree ledge mentioned for HERE COMES THE SUN.

1. Climb either the vertical jam crack on the left, or flakes on the right to reach the tree ledge. Move up, then traverse left for about 30 feet to a prominent, white birch tree and belay.

2. A short lead. Make difficult (5.9+) moves straight up, then face climb on large holds up to a tree ledge. 5.9+

3. Step right, then jam and layback a narrow corner which forms a perfect 7 (same as HERE COMES THE SUN) on the face above. Either exit straight up on knobs (5.7), or undercling around the left side (5.8). Belay under a short wall above. 5.7 or 5.8

4. Finish up the easier upper slabs to the woods.

FA: George Hurley & Steve Jagendorf   August 26, 1979
FFA: George Hurley, Al Bagdonas, & John Mitamura   April 2, 1980

STRAIGHT UP II 5.9+ R

The directissima of Humphrey's, with some excellent climbing and a finish on GIUOCO PIANO. Just left of the former route is a lower angled slab directly under the white birch tree of JAGEN DIE SIEBEN.

1. On the slab's left side, climb a shallow groove through a tiny overlap 15 feet up (bolt). Continue up a short, right-facing corner, then face climb just right of a corner over a bulge (5.9+ R) to the white birch. 70', 5.9+ R

2. Left of the birch, and above a hemlock, ascend a slightly overhanging wall past a small roof (5.8) to better holds and a tree ledge. 60', 5.8

3. Face climb directly up the face (5.8) 30 feet to the left of the 7 to a ledge with a juniper bush. 60', 5.8

4. Do 5.9 face moves off the ledge, and bee line up slabs and overlaps. 120', 5.9

FA: Todd Swain & Brad White September 27, 1980

VARIATION: **AFRICAN QUEEN** I 5.9

The smooth, gray slab to the right of the start of STRAIGHT UP.

1a. Face climb diagonally left over an overlap, move up to a second slender overlap, and step over it a little on the right to join STRAIGHT UP at the right-facing corner. 5.9

FA: Doug Madara & Kurt Winkler September 28, 1981

GIUOCO PIANO II 5.8 (5.7 R) or 5.9

The climb's name, Italian for "soft game", is a classic chess opening. Several large blocks and a poison ivy bush may also have influenced the title of this route. Forty feet to the right of SOUL SURVIVOR (the obvious, left leaning dike that runs up the center of Humphrey's Ledge) is a short, right-facing corner with a layback crack leading up to a tree.

334 THE MOUNT WASHINGTON VALLEY

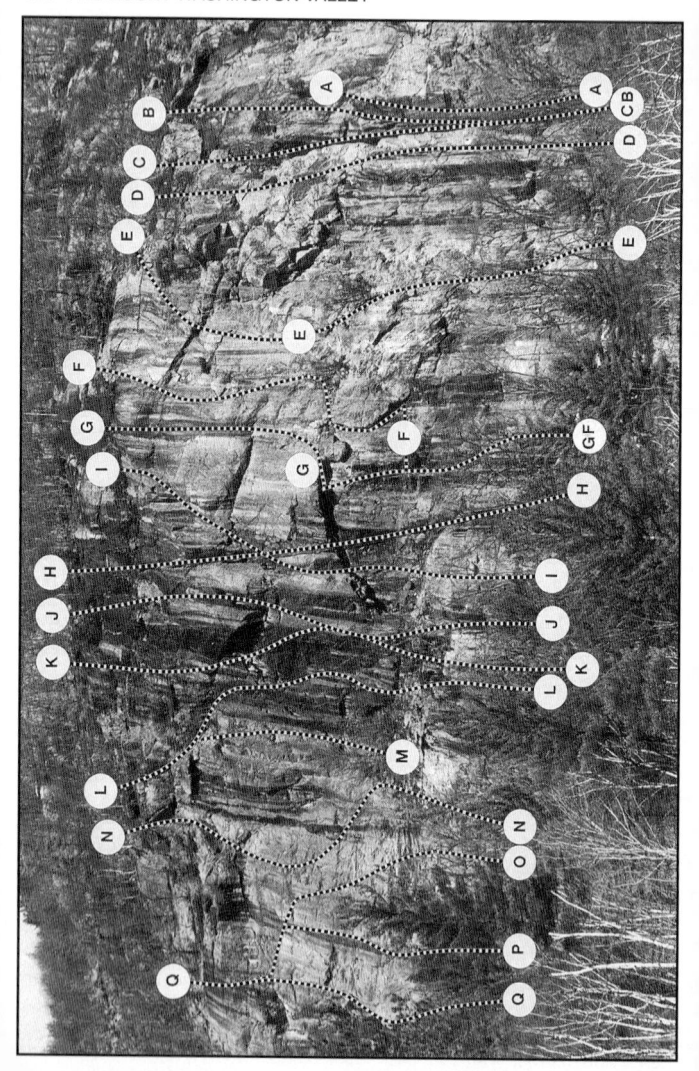

HUMPHREY'S LEDGE

A. *** **PROCESSION** I 5.12b (5.12c if you combine both pitches.)	Page 344
B. * **THE GUIDE'S ROUTE** II 5.9	Page 344
C. ** **WIESSNER ROUTE** II 5.8 R	Page 331
D. ** **THE GREAT ESCAPE** II 5.11d	Page 332
E. **HERE COMES THE SUN** II 5.8 R	Page 332
F. **GIUOCO PIANO** II 5.8 (5.7 R) or 5.9	Page 333
G. * **REGRESSION** II 5.9 (5.8 R)	Page 336
H. **SOUL SURVIVOR** II 5.11a	Page 336
I. *** **ROBINSON CRUSOE** II 5.10b R	Page 337
J. * **STICKY WICKET** II 5.8	Page 338
K. ** **ARIES** II 5.10b	Page 338
L. * **DEDICATION** II 5.7+	Page 340
M. * **DR. LEAKEY, I PRESUME?** I 5.9+ R	Page 341
N. **ECLIPSE** II 5.7	Page 342
O. **WANDERLUST** II 5.8 R	Page 342
P. * **THINK FAST, MR. MOTO** II 5.9 R	Page 342
Q. * **CAKEWALK** II 5.6+	Page 343

1. Gain the corner, layback up it to the tree, then move left up to a clump of trees on a higher ledge. 85'

2. An immense overlap is directly overhead. Climb over to the extreme right end of the overlap, then follow it back left past some poison ivy into a left-facing dihedral. Climb this to blocks beneath the roof, gingerly traverse around them to the right, and belay above at a ledge with a juniper. 70', 5.8

3. Thirty feet to the left of the 7, follow holds up the face with tricky nut protection to a flake. Belay above at another juniper tree. 80'

4. Step left into a shallow groove (5.7 R), or climb straight up (5.9) to a small wave in the summit slab. Fun slab climbing gains the top. 110', 5.7 R or 5.9

FA: George Hurley, Phil Erard, & Ed Mathews   June 16, 1979

REGRESSION II 5.9 (5.8 R) (*)

An impressive line up the massive slab in the cliff's center. The route's other main feature is a hanging block below the long overlap. Start the same as for GIUOCO PIANO, 40 feet to the right of SOUL SURVIVOR. Bring along some large sized protection for the overlap.

1. Layback the short, right-facing corner to a tree, and belay at the next tree clump up on the left. 85'

2. Step left 12 feet, then face climb up a steep wall to a unique cave belay (large Friends needed) under the ceiling 15 feet right of SOUL SURVIVOR. 70'

3. Traverse right beneath the overlap to the hanging block, make an exciting handtraverse right onto its front, then face climb up the wall above following a fairly prominent black water streak (5.8 R). Belay on a small stance below the right end of a horizontal crack. 140', 5.8 R

4. Head up the water streak to a blank bulge (5.9; bolt) and easy slabs. 140', 5.9

HISTORY: The reunion of two old friends, one time Colorado climbers George Hurley & Larry Hamilton, saw the first ascent of this bold climb made on June 15, 1979.

SOUL SURVIVOR II 5.11a

Upgraded from its original rating of 5.10, this is one of the cliff's most prominent lines: the long, left-slanting dike in the center of the crag. Keep your safety line handy if you think you might need to bail on the crux!

1. Follow a moderate corner to a tree ledge on the left.

2. At the large overlap, bolts protect 5.11a moves out the overhang, then easier climbing leads to the white birch on ROBINSON CRUSOE and a double ring bolt anchor. 5.11a

3. Follow the same crack line, bridging up a corner, to the top.

HISTORY: On the first ascent in the Summer of 1972, Joe Cote led the crux overlap on aid, and Paul Ross followed it free. In 1974, on the second ascent, Mark Hudon & Michael Hartrich did the first free ascent on the lead.

HUMPHREY'S LEDGE (SOUL SURVIVOR & ROBINSON CRUSOE)

ROBINSON CRUSOE II 5.10b R (***)
If you were stranded alone on a desert island and had only one climb to do—and this was it, you'd still be happy! Three leads of mostly 5.9 climbing, except for the challenging crux moves up the Pitch two dihedral (5.10b R; with tricky wired nut protection) make for a classic journey. ROBINSON CRUSOE is also the best rappel descent for all the routes in the center of Humphrey's Ledge, so bring a spare rope along. Around the corner to the left of SOUL SURVIVOR is a short, flaring dihedral rising above a ledge 20 feet off the ground.

1. Ascend the enjoyable, flaring corner past two pitons and a bolt (5.9+) up to a large tree ledge. A very enjoyable and popular pitch. 50', 5.9+

2. Climb easy rock to the prominent horizontal overlap on SOUL SURVIVOR. Swing to the left (bolt) out the overlap to a stance at a second bolt. Conquer the flaring groove above (5.10b R; tricky wired nut protection), then face climb up to a double ring bolt anchor on a stance beside a white birch tree. 90', 5.10b R

3. Climb easily up and right across SOUL SURVIVOR to the base of an unlikely headwall. Make 5.9 face moves (bolt) to moderate climbing up a huge, right-facing, flaring corner. At its top, finish up a 5.8 corner on the left (peg) to the summit slab and another double ring bolt anchor. 100', 5.9 Make three easy rappels back down the route using two ropes.

HISTORY: Michael Hartrich, Albert Dow, & Ed Webster made the first ascent of this historic climb on September 12 & 13, 1981. The bolt on Pitch one was placed from a top-rope; all the others were drilled free on the lead. The first bolt on the Pitch two overlap (which replaced the original fixed bong that had disappeared), plus the two, double ring bolt belay/rappel anchors, were added in 1995 with the consent of the first ascent party.

VARIATION #1: **LEFT ARETE** I 5.10b (Top-rope)
1a. Layback up the rounded, left-hand arete. 45', 5.10b
FA: Ed Webster & Brad White, top-rope April, 1982

VARIATION #2: **CENTER** I 5.9+ (Top-rope)
1b. Face climb up the center of the right-hand wall. 45', 5.9+
FA: Ed Webster & Brad White, top-rope April, 1982

VARIATION #3: **PUMPING ADRENALINE** I 5.11b R
What a way to train! There is virtually no protection.
1c. Climb the desperate, unprotected right-hand arete. 45', 5.11b R
HISTORY: Ed Webster made the first ascent on a top-rope in April, 1982, before Jim Surette led the climb in the Spring of 1985.

VARIATION #4: **MAN FRIDAY** I 5.9+ X
Another one to definitely avoid getting stranded on. Don't fall!
2a. From the 5.10b R crux in the flaring groove on Pitch two, escape left

around the arete onto the exposed face below STICKY WICKET. 100', 5.9+ X
FA: Michael Hartrich   September 12, 1981

CASTAWAYS I 5.11a (**)
The thin, vertical crack line just left of Pitch one of ROBINSON CRUSOE. A popular, well protected lead. Don't forget to wear your Hawaiian shirt.
1. Climb the thin, vertical crack (piton), then stay directly on the arete past two bolts (5.11a), climbing on small edges up to the large tree ledge. 50', 5.11a

HISTORY: After attempting the route with Kurt Winkler a week earlier, Ed Webster made a direct ascent up the arete on April 30, 1982, protecting the climb with several knifeblades. After the top two pitons broke, they were replaced with two bolts with the consent of the first ascent party.

STICKY WICKET II 5.8 (*)
Pitch two is indeed a sticky affair. Don't come unglued on the crux.
1. Climb the right-facing corner and layback crack 50 feet to the left of SOUL SURVIVOR to the large, tree-covered ledge.
2. The crux pitch ascends the right margin of the smooth face right of the upper pitch of DEDICATION. Face climb up and then diagonally right past two pins to 5.8 moves (bolt) leading to a small stance on the right at a fixed belay/rappel anchor 10 feet to the left of the white birch on ROBINSON CRUSOE. 5.8
3. Directly above, surmount an awkward, strenuous 5.8 bulge, then follow a groove and crack system to the top of the ledge. 5.8
FA: George Hurley & John Walsh   June 12, 1979

> The next two short climbs are located on the small, V-8 Buttress between the base of STICKEY WICKET and DEDICATION.

V-8 I 5.8 "I knew I should have had a V8!"
1. Climb the perfect V groove on the buttress's right side. 75', 5.8
FA: Kurt Winkler & Ed Webster   April 18, 1982

LITTLE BIG MAN I 5.7+ R
Begin on the left side of the V-8 Buttress.
1. From an oak tree, follow a thin crack up the arete. 75', 5.7+ R
FA: Todd Swain & Mark Wallace   April 7, 1983

ARIES II 5.10b (**)
A full length route up the center of Humphrey's Ledge, with sustained and challenging free climbing on good rock. Bring a modern rack.
1. Climb straight up the center of the lowest buttress, just left of V-8. Make a 5.9 move past a peg to good holds, and belay at trees. 5.9
2. On the left-hand side of the next buttress, make an extremely awkward mantleshelf move (5.10b; small wired nuts), then face climb past horizontal cracks up the arete to the tree-covered ledge. 5.10b

HUMPHREY'S LEDGE (CASTAWAYS & STICKY WICKET) 339

Ed Webster leading Castaways (5.11a) in 1982. Photograph by Alec Behr.

3. Face climb up the start of STICKY WICKET's second pitch past two pitons to a bolt. Belay on the left on a beautiful small ledge at a piton anchor. 5.9

4. Climb strenuously up an overhanging flake (5.9) just to the right of DEDICATION, then traverse left to another flake perched on the exposed, final bulge. Easy slabs lead to the woods and the top. 5.9

HISTORY: Kurt Winkler & Ed Webster did the first two pitches on April 23, 1982. Ed Webster & Rob Walker made the first ascent on June 11, 1982.

VARIATION: **BONDI BEACH** I 5.10b

Climbs the steep wall 10 feet to the right of ARIES' second pitch.

1a. Face climb up to a hard layback move (5.10b), mantle, then forge up the face just right of a small, right-facing corner. 40', 5.10b

FA: Doug Madara, George Hurley, & Ray Lasman (Australia) October, 1982

DEDICATION II 5.7+ (*)

Both this climb and its neighbor STICKY WICKET offer similar climbing on the upper wall: steep face climbing with tricky route finding. Walk about 100 feet to the left of SOUL SURVIVOR, around the base of a small buttress, until below a sharp-edged, left-facing dihedral.

1. Ascend the clean-cut, left-facing corner on good holds (5.4) to some trees. Belay about 25 feet higher on the next ledge at an oak tree. 5.4

2. Climb a slight weakness in the face above, aiming for a shallow groove 35 feet up. Step right into the groove, & follow it up & left onto a good ledge. 5.7+

3. Layback a short crack, surmount a bulge, and enter another shallow, tight-fitting groove. When thwarted by an overhanging wall, make a long traverse to the left. Make sure to protect the second.

4. Climb an easy corner on the left to the final slabs.

FA: Paul Ross & Bill Aughton July 9, 1973

VARIATION #1: **HALLOWEEN III** 5.10b

Start about five feet to the left of the first pitch of DEDICATION.

1a. Climb up the face, staying out of the corner. Get protection by a juniper before moving left, laybacking over a small overhang. 5.10b

FA: Doug Madara, George Hurley, Chris Noonan, David Stone
    & John Syrene October 31, 1982

VARIATION #2: **HALLOWEEN II** 5.9-

Begin roughly 25 feet left of DEDICATION's first lead. A three inch fin of rock with a tunnel marks the start. Bring a baby angle and a blade piton.

1b. Climb straight up and a bit left to a small roof. Pass it on the right (more direct), or the left, moving past a small birch to the top. 5.9-

FA: George Hurley, David Stone, Chris Noonan, John Syrene,
    & Doug Madara October 31, 1982

VARIATION # 3: **DEDICATION DIRECT** I 5.4
Below the big ledge at the top of Pitch one is a left-facing rib.
1c. Climb up the rib and the face to its left to a traverse. 50', 5.4
FA: Barry Nelson & Tim Donnelly   August 20, 1979

> The next five routes ascend the unlikely, steep face left of the top pitches of DEDICATION. Bring double ropes and a modern rack on each climb.

KEY LARGO II 5.10c
1. Climb the first 30 feet of DEDICATION's second pitch to a knifeblade, then face climb left past a bolt (5.9+) to better holds. Angle farther left to a second knifeblade, step over a bulge, and belay on a stance on the right. 5.9+
2. Undercling flakes up left to a difficult bulge (5.10b; peg). Hard face moves lead up the steep wall to a juniper on DEDICATION. 60', 5.10c
FA: Ed Webster & Todd Swain   May 28, 1982

EVEN CAVEGIRLS GET THE BLUES I 5.10a R
The improbable face between DR. LEAKEY, I PRESUME? and KEY LARGO. Prozac, a modern rack, and double ropes are all recommended—in that order!
1. Face climb up to an overhang between DR. LEAKEY and KEY LARGO (bolt). Pull through the center of the roof (5.9; bolt), then continue straight up, eventually passing a short, right-facing corner capped by a ceiling. Swing left on a flake and mantle (5.9+), then cruise up to another bolt. Finish straight up just to the left of the 5.10 moves on KEY LARGO, then angle left (peg) to a yew tree. 130', 5.10a R
FA: Todd Swain, Dick Peterson, & Kathy Beuttler   September 24, 1987

DR. LEAKEY, I PRESUME? I 5.9+ R (*)
Don't forget to introduce yourself to your partner. Takes an uncompromising line up the fingery steep face 30 feet left of KEY LARGO, above three stacked blocks sitting on the left end of the DEDICATION tree ledge.
1. Above the blocks, climb over a small overhang on good flakes to a narrow, right-facing corner with a stance at its top. Next, face climb straight up past several fixed pitons, traverse left to a tiny corner, handtraverse farther left, and pull up to the juniper on DEDICATION. 120', 5.9+ R
FA: Ed Webster & Todd Swain   May 27, 1982

EVOLUTIONARY THROWBACK I 5.9 R
Ascends the steep face between ROBUSTUS and DR. LEAKEY. Carry a modern rack including three skyhooks and many wired nuts.
1. Start up ROBUSTUS, climbing a brown water streak to the pedestals, then face climb up and right past several potholes, eventually reaching a short slab leading to a belay tree on DEDICATION. 140', 5.9 R
FA: Todd Swain & Mark Wallace   April 13, 1983

342 THE MOUNT WASHINGTON VALLEY

ROBUSTUS II 5.9+ (5.9 R)
Another brutish face climb with tricky protection and a spectacular roof crack to finish. Carry the tools of the trade. Chipped flint probably won't work! Start at the far left end of the DEDICATION tree ledge.
1. Climb up to a short, hanging corner facing left, then step up and right past the corner to the higher of two small pedestals. Step left on hollow flakes into a groove, and climb this and the corners above to a belay on ECLIPSE. 5.9 R
2. Above a slab, jam a hand crack out a wild, six foot roof. 5.9+
HISTORY: Paul Boissonneault & Kurt Winkler made the first ascent on May 18, 1982. Australopithicus Robustus was the evolutionary dead end, thick-skulled ancestor of modern man.

MACADAMIA II 5.10b
This little known route climbs the steep, black, left-facing corner between ROBUSTUS and ECLIPSE. Protection is adequate.
1. Off the left end of the DEDICATION tree ledge, climb up the back of the open, flaring dihedral to the right of ECLIPSE, exiting right at the top. 5.10b
FA: Mark Richey & Polly DeConto Autumn, 1982

> Humphrey's left side is a large, steep, open slab. Climbs here are face routes on angular holds with generally poor protection. Modern rack helpful!

ECLIPSE II 5.7
The DEDICATION tree ledge 80 feet above the ground is just right of the slab.
1. Third class an easy broken corner to the ledge's left end.
2. Traverse out left onto the wide slab, past one peg to a belay stance below a steep, bulging wall.
3. Escape through the band on the right, up a corner to a flake on the left. 5.7
FA: Joe Cote & Paul Ross June 17, 1973

WANDERLUST II 5.8 R
A dicey face climb up the center of Humphrey's left end slab.
1. Pick the easiest line through a steep headwall about 40 feet left of the start of ECLIPSE. Above, angle left on easier rock to a good belay ledge out in the center of the face. 5.8 R
2. Continue up and left with poor protection, face climbing up to a traverse ledge below the final, steep headwall. 150', 5.5 R
3. Traverse easily left, finishing up the CAKEWALK corner. 5.6+
FA: Albert Dow & Michael Hartrich Summer, 1981

THINK FAST, MR. MOTO II 5.9 R (*)
Don't get booberized by the morning movie, or you'll never do any climbing! Quick reflexes and a detective's cunning will be found useful on this fun face climb. The route ascends the black water streak up the slab's left side. Begin

25 feet to the right of the easily identifiable corner start of CAKEWALK, below a horizontal band of rotten overhangs just above the ground.
1. Face climb easily up a 15 foot slab to a knifeblade, then climb up to the overhangs, reaching good cracks (5.8). Make a few exciting moves out left onto the slab proper, and climb up and right to a layback flake. Belay at a small belay stance on the left at a fixed peg. 5.8
2. Step left and face climb up the black water streak (5.9 R) until finally reaching easier ground. Run the rope out to the traverse ledge at the slab's top. 5.9 R
3. Escape left up the final corner on CAKEWALK. 5.6+
FA: Kurt Winkler & Ed Webster April 23, 1982

A PIECE OF CAKE II 5.7+ (5.6 R)
Ascends the very thin slice of rock squeezed between MR. MOTO and CAKEWALK. The route has widely spaced protection.
1. Climb the groove immediately right of CAKEWALK's finger crack (peg) to a belay ledge with an oak bush. 30', 5.7+
2. Face climb straight up white rock, swinging over a large overlap at a hidden jug. Belay on ledges below the final headwall. 150', 5.6 R
3. Finish up either of the top dihedrals on CAKEWALK or LET THEM EAT CAKE to the final slab and the woods. 5.6+ or 5.7
FA: Todd Swain, Carole Renselaer, & Jim Ewing August 31, 1982

CAKEWALK II 5.6+ (*)
The cliff's easiest safe route. A nice climb ascending the left-hand margin of the slab with, for once, both good rock and good protection. A sloping buttress abuts the slab's left-hand side forming a 30 foot, flaring, right-facing corner.
1. Climb a right-slanting finger crack (5.6) up the buttress's right-hand side, stepping left around an awkward bulge, then scramble up to the large tree ledge above. 60', 5.6 (Climbing the awkward bulge directly is 5.7+)
2. Angle out to the right onto the main slab (exposed, but on good holds) and layback up a good flake to the base of a prominent, double, inside corner on the left side of the final headwall. Jam and layback up the right-hand of the two, steep corners (5.6+) to a belay stance at its top. 140', 5.6+
3. Finish up a short slab. 45', 5.5 Rappel from trees on the left using two ropes.
FA: Paul Ross & Joe Cote June 18, 1973

LET THEM EAT CAKE II 5.7 (*)
A tasty treat with good rock and a well protected 20 foot crux. Start as for CAKEWALK where Humphrey's left end slab & the sloping buttress meet.
1. Traverse left 20 feet across a narrow ledge, then climb the left edge of the buttress (5.4) to the tree ledge. 40', 5.4
2. There are two ways to start this pitch. Scramble up left to a narrow ledge and follow an easy traverse line diagonally back right beneath an overhanging wall,

or step right to a tiny pine and face climb straight up to the same overhanging wall. Above, climb the short dihedral (5.7) which is 15 feet to the left of the CAKEWALK corner to a good belay ledge on the left. 5.7

3. Step left and climb a slight groove (5.5) up a dark slab to the trees. 45', 5.5

FA: Bryan Becker, Cherra Wyllie, & Ed Webster   May 7, 1982

À LA MODE I 5.10b

Start 40 feet to the left of Pitch two of LET THEM EAT CAKE.

1. Climb an easy ramp to the base of a closed vertical flake. Protect here, then step down and back to the right up a weakness in the overhanging wall (5.10b). Belay at a knob and horizontal crack. 5.10b

2. Finish up a "square peg crack" to the left.

FA: Steve Larson, Chris Gill, & Kurt Winkler   August 7, 1983

> Climbs are now described from left to right across the right-hand side of Humphrey's, starting back at the WIESSNER ROUTE.

THE GUIDE'S ROUTE II 5.9 (*)

Good jamming up the steep crack system ascending the right-hand wall of the WIESSNER ROUTE chimney/corner. Bring a good sized normal rack.

1. Climb the first pitch of WIESSNER ROUTE (5.8) to a small stance (peg), then step right and follow the obvious, sustained jam crack (5.9) to the top of the pillar and a belay ledge. 150', 5.9

2. An unprotected slab leads straight up to a tree belay. 155'

3. Climb an easy V groove to the top of the cliff.

FA: George Hurley & Paul Ross   September 24, 1979

PROCESSION I 5.12b (5.12c if you combine both pitches) (***)

Well protected, fingery, and sustained face climbing up the steep, sunny wall to the right of WIESSNER ROUTE. The route dries quickly, and you can lower off the top of Pitch one with a 50 meter rope. Begin just to the right of THE GUIDE'S ROUTE at an obvious flake. Normal rack.

1. Climb up the easy, right-leaning, blocky detached flake until you can clip the first bolt. Then head left into a shallow, left-facing corner, and face climb straight up past six more bolts to a double bolt anchor. 80', 5.12b

2. Continue straight up the face (piton), and finish up a thin finger crack (5.12a; same as THE BREEZE Pitch two) to a tree on a ledge. 35', 5.12a

HISTORY: Jerry Handren made the first ascent of Pitch one, all free, in September, 1988. Todd Swain & Mike Hannon had previously climbed Pitch two on aid on January 28, 1983. Bob Parrott & Barry Rugo then free climbed Pitch two in July, 1989, and two weeks later, Bob Parrott & Rob Adair linked both pitches together at 5.12c.

Chris Gill leading Procession (5.12b) in 1988. Photograph by Nick Yardley.

THE BREEZE II 5.12a R (*)

A serious climb up the steep face right of PROCESSION. Modern rack.

1. Climb the flake up and right (same as PROCESSION) to a horizontal crack, traverse right, then move up and left to a bolt. Move left again to a second bolt, then face climb straight up (5.12a R), right to a pin, and past a bolt to a double bolt belay anchor on a ledge. 120', 5.12a R
2. Follow a crack left onto the beautiful wall right of THE GUIDE'S ROUTE, then climb a thin finger crack (5.12a) to a tree on top of the pillar. 40', 5.12a

HISTORY: This was Humphrey's first new winter rock climb. Todd Swain & Mark Robinson did the first pitch on December 31, 1982. The second pitch was aided on January 28, 1983, by Todd Swain & Mike Hannon. Jim Surette & Hugh Herr made the first free ascent of Pitch one in March, 1985, after prior attempts. Bob Parrott & Barry Rugo free climbed Pitch two in July, 1989.

TREETOTALERS I 5.9+

The face route just to the right of THE BREEZE. A little bit creaky.

1. Climb the flake 10 feet right of THE GUIDE'S ROUTE up and right, then wander up the steep, uncertain face past fixed pitons to a tree belay. 90', 5.9
2. Scramble up left to a double bolt belay on THE BREEZE 50', 5.0
3. Head up an exposed arete (pitons) to a pine on top of the buttress. 50', 5.9+

HISTORY: Dick Peterson & Todd Swain climbed Pitch one on August 16, 1982. Mark Wallace & Todd Swain finished the route on April 7, 1983.

THE OLD ROUTE I 5.2

The first climb on Humphrey's—the broken, gravel-covered ledges around the corner to the right of the WIESSNER ROUTE chimney. Mostly 3rd class.

HISTORY: The route was first climbed in 1931 by an unknown team.

ANGELS WITH DIRTY FACES I 5.8

A one pitch crack climb located partway up THE OLD ROUTE. Scramble up easy ledges until below a short, steep wall on the right.

1. Jam the obvious zig zag crack. 5.8 Rappel off from some trees.

FA: Doug Madara & Brooks Bicknell May, 1981

> The cliff's right side is generally indistinct, however a couple of lines stand out, including a trio of slight right-leaning, parallel corners 75 feet to the right of THE OLD ROUTE. Scramble up left to reach their base.

VERTICAL VENTURE I 5.10b The farthest left dihedral of the three.

1. Climb the left-hand, shallow corner for 60 feet (5.8) to a hanging belay (fixed peg) where another shallow dihedral branches off to the left. 5.8
2. Head up the corner to hard moves (5.10b; piton), then continue another 30 feet to a tree. 50', 5.10b Scramble to the top.

FA: Doug Madara & George Hurley November, 1980

PSYCHOKINETIC PRAXIS I 5.8 R
Bad protection and bad rock make this climb mentally fatiguing.
1. The center of the three parallel corners, up dark rock to a ledge.
2. Up the dihedral (poor protection) past a juniper to the top.
FA: Joe Cote, Gene Ellis, & Ajax Greene August 12, 1973

CASABLANCA I 5.9 R
1. Fifteen feet right of the former route, climb up a shallow green corner (with poor protection at the start) for 60 feet to a ledge on the left. 5.9 R
2. Climb down a few feet from the belay back into the crack, then follow it up and slightly left around a juniper to the top.
FA: Doug Madara & David Stone November, 1980

HUMPHREY'S HERBITUDE I 5.7
Climbs a right-slanting, black-streaked, open corner about 80 feet above the ground and 40 feet to the right of the previous route.
1. Follow a wide jam crack in the right-leaning corner for 50 feet to a fairly prominent orange overlap. Escape left up a lower angled slab and corner. 5.7
FA: Joe Cote & Tom Bates August 11, 1973

VARIATION #1: I 5.7
1a. The vague, shallow corner just to the left of the first pitch. 5.7
FA: Joe Cote & Tom Bates August 11, 1973

VARIATION #2: BEAT THE DEVIL I 5.10d
1. Climb the initial corner of HUMPHREY'S HERBITUDE, and belay on the right on a small ledge below the orange overlap.
2a. Step left and climb a desperate, short corner (5.10d) about 20 feet long through the overlap. Small wired nuts. 45', 5.10d
FA: Doug Madara & Brooks Bicknell June, 1981

TARNSMAN OF GOR I 5.9-
Begin just to the right of HUMPHREY'S HERBITUDE, below a clean corner with three trees below it and an arete on the right.
1. Climb a short wall and traverse right to the corner. 50', 5.7
2. Head right onto the arete, past a good horn, and climb the arete (bolt) to a slab. Finish up a corner/flake to a big pine tree. 100', 5.9- Rappel off.
FA: Todd Swain, Tiger Burns, Mark Wallace, & Randy Rackliff March 25, 1983

ELSA, DWARF DOG OF GOR I 5.6
Start 75 feet left of DARKNESS AT THE EDGE OF TOWN on a tree ledge below a short, steep wall with a small pine tree growing up against it.
1. Climb up onto the ledge, traverse right about 25 feet, then climb a layback flake and a chimney to an oak tree. 60', 5.6
FA: Tiger Burns & Todd Swain March 26, 1983

LAST RUNG ON THE LADDER I 5.9 (*)
On the ladder of success, the last rung is often the hardest to grab. Start 50 feet to the left of DARKNESS AT THE EDGE OF TOWN, directly below the chimney on DWARF DOG OF GOR at a buttress with a finger crack.
1. Climb up to a bush on the left, then step right (bolt) into the finger crack. Move up and right around a nose to steep flakes on the left and the top. 70', 5.9
FA: Todd Swain & Mark Wallace   March 31, 1983

THE WILD EYED AND THE INNOCENT I 5.10b (**)
Begin roughly 20 feet to the left of DARKNESS AT THE EDGE OF TOWN. Don't be too naive about what this climb has in store for you.
1. Climb broken rock until a traverse right gains a shallow, left-facing corner in orange rock just left of DARKNESS. Follow the corner to an overhanging crack (large Friend), move over it (5.10b), and finish left to the top. 5.10b
FA: Doug Madara & Kurt Winkler   April 7, 1983

DARKNESS AT THE EDGE OF TOWN I 5.8 (*)
The clean-cut corner/crack on the left side of a small buttress. Large gear.
1. Climb directly up the corner, hand jamming to a roof. Step left, then move past a detached block to a tree. 75', 5.8 Rappel off with one rope.
FA: Todd Swain & Brad White   November 5, 1980

PRUFROCK I 5.7
Ascends the steep prow of an orange buttress 50 feet to the right of the former route. A square-cut boulder sits at the base.
1. Climb the left side of a vertical flake to a tiny rectangular roof, step right a move, then jam up a thin, vertical finger crack. Enter a groove which slants left to a large pine growing at the top of the buttress. 5.7
FA: George Hurley & Les Gould   November 16, 1980

BOGEY I 5.9   The next prominent corner, slanting up and right.
1. Climb up the dihedral (old peg), exiting left at the top. 60', 5.9
FA: Doug Madara & David Stone   November 6, 1980

CONNECTICUT YANKEE I 5.9+
1. Climb up the slab 15 feet to the right of BOGEY. 5.9+
FA: Doug Madara & Brooks Bicknell   1981

FLAKE OF FEAR I 5.9 R
A flakey climb. Right of BOGEY is a steep crack with several shakey flakes.
1. Climb the awful-looking flake system just left of PETRIFIED FOREST. The flake trembles a bit at the top (so did the first ascent party!) 5.9 R
FA: George Hurley & John Papp   October 6, 1982

PETRIFIED FOREST I 5.9+
Just right of FLAKE OF FEAR is a right-diagonalling crack in an orange wall.

HUMPHREY'S GIRDLE TRAVERSES (SMALL CHANGE & BEAT THE CLOCK) 349

1. Jam the strenuous crack on good holds to the top. 5.9+
FA: George Hurley & Les Gould   June 7, 1981
FFA: Doug Madara & Brooks Bicknell   June, 1981

SMALL CHANGE II 5.8, A0 (One rappel)
The left to right girdle traverse across Humphrey's Ledge is characterized by sustained face climbing.
1. Climb the first pitch of CAKEWALK to the tree ledge. 5.6
2. Traverse right across a ledge to the stance at the top of Pitch two of ECLIPSE.
3. Climb the small corner on the right (pin) through the steep band (5.7; same as ECLIPSE) to a ledge with dead trees on the right. 5.7
4. From the right-hand end of the ledge, climb a shallow 5.8 crack onto the upper slabs. Belay at a tree near the cliff top.
5. Rappel 60 feet down the last pitch of SOUL SURVIVOR to the white birch and double ring bolt belay, top of Pitch two of ROBINSON CRUSOE.
6. Traverse straight right across the face (only 5.4!) to a ledge with a juniper tree at the top of Pitch two of GIUOCO PIANO. 120', 5.4
7. Traverse right past a loose corner to WIESSNER ROUTE.
8. Finish up WIESSNER ROUTE's top chimney pitch. 5.8
FA: Stoney Middleton & Dale Navish   November, 1978

BEAT THE CLOCK II 5.6+, A0 (One rappel) (*)
The reverse girdle traverse (right to left) of Humphrey's. Carry a 50 meter rope. A fun expedition. Punch in first, or you'll be disqualified!
1. Scramble up THE OLD ROUTE to THE GUIDE'S ROUTE. 200', 5.2
2. Down climb THE GUIDE'S ROUTE's chimney and step left onto the WIESSNER ROUTE belay ledge (piton anchor). 30', 5.6+
3. Go left to the tree ledge on HERE COMES THE SUN. 150', 5.5
4. Move left over to the next tree ledge. 50', 5.2
5. Traverse left above the central overlap along a horizontal crack to the double ring bolt anchor at the top of Pitch two of ROBINSON CRUSOE. 140', 5.5
6. Head straight to the left across a tricky traverse (5.6+) to the small and exposed belay ledge on ARIES (two piton anchor). 50', 5.6+
7. Rappel down to the tree-covered ledge on DEDICATION. 80'
8. From the ledge's left-hand end, traverse left onto the slab along a foot ledge to a nut belay on WANDERLUST. 40', 5.2
9. Climb the second pitch of WANDERLUST (5.5) to a belay at the top of MR. MOTO, below the steep, upper headwall. 150', 5.5
10. Traverse left to the final corner on CAKEWALK (5.6+), climb the corner, and finish left up the final slab on LET THEM EAT CAKE (5.5). 5.6+
HISTORY: Todd Swain & Ed Webster made the first ascent on April 9, 1983, racing across the cliff in just three hours car to car.

THE PIG PEN

Shaded by the forest and facing northeast, this short, severely overhanging, compact crag keeps its cool well into the sweltering summer months. Located down and to the left of the ice climb BLACK PUDDING GULLY, the cliff is also conveniently close to the Saco River swimming area. Park in the sandy pullout on the left two tenths of a mile north of Humphrey's Ledge on West Side Road. From the end of the guard rail beside the pullout, cross the meadow, and hike straight uphill through the woods for exactly six and a half minutes to reach the cliff base. A good destination on a hot day—if you crank the rads! The routes are now described from left to right.

ROBOT HEART I 5.13c
The farthest left-hand route starts just to the right of an obvious, wide, roof crack and under the left side of a curving, white overhang.
1. Clip a piton in a flake, then pull off some severe moves (5.13c) out the overhang past three bolts up to a double bolt anchor. 35', 5.13c
FA: Jerry Handren June, 1991

THIS MORTAL COIL I 5.13a (*)
According to Handren: the best route in the Pen. Start five feet right of ROBOT HEART under the same white overhang. Three bolts to the anchor.
1. Easy moves gain the first bolt, clip the second, too, then handtraverse left out the lip of the overhang to a short, vertical finger crack (bolt), and a two bolt anchor. 40', 5.13a
FA: Jerry Handren May, 1990

SULTANS OF SWILL I 5.13a
Swagger uphill to the right for 20 feet, and look confidently straight up. Five beefy bolts lead to a tree anchor on top of the cliff.
1. Above a ledge five feet off the ground (and just to the left of a block), face climb up a gently overhanging wall (5.13a) past five bolts to a steep slab and a tree anchor on top. 65', 5.13a
FA: Jerry Handren June, 1992

CURIOUS GEORGE LEAVES TOWN I 5.11c
The crag's right-hand route is 40 feet uphill and right of SULTANS OF SWILL, and 15 feet to the left of a small cave at the base of the cliff.
1. Climb up an overhanging wall of yellowish rock up flakes past two bolts (5.11c), make a big reach, then crank past a fixed piton up to a piton anchor in a vertical crack. 35', 5.11c
HISTORY: Peter Hovling & Dave McDermott made the route's first ascent in June, 1991, just as "Curious George" made a quick escape from the scene of the crime!

The next climb is found on a buttress buried in the woods between the Pig Pen and the Saco Crag. Around the corner to the north of Humphrey's is a house with a huge boulder in its front yard. Park opposite the next house north and walk straight into the woods for about 100 yards. The route ascends the first buttress north (or right) of the shallow cave called Pitman Arch. (You can't miss it.) Descend a stone staircase from the Arch back to the old right-of-way.

GENTLEMEN OF LEISURE I 5.10a (*)
A secretive crack climb with outstanding rock—a hidden gem!
1. A blocky wall leads to a rest beneath a six foot roof. Jam a hand crack out the roof (5.10a), then climb up a short wall to a belay ledge which has a belay/rappel anchor. 40', 5.10a
FA: Peter Lewis & Kurt Winkler September 8, 1984

THE SACO CRAG

This cute little crag above West Side Road is seven tenths of a mile north of Humphrey's Ledge and opposite the Saco River swimming area. Joe Cote predicted it 20 years ago: "Pretty soon they'll be doing new routes on that little cliff down by the river!" Although each route has been led, the cliff is a great top-roping area with its roadside locale, 40 to 50 foot climbs, and plentiful trees on top for anchoring. Park in the sandy pullout. A good trail traverses the base, looping around each side to the top. The routes are described from left to right.

SACO POTATOES I 5.10d
The short, hidden dihedral on the far, left-hand side of the cliff.
1. Climb a strenuous corner (5.10d) to a dirty face. 30', 5.10d
FA: Todd Swain, Dick Peterson, & Donette Smith September, 1994

ROADSIDE ATTRACTION I 5.9+ (*)
The shallow groove/finger crack above a slab on the cliff's left end.
1. Make bouldering moves off the ground up and over a bulge (5.9+), then follow the crack (bolt) to the top. 40', 5.9+
FA: Brad White & Todd Swain June 18, 1982

TERROR AT SEA I 5.10a Tricky Protection (*)
Begin just to the right of ROADSIDE ATTRACTION. Modern rack.
1. Face climb straight up past small overlaps and grooves. 50', 5.10a
FA: Tim Ashnault & Brad White October 27, 1987

FLAKE OUT I 5.9
Start 20 feet to the right of ROADSIDE ATTRACTION.
1. After a very awkward move off the ground (5.9), climb a layback flake to a sloping ledge, then head to the top. 45', 5.9
FA: Brad White & Tim Ashnault June 20, 1982

SHADOW AT NIGHT I 5.9- (**)
Begin 10 feet right of FLAKE OUT at the base of a U-shaped groove.
1. A hard move (5.9-) gains a nice finger crack, jammed to a small ledge. Exit left (easier), or stem up a corner against the arete on the right. 40', 5.9-
FA: Tim Ashnault & Brad White June 20, 1982

BLOODSPORT I 5.12c (**)
The round arete right of SHADOW AT NIGHT. Have a matching donor ready!
1. Climb up a shallow finger crack and seams in the arete (5.12c) past four bolts and one piton to the finish. 45', 5.12c
FA: Bill Lutkus July 21, 1990

TWO PINTS OF LAGER & A PACKET OF CRISPS I 5.12a (**)
The aesthetic V groove and slanting hand crack 10 feet to the right of BLOODSPORT. The route is much harder than it looks!
1. Stem up the groove (bolt) to gain a right-diagonalling hand crack. Above, step left past two bolts and face climb to the top. 45', 5.12a
HISTORY: Andy Ross, Tim Kelley, Rich Baker, & Jerry Handren all met up at the local pub before doing the first ascent of this thirst-quenching route in October, 1991.

SACO CRACKER I 5.12a (**)
A popular after work testpiece, but erosion is upgrading the route, so hurry!
1. The overhanging, bulging, finger/hand crack (5.12a) in the cliff's center. Erosion has upped the difficulty of the first moves getting started. 35', 5.12a
HISTORY: The first ascent is unknown. Rick Fleming made the first free ascent of this testing line in the Summer of 1979.

SWEATHOG I 5.12b
Pick a really nice, hot humid day to fully enjoy this route!
1. Start up SACO CRACKER, then move right past two bolts and over a desperate, rounded bulge (5.12b) to the top. 35', 5.12b
FA: Bob Parrott & Steve Damboise July, 1990

BIRCH TREE CORNER I 5.6 (*)
Forty feet right of SACO CRACKER is a nice dihedral with a ledge at its base.
1. Climb up a hand crack past a block in the corner (5.6) and a birch. 45', 5.6
FA: Todd Swain, free-solo June 7, 1982

HEMLOCK ARETE I 5.8 R
Should you fall, you'll suffer the same fate as Socrates!
1. Start on the ledge at the base of BIRCH TREE CORNER, and climb the arete (5.8 R) just to the right. 45', 5.8 R
HISTORY: Todd Swain & Brad White made the first ascent of this poorly protected route on June 18, 1982.

THE SACO CRAG - RIGHT SIDE

OVERTIME CRACK I 5.11b (**)
Start 50 feet to the right of SACO CRACKER, or 10 feet to the right of BIRCH TREE CORNER. Bring a normal rack, but be aware that the climb is very strenuous to protect. There is no fixed gear on the route.
1. Climb up an arete (5.10d) to gain discontinuous finger cracks, and finish up a thin, right-diagonalling finger crack (5.11b) on the final wave. 50', 5.11b
FA: Brad White, Tim Ashnault, & Todd Swain   October 18, 1987

MUSCLE BEACH I 5.12b (*)
Start just right of OVERTIME CRACK. Carry small wireds for the top crack.
1. Climb up the face (bolt), finishing up the thin crack (bolt) just to the right of OVERTIME CRACK. 50', 5.12b
FA: Bob Parrott, Barry Rugo, & Harry Brielmann   July, 1990

SO WHAT! I 5.12d
Literally a one move wonder. Climb the short, overhanging flake to the right of MUSCLE BEACH. Start on a sloping ledge 20 feet left of TRICYCLE.
1. Climb up a short, smooth slab past a cold shut and a bolt, then crank off a few power layback moves (5.12d) up a thin, vertical flake. 30', 5.12d
FA: Steve Damboise with Peter Hovling   July, 1990

TRICYCLE I 5.8
The left-hand of three short cracks on the crag's right side.
1. Climb the crack (5.8), heading up and slightly right. 25', 5.8
FA: Todd Swain & Brad White   June 18, 1982

HELPING HANDS I 5.8
The center crack, identified by its crystalline texture.
1. Jam the hand crack 15 feet left of THE V GROOVE past a block. 25', 5.8
FA: Ed Webster   November 4, 1985

MONARCH BUTTERFLY I 5.9 (*)
Just climb it! Nice jamming.
1. The pretty finger crack just to the left of THE V GROOVE. 25', 5.9
FA: Ed Webster   November 4, 1985

THE V GROOVE I 5.8 (**)
One of the cliff's most popular routes, the obvious, flaring corner. Hike to the crag's far, right-hand end. There is a large pine tree on top for top-roping.
1. Climb the corner (5.8) using a narrow hand crack on the left wall. 25', 5.8
FA: Unknown.

SLIGHTLY LESS THAN ZERO I 5.9-
Begin just to the right of THE V GROOVE.
1. Ascend the short, vertical finger crack up the arete. 25', 5.9-
HISTORY: Ed Webster cleaned and led the route on November 4, 1985.

THE CEMETERY CLIFF

An obscure cliff, discovered by the current generation. Drive north on West Side Road past the Saco Crag for half a mile up a small hill, and take your first left onto a narrow, hard to see dirt road. Park at the old cemetery. (If you're heading south on Route 302, drive south on West Side Road for two miles to reach the dirt road.) Hike uphill for a few minutes to the cliff. To descend, rappel off a tree, or hike around the cliff's left side. New routes will require large amounts of cleaning. There are many dangerously loose blocks and flakes, plus a cemetery conveniently close by, so beware! The climbs are described from right to left.

PSYCHOHOLIC SLAG I 5.9
Begin just downhill to the right of FOR DEAR LIFE.
1. Climb up 15 feet to a horizontal crack, step left, and follow a finger crack in a right-facing corner to an awkward move onto a small ledge. Finish straight up to the top of the cliff. 70', 5.9
FA: Karl Kruger & Bill Moratz September 18, 1994

FOR DEAR LIFE I 5.4
The easy, left-slanting ramp downhill and right of FOLLOW YOURSELF.
1. Climb easily up the low-angled ramp until it ends, then follow short hand cracks and blocks above (5.4) slightly up and right to the top. 70', 5.4
FA: Bill Moratz & Karl Kruger September 18, 1994

FOLLOW YOURSELF I 5.9+ R
A challenging, and potentially very dangerous undertaking. Above the main wall's right side and 45 feet to the right of THE SCYTHE, is a 25 foot long, horizontal roof/overlap. Be careful of loose rock, and bring a modern rack.
1. Jam a hand crack up the side of a flake to reach the right-hand end of the roof. Undercling and face climb left for 25 feet (5.9+ R in the center) beneath the overlap until you can turn the roof's left-hand end. Proceed up a flaring, left-facing corner to the top. 90', 5.9+ R
HISTORY: Hans Bern Bauer started up the climb, rope-solo, on July 15, 1995. When he fell from the crux halfway across the roof traverse, his self-belay failed, and he hit the ground from 30 feet up. Unhurt, but quite understandably shaken, Hans collected himself for an hour, went back up (still alone), and managed to complete the route's first ascent.

THE SCYTHE I 5.11b (*)
A grim face climb. Begin 45 feet to the left of FOLLOW YOURSELF or 30 feet to the right of HEAVEN CAN WAIT below a vertical, cleaned stripe of rock. A modern rack will probably be helpful.
1. Climb up a cleaned face to reach the base of a smooth, flaring corner (bolt; 5.11b) which is climbed to the top. 90', 5.11b
FA: Chris Davonport & Tyler Vadebonceur August 3, 1990

THE CEMETERY CLIFF

HEAVEN CAN WAIT I 5.9
It just barely did. In the center of the cliff above a large talus boulder are a series of shallow, black, left-facing corners. Modern rack.
1. Angle up from right to left to gain a shallow, left-facing corner which is followed up then left past a clean section to the top. 90', 5.9
HISTORY: This was the first route on the cliff—and almost Webster's last. Ed Webster & Harold Consentine did the first ascent in the Spring of 1982. An immense, teetering flake which had threatened the leader with almost certain death was dislodged on rappel after the first ascent.

A NAP ASIDE ELSIE I 5.7+
Farther left, just to the left of a short, smooth face, is a large birch tree growing against the wall in front of a vertical hand crack.
1. Jam and layback up the crack (5.7+) for 35 feet to a comfortable ledge with a birch tree. Continue up an awkward chimney (5.7+), step left to twin finger cracks, and finish up more cracks and a corner to the top. 100', 5.7+
HISTORY: After cleaning, a top-rope ascent, and a nap next to Elsie's grave, Hans Bern Bauer & Andrew Malcomb did the first ascent on June 28, 1995.

IMMORTALITY I 5.9
Start just around the corner to the left of A NAP ASIDE ELSIE.
1. Climb a 5.9 finger crack up the right side of a smooth, 20 foot face to a ledge, then continue up parallel cracks to a roof (#2 Friend). Pull over the roof, and finish up a 30 foot face to the top. 100', 5.9
HISTORY: Ed Webster & Harold Consentine climbed the 5.9 crack in the Spring of 1982—and retreated when Webster was attacked by bees. Harold Consentine & Owen Thompson completed the route on October 26, 1991.

WHERE SPIDERS HANG I 5.11c
The eye-catching, right-slanting dihedral capped by a roof on the cliff's far, left side. Protection is semi-reasonable, but is not above your head on the crux moves at the ceiling. Modern rack (and a broom for the spiders) helpful.
1. Climb up the right-facing corner to a short flare (or climb the face five feet to the right) to the roof. Then undercling, hang at the lip, and make an iron cross move (5.11c) to pull over. Finish up the groove up and right. 75', 5.11c
HISTORY: After a prior top-rope ascent and cleaning, Hans Bern Bauer & Scott Dicapio made the first ascent on July 6, 1995.

STONE COLD I 5.10d (*)
Start five feet left of WHERE SPIDERS HANG. Seven bolts lead to the top.
1. Face climb awkwardly up a series of right-slanting, left-facing shallow corners past seven bolts to the top. 75', 5.10d
HISTORY: Steve Damboise, Cindy Lehman, & Charley Bentley did the first ascent on November 10, 1991, placing all the bolts free on the lead.

Bob Parrott on the crux of Nightflyer (5.12a) on the first ascent in 1986. Photograph by Bill Holland.

THE CONWAY AREA

The following two cliffs are each located near the town of Conway. Both are also situated on private land, so please be courteous and considerate when climbing at either Band M Ledge or Albany Slab.

BAND M LEDGE

Band M Ledge is a 300 foot granite cliff located in Madison, New Hampshire, several miles from Conway. It is best seen from Route 113 past the gravel pits. Routes are described right to left, since the cliff is usually approached from the right, or up through the short talus slope below the ledge's center. Descend around either side of the cliff, or more easily via rappel. The original name for this complex cliff was B and M Ledge, for the Boston & Maine Railroad. Routes are now described from right to left.

FLEXIBLE FLAKE I 5.10a R
Sixty feet right of A DAY AT THE RACES is a cleaned face with a short, right-facing corner. Carry a modern rack.
1. Climb the right-facing corner, then move up left past a loose flake (5.10a R) to another undercling flake. Continue past horizontals to a desperate mantleshelf move, and the top. 60', 5.10a R
FA: Todd Swain, Peggy Buckey, & Dick Peterson September 5, 1987

A DAY AT THE RACES I 5.10b
Begin 30 feet to the right of the EREMITE Chimney. Modern rack.
1. Climb slightly loose flakes to a small tree ledge (possible belay here), jam up a finger crack, handtraverse to the left, and finish up another short finger crack to the top. 90', 5.10b
FA: Doug Madara & David Stone November 8, 1982

CAN IT CHALLENGE I 5.9+ R
Fifteen feet right of the EREMITE chimney is a left-facing corner.
1. Climb straight up the corner to the top. 90', 5.9+ R Don't fall!
FA: Doug Madara & David Stone November 8, 1982

ANIMAL CRACKERS I 5.9 (*)
Just to the right of EREMITE is an obviously cleaned flake system.
1. Climb the flake for 15 feet, stemming briefly into EREMITE, then move up right (5.9) to flakes and a left-facing corner (peg). Layback the corner, step left (piton), and climb straight up (5.9), finishing up a hand crack to the right of a pine tree. 90', 5.9
HISTORY: After cleaning the route, Dick Peterson, Brad White, & Jose Abeyta made the first ascent in September, 1985. While doing the climb, a flying squirrel and a tree frog leapt out at the climbers, landing safely from heights of 40 and 60 feet, respectively!

358 THE CONWAY AREA

EREMITE I 5.7
The most obvious route on Band M's right-hand side.
1. Climb up the chimney system past an immense, wedged block. 5.7
FA: Craig Seaver & Milt Camille October 8, 1973

IF DOGS RUN FREE II 5.11b (***)
One of the wildest short free climbs in the White Mountains, the route ascends disconnected cracks up the sheer face to the left of EREMITE. Double ropes are useful. A superb climb, well protected with some work!
1. Climb 20 feet up EREMITE, place a high nut, then traverse left with your feet hidden in a line of pockets, making a 5.10d move into a beautiful finger crack. Fire the crack (5.9+) up to a horizontal crack, then handtraverse left (two pegs) into another finger crack and up to an exposed stance (Piton & Friends) on the left wall of an arete. 90', 5.11a
2. This "out there" pitch moves left onto the overhanging wall, and jams up a short, testing hand/finger crack (5.11b) to a good belay ledge. 5.11b
3. Finish by scrambling up an easy chimney on the right.
HISTORY: Chris Noonan & Ed Perry made the first ascent in the Autumn of 1977. After earlier attempts, the first free ascent was accomplished by Paul Boissonneault & Felix Modugno, sharing leads, in October, 1982.

VARIATION: THE FLYING ENGLISHMAN I 5.11d R
1a. Instead of making the hard moves to gain the vertical finger crack, make even harder moves left around the prow onto a ledge. Finish left, merging with GENERAL HOSPITAL. Extremely strenuous and scary. 5.11d R
FA: (After getting severely lost) Chris Plant (UK) & partner 1984

GENERAL HOSPITAL II 5.7, A3
A difficult aid route up the bulging, overhanging wall to the right of BANDIT, the 5.9 corner/hand crack. Carry a big aid rack, including skyhooks and rurps.
1. Climb a crack on the left side of a prominent nose of rock to a ramp leading left to a bolt. Use thin aid and three more bolts to gain cracks on the overhanging wall above. When the cracks end, hook and free climb to a good belay ledge with a double bolt anchor. 100', A3
2. A fixed bashie gets you to an overhanging crack (A3) on the left. Follow this to an alcove, exit left, and free climb to the top. 50', A3
HISTORY: John Mallery & Mike Hass climbed Pitch one before John Mallery & Tom Callaghan finished the route in the Summer of 1981.

VARIATION: BECAUSE THEY CAN I 5.11d
2a. Off the right end of the belay ledge, make difficult moves (5.11d) past a bolt into an overhanging, finger and hand crack (5.11a). 40', 5.11d
FA: Bob Parrott & Rob Adair October, 1988

BAND M LEDGE - RIGHT SIDE (IF DOGS RUN FREE) 359

Paul Boissonneault leading the crux handtraverse during the first free ascent of If Dogs Run Free (5.11b) in 1982. Photograph by Dave Watowski.

360 THE CONWAY AREA

BANDIT I 5.9 (***)
Will steal your heart away! One of the best hand cracks around. To the left of IF DOGS RUN FREE is a round-edged crack in a left-facing corner.
1. Jam and layback up the sinker crack (5.9) in a left-facing dihedral past pitons. Exit left to a ledge (easier), or follow the crack straight up. 80', 5.9
FA: Michael Hartrich & Al Rubin Summer, 1973

PISTOLERO I 5.8
Just to the left of BANDIT is a dirty, left-facing dihedral.
1. Climb the corner and hand crack to a ledge.
2. Follow the upper dihedral to the top.
FA: Roger Martin & Joe Cote November 12, 1973

VEMBER I 5.6
Also overgrown. Begin on the same ledge as PISTOLERO.
1. Head up left over a block, then down left 40 feet to a stance.
2. Climb a corner up and left, then jam a hand crack over a chockstone to the top.
FA: Joe Cote, Milt Camille, & Roger Martin November 18, 1973

BLUEPOINT I 5.8 R
Begin at the large oak tree just to the left of VEMBER.
1. After surmounting a Gunks-style roof (5.8) onto a small ledge, climb a left-facing corner, and head up the right side of a jammed block to a tree ledge. 5.8
2. Walk right past a large, wafer-like flake sitting on the belay ledge to a narrow, left-facing corner. Stem up the corner, then balance left across the face (5.8 R) to better holds and the top. 5.8 R
HISTORY: Ed Webster & Kathryn Rogers made the first ascent in September, 1981, naming the route for Roger's favorite beach resort.

ALBERT'S SHUFFLE I 5.10d
Only some fast dancing will get you up this short pitch!
1. Layback the strenuous V groove/corner just to the left of BLUEPOINT, stemming against a good edge on the dihedral's right-hand arete. 30', 5.10d
2. Continue up a face and grooves to the top. 90'
FA: Albert Dow & Joe Lentini October 15, 1981

DHARMA BUMS I 5.8
A very dirty climb on crumbly rock. Meditate on this one first.
1. Twenty five feet to the right of THREE WOGS, face climb straight up on crumbly holds to a belay stance below an open groove.
2. Climb the last pitch of VEMBER up a seven inch wide corner/crack to a dangerous exit past loose blocks. Easier slabs gain the top.
FA: Kurt Winkler & Paul Boissonneault April 19, 1982

BAND M LEDGE - CENTER (THREE WOGS) 361

THREE WOGS I 5.10a (**)
One of Band M's best routes, the shallow groove with three bolts around the corner to the right of EVERYTHING THAT GLITTERS. Well protected.
1. Climb the deceptively easy-looking groove (5.10a), with the crux coming after the second bolt, up to a good belay ledge. 90', 5.10a
2. Move left, then step back right to an overlap. Climb the exceptional 5.7 dihedral around a roof to face climbing over the final overlaps (a little loose here; 5.7) to the top of the cliff. 120', 5.7
FA: Michael Hartrich, Joe Cote, Albert Dow May, 1981

MYSTERY ACHIEVEMENT I 5.11d (*)
Search diligently for three bolts 10 feet to the left of THREE WOGS. The route can be done in either one or two pitches, as desired.
1. Climb past the initial three bolts (5.11d crux mantling onto the slab after the third bolt), then traverse left at a ceiling to a crack. Climb this to a belay on the ledge at the base of the upper groove, or continue...
2. Stemming up a steep groove on the left past several more bolts (5.10), then swing out right on a jug, pull up to another bolt, then make scary face moves angling right up the final wall to join THREE WOGS. 150', 5.11d
HISTORY: Todd Swain, Dick Peterson, & Peggy Buckey placed the first three bolts on aid on the lead on September 4, 1987, but couldn't quite crack the crux moves. Jim Ewing & Steve Damboise did the first crux on September 21, 1987, but traversed right and finished up THREE WOGS. The next day, Swain cleaned the upper route and placed two of the groove bolts on rappel. Todd Swain & Kathy Beuttler made the first complete ascent on September 23, 1987.

EVERYTHING THAT GLITTERS IS NOT GOLD II 5.11d R (*)
Begin below the distinctively-shaped wall to the left of THREE WOGS.
1. Layback and undercling a left-leaning, 10 foot flake. Trend right up flakes (fixed protection) finally moving left to a hanging belay. Some of the fixed gear is of questionable value. 60', 5.11c R
1a. Twenty feet farther left, climb 25 feet up the face, then traverse right around the corner (5.9+), continuing on Pitch one. 5.9+
2. Move right, gaining a right-facing corner. At its top, step right around a roof, then move up beneath the large final overhang. Traverse left under the overhang to an arete, step left around it, and climb to the top. 60', 5.11d R
HISTORY: Steve Larson, Tricia Mattox, & Paul Boissonneault climbed the alternate first pitch, "an early reconnaissance", in the Spring of 1984. Paul Boissonneault, Steve Larson, & Scott Stevenson did the first ascent of the more direct first pitch in the Spring of 1985 before Scott Stevenson & Steve Larson made the route's first complete ascent on May 11, 1986.

THE CENTER ROUTE I 5.7
One hundred feet left is a face with a rounded groove on the right.
1. Climb the round-edged crack and groove past several small bushes. After a small ceiling, step left and belay on top of a spike. A bit dirty.
2. Climb the crack. When it ends, climb up and right (two bolts) past a flake to a hidden ledge around the corner to the right. Finish easily. 5.7

FA: Joe Cote & Larry Conrad   June 22, 1975
FFA: Joe Cote & Mark Whitton   June 29, 1975

TROUBLED WORLD II 5.9
Begin in the center of the face, just to the left of CENTER ROUTE.
1. Climb a narrow ramp leading left to a pointed pedestal. Continue left 30 feet on black rock to an overhanging, yellow wall and a two stepped block with a striking three inch crack on its right side. Jam this strenuous crack (5.9), and pull onto a belay ledge. 5.9
2. Step up and left, then climb a flake past a pine tree to a belay ledge.
3. Carefully climb up right on rotten rock to the top.

FA: Kurt Winkler & Barry Moore June, 1980

BEDO BEDO I 5.11c
Strenuous moves and tricky face climbing require a good balance of arms. Begin just to the left of the steep face of TROUBLED WORLD.
1. Climb thin flakes to a blank wall protected by two bolts. Balance left (5.11c) to a short crack climbed to a ledge (peg). Step back down, then left up to a second ledge, and follow a crack up the left side of the TROUBLED WORLD pillar to its top. 5.11c

HISTORY: After placing the second bolt on aid on the lead, Ed Webster climbed the crux with Chris Gill & Steve Larson in October, 1986. Chris Gill & Peter Gill completed the route on October 31, 1986.

MACHINA EX DEUS I 5.10d (**)
A theatrical ascent with a delicate introduction and an arm-blowing final act. Carry several medium to large Friends for the main dihedral. To the left of the previous two routes is a clean, open corner fitted with an overhanging crack. A streak of orange lichen beside a beech tree marks the start.
1. Slab climb diagonally left (peg; 5.10a) into a shallow groove to a ledge higher. Above, jam up parallel finger cracks to a rest, then go for broke up the overhanging corner and hand/fist crack (5.10d) to a big ledge with some trees. 90', 5.10d Due to rotten rock above, rappel off with two ropes.

HISTORY: Ed Webster, Michael Hartrich, & Albert Dow made the first ascent of the route in September, 1981.

Chris Gill on the crux of Bedo Bedo (5.11c) in 1986. Photograph by Ed Webster.

JUNGLE WORK I 5.11d
Named after a song by Warren Zevon, this very strenuous climb ascends the overhanging finger and hand cracks 20 feet to the left of MACHINA EX DEUS. Unfortunately, the crack is somewhat crumbly. Carry many cams.

1. Climb up a short corner (old peg) to a ledge with a large pine. Step right, then forge up the strenuous, overhanging, twin cracks, laybacking and jamming your way to the top. 60', 5.11d

HISTORY: Brian Boyd made the first ascent of the route on August 28 & 29, 1982. "Albert Dow and I were good friends and climbed together for four or five years. He sent me route topos of several of his climbs, and I went out to Band M to look for Machina Ex Deus, but noticed this line first. Albert had taught me crack technique on the wooden jam boards in the EMS attic. By 1982, though, I wasn't doing much climbing, but I did have a 40 foot plywood roof in my basement. I worked out on it every night for six months. Jungle Work did seem a lot harder than Airation or Vultures, so I don't know why I rated it 5.10 at the time. And since Albert had gotten me into Zevon, I thought the name was appropriate," remembered Brian Boyd.

VARIATION: THE DIRECT START I 5.10b
1a. Climb the lower twin cracks, left of the initial corner. 30', 5.10b
FA: Bob Parrott & Steve Damboise October, 1986

MALT THERAPY I 5.11a (*)
Fifty feet to the left of MACHINA EX DEUS is a short, right-leaning corner. A thirst quenching pitch. Bring a normal rack—plus a few cold ones.

1. Hard moves gain the base of the corner, then layback past a peg (5.11a) to a big ledge with trees. 50', 5.11a Rappel off.

HISTORY: The Budwieser Climbing Team (a.k.a.: Tom Callaghan, John Strand, & Al Rubin) made the first ascent on September 11, 1982.

DREAM TIME I 5.9+
A varied climb up the face 40 feet to the right of STANDARD ROUTE.

1. Mantle and face climb (thread) to an overlap, then step right to a bush (peg above an arch). Traverse right 20 feet along an overlap. At its end, make a hard pull (5.9+) onto a slab with a good ledge above, with a bolt and a horn for the anchor. 100', 5.9+ You can also finish left (5.8) to gain the STANDARD ROUTE ramp.

FA: Tom Callaghan, rope-solo July, 1983

STANDARD ROUTE I 5.5
The first route on the ledge, the prominent, right-diagonalling ramp near the middle of the cliff. The granite is decomposed at the start.

1. The bottom of the ramp is an easy scramble up to several ledges.

2. From a large ledge, continue diagonally right on easy ground, then head up a crack past an old piton (5.5) to the trees. Watch for loose rock. 5.5
FA: Unknown.

HEAVY WEATHER SAILING II 5.12a (***)

This is the obvious, overhanging flake system above the lower ramp on the STANDARD ROUTE. Hang tough on this one, and bring plenty of able-bodied mates, plus numerous Friends! Scramble up the bottom of the gully on STANDARD to a big ledge.

1. Follow the strenuous, undercling/jam crack flake (5.12a) up a pronounced overhanging wall into a squeeze chimney. Climb out of the chimney to a steep bulge with two parallel cracks, then climb the left crack to a belay above a crease in a shallow groove. 70', 5.12a

2. Angle diagonally left up a slab, then move back right following a finger crack to the top of the cliff. 70', 5.9

HISTORY: The route was first attempted and named by Doug Madara in the early 1980s. Several other top climbers had also been blown ashore before Steve Larson & Andy Tuthill sailed up the first ascent on May 29, 1983.

VARIATION #1: GALE FORCE I 5.10c X (*)

A deadly variation, offering no protection from the wind—or a mistake!

2a. Avoid the final finger crack by stepping left into a crack-less, unprotected, right-facing corner (5.10c X) leading up to a pine tree. 50', 5.10c X

HISTORY: Tom Callaghan & Chris Plant (UK) made the first ascent in September, 1983 on the second ascent of HEAVY WEATHER SAILING. "I really ran it out," said Callaghan. "You mean someone actually repeated it?"

VARIATION #2: THREE WAGS I 5.10b

A much more reasonable (and protected) alternate finish!

1a. After the crux of HEAVY WEATHER, traverse right under a roof to the base of a right-leaning dihedral. 65', 5.10b

2a. Climb the corner (5.10b) to the top. 5.10b

FA: Bob Parrott, Barry Rugo, & Harry Brielmann   October 20, 1986

VARIATION #3: ALTERED STATES I 5.12a

1b. Compass? Climb the crux of HEAVY WEATHER to the start of THREE WAGS, then head left across a prominent horizontal crack. 35', 5.12a

FA: Bob Parrott & Dan Hutchens   October 11, 1986

MOTHER OF INVENTION III 5.11d, A3 (**)

A difficult mixed climb. The blind, vertical crack on the overhanging wall 20 feet to the left of STANDARD ROUTE marks the start.

1. Aid the incipient vertical crack past two bolts and a rurp to a ledge. A3

Tom Callaghan hanging it out on the second ascent of Heavy Weather Sailing (5.12a) in 1983. Photograph by Dave Rose.

BAND M LEDGE - LEFT (SACRED SPACE)

THE VIRGIN II 5.11c (**)
The free finish to MOTHER OF INVENTION. The route is usually approached by starting up either NIGHTFLYER or THE STEPS.
2. From the right end of the large ledge, follow an obvious hand and finger crack to a fixed piton (same as BITING BULLETS, which goes left). Now move right around the arete to an exposed belay. 50', 5.11
3. Head right up a thin dihedral with a fingertip crack (5.11c). When the crack ends, grab a good square-cut and pull up to a horizontal crack. Belay here (#1 Friends useful.) 5.11c
4. Finish up and left on NIGHTFLYER's last pitch. 75', 5.9+
HISTORY: Bob Parrott & Jay Depeter made the first ascent of the climb on February 10, 1985. After Depeter had freed the second pitch to the fixed pin in September, 1984, Parrott free climbed the entire second pitch the next Spring. Later, Jay Depeter led the third pitch with some aid (under attack by black flies), and Bob Parrott followed it free.

> Around the corner to the left of STANDARD ROUTE and HEAVY WEATHER SAILING is a large amphitheater with a terrace one third of the way up and a stepped dihedral rising above. This is the highest section of the cliff, containing Band M's hardest multi-pitch routes: SACRED SPACE, SUNNY DAYS, and NIGHTFLYER.

SACRED SPACE II 5.12a (***)
A very high quality free climb up superb granite with mostly fixed protection.
1. Climb the narrow dihedral just to the right of NIGHTFLYER's first pitch, then make strenuous, fingery moves (5.12a) past a pin and three bolts up a slightly overhanging wall. Mantle onto an easy slab at the top, and belay at a large pine. 60', 5.12a Move up to a sloping ledge at the base of Pitch two.
2. Directly above Pitch one of NIGHTFLYER (and to the left of Pitch two of THE STEPS), climb up a large, left-facing corner to the top (sustained; 5.12a) past several fixed pitons. 60', 5.12a
HISTORY: The upper dihedral was cleaned and some protection was fixed on rappel. Bob Parrott & Steve Damboise climbed the final corner on August 22, 1986. After previewing and placing two bolts on rappel, Bob Parrott with Steve Damboise added the first pitch on August 30, 1986. The route's first continuous ascent was made by Jim Surette with Steve Larson in October, 1986. Parrott later added a third bolt to the first pitch, protecting what had been a dangerous mantleshelf.

VARIATION #1: HOSS COCK I 5.12a (*)
This bolted face just to the right of RAT'S EYE is a very overhanging face route, which fortunately has a couple of good rests on it.

1. You can start by climbing up either Pitch one of SACRED SPACE or NIGHTFLYER. 5.12a or 5.9+
2a. Head up an overhanging face on square-cuts past four bolts, just to the left of THE STEPS, and belay on that route. 50', 5.12a
HISTORY: Bob Parrott, Barry Rugo, & Rob Adair made the first ascent of the route on May 10, 1989, and named the climb in memory of Bill Holland.

VARIATION #2: **RAT'S EYE** I 5.12b (**)
The gently overhanging face 30 feet right of SACRED SPACE, Pitch two.
1. Depending on your mood and inclination, climb the first pitch of either NIGHTFLYER or SACRED SPACE. 5.9+ or 5.12a
2. Start up a shallow, rounded, left-facing flake, then climb the overhanging face (5.12b) past five bolts to a horizontal break & a two bolt anchor. 60', 5.12b
3. Finish up Pitch four of THE STEPS, or rappel off.
FA: Bob Parrott & Barry Rugo May 10, 1989

NIGHTFLYER II 5.12a (**)
The incredibly spectacular fourth lead is nothing you'll want to hang around on for very long! The full route is quite long and complex. Begin on a ledge located 25 feet to the right of SUNNY DAYS. Normal rack, with large gear.
1. Layback and jam up a left-slanting corner with a wide crack (big cams needed) to an easy slab and a large pine tree growing on a ledge. 60', 5.9+
2. Traverse to the right end of the belay ledge where two pull-ups on good holds allow a higher ledge to be reached. 100'
3. Climb an overhanging dihedral (5.8) to a large balcony. 25', 5.8
4. Handtraverse right along an exposed horizontal crack (5.12a) across a 100 degree wall past three fixed pitons to a belay. 40', 5.12a
5. Slab climb left to join the final crack on SUNNY DAYS. 75', 5.9+
HISTORY: Joe Cote & Jeff Pheasant made the first ascent of the entire route, with aid, on September 7, 1974. Cleaning on the lead, George Hurley & Kurt Winkler free climbed the first pitch on August 31, 1984. Bob Parrott, Barry Rugo, & Rob Adair made the first free ascent of the climb in May, 1986, after pre-placing three pitons on aid to protect the crux handtraverse.

BITING BULLETS I 5.12b (*)
This is the lower of the two handtraverse cracks, located 20 feet below the more obvious traverse crack on NIGHTFLYER. Sort of a ridiculous route, according to Surette—equally or more desperate than its neighbor!
1. Climb up THE VIRGIN to the top of the crack. At a piton, traverse left across the wall along a dead obvious flaring crack (5.12b) to reach the large balcony on NIGHTFLYER. 60', 5.12b
FA: Jim Surette October 23, 1986

BAND M LEDGE - LEFT (NIGHTFLYER & INTERROGATOR)

SUNNY DAYS II 5.11d (*)
A real solar collector on a warm day. Begin at the back of the amphitheater to the left of NIGHTFLYER. Scramble up 30 feet to a stance below a corner with a hand crack in it. Carry a normal rack.
1. Climb the overhanging dihedral (5.9+) to the large ledge. 5.9+
2. Move up easily to a large terrace and walk to its right end.
3. Make strenuous moves and lunges (5.11d; fixed pitons) up the right side of a flake system just to the left of NIGHTFLYER to a tree belay. 5.11d
4. Follow a crack diagonally right to the top of the cliff. 5.8

HISTORY: Jeff Pheasant & Joe Cote made the first ascent on August 31, 1974. Jim Dunn freed Pitch one in September, 1975. Romain Vogler (Switzerland) & Ed Webster accomplished the route's first free ascent on May 17, 1982.

THE STEPS II 5.10c
Another long free climb, up the dihedral in the back of the cliff's upper amphitheater. Begin on the left side of the amphitheater. Normal rack.
1. Climb up left a short ways, then straight up to the highest ledge.
2. Third class right to the back, to the base of a large, stepped dihedral.
3. Climb the impressive corner (5.10c) to a belay on a slab. 5.10c
4. An overhanging corner on the right leads to the top.
FA: Joe Cote, Richard Arey, Mike Macklin, & Alan Herschalag September 15, 1974
FFA: Jim Dunn, Doug Madara, & Eddie Beaudry September, 1975

FLESH FOR FANTASY I 5.13a (*)
Short, but desperate! The purple bolt marks the route.
1. Start up an overhanging undercling to a purple bolt, then make very hard face moves (5.13a) up and left to the top. 30', 5.13a
FA: Steve Damboise & Andy Blair May 23, 1989

INTERROGATOR I 5.9
Farther left one encounters a black, left-facing, 30 foot corner with a crack in the right wall that begins as fingers and widens to offwidth. Normal rack.
1. Climb the crack up the right-hand wall past a small tree (5.9), mantleshelf at the top of the corner, and continue to a piton on the left. The easiest escape from here is to step left from the piton into a dirty gully and boulder up 20 feet to a walk-off ledge. Otherwise, climb past the peg up and right to a corner that ends on a large ledge. Now either go up and left to a dead tree where the direct finishes WAY RADICAL and LEATHER & LYCRA start, or traverse right to the trees below the last pitch of SACRED SPACE, and rappel back to the ground (with two ropes) from there.
FA: Joe Cote & Roger Martin November 12, 1973

VARIATION: **BLACK PLAGUE** I 5.10c

There is no known cure for this size of crack. Carry some large protection
1a. Climb the painful hand/fist crack in the back of the black, overhanging corner just to the left of the start of INTERROGATOR. 5.10c
FA: Michael Hartrich & Albert Dow 1981

DIRECT FINISH: **WAY RADICAL** II 5.9+ R (*)

Especially if the expanding flake comes off! Not for the faint at heart.
1. Climb INTERROGATOR's first pitch to a ledge with a dead log. 5.9
2a. Head up to a bolt, step right, and layback an overhanging, expanding flake to a stance (bolt). Face climb to an overhanging hand crack, jam it face climb to a horizontal crack, awkwardly traverse right, and finish up another overhanging crack (5.9+) to the top. 125', 5.9+ R

HISTORY: Tom Callaghan, John Mallery, & Mike Cody made the very eventful first ascent of this route on July 16, 1981. Only 10 feet from completing the pitch, Tom Callaghan suddenly discovered that his rope had somehow gotten completely jammed somewhere below him. His last piece of protection, a Friend 30 feet lower, had inverted and the cams had jammed up the rope. Tom tried to down climb the overhanging 5.9+ crack beneath him back to the Friend (creating a huge loop of slack in the rope as he did so!), but he was too blown out—so he climbed back up to his high point. His partners couldn't hear his cries for help, and eventually, Tom realized he had only one option: to untie! Which he did, dropping his now useless rope—and free-soloed to the top. Severely dehydrated from his exertions (it was also a very hot day), Callaghan got lost in the woods while trying to descend to his belayer, John Mallery, who was sitting contentedly below, and still had him on-belay! But Tom couldn't find the cliff base, and now completely dazed, he stumbled through the thick forest up to a nearby house whose owners were in the midst of a rollicking afternoon cocktail party. "Here, want one?" said one of the revellers, handing Tom a beer. "You look kinda thirsty." Sometime later, after quaffing a couple of beers, Tom staggered back through the woods, up to the cliff, and finally told John that he was off-belay!

LEATHER & LYCRA I 5.12a (*)

Located above BUTCHER BLOCK and before WAY RADICAL. Bring a small Tri-cam and a big Friend. The crux on Pitch two is strenuous and technical.
1. Climb a short face to a shallow, right-facing dihedral capped by a roof. Swing over and mantle. 40', 5.11a
2. Climb left up twin dihedrals (5.12a), move past a bolt, then undercling left to a stance (bolt). Continue up an arch underclinging up its left side past bolts to a 5.11d mantleshelf at the top. 100', 5.12a

BAND M LEDGE - LEFT (WAY RADICAL & OVER DONE)

HISTORY: Bob Parrott & Steve Damboise climbed the top crux pitch on October 5, 1986, before Steve Damboise & Dan Hutchens added the first pitch, after placing two bolts on rappel, on April 20, 1987.

DOGGIE-STYLE I 5.11a
1. Climb the difficult, sustained arete (5.11a) just to the right of THE UNDERSTATEMENT, using a tree for protection. 45', 5.11a

FA: Bob Parrott, Steve Damboise, Barry Rugo, & Harry Brielmann
   October 21, 1986

THE UNDERSTATEMENT I 5.8
At the far left end of the cliff are three vertical jam cracks in good granite. Surprisingly, this is the easiest one.
1. Layback and jam up the right-hand crack. 50', 5.8

FA: Roger Martin & Joe Cote November 12, 1973

FINALLY DUNN I 5.10d (*)
The deceptively awkward center crack. Be forewarned!
1. The strenuous crux (5.10d) is just below a small alcove. Finish up a flared chimney to the top. 50', 5.10d

FA: Jim Dunn September, 1975

OVER DONE I 5.10a (**)
Although not the hardest of the trio, try not to over act on the final mantleshelf move. Protection is strenuous to place.
1. Climb the overhanging, left-hand crack using a variety of face holds, and mantleshelf left at the top. 45', 5.10a

FA: Doug Madara & Chris Noonan 1978

HERCULES I 5.11b (*)
1. Climb the bolted face (5.11b) just to the left of OVER DONE. 45', 5.11b

FA: Steve Damboise & Bob Parrott September, 1987

BUTCHER BLOCK I 5.12c (*)
You fingers will definitely be cooked after this one!
1. Above OVER DONE, climb the dramatic, overhanging finger crack (peg) out a body length roof. 30', 5.12c

FA: Bob Parrott with Jay Depeter June, 1985

FROSTY FINGERS I 5.7
This one pitch jam crack is located on a hidden wall high up on the far left-hand side of the cliff. To reach it, climb one of the previous routes, or up INTERROGATOR, or circle the cliff's left side, walking steadily uphill.
1. Climb the obvious, slightly right-leaning crack system. 5.7

FA: Roger Martin, Joe Cote, & Milt Camille November 17, 1973

Anne Rutter climbing The Tao Of Dow (5.8) in 1981. Photo by Ed Webster.

ALBANY SLAB

This south-facing, one pitch "sunshine slab" is located to the west of Conway. Ask a local. All the climbs at Albany were established on the lead using a minimum number of bolts, which were all drilled by hand. Accordingly, a modern rack is extremely helpful on nearly every route here. Hike in until below some talus blocks at the base, circle around these to the right, then scramble left (rope up first) onto a long, narrow belay ledge with a couple of large pine trees growing on it as anchors and route landmarks. Since the climbs at Albany Slab are now described from right to left, the first three routes are actually located on a shorter, steeper cliff that is approximately 150 feet horizontally to the right of the Main Slab.

VIRGO RISING I 5.10d
Walk 30 feet to the right of the GEMINI DREAM'IN finger crack, down a bit, past the easy CAPRICORN CORNER to a small, steep wall split in the center by an incipient, vertical crack with a white, triangular block jammed in the horizontal break 25 feet up. Bring a normal rack, including small wired nuts. The route can also be easily top-roped.
1. Jam up the incipient crack (5.10d). When the crack becomes too thin, step right to a convenient flake/hand crack leading up to the securely jammed block. Belay on the good ledge on the left. 35', 5.10d
FA: Michael Hartrich & Albert Dow July 30, 1980

CAPRICORN CORNER I 5.4
The easy, left-facing corner, blocks, and pine tree 20 feet to the left of VIRGO RISING, and 10 feet right of GEMINI DREAM'IN.
1. Climb a fist crack up the corner to two blocks and a large pine on a ledge. Finish up the nice hand crack (5.4) in the corner's right wall to the top. 60', 5.4
FA: Unknown.

GEMINI DREAM'IN I 5.10b (*)
One hundred feet right of the Main Slab, on the left side of the same small cliff as VIRGO RISING, is a very, very thin, short, right-leaning crack. Carry a modern rack, including a full set of RP nuts.
1. Make bouldering moves up the wall from the right to gain a horizontal break and the initial thin crack, which is climbed (5.10b) until a long reach and a mantleshelf (5.10a) gains the center ledge. Step left, finishing up a pretty, vertical finger crack (5.9+) to the pine tree growing on top. 75', 5.10b
FA: Tom Callaghan, John Strand, & John Mallery August 28, 1981

The following climbs, listed from right to left,
ascend Albany's Main Slab.

ZEN & NOW I 5.10c (*)

This is the right-hand route on the Main Slab. Belay at the small pine tree just to the right of the large, central pine tree.

1. Face climb up and right past a bolt on a smooth slab with perfect rock (5.8) to a wired nut placement, and higher, a possible belay on the right. Step left, clip a bolt, then face climb up an obvious, brown water streak (5.10c) to a dike (bolt), a pine tree, and the top. 140', 5.10c

FA: Albert Dow & Michael Hartrich May, 1980

THE TAO OF DOW I 5.8 (*)

The slab's easiest climb. Belay at a large pine tree below the center of the Main Slab. Modern rack helpful.

1. Climb up to a big hole large enough to stand in. Continue past a bulge (5.8; bolt), climb flakes up and right to the top, or finish left up a dike. 150', 5.8

FA: Michael Hartrich, Alec Behr, & Albert Dow May, 1980

STANDARD & POOR I 5.9 (**)

This popular route begins just left of the slab's center, below a long, horizontal overlap. Belay at the large pine. Protection is actually semi-reasonable!

1. Face climb straight up (wired nuts) to a good ledge (bolt) with a bulge above it. Continue straight up past a second bolt (5.9) to an overlap, a third bolt, and a 5.8 face leading to the top. 150', 5.9

FA: Michael Hartrich, Joe Lentini, & Albert Dow May, 1980

REELING IN THE FEARS I 5.10a X (5.9 R) (*)

A very serious lead. Bring a modern rack, including a double set of RP nuts, plus small and medium Tri-cams. Just to the left of STANDARD & POOR is a slanting pine tree leaning up close to the slab.

1. Move up and right along a seam (5.9 R) to a stance. (An off route bolt may be seen above.) Now angle up and left past a solution pocket (Tri-cam; the last protection!) and head for the final overlap and bulge which is climbed at a very thin flake (5.10a X) to a tree—and safety. 150', 5.10a X (5.9 R)

HISTORY: On his first attempt, on the morning of August 29, 1981, John Strand took a 70 foot leader fall from the final moves, broke three RP nuts—and was just saved from a groundfall by some quick reeling in of the rope and a very alert belayer. Several beers later, that same day, John Mallery, Tom Callaghan, & Strand drove over to Cannon and made the first complete ascent of SLIP-O-FOOLS. John Strand returned to lead the first ascent of REELING, unseconded, in September, 1981.

FOOLS FOR A DAY I 5.10b (***)

Seven bolts, seven quick draws! One of the White Mountain's best 5.10 slab routes, offering sustained climbing on excellent rock right up the cliff's center.

Just don't fall while clipping the second bolt, but if you're solid on 5.9, you'll be OK. The route takes an independent line between REELING IN THE FEARS and DEATH OF A SALESMAN. Begin just left of REELING.

1. Above the first bolt, face climb (scary 5.9) until you can clip the second bolt. Continue face climbing past four more bolts above, with the crux moves coming after the sixth bolt, climbing up a short, final headwall (5.10b; bolt) onto an easier slab. Belay at a pine tree on top. 150', 5.10b

HISTORY: The route was established in impeccable style. Gerry Lortie & Tim Kemple placed the first six bolts on the lead by hand on April 1, 1995. Gerry Lortie & Chris Small returned on April 30, 1995, added one more bolt (also on the lead), pulled their ropes and quick draws, then led the first ascent.

DEATH OF A SALESMAN I 5.10b R
Start as for REELING IN THE FEARS. Modern rack very helpful!

1. Using a runner placed in the REELING pine tree, face climb angling left to a bolt 30 feet up. Continue face and slab climbing straight up, eventually joining the top section of DOW JONES AVERAGE on the left. 150', 5.10b R

FA: John Strand & Rose O'Brien July, 1985

DOW JONES AVERAGE I 5.10a (5.7 R)
The farthest left-hand route on the cliff, with average length (read: long) Albany Slab runouts. Bring a modern rack.

1. Face climb up the left side of the slab to a pine tree 40 feet up, wrap a runner around the tree, then face climb up a 5.7 R face to the first bolt, 40 feet higher. Continue straight up the face past a natural thread and a wired nut placement to a second bolt (5.9), and finish by making a thin reach left (5.10a) to a flake. Belay at a tree on top. 150', 5.10a (5.7 R)

FA: Michael Hartrich, Joe Lentini, & Albert Dow May, 1980

376 THE KANCAMAGUS HIGHWAY AREA

Jim Dunn leading the first ascent of The Crack In The Woods (5.10d) in 1973, one of the best free climbs in the Kancamagus Highway area. Photo by Rick Wilcox.

THE KANCAMAGUS HIGHWAY AREA

West of the town of Conway on both sides of the Kancamagus Highway (Route 112) and the Swift River are many excellent, small crags tucked away in the woods. Most of these cliffs have become quite popular in recent years, particularly Woodchuck Ledge, each of the Sundown Ledges, Found Ledge, Rainbow Slabs, and The Crack In The Woods Cliff. High quality climbing, including many of the best sport climbs in the White Mountains, great rock, and pleasant approaches are just several of the positive aspects of "climbing on the Kanc." Camping is nearby at three State Forest campgrounds: next to Sundown at either the Covered Bridge Campground or Blackberry Crossing Campground, or farther west on Route 112 at Jigger Johnson Campground.

Kancamagus, The Fearless One, was the grandson of Chief Passaconaway of the Penacook Indians. About 1684, he succeeded his uncle Wonalancet as the third and last Sagamon, or Chief, of the Penacook Indian Confederacy. In 1686, Kancamagus led the raid on Dover, New Hampshire. Although he tried to keep the peace with white settlers moving into the White Mountain region, repeated conflicts eventually brought war. The Penacook tribes disbanded after 1691, and Chief Kancamagus and his kin finally left the White Mountains for northern New Hampshire or Canada, never to be heard from again.

The Kancamagus cliffs are described from east to west in the order they are approached from the highway when driving west from Conway. For first time visitors, approaches to most of the cliffs along the Kancamagus can be quite confusing. Follow the directions and mileage numbers carefully, and if possible explore the area first in the spring or autumn when the trees have lost their leaves. These are the only times of the year when you can even see a few of the cliffs! Getting descriptions for several Kancamagus climbs has been difficult, and some of the information is no doubt a little rough. My aim has been to give some historical documentation to these areas before all records are completely lost or forgotten. Sketchy descriptions should be taken with a large grain of salt.

WOODCHUCK LEDGE

The first cliff you'll see when driving west along the Kancamagus Highway is Woodchuck Ledge, a 250 foot crag on the southern slope of Mt. Haystack. The cliff is also visible when driving west on the Dugway Road from the meadow at the southern end of the Moat Mountain trail. The rock forming the cliff is syenite, a fine grained igneous rock that makes for unusual face climbs and smooth-sided parallel cracks. Drive west on the Dugway Road, and park at a small, dirt pullout on the right bordered by several small boulders, half a mile past the Dugway Picnic Area. From the Kancamagus Highway and the Albany

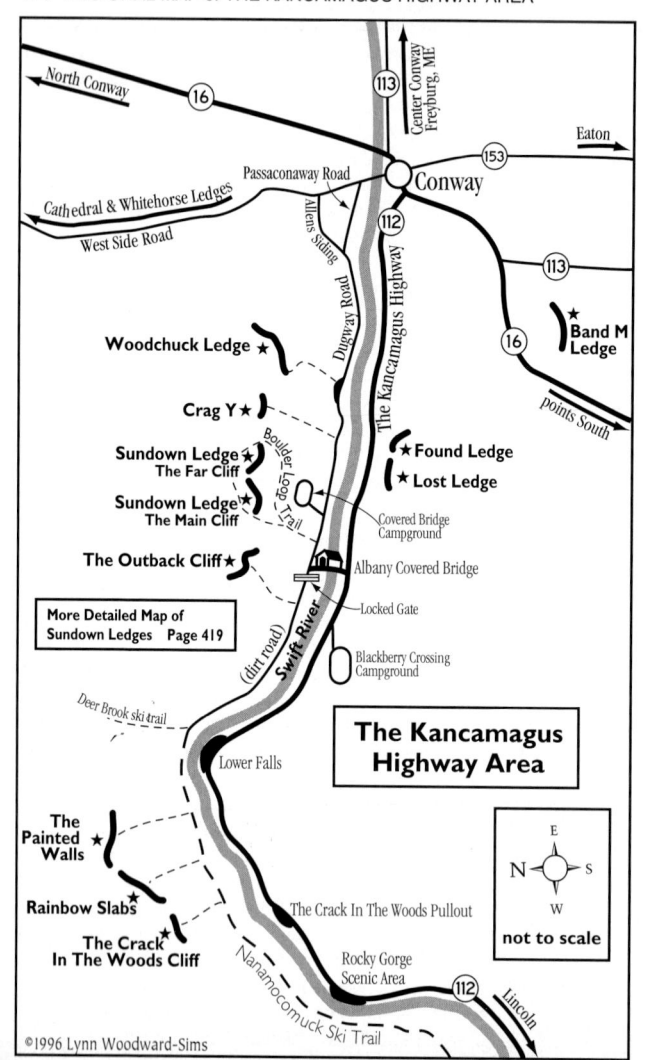

378 REGIONAL MAP of THE KANCAMAGUS HIGHWAY AREA

WOODCHUCK LEDGE - THE JURASSIC WALL 379

Covered Bridge, this pullout is 2.5 miles east, on your left. Follow an obvious lumber road straight uphill (north) which leads through raspberries to an overgrown thicket in an old clearcut below the cliff. At the clearcut, take the left-hand trail (cairn) into the woods on the left. Follow the trail gradually uphill, and you'll soon reach the cliff base 100 feet left of the farthest, left-hand route at Woodchuck, FORCES OF GRAVITY. This first cliff has a horizontal band of roofs halfway up, and offers the first two routes. The climbs at Woodchuck, which is a very complex cliff with several distinct sections, are now described from left to right. Allow 20 minutes for the hike in.

FORCES OF GRAVITY I 5.9+
Use double ropes to cut rope drag, or you may feel very tied down.
1. Thirty feet left of THE MADARA-DAMP ROUTE, climb a chimney to a difficult move right around a tricky corner. Wander up and right through the main overhangs, and finish up a crack and corner. Needs cleaning. 130', 5.9+
FA: Ed Webster & Kurt Winkler May 19, 1982

THE MADARA-DAMP ROUTE I 5.10
An impressive, rarely repeated route up the vertical crack system located just to the right of the cliff's center. Carry large protection.
1. Climb the crack through three roofs, and struggle up an offwidth. 130', 5.10
FA: Doug Madara & Eben Damp Summer, 1976

THE JURASSIC WALL
This short, steep face is 200 hundred feet right of THE MADARA-DAMP ROUTE, or about 100 feet down and left of the ZONKERS Wall. Walk to the right past THE MADARA-DAMP ROUTE, and in one minute, you'll be below the Jurassic Wall. After some cleaning on rappel, this 70 foot cliff yielded several noteworthy discoveries. Climbs here are generally decomposed and brittle for their first half—and absolutely brilliant above as on JURASSIC CRACK, the central finger crack. Sensible climbers may wish to top-rope the routes off the trees growing on the flat ledge at the wall's top (bring a short rope to extend out the anchor), otherwise, for the bold of heart and mind, carry a modern rack for these prehistoric routes which are now described from left to right.

TRIASSIC CRACK I 5.8
Start from a pile of blocks at the left-hand side of the wall.
1. Head up into an irregular, alcove/chimney topped by a small roof. Climb the crack out the right side of the roof, and finish up the same crack. 50', 5.8
FA: George Hurley & Rick Wilcox August 23, 1995

MASS EXTINCTION I 5.10b
This is the attractive, thin finger crack in the top half of the face midway between the TRIASSIC and JURASSIC cracks. The first 20 feet are on poor

380 THE KANCAMAGUS HIGHWAY AREA

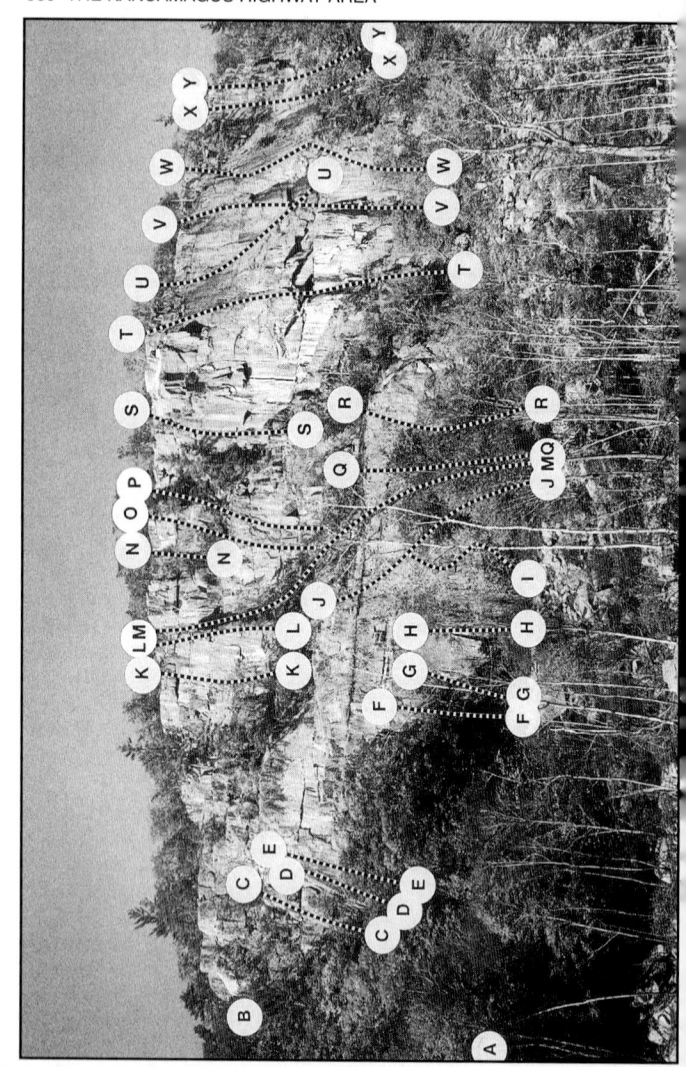

WOODCHUCK LEDGE

A.		The Jurassic Wall	Page 379	M.	ZERO GULLY I 5.6	Page 388
B.		The Playground	Page 382	N.	WOODCHUCK LODGE I 5.10a	Page 389
C.	**	RAPTURE OF THE STEEP I 5.10b	Page 384	O. **	MATHEMATICA II 5.10c	Page 390
D.	**	ZONKED OUT I 5.12b	Page 386	P.	STEP FUNCTION II 5.10b	Page 390
E.	***	SCREAMING YELLOW ZONKERS CRACK I 5.11c	Page 386	Q. **	DIAMOND EDGE I 5.10d	Page 391
F.		ROGER'S SPIRE I 5.5	Page 387	R. *	TERMINATOR I 5.11d	Page 391
G.	***	WINGED EEL FINGERLING I 5.12d (Top-rope)	Page 387	S. **	SLEDGEHAMMER I 5.10d	Page 392
H.	***	THE MISSION I 5.13b	Page 387	T. **	STONE FREE II 5.11b	Page 392
I.	**	STEAMROLLER I 5.12a	Page 387	U. **	PLEISTOCENE II 5.10c	Page 393
J.	*	BUCKET LOADER I 5.11d	Page 388	V.	DEADLINE I 5.9	Page 393
K.		CHINA I 5.10d R	Page 388	W.	THE ROUTE OF ALL EVIL I 5.7	Page 393
L.		WOODCHUCK EDGE I 5.8 R	Page 389	X. *	ZANZIBAR I 5.5	Page 394
				Y. *	OKTOBERFEST I 5.6	Page 394

WOODCHUCK LEDGE 381

rock, while the upper finger crack, once reached, is hard, but well protected.
1. Start as for either the TRIASSIC or JURASSIC CRACKS, and finish up the thin, vertical, finger crack (5.10b) above. 60', 5.10b
FA: George Hurley & Rick Wilcox   August 23, 1995

JURASSIC CRACK I 5.9 (*)

A classic from its age! The first route done on the wall is identified by its desirable, upper finger crack, easily seen from the approach trail. Start just left of the wall's center, 30 feet right of TRIASSIC CRACK, directly below the top, finger crack—with the crux being to get to the crack.
1. After climbing up a series of creaky flakes (5.8) to a horizontal crack, make a thin, balance move (5.9) to better handholds, and finish by jamming up the all-time, sinker finger crack (5.7) to the tree ledge on top. 65', 5.9
HISTORY: George Hurley & Ed Webster made the first ascent on August 18, 1995—with thanks to Butch for the crucial loan of his pruning shears!

VARIATION: PRUDENCE I 5.9

Start 20 feet right of JURASSIC CRACK where a tree grows near the cliff.
1a. Climb discontinuous features straight up for about 25 feet until you can traverse left to JURASSIC CRACK's top finger crack. 65', 5.9
FA: Joe Hayes & George Hurley   September 3, 1995

NATURAL SELECTION I 5.9

On the upper, right-hand side of the Jurassic Wall are a series of right-angling, discontinuous, thin cracks. Bring along a modern rack if you want to pass on your evolutionary advantages to future generations!
1. Climb straight up for 20 feet, then angle left to reach the line of discontinuous cracks, and follow them to their logical end (and your own) on top. 70', 5.9
FA: George Hurley & Joe Hayes   September 3, 1995

PRIMATES R US I 5.9

The route takes a straight line up the right side of the wall. Find a large tree growing near the cliff base with a triangular block resting against the tree.
1. Climb up short cracks and shallow grooves to a triangular hole. 70', 5.9
FA: George Hurley & Ed Ewald   September 24, 1995

SASHA I 5.8

On the tree ledge on top of the Jurassic Wall, walk left to the second of two, three foot high steps. The correct step has a boulder sitting on top of it.
1. Follow a finger, layback crack up the wall above the step. 25', 5.8
FA: George Hurley & Joe Hayes   September 3, 1995

THE PLAYGROUND

The next routes are located on a small cliff band above and left of the ZONKERS Wall. This short crag makes for a pleasant day's outing, giving

WOODCHUCK LEDGE - THE PLAYGROUND

routes of all grades. Although it faces south, the crag is shaded by several big trees. Several routes here were probably climbed before, but went unrecorded. Scramble up an easy gully 50 feet left of SCREAMING YELLOW ZONKERS CRACK. The climbs are now described from right to left.

EASY STREET I 5.4
The farthest right-hand route up the crag. Well protected.
1. This clean-cut, right-facing dihedral has a ledge halfway up it. 40', 5.4
FA: Unknown.

GEMINI I 5.6 (*)
Begin 75 feet left of the EASY STREET corner at the base of obvious twin finger cracks. Nice moves, but they're harder than they look!
1. Climb the twin cracks (5.6), finishing into a slot at the top. 40', 5.6
FA: Dick Peterson, Brad White, & Barbara Knight August, 1988

ZIG ZAG I 5.7+
The zig zag finger crack that splits the right wall of THE BULLY dihedral.
1. Climb the thin finger crack (5.7+) to a small ledge with a tree. 40', 5.7+
FA: Brad White & Dick Peterson August, 1988

THE BULLY I 5.9 (or 5.10b) (*)
The most obvious route on the cliff ascends the large, right-facing dihedral in the center of the crag. Bring several large cams.
1. Layback up an offwidth/fist crack (5.9) in a right-facing dihedral. If you offwidth up the crack, it's more like 5.10b. 40', 5.9 (or 5.10b)
FA: Brad White & Dick Peterson August, 1988

WITCHCRAFT I 5.10a (**)
Just around the outside corner left of THE BULLY is this spell-binding route, the Playground's best climb. Look for a shallow, left-facing corner with an overlap 12 feet up. Carry a modern rack.
1. Climb past the overlap, then up a thin, vertical crack system (5.10a) which gives several thought-provoking moves to the top. 40', 5.10a
FA: Dick Peterson & Brad White August, 1988

CRANKSHAFT I 5.9 (*)
Start 60 feet to the left of THE BULLY. Strenuous jamming.
1. Jam up a vertical finger crack into an alcove, followed by an overhanging 5.9 finger crack leading to a pine tree growing on top. 40', 5.9
FA: Dick Peterson & Brad White August, 1988

THE STING I 5.7
1. Just left of CRANKSHAFT, jam a finger crack to a ledge & V groove. 40', 5.7
HISTORY: Brad White, Barbara Knight, & Dick Peterson did the first ascent in August, 1988. A nest of angry yellow jackets made for a memorable ascent!

384 THE KANCAMAGUS HIGHWAY AREA

SQUEEZE PLAY I 5.3
1. Ten feet left of THE STING, squeeze up a chimney behind a block. 25', 5.3
FA: Dick Peterson, free-solo August, 1988

BUMBLE'S BOUNCE I 5.5
1. Eight feet left of SQUEEZE PLAY, jam up a short hand/fist crack. 20', 5.5
FA: Brad White & Barbara Knight August, 1988

THE ZONKERS WALL

The next climbs, all highly recommended, are on a 100 foot cliff 100 feet right of the Jurassic Wall and well to the left of Woodchuck's Main Cliff. A short, steep trail leads to a tree ledge at the base of a gently overhanging wall sliced by several vertical cracks. The obvious, central route is Woodchuck's famous testpiece: SCREAMING YELLOW ZONKERS CRACK, a straight-in, overhanging finger crack. These well protected climbs are described left to right.

FIREBIRD I 5.7+
Begin this vertical dance below the obvious corner/crack 15 feet around the outside corner to the left of QUEEN OF HEARTS. Normal rack.
1. Climb up a vertical hand crack to its top and a good tree ledge. 80', 5.6+
2. Face climb up (5.7+) into a six inch wide crack in the left wall of the upper, open book. Finish by a boulder that juts out over the crack's top. 45', 5.7+
FA: Joe Hayes & George Hurley June 7, 1987

VARIATION: I 5.4
2a. Climb directly up the back of the fold of the FIREBIRD corner. 45', 5.4
FA: George Hurley & Jon Norling August 8, 1987

RAPTURE OF THE STEEP I 5.10b (**)
Ascends the unlikely arete between FIREBIRD and QUEEN OF HEARTS. The name tells the story of this memorable and exciting climb. Modern rack.
1. Climb the easy chimney up the wall's left side, then finger jam straight up (same as QUEEN OF HEARTS) to a stance below the top overlap. Move left onto the steep arete, laybacking up (5.10a) into a hidden finger crack on the arete's left side. Climb the thin crack (5.10b) to a ledge on the right. 80', 5.10b
2. Step left and face climb up the final, steep wall (5.9+) using an incipient, vertical crack for protection, to a large tree at the top. 50', 5.9+ Rappel twice, with one rope, back down SCREAMING YELLOW ZONKERS.
FA: George Hurley & Ed Webster August 18, 1995

QUEEN OF HEARTS I 5.9+ (*)
A beautiful climb deserving of more attention. Well protected.
1. Just to the right of an outside corner, ascend a crack system up the wall's left side over the center of a small roof or overlap near the top. 80', 5.9+
FA: Jim Dunn, Peter Cole, & Rainsford Rouner 1975

Jim Dunn leading the first free ascent of Screaming Yellow Zonkers Crack (5.11d) in 1975. Photograph by Joe Lentini.

ACE OF SPADES I 5.9+
1. The cracks right of QUEEN OF HEARTS, up a left-facing corner. 80', 5.9+
FA: Henry Barber, Joe Cote, & Ric Hatch May 6, 1978

ZONKED OUT I 5.12b (**)
The first 5.12 route in the White Mountains could still leave you a bit dazed. Start five feet right of ACE OF SPADES. Bring small wired nuts and cams.
1. Layback and jam the thin, vertical crack (5.12b) just to the left of the central crack system (ZONKERS) up to a double bolt anchor on a stance. 60', 5.12b
HISTORY: After numerous prior attempts, Jim Dunn finally succeeded in mastering the climb on May 14, 1978. What made Dunn's ascent even more remarkable was that he did the climb with one bare foot and one EB!

SCREAMING YELLOW ZONKERS CRACK I 5.11c (***)
THE classic, overhanging finger crack. No clues from the popcorn gallery!
1. Finger jam up the appealing, overhanging central crack system. Save your strength—you'll need it. The crux is at the top. 90', 5.11c Two bolt anchor.
HISTORY: Joe Cote & Bruce Kumph aided the first ascent of the route on June 15, 1975. The first free ascent was a significant climb of the times when it was done by Jim Dunn in October of 1975.

CIRCUS TIME I 5.10b
The swinging dihedral just right of SCREAMING YELLOW ZONKERS.
1. Face climb and layback up into the main, left-facing corner. At a large, protruding block, handtraverse right onto a belay ledge. 75', 5.10b Since the flakes above are loose, rappel off with one rope.
FA: Ed Webster & Anne Rutter November 7, 1981

ASPIRING II 5.10b (*)
Ascends the front face of ROGER'S SPIRE before continuing to the top of the cliff. Begin 75 feet to the right of ZONKERS and CIRCUS TIME at a 20 foot high, right-facing corner leading up to a large roof.
1. Move up the corner, then fingertip layback and undercling out the roof's right edge (5.10b). Belay on the second ledge at a block. 45', 5.10b
2. Continue in the same line up cracks in the south face of the spire to its summit. Climb a crack in a small corner to a good ledge, step left, and jam another short crack to a large tree ledge. 60', 5.9
2a. Step right and climb a nice 5.9 arete to the spire's top. 5.9
3. Twenty feet right, an easy ramp leads up left to a large pine tree. Finish up a corner/crack with a chockstone to the woods. 70', 5.4
HISTORY: George Hurley & Tony Tulip made the first ascent on April 22, 1987, using one aid point on Pitch one. Hurley & Tulip free climbed the route, plus added the Pitch two variation, on April 25, 1987.

ROGER'S SPIRE I 5.5
Begin 30 feet to the right of ASPIRING at the base of an obvious chimney system behind a huge detached flake or spire, located at the left-hand end of a large, blank wall known as the Catipillar Wall.
1. Chimney your way up the right-hand side of the spire to a collection of rappel slings wrapped around the top of the flake. 75', 5.5 Rappel off.
FA: Roger Martin, solo April, 1972

THE CATIPILLAR WALL
Rev up your engines and bring plenty of extra fuel in reserve! The unabashedly steep, large, and mostly blank Catipillar Wall immediately to the right of ROGER'S SPIRE is home to Woodchuck's hardest and most fingery sport routes. From left to right, the climbs are:

WINGED EEL FINGERLING I 5.12d (Top-rope) (***)
The farthest left-hand route up the wall. A slippery proposition?
1. Climb 15 feet up a short, vertical finger crack in blocks 15 feet to the right of ROGER'S SPIRE. Then face climb up and right past two bolts, stepping right into a beautiful, vertical crack (5.12d) which slowly widens from thin fingers to hands. Fixed anchor at the top. 80', 5.12d
HISTORY: After bolting the route, Jerry Handren tried to lead the climb in 1991, but was understandably worried about hitting a spike of rock if he fell off the thin face moves at the start, so he top-roped it instead. (Although Jerry says that one more bolt "will probably" keep you from hitting the spike!)

THE MISSION I 5.13b (***)
This classic, hard-won sport route is located 75 feet to the right of ROGER'S SPIRE in the center of the Catipillar Wall. Find a 15 foot V groove 10 feet left of a natural spring at the cliff base. Modern rack.
1. Climb the V groove, then continue up a thin, vertical crack, following it left until it ends (bolt) in a blank face with black and white water streaks and a ring bolt. Face climb up and right (5.13b) past two more ring bolts into another crack that angles up and left to a stance with a two bolt anchor. 80', 5.13b
HISTORY: Jim Surette first attempted the route in September, 1987, placed only one bolt, and took several sizable leader falls, coming close to success before a hold broke. Steve Damboise added three additional protection bolts, and made the climb's first ascent with John Weaver in July, 1991.

STEAMROLLER I 5.12a (**)
Start 40 feet to the right of THE MISSION, or 40 feet to the left of ZERO GULLY. Sustained and very strenuous jamming and underclinging lead to the final, frustratingly thin face moves. Try to keep your momentum going uphill as long as you can! Normal rack. Pitons were pre-placed for protection.

1. Undercling an obvious, strenuous arch up and left to difficult face moves (peg; 5.12a) onto a narrow, belay ledge with a piton & bolt anchor. 80', 5.12a Rappel off from here, or if you have any energy left...
2. Continue up the left-slanting BUCKET LOADER finger crack (5.11a) to the large, tree-covered ledge just below the Upper Tier.
FA: Jerry Handren & Chris Gill October 15, 1986

BUCKET LOADER I 5.11d (*)
Begin 50 feet to the right of STEAMROLLER, or 15 feet to the left of ZERO GULLY. Carry a modern rack with RPs and small wired nuts.
1. Climb up a shallow, left-facing corner to two overlaps, undercling left to a knifeblade, then make hard moves (5.11d) up and left to the STEAMROLLER belay ledge with a piton & bolt anchor. 80', 5.11d
2. Finish up a strenuous (5.11a) left-leaning crack to the trees. 5.11a
HISTORY: Jim Ewing & Chris Gill did Pitch one on October 21, 1986. Jerry Handren, Chris Gill, & Andrew Ross finished the route the next day.

ZERO GULLY I 5.6
Woodchuck's most obvious route is the long, left-slanting dike in the center.
1. After tricky moves off the ground (5.6), the rest of the gully yields fairly easily. You can also walk off right after one pitch along a tree ledge. 100', 5.6
FA: Roger Martin & Joe Cote April 8, 1972

THE UPPER TIER
The next one pitch routes ascend Woodchuck's top, central cliff band directly above the Catipillar Wall and the Diamond Wall. These climbs can be approached from below via any of the central routes from ASPIRING on the left to DIAMOND EDGE on the right—for which they make short, aesthetic finishes. Another approach is to hike around the cliff's left side up the gully just to the left of the ZONKERS Wall to the summit, then rappel down to several large tree ledges at the base of the Upper Tier routes. EIGENVECTOR and STEP FUNCTION are multi-pitch climbs whose crux third pitches can be reached in two single rope rappels. The climbs are described from left to right.

CHINA I 5.10d R
Ascends brittle, white-stained rock 15 feet left of NEUROMANCER, and just to the right of a conspicuous, leaning jam crack. Bring a modern rack.
1. Jam a few moves up the wide, left-hand crack, then step right into the overhanging, white crack. Continue straight up over a bulge to less overhanging rock above (fixed piton). Face climb past an awkward small ledge until it's possible to move left and mantle on a larger ledge. Now go left a few yards to a clean, 10 foot layback crack that leads to the summit. 70', 5.10d
FA: Jim Ewing & Larry Hamilton October 9, 1988

NEUROMANCER I 5.12a (*)
Ascends the center of the overhanging face left of WOODCHUCK EDGE. Begin at the back of a concave area. Two bolts are visible far above.
1. Strenuous moves (with adequate, but hard to place wired nut protection) break through the concave area. Two bolts protect more technical climbing on thin flakes (5.12a) up to a narrow ledge with fixed pitons. Lower off from here, if desired (50', 5.12a), or traverse left and finish up CHINA.
FA: Jim Ewing & Larry Hamilton August 13, 1988

WOODCHUCK EDGE I 5.8 R
Left across the gully from WOODCHUCK LODGE is an arete on the Upper Tier's right boundary, at the cliff's upper left side above ROGER'S SPIRE.
1. Climb up the arete (5.8 R) past a fixed piton. 70', 5.8 R
FA: Alex Alvarez & Larry Hamilton June 19, 1988

WOODCHUCK LODGE I 5.10a
Several good bivi sites are on this half-pitch route. The climb ascends the large, left-facing corner forming the left boundary of the face climbed by SCALAR.
1. Climb easily up a wide flake/crack to a large ledge at the base of the main corner. A bolt protects boulder problem moves (5.10a) on the first smooth step, after which easy, pleasant climbing leads too quickly to the top. 70', 5.10a
HISTORY: Larry Hamilton & Scott Hobson climbed the route's first ascent without a bivouac in September, 1987.

SCALAR I 5.10c
About 30 feet left of the sloping dihedral up which EIGENVECTOR and STEP FUNCTION finish is a short wall topped by some ominous-looking blocks. SCALAR ascends the prominent, thin crack that ends just to the right of the right-hand block.
1. Climb the gently overhanging crack past two pitons to a blocky ledge. 30', 5.10c (The DEVIATION crux is just above this ledge on the right.)
2. Move left and finish up a short, layback corner. 20', 5.9.
FA: Larry Hamilton & Alex Alvarez June 7, 1988

DEVIATION I 5.10d
Belay at the large pine at the base of the V groove, final pitch of STEP FUNCTION. GRAND FINALE finishes up the right wall of this corner.
1. Climb 10 feet up the V groove, then turn left and jam up a wide crack (#4 Friend helpful) to a roof. Surmount the first roof (5.10d), climb a finger crack, and pull over a second roof. 60', 5.10d
HISTORY: George Hurley & Joe Hayes made the first ascent on June 7, 1987, using a couple of points of aid on the crux roof. Kris Hansen & George Hurley made the first free ascent on June 13, 1987.

EIGENVECTOR II 5.10c (*)

Variations upon a Mathematical Theme? Start as for STEP FUNCTION, or rappel in from above to the base of the Pitch three crux. Thirty feet left of STEP FUNCTION's wide crack is a finger crack, straight as a knife cut. Small cams.

1. Climb the first pitch of ZERO GULLY. 100', 5.6
2. Head straight up steep corners (5.7), aiming towards a prominent jagged crack. Belay on a flat ledge just below the crack. 60', 5.7 (Pitches one & two may be combined into a long pitch of 160', 5.7)
3. Thirty feet left of the jagged crack (STEP FUNCTION), climb steep flakes up and left into a clean, sharp-edged finger crack (5.10c; small cams useful) which is climbed to a tree ledge. 50', 5.10c
4. Move the belay up and right across the ledge to the large pine tree at the base of the final V groove/corner common finish of STEP FUNCTION and THE GRAND FINALE. Make tricky layback moves up the corner's first 15 feet, then use a horizontal hand crack to gain a steeper, bottomless dihedral on the left wall, and jam a finger crack up this corner to the top. 70', 5.9

FA: Larry Hamilton & George Hurley   June 10, 1987

MATHEMATICA II 5.10c (**)

A brilliant integration of three compact climbs. Begin up ZERO GULLY and EIGENVECTOR to reach the base of the second cliff band, or approach on rappel from above, to eliminate the easier climbing at the start.

1 & 2. Ascend the first two pitches of EIGENVECTOR. 5.6 & 5.7
3. Crank up EIGENVECTOR's first pitch, the knife-cut finger crack. 60', 5.10c
4. Climb SCALAR's first pitch, the overhanging, thin crack. 30', 5.10c
5. Finish up DEVIATION, stemming up a thin crack past a roof. 60', 5.10c

STEP FUNCTION II 5.10b

To a statistician, the jagged crux crack resembles nature's graph of a step function. Take some medium to large Friends. The first ascent party approached via ZERO GULLY up two uninspiring pitches of 5.6 and 5.7. The good climbing begins with the wide, jagged crack on Pitch three, which may also be accessed by rappelling in from above.

1. Climb Pitch one of ZERO GULLY to a tree ledge. 100', 5.6
2. Head straight up a series of short, steep corners (5.7), aiming towards a prominent jagged crack. Belay on a good ledge just below the crack. 60', 5.7 (Pitches one & two may be combined into a long lead of 160', 5.7)
3. On the second cliff band, ascend a wide, jagged crack (5.10b) that diagonals right across a steep wall to a tree-covered ledge. Belay at trees below a wide, open, low-angled corner—the finish of THE GRAND FINALE. 60', 5.10b
4. Layback up the groove, step left, and finish up a tiny corner. 70', 5.9

FA: George Hurley & Larry Hamilton   May 29, 1987

THE DIAMOND WALL

The very popular DIAMOND EDGE and the serious lines of JUDGEMENT DAY and TERMINATOR ascend the impressive, steep, smooth face of the Diamond Wall just to the right of the Catipillar Wall.

DIAMOND EDGE I 5.10d (**)
Start just to the right of ZERO GULLY below an appealing, sharp arete.
1. Climb up the face past two pitons to a small ledge at the base of a left-facing corner and hand crack. Jam and stem up the crack/corner (5.10d), step left at a peg, then finish up and right. Be careful of loose rock near the top. Tree anchor. 120', 5.10d Most parties rappel off with two ropes.
FA: Brad White & Dick Peterson July 30, 1988

JUDGEMENT DAY I 5.11a (**)
Start 10 feet to the left of TERMINATOR at a large block leaning against the cliff base. Very sustained moves, but the route is remarkably easier than TERMINATOR. Well protected with a modern rack and thin gear.
1. From on top of the block, step left to the base of a 15 foot high, shallow, right-facing corner. Climb the corner (5.9). When it ends, traverse left (pin; 5.11a) across a steep face to a welcome rest ledge. Next step back right and climb straight up thin cracks (5.10b), then move right again at a prominent horizontal crack to another thin seam before joining TERMINATOR at a fixed peg. Clip the bolt up and left (also on TERMINATOR), then at good flakes, climb past another piton on the left in orange rock (second crux; 5.11a) into a thin, left-facing flake system that leads to the top. 120', 5.11a
FA: Brad White & Ian Cruickshank August 28, 1996

TERMINATOR I 5.11d (*)
Begin 50 feet to the right of ZERO GULLY at the base of a steep, open face called the Diamond Wall. A modern rack including HB nuts, plus double ropes, and good route finding are all mandatory!
1. Face climb up to the right-hand of two, right-facing flakes, then step left to two side-by-side fixed pegs. Climb straight up past two more pitons to a horizontal crack just below a prominent overlap. Undercling left to a bolt (5.10b), then face climb up to big flakes. Move back right along the flakes, and continue up shallow grooves past two pegs (5.11d) to the top. 140', 5.11d
FA: Brad White & Tim Ashnault July 4, 1988

THE MAIN CLIFF
Woodchuck's Main Cliff is actually the farthest right-hand portion of the cliff—and its tallest section. It offers a wide variety of routes from difficult, multi-pitch free climbs like STONE FREE and PLEISTOCENE in the center, to moderates such as ZANZIBAR and OKTOBERFEST on the far right.

THE KANCAMAGUS HIGHWAY AREA

COUNTRY ROAD I Class 3 or 4

This long scramble up the middle section of Woodchuck gives a thrilling, moderate adventure with few technical difficulties.

1. Climb either of two, easy grooves up to the right end of a terrace.

2. Walk to the terrace's left end. Climb a short dihedral to the woods, or more directly, follow the upper part of ZERO GULLY.

FA: Unknown.

THE GRAND FINALE I 5.4

In the cliff's center, climb up left following either of two easy grooves to a tree-covered ledge. Walk left several feet, then climb a short corner and a series of easy ledges to the higher of two large pine trees easily seen from the base. The right-hand wall of a large V groove (5.4) gains the top. 70', 5.4

FA: Joe Cote & Dick Arey March 26, 1972

SLEDGEHAMMER I 5.10d (**)

This mighty route climbs an overhanging corner system at the left-hand side of the STONE FREE Wall, 40 feet to the left of a black streak in the center of this part of the face directly above TERMINATOR.

1. Climb up a sharp-cut, right-facing, overhanging dihedral past pegs and bolts (5.10d), then step left and follow a finger crack to the top. 100', 5.10d

FA: Brad White & Dick Peterson September 24, 1988

STONE FREE II 5.11b (**)

The best long, hard free climb on Woodchuck. Scramble uphill to the right of TERMINATOR, around the right side of the Diamond Wall, up some talus, until below a prominent overhang split in the center by a large flake system, with a flaring groove at its base.

1. Climb the indistinct groove to blocks under the main overhang. Pull over the lip on the left at a flake, then power undercling back right (5.11b) to an overhanging finger/hand crack leading to a stance (piton anchor). 125', 5.11b

2. From the belay, step left, and face climb straight up to the top. 70', 5.8 (The original second pitch traverses left across some ledges for 25 feet, and finishes up a right-facing corner to the top. 60', 5.6)

HISTORY: The FA party is unknown, as they didn't sign their new route entry. Pitch one was freed by Brad White, Ian Cruickshank, & Bruce Luetters on September 22, 1988, with a finish up the original second pitch. The 5.8 finish was added by Brad White & Dick Peterson on October 15, 1988.

RIGHT-HAND FINISH: **STONED FOR FREE** I 5.10d (*)

A harder and more fitting conclusion. Take a toke?

2b. From the belay at the top of Pitch two, step right 10 feet to a left-slanting finger crack that eventually fades into a smooth face. Climb up the crack to hard face moves (5.10d) leading to a blocky finish. 60', 5.10d

WOODCHUCK LEDGE - THE MAIN CLIFF

HISTORY: Dick Peterson & Brad White made the first ascent on October 15, 1988, naming the route for "a friend and former room-mate, who usually was."

PLEISTOCENE II 5.10c (**)
An exposed route up the left-hand edge of the steep, open slab on the upper, right-hand side of Woodchuck's Main Cliff. Recommended.
1. Climb the first pitch of THE ROUTE OF ALL EVIL, up the chimney on the left side of a blocky buttress (5.6), or the blocky face just to the right of the chimney (5.7+) to a small oak tree on a ledge on the left. 100', 5.6 or 5.7+
2. Head up a blank slab above the belay, about six feet left of Pitch two of DEADLINE. Above a stance (bolt), move up left (5.10c) to a thin overlap, then step left to a break. Move over the overlap at the break, then follow some discontinuous cracks (5.9) diagonally up left to the top. 140', 5.10c

HISTORY: After an earlier attempt by John Barley, Chris Gill & George Hurley made the route's first ascent on November 5, 1986.

DEADLINE I 5.9 (*)
Ascends the corner and arete just to the left of ROUTE OF ALL EVIL.
1. Climb the left-facing corner and crack (5.9), the latter becoming overhanging and offsize near the top. When the corner ends at a ledge, walk right and belay from trees. 75', 5.9
2. This pitch lies to the right of PLEISTOCENE and left of THE ROUTE OF ALL EVIL. Begin up the left-facing corner above the belay, but after 12 feet move right, making exposed moves onto an arete formed by the right wall of the corner and the slab to the right. Stay directly on the arete (amazingly only 5.6, well protected with a great situation), heading straight to the top. 100', 5.6
FA: George Hurley & Neil Hesketh   April 11, 1987

VARIATION: DARKENING OF THE LIGHT I 5.11b (*)
Ascends the bolted arete just to the right of Pitch one of DEADLINE.
1a. Start up the easy offwidth crack in the large block just to the right of DEADLINE. After 20 feet, step left onto a ledge at the arete's base. Face climb, crimp (5.11b at the second bolt), and layback up the arete past three bolts to a good tree ledge shared with DEADLINE and PLEISTOCENE. 75', 5.11b
FA: Brad White & Ian Cruickshank   October, 1993

THE ROUTE OF ALL EVIL I 5.7
On the right-hand side of the crag lies a large, broken blocky buttress whose left side forms a vertical chimney system.
1. Climb the chimney crack (5.6) to the top of the buttress. 5.6
2. From a blocky ledge, traverse 10 feet right and surmount a short, steep wall onto a large, open slab. Delicate face climbing leads up the slab to the top. 5.7
FA: Roger Martin & Joe Cote   April 2, 1972

VARIATION: **BLUE SKY DIKE** I 5.4
2a. From the top of the regular first pitch of THE ROUTE OF ALL EVIL, face climb left (exposed) along a left-slanting dike (5.4) which eventually intersects with Pitch two of DEADLINE. 5.4
FA: Paul Cormier & Jeff Campbell June, 1988

BIRCHFIELD BOOK I 5.5
The left edge of the ZANZIBAR face is marked by an inside corner just right of THE ROUTE OF ALL EVIL face. This corner is the route's major feature.
1. Begin 12 feet to the left of ZANZIBAR on an outside corner just to the left of the start of KAMPALA. Climb easily to the overlap below the large corner with many small birch trees growing in it. Swing past the overlap (5.5), climb the main dihedral, then continue up a smaller inside corner to a ledge 20 feet below the top of the cliff. 150', 5.5 Climb easily to the top.
FA: George Hurley & Bob Marquis April 27, 1987

KAMPALA I 5.5
Follows the parallel crack line 12 feet to the left of ZANZIBAR.
1. Begin by climbing up a right-facing corner, then follow a crack system up to a large, one foot diameter pine tree. 100', 5.5
2. The same crack leads up a slightly overhanging wall (5.5) on perfect holds to the top. Belay from another tree. 35', 5.5
FA: George Hurley & Jean Hurley April 26, 1987

ZANZIBAR I 5.5 (*)
For its difficulty, a classic climb on good rock, well protected, and in a scenic location. Walk right to the far, upper, right-hand side of the Main Cliff to the base of a two inch crack running up the entire face.
1. Start up a left-facing corner, then climb the crack to a nice ledge. 75', 5.2
2. Follow the crack (5.5) straight to the top (peg). 60', 5.5
FA: Joe Cote & Roger Martin April 8, 1972

OKTOBERFEST I 5.6 (*)
A nice line up Woodchuck's right-hand edge. Start from a large block 15 feet to the right of ZANZIBAR. Carry a #3.5 Friend.
1. Climb an easy face to a small notch in an overlap 30 feet up. Continue straight up to the good belay ledge on ZANZIBAR. 70', 5.6
2. Twenty feet right of ZANZIBAR, climb a thin crack in a slab, go left 10 feet, move over a bulge (5.6), and finish up a steep crack. 75', 5.6
HISTORY: Ed Webster & Kristina Kearney climbed the second pitch on October 26, 1985 as a variation to ZANZIBAR. George Hurley & Bob Marquis completed the full climb on April 27, 1987.

CRAG Y

By Larry Hamilton.

Amongst the most difficult to approach and obscure cliffs in the Kancamagus Highway area, Crag Y, located near Haystack and South Moat Mountain, offers a host of excellent cracks and free climbs. It has been said that if several of Crag Y's routes were at Cathedral, they would be instant classics! Geographically, Crag Y is the northwest extension of the cliff band that forms the south face of Haystack. The rock is the same fine-grained syenite found on Sundown and Woodchuck Ledges, an unusual volcanic rock that yields a profusion of thin, vertical cracks and dihedrals. Although small and compact, never quite reaching a full rope length in height, Crag Y nonetheless has a rich concentration of fine climbs.

THE APPROACH: The surest way to find Crag Y is to go along with someone who has been there before! The forested slopes surrounding the crag are almost featureless, so it is easy even for return visitors to discover that they are accidentally climbing Moat Mountain. Alas, the adventure of finding this cliff has now been considerably lessened by the appearance of fluorescent orange blazes on the trees. If you don't get lost, the approach takes about 45 minutes, however, a logging operation begun in 1996 has irrevocably altered the approach to Crag Y. The best advice is to ask a local about the approach, which at present is "in flux."

Begin at an old logging road that branches off the Dugway Road between Woodchuck and Sundown Ledges. The logging road starts 1.8 miles west of the Dugway picnic area, or 1.2 miles east of the Albany Covered Bridge. Hike west along this road until you cross Big Brook, a sizable stream. Continue about two hundred yards farther, to a point just before the logging road takes a sharp left turn and begins to climb. Head into the woods on the right here, quickly joining Big Brook. Walk alongside the brook a short distance until a huge mossy boulder, almost house-sized, can be dimly seen on its east bank. Cross over to the east bank at this boulder. A smaller stream descends the hillside from the east here, joining Big Brook beside the huge boulder. Begin hiking uphill along the right side of this small stream. Follow this streambed all the way to its head, choosing the wider branch every time it forks. From the stream-head, a faint trail continues up into the small valley which separates the crag (visible on your left) from the back side of Eagle Cliff. It is easy to miss this valley, and end up either too far left, climbing Moat Mountain, or too far right, on the slopes of Eagle Cliff. With some thrashing, you can reach the crag by traversing in the appropriate direction. If you find yourself on volcanic bedrock, you are likely too far left.

The crag's climbing history began on May 16, 1987 when the cliff was accidentally "discovered" by Paul Boissonneault and Jim Ewing after they had gotten lost while trying to find HYPERSPACE at Sundown's Outback Cliff. As Crag Y is several miles away from the Outback Cliff, Boissonneault and Ewing were indeed very, very lost! When they did finally stumble upon Crag Y, they found no trace of previous climbing. Since the crag is well hidden from nearly every vantage point, this was not much of a surprise, and the cliff's exact location remained secret through the early summer of 1987. It was Jim Ewing who coined the name "Crag Y"—a spoof on other North Conway climbers who were calling their own secret cliffs "Crag X".

Slowly, the discovery of Crag Y spread to a wider circle. As lasting testimony to the cliff's quality, many in this group returned repeatedly, despite the long, humid approach to work out new routes during the height of bug season. There was a sense of conspiracy about the work, as other climbers pried for information about the mysterious new crag. The conspiracy was not particularly quiet, however, because even during this "secret" phase of development, there were occasionally four parties on the cliff at once! The crag's early history involved extensive gardening and Sunday afternoon boulder trundling, this activity focusing particularly on the left and central parts of the cliff. Determined effort went into uncovering the clean crack lines now characterizing these sections. Within two months, 25 routes had been established—many of which, for still unexplained reason, were named for Saturday morning cartoon shows. Walking along the base of Crag Y, the rock changes character several times. The cliff's natural sections are used to help organize the descriptions below. From left to right, the various parts of Crag Y are:

- **The Left Side** Broken by ledges, it also has several clean crack systems and dihedrals on its upper half.
- **The Sunkist Wall** This is the crag's steep, central section, rising above the approach trail. This portion gets its name for the sunny orange slab, seamed by a dozen or so perfect cracks, on which all of the routes finish.
- **The Recess** Right of the Sunkist Wall area, a small talus field descends from a recess, bounded by dihedrals on both its left and right sides.
- **Decepticon Buttress** Forms the right-hand boundary of the Recess. While not really an actual buttress, it looks like one when approached from the left.
- **The Red Walls** This obviously named section of steep, water-stained slabs and ledges is located below and to the right of the Decepticon Buttress.
- **The Far Right** To the right of the Red Walls, the rock goes on and on, although it is nowhere very impressive.

CRAG Y - THE LEFT SIDE 397

Carry some traditional gear including small wired nuts and camming units for all climbs on Crag Y. Most routes were established in 1987, during the transitional period between the traditional ethics of the 1970s and '80s, and the rap-bolting spirit of the '90s. Crag Y routes were established in a variety of styles from pure traditionalism to rappel-cleaning and pre-protection. Climbers who are now confirmed sport addicts had not yet fully embraced the top-down, bolt protection concept in 1987, and the fixed protection they often placed was a piton. Both trad and rad first ascentionists had a good idea of how far they could trust their freshly-hammered pitons. Some of these fixed pins are by now rusting and/or loose. Larry Hamilton proposes, "If experienced future parties agree that fixed protection is still justified where Crag Y first ascentionists left pitons, then they should feel free to remove those pitons and replace them one-for-one with stainless steel bolts. Where the original climbers ran it out, or used natural protection, leave the route as it is." The routes at Crag Y are now described from left to right.

THE LEFT SIDE

TONIGHT I 5.11a

The second pitch, up a deep, smooth-walled V groove, is brief but quite captivating. Begin in the mossy crack just to the left of the initial groove of V.
1. Climb up to the large, sloping Doormat ledge (common to V, THE DOORS, and SPIDERLINE). Follow a short dihedral on the left to a stance, and step left onto another wide sloping ledge at the base of a deep corner. 80', 5.8
2. Start with moves up the corner's right wall and arete, then swing back left into the tight crack at a second fixed piton (5.11a). Exit carefully straight up, past a suspicious-looking jammed block to easier climbing and the top. 40', 5.11a
FA: Larry Hamilton & Scott Hobson   August 7, 1987

V I 5.9

Good rock, but needs more brushing. Begin in a small, but distinctive right-leaning, V groove with a finger crack, at a high point in the base trail. The groove is actually a lower extension of the crack forming SPIDERLINE.
1. Climb the V groove directly. At its top, move right a bit and join the first pitch of THE DOORS, following cracks to the sloping Doormat ledge. 70', 5.9
2. About 15 feet left of the dihedral pitch of THE DOORS is a second smaller corner system. Follow these steep, inside corners straight up, finishing with an overhang at the top. 60', 5.9
HISTORY: George Hurley & Larry Hamilton did the first ascent on June 16, 1987, inadvertently taking advantage of Andy Ward's trundling work on Pitch 2.

THE DOORS I 5.9

The second pitch follows a large, right-leaning corner with a hand crack, conspicuous from the ground. Some of the climbing motions in this corner may feel like opening (or trying NOT to open) doors. Begin in a crack about 20 feet right of V's V groove.

1. Moderate cracks and grooves (5.5) lead up to the large, sloping ledge (the Doormat) at the base of the main corner. 70', 5.5

2. Start up the overhanging left wall, using a flake to reach a horizontal crack. Then move right into the corner (5.9), and climb it to the top. 60', 5.9

FA: Larry Hamilton & Andy Ward May 31, 1987

SPIDERLINE I 5.10a (*)

On the wall just right of THE DOORS' dihedral, a very thin, short vertical crack can be seen. Small nuts provide good protection.

1. Climb the first pitch of either V (5.9) or THE DOORS (5.5) to reach the sloping Doormat belay. 70', 5.9 or 5.5

2. Step right to a fixed piton in a small inside corner. Good holds lead up the corner to a pedestal, where the summit seems inches away. Continue up the final, thin (5.10a) crack. 60', 5.10a

FA: Larry Hamilton & Jim Ewing June 13, 1987

BRUSHMASTER I 5.6

1. Climb Pitch one of THE DOORS to the Doormat ledge. 70', 5.5

2. Step right and climb the right side of a pillar (the left side is SPIDERLINE) to a ledge with a small tree. Finish up an easy arete to the top. 5.6

FA: Andy Ward June, 1987

BIG DOGS DON'T CRY I 5.8

The first route climbed on Crag Y. Begin behind a big birch tree and below a ledge 12 feet up, 20 feet uphill from the base of the main Sunkist Wall.

1. Off the ledge's left end, climb parallel cracks to a corner and the top. 100', 5.8

HISTORY: Paul Boissonneault & Jim Ewing made the first ascent on the day they got lost looking for HYPERSPACE: May 16, 1987.

THE SUNKIST WALL

From OOH MOW MAO to HARMONIC CONVERGENCE, the Sunkist Wall offers an unbroken series of high quality climbs.

OOH MOW MAO I 5.10a (**)

Starting either from the ground or from the same ledge as BIG DOGS DON'T CRY, this route ascends the smoother roofed dihedral to its right.

1. Climb the dihedral until a few feet below the roof, then make a tricky move out right (5.10a), before stepping up into a hand crack that shoots straight to the top. 100', 5.10a

HISTORY: Paul Boissonneault & Alan Cattabriga made the first ascent of this pleasing, eye-catching line on June 7, 1987.

CENTURION I 5.9+ (*)
This climb ascends a prominent V groove that begins halfway up the wall, after stepping into this groove from the left. Start on the same ledge as on BIG DOGS DON'T CRY. Crag Y's second route.

1. Step right around the corner and struggle up into the short, V groove (5.9+). Pull over a small overhang at its top, and follow cracks with good holds to the top of the cliff. 100', 5.9+

FA: Jim Ewing & Paul Boissonneault May 16, 1987

AARP CHALLENGE I 5.9+ R (*)
The crack just right of CENTURION's V groove. Like other full length routes on Sunkist Wall, AARP CHALLENGE has a personality change in midlife.

1. Start atop a small blocky pillar toward the left side of the main Sunkist Wall. A few feet higher, a knifeblade protects awkward moves up left and over a roof (5.9+). The clean face just above the roof is climbed at a very thin, vertical crack that soon fades. At a horizontal crack, move right into a shallow jam crack leading through another roof up to a sloping ledge at the base of the V groove (on CENTURION) halfway up. Now step right, and climb a thin crack just right of the V groove for 20 feet until the two crack systems merge. 120', 5.9+

HISTORY: This pitch was first led by card-carrying senior citizen George Hurley, accompanied by the youthful Larry Hamilton, on June 16, 1987.

AUTOBOT I 5.10a (**)
Just to the right of AARP CHALLENGE is a shallow corner with some loose-looking rock above. After this unpromising start, AUTOBOT races up what might be the nicest finger crack on the crag.

1. Ascend the corner and pass a small overhang to better holds (5.10a). Continue to a hand crack, then follow the obvious, and slightly left-angling finger crack above. The crack thins near the top, but can be climbed to its end without stepping left onto CENTURION. 120', 5.10a

HISTORY: Jim Ewing & Paul Boissonneault couldn't wait to come back the very next day after they'd gotten lost to make the first ascent on May 17, 1987.

WHITE SNAKE I 5.11c R (**)
Protection is adequate, but hard to place on Pitch two.

1. Climb AUTOBOT to a small stance at mid-height. 40', 5.10a

2. Follow thin cracks between the more substantial cracks of AUTOBOT and SHE-RA. After 15 feet in the first crack, make hard face moves (5.11c R) right to a bolt, then head up a second thin crack. 70', 5.11c R

HISTORY: Scott Stevenson & Alan Cattabriga first climbed this route on June 14, 1987, placing the bolt on the lead.

SHE-RA I 5.10d (***)
THE Crag Y classic. A few feet to the right of AUTOBOT is a triple set of corners and overhangs, leading up and right.
1. Climb straight up to the first overhang. Move up right into the next corner, and again into the next. After passing a peg (5.10d), easier climbing leads up to a small stance. Jam the crack on the right until it ends, then step right into another crack which is followed to the top. 120', 5.10d
FA: Jim Ewing & Paul Boissonneault May 30, 1987

LEGIONS OF POWER I 5.11d (**)
This route follows the obvious, overhanging, shallow crack line just above the approach trail, and about 15 feet to the right of SHE-RA.
1. Jam up to a horizontal break. The crack fades, but positive holds can be found. Continue past two pins (5.11d) to easier moves into a V groove, mostly using a crack on the left. When the groove ends, finish up the crack. 120', 5.11d
HISTORY: Jim Ewing led the first ascent on June 18, 1987, belayed by Chris Gill—who chose instead to follow George Hurley on MODERN MATURITY.

MODERN MATURITY I 5.9+ (*)
The route begins to the right of LEGIONS OF POWER. It ascends an inside corner to an overhang, moves left to briefly join the LEGIONS OF POWER crack system, then heads right again above the overhang.
1. Climb to the large ledge 15 feet up, then climb up the crack in the V corner on the right. Angle left under the large roof (bolt), then traverse left to the prominent notch that breaks through the overhang (5.9+). Immediately above the lip, move right and improvise a belay. 60', 5.9+
2. Follow the crack just right of the V groove, which angles slightly right, then left. The crux moves are about 15 feet below the top. 60', 5.8
HISTORY: George Hurley was the route's senior partner, established with Chris Gill on June 18, 1987. The bolt on Pitch one was placed on rappel.

TRAPEZIUS I 5.10d (**)
This climb diverges at MODERN MATURITY's athletic crux.
1. Climb up MODERN MATURITY until below the left side of the biggest overhang. Make trapeze moves out under the roof to the right, then pull over the apex with difficulty (5.10d), heel-hooking and laybacking over the lip, before moving up to the belay. 60', 5.10d
2. Jam up the hand crack (5.7) on the right. 60', 5.7
HISTORY: On the first ascent by Chris Reveley & George Hurley on July 5, 1987, a huge pine next to the cliff made the crux somewhat easier, plus provided an unusual belay stance. The pine was subsequently felled—not by any of the climbers involved—and the route was reascended by Kris Hansen & George Hurley in its present, harder, tree-less state on November 4, 1987.

CRAG Y - THE SUNKIST WALL (SHE-RA & LAST LAUGH)

SWORD OF OMENS I 5.11d (**)
Off to the right of the large, MODERN MATURITY / TRAPEZIUS corner system, a steep arete cuts through the overhangs. Begin in an open corner just below this arete, and right of the MODERN MATURITY start.
1. Climb the open corner to a ledge 15 feet above the ground, then step right into a thin dihedral (pin) at the base of the arete. Tricky climbing leads up this corner to a good stance. Just above is a second stance at a notch in the blade-sharp arete. A difficult sequence continues up the overhanging arete (5.11d) past two more pitons. There is a thin hold on the left that requires gentle treatment, and solid hand jams at the very top. Belay at a wobbly pine. 60', 5.11d
2. Grunge climbing (5.6) leads to the top. 60', 5.6
FA: Jim Ewing & Larry Hamilton July 26, 1987

LAST LAUGH II 5.12c (***)
This climb has great variety and perfect rock. Begin below a large, roofed dihedral near the right-hand side of the lower Sunkist Wall.
1. Traverse 10 feet right under a huge flake, then handtraverse back left again on top of the flake to gain entrance to the dihedral. A bolt protects stemming up to the main roof, then traverse right to a ledge with pitons. 60', 5.10d
2. Step left off the belay onto an exposed, bulging wall. Wicked moves lead up past two bolts (5.12c) to a rest at a horizontal crack. Easier thin cracks (5.9) continue straight to the top. 60', 5.12c
HISTORY: After Jim Ewing & George Hurley did Pitch one in June, 1987, Jim Ewing & Larry Hamilton made the first complete ascent on July 30, 1988.

HARMONIC CONVERGENCE II 5.8, A1 (3 Points of Aid) or 5.11b, A0 (*)
An obvious and attractive line—and if done with three aid points, the Sunkist Wall's easiest route. Begin below the large, broken corner of HONEMASTER.
1. A few moves up the HONEMASTER corner, handtraverse left, then face climb up & left across a steep wall (bolt & peg) to a belay at a tiny birch. 50', 5.8
2. Climb an overhanging crack above the belay. After 15 feet the angle relents, and the crack continues merrily to the top. This pitch has a variable rating: 5.8, A1 (with three points of aid), or 5.11b, A0 with one point of aid—and 5.??? for someone with strong enough fingers. 60'
HISTORY: This route has the longest history of any climb at Crag Y. Chris Reveley & George Hurley made the first ascent of the second pitch on July 5, 1987, after approaching via the first pitch of LAST LAUGH (which had been led earlier by Jim Ewing). On June 25, 1988, Hurley & Mike Daly found an easier approach, traversing to the belay ledge from the large, HONEMASTER dihedral on the right. Finally, on May 17, 1989, George Hurley, Larry Hamilton, & Alex Alvarez established a direct start to make HARMONIC CONVERGENCE independent of its neighbors.

THE RECESS

HONEMASTER I 5.7
Around a corner, right of the start of HARMONIC CONVERGENCE, is a prominent, inside corner/crack system with a large roof at its top.
1. Follow the obvious line until about 20 feet below the big roof, and step right into another major crack. Follow this second crack to the right edge of the roof and a comfortable belay ledge. 80', 5.7
2. From the belay, which is to the left of the California block (see below), follow the crack and ledges up and left to a large pine tree growing at the top of the cliff. 35', 5.7 (Same as Pitch two of CALIFORNIA DETOUR.)
HISTORY: George Hurley & Jon Norling made the first ascent of this quite facetiously-named route on August 15, 1987.

HONEMASTER DIRECT I 5.9+
The route climbs a detached pillar to the right of the big HONEMASTER corner, then follows a prominent arete.
1. Climb to the top of the pillar by any of several routes, then follow cracks up the steep arete (5.9+) to its top. 80', 5.9+
2. Finish on HONEMASTER, up cracks and ledges up and left. 35', 5.7
FA: George Hurley, Alex Alvarez, & Larry Hamilton May 17, 1989

HOTEL CALIFORNIA II 5.11a (*)
Takes a direct line up the water-stained dihedral forming the left boundary of the main Recess. It is named for the huge, California-shaped block partway up.
1. Climb the initial corner directly, with one awkward move (5.11a; fixed pins). Above, thin cracks on the right wall assist progress up the corner. Climb the wide crack on the right side of the California block, and belay on an airy ledge at its top. 80', 5.11a
2. Check out of the hotel with difficulty, cruising straight up. A bolt and two pins protect a steep, open groove. Step left to avoid dirty rock at the top. 60', 5.10c
FA: Jim Ewing & Larry Hamilton July 18, 1987

CALIFORNIA DETOUR I 5.9
Begin 10 feet right of the HOTEL CALIFORNIA corner.
1. A moderate layback leads up to a stance. Now move left onto a slab, and jam up wide hand cracks to a fixed piton. From the peg, move left and up the left side of the main HOTEL CALIFORNIA corner. Climb the left side of the California block to a belay stance situated below and left of its top. 60', 5.9
2. Angle left, heading to the top of the cliff and a large pine tree. 35', 5.7
HISTORY: This route began as an attempt on the obvious line of HOTEL CALIFORNIA. When their original goal seemed impractical, Jim Ongena & George Hurley climbed this line of least resistance on June 17, 1987.

RIGHTEOUS SLAB I 5.9 (*)
To the right of the California block is an attractive slab.
1. Start as for CALIFORNIA DETOUR, but stay on the slab as it curves right. At its top is a comfortable belay ledge. 80', 5.9
2. Traverse horizontally to the next major corner left of the belay, & follow it to the top. This dihedral is the next corner right of the HOTEL CALIFORNIA finish, and is directly above the start of CALIFORNIA DETOUR. 40', 5.7+
FA: George Hurley & Joe Hayes July 23, 1987

RISKY BUSINESS I 5.9
Locate the deepest V dihedral in the Recess.
1. Stem and jam up the dihedral (5.6) to a sizeable belay ledge (an area of large blocks) at its top. 40', 5.6
2. Climb the overhanging left wall above the large blocks, aiming for a nice-looking, short dihedral at the top of the cliff. This final corner is the first one to the right of the finish of RIGHTEOUS SLAB. 70', 5.9
FA: George Hurley & Randy Gagne July 25, 1987

SAINT GEORGE I 5.9 R (*)
The route ascends the arete immediately to the left of DRAGON CURVE, then continues in the same line up the final dihedral.
1. Climb the arete on its right side for several feet, then move a few inches left to a crack system which soon returns to the right. Gain a small triangular niche, level with and about eight feet left of the third piton on DRAGON CURVE. Continue straight above the triangular niche to a good ledge. 50', 5.9
2. The major dihedral of the Recess is above the belay stance. At first, it begins as three closely-spaced dihedrals. Climb the right-hand corner to its top where the three dihedrals become one, and follow it to the top. Protection is mostly with hard-to-place small wired nuts. 60', 5.9
FA: George Hurley & Joe Hayes July 23 1987

DRAGON CURVE I 5.9+ (*)
Ascends the clean, left-facing dihedral on the right side of the Recess. Above an obvious layback, DRAGON CURVE strikes out right onto the face of the DECEPTICON Buttress.
1. A few feet of poor rock leads into the dihedral. Continue up this corner past two pitons to a stance (third pin) above the leaning, layback section. Make a wild step up and right (5.9+) onto a narrow, sloping ledge, then move further up right, around a corner and onto the DECEPTICON Buttress. Climb up into some parallel finger cracks, above the regular finish of DECEPTICON, and follow these finger cracks to the top. 120', 5.9
FA: Larry Hamilton & Scott Hobson July 2, 1987

DECEPTICON BUTTRESS

To the right of the cliff's main section, and right of HONEMASTER, is a smaller wall with a big oak growing tight up against the rock. PUFF, RASTER SCAN, DECEPTICON, and THE TAO OF POOH are all located here.

PUFF I 5.9 (*)

This route climbs the thin crack system parallel to and just right of the arete which marks the left edge of the DECEPTICON Buttress.

1. Climb up the white birch at the lower left edge of the Buttress. Ten feet up in the tree, place protection in a good crack, then step onto the rock. Follow thin finger cracks (5.9) which are a couple of feet right of the arete. At one point DRAGON CURVE comes in from the left and crosses this line. Belay on the low-angled area above the left side of the Buttress. 50', 5.9

2. An easy, indistinct groove heads past a small pine to the top. 50', 5.4

HISTORY: This route was first climbed with the birch tree start by George Hurley & Randy Gagne on July 25, 1987.

VARIATION START: **HUFF** I 5.10d

You may very well have to HUFF & PUFF on this one!

1a. To free the route's start (5.10d), awkwardly avoid using the tree. 15', 5.10d

FA: Jim Ewing, Larry Hamilton, & Rich Baker July 3, 1988.

RASTER SCAN I 5.11c

If you know computers, you'll know why the climb got its name. An easy route with a hard start, RASTER SCAN requires rapid sideways movement. Start at a break below a short overhanging corner 20 feet right of the buttress's left edge.

1. Use buckets to leave the ground, then immediately move left along a thin traverse crack (5.11c; piton), then climb up 10 feet to a stance at the base of a peapod groove (pin). Easier climbing surmounts the groove and follows cracks to the top, merging with the finish of DECEPTICON. 110', 5.11c

HISTORY: On June 19, 1987, Larry Hamilton and Scott Hobson did the climb with one aid move. On June 25, 1987, Larry Hamilton & George Hurley returned to make the first free ascent.

DECEPTICON I 5.10c (*)

You too may be transformed! Locate a clean thin crack up an 80 degree face, just to the right of RASTER SCAN's peapod groove. Begin a few feet right of RASTER SCAN, on a more gently overhanging short wall.

1. Climb buckets up the short overhanging face. Step up left to footholds at the base of a thin crack, and puzzle out its initial moves (5.10c). After 15 feet, the crack widens slightly, and easier climbing leads to the top. 100', 5.10c

HISTORY: On the first ascent, climbed on May 31, 1987, Jim Ewing & Larry Hamilton thought the route would be easy, hence the name.

SLIMOR I 5.6
When every route on the crag is soaking wet, you might as well climb SLIMOR. Begin in the crack system seven feet left of the large oak tree.
1. Climb the mossy corner and crack to the top. 50', 5.6
HISTORY: George Hurley first led this natural drainage on June 24, 1987, but his partners wisely refused to follow. Subsequent cleaning of the route may have reduced its uniquely soggy character.

THE EFFECTS OF WOODEN TOYS ON LATER LIFE BEHAVIOR I 5.6
Ascends the crack directly behind the big oak tree mentioned above. The route name deserves a star, but not the route!
1. Tie off the oak for protection, then climb the crack until you can join SLIMOR atop its final pedestal, and scramble off right. 50', 5.6
FA: Kurt Winkler & Kevin Hall August 24, 1987

MIGHTY TONKA I 5.5
This route is much cleaner than its neighbors.
1. Ten feet right of the big oak, follow one crack to the top. 50', 5.5
FA: George Hurley & Jean Kosits July 1, 1987

THE TAO OF POOH I 5.6 (*)
This route follows the right-hand arete of the DECEPTICON Buttress. Start down at the level of the bottom of the Red Slabs.
1. Climb the left-most small dihedral, which is directly below the arete that forms the right edge of the DECEPTICON Buttress. (You can also avoid this bottom section, and start 20 feet higher on the same ledge as the other DECEPTICON Buttress routes.) Stay on the arete, with some excellent climbing on good holds. When the arete finally meets the crack to its left, follow that crack to the top. 100', 5.6
FA: George Hurley & Jon Norling August 15, 1987

RED BETWEEN THE LINES I 5.8
This route ascends the middle of the small buttress which is directly below the DECEPTICON Buttress. The difficulties are sustained.
1. Traverse onto the buttress from the left using a foot ledge. Make interesting moves to connect the horizontal cracks (5.8), the climb's major feature. 45', 5.8
FA: Kurt Winkler & George Hurley August 24, 1987

THE RED WALLS

WET DIHEDRAL I 5.7
Red Wall routes begin below and right of the DECEPTICON Buttress. About 25 feet right of the oak mentioned above is an obvious dihedral with cracks that curve up and right. Start from the cliff's lowest part, directly below the corner.

1. Climb a line of weakness below the dihedral, then the corner. 110', 5.7
HISTORY: George Hurley & Jean Kosits first climbed this route, running with water, on July 1, 1987—but later parties found that attraction missing.

SUPERFRIENDS I 5.10a R
Just right of WET DIHEDRAL's broken start are some steep, red-stained slabs. Near the center of the leftmost red slab is an obvious, straight-in crack that fades out just before it reaches a ledge 40 feet up. There are several short cruxes.
1. Start just right of the straight-in crack, and climb up using the face and crack to the first obvious ledge. Go a few moves up a dihedral on the right side of this ledge, then step right around a blind corner onto another steep face. Thin parallel cracks lead up this face to a second ledge. Climb a short broken headwall, just left of some white streaks, and continue to the trees. 110', 5.10a
FA: Jim Ewing, Peter Yost, & Larry Hamilton   July 13, 1987

RED FLASH I 5.7
Follows the main line of weakness which runs up the entire Red Walls face. Start about 15 feet to the right of SUPERFRIENDS.
1. Climb a wide, easy crack, following it slightly right, then climb straight up through a small overhang. Above the overhang, the route is a few feet right of the thin parallel cracks on the second face of SUPERFRIENDS. The routes join at a belay ledge above this face. Rappel off of a tree on top. 110', 5.7
FA: George Hurley & David Hall   August 24, 1987

THE FAR RIGHT

THE MANTLE BLOCK I 5.5 R
Walk past RED FLASH for a ways until it is easy to hike uphill to the cliff. Find a large rectangular block lying squarely beside the main wall of the cliff. Start by climbing the fist crack on the block's right-hand side.
1. Jam up the block, mantleshelf a few feet higher, then traverse left (short runout; nasty fall possible) before heading to the top. 50', 5.5 R
FA: Kurt Winkler & Kevin Hall   August 24, 1987

SINISTER GROOVE I 5.5
Walk past the Red Walls, then straight uphill to the cliff at a point midway between a large rectangular block (THE MANTLE BLOCK) and the hand crack of PORTUGUESE APPLE. Look for a shallow, square groove 15 feet up.
1. Climb easily up into the shallow, square groove, and chimney up it to a ledge. Continue straight up the final dihedral to the top. 50', 5.5
FA: George Hurley & David Hall   August 24, 1987

KENNEBUNK BOGGLE I 5.8
Ascends the slightly overhanging crack midway between SINISTER GROOVE and the more distinct hand crack of PORTUGUESE APPLE.

1. Above the crack's steepest part, head directly to the top. 60', 5.8
FA: George Hurley & Jon Eagleson   September 27, 1987

PORTUGUESE APPLE I 5.6 (*)
To find this route, walk along the climbers' trail under the Red Walls, past SUPERFRIENDS, until it is easy to hike straight uphill to the cliff. Look for an attractive hand crack which angles slightly to the right.
1. Climb the hand crack to its top, and finish up the final dihedral. 60', 5.6
FA: George Hurley, Mike Arsenault, & Bill Appleton   August 13, 1987

EAGLES' DARE I 5.10d (Top-rope)
The next crack right of PORTUGUESE APPLE heads right behind two trees.
1. Follow right-slanting crack to a steep, left-angling dihedral. 70', 5.10d
FA: Jon Eagleson, top-rope   September 27, 1987

FOREST OF DOOM I 5.7
About 20 feet left of TAKE MY TUNA's small inside corner is a blocky arete.
1. Start up the ragged, outside corner. After about 15 feet, move left to a large ledge with trees. Climb the crack which is a few feet right of the major inside corner that rises from the right end of the tree ledge. 90', 5.7
FA: George Hurley & John Cederholm   October 31, 1987

PETUNIA I 5.7
Start as for FORESTS OF DOOM, 20 feet to the left of TAKE MY TUNA.
1. Climb the ragged arete to a lower angled face. The arete becomes the left edge of the face also climbed by TAKE MY TUNA. Stay on the left edge until a finger crack angles up and right across the face to end near the top of the dihedral marking the face's right boundary. Small pine anchor. 90', 5.7
FA: George Hurley, Mike Arsenault, & Bill Appleton   August 13, 1987

TAKE MY TUNA I 5.8
Walking along the base of the broken rock to the right of the Red Walls, you'll reach a nice-looking little dihedral, facing left, with a finger crack in it.
1. Layback up the short corner (5.8), then climb easier rock til you can venture out left onto a steep face with cracks. Above, follow your best judgement to the top. 90', 5.8   The crack would be a classic if only it were longer.
HISTORY: Hobson has a long story about a poker game that inspired the name. Scott Hobson & Larry Hamilton did the first ascent on July 7, 1987.

ANTE I 5.10b
1. Climb the small arete just right of TAKE MY TUNA. Near the top of the arete, reach left, making two layback moves in the TAKE MY TUNA crack. Then move right, jamming up an obvious, overhanging finger crack (5.10b) past a small overhang to a belay at the small pine on PETUNIA. 90', 5.10b
FA: George Hurley & Jon Norling   August 15, 1987

408 THE KANCAMAGUS HIGHWAY AREA

Andy Ross on Lumberjack Crack (5.11c) in 1987, on the popular Lumberjack Wall at Found Ledge. Photograph by Rich Baker.

FOUND LEDGE

A hard-to-find cliff recently revitalized by several recommended sport climbs on the Lumberjack Wall. To reach the crag from Conway, drive 4.9 miles west along Route 112, the Kancamagus Highway, and park on the south side of the highway on the sandy shoulder. A large, blown-down tree marks the correct start. Driving east from the Albany Covered Bridge, the parking spot is 1.2 miles east of the bridge. From the fallen tree, hike diagonally left into the woods along a level path for several minutes before turning right, heading uphill, following the right bank (west side) of a small streambed. When the stream forks, bear slightly right, following the stream which gradually deepens into a cleft. Fifteen minutes more and you should see the cliff and several huge boulders on the right. If you don't get lost (but you probably will), the approach takes 30 to 40 minutes. Found Ledge has three separate sections: the Main Cliff (about 600 feet wide and split by half a dozen vertical cracks), the Little Slab, and the Lumberjack Wall, home to some excellent sport climbs. The routes are now described from right to left.

THE MAIN CLIFF

COTE'S CHIMNEY I 5.8
The chimney at the crag's right end, 75 feet right of SHORT BUT SWEET.
1. Climb up an obvious, tight chimney with a hand crack in the back. 60', 5.8
FA: Kit Dover & Joe Cote August 11, 1975

PRIME MERIDIAN II 5.8, A2
The set of mossy, vertical cracks 30 feet to the left of COTE'S CHIMNEY.
1. Climb the first crack up the face. When it ends, connect (A2) with the upper crack. The only aid moves are in the middle. 60' 5.8, A2
FA: Joe Cote & Kit Dover May 4, 1975

RICE CRISPIES I 5.8
Twenty feet right of SHORT BUT SWEET is another vertical chimney.
1. Climb up a chimney with flakes inside it. Although rotten looking, it's actually a fairly nice climb. 60', 5.8
FA: Joe Cote & Kit Dover May 3, 1975

SHORT BUT SWEET I 5.10d (*)
A famous, extremely difficult, and seldom-if-ever repeated roof problem. The obvious corner/roof crack at the Main Cliff's left end.
1. Climb up a slab, then undercling and jam up a left-facing corner to a painfully obvious and strenuous roof/fist crack at the lip. 60', 5.10d
HISTORY: Jim Dunn, with Rick Wilcox & Joe Cote, made the first ascent of this uniquely difficult crack climb in 1975. Don't forget: protection back then was just with Hexentrics and Tube Chocks!

Jim Dunn on the first ascent of Short But Sweet (5.10d) in 1975.
Photograph by Rick Wilcox.

LOOKING FOR GOLDILOCKS I 5.11b (**)
The left-facing, story book corner 30 feet to the left of SHORT BUT SWEET. Excellent overhanging rock, with golden locks. Bring a normal rack up to a 3.5 Friend.

1. Tip toe up a slab, pull over a roof (piton; 5.11b), then stem and layback up the corner and past a bulge into a hand crack. 75', 5.11b

HISTORY: After cleaning the climb on rappel, and pre-placing the piton, Rich Baker, Mark Wilson, & Andy Ross made the first ascent of this fine route on June 7, 1987.

GRANITE STATE I 5.9 (*)
On the left side of the cliff, 30 feet to the left of LOOKING FOR GOLDILOCKS, locate a narrow, right-facing dihedral. One wall of the inside corner resembles in shape the outline of the state of New Hampshire.

1. Climb up the corner/fist crack into a nice hand crack. 50', 5.9

FA: Kit Dover & Joe Cote May 3, 1975

NO GRIPPAGE I 5.0
Begin on the cliff's far, left side, 20 feet to the left of GRANITE STATE.
1. Climb a perfectly parallel-sided chimney crack. 45', 5.0
FA: Joe Cote, Kit Dover, Joe Steele, & Bill Steele May 3, 1975

THE DUNN BOULDER
At the left end of Found Ledge is a house-sized, granite block, the Dunn Boulder, which has a couple of tough routes up it. If you're facing the low-angled side of the boulder, off on your right is the overhanging, north face.

DUNN'S DECEPTION I 5.10d (Top-rope)
1. Face climb up the right side of the north face. 30', 5.10d
FA: Jim Dunn, top-rope 1975

LITTLE RAGE I 5.12a (Top-rope)
1. Climb the arete (5.12a) to the right of DUNN'S DECEPTION.
FA: Steve Damboise, top-rope Autumn, 1987

THE LITTLE SLAB
This is the short, yet appealing friction slab to the left of the Main Cliff and the Dunn Boulder, and just downhill and right of the Lumberjack Wall.

A LITTLE SLABBA DO YA I 5.8+ (*)
A fun, well protected friction climb up a clean slab. Could be this is just what the doctor ordered! Seven bolts lead to the tree anchor.
1. After making the hardest moves at the start (5.8+), face climb straight up the middle of the slab past seven bolts to a tree anchor at the top. 125', 5.8+
HISTORY: Dick Traverse & Karen Traverse made the first ascent of this enjoyable route on July 2, 1994, hand-drilling the bolts on rappel.

THE LUMBERJACK WALL
Hike uphill and left of the Little Slab and the Main Cliff to this popular 60 foot sport crag offering several desperately thin face routes, plus a couple of strenuous cracks thrown in for good measure. The trail to the top circles around the cliff's left end. Routes are described from right to left.

STARVING FOR STARS I 5.10d
This climb will probably keep on starving. The farthest right-hand route on the crag. Start 15 feet to the right of POKEMAN CRACK.
1. Jam up the wide, crumbly fist crack to a white birch tree. 45', 5.10d
FA: Ward Smith & Chris Smith October, 1988

POKEMAN CRACK I 5.11a
Begin 10 feet to the left of STARVING FOR STARS.
1. Climb up a dirty face with a short finger crack to a tree at the base of a wider crack (large Friends needed). 50', 5.11a
FA: Andy Holmes & Sam Morganti September 18, 1987

> Thursday afternoon Fossil Club meeting at the Lumberjack Wall in 1995. Charter members Nick Yardley (leading) & Rob Adair are on Hangerlane (5.12b). Rick Wilcox, standing below on the right, gets ready to hand out the post-climb refreshments. Photograph by Ed Webster.
>
> Membership requirements for the Fossil Club:
> 1. Age 39 (or older).
> 2. Married (or divorced).
> 3. A mortgage.
> 4. Children.
> 5. All of the above.

WALKABOUT I 5.12b (**)
Start 15 feet right of LUMBERJACK CRACK. A popular route—unless you spend hours wandering around lost in the woods trying to find the cliff!
1. Zig zag up the steep face (5.12b) past six bolts. 60', 5.12b
HISTORY: Andy Ross, Jim Ewing, & Mark Pelletier made the first ascent of this classic line in July, 1988.

FOUND LEDGE - THE LUMBERJACK WALL

LUMBERJACK CRACK I 5.11c (*)
The sustained, left-slanting finger/hand crack just to the right of the center of the Lumberjack Wall, or 20 feet to the left of WALKABOUT. Carry a normal rack with cams up to a #4 Friend.
1. Jam up the strenuous (5.11c) finger/hand crack. 60', 5.11c
HISTORY: Probably the most obvious route on the wall, Chris Gill climbed the first ascent on May 18, 1987.

THE BIG WHOOP I 5.12b (*)
The steep face eight feet to the left of LUMBERJACK CRACK.
1. Face climb up and right to reach the first bolt, then move up (5.11) and trend slightly left past five more bolts on enjoyable but sustained ground. The last 20 feet is the 5.12b crux, "involving side pulls, layaways, and high steps to a slap over a bum-smooth top." 60', 5.12b
HISTORY: Barry Rugo, Harry Brielmann, & Greg Child made the first ascent of the route in October, 1993.

JAZZ SLIPPERS I 5.12b
Start this graceful dance 20 feet to the left of LUMBERJACK CRACK.
1. Start up the HIP-HOP crack system, then face climb straight up (5.12b) with difficulty past three bolts. 60', 5.12b
FA: Jerry Handren Summer, 1989

HIP-HOP-BE-BOP, DON'T STOP I 5.12a (**)
Start the same as JAZZ SLIPPERS, 15 feet right of HANGERLANE.
1. Climb up the crack. When it ends, step left to a thin finger crack, which angles up and right at the top. 60', 5.12a Carry a modern rack.
FA: Jerry Handren May 18, 1987

HANGERLANE I 5.12b (**)
Just try to hang on! Classic thin face moves. Commence 15 feet to the left of JAZZ SLIPPERS. Bring a #.5 Flex Friend, plus five quick draws.
1. Ten feet to the right of the flaring groove of THE INQUISITION, face climb up an unrelentingly steep, smooth wall past five bolts. 60', 5.12b
FA: Duncan McCallum (Scotland) April 27, 1988

THE INQUISITION I 5.11d (*)
Start five feet to the left of HANGERLANE. To lead this super pumpy inquiry, bring a variety of Friends for your defense, including two #4 Friends, plus a #5 Camalot for the crack's top wide section.
1. Face climb up an incipient, vertical crack to the only bolt on the route, then step left to gain the base of a flaring water groove at the cliff's left-hand end. Continue with grave difficulty to the top. 60', 5.11d
FA: Chris Gill & Andy Ross July, 1987

LOST LEDGE

The cliff's sunny atmosphere, friendly slab climbing, unusual potholes, and moderate, bolted routes make this an ideal area for new leaders to gain experience and confidence. Located just to the west of Found Ledge, this outcrop is the second cliff on the left or southern side of the Kancamagus Highway when driving west from Conway. Approach by parking half a mile east of the Albany Covered Bridge at a large pullout by a stream at a sign for Ham Brook. Hike upstream (south) until you reach an old fishing camp with a fire ring on the brook's east side. Cross the stream here, and follow the high ground to the right of a gully up to the cliff, which takes roughly another 20 minutes from the fishing camp. A tree-lined gully splits the cliff into two halves. The right half, the Carpet Slab, is a low-angled novice area. The clean granite of the Main Slab is noted for high-angled friction climbs similar to those on Whitehorse. The broad range of climbs here means there is something for everyone. Carry an extra rope to rappel off with. Most of the routes are protected by bolts, all of which were placed on the lead. The climbs are now described from right to left.

THE CARPET SLAB

CARPET SLABBER I 5.3
A moderate and recommended climb for your first lead on friction.
1. Friction up the right side of the Carpet Slab past several bolts. 5.3
FA: Joe Cote, Bob Fraser, Jeff Fraser, & Al Lapradde December, 1973

THE HOLE TRAVERSE I 5.5
Start 25 feet to the left of CARPET SLABBER below some broken rock.
1. Head straight up on easy friction past two bolts to a large flake with a bush growing out of its right side. Belay from Friends and one bolt. 90', 5.4
2. Step right to a left-diagonalling dike full of holes. Climb the dike for a short distance beneath a white streak going through the headwall above, then friction straight up the wall (bolt), joining FOUR HOLES (bolt) to the top. 70', 5.5
HISTORY: Dick Traverse & Karen Traverse made the first ascent, hand-drilling the protection bolts on the lead on July 18, 1993.

FOUR HOLES I 5.5
Start in the middle of the Carpet Slab below a vertical row of four potholes, each about three inches in diameter.
1. Climb past the four solution pockets to clip a bolt 30 feet up, then friction diagonally up and right to reach a good belay ledge. 5.5
2. Follow a ridge up right, finishing straight up a clean white streak.
HISTORY: Bob Fraser, Jeff Fraser, Mark Baglini, Joe Cote, Dick Arey, & Chuck Zaikowski made the first ascent on December 2, 1973.

COVER GIRL I 5.5 (*)
Begin 10 feet to the left of FOUR HOLES. There is a "champagne bucket" sized pothole on this route, plus fun slab moves.
1. Climb up a vertical, incipient corner to a left-facing corner, and protect. Continue up, trending left to a large pothole several feet deep (bolt). Angle farther left, then slab climb up beautifully sculpted rock past three more bolts to a double bolt anchor on a half moon ledge. 125', 5.5
2. Rappel off from here, or continue without protection to the top.
HISTORY: Cathy Connell & Sue Deming made the first ascent on May 12, 1990, without placing any bolts. This is the only route in the White Mountains whose first ascent party was all-women! (This was their route name, too.) The bolts were added by another team, who were unaware of the previous ascent.

THE MAIN SLAB
The next climbs ascend the left-hand or Main Slab of Lost Ledge to the left of the central descent gully. The routes are described from right to left.

WEAK NUTS I 5.6
The left-slanting crack up the slab to the left of the descent gully.
1. Face climb past two bolts (5.6) into the crack system. 5.6
FA: Milt Camille & Joe Cote November 24, 1973

RHUMB LINE I 5.8
Start about 30 feet to the left of WEAK NUTS below a bolt.
1. Head up 20 feet to the bolt, then continuously delicate footwork leads straight up (5.8) until both the angle and difficulty eases. 5.8
FA: Bruce Kumph & Joe Cote September 1, 1975

VECTOR I 5.8
The sister slab climb to RHUMB LINE ascends the central blank wall. Begin below another bolt 30 feet farther to the left.
1. Face climb up the line of least resistance (bolt; 5.8), heading straight up. 5.8
FA: Joe Cote & Bruce Kumph September 1, 1975

LOST ARCH I 5.8 (*)
Start halfway between VECTOR and GROOV'IN. The upper belay bolts are situated next to an unusual, exfoliating flake or arch.
1. Pick a line straight up past two bolts (5.8) to a pocket with a small maple tree growing in it (bolt). Continue up a clean streak past another bolt to a double bolt anchor beside the arch. 100', 5.8
2. Rappel off from here, or continue easily to the trees. 150', 5.0
HISTORY: George Hurley, Bill Appleton, & Mike Arsenault made the first ascent on August 11, 1987, without placing any fixed protection. The bolts were added by a subsequent ascent.

GROOV'IN I 5.4
Look for an obvious, left-leaning crack to the left of LOST ARCH.
1. Climb the crack past four bolts. Belay on the fifth bolt. 5.4
FA: Joe Cote & friend June 8, 1974

EROSION GROOVE I 5.6
Begin at the cliff's left end at the base of an obvious apron.
1. Climb up the apron and a flake to the base of an obvious, eroded groove. Follow the groove straight to the top. 5.6
FA: Joe Cote & Roger Martin November 11, 1973

OLD NASHUA ROAD I 5.5
Twenty feet farther left of EROSION GROOVE is a crack which begins at the lowest point of the face. The route climbs this crack to the top in two leads, but you must simul-climb on the first pitch so that the leader can reach the next belay anchor! The crack blanks out 150 feet up at a steeper section, which is the 5.5 crux, then starts again higher.
1. Follow the crack to its end at 150 feet. The only anchor here is a Tri-cam in a small pocket, so have the belayer move up until the leader can reach a clump of birches growing in a large solution pocket. 190', 5.5
2. Easy climbing up the top crack gains the woods. 150', 4th class.
FA: George Hurley, Bill Appleton, & Mike Arsenault August 11, 1987

SUNDOWN LEDGES

This long, increasingly complex escarpment of cliffs grows in number with every new guidebook. The Sundown Ledges are located just behind the Albany Covered Bridge and the Covered Bridge Campground, six miles to the west of Conway and just off the Kancamagus Highway on the Dugway Road. Newly developed crags described in this 1996 edition include Lost Horizon, a small cliff band up and left of Sundown's Main Cliff, plus the Alcohol Wall, a popular sport climbing area located at the far, right-hand end of the Main Cliff. From left to right, the various cliffs and ledges at Sundown are: the Outback Cliff, Lost Horizon, the Main Cliff, the Alcohol Wall, Call Of The Wild Cliff, Gill's Groove Crag, and the Far Cliff. The three principal ledges are the Main Cliff behind the Covered Bridge Campground, the Far Cliff on the right (or east), and the Outback Cliff behind and to the left (or west) of the Main Cliff.

The variety and texture of the rock climbing on these ledges is remarkably different from the granite climbing on Cathedral and Whitehorse Ledges. The reason is the rock: porphyritic quartz syenite, a fine-grained volcanic rock emplaced just beneath the earth's surface at the time of deposition. Due to its very fine grain, the rock's surface at Sundown is smooth, yet fractures and handholds are sharp and angular, and the rock surface is split in many places by excellent, parallel-sided cracks. There are also many large roofs. Add these qualities up, and you can easily see why Sundown's Main Cliff has become a world-class sport climbing area.

To reach any of the above mentioned cliffs, from Conway, drive west along the Kancamagus Highway for 6.1 miles, and turn right at the Albany Covered Bridge onto the Dugway Road. Drive through the old wooden bridge, and park in the Boulder Loop Trailhead parking lot on the right. You may also drive here from North Conway, or by the back roads from Conway: from the West Side Road, turn west onto either Allens Siding or the Passaconaway Road which both merge with the Dugway Road. The Boulder Loop Trail, a popular, scenic hike, makes a 2.9 mile circuit around Sundown's Main and Far Cliffs, and is the approach trail to the Main and Far Cliffs—but not to the Outback Cliff, which has a different approach. To reach Sundown's Main Cliff, cross the Dugway Road, and hike (signpost) along the Boulder Loop Trail heading straight through a second signposted junction (DO NOT go left here, as this trail leads to the top of Sundown's Main Cliff), but continue straight ahead, finally crossing over a dry streambed. When you see a talus slope on the left through the trees, turn left on a climber's path marked by a cairn, and follow the trail up through the short talus slope to the cliff base. The approach takes about 15 to 20 minutes.

418 THE KANCAMAGUS HIGHWAY AREA

Steve Larson on Romper Room (5.12a) in 1995, one of the most popular sport routes on the Main Cliff at Sundown Ledge. Photograph by Joe Lentini.

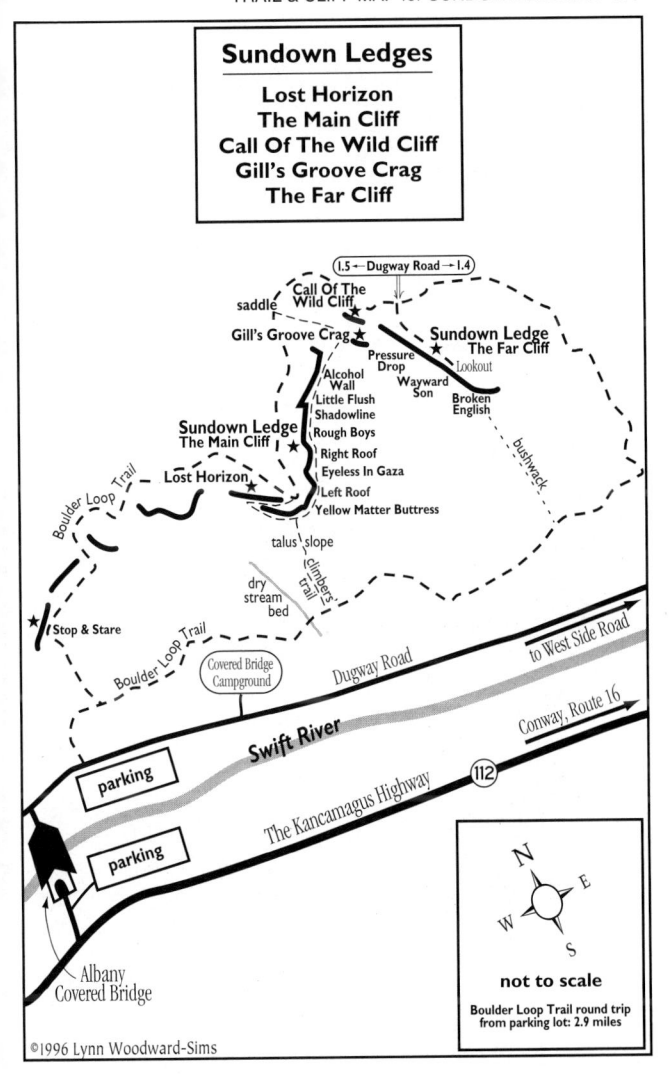

TRAIL & CLIFF MAP for SUNDOWN LEDGES 419

Sundown Ledges

Lost Horizon
The Main Cliff
Call Of The Wild Cliff
Gill's Groove Crag
The Far Cliff

1.5 ← Dugway Road → 1.4

Call Of The Wild Cliff
saddle
Gill's Groove Crag
Sundown Ledge
The Far Cliff
Pressure Drop
Lookout
Wayward Son
Broken English
Alcohol Wall
Little Flush
Shadowline
Rough Boys
Sundown Ledge
The Main Cliff
Right Roof
Eyeless In Gaza
Lost Horizon
Left Roof
Yellow Matter Buttress
Boulder Loop Trail
talus slope
climbers' trail
bushwack
dry stream bed
Stop & Stare
Boulder Loop Trail
Covered Bridge Campground
Dugway Road
to West Side Road
Swift River
parking
Conway, Route 16
The Kancamagus Highway
112
parking
Albany Covered Bridge

not to scale

Boulder Loop Trail round trip
from parking lot: 2.9 miles

©1996 Lynn Woodward-Sims

420 THE KANCAMAGUS HIGHWAY AREA

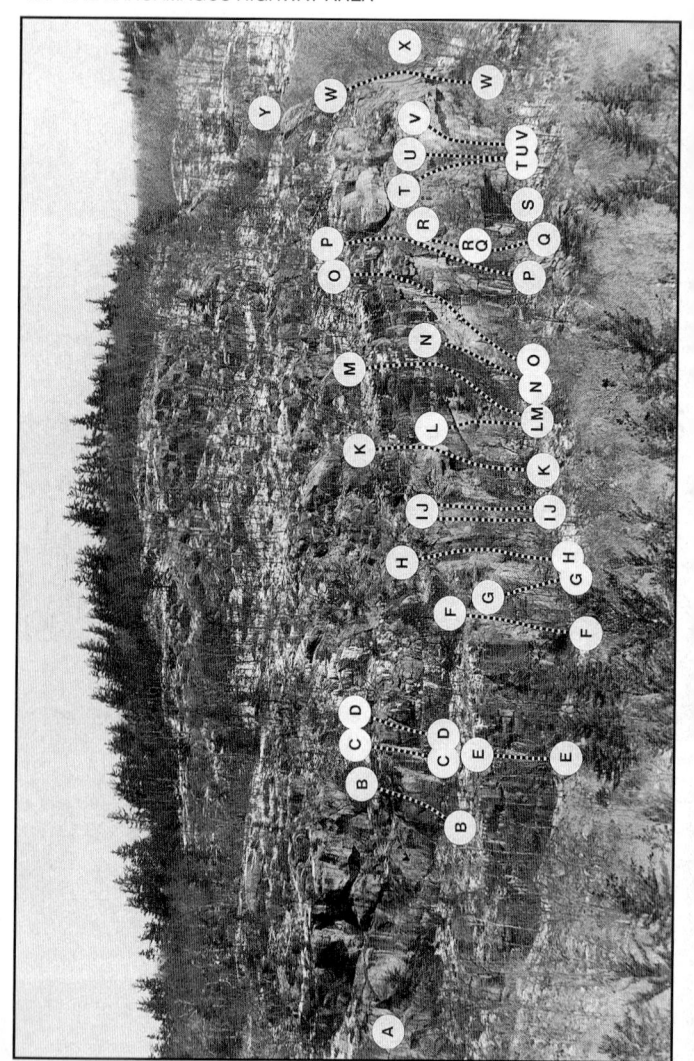

SUNDOWN LEDGE - LOST HORIZON & THE MAIN CLIFF

A.		LOST HORIZON	Page 422	N.	*	BIG BANANA I 5.13c	Page 432
B.	*	FINGER FOOD FROM THE FUTURE I 5.9+	Page 423	O.		BLACK SUNDAY I 5.7 R	Page 432
C.		BIGGER THAN A BREAD BOX I 5.11c	Page 423	P.		MIDNIGHT GROOVE I 5.8	Page 436
D.	*	STRAY CATS I 5.11b	Page 423	Q.	***	VULTURES I 5.10d	Page 436
E.		RUNNING HANDS I 5.9+	Page 425	R.	**	CARRION I 5.11d	Page 436
F.		THE TOMB I 5.9	Page 427	S.		The Left Roof	Page 436
G.	**	DIKENSTEIN I 5.11c	Page 428	T.	*	FLIRTING WITH DIKES I 5.10c R	Page 439
H.		THE CAPTAIN I 5.10a	Page 428	U.	***	EYELESS IN GAZA I 5.12b	Page 439
I.	***	YELLOW MATTER CUSTARD I 5.13a	Page 430	V.	***	CONFEDERACY OF DUNCES I 5.12c	Page 442
J.	***	ROMPER ROOM I 5.12a	Page 430	W.	***	END OF THE TETHER I 5.12a (or 5.11d, A0)	Page 443
K.		GRAVE DIGGER I 5.8	Page 430	X.		The Right Roof	Page 443
L.	**	BETE NOIR I 5.11b	Page 431	Y.		The Little Flush (Descent Route)	Page 425
M.	*	DAVY JONE'S LOCKER II 5.10b	Page 432				

The first described route is located on a separate 40 foot outcrop on the left side of the Boulder Loop Trail, several minutes uphill and left from the sign-posted trail junction before you reach the dry streambed and the climber's trail to Sundown's Main Cliff.

STOP & STARE I 5.10d
Look for two bolts on a steep, cleaned strip of rock eight feet to the right of the #1 trail marker. Don't strain your neck!
1. Undercling and layback up a flake to the first bolt, step left onto a small ledge, and face climb past one more bolt to the top. 40', 5.10d

FA: Joe Perez, Ben Onachila, & Judy Perez November 3, 1991

LOST HORIZON

This one pitch cliff located up and to the left of Sundown's Main Cliff offers a variety of short routes. Hike up to the base of the Main Cliff, then traverse horizontally left around the corner, up and left along a good trail for several minutes to reach the left end of Lost Horizon.

ROCK GARDEN I 5.4 (**)
One of the easiest crack climbs around, the route should become popular. Start 10 feet right of the prominent roof/overlap at the crag's left end. Rock out!
1. Face climb, jam, and layback up a fairly prominent, left-slanting finger crack onto a resting ledge. The short chimney above yields after several awkward moves to good holds and more ledges on the right. Belay at a two bolt belay/rappel anchor on a good ledge. 60', 5.4
2. Friction up a slab to the top (5.4) and trees, or rappel off. 50', 5.4

FA: Ed Webster & Billy Squier July 22, 1995

FORE PAWS I 5.7 (*)
This is the thin flake system immediately to the right of the middle section of ROCK GARDEN. Well protected with wired nuts.
1. Climb the first 20 feet of ROCK GARDEN (5.4), then head up a short, thin crack (5.7) on the right onto a good ledge. Now paw up the thin flake above (5.7), laybacking and face climbing to the same ledge and double bolt anchor as on ROCK GARDEN. 60', 5.7

FA: Ed Webster & Billy Squier July 22, 1995

> On the right-hand side of Lost Horizon, 300 feet right of ROCK GARDEN, is the Breadbox, an easy to identify brown, rectangular buttress.

FINGER FOOD FROM THE FUTURE I 5.9+ (*)
This mouth-watering finger crack splits the center of the Breadbox.
1. From the detached block jutting out at the cliff's base, step up onto the face at horizontal cracks (5.9+), then move right into the finger crack. Climb past a bulge on fantastic jams, then reach up and left (5.9+) to good holds. Easier climbing gains the top. 75', 5.9+ Another classic Winkler route name!
HISTORY: After a previous try and some more cleaning, Kurt Winkler & Ed Webster made the first ascent on July 15, 1995.

BIGGER THAN A BREAD BOX I 5.11c
Climbs the right-facing corner 40 feet to the right of FINGER FOOD.
1. Jam up an overhanging finger crack in a right-facing dihedral (5.11c), past a small roof at the start, to the top. 40', 5.11c
FA: Steve Damboise & Bob Parrott Summer, 1989

STRAY CATS I 5.11b (*)
The brown and white arete 10 feet to the right of BIGGER THAN A BREAD BOX. Short, but well protected, with nice-looking moves.
1. Climb a short, attractive arete with a roof at the base, protected by a bolt, a pin, and a bolt. 40', 5.11b
FA: Bob Parrott & Dave Lattimer May 15, 1989

424 THE KANCAMAGUS HIGHWAY AREA

Jerry Handren on the second free ascent of Police & Thieves (5.12c) in 1988. Photograph by Nick Yardley.

SUNDOWN LEDGE – MAIN CLIFF

The first climbs are located above the talus slope up the ledge's left-hand end, straight left of some shattered rock and a prominent right-facing corner with a pine tree at its top, the line of THE TOMB. Descent from the Main Cliff involves rappelling off the route you just climbed, usually off a fixed anchor, hiking left on top along an easy trail below Lost Horizon and around the west (left) end of the Main Cliff, or rappelling down the Little Flush, the small gully located around the corner to the right of the Right Roof, next to SHADOWLINE, making a one rope rappel from a tree to the ground.

OGBP I 5.10c
The farthest, left route on the Main Cliff. Short, but not to be underestimated! When the trail reaches the cliff base, hike 300 feet straight left of THE TOMB.
1. Climb a short finger crack (5.10c) out a roof 10 feet up. 35', 5.10c
FA: Mack Johnson, Mike Guravage, Paul Boissonneault, & Mike Hartrich April 26, 1987

RUNNING HANDS I 5.9+
The right-facing corner at the Main Cliff's left end, 20 feet right of OGBP.
1. Climb up the corner, then handtraverse left (5.9+) through some dirty roofs to a crack and the top. 50', 5.9+ Needs more cleaning.
FA: Kurt Winkler with Shraddha Howard & Sunil Davidson July 15, 1995

UP ON THE ROOF I 5.9
The first climb to the left of THE SEVEN YEAR ITCH.
1. Climb past a short crack/corner to a bolt (5.9), and continue up a steep slab to a roof. Step right around a roof onto a face (also 5.9), and finish past a piton to the top of the cliff. 60', 5.9
FA: Joe Perez, Judy Perez, Mona L'Heureux, & John Snyder September 1, 1995

THE SEVEN YEAR ITCH I 5.8- X
A dangerous lead. Don't scratch and make it worse. Begin 40 feet to the left of ALLERGIC REACTION at a clump of trees.
1. Climb the slab on the left, then face climb straight up to the unprotected crux, 45 feet up. Finish up a left-facing corner. 75', 5.8- X
HISTORY: Todd Swain, Randy Schenkel, & Andy Schenkel did the first ascent on September 3, 1986—the Schenkel's lucky 7th wedding anniversary.

LE GRANDE ÉCART I 5.10a
Begin as for THE SEVEN YEAR ITCH. Be careful of some loose blocks wedged below the upper overhangs.
1. Climb up and right to a bolt and a piton (5.10a), then continue up through two overhangs to the top. 70', 5.10a
FA: Joe Perez, Judy Perez, Mona L'Heureux, John Snyder September 30, 1994

Peter Beal leading Dikenstein (5.11c) in 1992. Photo by Caolan MacMahon.

ALLERGIC REACTION I 5.10b R
Have a bad reaction to insecure, dirty, hard to protect 5.10 cracks? Then avoid this climb like the plague. Ascends the V groove/crack 40 feet to the left of the shattered area at the cliff base. Definitely carry a modern rack.

1. Beginning on the right, climb a series of easy ledges back left, then make poorly protected moves into the crack. Climb strenuously up the groove (5.10b R) to the top of the cliff. 75', 5.10b R

FA: Ed Webster & Steve Larson August 28, 1981

DAY FOR NIGHT I 5.9 R
An extremely dirty, scary climb up the left-facing corners just to the right of ALLERGIC REACTION. Seldom, if ever, repeated.

1. Climb the same stepped ledges, then up a crack to the base of the corners. Move by an awkward, rounded arete, past a bulge on flat handholds, and up the final corner, the crux. 75', 5.9 R

FA: Ed Webster & Michael Hartrich August 26, 1981

ARETE-Z-VOUS I 5.10b
A bold route up the exposed arete to the left of THE TOMB. It could stop you dead in your tracks. Carry a modern rack—and high levels of nerve.

1. Start up THE TOMB, then break left (5.10b) onto the arete. Sustained moves lead up the sharp ridge (more 5.10b) with tricky protection to the top. 75', 5.10b

FA: Michael Hartrich, Albert Dow, & Ed Webster September 4, 1981

THE TOMB I 5.9
When the climber's trail first meets the base of the cliff, this is the large inside corner with a slab at its base and a large pine at its top—a key landmark.

1. Tricky bouldering moves off the ground (5.9) gain the slab, then surmount a small overlap, and climb up the final corner. 75', 5.9

FA: Joe Cote, Dick Arey, & Tom Bates May 6, 1972

VARIATION: KING TUT'S TREASURE I 5.9
The start is 5.9, while the variation itself is only 5.7 in difficulty.

1a. After the initial boulder moves (5.9), climb the center of the slab to an overlap. Traverse right (5.7), and finish up a dike. 85', 5.9

FA: Ed Webster, rope-solo September 4, 1981

CHARLATAN I 5.12c (*)
Ascends the short, overhanging wall located just to the right of THE TOMB and 60 feet to the left of the YELLOW MATTER Buttress. Stick-clip the first bolt, then crank like a fiend. Three bolts lead to the anchor.

1. Beginning on the wall's left side, face climb with great difficulty past three bolts (5.12c) to the fixed anchor above. 20', 5.12c

FA: Andy Ross May, 1991

DIRECT FINISH: **ATROSSITY** I 5.13a (*)
Avoids grabbing for the CHARLATAN belay anchor by forging up the arete above on the right, joining DIKENSTEIN. The crux moves are to not use the original anchor. A small modern rack is needed.
1a. Climb up CHARLATAN (5.12c), clip its anchor, then head up (5.13a) onto the exposed arete (TCU), merging (5.11a) with DIKENSTEIN. 40', 5.13a
FA: Peter Beal with Kris Hansen May, 1993

DIKENSTEIN I 5.11c (**)
Just right of CHARLATAN is an obvious, overhanging, left-slanting dike. Popular, pumpy, & absolutely incredibly awkward—unless you're really short!
1. Climb up the overhanging, left-angling dike on large angular holds past three bolts (crux after the second bolt) to reach the fixed anchor. 35', 5.11c
FA: Andy Ross April, 1991

(Open Project)
The overhanging bolted face just right of DIKENSTEIN. Six bolts to the anchor.
1. Above DIKENSTEIN's first bolt, climb up the overhanging face. 40'
HISTORY: Andy Ross bolted the climb in 1991, but after a flake came off, the route has yet to be free climbed.

THE CAPTAIN I 5.10a
The right-slanting crack 30 feet right of DIKENSTEIN. Formerly El Cap Tree Route, the small pine growing out of the triangular recess is long gone.
1. Follow the crack (5.10a) past a triangular recess to a slab. 80', 5.10a
FA: Joe Cote & Jean-Claude Dehemel   May 14, 1972
FFA: Henry Barber & John Bragg   August 18, 1973

THE YELLOW MATTER BUTTRESS
This steep, smooth buttress 80 feet to the right of DIKENSTEIN boasts an extremely popular set of five high-energy sport routes.

PASTRYWORKS I 5.13b (***)
La Creme de la Creme? The hardest route on the buttress. Several of the holds were enhanced prior to the first ascent. Start 80 feet to the right of DIKENSTEIN, and 15 feet to the right of a large oak tree.
1. Begin as for YELLOW MATTER CUSTARD, then go left to the first bolt on an arete on the left side of the buttress. Extreme face moves lead straight up on hideous crimpers (5.13b) past several more bolts, joining THE BIG PICKLE at the top. 60', 5.13b
HISTORY: Duncan McCallum (Scotland) climbed the route in September, 1990, and named it for what was then North Conway's most popular climber's breakfast spot. Pastryworks went out of business not long after they had awarded McCallum a lifetime supply of coffee for his superlative efforts.

SUNDOWN LEDGE - MAIN CLIFF (DIKENSTEIN & PASTRYWORKS)

Duncan McCallum (Scotland) on Yellow Matter Custard (5.13a) in 1988.
Photograph by Nick Yardley.

THE BIG PICKLE I 5.13a (*)
The direct finish to YELLOW MATTER CUSTARD.
1. Climb up YELLOW MATTER for the first four bolts, then move left, and face climb up and left past three more bolts to a fixed anchor. 60', 5.13a
HISTORY: Steve Damboise made the first ascent on May 4, 1990. The Big Pickle was the old breakfast hangout next to IME's original store.

YELLOW MATTER CUSTARD I 5.13a (***)
This mega-classic ascends the shallow, yellow-colored groove in the center of the buttress. One of the best 5.13s in New Hampshire. Just try and eat it all at once! Carry a #1 and a #1.5 Friend for the upper flake.
1. Climb up the unrelenting groove, following six bolts up and right (5.13a) to a flake and eventually a double bolt anchor. 45', 5.13a
HISTORY: After Duncan McCallum bolted and first attempted the route in May, 1988, the weather turned bad, and finally he had to fly home to Scotland. Jason Stern made the notable first ascent on July 20, 1988.

FRIGID RELATIONS I 5.12b (*)
Start on ROMPER ROOM, several feet to the right of YELLOW MATTER CUSTARD. Bring a #1 and a #1.5 Friend for the top flake.
1. Climb past three bolts, move left, and finish up the top flake on YELLOW MATTER CUSTARD to a two bolt anchor. 50', 5.12b
FA: Steve Damboise, Charley Bentley, & Mark Pelletier October, 1988

ROMPER ROOM I 5.12a (***)
A wild romp and the first route on the buttress, ascending the steep, very sustained bolted face just to the left of the GRAVE DIGGER dihedral. Extremely popular. Start the same as for FRIGID RELATIONS.
1. Above the first bolt, hard climbing lead up to and over a small roof, then make a gymnastic series of moves up a smooth, inviting face past three bolts to fixed pitons and the anchor. 60', 5.12a
HISTORY: The all-star team of Steve Damboise, Jerry Handren, Duncan McCallum (Scotland), Nick Yardley (UK), Greg McCausland, Andy Ross, & Ronald Reagan made the first ascent of this classic sport route on May 13, 1988. (The new route book said Ronnie flashed it—honest!)

GRAVE DIGGER I 5.8
This is the dark, wet crack just right of the YELLOW MATTER Buttress.
1. Above some ferns in an alcove, chimney past two old pegs, then squeeze out to a stance on the right. Traverse right again to an easy dike and the top. 5.8
FA: Joe Cote & Alan Herschalag July, 1974

DIRECT FINISH: TRAPEZE I 5.10a
An atrociously dirty, strenuous, and deservedly unpopular pitch.

SUNDOWN MAIN (YELLOW MATTER, ROMPER ROOM, & BETE NOIR) 431

1a. After the initial chimney, climb out left on an overhanging wall on good holds, finishing up a thin, vertical crack, the crux. 5.10a
FA: Ed Webster & Susan Patenaude August, 1980

BETE NOIR I 5.11b (**))
This unusual and popular face climb begins five feet to the left of the start of DAVY JONE'S LOCKER in the center of an open face seamed by numerous overlaps 75 feet right of the YELLOW MATTER Buttress. Carry quick draws, plus several Friends and a few wired nuts. Five bolts lead to the anchor.
1. Face climb up to and over a small overlap to a blank face protected by two bolts (5.11b). Above a second overlap, climb a blank, black slab (5.11b) past two more bolts. Swing past the final, large overlap (bolt; 5.11a) on good holds to reach a small stance with a double bolt anchor. 60', 5.11b
FA: Rich Baker & Ann Yardley May, 1992

Chris Noonan on the crux of Bete Noir (5.11b) in 1995. Photo by Ed Webster.

DAVY JONE'S LOCKER II 5.10b (*)
The position of this imaginative face climb will send you right off the deep end. Well protected. Right of BETE NOIR is a steep, slabby face layered by overlaps. Start at an incipient vertical crack in black rock below an overlap.
1. Climb the crack up onto a narrow, sloping ledge. Walk and traverse right 20 feet to where a hard move (peg) gains a thin, vertical crack on the right. Face climb up a smooth, black face (several pitons; 5.10b) to a good belay ledge beside a tremendous block. 100', 5.10b
2. Standing on top of the block, make a strenuous series of moves (5.10b) to good holds, and pull up to the top. 35', 5.10b
FA: Ed Webster & Michael Hartrich   August 26, 1981

BANANA HEAD I 5.13b (**)
This unusually powerful route ascends angular, slanting holds up the severely overhanging, yellow wall 150 feet to the right of the YELLOW MATTER Buttress, and 100 feet left of VULTURES. Practice your one arm pull-ups (while eating some bananas) first! Six bolts lead to the lower of two anchors.
1. Follow a right-angling line using underclings and sidepulls past six bolts up the left side of the wall, making wild, dynamic moves (5.13b) to reach the lower, fixed anchor. 40', 5.13b
FA: Jerry Handren   Summer, 1992

DIRECT FINISH: BIG BANANA I 5.13c (*)
Don't let your head swell over this one! Handren claims this is "probably the most fun hard sport route in the White Mountains." And controversial.
1. Above the lower double bolt anchor on BANANA HEAD, use a bolted-on artificial hold to cruise the next 15 feet past a couple of bolts (5.13c) to the highest fixed anchor. 55', 5.13c

HISTORY: Finding that he was too weak to complete the moves, Jerry Handren added the artificial handhold, and eventually, after many attempts made the first something ascent in the Summer of 1993. The addition of the man-made hold on this route, and a power-drilled finger pocket on the crux of TOTALLY SAVAGE prompted the December, 1991, "Climber's Town Meeting" in North Conway amongst local climbers where both practices were discussed, voted upon, and unanimously condemned.

BLACK SUNDAY I 5.7 R
The first climb on Sundown's Main Cliff. Protection is widely spaced. The route ascends the prominent, right-diagonalling dike bordered by an overhanging yellow wall (BANANA HEAD) on the left.
1. Climb up the dike, then traverse right to a belay cave.
2. Continue up the chimney over a chockstone to the top.
FA: Joe Cote & Dick Arey   November 28, 1971

SUNDOWN LEDGE - MAIN CLIFF (BANANA HEAD & AGENT ORANGE)

AGENT ORANGE I 5.11b (*)
Start five feet right of BLACK SUNDAY below a large block/flake at the cliff base. Bring a normal rack. The bolted start up the 5.11a face is popular.
1. Above the block, face climb past three bolts up a short, testing face (5.11a) to a stance on BLACK SUNDAY. Now move up and left (cold shut; 5.11b) into the prominent, orange, right-slanting dihedral above (5.9+). Continue up and right out a series of unlikely roofs until you can escape up to a stance near the top of the cliff with a double cold shut anchor. 90', 5.11b
FA: Brad White & Ian Cruickshank June, 1993

TAR & FEATHER I 5.11d (*)
Start 15 feet to the left of BLOODY SUNDAY. There is difficult protection on the crux with small wired nuts. Modern rack helpful.
1. Climb up a dark-colored arete following a thin crack to a stance. Next move up a short, steep wall that ends at a horizontal crack, and belay on the right at fixed anchors under a roof. 5.9+
2. Jam up a slot on the left, and diagonal up along a tapering crack over the crux bulge at its top (5.11d) to a belay off of large Friends. 5.11d
FA: Tom Callaghan & John Strand June 6, 1985

BLOODY SUNDAY I 5.9
The right-leaning crack system just to the right of TAR & FEATHER.
1. Climb a crack up a right-facing corner, move over an overhang, then head off left, finishing up BLACK SUNDAY to the top. 5.9
FA: Henry Barber & Bob Anderson October 15, 1972

AFTER THE FOX (Open Project) I 5.13
This former nail-up is essentially free. Start 15 feet left of MIDNIGHT GROOVE at two, right-leaning, thin cracks in an overhanging wall.
1. Make a series of fingerlocks, lay-aways, and extreme face moves (5.13) past six bolts to a fixed anchor on a good belay ledge. 45', 5.13
2. After a boulder problem, scramble up the final groove to the top.
HISTORY: Brooks Bicknell & Chris Gill nailed the first ascent in September, 1982. Jerry Handren bolted and nearly freed the route in 1995.

CRANK CASE I 5.11a
Start just to the left of MIDNIGHT GROOVE at a narrow dihedral.
1. Follow the corner past two knifeblades to a mantleshelf move on the right. Step back left and climb up under a triangular roof to a semi-hanging belay off large Hexes or Friends. 5.10b
2. Pass the roof on the left with a Herculean reach (5.11a), then finish up a 5.7 groove to the woods. 5.11a
FA: Mike Kenney & Dave Anderson July 29, 1983

434 THE KANCAMAGUS HIGHWAY AREA

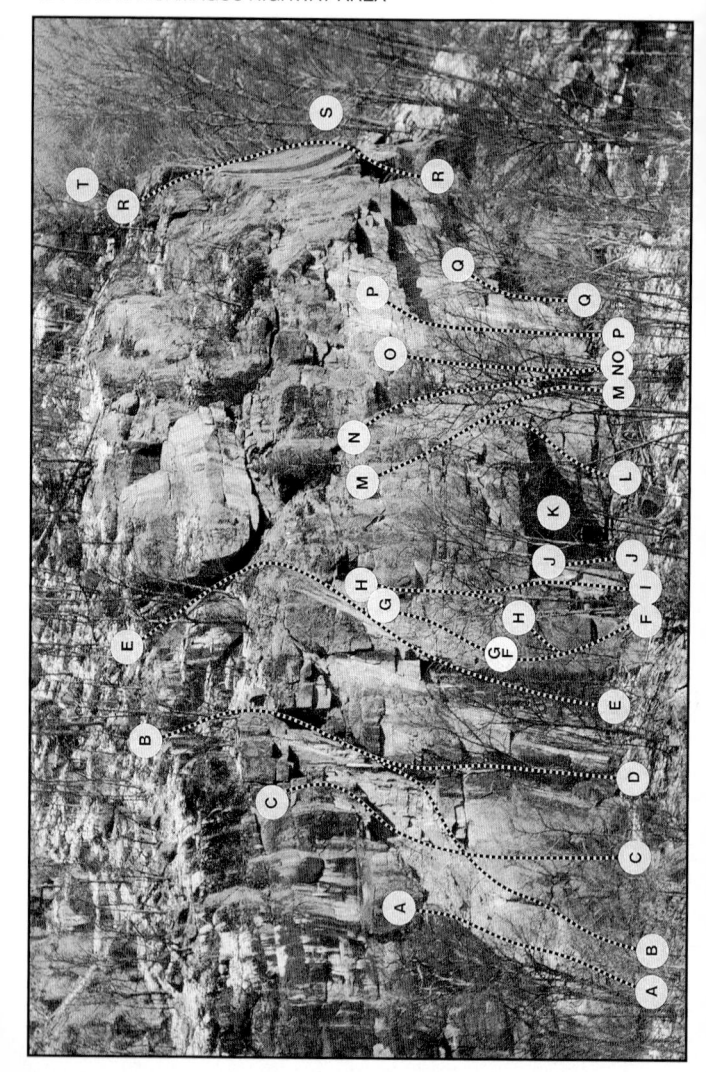

SUNDOWN LEDGE - THE MAIN CLIFF (CLOSE-UP)

A.	* **BIG BANANA** I 5.13c	Page 432	L.	** **EXODUS** I 5.12c	Page 439
B.	**BLACK SUNDAY** I 5.7 R	Page 432	M.	* **THE PROMISED LAND** I 5.12c	Page 439
C.	* **AGENT ORANGE** I 5.11b	Page 433	N.	* **FLIRTING WITH DIKES** I 5.10c R	Page 439
D.	**BLOODY SUNDAY** I 5.9	Page 433	O.	*** **EYELESS IN GAZA** I 5.12b	Page 439
E.	**MIDNIGHT GROOVE** I 5.8	Page 436	P.	*** **CONFEDERACY OF DUNCES** I 5.12c	Page 442
F.	*** **VULTURES** I 5.10d	Page 436	Q.	* **UNFINISHED SYMPHONY** I 5.12c	Page 442
G.	** **CARRION** I 5.11d	Page 436	R.	*** **END OF THE TETHER** I 5.12a (or 5.11d, A0)	Page 443
H.	* **FLIGHT OF THE FALCON** I 5.10d	Page 436	S.	**The Right Roof**	Page 443
I.	** **POLICE & THIEVES** I 5.12c	Page 436	T.	**The Little Flush** (Descent Route)	Page 425
J.	* **SHE'S CRAFTY** I 5.12c	Page 438			
K.	**The Left Roof**	Page 436			

MIDNIGHT GROOVE I 5.8

The black corner and crack, a little rotten and usually wet at the start, 15 feet to the left of VULTURES, the vertical finger crack in a steep, clean face.
1. Climb the awkward, vertical crack system to an alcove. 5.8
2. Continue up the crack, over blocks, trending right to the top.
FA: Dick Arey & Joe Cote Summer, 1972

THE LEFT ROOF

The next climbs are in the vicinity of the Left Roof, the first major horizontal roof you'll encounter when walking right following the base of the Main Cliff.

VULTURES I 5.10d (***)

The strikingly obvious, vertical finger crack just to the left of the Left Roof. Well protected, popular, hard for its grade—and frustratingly tricky.
1. Climb the deceptively strenuous finger crack (5.10d) up to a fixed anchor. Lower off, or continue up CARRION (5.11d). 40', 5.10d
FA: Joe Cote, Dick Arey, & Jean-Claude Dehemel   May 13, 1972
FFA: Henry Barber & John Bragg   August 18, 1973

DIRECT FINISH: **CARRION** I 5.11d (**)

The meaty direct finish to VULTURES—and a popular feast. This route is also tough for its grade, with a strenuous crux. Bring wired nuts, small cams, and steel fingertips, or you'll be DOA on the crux!
1. Climb the VULTURES finger crack (5.10d) to the fixed anchor, move up and step right (bolt), then face climb past horizontal cracks (piton) to the final, desperate 5.11d headwall (bolt), and a fixed belay/rappel anchor above on MIDNIGHT GROOVE. 75', 5.11d
FA: Nick Yardley (UK) & Andy Ross April 21, 1988

FLIGHT OF THE FALCON I 5.10d (*)

An airy, challenging face climb up the steep face and exposed arete to the right of VULTURES and above POLICE & THIEVES. Modern rack.
1. Climb the first 30 feet of VULTURES (5.10d), then angle right across the face past two pitons into a short, vertical finger crack. Jam up this, step right onto the arete, and climb up another finger crack (peg), finally stepping back left onto a good ledge with fixed anchors. 115', 5.10d Rappel with two ropes.
FA: Ed Webster & Susan Patenaude September, 1980

POLICE & THIEVES I 5.12c (**)

Seldom repeated. Just don't get caught in the act! The route free climbs the original aid start of LUCIFER'S LIP before breaking out left around the roof onto FLIGHT OF THE FALCON. An exceedingly strenuous pitch with very tricky protection. Start 10 feet to the right of VULTURES. Modern rack.
1. Layback up the thin crack, moving up (5.12a) to the undercling.

SUNDOWN LEDGE - MAIN CLIFF (VULTURES & CARRION)

John Harlin III leading Vultures (5.10d) in 1980. Photograph by Ed Webster.

Undercling right (also 5.12a; piton), then climb a finger crack leading up to the main roof and a two bolt anchor. 35', 5.12c Lower off, circle left around the roof up FLIGHT OF THE FALCON, or finish up TOTALLY SAVAGE.
HISTORY: This is the original start of the aid route LUCIFER'S LIP which is now completely free. Jim Surette made the first free ascent after two days of effort, on March 29, 1986.

DIRECT FINISH: **TOTALLY SAVAGE** I 5.12d
Rope drag, a drilled finger pocket, and the slightly overhanging nature of the route make for a very primitive adventure.

2. From the double bolt anchor under the roof on POLICE & THIEVES, climb out underneath the Left Roof, and then right over the lip of the roof, making extreme moves (5.12d) using a controversial drilled finger pocket to reach the double bolt anchor up above. Beware of rope drag. 40', 5.12d

HISTORY: Brad White & Jim Frangos aid climbed this variation to LUCIFER'S LIP in December, 1982. After enhancing a finger pocket on the route, Steve Damboise made the first "free" ascent on May 11, 1991. This was one of several rock-altering incidents that prompted the landmark 1991 "Climber's Town Meeting" held on December 13, 1991 in North Conway so that local climbers could discuss and vote on rock defacement and route alteration. The vote was unanimously against these damaging practices.

SHE'S CRAFTY I 5.12c (*)
Always dry! The short face and V groove 20 feet to the right of POLICE & THIEVES. Four bolts lead to the anchor under the Left Roof.
1. Crank up the thin, crimpy face (5.12c) into a shallow, vertical groove, and finish at a horizontal crack with a fixed anchor. 30', 5.12c
FA: Steve Damboise & Bob Parrott May 7, 1988

THE ARGONAUT I 5.13a
Start 10 feet to the right of SHE'S CRAFTY, under the Left Roof.
1. Face climb up a steep wall past three bolts to a two bolt anchor. 25', 5.13a
FA: Steve Damboise & Charley Bentley September 22, 1991

HIGH & DRY II 5.9, A3 (*)
The route stays dry even in a downpour. Start five feet to the right of THE ARGONAUT at the back of the Left Roof. Bring aid gear, KBs, and blades.
1. Free climb a right-facing corner (5.9) for 20 feet (peg), then move up to the large roof. Fine, awkward aid moves (A3) lead out a thin crack splitting the large, horizontal roof. 100', 5.9, A3
HISTORY: Bill Holland, Harry Tucker, & Dan Hutchens made the first ascent of this wild aid climb in the mid-1980s in a torrential rainstorm, yet somehow managed to remain high and dry the entire time!

SUNDOWN LEDGE - MAIN CLIFF (EYELESS IN GAZA)

EXODUS I 5.12c (**)
Escape at all costs. Start 35 feet left of EYELESS IN GAZA underneath the right side of the Left Roof. The first bolt has a long sling for the clip.
1. Face climb up and right out around the roof's right side past four bolts (5.12c) to a double bolt anchor just above the lip. 30', 5.12c
FA: Andy Ross & Jerry Handren October 25, 1991

KILT FLAPPER I 5.12b
This overgrown boulder problem ascends the steep wall five feet to the left of FLIRTING WITH DIKES. Wait for a windy day!
1. Climb the face past horizontal cracks (bolt stud), then up a short fingertip crack to a hidden peg. After a second bolt, grab the EXODUS anchor. 35', 5.12b
FA: Jerry Handren, Nick Yardley (UK), & Chris Gill April, 1989

THE PROMISED LAND I 5.12c (*)
This impressive, sustained route was upgraded from 5.12a after a handhold broke. Bring small and medium Friends, plus seven quick draws.
1. Start up the dike on FLIRTING WITH DIKES for 10 feet, head left past the EXODUS bolt anchor, and continue up and left (5.12c) past more bolts to cracks in the steep, upper headwall above. Fixed anchor. 75', 5.12c
FA: Andy Ross & Ken Reville October, 1991

FLIRTING WITH DIKES I 5.10c R (*)
Thirty feet to the right of the Left Roof, this unlikely route ascends a very prominent, left-slanting, eroded dike up a gently overhanging orange wall. Double ropes and a modern rack are both helpful.
1. Face climb up the dike with nut and Friend protection on either side of it (5.10c R). Protection is strenuous to place. After the angle relents, easier climbing leads to a tree belay. 90', 5.10c R Rappel off with two ropes.
FA: Steve Larson & Paul Boissonneault June, 1986

EYELESS IN GAZA I 5.12b (***)
Sundown's world-class sport route offers incredibly sustained moves in a tremendous situation. The route ascends the overhanging, always dry face just to the right of FLIRTING WITH DIKES. Highly recommended. Six bolts lead to the fixed anchor. Save your strength for the last clip!
1. Start up the first 10 feet of FLIRTING, then lay-away up a series of thin, vertical flakes in the center of the wall (5.12b), face climbing strenuously up to the fixed anchor at the overlap above. 65', 5.12b

HISTORY: In April, 1988, just as the sport climbing boom was about to hit Sundown, Chris Gill & Nick Yardley (UK) conceived of and began the climb from the ground-up, placing natural gear "until we were finally forced to place a piton for protection in the crux layback flake," related Nick Yardley.

440 THE KANCAMAGUS HIGHWAY AREA

Nick Yardley off Eyeless In Gaza (5.12b) in 1988.
Photograph by Greg McCausland.

Jerry Handren on the first ascent of Confederacy Of Dunces (5.12c) in 1989.
Photograph by Nick Yardley.

"Unfortunately each time one of us fell, the piton moved a little, which was pretty entertaining, so on the next effort, we'd have to hammer the pin back in, then try and keep going." Gill & Yardley eventually did the crux that day, and placed one bolt on the lead from a hook, but since they didn't have another bolt with them, they never completed the pitch. After Gill left town on a trip out West, Duncan McCallum bolted the route on rappel, and on June 1, 1988, Jerry Handren made the first ascent of this superb climb. "The next time I went back out to Sundown, the bolts were in, and the route was climbed," said Yardley.

MITHRAS I 5.12d (**)

The Sun God—or is it Clod? Climbs the aesthetic arete 15 feet to the right of EYELESS IN GAZA, with an added bonus: a couple of no-hands rests between the hard parts. Eight bolts lead to the anchor. Another popular line.
1. To the right of EYELESS IN GAZA, climb past three bolts, then move right around a small roof (the first crux). Continue up the CONFEDERACY arete to a rest, step out left, and face climb straight up past several more bolts (the second crux) to the fixed belay/rappel anchor. 65', 5.12d
FA: Steve Damboise & Jerry Handren   October 5, 1991

CONFEDERACY OF DUNCES I 5.12c (***)

Another visionary route. Begin 30 feet to the right of EYELESS IN GAZA as for UNFINISHED SYMPHONY at the base of a large, right-facing corner.
1. Start up UNFINISHED SYMPHONY, then step left into a thin, vertical crack (5.11b). Jam the crack over the left side of the roof above, then face climb diagonally right (5.12a; exposed) just above the lip of the huge roof past bolts (5.12c) to a double bolt anchor. 90', 5.12c
HISTORY: Chris Gill & Andy Ross got above the first roof and called their creation Tits Out For The Lads, in July, 1988. Jerry Handren completed the first ascent in April, 1989—"with some help from the usual dunces."

SUNDOG DELIGHT I 5.12d (*)

This multi-climb combination sport route should challenge even the most ardent hangdoggers! The logistics, however, are a bit complicated if your second can't follow. Have a spare rope handy just in case.
1. Climb all of EYELESS IN GAZA (5.12b), continuing above the anchor to a horizontal crack. Rest here off hand jams, then traverse straight right, across MITHRAS, clipping the anchors, and finish to the right (5.12c) up CONFEDERACY OF DUNCES to its double bolt anchor. 140', 5.12d
FA: John Mallery   July, 1990

UNFINISHED SYMPHONY I 5.12c (*)

Begin 30 feet to the right of EYELESS IN GAZA at an obvious, right-facing, corner/flake beneath the left side of the Right Roof. Small normal rack.

SUNDOWN LEDGE - MAIN CLIFF (CONFEDERACY & TETHER)

1. Climb up the right-facing corner until below the main roof, then face climb out right to the higher of two fixed anchors, to a bolt, and then up to a piton. 60', 5.12c Down climb back to the highest double anchor to descend.
2. Aid to the lip of the roof, then...?

HISTORY: Todd Swain & Mike Hannon climbed the first pitch and reached the roof's lip in the pouring rain in March, 1983. After Chris Gill & Steve Damboise had free climbed the pitch in July, 1988, a key handhold broke, but Jerry Handren with Greg McCausland soon re-free climbed that section. The single bolt above the main roof was placed on an exploratory free attempt.

THE RIGHT ROOF

One hundred yards to the right of the Left Roof is the Right Roof, a huge series of jutting roofs and overhangs, and the location of two extremely strenuous free climbs, END OF THE TETHER and TOOTHLESS GRIN. Below the Right Roof is a clutter of large, fallen blocks.

END OF THE TETHER I
5.12a (or 5.11d, A0) (***)
This gymnastic route will shock you right to your wit's end. Easily identified as the painfully strenuous, layback and undercling crack around the corner to the left of TOOTHLESS GRIN. Begin on top of a large, rectangular block 40 feet to the right of the UNFINISHED SYMPHONY dihedral. About eight feet up, above the lower lip of the roof, slants an overhanging, right-

Michael Hartrich on the free ascent of End Of The Tether (5.11d, A0) in 1981. Photo by Ed Webster.

facing corner. Bring many Friends for protection, others to stand on! The first moves to gain the crack now go free at 5.12a, involving both a one arm pull up and a huge reach—pretty much impossible for anyone under six feet tall. Most will want to use the traditional shoulderstand, which makes the route 5.11d, A0.

1. Gain the base of the crack off the boulder, then layback up to a stance. Undercling right (5.11d) into an alcove (pegs), rest, then attack the last 15 feet of the roof (5.11d), underclinging right again to a belay ledge. Fixed anchors. 5.11d, A0 or 5.12a Most parties usually rappel off from here. Or, if wanted:
2. Climb up a vertical crack (5.9) on the left to the top. 5.9

HISTORY: Pitch one was aided by Chris Smith & Gary Peterson in October, 1978. Todd Swain & Curt Robinson did the climb's first complete ascent in June, 1979. Ed Webster, Albert Dow, & Michael Hartrich made a free ascent of the route except for using a shoulderstand off the block in September, 1981. Russ Clune free climbed the difficult 5.12a start on August 30, 1985.

TOOTHLESS GRIN I 5.12a (***)
Don't loose any teeth (or sleep) over this one. A desperate free climb up the large dihedral under the Right Roof, 40 feet right of END OF THE TETHER.
1. Free climb the strenuous, flaring corner past two pitons. After an intricate start (5.12a), layback and jam up to the fixed anchor underneath the roof. 45', 5.12a Lower off, or escape left to a ledge, finishing up the top 5.9 crack on END OF THE TETHER.

HISTORY: Ward Smith & Jim Ainsworth aided the first ascent in October, 1978. Felix Modugno, Harry Brielmann, Jim Damon, & Mick Avery made the first free ascent on Memorial Day Weekend in 1983.

VARIATION: **THE DIRECT START** I A4
Start below the huge roof to the left of TOOTHLESS GRIN.
1a. Aid out a thin crack splitting the horizontal roof on tricky aid (A4) to an incipient, vertical crack in the smooth face just left of TOOTHLESS GRIN. When the crack ends, aid left to the belay on END OF THE TETHER. 60', A4
FA: Unknown.

DIRECT FINISH: (Open Project)
The final, culminating overhang on TOOTHLESS GRIN.
1a. Above the fixed anchor on TOOTHLESS, continue up and left following the crack system out the lip of the huge roof past several bolts to a higher, chained double bolt anchor. Fifteen very wild feet!

HISTORY: In October of 1986, Jim Surette (and more recently, Jerry Handren) both worked on this desperate direct finish, without completing it.

RAZOR CRACK II A1 (With a possible 5.11 Finish) (*)
The perfect, thin aid crack out the right side of the Right Roof, 40 feet to the right of TOOTHLESS GRIN. It'll be a while before anyone frees this one! One of the area's best practice aid routes. Carry wired nuts and blade pitons.
1. Aid climb the gently overhanging, thin vertical crack (fixed pitons) over a small bulge to a small, exposed belay stance just above the lip. 60', A1
2. The same thin crack leads directly to the top. 80', A1 or 5.11

SUNDOWN LEDGE - MAIN CLIFF (TOOTHLESS GRIN) 445

Jim Surette attempting the Direct Finish to Toothless Grin in 1986.
Photograph by S. Peter Lewis.

HISTORY: Joe Cote & Dick Arey made the first ascent on April 30, 1972. Pitch two was free climbed by Michael Hartrich in 1983.

FAT GIRLS WITH ACNE I 5.11c (*)
No blemishes on this hormone-producing route! Start as for ROUGH BOYS.
1. Climb to the base of the ROUGH BOYS corner. Protected by a peg in the dihedral's left-hand arete, swing out left & mantle (5.10b) into a shallow groove. Climb the roof crack (5.10d) to the ROUGH BOYS anchor. 60', 5.10d
2. Follow a thin crack up the wall directly above the belay. When it ends, traverse left five feet (5.11c), and climb straight up, finishing directly through the final roofs to the top. 80', 5.11c Bring a modern rack.
FA: Andy Holmes & Steve Larson September, 1986

ROUGH BOYS I 5.10a (***)
Since the first ascent, the climb has developed something of a cult following. Popular. The route ascends the upper part of the smooth dihedral 40 feet right of RAZOR CRACK. Wild, street-smart maneuvers, with adequate protection.
1. Climb onto a moderate slab, protect under a thin arch, then face climb (5.9+) up to a small, horizontal ledge six feet right of the actual dihedral. Clip a piton (with relief), step left, and stem up (5.10a) to good holds and a stance. Escape left around a small roof to a belay/rappel anchor. 60', 5.10a
2. Traverse 15 feet right and climb a crack with a peapod slot (5.10a). 80', 5.10a (Pitons used on the FA were not left fixed.) A better protected, easier finish is to traverse 25 feet right, and jam up WOMBAT's upper finger crack. 100', 5.9+
FA: Doug Madara & Choe Brooks (UK)   April, 1981

WOMBAT I 5.12a (*)
Now free—but still kinda hairy. I'd be very suspicious. Start 15 feet to the right of ROUGH BOYS. Modern rack quite helpful.
1. Climb the first crack to the right of ROUGH BOYS past two fixed knifeblades to a bulge (5.12a). Belay above on a small stance. 60', 5.12a
2. Finish up an aesthetic, vertical finger crack (5.9+). 80', 5.9+
FA: Todd Swain & Brad White   October, 1980
FFA: Jim Surette   October 21, 1984

BLACK WOLF I 5.10c
Tackles the unlikely bulge 15 feet right of WOMBAT. Tricky protection.
1. Climb up an easy corner until beneath an overlap, then step left (5.10b) around the arete, and up to the belay. 60', 5.10b
2. This good pitch ascends a very thin, nice crack straight up (5.10c). Near the top, escape left, or persevere straight up to the trees. 80', 5.10c
FA: Brad White & Todd Swain   October, 1980
FFA: Choe Brooks (UK) & Doug Madara   April, 1981

STILETTO I 5.6 (**)
The easiest route on Sundown's Main Cliff, and a good intro to crack and chimney climbing, but psychologically it's a 5.6 route for 5.8 leaders. Begin 60 feet right of the Right Roof. A 30 foot high triangular flake marks the start.
1. Chimney behind the flake to its top, climb a short corner, step left on secure holds to a pair of cracks, and jam up these steeply to a stance. 80', 5.6
2. The same crack system leads straight up to the woods. 40', 5.3
FA: Dick Arey & Joe Cote   May 6, 1972

VARIATION: **BON TEMPS ROULER** I 5.9- "Let the Good Times Roll!"
1a. At the top of the STILETTO chimney, continue straight up a crack (5.9-) to the top, instead of stepping off to the left. 5.9-
FA: Steve Larson & Tricia Mattox   September, 1983

SUNDOWN LEDGE - MAIN CLIFF (ROUGH BOYS & SHADOWLINE)

TODD FOOLERY I 5.8 (*)
On the steep wall right of STILETTO are several parallel vertical cracks.
1. Climb roughly 30 feet of STILETTO until it's possible to step right into the first vertical crack. Follow it to the top. 5.8
FA: Todd Swain & Brad White   April Fool's Day, 1981

THE BRITISH ARE HERE I 5.7 (*)
They're coming, they were here—and now they've left again!
1. Climb STILETTO to TODD FOOLERY, but step further right beneath a small overhang, and climb the right-hand, parallel crack system to the top. 5.7
FA: Todd Swain & Nick Donnelly (UK)   March 31, 1981

ASSAULT & BATTERY I 5.10b
A vicious, bruising line roughly 35 feet to the right of STILETTO.
1. Climb up broken blocks, step left, and groan up a one foot wide crack to a cramped niche. Exit out right (5.10b) to a belay stance (peg). 5.10b
2. Step back left over a bulge to a friction slab and the top.
HISTORY: Doug Madara & Kurt Winkler did Pitch one on September 25, 1981. The climb was completed by John Bragg & Ric Hatch on May 1, 1982.

SHADOWLINE I 5.11d (***)
A hidden gem, with a traditional grade. Most climbers, if they get up the route, find it harder. Hike 300 feet uphill and right of STILETTO to a small gully called the Little Flush. The beautiful, desperate finger crack on the left is SHADOWLINE. Scramble onto a ledge at its base. Wired nuts, small cams, and Flexible Friends are all useful if you can hang on long enough to place them.
1. Finger jam up the continuously intricate crack. 45', 5.11d
HISTORY: Michael Hartrich & Albert Dow made the first ascent of this historic route on October 30, 1980. They originally graded the climb 5.11b.

EDGE OF NIGHT I 5.8
A good, short climb for the grade.
1. Ascend the sharp arete just right of SHADOWLINE, stepping out right onto a slab at mid height. 45', 5.8 Rappel off a tree back down the Little Flush.
FA: Ed Webster, rope-solo   September 4, 1981

> The next section of the Main Cliff at Sundown is, in general, crumbly, loose, and lichen-covered. Care is needed on the following four routes.

BORBETOMAGIC ELUSION I 5.8
The route climbs a vertical chimney crack, the first, obvious-looking line about 100 feet to the right of the Little Flush.
1. Climb up the chimney past loose rock to an awkward exit move. Follow cracks through a bulge to a tree ledge. 5.8 Rappel off with one rope, barely.
FA: Joe Cote & Roger Martin   1972

448 THE KANCAMAGUS HIGHWAY AREA

Michael Hartrich on the first ascent of Shadowline (5.11d) in 1980. Photograph by Joe Lentini.

SUNDOWN LEDGE - MAIN CLIFF (SLIPPING INTO DARKNESS)

SOMETHING FOOLISH I 5.9
The left-facing corner 20 feet right of BORBETOMAGIC ILLUSION.
1. Climb the corner, stemming past a steep bulge with protection below your feet. Some crumbly rock. Belay on a sloping, tree ledge. 50', 5.9
2. Head up a short slab above, then continue through trees to the steep upper wall above the tree-covered ledge. 40', 4th class.
3. Climb the large, right-facing dihedral with broken rock to a roof 35 feet up. Traverse right just below the roof (5.9), then on up to the top. 65', 5.8
FA: George Hurley & Ray Franzem   August 18, 1982

QUITS COMPLETELY I 5.8
If you're going to stop, you might just as well completely give up! Start at the short jam crack 85 feet right of SOMETHING FOOLISH.
1. Up the straight crack, easily at first, but harder higher up, to trees. 45', 5.8
2. Scramble up to the large, tree-covered ledge.
3. About 50 feet to the left of the top pitch of OH XANA, marked by a 10 foot, free-standing boulder, climb up a steep wall, angling left to the top.
HISTORY: George Hurley & Ray Franzem did Pitch one, QUITS, on August 18, 1982. George Hurley & Brian Mauro finished the route on June 10, 1983.

OH XANA II 5.8+
Hike 250 feet to the right of the Little Flush (or 40 feet right of QUITS COMPLETELY) to a 10 foot high, friable pillar that marks the route's start.
1. Climb the left side of the pillar, stand on top, traverse a foot ledge 12 feet left, then climb up and left to an open, left-facing corner. Good ledges left of this corner and the corner itself lead to a tree ledge. 70', 5.7+
2. Above is a low-angled slab. Walk right, then climb up a groove through a steep, blocky loose wall 15 feet high to a left-angling ramp of good rock that leads to a birch tree and good ledges below the prominent, final crack. 60', 5.7
3. Finish up the slightly overhanging (5.8+) jam crack. 40', 5.8+
HISTORY: George Hurley, Paul Ross, & Marc Chauvin did the first ascent on November 9, 1982, and named the climb for Chauvin's daughter, Xana.

SLIPPING INTO DARKNESS I 5.11d (*)
The location of this route is approximately 150 feet to the left of the Alcohol Wall. Just to the north of the #5 lookout on the Boulder Loop Trail, rappel 70 feet to reach a good ledge at the climb's base. Pumpy moves with a few long reaches. Start on the arete's left side.
1. Clip the first two bolts, then make reachey moves (5.11d) up and left to a shallow, right-facing corner with two pegs. Exit right onto the steep arete, climbing up the arete's right-hand side for 20 feet, then finish left past the final two bolts (5.11a) to the top. 60', 5.11d
FA: Brad White, Ian Cruickshank, & Dick Peterson   October 17, 1991

450 THE KANCAMAGUS HIGHWAY AREA

Bill Bentley hanging 10 on Surf Psycho (5.13a) in 1992. Photo by Charley Bentley.

THE ALCOHOL WALL

This twelve pack of sport routes is located on the far, upper, right-hand tier of Sundown's Main Cliff. All the routes here are bolted clip-ups except STANDARD ROUTE. Hike past the Roof Routes to the Little Flush, the small gully just to the right of SHADOWLINE. From here, walk right along the cliff base beneath several small overhangs until you can see the orange-white colored wall up above. Scramble up and right, then up a dirty, vertical gully (located very close to the actual right end of the cliff) to reach the right-hand end of the narrow access ledge below the climbs. Care is needed when walking around on this potentially dangerous ledge which is about 100 feet above the ground! To descend, carefully down climb the approach gully, or rappel off with one rope from the double bolt OUTSHINED belay/rappel anchor halfway across the access ledge. The routes, which were all cleaned and bolted on rappel, are now described from right to left:

HAVANNUTHA DRINK I 5.11b (**)
The first route on the wall. Start at a one bolt belay anchor about 50 feet left along the access ledge from the approach gully. Well protected, sustained—and a very popular idea. Nine bolts lead to a double bolt anchor.
1. Above the belay bolt, scramble up broken ledges to the first bolt, on a clean face with a left-arching, finger traverse flake just above. Face climb straight up over a yellow bulge, then continue directly up the face over a small overlap onto the upper face to a two bolt anchor. 80', 5.11b
FA: Ken Reville & Jamie Cunningham June 15, 1991

CLAMBAKE I 5.12b
Be careful your fingers don't get overcooked. Ascends overhanging, orange rock up through a roof split by a right-facing corner. Start 30 feet to the left of HAVANNUTHA DRINK at a pine tree growing directly below the roof. Four bolts and a fixed nut lead to a double bolt anchor.
1. At the base of the roof (the 5.12b crux), hang in there to make a long reach up into the crack in the corner above the roof. Crank to the anchor. 50', 5.12b
FA: Bill Bentley & Ken Reville June, 1992

JING & TONIC I 5.10b (***)
The wall's easiest and most popular climb. This route yields good, steep face climbing with handy rests between the hard moves. Start 40 feet to the left of the CLAMBAKE pine tree. Six bolts lead to a double bolt anchor.
1. Climb up a narrow, right-slanting ramp formed by an orange dike through the initial bulge, the first 5.10b crux. Continue up the steep face above, with one more hard move for good measure near the top. 80', 5.10b
HISTORY: Ken Reville & Holly Reville made the first ascent on May 20, 1992. Holly was 6 months pregnant when she did the route—and she flashed it!

(Open Project)
One hundred feet to the left of JING & TONIC is a 100 degree, overhanging wall with zebra-like, black and white stripes.
1. Face climb up a narrow vertical dike past several bolts to a bolt anchor. 25'
HISTORY: First bolted and attempted by Dean Potter in September, 1992.

THE LEATHERFACE WALL
The next routes climb the LEATHERFACE Wall, the left side of the Alcohol Wall.

SURF PSYCHO I 5.13a (**)
This very popular route cranks up the smooth, orange-white face just the right of an obvious prow approximately 150 feet to the left of JING & TONIC. A safe route for blowing clips. Six bolts lead to a two bolt chained anchor.
1. Surf the psychotically smooth, overhanging face past six bolts. 35', 5.13a
FA: Corbin Marr June, 1992

OUTSHINED I 5.13b (*)
This climb blazes up the center of the orange, overhanging prow just to the left of SURF PSYCHO. There is a two bolt belay/rappel anchor at the base. After clipping PSYCHO's first bolt, stick clip the second bolt, too, and yard up until you're at the lip of the roof. Eight bolts lead to a two bolt anchor.
1. Starting at the roof on square-cut holds, crimp straight up a 115 degree orange face past several bolts (5.13b) to a double bolt anchor on an arete below and right of the STANDARD ROUTE Roof. 50', 5.13b
FA: Bill Bentley June, 1992

STANDARD ROUTE I 5.11d (*)
Undoubtedly the hardest of all the STANDARD ROUTES in New Hampshire, this route ascends the enormous dihedral and flaring chimney just to the left of OUTSHINED, then follows the roof's left-hand crack up the steep upper face. Bring a full rack, including a good selection of Friends. There are no bolts. Start 15 feet to the left of OUTSHINED.
1. Head up a short, striped face, climb the giant dihedral, then move out the spectacular, left-hand side of the roof (5.10c) into an overhanging, flared chimney. Climb up out of the flare, face climbing (5.11d) to undercling and traverse moves leading left, eventually to good hand jams. Then continue straight up the crack (5.10b) to the top of the cliff. 120', 5.11d
HISTORY: Ken Reville & Maury McKinney first climbed most of this route mixed free and aid in July, 1993, traversing left above the main roof to finish at LEATHERFACE's double bolt anchor. After a previous attempt that ended with a spectacular leaderfall by Larson, Steve Larson & Rob Adair returned to make the first complete ascent and first free ascent of this challenging climb in October, 1995.

> The next three routes ascend the steep orange wall (with a belay platform below it) located up and to the left of OUTSHINED and STANDARD ROUTE. From the two bolt OUTSHINED anchor, scramble carefully left across an exposed, narrow section of the access ledge to reach a single bolt anchor 30 feet to the left, and directly below LEATHERFACE's first pitch — the short, thin, vertical crack (5.11c) which is the usual way to reach the main belay platform above. The climbs are described from right to left.

NAUGAHYDE I 5.13a (***)

One of the best 5.13a's in New Hampshire. The route is essentially a direct start to LEATHERFACE's second pitch.

1. Climb Pitch one of LEATHERFACE up the thin, vertical crack (5.11c) with three bolts to a good ledge and a double bolt anchor. 40', 5.11c

2. Continue face climbing straight up past several bolts (5.12d) until joining LEATHERFACE just above the alcove. Two bolt anchor at the top. 60', 5.12d

FA: Bill Bentley August, 1992

LEATHERFACE I 5.12c

Toughen up those tips! Begin below a 10 foot high thin, vertical crack. The Pitch two alcove, often wet, needs to be completely dry. Modern rack.

1. Climb past three bolts up the thin, vertical crack (5.11c) to a good ledge with a two bolt anchor. 40', 5.11c

2. Head up a small corner into an alcove, then climb a crack system onto the face above. Continue past several bolts (5.12c) to a two bolt anchor. 60', 5.12c

FA: Bill Bentley October, 1991

INDIAN SUNBURN I 5.12a (**)

Rave reviews, but bring plenty of chalk — and sunblock. Begin 20 feet to the left of LEATHERFACE's second pitch.

1. Climb Pitch one of LEATHERFACE to a two bolt anchor. 40', 5.11c

2. Face climb up the steep, bolt-protected face (5.12a) just to the left of LEATHERFACE to another double bolt belay/rappel anchor. 60', 5.12a

FA: Bill Bentley July, 1992

George Hurley on the first ascent of Wild Calling (5.10b) in 1990. Photograph by Bruce Borylo.

SUNDOWN – THE FAR CLIFF

This long and complex cliff has slowly but surely become a more popular destination, but locating the base of routes is still difficult, especially on the cliff's right-hand side. There are several ways to reach the Far Cliff. While the first approach is definitely longer, it promises certain success for the first time visitor. With increased use, the shorter, second approach trail will undoubtedly become easier to follow and the route of choice.

- **Approach #1:** Hike along the Boulder Loop Trail, turning left and uphill at the first signposted trail junction so that your are walking the loop in a clockwise direction. Hike past the first overlook (located on top of Sundown's Main Cliff), continuing along the path through the woods. About four minutes later, below the level of the overlook at a small col or saddle in the woods, you will see Sundown's Far Cliff on your right. Head east, bushwhacking downhill, then traverse along the base of the Far Cliff until you spot your climb.

- **Approach #2:** Faster, but slightly harder to follow. Hike along the base of Sundown's Main Cliff past the Roof Routes and the Alcohol Wall until the Main Cliff finally peters out. Straight ahead is Gill's Groove Crag, home to GILL'S GROOVE and its companion route, SCORPION ARETE. Hike uphill and past this cliff to the right—once on top, bear up and slightly left for five minutes and you'll reach the base of Sundown's Far Cliff in the vicinity of PRESSURE DROP and the Orange Wall.

- **Approach #3:** To reach any of the climbs on the right side of the Far Cliff, hike in along the right-hand, counterclockwise portion of the Boulder Loop Trail. When you finally see the Far Cliff on your left through the woods, bushwhack over to it.

Routes are now described from left to right across the Far Cliff, starting with the climbs located on two small cliffs, Call Of The Wild Cliff and Gill's Groove Crag, which are situated just below the left end of Sundown's Far Cliff, below (and to the east) of the forested saddle between Sundown's Main Cliff and the Far Cliff. The Call Of The Wild Cliff is the higher of the two outcrops, while Gill's Groove Crag, identified by its striking dihedral, is the lower cliff.

CALL OF THE WILD CLIFF

CALL OF THE WILD I 5.8
Start on the left side of the cliff at the base of a left-facing dihedral.
1. Climb up a blocky, left-facing corner, moving over a small roof at mid height, to the top. 90', 5.8
FA: Ed Webster & Kurt Winkler May 18, 1982

WILD CALLING I 5.10b

Begin 15 feet downhill and to the right of CALL OF THE WILD at the left side of the highest part of a small, blocky buttress.

1. Climb up the buttress until you can traverse right to a rectangular block sticking at an angle out of a horizontal crack 30 feet above the ground. Stand on top of the block, then climb up and right through a roof (5.10b) before heading straight up a face to the top. 65', 5.10b

FA: George Hurley & Bruce Borylo April 19, 1990

WILD JOURNEY I 5.10b

Thirty feet right of WILD CALLING's blocky buttress is a right-pointing flake.

1. From on top of the flake, traverse left five feet, climb up to a roof, then traverse right under the roof to a prominent, blocky handhold on the lip of the roof. Pull past the roof, then angle left up the face to a good ledge. 50', 5.10b

2. Finish up edges and horizontal cracks to the top. 15', 5.7

FA: George Hurley & Bill Jurney April 14, 1990

GILL'S GROOVE CRAG

GILL'S GROOVE I 5.12b (**)

A difficult route up the clean-cut, overhanging dihedral splitting the center of the small crag downhill and to the right of the Call Of The Wild Cliff. Bring a modern rack with many small wired nuts and small cams.

1. After traversing in from the left, stem and layback up the dihedral (5.12b) using a fingertip crack for progress. 70', 5.12

FA: Jerry Handren & Chris Gill October 29, 1986

SCORPION ARETE I 5.11a (**)

The sharp, attractive-looking arete just to the right of GILL'S GROOVE. Normal rack—but watch out for the sting in the tail!

1. Starting below GILL'S GROOVE, traverse right to get established on the arete. A series of hard layback moves (piton; 5.11a) lead up the spectacular arete, including a few more difficult moves near the top. 70', 5.11a

FA: George Hurley & Andy Ross November 18, 1989

SUNDOWN – THE FAR CLIFF

PANORAMA I 5.5
This is the first climb you'll see when walking down from the saddle below the left end of Sundown's Far Cliff. A sharp, jutting flake forms a triangular recess at the base next to two white birch trees.
1. Climb the crack up the right side of the recess (5.5), layback a flake on the left to ledges, and climb sharp flakes up two final walls. 125', 5.5
FA: Kurt Winkler & Ed Webster May 18, 1982

MISS SCARLET WITH THE ROPE IN THE CONSERVATORY I 5.6
A mysterious climb whose true identity is seldom revealed. Could it also have been Colonel Mustard? Around the corner to the right of PANORAMA is a small face bounded by a gully on the right. The route still needs cleaning.
1. From the gully, step left onto the face, and climb a right-slanting corner past a pine tree. Fun moves up a flake system on the right gain a ledge on the left, then a shallow corner leads to the top. 125', 5.6
FA: Cherra Wyllie & Ed Webster May 25, 1982

GREEN DIHEDRAL I 5.5
Most of the Far Cliff's left side overhangs quite dramatically. A big V corner slices through this overhang, making a natural (if dirty) line of ascent.
1. Climb the back of the groove, making interesting moves (5.5) past small overhangs on the left wall near the top. 130', 5.5
FA: George Hurley, Ray Franzem, & David Cadorette May 11, 1982

GREEN DIHEDRAL BYPASS I 5.6
If this route is ever cleaned, it could be much easier.
1. Climb the parallel crack system on the groove's right wall. 130', 5.6
FA: George Hurley & Kathryn Rogers May 8, 1982

CANNIBAL CRACK I 5.10b
Don't be eaten alive. Bring some Friends for protection.
1. Jam up the awkward, strenuous, overhanging offwidth/hand crack (5.10b) just to the right of GREEN DIHEDRAL to a tree. 35', 5.10b
FA: Ed Webster May 25, 1982

OMINOUS CRACK I 5.7
The unsettling-looking chimney crack to the right of CANNIBAL CRACK. The wedged blocks are secure, luckily. They're big!
1. Climb up to a piton deep within the chimney below the chockstones, then move out horizontally around the outside of the blocks. 80', 5.7
2. Mantle onto the next block, and offwidth up the crack to the finish.
HISTORY: George Hurley, David Cadorette, & Ray Franzem made the route's first ascent on May 11, 1982.

458 THE KANCAMAGUS HIGHWAY AREA

SUNDOWN LEDGE - THE FAR CLIFF

A.		The Orange Wall	Page	460
B.		**LITTLE ROCK LINE** I 5.10a	Page	460
C.	*	**BLANK ON THE MAP** II 5.10a	Page	461
D.	*	**PRESSURE DROP** II 5.11b	Page	461
E.	**	**THWARTHOG** II 5.9	Page	461
F.	*	**REBELLIOUS YOUTH** I 5.10b or 5.10c	Page	462
G.	**	**WAYWARD SON** I 5.11b	Page	463
H.	*	**BAD TO THE BONE** I 5.11b	Page	463
I.	*	**THE BLACK CORNER** I 5.6	Page	463
J.	*	**BROKEN ENGLISH** II 5.9 (or 5.10b)	Page	467

REGGAE PARTY I 5.11b, A2
This aid climb ascends the wild roof to the left of THE GASH. Care is needed when touching some semi-loose, VW-sized blocks!
1. Start free (5.11b), then aid climb an obvious crack system (A2) out the large roof/wall over the lip to a ledge on the left. 60' 5.11b, A2

FA: Bob Parrott & Dave Lattimer May 15, 1989

THE GASH I 5.10b
Guaranteed to bring out the punk in you, if you're blonde or black. Carry big gear for what little protection there is. Start 60 feet right of OMINOUS CRACK.
1. Climb the awesome, overhanging chimney/offwidth crack to the top. 5.10b

HISTORY: Two British climbers nicknamed "Blonde Nick" & "Black Nick" (Nick Donnelly & Choe Brooks) made the first ascent in the Spring of 1981.

ORANGE PEEL I 5.8
Ascends the prominent outside corner, with some very bad rock in the beginning, 30 feet to the right of THE GASH.
1. Climb an easy slab for 20 feet, then traverse right along a narrow, down-sloping shelf just above a small overhang to a stack of loose, square blocks on the cliff's outside corner. From on top of the blocks, climb up and right into the route's first good crack, laybacking & jamming to a good ledge. 75', 5.8
2. Follow a dihedral straight up (5.4) to a tree ledge. 45', 5.4
3. Continue the route's straight line up yet another corner (which has a large tree in it 30 feet up), and finish left up a short buttress to the top. 80', 5.2

FA: George Hurley & Mike Guravage July 2, 1982

THE ORANGE WALL
This superb, fantastically steep, clean, orange face is located 40 feet left of LITTLE ROCK LINE, and 200 feet left of PRESSURE DROP.

WHIPPING POST I 5.11c (**)
This spectacular route ascends the right side of the Orange Wall. Belay at a birch tree growing at the cliff base. Bring a small normal rack.
1. Climb carefully up blocky bulges (5.7) for 40 feet to a large ledge system, and climb an overhanging, right-facing corner up to the second bolt. Pop right, then do the mantleshelf-from-hell (5.11c) to reach the third bolt. Continue straight up to the overlap above, clip the top bolt (above the lip), and pull past the exposed overlap (5.10b) to a two bolt anchor. 80', 5.11c

FA: Ken Reville, Maury McKinney, & Jeff Montgomery June, 1992

LITTLE ROCK LINE I 5.10a
Around the corner to the right of the Orange Wall (and roughly 200 feet to the left of PRESSURE DROP), at the left-hand end of a band of roofs, is a 20 foot V corner 45 feet off the ground.

SUNDOWN LEDGE - FAR CLIFF (WHIPPING POST & PRESSURE DROP)

1. Climb a vertical crack to a loose flake, then step right onto a stance below the dihedral. Climb up the clean-cut corner (peg), then make several difficult stemming moves over a roof (5.10a). Belay on one of several stances. 80', 5.10a Watch out for rope drag at the roof.
2. After 40 feet of 5.5, scramble diagonally right to the top. 5.5
FA: George Hurley & Kevin Short   May 20, 1982
FFA: Ed Webster & Kurt Winkler   May 21, 1982

BLANK ON THE MAP II 5.10a (*)
Not as alluring as previously thought, it's still an exotic adventure. At the right-hand end of the roofs, 40 feet to the left of PRESSURE DROP, a left-facing V corner breaks out two separate roofs. Carry a modern rack.
1. Stem and layback up the corner to the first roof (5.10a), move by it, then step right onto the face. Surmount another overhang and belay on a small stance under a roof at the top of a narrow corner. 5.10a
2. On the right, climb an awkward, flaring slot (5.9) to good holds, then make a series of tricky mantleshelfs (one is 5.9+) diagonally right to the top. 5.9+
FA: Todd Swain & Ed Webster   May 26, 1982

VARIATION: BLANK IN THE HEAD I 5.10b
2a. Before the 5.9+ mantleshelf, traverse easily left 15 feet across a ledge to a thin, vertical crack. Protect, then make a difficult mantle (5.10b) to better holds. Another mantle and a short chimney behind a block gains the top. 50', 5.10b
FA: Dick Peterson, Brad White, & Jose Abeyta   September, 1985

PRESSURE DROP II 5.11b (*)
A real heart stopper. From a distance, the centerpiece route of the Far Cliff is also the easiest climb to locate: the central, dihedral system in white rock. Carry some large gear—plus lots of nerve.
1. From below the corner, layback up the side of a block (5.8), then, staying left of large blocks, climb a corner to a belay ledge on the right. 5.8
2. Handtraverse out left, then follow the main dihedral to a painfully obvious, overhanging hand/fist crack. Jam around a large, wedged flake (scary) to a poor rest in a flared slot. After a long reach to a bucket, make another handtraverse left to a vertical crack and the top. 5.11b
HISTORY: Pitch one had been climbed earlier. Rick Fleming & Bob Rotert made the first complete ascent in May, 1980.

THWARTHOG II 5.9 (**)
A recommended climb up the steep wall below the scenic overlook on the hiking trail. Start 15 feet to the right of PRESSURE DROP.
1. Climb up a slab to a short dihedral (5.9; bolt) to square-cut holds leading to a roof, then traverse right to a good ledge. 80', 5.9

2. Diagonal up left past a fixed warthog to a yellow, right-facing corner capped by a roof. Pull over it, then move out left along a thin seam (5.9) to a ledge. A short finger crack leads to a white birch tree. 140', 5.9 Scramble off left into the forest.

HISTORY: Todd Swain & Jim Frangos climbed Pitch one on aid on April 27, 1983. Todd Swain, Pete Yost, & Pete Axelson returned the next day and free climbed the route's first complete ascent. The bolt on Pitch one was added later.

THE BLACK WALL I 5.7+ R

Scramble up left from THE BLACK CORNER to an obvious, left-facing flake above a tree ledge to the right of THWARTHOG.

1. Climb the flake to a small pine tree, then diagonal left to a right-facing flake. Continue up left across a steep, lichen-covered wall on some scary flakes to a traverse ledge, and escape left to THWARTHOG. 150', 5.7+ R

FA: Todd Swain & Jim Frangos   April 27, 1983

DRAGGIN I 5.8+

Start this scenic tour at two large pines on the tree ledge at the base of the upper face below the Far Cliff lookout, left of THE BLACK CORNER.

1. Face climb up and right from the left-hand pine, then move left to a prominent alcove with a small birch. Move left again from the top of the alcove, and traverse horizontally left 50 feet to the face's left-hand shoulder, then climb the final 30 feet to the summit. 150', 5.8+

HISTORY: George Hurley, Gail Effron, & Larry Knicely climbed the first ascent using two points of aid on June 8, 1982. George Hurley & Ted Stryker made the first free ascent on June 18, 1982.

THE LOOKOUT WALL

The next four routes share the same approach. Hike clockwise along the Boulder Loop Trail to the top of the Far Cliff and an obvious, open granite slab lookout at the top center of the cliff. Find a double, welded cold shut anchor in a bathtub-shaped depression near the edge. REBELLIOUS YOUTH rappels from the cold shuts 140 feet down and slightly left (or right, facing out) to a small pine growing on a ledge, while WAYWARD SON, WILD AT HEART, and BAD TO THE BONE rappel 100 feet straight down to reach a good ledge at large, twin pine trees. From left to right, the routes on the Lookout Wall are:

REBELLIOUS YOUTH I 5.10b or 5.10c (*)

Rappel 140 feet from the bathtub to a small pine tree that is down and left of the twin pines which are the communal anchor and starting point for the next three routes. This climb is easier than its right-hand neighbors.

1. Climb straight up vertical cracks to a roof (bolt), pull over, then face climb steeply to the traverse ledge on DRAGGIN. Continue straight up into

a large, left-facing dihedral with a peg in the right wall. From here, either step left, climb up, and cut back right (5.10b), or stay in the corner (5.10c), climbing a series of strenuous flakes. Finish more easily to the top, and belay in the bathtub on the right. 140', 5.10b or 5.10c
FA: Ian Cruickshank, Dick Peterson, & Brad White   October 23, 1991

WAYWARD SON I 5.11b (**)

The hardest and best quality route on the Lookout Wall. Rappel down to the large, twin pine trees, and begin at the left-hand pine. Bring small Flexible Friends. There are six fixed pitons en route.

1. From the left pine, move up and left to a ledge below a short, steep wall (5.8). Now move up and left to a vertical corner capped by a roof. Boulder up the corner's right-hand arete (pin), then step right to a right-facing flake/corner (peg). Climb straight up to an overhanging block (piton), then make a hard move up and left (5.11b) onto a continuously overhanging wall. Face climb straight up the wall's center past horizontal breaks and edges, protected by three more pitons, to the top. Belay in the bathtub. 100', 5.11b
FA: Brad White, Ian Cruickshank, & Dick Peterson   October 23, 1991

WILD AT HEART I 5.11a (*)

Rappel down to the two, large pines, and start as for WAYWARD SON at the left-hand pine tree. Modern rack required.

1. From the pine, move up and left to a ledge below a short, steep wall (5.8). Above a big ledge, head right up several blocks on good holds, then step left into an overhanging alcove. Crank up (5.11a) onto a slab under a roof, then exit out the roof's left side into a left-facing corner followed to the top. 100', 5.11a
FA: Brad White & Ian Cruickshank   November 6, 1991

BAD TO THE BONE I 5.11b (*)

Rappel down to the twin pine trees as for WAYWARD SON, and start at the right-hand pine. Bring a modern rack. Steep, strenuous, and sustained.

1. Climb 30 feet up and right to the base of a steep wall, continuing past a pin, a bolt, and another peg up a slightly overhanging face to a second bolt. Snap right (5.11b) to a good hold, and at the horizontal crack above, handtraverse left, then move up and left to an awkward, overhanging corner. 120', 5.11b
FA: Brad White with Mike Hardert   November 9, 1991

THE BLACK CORNER I 5.6 (*)

Right of PRESSURE DROP and the Lookout Wall is one of the Far Cliff's fairly major features: a left-leaning corner system with a broken gully below it. The next four climbs all start by scrambling up this gully.

1. Climb straight up the back of the main corner, past a small overhang halfway up, to the top. 90', 5.6

HISTORY: This was probably one of the first climbs at Sundown's Far Cliff. It could be BLACK FLY (5.6), done by Mark Hudon & partner in 1974. The first recorded ascent was by George Hurley & David Cadorette on May 6, 1982.

BON VIVANT'S WALL I 5.6 (*)
1. Climb to the top of a pointed flake about 12 feet to the right of THE BLACK CORNER. From the top of the flake, follow a crack system straight up to a chimney and the top. 70', 5.6

HISTORY: Another possible early climb on the cliff, George Hurley & Kathryn Rogers made the first recorded ascent on May 8, 1982.

RHODE ISLAND MEMORANDUM I 5.7 Another little known climb.
1. The vertical crack system (5.7) just right of BON VIVANT'S WALL. 5.7
FA: Ed De Santo & partner

RAVEN'S WAY I 5.7
Ascends the steep wall 30 feet to the right of THE BLACK CORNER. The second pitch begins under an overhang 15 feet to the right of the pointed flake on BON VIVANT'S WALL.
1. Start up the easy corner approach to THE BLACK CORNER, or staying about 30 feet to the left, climb up three, short, steep faces and cracks. 150', 5.7
2. Climb an inside corner to the left edge of the overhang, traverse left several feet (past a raven's nest, in which there were three chicks on the FA), and move up to a clump of birch trees. Step right, climb a lichen-covered face on sharp holds to a horizontal finger crack, traverse right, and follow an exposed edge to the finish. 5.7
FA: George Hurley, Tom Scofield, & Bob Mayo May 16, 1982

> The Far Cliff's next section right of the preceding climbs has trees and blocky outcrops. The farther right you hike, the better the rock becomes until finally you'll reach a steep nose or buttress offering the following climbs.

HURRY UP SUNDOWN I 5.5
As the rock begins to improve in quality, scramble up to a ledge system one third of the way up the cliff. This seldom climbed route ascends a vertical crack system to the left of two, small pine trees growing side-by-side on a steep, blocky wall. There is a long, thin flake or block on the ledge at the crack's base.
1. Starting behind the block, climb a crack to corners and a gully, then move up the gully to a belay at trees on the left.
2. Continue up more grooves and cracks to the top.
FA: Kurt Winkler, Dick Greenwood, & Joe Perez September, 1979

SPIDERS ON HOLIDAY I 5.7+
Left of CIRCADIAN RHYTHM is a buttress with a large block at its base.

1. From the left end of the block, step onto a horizontal finger crack and foot ramp. Follow this left for 12 feet to a break at a hanging flake. Move up and left, mantling onto a shelf (5.7+), and belay off the right-hand pine mentioned in HURRY UP SUNDOWN. 5.7+

2. Directly above, surmount a loose-looking roof at a V notch. Loose 5.6

FA: Kurt Winkler, Steve van Donselaar, & Dominick Palmer April 23, 1983

ARE YOU EXPERIENCED? I 5.9, A3

The experience may well lie in finding this route. Amidst the blocky section of the Far Cliff is a prominent, eight foot roof on the left side of a small gully.

1. Tricky aid on thin pegs (one fixed) leads out the roof (A3). After the crack widens to fingers, jam up to a tree ledge. 5.9, A3 Rappel off of a unique tree on the right, or finish up dirty cracks to the top of the cliff.

FA: Jay Depeter & Rob Adair November 24, 1984

CIRCADIAN RHYTHM I 5.7

This and the next three climbs are located roughly 300 feet to the right of HURRY UP SUNDOWN. Start at a right-facing dihedral which has a roof in it 40 feet above the ground. You can rappel off the top with one rope.

1. Climb the corner to a cramped position below the roof, then exit right onto a small ledge. Be careful of jamming the rope at the lip of the roof. 50', 5.7

2. Move up left to a small birch, step right, and finish straight up. 45', 5.5

FA: George Hurley & Kurt Winkler June 1, 1982

PENTATONIC SCALE I 5.8

Ascends the crack between CIRCADIAN RHYTHM and CIRCADIAN CRACK. Large and small spruce trees grow four feet up in the crack.

1. Climb easily up the crack system for about 50 feet to a small overhang. Hand jam and face climb (5.8) over this steep section. 75', 5.8

FA: George Hurley, Cleve Pozar, & Mingus Pozar June 27, 1982

CIRCADIAN CRACK I 5.8 (*)

A recommended hand crack 25 feet right of CIRCADIAN RHYTHM, which is also the rappel route back down. Good nut protection.

1. Climb straight up the crack without much trouble until it becomes shallow and overhangs for 10 feet—which is, not surprisingly, the crux. 75', 5.8

FA: George Hurley & Kurt Winkler June 1, 1982

THE HAWK I 5.7

Just to the right of CIRCADIAN CRACK are two neighboring routes, ascending either one of a pair of left-facing corners.

1. Climb up the left-hand, left-facing dihedral to a large block. Surmount the block (5.7), and continue to the top. 125', 5.7

FA: Joe Perez & Judy Perez Summer, 1974

PEREZ DIHEDRAL I 5.4 (*)
This is the right-hand of the two corners, just right of THE HAWK.
1. Climb up the face to an old piton, then continue up the right-hand of the two dihedrals to a long, narrow cave with a boulder sitting in it. Climb over the cave opening, or go through the cave, move back left to the corner, and continue to the top. 130', 5.4

HISTORY: The route had an old peg on it. Joe Perez & Judy Perez made the first recorded ascent in the Spring of 1974.

HIDDEN CHIMNEY I 5.0
This straightforward chimney to the right of PEREZ DIHEDRAL is all too easy to miss—plus the simplest route up Sundown's Far Cliff.
1. The climb is an easy, unexposed, well protected route to the top. 125', 5.0
FA: Joe Perez & Judy Perez Summer, 1974

SUPERBA I 5.5 (**)
A nice outing for its grade, with secure protection. The climb ascends the nose of the small buttress to the right of PEREZ DIHEDRAL. To reach the start, scramble up a 30 foot cliff band onto a tree ledge.
1. Climb a crack up the left side of a large block to a pine tree on a ledge 30 feet up. Continue to a birch growing beneath an overhang, step right, and climb a shallow, flat-sided slot to the top. 125', 5.5
FA: George Hurley & Stuyvesant Bearns June 4, 1982

GYMCRACK I 5.8 (*)
A variety of jamming is required for this exercise. Follows the slightly, right-leaning corner 15 feet to the right of SUPERBA.
1. Layback the strenuous corner (5.8) for 40 feet to a ledge. Belay here, or surmount a roof on the right, and climb more easily to a birch tree. Finish up an offwidth crack to the top of the cliff. 110', 5.8
FA: George Hurley, Wendy Anderson, & Stuyvesant Bearns June 4, 1982

GUILLOTINE I 5.8+
Midway between GYMCRACK and TRIPTYCH, find an oak tree growing out of a 10 foot tall dead tree stump. Above, a crack leads to a small cave.
1. Climb easily into the cave, exit left to ledges, then climb the face above the cave (5.8+) to a good ledge. Mantleshelf onto a higher ledge, then make a hard move right before reaching a belay ledge beside a large, wedged block in a corner (the GUILLOTINE). 80', 5.8+
2. From on top of the block, jam up a steep crack to the top. 25', 5.7
FA: George Hurley & Jean-Charles Lamoureux July 31, 1982

TRIPTYCH I 5.9
Forty feet to the right of GYMCRACK, and left of BROKEN ENGLISH,

look for a steep crack and inside corner beginning 30 feet above the ground and running up the cliff for 50 feet.

1. Climb to an overhang 20 feet up with a fixed pin at its right edge. A hard move (5.8) gains easier climbing that leads to a large belay ledge. 30', 5.8
2. Head up the crack/corner (5.9) for 50 feet to where it ends. 50', 5.9
3. Above, climb past small trees and the flat top of a small, pointed prow of rock just to the left of a major overhang to reach the cliff's top. 70', 5.4
FA: George Hurley & Kathryn Rogers   June 19, 1982

VOODOO CHILE I 5.11d
Fifty feet to the left of BROKEN ENGLISH is a razor thin, vertical crack. Small wired nuts, small Friends, & TCUs all are helpful.
1. Climb the thin crack system (5.10b) to detached blocks. 50', 5.10b
2. Head past a small roof following the same thin crack diagonally left. Belay up and right on a good ledge. 80', 5.11d
3. Finish as desired, up BROKEN ENGLISH or THE PUB CRAWL.
HISTORY: Jay Depeter & Rob Adair made the first ascent on November 24, 1984. After Rob Adair & Jerry Handren had earlier free climbed Pitch one, Jerry Handren & Chris Gill made the route's first free ascent on October 24, 1986.

BROKEN ENGLISH II 5.9 (or 5.10b) (*)
The right-hand side of the Far Cliff forms a distinctive, steep buttress or nose of rock. Two obvious dihedrals can be seen in profile when this buttress is viewed from the top of the Main Cliff at Sundown. BROKEN ENGLISH is the left-hand of these two corners, which is located about 100 feet to the right of GYMCRACK.
1. Jam and layback the right-diagonalling corner past a small roof at the start to a comfortable ledge with a small birch tree. 5.9
2. Layback a thin overlap on the left, and mantle onto a ledge (5.10b), or climb up to a horizontal crack above the belay, then traverse left (5.9) to reach the same ledge. Tree belay on the left. 5.9 or 5.10b
3. A 5.9 chimney crack leads to the top of the buttress. 5.9
FA: Michael Hartrich, Nick Donnelly (UK), & Albert Dow   Spring, 1981

VARIATION #1: **BODY ENGLISH** II 5.9+
1. Climb Pitch one of BROKEN ENGLISH, up the 5.9 leaning corner.
2a. Go horizontally left 20 feet, then climb up good, small edges to a birch tree on a big ledge (the same ledge as on BROKEN ENGLISH). 5.6
3a. Climb 20 feet up to a large pine tree, and finish up an offwidth crack (5.9+) 20 feet right of Pitch three of BROKEN ENGLISH. 5.9+
FA: Larry Hamilton & George Hurley   December 5, 1982

Michael Hartrich on the first ascent of The Pub Crawl (5.10d) in 1982. Photograph by Ed Webster.

DIRECT FINISH: **THE PUB CRAWL** I 5.10d (*)

Avoid guzzling too many pints at the pub—and use double ropes to avoid rope drag—or you could become paralytically drunk and unable to move.

1. Climb the first pitch of BROKEN ENGLISH, the 5.9 corner.
2b. Head up a small V groove to the left side of a large, jutting roof. Make an airy, strenuous handtraverse (peg) back right above the lip of the overhang (5.10d) to easier climbing up a face and a large, detached flake. 100', 5.10d
FA: Ed Webster & Michael Hartrich April 30, 1982

PINS & NEEDLES I 5.9 (*)

The right-hand of the two inside corners, located about 80 feet to the right of the BROKEN ENGLISH dihedral.

1. Layback the corner past a bulge (5.9; two pegs) to a tree. 5.9
2. Finish diagonally left up a face (5.7). Easier than it looks! 5.7

HISTORY: The first ascent is unknown. Michael Hartrich & Albert Dow free climbed the route in the Spring of 1981.

CHILLY WILLY I 5.8

On the far, right-hand end of Sundown's Far Cliff is a right-leaning ramp bordered by a steep yellow wall.

1. Climb up the ramp (5.8) to a good ledge with small birches. 5.8
2. Surmount a short, dirty headwall to the top of the cliff.
FA: Jay Depeter & Bill Holland November 18, 1984

SUNDOWN – THE OUTBACK CLIFF

Located to the west of Sundown's Main Cliff is the Outback Cliff, a much less frequently visited 150 foot crag. Even when the trees have lost their leaves, the cliff is only briefly visible from the Kancamagus Highway. When the foliage is full, you'd never guess the cliff existed. Luckily, the approach is not as mystifying as for Lost and Found Ledges, but directions should be followed carefully. Park in the lot next to the Albany Covered Bridge and walk west along the dirt logging road following the northern bank of the Swift River. Six or seven minutes from the bridge, turn right on the first old logging road. Follow this across a stream, continue parallel to the stream, and when the road turns right, bushwhack alongside the stream for another 20 minutes uphill to the base of the cliff. Avoid getting sidetracked by scruffy looking cliffs on the left. From the Covered Bridge, the approach should take about 30 minutes. The routes are now described from left to right.

UP FRONT I 5.8
The left-most climb on the cliff, farther left of ADAGIO.
1. Climb up a prominent, shallow corner. Move right when the corner ends, then back left, and up to the top. 5.8
FA: Michael Hartrich & Al Rubin October 16, 1983

ADAGIO I 5.8
Start 10 feet to the right of a descent gully at the cliff's far, left-hand side, at a series of small corners and overhangs angling right.
1. Climb these features diagonally right to the top. 60', 5.8
FA: George Hurley & Paul Ledoux September 9, 1984

CULTURE SPONGE I 5.10d R (**)
Begin 10 feet to the left of a detached flake at the base of the cliff.
1. Layback a right-curving flake, undercling up to a tiny overlap, then step left onto an improbable slab. Above a horizontal crack, face climb straight up the face (5.10d R) to the top. 90', 5.10d R
HISTORY: Michael Hartrich & Al Rubin climbed most of the route on September 9, 1984, before exiting left onto ADAGIO. In the Summer of 1985, Michael Hartrich & Joe Lentini completed the direct line.

COUNTER CULTURE I 5.10d (**)
Start as for CULTURE SPONGE.
1. Climb up a crack to an overlap, pull over it (5.8), and face climb straight up past a bolt (5.10d) to the top. 90', 5.10d
FA: Dick Peterson & Brad White October 9, 1989

PHANTOM OF THE WOODS I 5.8 or 5.9 (*)
With its interchangeable finishes, this climb begins directly behind the detached flake sitting on the ground on the left side of the cliff.

1. Climb a scoop-like depression up and right past a small ledge, exiting right below the top at a one foot wide overlap. Another shallow groove and a layback flake gains the top. 5.8 An alternate finish stays left on the face near the top, climbing up edges and flakes (5.9), then merging. 5.8 or 5.9

HISTORY: Michael Hartrich & Rob Walker made the first ascent using the right-hand finish in the Summer of 1982. The following Summer, Michael Hartrich & Lee Spiller added the harder direct finish.

THE SUMMER OF '82 I 5.9

To the right of the detached flake is a large ash tree.

1. Climb a finger crack to the right end of a small roof 15 feet up. Jam over the roof (5.9) then, when the crack peters out, face climb up left to a stance. Finish 15 feet to the right of PHANTOM OF THE WOODS, following indistinct grooves (5.7) straight up. 120', 5.9

FA: Michael Hartrich & Lee Spiller Summer, 1982

WALKABOUT I 5.9

Five feet to the right of the ash tree is a right-diagonalling flake.

1. Layback to the top of the flake (5.9), then climb a short face via thin finger cracks up and right to more flakes and a small, flat ledge. 80', 5.9
2. Climb up to a small roof, and exit right to the top. 35', 5.7

FA: Michael Hartrich & Al Rubin October 16, 1983

SUSPENDED SENTENCE I 5.11d (**)

Superb climbing, but with strenuous, committing moves. Exactly in the middle of the main face is a clean, shallow groove with several small roofs.

1. Climb the face directly (pitons) to reach the first roof, move up to a bolt, then hard climbing leads up a thin crack (5.11d) past pitons to a stance (bolt). Climb to a higher bolt, then traverse right (piton) to good holds (bolt). Easier climbing takes you to a good ledge with a two bolt anchor. 75', 5.11d

HISTORY: Bill Lowther & Gerry Lortie made the first ascent over four days in October, 1995, finally completing the pitch on October 12, 1995.

FALL CLEANING I 5.8+

Start 20 feet to the right of SUSPENDED ANIMATION up on a higher tree ledge with a clump of trees.

1. Climb up to a roof, then traverse left to the base of a finger crack that widens to hands. When the crack ends, traverse right to a stance. Steep climbing on good holds gains a good belay ledge with a piton & bolt anchor. 40', 5.8+

FA: Bill Lowther, rope-solo October 17, 1995

PARALLEL WORLDS I 5.11b

Fifty feet to the right of the detached flake below the start of PHANTOM OF THE WOODS are twin dihedrals. Modern rack. PARALLEL WORLDS is the left-hand corner, REPEAT PERFORMANCE is the right corner. Bring a modern rack with small wired nuts.

1. Climb the shallow, left-hand corner to its end (5.11b), step up and right, then back left, face climbing to a layback flake, and up to a good ledge. 70', 5.11b

2. Finish up flakes to the top of the cliff.

HISTORY: Michael Hartrich & Lee Spiller climbed the initial corner, exiting right up REPEAT PERFORMANCE in the Summer of 1982. Chris Gill & Michael Hartrich did the route's first complete ascent in the Summer of 1987.

REPEAT PERFORMANCE I 5.10b (*)

The right-hand dihedral, the full length line. Standing room only!

1. Climb the corner past an overhang into a small sentry box, then exit (5.10b) by circling up to the right. Easier climbing gains a small ledge. 80', 5.10b

2. Face climb up to a jutting block or roof, pass it to the right, then move left to easy ground and the top. 45', 5.8

FA: Michael Hartrich & Rob Walker Summer, 1982

VARIATION FINISH: **HAT TRICK** I 5.9+ Three times a charm?

2a. Climb ramps out to the right, making a long traverse across an angling crack in the steep wall above the cliff's overhanging center. Finish up an exposed outside corner below the right-hand of two large pines growing on top. 75', 5.9+

FA: Michael Hartrich & Mack Johnson September 2, 1984

INTERZONE I 5.12c (***)

You might ozone out on how much the route overhangs the base: by 35 feet, and the climb's only 70 feet long! One of the best and certainly amongst the most overhanging free pitches in the White Mountains. Scramble up onto a ledge 40 feet above the ground, to the left of HYPERSPACE. INTERZONE begins off the left-hand end of this ledge. Nine bolts lead to the anchor.

1. Face climb slightly right, then up the center of a radically overhanging wall past nine bolts (5.12c) to a double bolt belay/rappel anchor. 70', 5.12c

FA: Jerry Handren 1993

BEATING A DEAD HORSE I 5.11c (**)

Another perfectly good sport route ruined by all natural protection! Begin from the right side of the INTERZONE starting ledge 40 feet up, 50 feet to the right of INTERZONE. Modern rack. Chances are pretty good that there won't be any life left in your arms at the top of this pitch!

1. Climb through a series of strenuous overhangs, protected by natural gear (5.11c), before traversing left to the INTERZONE two bolt anchor. 70', 5.11c

FA: Steve Larson & Chris Gill August, 1993

THE PORTALEDGE ROUTE I 5.9

The central free climb up the cliff's tallest section. Begin below a prominent, right-diagonalling ramp, just to the right of a smooth, overhanging, white buttress called the Nose. Scramble onto a shelf 15 feet up.

1. Make a hard 5.9 boulder move to avoid some poison ivy on the left, then trend right up an overhanging wall past blocks. Above, step out left, then climb a vertical, finger crack out onto the upper ridge and to the top. 125', 5.9

HISTORY: Michael Hartrich & Mack Johnson made the first ascent on September 2, 1984. Mack forgot his climbing shoes, and followed in sneakers!

HYPERSPACE II 5.10b (***)

This exhilarating, well-named voyage through a succession of roofs and overhangs could easily launch you into space at warp speed. Very popular. Fifty feet right of THE PORTALEDGE ROUTE, locate two large trees (an oak and maple) growing inches from the cliff, and 12 feet apart. Above looms an impressive array of unlikely-looking overhangs. Protection is good, with work.

1. Starting between these two trees, face climb up and slightly left, around a small overlap, then back diagonally right up a steep slab or ramp (5.9) to reach a small belay ledge beneath an overhang. 100', 5.9

2. Traverse left a few feet, then climb an awkward V chimney to a roof. Reach out left over the lip and pull into yet another short V chimney. When trapped again by another roof, launch left (exciting 5.10b), and mantleshelf to easier climbing up a ridge and corners. 50', 5.10b

FA: George Hurley & Paul Ledoux   September 9, 1984

> Uphill to the right of HYPERSPACE are a series of stacked slabs, large right-facing, inside corners, and sharp aretes.

THE POTATO CHIP I 5.5

Eighty feet to the right of HYPERSPACE is a jutting buttress.

1. Jam up a pair of parallel, fist cracks to a birch tree, then angle right onto an arete. Belay at a tree above. 30', 5.5

2. Climb a right-facing flake/corner to the top of the cliff. 60', 5.5

FA: Todd Swain & Tiger Burns   Palm Sunday, 1983

DEPTHS OF DOOM I 5.4

On either side of THE POTATO CHIP are two dirty chimneys.

1. Climb the right-hand chimney (5.4) to the trees. 5.4

FA: Unknown.

PALE MARY I 5.8 R

Tread gently, and try not to blanch. A scary route with some loose blocks. Right of DEPTHS OF DOOM are two, parallel, right-facing corners.

1. Climb the first third of the right-hand dihedral. At a break, traverse left into the left corner, and move up this past two blocks, bridging and jamming up wide cracks, finally escaping left to a ledge. 5.8 R

SUNDOWN LEDGE - OUTBACK CLIFF (HYPERSPACE) 473

George Hurley leading Hyperspace (5.10b) in 1986. Photograph by Ed Webster.

474 THE KANCAMAGUS HIGHWAY AREA

2. Above, climb up the face to an arete and the top.
FA: Michael Hartrich & Rob Walker Summer, 1983

REPTILIAN RESPONSE I 5.8
Start 35 feet to the left of the wet cave at the base of BELFRY.
1. Climb good face holds up to a small birch tree 12 feet above the ground, then follow the line of least resistance up to the right edge of a large roof. Stay in the corner above to an excellent flat ledge (same as BELFRY). 90', 5.7
2. Move right and down slightly through a crawlspace between blocks to the base of the next corner on the right. Climb this dihedral (5.7) to another good belay ledge with trees. 70', 5.7
3. Escape easily to the right, or move up and left into a V chimney. 40', 5.8
FA: George Hurley & Joe Hayes June 3, 1985

BELFRY I 5.8
To find the start of this route, locate a wet cave at ground level with a 5.5 right-facing, layback corner above it. This corner is a major feature of the cliff, up a steep wall separated by descent gullies on the left and right, roughly halfway between HYPERSPACE and the CANNON FODDER Buttress. Begin 10 feet left of the cave. BELFRY and its sister route, REPTILIAN RESPONSE, criss-cross at the top of their first pitches. Beware of bats!
1. Climb a right-facing corner rising above a maple tree. When the corner curves right and becomes unfriendly, angle slightly left up the face heading for a clump of sumac in a major inside corner (the corner above the sumac being Pitch two of REPTILIAN RESPONSE). Just below the sumac, climb up and left through a crawlspace between jutting blocks to an excellent, flat belay ledge (that is also shared with REPTILIAN RESPONSE). 85', 5.7
2. Climb directly up the corner (5.8) above the belay. Cracks on the left wall make the corner easier than it looks. 50', 5.8
HISTORY: Michael Hartrich & Lee Spiller climbed the initial flake, and finished up and right (5.8) in the Summer of 1983. George Hurley & John Tremblay climbed the route described above on June 2, 1985.

SLIP'N SLIME I 5.5 (*)
Start just to the right of the wet cave.
1. Layback up the prominent, moderate, right-facing corner (5.5) to an easy descent gully that angles back down to the right through the woods. 100', 5.5
FA: Paul Ledoux, Al Rubin, & George Hurley September 9, 1984

SHAKE'N BAKE I 5.6
Forty feet to the right of SLIP'N SLIME is a 30 foot crack/flake.
1. Climb the flake to an overlap, then layback up right to the trees. 5.6
FA: Michael Hartrich & Lee Spiller Summer, 1983

> The next two routes are located on the steep and impressive buttress between SHAKE'N BAKE and CIRCUS.

IRON LUNG I 5.10d (*)
Begin 100 feet uphill to the right of HYPERSPACE. Wired nuts, large size Friends, and double ropes are all a must. A complex route.
1. Start up a slab to a small roof, pull past the roof on the left, then traverse right just above the lip (5.10d) past two bolts to a thin hand crack on an arete. Follow the arete to the belay anchor. 75', 5.10d
FA: Bob Parrott & Dave Lattimer   Spring, 1990

LOVE CRACK I 5.12b (***)
Start 50 feet to the right of IRON LUNG. Superb crack and face climbing up the right-hand side of the buttress. Bring a wide selection of Friends, and make sure you start at the very bottom of the crack!
1. Jam up the right-diagonalling crack (5.11a) to a rest on the right at a horizontal break, then when the crack ends, face climb straight up (bolt; 5.12b) to a double bolt anchor at the top of the arete. 80', 5.12b
HISTORY: Bob Parrott & Barry Rugo climbed the initial part of the crack in October, 1989. A month later, Bob Parrott & Rob Adair added the upper crux, utilizing an easier start on the right. Barry Rugo & Andy Ross made the first continuous ascent of the entire line, without using the rest, in July, 1990.

> Farther uphill to the right is the 100 foot high CANNON FODDER Buttress, bordered on both sides by wooded descent gullies.

CIRCUS I 5.9
Walk halfway up the left-hand gully until below a large pine growing on top.
1. Climb up a shallow, white, right-facing corner, following a good hand crack in the middle section of the pitch. 75', 5.9
FA: George Hurley, Al Rubin, & Paul Ledoux   September 9, 1984

CANNON FODDER I 5.11b (*)
Twenty feet to the right of CIRCUS is a bomb bay flake.
1. Layback a thin flake on the right into a right-facing corner with some loose rock. Move up into an overhanging flaring V (5.11b), gaining the wide crack up above. Belay on a sloping ledge. 90', 5.11b
2. A short dihedral leads to the top of the cliff.
HISTORY: After Hartrich sacrificed himself to place the pro, Neil Cannon, Michael Hartrich, & Al Rubin blasted up the first ascent on October 10, 1983.

VETERAN'S DAY I 5.10b
Ascends a series of flakes up the steep face between the CANNON FODDER corners and the jutting roof on the right.

1. Just right of a maple, layback a flake, then face climb to where the angle steepens just to the left of the roof. Now step up and left (5.10b) to a small belay stance just to the right of CANNON FODDER. 90', 5.10b
2. Climb to horizontal cracks, then right up an exposed finger/hand crack. 40', 5.9
FA: Michael Hartrich & Al Rubin   September 9, 1984

UNDERCOVER AGENT I 5.8
A shadowy climb up the right-hand side of the CANNON FODDER Buttress, approached via the right-hand descent gully. Begin by a birch tree below the left end of a large slanting roof, the biggest roof on this part of the cliff.
1. Climb to the lower, left end of the roof, then follow it diagonally right, eventually using face holds on the right wall to reach the top. 60', 5.8
FA: George Hurley & Jerry Handren   October 3, 1984

THE OBJECT OF GREAT DESIRE I 5.9
Real or imagined—only you can decide!
1. Follow obvious, shallow flakes to the jutting roof. Step right (5.9) around the roof, then follow a dihedral and crack to the top. 5.9
FA: Michael Hartrich & Joe Perez   1983

MATA HARI I 5.9-
Start below the right end of the roof on UNDERCOVER AGENT.
1. Climb straight to the top (5.9-), in line with the roof's right edge. 50', 5.9-
FA: George Hurley & Alison Osius   October, 1984

CORIANDER I 5.8
Right of the UNDERCOVER AGENT roof is a right-angling, layback crack.
1. Climb up a small, irregular, inside corner to reach the base of the layback crack, then follow it to the top. 45', 5.8
HISTORY: Aid top-roped by Christopher Griffin & Pat Davis on September 30, 1984, the free ascent was by George Hurley & Bob Marquis on October 6, 1984.

OREGANO I 5.9
A few feet to the right of CORIANDER is a similar climb.
1. A vertical crack leads to a right-facing layback up above. 35', 5.9
HISTORY: First top-roped on aid by Pat Davis, Esperanza Recio, & Christopher Griffin on September 30, 1984, the first free ascent was done by George Hurley & Bob Marquis on October 6, 1984.

RAPTOR I 5.9
About 100 feet right of the right-hand descent gully is a dike below a prominent roof 40 feet up, split by a nasty four inch crack (THE RAPTOR ROOF).
1. Head up the dike and easier ledges, then climb just to the right of the roof (5.9), around it to a jam crack with a birch tree, and the top. 85', 5.9
FA: George Hurley & Bill Supple   September 18, 1984

THE RAPTOR ROOF I 5.11d (*)
This roof crack will eat you alive, spit you out, or both! Carry large Friends, large Camalots, and big biceps. "Fat hands also helpful."
1. Using deep hand & fist jams, jam out the spectacular, body length roof. 5.11d
FA: Steve Larson & Chris Gill August, 1992

THREE STARS I 5.7
Begin 35 feet right of RAPTOR on the right side of an enormous, flat flake.
1. Climb up a shallow crack until the angle eases below a large overhang. Traverse left, climb up under the overhang, then traverse right, moving around the overhang's right side. Continue up to the left bypassing some large blocks, then up the summit crack, 25 feet right of the top crack on RAPTOR. 85', 5.7
FA: George Hurley & Bob Marquis October 6, 1984

> Walk a couple of hundred yards to the right to reach to reach a 25 foot tall gray flake or pillar leaning up against the cliff base.

A SCHOLARLY PURSUIT I 5.8
Just to the left of the flake is a birch tree 20 feet above the ground.
1. Gain the birch from the left. Climb up until a traverse left (piton) leads up to a horizontal crack, then make a long reach to a flake and a ledge. 65', 5.8
2. Move off the belay to the right, then back left to a crack through a small ceiling. Finish up the arete left of the ceiling to the top. With lots of long slings, the two pitches may be combined. Rappel off with two ropes.
FA: Kurt Winkler & Reg Woolard, with Ann Woolard June 30, 1983

THE SQUIRM I 5.9
1. Squeeze up the flake's left side, then up A TALE OF THREE CITIES. 30', 5.9
FA: Kurt Winkler April 23, 1983

A TALE OF THREE CITIES I 5.8+
1. Climb the right side of the pillar or flake to a tree. 30', 5.4
2. Follow a diagonal crack or ramp left until cracks lead to a pedestal on top of the flake. Make a hard move (5.8+) over the short, steep wall above onto a slab, then head right with no protection to a final flake and the trees. 5.8+
FA: Kurt Winkler, Karen Moffat, & Polly DeConto April 23, 1983

TERROR INFIRMA I 5.6
About 300 feet right of the previous climb is a broken, but attractive gray face.
1. Layback a five foot, slanting corner on the right side of a large, fallen block, then zig zag up the upper face. 100', 5.6
HISTORY: Michael Hartrich & Bob Fraser made the first ascent in 1983. After the rope got stuck in a crack, Fraser climbed up to free it, slipped on a greasy slab, and hit the deck—but fortunately was unhurt.

Tom Callaghan on the crux of Windjammer (5.11b) on the Painted Walls in 1983. Photograph by Dave Rose.

THE PAINTED WALLS

The Painted Walls, the large, black-streaked cliff to the right of Rainbow Slabs, is one of the least visited larger cliffs along the Kancamagus Highway, but offers several good climbs, particularly the popular 5.11, WINDJAMMER. Other routes on the cliff have crumbly granite and can only be recommended for true, loose rock connoisseurs. The cliff's three hundred foot height is considerably foreshortened when seen from the road.

PEREGRINE FALCON ALERT

The NH Fish & Game Department requests the cooperation of all rock climbers in their effort to re-establish one of nature's most elegant birds of prey, the peregrine falcon, back to its natural habitat. Peregrine falcons are a federally listed endangered species. In the last 10 years, mating pairs of peregrines have nested at the Painted Walls. Please read the seasonal cliff closure notices! ALL ROCK CLIMBING SHOULD BE AVOIDED on the Painted Walls during the nesting season, from APRIL 1ST UNTIL THE END OF JULY, each year, until further notice. Thanks for your attention to this important program!

There are two approaches to the Painted Walls: crossing the Swift River from THE CRACK IN THE WOODS pullout, or hiking in on the Nanamocomuck ski trail. For the Nanamocomuck ski trail approach, start at the dirt logging road running west from the Albany Covered Bridge on the north side of the Swift River. Walk upstream following the road, turn left on the ski trail, and follow the path west along the north bank of the Swift River over four small wooden bridges. At the fourth bridge, turn right into the woods and bushwhack uphill following a small stream. An overgrown lumber road eventually leads very close to the cliff base. The alternate approach is to park at THE CRACK IN THE WOODS pullout, 1.3 miles beyond the Covered Bridge alongside the Kanc. Cross the river, walk a short ways right along a lumber road following the bank, then join the Nanamocomuck ski trail. Continue downstream (east) along the ski trail to a junction marked by a small, wooden ski trail marker nailed to a tree. (The sign reads 9 km/5.6 miles on one side; 2 km/1.2 miles on the other.) Turn north here, following the right-hand of three logging roads to join a climber's trail marked by orange ties that leads toward Rainbow Slabs, then bushwhack diagonally right towards the Painted Walls. Neither approach is easy, so don't be surprised if you get lost. If you follow your nose right, the first approach is the easiest. Rappel down the route you've just climbed, or descend around the cliff's closest side. The routes are described right to left.

NORTHWEST PASSAGE I 5.7

The far, right side of the cliff is an immense, overhanging blank wall painted with black water streaks. The left side of this wall is bordered by a large buttress. NORTHWEST PASSAGE ascends the large, left-leaning corner formed by these two features. While the rock and protection are good, the route also has some grassy cracks.

1. Climb up the corner, stemming and jamming to a stance below some blocks. Move right, face climbing up to a good ledge with a piton anchor. 5.7
2. Continue up the dihedral (5.7). Small stance with a pine. 5.7
3. A short lead gains the top. Rappel the route with two ropes.
FA: Janot Mendler Comeau & Alain Comeau October 12, 1981

THE ARCH I 5.8 R

Begin between NORTHWEST PASSAGE and BROKEN ARROWS. It is recommended that a bolt be placed to protect the final crux.

1. Climb a left-angling crack for 40 feet. When the crack gets crumbly, face climb on the left to a belay at an oak on a good ledge. 70', 5.6
2. Head up the left side of a large arch, traverse right over the arch's top, then move up to a small clump of maples. Climb a crack and the face above (5.8 R) to a final crack and the top. 125', 5.8 R
FA: George Hurley & Les Gould June, 1983

BROKEN ARROWS I 5.8

The crack system up the center of the face left of NW PASSAGE.

1. Follow a diagonalling, root-filled crack to a pine tree in a large niche. Climb through the niche, moving left to a small stance with a piton anchor. 5.7
2. Surmount a small roof, and continue up the main crack to some large blocks, move slightly right, and up to the top. 5.8 Rappel back down NORTHWEST PASSAGE with two ropes.
FA: Alain Comeau & Janot Mendler Comeau April, 1982

CENTRAL EPIC I 5.8

The name says it all. The first climb on the cliff, but that's about it. Crumbly rock. From the base of the buttress, scramble left to a strange rock spike.

1. Climb straight up from the spike to a good belay. 65'
2. Move left to small oaks in a rotten groove. Climb this for 20 feet, then traverse left past a loose flake to a belay ledge (piton). 60', 5.8
3. A jam crack leads to the top. 70'
FA: Paul Ross, Julia Blake, Carl Brown, & Bob Newton September, 1975

RHYME OF THE ANCIENT MARINER III 5.9, A3

Locate an incipient, vertical crack that bisects the lowest toe of the main buttress to the right of THE STRAITS OF MAGELLAN. Bring a variety of aid gear, including bashies and pointed skyhooks.

1. Above a short slab, aid the incipient vertical crack (A3) to its end, then mantleshelf onto the belay ledge. 5.7, A3

2. Move left up a small flake, then bolts and skyhooks lead up to a right-diagonalling crack. When it ends, climb up to a big ledge. 5.7, A3

3. Traverse left past a large, left-facing corner to a steep, vertical crack. Aid this to a roof, traverse left, then free climb up to the next belay ledge. 5.9, A2

4. Move left again, finishing up the last pitch of WINDJAMMER.

FA: Alain Comeau & Janot Mendler Comeau August, 1981

THE STRAITS OF MAGELLAN III 5.9+ R

A long and arduous voyage, with crumbly rock making for rough seas. The route traverses left under a series of left-arching roofs at mid height on the buttress. Locate the obvious, left-facing corner to the right of WINDJAMMER.

1. Climb the corner to an aesthetic finger crack in the right-hand wall. Jam up this nice crack (5.9) to a stance with two bolts. 5.9

2. Continue up the main corner for 20 feet (5.8) to a possible belay at the roof at a triple bolt anchor. Traverse sloping ledges left below the overlap until you can circle around its left end up a shallow, left-facing corner to face climbing and a large belay terrace with a double bolt anchor. You may want to break the pitch in half because of rope drag. 5.9+ R

3. Twenty feet left, climb up a steep, shallow groove (bolt), step left under a small roof, and mantleshelf to the belay. 5.9

4. Traverse left, and again climb the last pitch of WINDJAMMER.

HISTORY: Alain Comeau & Janot Mendler Comeau did the first ascent in September, 1981. Pitch two was free climbed by Doug Madara. Chris Gill, Steve Larson, & Chris Noonan made the first free ascent on October 12, 1986.

WINDJAMMER III 5.11b (***)

By popular acclaim, this is one of the best hard free climbs on the Kancamagus. But don't ruffle your sails if you can't get the crux first try. The climb ascends the deceptively overhanging inside corner system to the right of WAY IN THE WILDERNESS. Good granite, good protection, and absolutely great anchors! Rappel the route with two ropes to descend.

1. Climb a narrow, overhanging dihedral (5.10b) past several bolts to a belay stance at the base of a flaring V groove. Fixed anchor. 80', 5.10b

2. Make very technical chimney moves up the groove (5.11b crux; bolt) to reach better holds. Belay above on a sloping ledge on the left at a double bolt anchor. 60', 5.11b

3. An airy pitch jams an enjoyable hand crack up the back of a large, overhanging dihedral (5.10a) past a small roof near the top. Belay on a good ledge on the left at another fixed anchor. 5.10a

4. Step left and climb a vertical, rotten groove past several fixed pitons. You can rappel back down the route easily with two ropes.

482 THE KANCAMAGUS HIGHWAY AREA

THE PAINTED WALLS

A.		NORTHWEST PASSAGE I 5.7	Page 479
B.		RHYME OF THE ANCIENT MARINER III 5.9, A3	Page 480
C.		THE STRAITS OF MAGELLAN III 5.9+ R	Page 481
D.	***	WINDJAMMER III 5.11b	Page 481
E.		VIA COGNOSCENTI II 5.9+	Page 484
		with THE DIRECT FINISH II 5.10d	Page 484
F.		PHYLOGENY II 5.9	Page 484
G.		WAY IN THE WILDERNESS II 5.9	Page 484

HISTORY: Alain Comeau & Janot Mendler Comeau did the first ascent over several days in August, 1981. Ed Webster & Romain Vogler (Switzerland) made the first free ascent on May 18, 1982, but repeated dive-bombing by a hawk forced a hasty retreat from the top of Pitch three.

VIA COGNOSCENTI II 5.9+
with THE DIRECT FINISH II 5.10d

Crumbly granite and sustained difficulties call for sound judgment and prior experience climbing bad rock. A classic of its kind. Start 40 feet right of WAY IN THE WILDERNESS, below a long, right-leaning crack.

1. Follow the crack past two pitons to a good ledge. 5.9+

2. Stay in the same crack for another 70 feet (also 5.9+). Belay at a stance about 20 feet to the right of the clump of maples at the top of the first pitch of PHYLOGENY. 5.9+

3. Follow the crack system (more 5.9+) to where the crack makes a 90 degree left turn. A difficult finish (peg; 5.10d) climbs the thin crack straight to the top. Or, step 10 feet right, then climb a parallel crack to the top (5.9+). Or follow yet another parallel crack several feet further right (5.5).

HISTORY: George Hurley & Ray Franzem made the first ascent up the 5.9+ finish on May 12, 1982. The 5.10d direct finish and the 5.5 finish were added by Kurt Winkler & George Hurley on August 30, 1984.

PHYLOGENY II 5.9

Begin at the base of WAY IN THE WILDERNESS.

1. Climb the first 20 feet of WAY IN THE WILDERNESS (a veritable waterfall on the first ascent), then angle up and right for 30 feet to a small stump. Climb straight up a crack (5.8). When progress is blocked by an overhang, step left into an easy chimney, and belay on a ledge with several maple trees. 5.8

2. Jam a difficult crack (5.9) straight to the top. 5.9

FA: George Hurley, Alain Comeau, & Janot Mendler Comeau May 7, 1982

WAY IN THE WILDERNESS II 5.9

Perhaps the most striking feature on the cliff, this large corner/chimney system is located just to the left of center. A prominent, difficult, and renowned ice climb in winter, this is an often wet rock climb in summer, demanding refined chimneying technique. Friends and large nuts will be found helpful.

1. Climb the main dihedral, then chimney up to a comfortable belay ledge on the left with a two piton anchor. 80', 5.9

2. Continue chimneying up the corner until the difficulties lessen, and easier climbing leads up a low-angled gully to the top. 130', 5.8

FA: George Hurley & Les Gould May 26, 1982

ONTOGENY II 5.9+
ONTOGENY recapitulates PHYLOGENY. Begin 150 feet left (west) of WAY IN THE WILDERNESS, and 40 feet right of STORMY MONDAY, below a steep dihedral starting 35 feet above the ground.
1. Climb ledges for 35 feet to a small cave below the corner. Sustained, moves (5.9+) ascend the dihedral and the face to the left to a white birch. 115', 5.9+
2. Up & right 30 feet on a grassy ramp, then climb a right-angling crack. 65', 5.7
FA: George Hurley & Larry Hamilton August 14, 1982

STORMY MONDAY I 5.7 (*)
The inside corner about 300 feet left of WAY IN THE WILDERNESS. A well protected route on good rock.
1. Climb the corner until vegetation forces you to climb the face just to the left. Step back right into the corner to a ledge with a tree stump. 5.7
2. Step right again, and climb an enjoyable dihedral (5.7) using some face holds on the left-hand wall. 5.7
FA: George Hurley, Alain Comeau, & Janot Mendler Comeau May 3, 1982

THE DARK FORCE II 5.10b
The next line to the left of STORMY MONDAY is a deep squeeze chimney and offsize crack in a right-facing corner. The route is reminiscent of The Crack Of Fear in Colorado, so take heed!
1. Climb the chimney crack up and slightly right past a bolt to a belay in a cave-like recess. 100', 5.10b
2. Face climb up then right (bolt) to the right edge of a large roof. Continue to a belay at a large pine stump. 60', 5.7+
3. Finish up an obvious crack on the left. 30', 5.6
HISTORY: George Hurley & Les Gould made the first ascent with a small bit of aid, including a bat hook move, on July 9, 1983. George Hurley & Jim Frangos did the first free ascent on September 28, 1983.

ALPINE DIVERSIONS II 5.8
Mixed climbing, New Hampshire style!
1. An obscure route that apparently climbs the right-facing corner and hand crack to the left of THE DARK FORCE. 5.8
2. Finish up a very rotten chimney, or rappel off.
FA: Doug Madara & Casey Newman Spring, 1977

FAMILY MATTERS I 5.8
The shallow, left-facing corner to the left of ALPINE DIVERSIONS.
1. Climb the corner past two short walls, and finish at a ledge with a tree. 5.8 The first ascent party rappelled off due to poor rock above.
FA: Barry Moore & Chris Moore 1980

Ed Webster on the first ascent of Cruise Control (5.7+) on the Perfect Wave at Rainbow Slabs in 1995. Photograph by Matt Harris.

RAINBOW SLABS

The Rainbow Slabs are the prominent, water-stained slabs located on the opposite side of the Swift River from the Lower Falls parking area on the Kancamagus Highway. Both Rainbow Slabs (on the left) and the Painted Walls (on the right) may be seen from here. Situated on the sunny side of a secluded, wooded amphitheater, Rainbow's 200 foot slabs give many pleasant two pitch friction climbs. The clean, white slab on the cliff's right side, known as the Perfect Wave, offers several of the best routes, such as TAKE A GIANT STEP, THE PERFECT WAVE, and CRUISE CONTROL. Protection on Rainbow, however, is usually even more sparse than on Whitehorse. Indeed, several pitches have no protection at all. While many of the newer climbs have protection bolts, in general be forewarned of some very long runouts. Carry a modern rack with Tri-cams and small wired nuts.

If the Swift River is low, park at a dirt pullout on the right, 1.3 miles west along the Kancamagus Highway from the Albany Covered Bridge (six tenths of a mile west of the Lower Falls parking area). Lined with several granite boulders, this pullout can be used at low water to approach Rainbow Slabs, the Crack In The Woods Cliff, or the Painted Walls. Ford the Swift River, walk a short ways right along a lumber road following the bank, then join the Nanamocomuck ski trail. Continue downstream (east) along the ski trail to a junction marked by a small, wooden, Nanamocomuck ski trail marker nailed onto a tree. (The sign reads 9 km/5.6 miles on one side; 2 km/1.2 miles on the other.) Turn north here (toward Rainbow Slabs and the Painted Walls), and at the start follow the right-hand of three logging roads to join a climber's trail marked by orange ties that leads up through the woods to the base of Rainbow: the large, long, easy-angled granite slab.

If the river is high, then your only possible approach is from the Albany Covered Bridge via the Nanamocomuck ski trail. Park at the Covered Bridge, follow the dirt lumber road west along the northern bank of the Swift River to the ski trail junction (signposted), turn left (west), and hike along the trail just past the Lower Falls to the wooden Nanamocomuck ski trail marker nailed onto a tree, as mentioned above. Now turn right (north) on an old logging road and the climber's trail to reach the cliff base. The Albany Covered Bridge approach takes about 40 minutes (provided you don't get lost), and although it's a much longer hike than fording the Swift River—at least you won't get completely soaked!

Descent off Rainbow Slabs is commonly made by rappelling down your route of ascent, or a nearby climb, using two ropes. Look for fixed anchors on the way up. Well-used rappel routes include: INSPECTRUM on Rainbow's far left side; the large pine tree above HERMAPHRODITE

FLAKE near the Height Of Land, and THE PERFECT WAVE on the slab's right-hand side. The routes are now described from left to right.

INSPECTRUM I 5.6 R
Fifty feet to the left of POT OF GOLD is a shallow, right-facing corner interrupted partway up by a horizontal ceiling.

1. Climb up the corner, underclinging the ceiling, and step left out of the top of the corner before it ends to good holds on a slab. Finish up and right (crux) to an overlap, protection, and the top. 80', 5.6 R A one rope rappel just makes it back down to the ground.

FA: Kurt Winkler & Karen Moffat September 3, 1983

POT OF GOLD I 5.6
A two pitch climb up Rainbow's far left-hand side. Begin below an obvious, horizontal ceiling where it turns into a right-facing corner.

1. Square-cut holds gain the ceiling. Move right and belay.

2. Diagonal out right, then head up a clean slab to the top.

FA: Paul Ross, Hugo Tosco, & Isabella Tosco September, 1980

TREASURE HUNT I 5.9
1. Climb the vertical crack system (5.9) between POT OF GOLD and WIT'S END past a steep headwall at the start. 5.9

2. Finish up the easier friction slabs above.

FA: Michael Hartrich & Joe Cote 1975

SOL I 5.9 Begin 40 feet left of WIT'S END at a steep headwall.

1. Climb up the headwall past two pockets five feet above the ground (5.9) to a crease. Friction up easier slabs to horizontal cracks and belay. 145', 5.9

HISTORY: Kurt Winkler & Lee Gerstein made the first ascent on October 15, 1991, and named the route for Kurt's youngest son.

THE WATERMELON I 5.8
Start 20 feet to the left of WIT'S END at a shallow, circular indentation which resembles the size and shape of a watermelon.

1. Stand up on top of the watermelon, surmount the headwall, and climb easier slabs to horizontal cracks and belay. 145', 5.8

FA: Kurt Winkler & Lee Gerstein October 15, 1991

WIT'S END I 5.6 R (*)
Lovely slab climbing, but poor protection. Start on a ledge where a tree branch leans up against the slab.

1. Step off the branch onto the slab and make a thin move (5.6 R) up to a flake. Belay on a higher stance with a bolt. 5.6 R

2. A beautiful, unprotected slab gains the top. Rappel the route with two ropes.

FA: Paul Ross, Hugo Tosco, & Isabella Tosco September, 1980

LUCKY CHARMS I 5.7 R
Bring your rabbit's foot, because protection is again poor. A fixed pin at stepped ledges 40 feet left of WHAT'S UP YANKEE marks the start.
1. Climb up to the peg, make tricky moves up to a horizontal crack, then diagonal right to a flake. Angle back left across a thin friction slab to a large solution pocket, and belay here from Friends. 5.7 R
2. Face climb left, then run out the rope to small trees. Rappel WIT'S END.
FA: Ed Webster & Kathryn Rogers   September, 1981

THE HEIGHT OF LAND
On the cliff's left-hand side is a tree-covered height of land (a rise in the level of the woods) where the slab becomes the shortest.

WHAT'S UP YANKEE? I 5.5
Above the left side of this tree ledge is a dirty, 20 foot corner.
1. Climb the corner. Belay on sloping ledges on the right (tree). 40', 5.5
2. Head left across a slab to flakes. Friction to the top. 165'
FA: Paul Ross & Tana Cathcart   August 7, 1973

SLAB OF THE WOODS I 5.3 X
There is no protection at all on this route.
1. From the height of land, traverse out left across a slab and surmount a bulge at solution pockets, roughly 30 feet right of WHAT'S UP YANKEE? An easier slab leads to the top. 200', 5.3 X
FA: Michael Hartrich & Paul Ross, tandem free-solo   November 12, 1973

YAK BETWEEN WORLDS I 5.8
Feed him a ball of tsampa if he's hungry. The climb ascends the obvious, flaring corner above the height of land's left-hand end.
1. Make an undercling move up to better holds at the top of the corner about 20 feet up, move left to a bolt, then make 5.8 face moves to an easy streak and the top. 100', 5.8 Rappel the route with two ropes.
FA: Alain Comeau, Janot Mendler Comeau, & Ed Webster   May 16, 1982

SUMMER BREEZE I 5.2
Thirty feet above the height of land, a small spruce grows on a ledge.
1. Follow an easy line left to the spruce tree, step left then back right to a stance, and finish up an easy slab past flakes. 100', 5.2
FA: Unknown.

ROAD TO LHASA I 5.7 (*)
It's a long and dusty road to the golden roofs of the Potala in Tibet, but try hard enough, and you might get there someday. At the center of the height of land ledge is a white birch tree. Carry a #1 Friend.
1. Above the birch, face climb straight up the face on hidden holds (5.7)

490 THE KANCAMAGUS HIGHWAY AREA

RAINBOW SLABS

A.	*	**WIT'S END** I 5.6 R	Page	488
B.		**SUMMER BREEZE** I 5.2	Page	489
C.		**HERMAPHRODITE FLAKE** I 5.4	Page	492
D.	**	**FACE DANCES** I 5.6+	Page	492
E.	*	**COLORING BOOK** I 5.7	Page	493
F.		**DEAD EASY** I 5.1	Page	493
G.	*	**PENCILNECK GEEK** I 5.7	Page	494
H.	***	**TAKE A GIANT STEP** I 5.8+	Page	494
I.	***	**THE PERFECT WAVE** I 5.7	Page	495
J.	***	**CRUISE CONTROL** I 5.7+	Page	496
K.		**SUPER SLAB** I 5.7 R	Page	497

with nut protection. When the angle eases, head up to a clump of trees at the top. 100', 5.7 To descend, rappel off the trees using two ropes.

HISTORY: Ed Webster, Janot Mendler Comeau, & Alain Comeau made the first ascent on May 16, 1982.

MISSISSIPPI RAMBLE I 5.4 (*)

Protection at last! Above the right side of the height of land is a prominent flake system, the HERMAPHRODITE FLAKE. A tall, obvious pine tree grows directly above it. Normal rack.

1. Layback up a right-arching, mossy flake, step left to the main flake, and jam a hidden crack up the flake's left side to a belay at the big pine. 140', 5.4 Rappel easily back down off the pine tree with two ropes.

FA: Paul Ross & Tana Cathcart August 7, 1973

HERMAPHRODITE FLAKE I 5.4

The large, obvious exfoliation flake, a good landmark.

1. Layback up a dirty arch, step left into the flake, and layback its right side (also dirty) to the pine tree. 140', 5.4 Rappel off easily with two ropes.

FA: Joe Cote, Roger Martin, & Bob Fraser October 28, 1973

THE MID SECTION

The middle portion of Rainbow Slabs is where the central, open slab descends the farthest into the woods. This central slab is fairly low-angled, broken by a series of steps, and marked by several water streaks. The height of land is now on your left, and just to its right, in the slab's center is the long, vertical white streak of FACE DANCES.

FACE DANCES I 5.6+ (**)

A high quality friction and face route directly up the central white streak.

1. This enjoyable lead ascends the bottom, lower angled slab, then face climbs straight up the white streak on "moon scoops" to a 5.6+ bulge (bolt). Continue straight up to a double bolt belay in the center of the slab. 5.6+

2. An easy pitch leads to the top. Rappel the route with two ropes.

FA: Alain Comeau & Janot Mendler Comeau October, 1981

FIFTY CENTER I 5.4

Briggs Bunker's favorite climb! Easier than its neighbor, FACE DANCES.

1. Head up the white streak (5.2) to a prominent horizontal break. 5.2

2. Diagonal right to a small, right-facing corner, then friction up slabs on the left to the two bolt belay on FACE DANCES. 5.4

3. Take the easiest line up to the woods at the top of the slab.

HISTORY: Paul Ross & Tana Cathcart climbed the route's first ascent on August 7, 1973. Extra points if you know who Briggs Bunker is—and why the route got its name!

RAINBOW SLABS (HERMAPHRODITE FLAKE & FACE DANCES)

COLORING BOOK I 5.7 (*)
Walk out onto the white streak and head up right on an easy, low-angled slab. Twenty feet right of the streak and at the top of a blocky area is a one foot by six foot sloping stance. A rope length above and roughly 20 feet right of the upper corner on FIFTY CENTER is a 35 foot long, right-facing corner, the route's major feature. Normal rack.
1. Climb a 15 foot diagonal flake/overlap (5.7) to the right, then head easily up to the right-facing corner. Belay on a small stance at the corner's top. 155', 5.7
2. Continue straight to the top and the woods. 160', 5.2
FA: Kurt Winkler & Karen Moffat Winkler August 16, 1984

BRUIN I 5.4 X
Walk 40 feet to the right on easy ledges to a piton. No brawn here.
1. Climb straight up the left side of a prominent, brown water streak directly above (5.4 X). Belay on the right at a right-facing flake with a double piton anchor (same stance as on TRUE COLORS). 125', 5.4 X
2. Follow TRUE COLORS easily to the top of the slabs. 140', 5.1
FA: Kurt Winkler & Karen Moffat Winkler October 22, 1984

TRUE COLORS I 5.7 X
Thirty feet right of BRUIN is a flat ledge with a large horizontal crack at its back (#4 Friend or big Hex). The slab's lowest point is now directly below you.
1. Head straight up an obvious orange streak to a short bulge 60 feet up, which is climbed with no protection (5.7 X) to a small, right-facing flake and stance. Above the flake, step left, and belay at another right-facing flake with a two piton anchor. (Same stance as on BRUIN.) 120', 5.7
2. Gallop straight to the top. 140', 5.1
FA: Karen Moffat Winkler & Kurt Winkler October 22, 1984

L'ANNIVERSAIRE I 5.8
A nice climb up the center of the slabs near DEAD EASY.
1. Above a dowel, climb sloping ledges then up excellent brown rock (bolt) to a swell (5.8). Belay at two bolts 15 feet to the right of TRUE COLORS. 5.8
2. Finish up easy rock, or rappel off with two ropes.
FA: John Strand & Rose O'Brien July 20, 1985

RHINO SKIN I 5.6 R
You'll need a tough hide to climb this route, especially if you slip!
1 & 2. Climb the unprotected slab just to the left of DEAD EASY. 200', 5.6 R
FA: Jim Shimberg & Bradley White October 18, 1987

DEAD EASY I 5.1
Well to the right of FACE DANCES, and to the right of the slab's lowest point is a tree ledge 100 feet up.

1. Scamper up an easy slab to the left end of the tree ledge.
2. Follow a series of steps leading left across the upper slab.
FA: Paul Ross & Tana Cathcart August 7, 1973

PENCILNECK GEEK I 5.7 (*)
Rainbow's steepest climb! Start under the middle of the RUBBERNECK overlap. One wonders which of the first ascentionists the route was named for...?
1. Head straight up an easy slab to flakes in the overlap eight feet right of a right-facing corner. Swing over the overlap (5.7) and belay on the highest tree ledge. 150', 5.7
2. Above the tree ledge, climb left-leaning flakes, then move back right, finally climbing up green moon scoops to the top. 170', 5.2

HISTORY: Todd Swain, Brad White, & Dick Peterson made the first ascent of the climb on September 18, 1982.

RUBBERNECK I 5.6
Begin under the long, narrow overlap located to the left of the large, white slab (the Perfect Wave) on the cliff's right-hand end.
1. Climb easy slabs to the overlap, then head around its right side, stepping over it at a flake. Belay in the last crack (piton). 5.6
2. Continue up a steepening slab to a good thread a third of the way up the pitch, then friction straight up to the top.
FA: Paul Ross & Tana Cathcart August 7, 1973

THE PERFECT WAVE
The large, steep white slab on the right-hand side of Rainbow, the Perfect Wave, offers the highest concentration of quality routes on the cliff. Protection can be mostly good, as on TAKE A GIANT STEP, THE PERFECT WAVE, or TSUNAMI, excellent as on CRUISE CONTROL, or almost zero, as on CRAZY WOMAN DRIVER. The sling-draped belay flake at the top of the second pitch of THE PERFECT WAVE is the standard midway rappel anchor for all the routes on this section of Rainbow. Routes are now described from left to right across the Wave.

TAKE A GIANT STEP I 5.8+ (***)
The immaculate, white granite of TAKE A GIANT STEP yields a delicate face climb straight up the Wave's left margin. Start at the left-hand base of the Perfect Wave, below a small overlap 40 feet up. Carry a couple of medium to large cams for Pitch two. The bolts were placed free on the lead.
1. Scramble straight up a brown slab to a small corner and narrow overlap (with a small birch tree), and a couple of belay ledges just above. 70', 5.4
2. Move from right to left up past a solution pocket to a bolt at the base of a steeper, blank white slab. Face climb slightly left past a second bolt (5.8+)

with classic moves over the crest of the wave, then friction more easily up and left to a good horizontal crack, and a nut belay. 90', 5.8+
3. Finish up and right quite easily, but with no protection, to the top.
FA: Ed Webster, Susan Patenaude, & Bob Rotert November, 1980

SILVER SURFER I 5.8 X
The almost completely unprotected slab/face climb between TAKE A GIANT STEP and THE PERFECT WAVE. Hang 10!
1. Climb Pitch one of GIANT STEP up the brown slab past a narrow overlap and a small birch tree to a couple of belay ledges. 70', 5.4
2. Off the far right end of the belay ledges, climb up past a bombproof #7 Hex placement to a small ledge, then head straight up and over the wave (5.8 X) between TAKE A GIANT STEP and THE PERFECT WAVE to a ledge. 5.8 X
3. Finish easily to the top up a short flake and a left-leaning dike.
FA: Ward Smith & Chris Smith August, 1984

THE PERFECT WAVE I 5.7 (***)
An excellent route, one of the best on the Kanc. Ride this one for as long as you can. It even has protection! The route ascends the center of the white wave to thin, vertical flakes about two thirds of the way up. Start the same as for TAKE A GIANT STEP at the lower, left side of the Wave.
1. Friction straight up a brown slab past a small corner and narrow overlap (small birch) to the right-hand of two, sickle-shaped ledges. 70', 5.4
2. Follow a short groove up and right, then face climb diagonally right into the center of the slab. Protect under a flake, then face climb straight up a very faint, vertical dike (5.7) past two bolts which are hard to see from below. Then move delicately right to a thin, vertical flake, and belay on the small stance above at a secure flake (slings). 100', 5.7 (This flake is the midway rappel anchor for all the routes on the Perfect Wave.)
3. Climb easy friction to the top, the same as TSUNAMI.
HISTORY: Ed Webster & Susan Patenaude climbed the first ascent in November, 1980. The two bolts were drilled by hand, free on the lead.

TSUNAMI I 5.6 (**)
The most obvious line on the Perfect Wave is the left-leaning dike in the very center of the slab. Right of TAKE A GIANT STEP and THE PERFECT WAVE, scramble 40 feet up onto a narrow, tree ledge. Modern rack helpful.
1. From the tree ledge, face climb up and left along the left-slanting dike on good holds (piton) past two natural threads (5.6) to the upper layback flake, and the belay stance and slings on THE PERFECT WAVE. 140', 5.6
2. Slab climb easily, but with no protection, up to the woods.
FA: Joe Cote & Michael Hartrich 1975

Billy Squier on Tsunami (5.6) on the Perfect Wave in 1995. Photo by Ed Webster.

CRUISE CONTROL I 5.7+ (***)

Good protection and moderate climbing make for a fun outing. The route takes a relatively straight line up the smooth slab (look for three bolts) between TSUNAMI and CRAZY WOMAN DRIVER. Scramble to the top of the tree ledge right of THE PERFECT WAVE—the same start as for TSUNAMI.

1. From the tree ledge, climb up easily for 40 feet to a flake, and belay. (TSUNAMI ascends the left-diagonalling dike just to the left.) 40', 5.4

2. Climb up stepped rock (or friction up the smooth slab on the left; harder) to reach the first bolt. Continue face climbing straight up past several handy pockets (5.7+) and two more bolts onto the easier final slab. Run the rope out to the trees. 165', 5.7+ All the bolts were placed free on the lead.

FA: Ed Webster & Maria Hannus (Sweden) May 27, 1995

BONSAI I 5.9 R
A diagonal line from left to right all the way across the Perfect Wave. Typically scary. Begin down and right of the TSUNAMI tree ledge.
1. Climb the center of the steep wall at the wave's base (5.9 R), above a bush and tree stump. Belay at a dwarfed tree once the angle lessens. 5.9 R
2. Diagonal right past another small tree to a clump of bushes growing on the slab's right-hand margin.
3. Head straight up, taking the easiest way to the woods.
FA: Michael Hartrich & Joe Cote 1975

CRAZY WOMAN DRIVER I 5.9 X (*)
Protection on this slab route is virtually nonexistent. Begin at the base of the far, right side of the Perfect Wave beside a broken tree stump. This start is the same as for BONSAI, below and to the right of the TSUNAMI tree ledge.
1. Make unprotected 5.9 face moves straight up the steep initial headwall (as for BONSAI), aiming towards a shallow, rounded pocket. Move up the lower angled slab to the SUPER SLAB belay at a small ledge (piton). 90', 5.9 R
2. Continue the straight line of the climb up the white slab above, making thin, sustained moves over a slight swell (5.9 X) up to a narrow, horizontal overlap. Protect here, then run the rope out to the top. 140', 5.9 X
HISTORY: Susan Patenaude, Ed Webster, & Bob Rotert made the first ascent in November, 1980. With impressive self control, Patenaude led the route's crux. She'd never placed a bolt before, decided not to stop and try to drill—and as a result, led the entire 5.9 crux with virtually no protection.

SUPER SLAB I 5.7 R
The right margin of Rainbow is formed by a very large, conspicuous white slab (the Perfect Wave) bordered by large, black water streaks on the right. Start 25 feet to the right of a bush growing at the base of the steeper, bottom portion of the black-streaked slab.
1. Face climb slightly left on small holds up a faint dike to a fixed pin at 40 feet. Continue along the dike up a steep slab to a small ledge (peg). 100', 5.7 R
2. Climb up a steepening slab, then slightly left to a hidden solution pocket. Easy friction (with no protection) leads to the top.
FA: Paul Ross & Tana Cathcart August 7, 1973

THE PETROGLYPH I 5.8+ X
One hundred feet to the right of SUPER SLAB are two solution pockets six feet off the ground with a two foot long horizontal foothold below. Follow the clean, brown slab straight above the odd-looking mask. Bring a modern rack—including a roll of duct tape and a few different sized skyhooks!
1. Climb to a gray band at 45 feet. Step right to ledges, then move back left to the top of a shallow flake. Make a difficult move to gain a pocket in

lichen on the right, then continue more easily to a narrow belay ledge above. 125', 5.8+ X (Two duct-taped skyhooks for protection.)

2. Continue up the brown friction slab to the trees. 140', 5.3

FA: Kurt Winkler & Karen Moffat Winkler September 18, 1983

THE GIRDLE TRAVERSES OF RAINBOW SLABS

AURORA III 5.6 X

The left to right original girdle traverse of Rainbow is over 1,000 feet long, with random protection. Carry a modern rack and two ropes.

1. Starting up POT OF GOLD, traverse horizontally right to a shaky nut belay below an overlap.

2. Traverse right under an overlap (don't fall) to a good belay ledge at the large pine tree above HERMAPHRODITE FLAKE.

3. Down climb the HERMAPHRODITE FLAKE. 5.4

4. Traverse right across FACE DANCES to tree ledges on DEAD EASY, and walk to the ledge's right-hand end.

5. Traverse right on good rock past TAKE A GIANT STEP.

6. Diagonal up and right, finishing up SUPER SLAB.

HISTORY: Todd Swain & Peter Beal did the route's first ascent on July 27, 1982, but chose to rappel down HERMAPHRODITE FLAKE. Kurt Winkler & Shraddha Howard made the first free ascent by down climbing the same flake (at 5.4) in July, 1993. Aurora is Kurt & Karen Winkler's daughter.

ORION III 5.7 X

The right to left girdle traverse of Rainbow offers delicate and occasionally dicey slab climbing. Bring a modern rack and double ropes. Start on top of the small tree ledge at the beginning of TSUNAMI. A beautiful route to do on a sunny autumn day when the leaves are turning color!

1. Face climb up and then left to the piton on TSUNAMI. Continue up and left (5.5) to the second bolt on PERFECT WAVE, traverse farther left (5.6), and belay off Friends at a stance between SILVER SURFER and TAKE A GIANT STEP. 150', 5.6

2. Climb up 15 feet, then traverse farther left, down climbing the slab just to the left of the crux wave on TAKE A GIANT STEP to a traverse line that leads left across a dark streak and under an overlap. Continue left past a good thread to some tree ledges. 160', 5.4

3. Move down and left along the tree ledge, then head up and left on good horizontal cracks and ledges at the start of PENCILNECK GEEK, heading left (5.4) past the double bolt L'ANNIVERSAIRE belay to reach the two piton belay on BRUIN. 160', 5.4

4. Traverse straight left to the right-facing corner on COLORING BOOK. Down climb this corner for 20 feet, then traverse left to a horizontal crack on FIFTY CENTER, and belay. 100', 5.3

5. Continue left across FACE DANCES, then move up and left to the Exxon Valdez Slab, a black, algae-covered nightmare. (Better hope you don't get caught here in the rain!) Climb up brushed-off "moon scoops" onto this slab, then traverse down and left (5.7 X) onto a ledge. Continue up and left, climbing the HERMAPHRODITE FLAKE (5.4) to the big pine on top. 130', 5.7 X

6. Traverse left, slightly up, back down, then back up, taking advantage of protection possibilities until you reach a big, horizontal crack. 90', 5.4

7. Traverse left across a black streak until below an obvious ceiling, then continue left along holds under the ceiling until it's possible to down climb diagonally left to a ledge below a bush clump. 130', 5.4

8. Diagonal up and left to a bolt on TREASURE HUNT, then traverse straight left across another black streak onto a clean slab which is climbed straight up to a horizontally growing red pine tree. 100', 5.4 Rappel off the tree with two ropes back to the ground.

HISTORY: Kurt Winkler & Shraddha Howard climbed the first ascent on July 8, 1993, and named the route for Kurt's son Orion.

500 THE KANCAMAGUS HIGHWAY AREA

Tom Callaghan on the first ascent of Pumping Station (5.11b) in 1985. Photograph by Haydie Donahue.

THE CRACK IN THE WOODS CLIFF

Joe Cote discovered this remarkable cliff after getting lost hiking to Rainbow Slabs. THE CRACK IN THE WOODS is one of New Hampshire's best crack climbs, a perfect hand crack in the back of a dramatically overhanging, clean-cut dihedral. This classic exercise in jamming is also one of the hardest climbs in the White Mountains to find. Many climbers have never managed to locate the cliff, spending hours instead wandering aimlessly around in the forest. Face it, getting lost in the woods is occasionally an integral (and extremely important!) part of doing a route in the White Mountains.

The Crack In The Woods Cliff is a small, nearly invisible cliff tucked away in the forest just west of Rainbow Slabs. Park at the dirt pullout on the right (north) side of the Kancamagus Highway, 1.3 miles west of the Albany Covered Bridge (six tenths of a mile west of Lower Falls). Cross the Swift River to a lumber road, walk right—but not very far right—and turn left into the woods, up a small drainage. Hike a short ways more, turn slightly left, and walk gradually uphill, looking hard for the cliff. If the river is high, park at the Covered Bridge, follow the Nanamocomuck ski trail past Rainbow Slabs, then turn right at the drainage. Better yet, get a local to show you the way! The routes are described from right to left.

PUMPING STATION II 5.11b (*)

One of the steepest free climbs in the state: the top of the route overhangs the base by 30 feet! The route ascends the diagonal crack system 70 feet to the right of THE CRACK IN THE WOODS. Strenuous and sustained.

1. Hard jamming off the ground leads to a small, left-facing corner and a sit-down rest on the right. Handtraverse out left (piton), then face climb straight up past a second peg (5.11b). Follow cracks and ramps until you can belly flop onto a sloping ledge with fixed anchors (which makes a reasonable belay stance, if desired). Now step left, and climb up a stupendous, overhanging corner/crack (5.10b) to the top. 5.11b

HISTORY: Tom Callaghan with Haydie Donahue did the first ascent in July, 1985. After two attempts, the climb was led in one pitch, with one fall.

THE CRACK IN THE WOODS I 5.10d (***)

Strenuous, classic hand jamming up perfect granite. Carry a good-sized rack of Camalots and Friends. In the center of the cliff is a hand-width crack splitting the back of a beautiful, but very overhanging dihedral.

1. Start up the crack, jam left under and around a roof, then struggle up the parallel sided hand crack (5.10d) into a niche. Take a well-earned rest, then exit the crack with difficulty, and traverse left across a ledge to a tree belay. 80', 5.10d Rappel off the tree with one rope to descend.

HISTORY: After first attempting the crack with Donn Stahlman, Joe Cote recruited Jim Dunn to try it free. "The weather was too cold to climb that day, so we just hiked in instead. I had told Jim about the crack and he couldn't wait to see it," said Cote. "When we finally got to the base, he could hardly believe his eyes." Several days later, in October, 1973, Jim Dunn and Michael Hartrich did the first ascent.

VENUS VERMICULATE I 5.8
The corner 40 feet to the left of THE CRACK IN THE WOODS.
1. Layback and stem up the corner (5.8) to a tree on a ledge. 5.8
2. Climb the face above (5.7) to the woods. 5.7
FA: Joe Cote & Donn Stahlman   October 14, 1973

LOST & FOUND I 5.10a
The broken cracks 30 feet left of VENUS VERMICULATE.
1. Follow a thin finger crack to a groove, traverse right, and finish past a tree growing on the ground up to a grass ledge. 5.10a
2. Climb a short 5.7 face. Rappel off on the left with two ropes.
FA: Michael Hartrich, Joe Lentini, & Albert Dow   May 22, 1980

TABLE MOUNTAIN SLAB

This nice backcountry slab at the head of the first drainage to the northwest of Rainbow Slabs offers a pleasant approach, fine views, and steep friction climbing up scooped-out pockets. The history of the cliff is unfortunately vague. Several teams have visited here, enjoyed the routes, and left with hardly a word. The first climb was probably DRAGON FLY (5.6), done in 1975 by Paul Ross & Julia Blake. Other routes were climbed in the early 1980s without bolts by Michael Hartrich & Albert Dow prior to the next ascents which were done in 1982 and 1983. Since it's a very long hike in from the Kanc, the best approach is from Bartlett on Route 302. Drive south up Bear Notch Road and park on the east (or left side, driving this direction) of the road at a dirt pullout below the crest. Hike up the Attitash Trail for two miles to the top of Table Mountain, which takes about an hour. (The actual summit of Table Mountain is a short bushwhack off the hiking trail.) Where the trail crosses the top of a large, open slab—the top of Table Mountain Slab—note the tree clump 100 feet below and right which was spared during the October, 1984 fire that burned 105 acres in this vicinity in one of the worst forest fires in recent White Mountain history. From the summit slab, walk back down the trail 25 feet to a cairn, turn left into the woods, and follow a short climber's path to a large pine. Rappel off the tree with two ropes for 140 feet to a two bolt anchor on BUGS EAT FROGS, then another 80 feet to the ground. Most of the way up the slab's left-hand side is a small, horizontal overlap. Farther right, there is a larger, main overlap near the cliff's center, and a cave at the base on the far, right side. The routes are now described from left to right.

KNIGHTS IN WHITE SATIN I 5.7
Ascends the slab's left-hand side. Start just left of THE HOLY GRAIL.
1. Diagonal left (5.7) to a nut belay at a flake. 5.7
2. Wander up the upper slab to the trees.
HISTORY: Matt Peer & Mark Hanson made the first recorded ascent of the climb in the Autumn of 1982.

THE HOLY GRAIL I 5.7
A bit easier than its neighbor, MERLIN. This route offers nice friction, epoxied bolts, and is very direct. Begin 50 to 60 feet to the left of MERLIN.
1. Face climb straight up past a bolt to a double bolt anchor. 5.7
2. Continue up an easier slab to the top of the cliff.
FA: Matt Peer & Mark Hanson Autumn, 1982

HOLY SMOKE I 5.5 (*)
Start this route 40 feet to the left of MERLIN below two curving flakes that are 20 feet above the ground. The climbing was somewhat easier than expected, and the no-bolt protection better than anticipated.
1. Climb up white rock to the right-hand of the two flakes, then head straight up a dike, eventually angling right on easier rock to a belay stance below the MERLIN overlap. 160', 5.5
2. This pitch climbs the upper part of MERLIN's top pitch. Traverse right around the overlap, then climb up a dike toward a bush. Step out right and friction up a white slab, then head back left, finally climbing straight up a darker colored slab to the pine tree at the top of MERLIN. 150', 5.4
FA: Doug Burnell & Doug Teschner October 11, 1993

MERLIN I 5.8 (*)
The cliff's most popular route begins just to the left of the slab's center. Start 50 to 60 feet to the right of THE HOLY GRAIL at a black water streak, the route's identifying feature.
1. Friction and face climb up the black streak, climbing up to and over a small, horizontal overlap, to a double bolt belay anchor. 5.8
2. Fly up the top slab to the woods.
FA: Mark Hanson & Matt Peer Autumn, 1982

SIR BOR'S DREAM I 5.7 R
About 20 feet to the right of MERLIN is a white streak.
1. Friction up the white streak past a narrow, right-facing flake, then move over a swell to reach a belay stance either at two pitons in a flake on the left, or slightly higher, under the MERLIN overlap. 165', 5.7 R

504 THE KANCAMAGUS HIGHWAY AREA

2. Finish easily to the top of the slab.
FA: Kurt Winkler & Bunny Goodspeed July 31, 1989

GENEVIEVE I 5.8 R (5.6 X)
Forty feet to the right of SIR BOR'S DREAM is a wide, gold stripe.
1. Up the streak (5.6 X) to a hollow flake. Belay left of a tree clump. 135', 5.6 X
2. Move up left of the trees following the same gold streak to an overlap with horizontal cracks. Move past the overlap on the left (5.5), or on the right (5.8 R), to another hollow flake belay. 100', 5.5 or 5.8 R Scramble from here to the top.
FA: Kurt Winkler & Bunny Goodspeed July 31, 1989

NOBLE GESTURE I 5.9- R
Start below the very center and tallest section of the slab.
1. Thin face climbing past a bolt (5.9-) leads to a poor belay at twigs.
2. Easier friction straight up gains the top.
FA: Mark Hanson & Matt Peer Autumn, 1982

TABLE SCRAPS I 5.9 (**)
Start 30 feet right of NOBLE GESTURE or 25 feet left of BUGS EAT FROGS below two holes with shrubs in them. The crux overlaps are height dependent.
1. Climb up obvious steps left of the shrubs, then straight up sculpted rock to the right end of an upward-curving flake. Belay at a double bolt belay at the flake's highest right-hand point. A fun pitch. 80', 5.3
2. Head straight up to the main overlaps. Climb by the first overlap (bolt), past the second step (#2 Friend), and over the third overlap (bolt) before angling up and right to a double bolt anchor above a narrow ledge. 80', 5.9
3. Move up, trending right (bolt) to the trees. 80', 5.7
FA: Dick Traverse & Karen Traverse August 19, 1995

THE CITY OF LOST CHILDREN I 5.8
Fifteen feet to the left of the three bolts at the start of BUGS EAT FROGS, look for a lonely, old bolt up on the slab above.
1. Climb straight up past the bolt (5.8), then angle right to the two bolt anchor on BUGS EAT FROGS below the overlap's right end. 90', 5.8
2. Circle around the right-hand side of the main overlap, and finish up a left-diagonalling dike to the top and the woods.
FA: Brad White & Jim Frangos Summer, 1983

BUGS EAT FROGS I 5.8 (*)
Takes a direct line to the double bolt rappel station on the main slab's right side. Begin 15 feet to the right of an old bolt well above the ground (the first bolt on CITY OF LOST CHILDREN). Carry several Tri-cams along.
1. Ascend several steps past three bolts to an expanding flake, and continue up to the double bolt belay/rappel anchor. 80', 5.8

2. Angle up and right to where a dike goes through an overlap (#2 Friend), then climb the dike, trending left to the trees using Tri-cams in pockets. 150', 5.5

HISTORY: Dick Traverse & Karen Traverse made the climb's first ascent in swelteringly hot weather amidst a monstrous swarm of black flies on July 2, 1995—but still managed to place all of the bolts on the lead by hand.

VARIATION: **THE HORNET** I 5.7 R
Begin just to the left of a pine stump leaning up against the cliff.

1a. Friction up to a right-facing flake system. Follow a series of hollow flakes to the two bolt belay on BUGS EAT FROGS. 80', 5.7 R Be very wary of creaky flakes—and the hornets living under them!

FA: Dick Traverse & Karen Traverse July 16, 1995

DICK TO THE RESCUE I 5.10c (*)
The slab's hardest route. Start 20 feet to the right of BUGS EAT FROGS, just to the right of a large pine stump leaning against the cliff.

1. Climb up to a right-facing flake (small TCUs), then go straight up smooth rock past three bolts (5.10c; but easier to either side of this clean streak) to a break in the slab. Belay from the highest flake at a two bolt anchor. 90', 5.10c

2. Move up to thin flakes and follow them left. Finish up 5.9 friction past three more bolts, trending left as the cliff eases (bolt) to the rappel pine. 140', 5.9

HISTORY: Dick Traverse & Dick Tucker did the first ascent on July 16, 1995, following a serious gardening effort to clean lichen. Most of the bolts were eventually placed on rappel after Tucker had to rescue Traverse from certain heat stroke while he was valiantly drilling bolts on the lead.

TABLE TALK I 5.10b
Begin 20 feet right of DICK TO THE RESCUE, and just to the left of the base of a dike that diagonals up this far, right-hand side of the slab.

1. Head up horizontal steps to a shrubbery-lined ledge. Step right of the dike, and climb up a green streak past four bolts (5.10b) to a break in the slab on the left. Belay at the two bolt anchor on DICK TO THE RESCUE. 90', 5.10b

2. Climb Pitch two of DICK TO THE RESCUE (the preferable finish: 140', 5.9), or wander right up poorly protected, lichen-covered slabs.

FA: Dick Traverse & Linda Sugiyama September 30, 1995

PICNIC TABLE I 5.6
The farthest right-hand route ascends the length of the left-slanting dike up the slab's right side. Start just right of TABLE TALK and just left of the cave.

1. Follow the long, left-diagonalling dike up and to the left across the bushy shelf on TABLE TALK, left across DICK TO THE RESCUE, and belay. 5.6

2. Continue left up the dike to the summit.

FA: Brad White & Jim Frangos Summer, 1983

BEAR MOUNTAIN SLAB

Driving west along the Kancamagus Highway past Rainbow Slabs, this is the first large cliff on the right, the south-facing granite slab or wall just above the Swift River. Over the years, a few climbers have occasionally climbed here, but no records were kept of their ascents. Hopefully the following notes will establish a basic historical record. The approach across the Swift River then bushwhacking up through the woods takes 20 to 25 minutes, unless you get lost (and you probably will). Routes are described from right to left.

SAY MR. CONGRESSMAN II 5.8
The obvious, diamond-shaped face on the slab's far right side. Attempts by experienced climbers to find this climb have failed, so be forewarned!
1. Face climb up sloping ledges to a small overhang split by a flaring crack (5.8). Belay just above. 5.8
2. Face climb straight up to the top of the cliff.
FA: Michael Hartrich & Ed Smith 1971

THE UNINVITED I 5.8
A nice intermediate route on good rock. The far, right-hand side of the cliff is formed by a large, easy-angled slab with rockfall debris at the base. Start 80 feet to the left of this slab below a thin, vertical flake and a bolt 30 feet up.
1. Make bouldering moves up the flake to a ledge (bolt). Move left past two more bolts (5.8), then run it out up an easier slab to a tree. 90', 5.8
FA: Harvey Weener & John Strand June, 1992

DYKES TO WATCH OUT FOR I 5.11d (5.9 R) (*)
This is probably the most obvious and easiest route to locate on the cliff. Look for a left-diagonalling dike with a lonely bolt 20 feet up.
1. Do an extremely hard boulder problem off the ground (5.11d) to clip the first bolt, then follow the left-leaning dike until it ends, moving left (5.9 R) to reach a two bolt belay. 110', 5.11d (5.9 R)
FA: Gerry Lortie & John Strand June 3, 1990

PIERCED BOYS I 5.10c
Start 40 feet to the left of DYKES TO WATCH OUT FOR at a dark slab.
1. Slab climb past a bolt to a rest, then move up and left past two more bolts (5.10c) to the double bolt belay on DYKES. 60', 5.10c Rappel off.
FA: Chris Small & Dan Pacheco July, 1995

> In 1980, English climber Choe Brooks climbed two other routes here, one on either side of SAY MR. CONGRESSMAN. One had a big layback flake.

HOBBITLAND

This unusual collection of outcrops and large granite boulders is located on the northwest shoulder of Mt. Chocorua (3,475') near Champney Falls, named for the famed White Mountain landscape painter, Benjamin Champney. Mt. Chocorua was named for Chief Chocorua of the Pequawket Indians. The tallest routes at Hobbitland are 60 feet high. Temperatures between the boulders stays cool in midsummer (there can be ice here in June!), and the views of the nearby Three Sisters (3,330') from on top of the rocks is superb. From Conway, drive 10.4 miles west along the Kancamagus Highway to the Champney Falls Trailhead parking area on your left.

Hike along the Champney Falls trail for about 30 minutes to the falls (at low water during the summer), then walk left through a narrow, rock-walled gorge. Hike up the steep, dirt incline at the end of the cleft past a wire fence, and up to another small waterfall. From here, hike steeply uphill, up and left until you see several granite outcrops, with the largest boulders (and the passageway) just to their left. From Champney Falls, it should take you another 15 minutes to reach the rocks. The entire approach takes from 30–45 minutes. When you first get to the outcrops, there is a short face on the right with the next several climbs. The routes are described from right to left.

SILENT LUCIDITY I 5.7 R
Ascends the center of the right-hand small face.
1. Climb up 15 feet to a small ledge, then another 15 feet to a second stance. Continue to the top with tricky protection. 50', 5.7 R
FA: Harold Consentine & Bud Dubey Summer, 1980

TOLKIEN HIGHWAY I 5.7 R
To the left of SILENT LUCIDITY is a rounded arete.
1. A hard move gains a small stance. Continue up the arete proper for another 25 feet, running it out to another stance, then meander to the top. 50', 5.7 R
FA: Harold Consentine & Bud Dubey Summer, 1980

CALIMARI I 5.10c (*)
On the left-hand side of the first outcrop, to the left of TOLKIEN HIGHWAY, is a narrow, right-facing corner/flake about 15 feet tall.
1. Stem up a short, bottomless, rounded corner (5.10c) to gain the flake, then make another hard move up the face into the left-facing flake above, which is followed to the top of the cliff. 50', 5.10c
FA: Paul Camari & Harold Consentine Summer, 1981

> Hike left to another 45 foot outcrop. Harold Consentine & a friend top-roped two 5.8 routes up this pockmarked wall in 1979. Walk another minute left to reach the largest, orange, granite boulder at Hobbitland: the Brain.

THE CINDERELLA THEORY I 5.12c (**)
Several bolts on the right side of the Brain mark this challenging sport route. Bring small wired nuts and TCUs for the top corner.
1. Climb gymnastic moves (5.12c) up a thin seam past three bolts, then make a wild step left into a shallow, arching, left-facing corner (5.11b), which is laybacked to the top. 60', 5.12c
FA: Barry Rugo & Craig Smith June, 1993

FRODO I 5.7+
To the left of THE CINDERELLA THEORY, and above and right of the entrance to the inner passageway is this short, hand crack/corner.
1. Just to the right of the passage, climb a short, vertical finger crack onto a ledge, then jam up a beautiful hand crack (5.7+) in a flaring corner. 50', 5.7+
FA: Ed Webster & Harold Consentine August 19, 1995

THE THUMB I 5.7
Crawl through the initial part of the passageway, and behind you, on the left, is a sharp arete leading to the top of a small pinnacle.
1. Climb the left-hand arete to the thumb's top. 45', 5.7
FA: Harold Consentine, free-solo barefoot 1979

FRAGALROCK I 5.7+
Chimney through both tunnels into the magical, inner passage. Thirty feet left of HOBBITLAND, between two huge boulders, is a right-facing corner.
1. Climb up into the right-facing, dihedral/groove, finishing with tricky moves (5.7+), jamming and laybacking to the top. 50', 5.7+
FA: Harold Consentine, free-solo Autumn, 1979

HOBBITLAND I 5.9 (*)
The vertical finger/hand crack in the center of the far wall in the passageway.
1. Jam and layback up the very steep crack on great jams. 45', 5.9
FA: Ed Webster & Harold Consentine August 19, 1995

MAGIC EARTH I 5.5
Across from HOBBITLAND, on the opposite side of the passageway, and at its far end, is a short face with some good holds.
1. Climb up the face. 40', 5.5
FA: Harold Consentine, free-solo Autumn, 1978

BARTLETT HAYSTACK

To reach this remote cliff, from Conway, drive west along the Kancamagus Highway for 12 miles, then turn north onto Bear Notch Road. Park 3.45 miles north of the Kancamagus Highway, on the left at the start of a logging road. Hike along the main logging road until it ends, from where you can see the cliff. Bushwhack for several minutes up to the crag's left end. The approach should take about 40 minutes, but watch out for bears!

THE FLARE I 5.10d (5.7 R) (**)
At the cliff's left-hand end, locate an 80 foot, overhanging offwidth crack above a 40 foot slab. Bring a full set of Friends, including three or four #4s. Plenty of gymnastic tape—or a full body neoprene suit—advisable!
1. Climb up the slab (5.7 R) to a short headwall and the base of the crack. Jam awkwardly up the overhanging, flaring offwidth crack (5.10d) to a fixed belay anchor at a bong. 80', 5.10d
2. Continue up a nice finger and hand width crack (5.9) to the top. 40', 5.9
Rappel off a tree with two ropes back to the ground.
FA: George Hurley & Joe Hayes   May 30, 1989
FFA: George Hurley & John Strand   July 29, 1989

VARIATION: FEAR OF EJECTION I 5.11b (*)
1a. Climb the very thin crack in a flare (5.11b) in the headwall, halfway up the first pitch, just to the right of the regular route. 15', 5.11b
HISTORY: John Strand top-roped this short variation on July 29, 1989, before returning to lead it in 1991.

GREEN'S CLIFF

Perhaps the most remote cliff along the Kancamagus Highway (and that's really saying something), this 300 foot high granite escarpment remains one of the White Mountain's hardest to reach, least explored cliffs. The ledge is located about as far west along the Kancamagus as Mt. Hedgehog, but to the north of the highway, visible in the distance as the horizontal band of rock rising above an ocean of trees. Lest we forget the exploring spirit of AMC rock climbers of the 1920s, the following is quoted from the 1928 AMC Bulletin: "Excellent opportunities will be offered those interested in rock climbing. Experienced rope leaders will lead parties on the known courses of Hedgehog and Potash Mountains, while groups of experienced climbers reconnoiter Square Ledge and the imposing faces of Owl's Head and Green's Cliff." To this very day, these latter three cliffs, located southwest of Bartlett off the Bear Notch Road, are still amongst the least visited crags in the entire White Mountain region! Newly discovered evidence confirms that Lincoln O'Brien actually did make an attempt to climb Green's Cliff in 1928. (See next page.)

There are two ways to approach Green's Cliff: one is very long, starting from the Kancamagus Highway, while the other is even longer, beginning from Bear Notch Road. However, the Bear Notch Road approach is undoubtedly the easiest, but use that term advisably, and bring your mountain bike.

- **The Kancamagus Highway Approach:** A sizable bushwhack (even by New Hampshire standards) leads through almost impenetrable forest up to the cliff base. Bring a compass, bivy gear, extra food and water, bear repellent—and good luck!

- **Bear Notch Road Approach:** From Conway, drive west along the Kancamagus Highway for 12 miles, then turn north up Bear Notch Road driving another nine tenths of a mile to Fire Road #35 (Rob Brook Road). Park in a dirt pullout on the left at an information kiosk. From the gate at the start of the road, mountain bike one hour and 15 minutes along the road through enjoyable, rolling terrain (watch out for moose and bears!) until you reach the start of the first and only steep uphill section of the road, and a wooden snowmobile bridge. (After roughly 20 minutes of biking, you can see Green's Cliff up ahead.) From the snowmobile bridge, bushwhack uphill looking for occasional pink surveying tape for another 45 minutes (if you don't get lost) to reach the cliff base. By bike, the entire approach takes roughly two hours. If you hike in, allow four hours. Either way, it's a good 15 miles round trip! Above a slight clearing at the cliff base is the following route:

BLACK FLIES CONSUME JIM DUNN II 5.12d (**)
It may look like a 5.10 slab, but it is definitely not! Just left of a dirty ramp/corner (100 feet left of STEWART'S CRACK) is a large, steep, dark gray slab. There are six protection bolts. Bring a normal rack.

1. Head up black rock (5.11a) past a bolt to a good ledge. Move right (5.11b) to a short, left-facing corner (bolt). Climb up the corner to another bolt, then step right onto the crux (5.12d), an incredibly difficult iron cross move on a steep slab (bolt). Mantleshelf above (bolt), and rest. More sustained 5.11 face climbing (bolt) gains a sloping belay ledge with a double bolt anchor. 100', 5.12d

HISTORY: After considerable effort, Gerry Lortie & John Strand made the route's first ascent in the Summer of 1993. On August 28, sharing the lead, they placed the first two bolts—after a long hike in to the cliff. On September 6, after a much faster bike ride, they drilled the last four bolts and completed the pitch. All six bolts were drilled free on the lead by hand.

STEWART'S CRACK II 5.9 (*)
The first route on the cliff: the obvious, vertical crack system in the cliff's center. Look for a 300 foot hand crack with several trees growing in it, that begins in a left-facing corner 100 feet to the right of BLACK FLIES CONSUME JIM DUNN. Bring a normal rack.

1. Climb up the corner (5.9), then jam up an easier angled hand crack to a tree belay. 100', 5.9
2. Continue up the crack (5.9) to a large belay ledge. 110', 5.9
3. Finish up the hand crack, which finally relents, to the top of the cliff. 90', 5.8 Rappel back down the route off tree anchors.

HISTORY: Jim Dunn & Michael Macklin made the first ascent of the cliff in 1975, naming the climb for Dunn's old friend from Colorado, Stewart Green.

O'BRIEN'S ROUTE I Grade Unknown.
The following is quoted from a 1928 typed report signed by Lincoln O'Brien (who was Miriam O'Brien Underhill's brother) which he submitted to Robert Underhill, who was interested in compiling a rock climbing guidebook to the White Mountains: "The Albany Intervale was thoroughly explored for its rock climbing possibilities by the several climbing caravans of the (AMC) camping party of October 12–14, 1928. Green's Cliff is some two and one half hours from the campsite over a trail recently cut out. A caravan led by Lincoln O'Brien ascended the cliff at its right-hand (east) end for 100 feet, but were unable to find a route to the top of this magnificent cliff. No other route could be found; the smooth, massive slabs seem impregnable."

MT. HEDGEHOG

Surprisingly, this isolated cliff boasts the first rock climbs on the Kancamagus. Mt. Hedgehog was the goal of two separate AMC climbing parties in 1928. As Lincoln O'Brien wrote, "Two caravans on different days found excellent sport here." In the intervening years, visitors to the cliffs have been few and far between. While there are four separate granite ledges, only three have apparently been climbed on. All the ledges get plenty of sunshine and enjoy the same beautiful, quiet setting. Drive one and a half miles west of the Passaconaway Historical Site and park at the Mt. Potash / UNH Trail. Hike up the trail's left branch, the UNH / Mt. Hedgehog Trail, for two more miles to the summit of Mt. Hedgehog. There is a stream for water three tenths of a mile before the cliffs.

Passaconaway, Child of the Bear, was the peace-loving chief of the Penacook Tribe. In 1627, he united over 17 Indian tribes living in central New England into the Penacook Indian Confederacy. Appointed its first Sagamon, Chief Passaconaway ruled compassionately until his death in 1669. The first white settlers built homes in Passaconaway, also known as Albany Intervale, in 1790. They made a slender livelihood from farming, and later logging, which reached its peak about 1900. The first road was built between Conway and Passaconaway in 1837, while the Kancamagus Highway opened in 1959.

THE EAST LEDGES

The following is quoted from Appalachia, 1928: "The east loop was taken to the top of the east cliff where trees to furnish a belay for roping down were readily found. After two rappels, the rest of the descent was made on easy ledges. The party started up from a birch stump somewhat to the right of the middle of the cliff, and ascended a slope with only friction holds to a stance 30 feet from the ground. Here it was necessary for the second man to unrope while the leader found a route to the next stance on a shelf some 70 feet above and to the right. This pitch started with a narrow vertical crack, followed by an inconvenient bulging rock and a diagonal traverse right on an ascending series of minute ledges to a three foot shelf. From here it was necessary to pass to the left 15 feet to a six foot layback crack which led to another ledge. Twelve feet to the left of this ledge, a more difficult vertical crack of 20 feet was found and climbed to a shelf. A slanting scrabble upward to the right, behind trees, was followed by 10 feet of delicate climbing to a single tree. An easy diagonal upward to the left led to a small platform. The final pitch was long and exposed, so the second man unroped and belayed the leader around a point of rock just below the platform. The wall above offered no holds, necessitating a traverse to the left with a long stride to a narrow ledge, whence a two inch crack was climbed straight up about 60 feet to the top of the cliff.

MT. HEDGEHOG - THE EAST LEDGES

Height: over 200 feet. Average angle: 60 degrees. Time: two hours."
FA: G. L. Stebbins, Marjorie Hurd, & Avis E. Newhall, Henry E. Childs, Hester L. Bassett, & Mrs. R. E. Bates   October 14, 1928

On the preceding day, a second group did two other climbs on the East cliff, to the left and right of the former route, but the details were not recorded.
FA: Lincoln O'Brien, Edith D. Sprague, & Frances E. Clarke; and Park Carpenter, James B. Herron, & Edith Lamprey   October 13, 1928

> It has been impossible to determine how modern routes relate to these early endeavors. The 1928 routes probably ascended the lowest band of rock below the middle tree ledge. Another route, CLOUDS, was done here in the early 1980s. The next routes all ascend the top face above the center ledge.

STONE'S THROW I 5.5
At the left end of the cliff (facing out) is a small clearing in the trees. Rappel from here down to a tree ledge, and start the climb from there.
1. Climb a flake and dirty chimney to a finger crack. 130', 5.5
HISTORY: Todd Swain & Curt Robinson did the first ascent on September 11, 1977. A big boulder dislodged from the chimney narrowly missed Robinson.

DAG-NABIT I 5.5
About 50 feet to the right (when facing out) of STONE'S THROW is a small buttress. Rappel down to a tree ledge from here.
1. Start up a rotten dike, then head up the left side of the buttress. 140', 5.5
FA: Todd Swain, Rich Couchon, & Ned Getchell   September 3, 1977

RINGWRAITH I 5.4
1. The obvious crack just to the left of DAG-NABIT. 130', 5.4
FA: Rich Couchon, Ned Getchell, & Todd Swain   September 3, 1977

18 HOLES I 5.5
1. Climb up pockets 25 feet to the left of RINGWRAITH. 5.5
FA: Todd Swain & Curt Robinson   September 11, 1977

PB & J I 5.5   The favorite food of every red-blooded American climber!
Facing out, 40 feet right of RINGWRAITH, rap off the right center of a ledge.
1. Ascend short cracks and friction up to a short, vertical wall near the top with few good holds—the crux. 130', 5.5
FA: Rich Couchon, Ned Getchell, & Todd Swain   September 3, 1977

MacDOUGAL'S VARIATION I 5.7 (*)
1. Climb the obvious thin crack to the right of PB & J to the top bulge, then up the left crack (5.7), or up a finger crack (5.6).
HISTORY: Don MacDougal, Mark Robinson, Ned Getchell, & Todd Swain made the first recorded ascent on May 28, 1978.

CATCH-22 I 5.7 (5.6 R)
Rappel from the right end of a tree ledge (facing out), just to the left of the trees on top down to the tree ledge below.
1. Angle up and left to a shallow, right-facing corner, protect, then head right up a vertical seam (5.6 R) to a ledge. Finish up a short, left-facing corner (5.7).
FA: Todd Swain & Curt Robinson September 11, 1977

VARIATION #1: **IMAGINATION** I 5.8+
1a. Head up the face (5.8+) to the left of the final corner. 5.8+

VARIATION #2: **CASEY'S VARIATION** I 5.4
1a. Climb a block and a flake (5.4) to the right of the final corner. 5.4

SPINEY NORMAN I 5.2
Named after a Monty Python character, the Hedgehog.
1. Start as for CATCH-22, but move left past the corner into a vertical finger crack, and climb this to the top. 100', 5.2
HISTORY: Curt Robinson & Todd Swain made the first recorded ascent on September 11, 1977. The Hedgehog, Spiney Norman, was "100 feet long from his nose to his anus."

THE GIRDLE OF THE EAST LEDGES II 5.6+
Start at the top of SPINEY NORMAN.
1. Climb down and right across CATCH-22 (5.6+), then down farther and right to the PB & J / RINGWRAITH alcove. 5.6+
2. Continue right to an awkward down climbing move, then head over to the crux of DAG-NABIT (5.5) and the finish. 5.5
FA: Todd Swain, Sharon Casey, & Ned Getchell September 24, 1978

HELMS DEEP GULLY

Sixty feet beyond the East Ledges heading towards the summit is a wide gully leading down to the right. Scramble down it to reach:

TREEBEARD I 5.6
1. On the right wall of the gully (facing uphill), climb straight up the large crack at the bottom (5.6), or the arete to its left (5.5). 40', 5.6
FA: Todd Swain, Ned Getchell, & Sharon Casey September 24, 1978

THE NORTH LEDGE

Continuing 150 feet west on the trail towards the summit, one emerges on top of a steep cliff. Hike down around the cliff's right side (facing out) to the base.

AVATAR I 5.8+ (**)
The enjoyable, left-facing dihedral on the right-hand side of the cliff.
1. Jam and stem up the one wizard of a corner to the top. 70', 5.8+

HISTORY: Michael Hartrich & Albert Dow, and Todd Swain all appear to have done the climb during the late 1970s.

AND THEN THERE WERE TWELVE I 5.6
Begin to the left of AVATAR at a dirty corner with a large pine tree.
1. Up the dihedral 30 feet, step right, and finish up another corner. 70', 5.6
FA: Todd Swain & Ned Getchell April 7, 1979

THE SUMMIT CLIFF

This is the highest cliff at Mt. Hedgehog. Lincoln O'Brien's 1928 team also climbed the north end of this ledge via "an amusing climb of 40 minutes. Other routes looked possible." From the open top of the East Ledges, one has a clear view of the upper-most cliff. Bushwhack to the right side of the summit ledge, aiming for a prominent, right-facing corner. From this feature continue left, first uphill then back down, following the crag's base until below to a solitary pine growing 20 feet up, and just above a shallow, right-facing corner or ramp, the line of PONDEROSA. The routes are now described from left to right.

THE LOST DUTCHMAN I 5.10b
Start at the left-hand side of the cliff, to the left of PONDEROSA.
1. Climb a striking corner/crack up to and over a small roof (5.10b), then continue following the same crack system to the top. 5.10b
FA: Mike Hartrich, Al Rubin, & Guus Lambreghts (Holland) June, 1980

PONDEROSA II 5.7
The central route up the Summit Cliff.
1. Climb the right-facing ramp to the solitary pine 20 feet up, then head up and right towards a bulge. Move over this on solution pockets, then trend back left to a smooth block. Belay above on a ledge with stunted pine trees. 5.5
2. From the left end of the belay ledge, step across a gully to a crack that leads to an obvious, left-facing corner and ceiling. Exit right out of the corner's top, then continue past a small pine to a belay. 5.7
3. Head up and left to reach the UNH Trail and the summit.
FA: Joe Perez & Kurt Winkler December 31, 1979

THE JOPLIN-HENDRIX ROUTE I 5.9- R
Start at the right-hand end of the cliff. Modern rack.
1. Climb up a shallow, right-facing corner/arch until it ends, then face climb up a steep wall over a bulge (5.9- R) to easier moves leading up to a belay stance (piton anchor). 110', 5.9- R
2. Climb up and left towards a block, circumnavigate around the block (5.6), and head for the trees on top. 80', 5.6
FA: Kurt Winkler, Shraddha Howard, & Dhrubbha Hein September, 1993

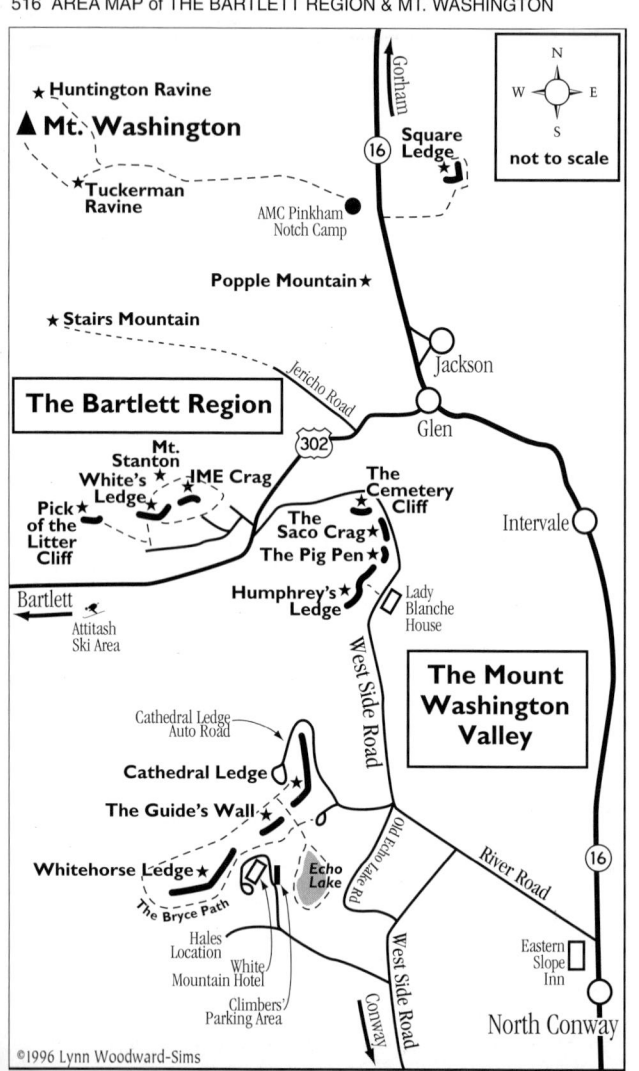

516 AREA MAP of THE BARTLETT REGION & MT. WASHINGTON

THE BARTLETT REGION

In recent years, the cliffs near the town of Bartlett have been the focus of increasing attention by local climbers. The largest cliff, White's Ledge, climbed upon since 1929, boasts the popular, multi-pitch routes ENDEAVOR and THE WHITE STREAK. Several nearby smaller cliffs such as the IME Crag, the Pick Of The Litter Cliff, the Attitash Crag, and Cave Mountain, offer challenging one pitch routes. In the Remote Crags Category are Hart's Ledge, and Stairs Mountain, with its hidden assortment of back country cliffs. Modern climbers looking for new adventures, especially on some of the Bartlett area cliffs, might tend to think, "No one could have possibly been up here before." Not necessarily true! This intriguing quote from the 1929 AMC Bulletin should refute that notion: "Objectives will be selected from among the many fine, rugged mountains, etc., immediately adjacent to the Rocky Branch Valley... including also certain other points of interest outside the valley: Mts. Stanton and Pickering, Stairs Mt., White's Ledge, Cave Mt., Hart's Ledge, and Silver Spring Mt. (exploration). These do not exhaust the possibilities."

STAIRS MOUNTAIN

Stairs Mountain (3,460') in Sargent's Purchase is a complex set of cliffs located in a true wilderness setting. No doubt because of their lengthy approach, it has only been in the past decade that the area has been thoroughly explored. There are several distinct cliffs, including the Back Stairs and the Upper Tier of the Giant Stairs. These features, "the stairs of the Giants", were named by Dr. Samuel Bemis, a Boston dentist who lived each summer in Hart's Location from 1827 to 1840. It was Dr. Bemis who built and resided in the granite block home (now an inn) on Route 302 known as Notchland.

From Glen, drive west on Route 302 less than a mile to the Jericho Road on the right. Follow the Jericho Road to its end, then walk (or mountain bike) 2.3 miles up an old railroad bed to the first shelter on the Rocky Branch Trail. To reach the Upstairs, hike west up Stairs Col Trail to the col. To approach the Giant Steps, hike up Stairs Col Trail until just before Stairs Col and bushwhack right for five minutes to the cliff base. For the Back Stairs, turn right after about a mile and a half up the Stairs Col Trail, and bushwhack 20 minutes north to the base of the 300 foot high, south-east facing, main cliff. The approach to any of the Stairs cliffs takes from one and a half to two hours. Riding a mountain bike in is extremely helpful—especially riding downhill on the way out!

THE UPSTAIRS

Hike to Stairs Col (located between Stairs Mountain and Mt. Resolution) to a trailhead marked "Stairs Lookout". Follow this trail for 20 minutes to reach the viewpoint, with its spectacular panorama. Directly below is a fun, 60 to 80 foot crag with routes that can be either led or top-roped. A one rope, 80 foot rappel off a tree gains the cliff base. The routes are now described from left to right.

HERE'S STAIRING AT YOU I 5.7 (*)
1. Climb thin cracks (5.7) up the slab's left side. 60', 5.7
FA: John Strand & Rose Strand   October 3, 1987

EASY ENOUGH I 5.6
1. Climb the face 20 feet right of HERE'S STARING AT YOU. 60', 5.6
FA: John Strand & Rose Strand, top-rope   October 3, 1987

NATURAL ORDER I 5.8 (*)
The first route on the cliff ascends the central, thin, flaring hand crack just to the left of a nice arete.
1. Above a pine tree, jam up a 60 foot tall, thin hand crack past a block into a V slot corner, then face climb to the top. 80', 5.8
FA: Michael Hartrich & Albert Dow   September 22, 1980

ROSEBUD I 5.9 R (*)
The attractive arete just to the right of NATURAL ORDER.
1. Climb up the arete (5.9 R) until it eases towards the top. 80', 5.9 R
FA: John Strand & Rose Strand   October 3, 1987

STARRY, STAIRY NIGHT I 5.9+ (*)
The Upstair's right-hand route is a real masterpiece.
1. Climb the steep, rough slab 20 feet right of NATURAL ORDER. 70', 5.9+
FA: John Strand & Rose Strand   October 3, 1987

THE GIANT STEPS

HEAVENLY LIGHT I 5.10c
A remote free climb up the 200 foot tall precipice of the Giant Steps. Look for a vertical crack system just to the right of a ramp area.
1. Climb a 5.10c finger crack (fixed nut) for 35 feet until the crack widens at a rotten pinnacle. Easy face climbing gains some left-facing corners, then layback a 5.9 flake to a bush. 130', 5.10c
2. Easier climbing leads to the top. 50'
FA: Albert Dow & Michael Hartrich   September 22, 1980

FINAL FRONTIER II 5.11d (***)
Stairs' best route, with excellent steep climbing in a truly beautiful setting. Start below the cliff's tallest section on a small ledge 15 feet up with a peg anchor.
1. From the belay, move left to a rotten pillar before thin moves (5.9+; peg) lead to slightly left-diagonalling cracks. Now move right over a bulge (5.9+; piton) to a double bolt belay. 100', 5.9+ R

2. Climb past two bolts to a left-leaning arch with two pitons, then reach left (5.11d) to a lovely jug (bolt). Traverse left, then face climb back right (scary) to better holds, and up a final, thin crack (5.9+) which leads to another double bolt belay. 90', 5.11d Rappel back down the route with two ropes.

HISTORY: John Strand & Gerry Lortie climbed Pitch one on October 5, 1989, before Tom Callaghan & John Strand completed the route's first ascent on November 3, 1989. A total of six days of effort were required—with snow! On the actual first ascent, Callaghan completed the crux moves, reached huge buckets above, but was so exhausted that he couldn't hold on any longer. After some agonizing moments, he melted off, taking a dramatic swinging fall, and bruising his hands so badly that they swelled up like balloons. After a good rest, he led the pitch successfully.

THE BACK STAIRS

A massive cliff, first explored in 1976 when the cliff was stumbled upon after a lengthy bushwhack. BACK STAIRS DIRECT is the best landmark to find first. The cliff's standard descent route is to rappel down VETERANS OF FOREIGN WALLS in two rappels, of 150 feet and 70 feet, to return to the ground. The climbs are now described from left to right.

THE SLASH III 5.9+, A2

Start on the same tree ledge as BACK STAIRS DIRECT. Scramble up carefully to the ledge and belay below an open V corner 30 feet to the left of BACK STAIRS DIRECT.

1. A thought-provoking lead: stem up the V dihedral for 20 feet, protect, then step down and traverse left (5.9) on small holds for 20 feet to a small corner. Climb the corner and the face to its right to reach a semi-hanging belay at a piton anchor. 110', 5.9+

2. Climb straight up past a difficult unprotected move to a bolt 20 feet above the belay. Aid the overhanging, diagonal crack above (THE SLASH) to a belay at the top of a horizontal flake on the left near the crack's top. 70' 5.9, A2

3. Aid and free climb up to a roof, then move left out from under it, climbing up a crack, and exit left to a tree ledge. 70' 5.9, A2

FA: Kurt Winkler & George Hurley November 8, 1984

FIVE MINUTES LATER III 5.7, A3+

This mixed route ascends the slanting crack system between THE SLASH and BACK STAIRS DIRECT. Get a very early start if you don't want to sleep out under the trees. To begin, scramble up a rotten corner past a four-trunked birch tree to a good belay ledge shared by both of the aforementioned routes.

1. Stem up a V dihedral (as for THE SLASH) until a bulging headwall forces you to aid left (bolt). Continue up a left-slanting corner (A3) past a second bolt to a two bolt anchor at the base of the upper headwall. 110' 5.7, A3

2. Spicy A3+ skyhooking leads up the slightly overhanging headwall past fixed protection before a couple of moves in an incipient crack lead to a long, enjoyable A1 crack system. Belay at a two bolt anchor. 100', A3+

3. Nail up and left through light-colored granite roofs to a bolt. Hook across a short slab to a right-facing corner, then free climb onto a very narrow ledge. Finish by traversing right past a dead tree to a two bolt anchor. A3

HISTORY: Jason Laflamme & Brady Libby completed the first ascent of the route over several days, using fixed ropes, in the Spring of 1995.

BACK STAIRS DIRECT II 5.9+

An obvious and continuous line up the highest part of the face.

1. Scramble onto a tree ledge 25 feet up. Climb a narrow, blueberry bush-filled groove to a birch, then hand jam a perfect crack for 30 feet to a horizontal break, and climb double cracks (5.9+) up right onto a flat belay ledge. 75', 5.9+

2. Follow the single crack up a chimney, then layback up a corner/crack, first left then right, to a big tree ledge and belay. 90', 5.9

3. Scramble up right to a moderate offwidth crack (5.6). Climb this and another similar crack higher to the top of the cliff. 65', 5.6

FA: Michael Hartrich & George Hurley October 14, 1984

WEBSTER–ROSS ROUTE I 5.10b (Unfinished)

To the right of BACK STAIRS DIRECT lies the earliest, attempted line on the cliff. The leader (Webster) climbed about 80 feet up a difficult, left-facing, flaring corner (5.10b) before retreating in the face of extreme difficulty, and attacks on the belayer (Ross) by squadrons of man-eating black flies!

1. A fading retreat sling on a peg marks the high point. 80', 5.10b

HISTORY: Ed Webster, Paul Ross, & Cindy Ross attempted the first ascent of Ross's mythical "secret cliff" in the Summer of 1976. The hike in was the crux!

TO THE TERRITORY II 5.9

One hundred feet to the right of BACK STAIRS DIRECT is a big, left-facing corner that doesn't reach the ground. Below the corner is an arch.

1. Layback and undercling up the small arch to its end. Make a long reach to a thank-god hold, then follow the corner/crack as it curves up and left to a partially hanging belay where the corner changes direction. Belay above a birch tree beneath a protective roof. 90', 5.9

2. Climb up a dihedral (5.8) to a tree-covered ledge. 50', 5.8

3. Scramble up right to the final wall just to the left of a big roof. Thirty feet left of the roof, climb up and left to gain right-leaning double cracks. Follow them to a ledge, then climb up a short wall to the top, finishing 20 feet to the left of VEEDAUWOO EAST.

FA: Kurt Winkler & George Hurley October 24, 1984

STAIRS MOUNTAIN - THE BACK STAIRS (TO THE TERRITORY) 521

George Hurley on the first ascent of The Slash (5.9+, A2) in 1984. Photograph by Kurt Winkler.

VEEDAUWOO EAST II 5.10b

Hike right from the continuous line of BACK STAIRS DIRECT for about 100 feet until below the large, uneven, left-facing corner of TO THE TERRITORY. Walk right another 20 feet to a hand crack with a small birch tree growing seven feet up the crack, and a spruce 60 feet up.

1. Climb the crack past a dirt-filled section to the large spruce. Continue up the crack past a large flake to where the crack widens to offwidth. Use holds and protection to each side of the wide crack, and belay on a tree ledge. 125', 5.9

2. Scramble up and right across the tree ledge and arrange a belay below and left of a large roof. Climb the face easily up to a short, difficult dihedral (5.10b) just to the left of the roof, and follow the corner to the top. 50', 5.10b

FA: George Hurley & Michael Hartrich   October 14, 1984

ROAD TO SHAMBALA II 5.10d, A2 (Five Points of Aid)

From the highest part of the face, walk right until below the right side of a large overhang near the top of the cliff. The route follows a corner that angles up and slightly left toward the crack splitting the center of the large overhang. Bring along a small selection of pitons.

1. Climb a dihedral with trees to a small overhang 60 feet above the ground. Avoid the overhang on the left by climbing a short arete (5.10b), then continue up the crack to a hanging belay at a small V. 100', 5.10d

2. Move left to a right-facing corner with a crack. Follow the dihedral up to a comfortable belay stance (with a piton anchor) on a long, narrow ledge 20 feet below the main roof. 60', 5.10b

3. Follow the same crack to the overhang, aid out the roof (A2) past two fixed pitons (five points of aid) to a good ledge just over the lip (possible belay here if two bolts were placed), then jam up a nice hand crack that slants left to the top of the cliff. 80' 5.9+, A2 Beware of rope drag at the roof and above.

FA: George Hurley & Kurt Winkler   October 30, 1984

FFA, Pitch One: Jerry Handren, Kris Hansen, & Mark Wilson   August 14, 1987

SHAMBLE ROAD I 5.10b

1. Climb the face just to the left of the crack system on ROAD TO SHAMBALA for 40 feet, step right into the crack, and belay at the overhang. 60', 5.7

2. Angle up right, at first very easily, then climb up an excellent, left-facing, open book (5.10b) to a good belay ledge. 150', 5.10b

3. Off the ledge's right end, jam an offsize crack (5.7) and angle right to the top, ending 20 feet left of VETERANS OF FOREIGN WALLS, the rap route. 80', 5.7

FA: Michael Hartrich & George Hurley   November 1, 1986

MICHAEL'S WAY II 5.9

Find the tree-filled crack/dihedral of THE ROAD TO SHAMBALA below the giant roof to the right of the center of the cliff. Twenty five feet farther right is

another crack with a triangular-shaped block sitting in it just above the ground.
1. Above the block, climb the crack (5.9) to a ledge 15 feet up. Above, climb the same crack through a blueberry patch to a tree clump, then angle up and right to a large, tree-covered ledge. 90', 5.9
2. Walk left, and from the left end of the tree ledge, climb up into a left-facing corner following a great finger crack a short distance before moving left into a dirty offwidth crack which leads to a cave. 75', 5.9
3. Traverse right (5.7) to a good ledge. 40', 5.7
4. Finish up the top pitch of SHAMBLE ROAD. Off the right end of the belay ledge, climb an offsize crack (5.7), then angle right to the top, ending 20 feet to the left of the finish of VETERANS OF FOREIGN WALLS, which is the usual rappel route back to the ground. 80', 5.7
FA: Michael Hartrich & George Hurley September 3, 1994

MERLIN'S WAY II 5.10b (5.9 R)
Begin 15 feet right of MICHAEL'S WAY, looking for two comma-shaped grooves 12 feet above the ground. This start is also 25 feet to the left of the initial V groove of VETERANS OF FOREIGN WALLS. Modern rack.
1. Getting past the commas is the crux of the pitch (5.9 R). Continue up more discontinuous features to gain a large, tree-covered ledge. 80', 5.9 R
2. Again walk to the left end of this tree ledge, then climb up the left-facing corner following the great finger crack. When the crack ends in a steep face, climb the face to a good tree ledge. 60', 5.10b (This pitch shares the last 60 feet of SHAMBLE ROAD.)
3. Climb Pitch three of SHAMBLE ROAD, up the right-slanting offwidth crack (5.7) to the top of the cliff. 80', 5.7
FA: George Hurley & Michael Hartrich September 3, 1994

VETERANS OF FOREIGN WALLS II 5.10b (******)
From below the cliff's highest section, walk right until beneath the right edge of the enormous roof to the right of the main face. Hike another 60 feet further right to a 20 foot V groove. Since this climb is the normal rappel line down the Back Stairs, it's also a good introductory route to the cliff.
1. Climb the initial V groove, then follow small, discontinuous cracks straight up the face (5.8) to easier climbing and a tree ledge. 70', 5.8
2. Climb the obvious crack which passes just left of a long, three foot roof before becoming a left-facing dihedral (5.9). Above a narrow ledge, climb a short, difficult corner (5.10b) to easier ground and the top. 130', 5.10b (Possible belay on the narrow ledge at 80 feet.) Rappel twice back down the route, for 150' and 70' respectively, using two ropes to reach the ground.
HISTORY: George Hurley & Kurt Winkler made the first ascent on October 18, 1984, doing a massive gardening effort, all on the lead.

524 THE BARTLETT REGION

Ed Webster climbing Especially When The October Wind Blows (5.8) on White's Ledge in 1981. Photograph by Anne Rutter.

WHITE'S LEDGE

Located on the sunny, south face of Mt. Stanton northeast of Bartlett, White's Ledge lies on the opposite side of the fertile Saco River valley from the Attitash Ski Area. A pleasant wooded approach, enjoyable free climbing, solvable route finding, and good granite all contribute to this cliff's relaxing atmosphere. Although some small crags near the summit of White's Ledge were ascended by AMC climbers led by Herbert C. Towle in August, 1929, the first ascent of the main cliff via the general line of THE WHITE STREAK was made by Leland Pollock, Fritz Wiessner, & Robert Underhill in the Summer of 1933. From the intersection of Routes 16 & 302 in Glen, drive west on Route 302 Glen for 1.6 miles to Covered Bridge Lane on your right. (If you're driving east on Route 302 from Bartlett, Covered Bridge Lane is on your left, half a mile past West Side Road.) Turn onto Covered Bridge Lane and follow it for one mile, first bearing left at a Y, past houses, then past White's Ledge Lane before parking on the sandy shoulder on the left. From here, hike left (west) through the woods toward the cliff, keeping the steeper scree slopes of Mt. Stanton on your right. Eventually, scramble up through a small talus field to the cliff base. The approach takes about 30 minutes.

A shorter approach is along a dirt road which is gated and sometimes locked. From Route 302, turn onto Covered Bridge Lane, go left at the Y, and look for a metal pipe, gated dirt road on the left (four tenths of a mile from the Y at Covered Bridge Lane, or six tenths of a mile from Route 302). The dirt road follows the Saco River's northern bank west toward the cliff, and eliminates the traditional, forested approach. *The dirt road is always open to public access by foot. If the pipe is NOT locked, the road is open to drive on, too.* (The gate is locked during mud season and sometimes in the autumn as it does access private land.) Drive or walk along the road past a brushy logging area until even with White's Ledge. Just beyond are two dirt pullouts on the right. Park here. Hike left (west) on an old logging road, then when another logging road cuts off right (north), follow it to reach the talus below White's Ledge. To descend, scramble to the summit of Mt. Stanton, then down a hiking trail back to the housing development. Routes are described from left to right.

NEBULOUS II 5.6 (*)
If you thirst for adventure and don't mind following a vague, 25 year old route description, this could be your route! From the lowest toe of the cliff, walk uphill (left) for roughly 150 feet to a tree-covered section, then traverse out right across several sandy ledges (the higher, the easier) to the climb's start.
1. From a gully, diagonal up right to a square block topped by a tree ledge.
2. From the base of a large, low-angled face, climb an inside corner with trees, and belay behind the third tree.

526 THE BARTLETT REGION

WHITE'S LEDGE

A.	*	**NEBULOUS** II 5.6	Page	525
B.	**	**ENDEAVOR** III 5.7+	Page	528
C.	*	**TEN YEARS AFTER** II 5.9	Page	528
D.	*	**THE WHITE STREAK** II 5.8	Page	529
E.	**	**GRENDAL'S LAIR** I 5.10a	Page	530
F.	**	**INSIDE STRAIGHT** I 5.10a	Page	531
G.		**GIMP CRACK** I 5.9 (5.8 X)	Page	531
H.		Mt. Stanton (Descent Route)		

3. Face climb straight up, avoiding poor rock on the left.
FA: Joe Cote & Bob Fraser September 19, 1971

ENDEAVOR III 5.7+ (**)

A superior route offering good rock and nice moves—but a climb not to be underestimated. Along with THE WHITE STREAK, this is the cliff's other best intermediate route, but route finding and protection on the Pitch two crux requires patience & determination. Begin 30 feet left of the cliff's lowest point.
1. A short pitch gains the right end of a solitary tree ledge 30 feet up.
2. Intricate climbing heads straight up (5.7+) to a good belay at a large pine tree, the lower of two pines when the route is seen from the ground. 5.7+
3. Climb up and right to the higher pine tree. Belay at bushes just above.
4. A short lead gains several possible belay stances below the top slab.
5. Climb up the low-angled upper face into the start of a beautiful, toe-width crack, superb at only 5.5, that slices up the center of the clean, exposed final slab. Belay at a small stance halfway up the crack system. 90', 5.5
6. Continue up the Toe Crack (more great 5.5) until it ends, then face climb off to the right to a tree-covered ledge. 80', 5.5
7. An easy pitch leads up a crack over some bulges. 140', 5.3 Finish by scrambling up a gully, heading up and right to the top of Mt. Stanton.
FA: Joe Cote & Roger Martin November 6, 1971

TEN YEARS AFTER II 5.9 (*)

The quality directissima of White's Ledge. Carry a normal rack.
1. Just left of the cliff's toe, climb a vertical crack to a tree, then move right into the shallow, right-facing dihedral. When it ends, move over a bulge (5.9), and climb up a finger crack to a belay stance under a large overlap/roof. 5.9
2. Circle around the left side of the overlap, then climb disconnected finger cracks straight up to a block, and belay. 5.8
3. Climb a corner (5.6), then step right to a pine tree and a rounded arete. Follow the ridge (nice moves, but little protection) up to a pine tree belay. 5.6
4. A short, right-facing corner (5.9) gains a ledge. Step left and extend the straight line of the climb up an unprotected 5.7 arete just to the right of the ENDEAVOR Toe Crack. Belay at a tree above. 5.9
5. Scramble to the top, finishing as desired.
HISTORY: Jeff Pheasant & Mike Hartrich did Pitch one in 1975. Ed Webster & Mike Hartrich made the first complete ascent on October 31, 1981.

THE PRIMROSE PATH II 5.8

The route takes a slightly right-leaning path up the middle of White's Ledge, crossing over several other routes in the process.
1. Climb the first crack on TEN YEARS AFTER for 30 feet, then face climb

up and slightly left (5.8) to a stance. 5.8
2. Face climb up and right to a detached block.
3. Continue diagonally right to the base of a groove system.
4–6. Follow the long groove up and right to the top.
FA: George Hurley & Bill DeMallie   September 27, 1979

THE WHITE STREAK II 5.8 (*)

The first climb on the cliff. Ultimately this fine route ascends the prominent white streak near the summit of the ledge. A serious accident caused by an unexpected leader fall during the first ascent in 1933 turned the route into quite an ordeal. Start just to the right of the toe of the cliff, above the talus.

1. Climb a flake up right to a large tree 20 feet up, then follow a right-slanting crack to another tree, and belay.
2. After a 5.8 move, face climb left into a dihedral. Climb it past grass clumps and two fixed pitons, then undercling right to a pine tree belay. 5.8
3. Climb the corner above, overcome a short headwall, and enter a wide chimney. Belay at the base of a shattered pillar.
4. Traverse out left across an easy slab, then face climb past a group of white birches on the left. Belay on top of a large, detached spike.
5. Step left past a small pine tree, then head up and traverse left onto the upper face. From the base of the White Streak, face climb straight up (left of the ENDEAVOR Toe Crack) to one of several belay stances.
6. An easy lead gains the summit of the ledge.

HISTORY: Leland Pollock, Fritz Wiessner, & Robert Underhill did the first ascent in the Summer of 1933. "There was a fellow who was with us on White's Ledge: Leland Pollock. Everyone thought he was very good, and very daring, too," recalled Wiessner admiringly. "We went up to the cliff, which had never been climbed before, where Leland thought he knew of a good route. I led the first rope length, Leland led the second, and so on. After we changed the lead, Leland made a stretch—and has a fall and came off, maybe broke a handhold that wasn't very good. He was hurt, so we traversed right, I helped him up carefully, and we took him to the hospital. He had broken some bones."

"I can't remember why Fritz wasn't leading that section," Robert Underhill added. "I think he thought it was going to be even more difficult above, and was saving himself. We finally got Leland down safely, and Fritz did a wonderful job throughout. I thought to myself, 'Now here is a man I would go anywhere with.' I was very impressed with how expertly Fritz had managed Leland, who was badly hurt." Due to the accident, the line of ascent near the top differed from the now usual line taken today. The complete route was eventually climbed by Joe Cote & Eric Radack on October 31, 1971.

ESPECIALLY WHEN THE OCTOBER WIND BLOWS II 5.8
An enjoyable and intricate climb with several possible variations. Uphill to the right of THE WHITE STREAK is a right-facing corner.
1. Climb up to the top of the right-facing dihedral. Make several unprotected moves up a slab, then traverse right to a pine tree belay. 5.8
2. Step onto the face on the right, climbing a very shallow corner (5.8) past a peg and around a fir tree. Belay under a short wall. 5.8
3. Traverse easily left up over flakes to a blocky, left-facing corner. Climb the corner, and continue past the ledge at its top to good rock and a right-facing corner. Belay here.
4. Climb up right onto slabs. Belay beneath another short, dirty wall.
5. Move left up a mossy, right-facing dihedral to a tree ledge.
6. Climb 30 feet of delicate 5.7 to the finish.
FA: John Porter & Dave Masury   October 31, 1971

CRY FOR YESTERDAY I 5.11d (**)
This clean, aesthetic, well protected slabfest ascends the arete to the right of WHEN THE OCTOBER WIND BLOWS, 50 feet to the right of the toe of rock at the cliff base. Gear needed: eight quick draws! Popular.
1. Climb up the arete past seven bolts and one piton. 60', 5.11d Rappel off a white birch tree with one rope.
FA: Brad White & Ian Cruickshank   October, 1994

EL CAMINO NON REAL II 5.8+
Translation (with a Spanish accent): Not The Golden Road. A lengthy route, more or less a direct finish to WHEN THE OCTOBER WIND BLOWS.
1. Climb the initial corner of OCTOBER WIND, then traverse right (5.8+) to grass-filled cracks and a large pine tree. 5.8+
2. Same as WHEN THE OCTOBER WIND BLOWS: climb up shallow, 5.8 grooves (peg) and an arete on the right, around the right side of a fir tree. Continue straight over a rotten 5.7 overhang to a tree ledge. 5.8
3. Off the ledge's left-hand end, climb up a slab to the middle of three inside corners. Head up the central dihedral, then climb a right-facing corner formed by a large flake, and belay from a small pine tree on a ledge. 150', 5.7
4. Climb a flake on the left to an open chimney. Face climb up this, and belay on another tree-covered ledge. 80', 5.7
5. At the ledge's back, climb corners (5.7) past junipers to the top. 160', 5.7
FA: George Hurley & Paul Boissonneault   November 3, 1980

VARIATION: GRENDAL'S LAIR I 5.10a (**)
This fun pitch ascends the narrow, left-facing corner 30 feet to the right of WHEN THE OCTOBER WIND BLOWS up to the pine tree at the top of its first pitch. Wired nut protection is excellent.

1a. Stem up past a bolt to a ledge on the right (piton). Move up to a white birch, gain the base of the sharp-edged dihedral, then follow it (5.10a) to the pine. 5.10a Finish, or rappel twice down THE WHITE STREAK with one rope.
FA: Ed Webster & Cherra Wyllie   May 12, 1982

INSIDE STRAIGHT I 5.10a (**)
A popular, winning deal. Although a total of six pitches were climbed on the first ascent, the upper four are incongruous with the first two which give splendid climbing. About 100 feet to the right of WHEN THE OCTOBER WIND BLOWS is a short, clean-cut finger and hand crack.
1. Climb the crack (5.10a) to a ledge with two trees. 50', 5.10a
2. Face climb past two bolts (5.10a) to a flake which is laybacked up to another tree belay. 60', 5.10a Most parties rappel off twice with one rope.
3–6. The upper pitches, between 5.5 and 5.8, are mostly quite bushy.
FA: George Hurley & Les Gould   June 21, 1981
FFA: Paul Boissonneault & Ed Perry   June 26, 1981

VARIATION #1: **JOKER'S WILD** I 5.10c R (*)
Links Pitch two of INSIDE STRAIGHT with TRUMP CARD. Bring along a modern rack with RP nuts and tiny cams.
2a. At the second bolt on Pitch two of INSIDE STRAIGHT, face climb straight up (5.10c R) to a junction with TRUMP CARD. Continue face climbing up an incipient vertical crack (bolt; 5.10a) following TRUMP CARD up to a good ledge with a double ring bolt anchor. 140', 5.10c R
FA: Tom Callaghan & Paul Nager October, 1995

DIRECT FINISH: **TRUMP CARD** I 5.10a (*)
A more appropriate third pitch to INSIDE STRAIGHT.
3a. Step left with difficulty (5.9+) onto a ledge, then traverse left out into the center of a smooth wall (bolt). Face climb up an incipient, vertical crack past a second bolt (5.10a) to a good ledge with a double ring bolt anchor. 90', 5.10a Rappel off easily from the fixed anchor using two ropes.
FA: Brad White & Dick Peterson   August 20, 1983

GIMP CRACK I 5.9 (5.8 X)
The smooth slab just to the right of INSIDE STRAIGHT. To be, or not to be a gimp, that is the question! Scramble up to a ledge 40 feet up.
1. Make 5.9 moves past a peg into a shallow finger crack. A groundfall runout (5.8 X) reaches good holds and some protection. Tree belay. 5.9 (5.8 X) You can rappel off from here with one rope.
FA: Ed Webster & Cherra Wyllie   May, 1982

THE IME CRAG

The next routes are located on two small crags situated immediately to the east (or right) of White's Ledge. Begin from the northwest corner of the housing development. Hike west towards White's Ledge to a south-jutting spur of the main, east-west running ridge. small, open talus slope on your right. The two IME cliffs are 200 feet north (uphill) of the saddle between the spur and the main ridge. The Lower Tier is 70 feet high while the upper crag, home to INTERNATIONAL MOUNTAIN CRACK, is nearly a full pitch.

5TH AVENUE I 5.8
The farthest left route up the Lower Tier. Begin a few feet right of the DIRECT.
1. Climb up and right to the top of a small block, then traverse horizontally left to gain the right-hand end of a prominent, left-slanting groove. Finish up the groove past a pine tree to the top. 5.8
FA: George Hurley, Les Gould, & Peter McCorrmack August 2, 1981

VARIATION #1: 5TH AVE DIRECT I 5.9, A1 (2 Points of Aid)
Start under the right end of a prominent groove angling up and left to a pine.
1a. Above a hand-width slot, use side clings and two points of aid to reach better holds and the groove. Finish up and slightly right of the pine. 5.9, A1
FA: Mike Kahn & George Hurley September 20, 1996

VARIATION #2: 5TH AVE BYPASS I 5.8
1b. From on top of the small block at the start, move up and right to a small pedestal and crack, then angle left into a corner leading to the top. 5.8
FA: George Hurley & Brian Mauro September 22, 1996

NEW YORK TIMES I 5.7+ (**)
Begin a few feet to the right of 5TH AVENUE at an obvious, orange corner.
1. Layback up the right-slanting corner to its top, step left, and follow a higher corner to the woods. 5.7+
FA: George Hurley, Les Gould, & Peter McCorrmack August 2, 1981

YOU CAN TAKE IT WITH YOU I 5.8
Just to the right of NEW YORK TIMES are twin finger cracks.
1. Climb awkwardly through a short blocky section, step right using some cracks, and finish up an unprotected arete to the trees. 40', 5.8
FA: Peter Yost & Izzie Yost July 17, 1983

HEAT PAIN I 5.10b
Begin about 30 feet to the right of NEW YORK TIMES.
1. Climb up orange blocks, then jam a strenuous finger crack (5.10b) to reach a big pine tree at the top. 40', 5.10b
HISTORY: Doug Madara & Rob Walker made the route's first ascent on a very cold March 27, 1983. If you've ever experienced March rock climbing temperatures in New Hampshire, you can certainly appreciate the name!

THE IME CRAG - UPPER TIER (INT'L MTN CRACK) 533

THE MOUNTAINEER'S ROUTE I 5.6
1. To the right of the previous routes, climb up a left-diagonalling crack or groove, then scramble up through trees to reach the base of the Upper Tier.
2. Forty feet to the right of INTERNATIONAL MOUNTAIN CRACK is a narrow ledge system that slants left all the way to the top. Follow this past several small pine trees to a large pine tree at the finish.
FA: George Hurley, Gail Murphy, & Sean Murphy   August 9, 1981

BIG LICKS I 5.8
Begin 40 feet to the left of INTERNATIONAL MOUNTAIN CRACK.
1. Face climb up to a cleaned-off finger crack, avoid the undercling on the left, and jam all the way up the crack to the top. 50', 5.8
HISTORY: Doug Madara & Rob Walker climbed the first ascent on March 27, 1983. The Big Licks ice cream shop was next to IME's old location.

GROOVEDOGS I 5.10d
Start eight feet to the right of BIG LICKS.
1. Climb a shallow groove/corner past a bolt to small overlaps, step left, and make a hard move (5.10d) up to a rounded, brown groove. Above, climb a flake and an inverted V to the top. 60', 5.10d
HISTORY: Tom Stryker & Tony Tulip made the first ascent on June 29, 1986, placing the bolt on the lead from a skyhook.

NO SELF CONTROL I 5.11d (*)
Start just to the left of INTERNATIONAL MOUNTAIN CRACK.
1. Face climb past three bolts on an overlap (5.11d) to a finish up the top section of INTERNATIONAL MOUNTAIN CRACK. 90', 5.11d
FA: Paul Cusar & John Tremblay   August 5, 1989

INTERNATIONAL MOUNTAIN CRACK I 5.10b (**)
The beautiful, left-leaning finger crack on the Upper Tier. The route is well worth the long approach. Clean, sustained, and well protected.
1. Layback and jam the thin crack up to a piton. Step left onto the face (5.10b), reach a good hold, then climb the rest of the crack to the top. 100', 5.10b
FA: Brooks Bicknell & George Hurley   August 6, 1981
FFA: Brooks Bicknell, Alain Comeau, & Kurt Winkler   August 21, 1981

TOO THIN TO BE FUN I 5.11c (Top-rope)
The blank face 10 feet to the right of INTERNATIONAL MTN. CRACK.
1. Top-rope the smooth face on incredibly tiny crimpers. 90', 5.11c
FA: Ian Cruickshank, Dick Peterson, & Brad White   October 5, 1991

MOHEGAN I 5.9 R
The obvious, right-facing dihedral to the right of MOUNTAINEER'S ROUTE.
1. Hard moves gain the top of a fragile-looking pedestal. Move into the right-

facing corner (5.9 R), and continue on better jams to the top. 80', 5.9 R
FA: Kurt Winkler, George Hurley, & David Stone August 21, 1981

MIDLIFE CRISIS I 5.10c (**)
Start 12 feet to the right of MOHEGAN at a small, left-facing flake 10 feet off the ground. Bring a normal rack, including RP nuts.
1. Make hard moves off the ground (nut) up to a small, sloping ledge and a mantleshelf move. Then step left (peg) before climbing straight up past a bolt to a very shallow, left-facing corner. Climb this corner (5.10b), then diagonal right across the face (bolt) to small ledges which lead up onto an outside corner on the right (5.10c) with two bolts. Belay at a double cold shut anchor on the small ledge above. 80', 5.10c
HISTORY: Dick Peterson, Brad White, Ian Cruickshank, & Ken Parker made the first ascent of this fine route on October 5, 1991.

THE ROTTEN LOG I 5.9- R
The rotten log used to gain the corner has fallen, making the start harder.
1. Face climb (5.9- R) up into a left-facing, hanging corner 20 feet downhill and right of MOHEGAN. At the corner's top, make a rising traverse left, crossing MIDLIFE CRISIS (bolt), to a finish up MOHEGAN. 5.9- R
FA: George Hurley, Frank Matta, & Phil Erard June 13, 1981

MEAN LINE I 5.10b or 5.9 (**)
A few feet right of THE ROTTEN LOG are two maple trees. Nice moves.
1. Face climb straight up (5.10b; bolt—or 5.9 farther right) to reach the right edge of the large block that forms THE ROTTEN LOG corner. Climb the block's right side to reach the top. 50', 5.10b or 5.9
HISTORY: On September 22, 1996, George Hurley & Brian Mauro led the 5.9 version and top-roped the 5.10b direct start. After placing a bolt on rappel, George Hurley & Jean Hurley led the harder start on September 24, 1996.

MOUNT STANTON

The North Buttress of Mount Stanton is a one pitch slab. Follow the trail up over the summit of Mount Stanton. Continue on the path downhill until the first fork, bear right, and continue a few hundred feet farther to an overlook with a big boulder. Rappel down or hike around either side of the cliff to the base.

LOOK MA, NO HANDS I 5.9
Two bolts 30 feet up a blank slab mark the route.
1. Climb past the two bolts (5.9) to a third bolt, then continue to two hollow flakes. Step left to a narrow, but solid flake, and layback it to a fourth bolt, and the top of the slab. 120', 5.9
FA: Joe Perez, Judy Perez, & Ben Onachila May, 1993

THE PICK OF THE LITTER CLIFF

The Pick Of The Litter Cliff is a steep slab sitting on top of a separate knoll just to the west of White's Ledge. Contrary to popular belief, it is not really a sport crag. Be sure to bring a reasonably sized modern rack to protect the routes. Drive in as for White's Ledge from Route 302, and look for a metal pipe, gated dirt road (four tenths of a mile from the Y at Covered Bridge Lane, or six tenths of a mile from Route 302) on the left before the "sandy shoulder" parking area. This dirt road follows the northern bank of the Saco River west toward the cliff, and eliminates a long hike in. *The dirt road is always open to public access by foot. If the metal pipe is NOT locked, then the road is open to drive on.* (The gate is locked during mud season and sometimes during the autumn since it eventually does access private land.) Drive or walk along the road past a brushy logging area until even with White's Ledge. Just beyond the logging area are two dirt pullouts on the right. Park here. Hike left (west) on an old logging road. (Where another logging road cuts off to the right or north, you can also follow this to the talus below White's Ledge.) For the Pick Of The Litter Cliff, continue straight ahead (west) along the logging road until it begins to fade, then diagonal right into the woods to pick up a drainage that leads uphill to the cliff base. From the two dirt pullouts, it's a 20 minute approach if you don't get lost. The routes are now described from right to left.

HAIRLINE I 5.9 R
The crag's right-hand route. Start at a short, right-facing corner. Modern rack.
1. Head up the corner (poor peg; 5.8 R), then step left to a thin, vertical seam. Climb the seam (5.9) past a strange angle piton until it fades out, then finger traverse right (5.9 R) for 15 feet (piton), and finish straight up. 60', 5.9 R
FA: Brad White & Dick Peterson   June, 1988

TOP DOG I 5.11a (or 5.10c) (*)
Start 15 feet left of HAIRLINE. Modern rack required. There are two ways to climb into the crux "scoop" just above the second bolt.
1. Face climb up a series of holds past two bolts. The first ascent stepped right, then underclung an arch back left into the scoop (5.10c). The normal method now is to do a 5.11a mantleshelf up left into the scoop. Then face climb up and right (tricky pro) with funky moves to a big tree. 70', 5.11a (or 5.10c)
HISTORY: Dick Peterson & Brad White made the first ascent in June, 1988 using the right-hand undercling. Several days later, Jim Merchant & Bruce Luetters "greased up" the 5.11a mantleshelf move.

K-NINE I 5.9 (*)
Start by a prominent hemlock tree growing near the center of the cliff. The route ascends the steep, bolted face just behind the tree.

1. Face climb up a steep headwall past two bolts (5.9), then diagonal out right across the steep slab to a third bolt. Move up onto a ledge, and finish up a left-slanting hand crack (5.8) to the top. 80', 5.9
FA: Brad White & Dick Peterson   June, 1988

BY BOSCH, BY GOLLY! I 5.11c (**)
Begin about 30 feet to the left of the hemlock tree at the base of a shallow, left-facing corner/block 10 feet tall, below two bolts. Carry a modern rack with small wired nuts and cams. Sustained.

1. Make a couple of moves up the corner, step left onto the face, then climb straight up (5.10b) to the first bolt. Now make hard moves right (5.11c) to reach the second bolt, and angle right to a series of left-slanting, incipient finger cracks leading to the horizontal break running across the top of this part of the cliff. Finish straight up (5.10b; bolt) to the top. 90', 5.11c
FA: Brad White, Dick Peterson, & Tim Jepson (UK)   July, 1988

PUMPING POCKETS I 5.10b (*)
The obvious line of pockets five feet to the right of PICK OF THE LITTER, and just to the left of a blunt arete to the left of BY BOSCH, BY GOLLY! Take a modern rack with flexible cams.

1. Climb from pocket to pocket (5.9) straight up to a poor bolt, then make a very awkward move (5.10b) to gain the horizontal break above. Finish up and left, up the top corner on PICK OF THE LITTER. 70', 5.10b
FA: Dick Peterson & Brad White   June, 1988

PICK OF THE LITTER I 5.8+ (**)
The original and easiest route on the cliff. Very popular.

1. Face climb past four bolts (5.8+). After a peg, make a long reach to the horizontal crack, step right, and climb a right-facing corner to the top. 70', 5.8+
FA: Matt Peer & Elaine Stockbridge Peer   October 26, 1985

FORCHRISAKE I 5.10c
Begin 20 feet left of PICK OF THE LITTER in front of another hemlock.

1. Thin face moves (5.10c) lead past two bolts to gain the horizontal break, then traverse right a couple of moves, and head straight to the top. 60', 5.10c
FA: Dick Peterson, Brad White, & Jose Abeyta   September 29, 1990

THE ATTITASH CRAG

You've driven by this small cliff a hundred times, but never stopped! This is the short, steep granite outcrop rising just above the trees on the opposite bank of the Saco River from the Bartlett town cemetery. Drive north on Route 302 past the Attitash ski area to the railroad tracks. (Attitash, by the way, is the Abenaki word for blueberries.) The cliff is clearly visible to your right, on the north side of the Saco. Hike through the woods to the river, wade across it (easy or impossible, depending upon the time of year), and bushwhack uphill to the cliff base. The approach takes about 30 minutes. Michael Hartrich & Lee Spiller did some climbing here in years past, but there is no record of their routes. The climbs are now described from left to right.

THREE GEMS I 5.9
The farthest left-hand route on the crag is located just to the left of an easy, but very dirty vertical groove.
1. Layback a thin crack up a left-facing corner to a block/overhang (bolt), which is the crux. 90', 5.9
FA: Judy Perez, Joe Perez, & Ben Onachila May, 1994

HOW GREEN WAS MY VALLEY I 5.8
The route ascends the steep slab/face just to the right of the dirty, vertical groove. Carry several small Friends.
1. Above a small diagonal ledge, face climb on tiny nubbins (5.8) straight up the face past three bolts. 90', 5.8
FA: Joe Perez & Judy Perez April, 1994

GOLDEN SLIPPERS I 5.8 (*)
This is the bolted face climb just to the right of HOW GREEN WAS MY VALLEY. Again, bring a few small Friends.
1. Follow the line straight up past two bolts to a small, sloping ledge, one more bolt, and the top. 90', 5.8
FA: Judy Perez & Joe Perez April, 1994

A BOLT TOO FAR I 5.9
Start at a large oak tree growing near the cliff base at the slab's center.
1. Face climb straight up the steep slab past three bolts (5.9), staying just to the left of a shallow, vertical gully. 90', 5.9
HISTORY: Judy Perez, Joe Perez, & Ben Onachila made the route's first ascent in May, 1994.

IT'S TIME I 5.10a (*)
The well protected face climb just to the right of A BOLT TOO FAR.
1. Face climb straight up past four bolts to the crux bulge. 70', 5.10a
FA: Ben Onachila, Judy Perez, & Joe Perez April, 1994

LICHEN RUNS THROUGH IT I 5.10a
The route ascends the right side of the main slab, taking a line just to the left of a prominent, left-facing corner.

1. Face climb straight up the clean slab past three bolts, with the 5.10a crux coming just after the top bolt. 70', 5.10a

HISTORY: Joe Perez, Judy Perez, Ben Onachila, & Scott McIntyre made the climb's first ascent in March, 1994.

MENETHESIS I 5.8 or 5.9
The farthest right-hand route on the cliff is located roughly 300 feet to the right of the main, bolted slab routes. Walk up a slight ramp, and look for a short, horizontal crack with a bolt above it. The route is either 5.8 or 5.9, depending on the route you take. Bring a small normal rack.

1. Face climb past two bolts, then zig-zag up to and past a fixed piton at the top. 80', 5.8 or 5.9 (Depending on the route you choose.)

HISTORY: Joe Perez, Judy Perez, Mona L'Heureux, & John Snyder climbed the first ascent of the route in July, 1995.

CAVE MOUNTAIN

An excellent, short crag, Cave Mountain is located just a mile or two from the center of Bartlett. At the blinking yellow light on Route 302 in the middle of town, turn north, cross the Saco River, and park on the right at the Mt. Langdon trailhead (signpost). About a quarter of a mile up the Langdon Trail (actually a dirt road), turn left on an obscure trail. "Cave" is painted on a rock. Hike through the woods and up a steep hill to the cliff base. Allow 15 to 20 minutes to walk in. Cave Mountain is roughly 150 feet long and 50 to 75 feet high. A bottom layer of decomposing rock cushions a capstone of solid granite to form a long, horizontal roof ranging from four to twenty feet in width, that is also split regularly by a series of vertical cracks. If you like roof cracks, this is the place! Use caution climbing up to the roofs, however, because the bottom layer is quite rotten. The routes are now described from right to left.

CLING FREE I 5.9
On the cliff's upper, right end is a clean, horizontal crack.

1. Beginning on the right, hand and finger traverse straight left (5.9) along the full length of the crack system. 50', 5.9

FA: Peter Lewis, rope-solo   September, 1982
FFA: Peter Lewis & Dennis Goode   May, 1984

ROOFER MADNESS I 5.11d (*)
One of the hardest roof cracks in New Hampshire. Tape up unless you want skin grafts later. Carry a sizable rack of Friends. On the cliff's right side is a deep cave with two hand cracks splitting a 20 foot roof.

1. Very strenuous hand jamming (5.11d) leads out the longer, right-hand crack to the lip of the cave—the crux. 50', 5.11d

HISTORY: John Tremblay aided the first ascent in August, 1982. Dave Anderson, Mike Kenney, & Herman Gollner made the first free ascent on August 29, 1984. "It was not exactly an on-sight flash!" Two days of effort, numerous falls, and gear left in place were all required prior to success.

ALL BANGED UP I 5.11d

1. The equally strenuous, left-hand roof crack. 50', 5.11d

HISTORY: After attempts had been made by a variety of climbers (himself included), Michael Hartrich made the first ascent in 1982.

LEAVES OF GRASS I 5.8 (*)

Walk left, squeezing behind an immense oak tree until you are below the right-hand of two parallel cracks above a pedestal of rock.

1. Above the pedestal, jam up a sustained (5.8) hand crack. 50', 5.8

FA: Albert Dow & Michael Hartrich Summer, 1981

TAPE WORM I 5.8

The first crack, easily identified by its bomb bay, squeeze chimney.

1. Climb up broken rock to the bomb bay, making a wide stem to enter it. After a rest, climb the fist crack/squeeze chimney above to the top. 50', 5.8

FA: Michael Hartrich & Albert Dow August 25, 1981

FRIENDLY ADVICE I 5.8, A2

1. From a pedestal, traverse left on rotten rock, aid out the roof (A2), and climb up the right-facing corner/crack (5.8) that is eight feet to the left of TAPE WORM to the top. 45' 5.8, A2

FA: John Tremblay & Peter Lewis September 3, 1982

HARTRICH'S HORROR I 5.11c

To the left of FRIENDLY ADVICE is a yet another hideous-looking offwidth. Tube chocks or very large Friends will definitely come in handy!

1. Struggle and groan up the crack to your heart's content. 45', 5.11c

FA: Michael Hartrich & Albert Dow 1981

SLAM DANCE I 5.8

The cliff's farthest left crack. Again, large protection is needed.

1. Climb up and out the roof (5.8), then jam the crack to the top. 45', 5.8

FA: John Tremblay & Peter Lewis September 3, 1982

Brad White leading the first ascent of Hart Attack (5.10d) on Hart's Ledge in 1986. Photograph by Dick Peterson.

HART'S LEDGE

Another obscure cliff, quite visible from the road, yet seldom visited until recently. The cliff and surrounding area of Hart's Location were named for Colonel John Hart of Portsmouth as a reward for his military service during the French and Indian Wars. The ledge is characterized by three rock bands or tiers. The lowest band has the poorest quality rock with the exception of a small buttress on its left end which looks like a yellowish face from a distance. There are several routes on this buttress, as well as interesting boulder caves on its left side. When seen in profile from Silver Springs as you drive north on Route 302, the Upper Tier is the rounded nose high on the wooded hillside.

From Bartlett, turn north at the blinking light, cross the Saco River, and drive left (west) along a road for approximately two miles past houses to a right turn onto a dirt road. Follow this over RR tracks for about one quarter of a mile to a home development. Park at the end of the road, then follow logging roads west until they end. Locate a 15 foot high split boulder, and bushwhack diagonally up right to reach the base of the first tier, a walk of roughly 15 minutes. The landmark climb on the left-hand buttress of the Lower Tier is HART ATTACK, a prominent, overhanging, right-facing dihedral starting about a third of the way up the cliff. Approach the following climbs starting from a path below the buttress, but above a smaller cliff with talus blocks below it. Routes are described from right to left.

HEART OF THE NIGHT I 5.12c (***)
Sore arms guaranteed! This is the superb, overhanging right-facing corner in the center of the buttress. Now a phenomenal sport route—of sorts, with fixed wired nut protection. Carry a modern rack, too.
1. Starting between two large blocks at the cliff base, jam up a vertical hand/finger crack that splits a roof and enters the base of the severely overhanging, right-facing dihedral—which overhangs every inch of the way, and has a thin finger crack in the back. The technical crux is down low in the corner, with wild stemming, finger jamming, and "shoulder scumming" above! There is a fixed piton anchor just below the top. 80', 5.12c
HISTORY: Brad White, Dick Peterson, & Jose Abeyta aid climbed the first ascent of the route on October 19, 1986. After several previous days of attempts, Andy Ross & Chris Gill made the first free ascent in September, 1990. On the first ascent, White, Peterson, & Abeyta did climb the extra 40 feet to reach the very top of the cliff.

ANGEL HEART I 5.13a (***)
One of the White Mountain's wildest sport routes, with bolt protection. The climb ascends the left side of the hanging block/roof on HEART OF THE NIGHT. Begin 15 feet left of that route—and think pure thoughts.

1. Climb a crack up a slab (5.5) to a right-facing corner. Swing left (5.11) pulling around the corner into a left-facing corner. Stem up the dihedral until it ends, step right to a hueco, then face climb up a very steep wall on more pockets, over a bulging wave (5.13a at the top) to a two bolt belay/rappel anchor. 80', 5.13a

HISTORY: After earlier attempts with Andy Ross, Bob Parrott & Chris Misavage made the first ascent of this outrageous sport route on July 26, 1992. Rob Adair's son Torrey was born the same time that Bob was pulling through the crux!

HART ATTACK I 5.10d (**)

Twenty five feet left of HEART OF THE NIGHT is an old birch tree and a thin crack leading up to an overhanging, right-facing corner. Recommended.
1. Climb the birch tree to reach a shelf (piton), and mantleshelf (5.9). Continue up the short corner on the left to an overhang, step right around the roof to broken rock, then follow the main crack diagonally left. Climb the prominent, overhanging dihedral past two fixed pitons (5.10d), laybacking and stemming to its top. At a small roof, step left to a shelf (bolt), then make a long reach to a final mantleshelf move. 140', 5.10d

FA: Brad White, Dick Peterson, & Jose Abeyta November 1, 1986

PACE MAKER I 59+

Twelve feet to the left of the birch tree start of HART ATTACK is another old hollow tree, with a V groove/corner rising above it.
1. Climb the tree to a stance, step left into the main corner, and climb up through the V groove (5.8; piton), exiting right onto a big ledge. 40', 5.8
2. Make a hard 5.9 move to gain the bottom of a narrow, expanding flake above the belay. Jam up a clean finger crack (5.9+) to a large ledge with a birch tree, and finish up an overhanging, layback crack to the top. 70', 5.9+

FA: Dick Peterson & Jose Abeyta October 26, 1986

THROMBOSIS I 5.8

Below the former climbs is a 60 foot cliff band with a small talus field at its base. Start THROMBOSIS at a thin, left-facing layback flake in the center of this lower cliff.
1. Layback up the flake to a good stance. More laybacking and stemming in the upper corner lead to bushes (5.5), then continue the straight line of the climb to a difficult mantle (5.8) on a short, final wall. Belay at an oak. 60', 5.8

FA: Dick Peterson & Paul Swingle November 16, 1986

HART TO HART I 5.6

Ten feet to the right of THROMBOSIS is a short, left-leaning crack with a small recess or cave at its base.

1. Step left to an incipient, vertical fault. Follow this to a horizontal crack, then go straight up past flakes and knobs (5.6) to a big ledge. Step left to surmount a final, short wall at a left-facing, pointed flake. 60', 5.6
FA: Dick Peterson & Paul Swingle November 16, 1986

THE UPPER TIER

CHRONOLOID CONTINUUM I 5.5
The left-hand of a pair of cracks at the left end of the Upper Tier. Start below a four foot triangular roof 30 feet above the ground. Just below the right end of the roof is a pinnacle of rotten rock.
1. Climb up to the roof's left side, step right around a corner, and move over the roof, up a two foot corner to its top. 5.5
2. Scramble up to the summit of the ledge.
FA: Joe Cote & Bob Fraser August 5, 1973

HEART OF GOLD I 5.9+ R
An obvious hand crack begins 80 feet above the ground on the Upper Tier. Belay at an oak tree on a ledge above a 15 foot face with a dike.
1. Step left (5.9+) to a pod (threaded runner). Beautiful face climbing leads to a second natural thread, then jam a hand crack in a slot straight up past a bush to the top of the cliff. 120', 5.9+ R
FA: Michael Hartrich & Albert Dow September 19, 1980

THE JACKSON AREA

There are two cliffs near the village of Jackson north of Glen that climbers have frequented over the years. These include the better known traditional routes on Popple Mountain, and the more recently discovered sport climbs at the Jackson Crag.

THE JACKSON CRAG

This very hard to see cliff (except in autumn or winter) is located just to the northwest of Jackson. Ask a local. The routes are described left to right.

THE LEFT WALL

DEBASER I 5.11d
Look for four bolts on a blocky basalt section of the Left Wall.
1. Climb past four bolts on good holds (5.11d) up a 100 degree wall to a double bolt anchor. 40', 5.11d
FA: Rich Baker & Alex Drummond July, 1992

VLADD THE IMPALER I 5.12b (**)
The harder companion route to DEBASER. Seven bolts lead to the anchor.
1. Climb past the first four bolts on DEBASER (5.11d), then traverse right, grab a spike (bolt), and handtraverse right across the spike to a blocky section. Now move up (bolt), making hard face moves (5.12b) past one final bolt to reach a double bolt anchor. 50', 5.12b
FA: Rich Baker July, 1994

THE RIGHT WALL

Hike uphill and right another 150 feet to the base of the Right Wall.

EL ROSCO I 5.12a (*)
The wall's left-hand sport route.
1. Face climb up to a seam (bolts), then make hard moves (5.12a) traversing up and left, up a face to the top. 50', 5.12a
FA: Andy Ross & Caroline Cline Spring, 1991

EL JORRO I 5.12c (Top-rope)
1. To the right of EL ROSCO, face climb straight up. 50', 5.12c
FA: Jerry Handren, top-rope Spring, 1991

POPPLE MOUNTAIN

Driving north on Route 16 from Jackson into Pinkham Notch, you'll have a brief glimpse of an attractive cliff high on a hillside to the left. Park on the side of the road, ford the Ellis River, and bushwhack up to the base. Not an easy approach. The history of this worthwhile crag is sketchy. Most of the routes were climbed by those "phantoms of the woods", Michael Hartrich and Albert Dow. The climbs are now described from right to left.

LACERATION GULLY I 5.7

Start to the right of ALPHA ARETE on the crag's far right-hand side.

1. Scramble up a low-angled slab (5.3) to a large platform, then continue up a friction gully to a tree. Step left, and climb past an overhang (5.5) up to a good belay ledge with a large tree. 80', 5.5

2. Step onto the face, & climb straight up for 30 feet to easier ground. 75', 5.7

FA: Michael Coyne, Christine Coyne, & Anne Marie Hayes April, 1995

ALPHA ARETE I 5.8

Start on the cliff's far, right side at a groove just to the left of a ridge, and directly below a bomb bay chimney with a spruce tree growing in it. Much of the cliff to the left overhangs near the ground, while to the right is a giant amphitheater with a low-angled, striped slab on its right side.

1. Climb the groove, past blocks, then move right to the ridge, finishing over the bomb bay chimney/roof on the right (5.8). Tree belay. 110', 5.8

2. Go left, climb a face, and follow a ramp up left, finally stepping left onto another face. Move left into a big corner which is climbed to the top. 100'

FA: Michael Hartrich & Dave Cilley April 23, 1973

THIRTY SECONDS OVER TOKYO II 5.10b (*)

The strenuous, bomb bay offwidth out the left side of the same roof.

1. Climb up the corner past the tree (5.8; a bit unprotected), stemming higher to a belay under the large roof. 5.8

2. Stem and fist jam out the bomb bay chimney to the lip (5.10b), then struggle up a fist/offwidth crack past a tree to a belay ledge. 5.10b

3. Finish up left as desired, or up Pitch two of ALPHA ARETE.

FA: Michael Hartrich & Albert Dow September 16, 1980

EASTER ISLAND REUNION I 5.10b (*)

Start between THIRTY SECONDS OVER TOKYO and AKU AKU.

1. Climb a shallow corner, make a difficult step left, then work your way up to an orange wall. Climb this steep wall (5.10b) at some thin cracks, and move up to a belay ledge on the right below a small roof. 90', 5.10b

2. Bypass the roof to the left, up to the trees. 35', 5.7

HISTORY: Kurt Winkler & Michael Hartrich had tried the route before they eventually made the first ascent with Chris Gill in the Autumn of 1986.

AKU AKU I 5.6 (**)

Heading uphill and left, you'll go under a big, horizontal overhang to a section with many parallel inside corners. Prominent is a right-facing dihedral capped by a large overhang split by a fist crack (WHERE EAGLES DARE). Ascending this same section, AKU AKU offers spectacular free climbing at 5.6. Begin below a pine growing up and right of a short, right-facing corner at the base.

1. A finger crack gains the right-facing corner. Level with the pine, step left on the face, then climb ledges and a groove up and slightly right to the base of the large, right-facing dihedral and traverse right to a ledge with a bush. 110', 5.6
2. An obvious fist and hand crack (5.6) leads to the top. 60', 5.6
FA: Michael Hartrich & Albert Dow October 6, 1980

WHERE EAGLES DARE II 5.11a (**)

An outrageous roof problem, and a great lead by Albert Dow. Large cams.

1. Halfway up AKU AKU's first pitch, move up to the roof. Belay a little higher at the base of a left-angling, chimney system. 100'
2. Stem up to chockstones in a wide crack. Step right into a five foot deep, right-facing corner, then face climb right across an exposed face below the crux roof. Jam the spectacular fist/offwidth crack (5.11a) out the roof just left of a 90 degree edge and a right-facing corner. Climb around the lip, up the crack (a bit rotten) to a ledge with a small tree. Large nut for the anchor. 50', 5.11a
FA: Albert Dow, Michael Hartrich, & Alec Behr October 9, 1980

CHIMNEY ROUTE I 5.7

Another of the cliff's more moderate lines.

1. Start up AKU AKU, then stay left, climbing a prominent chimney. 5.7
FA: Michael Hartrich & Kurt Winkler 1980

WALKING MAN I 5.9 (Top-rope)

1. Just right of ALPHA ROUTE, climb up a face with horizontal cracks. 5.9
FA: Rob Walker, top-rope 1982 or 1983

ALPHA ROUTE I 5.4

Obscure at best. At the cliff's far, left end is a south-facing wall—the first section from the left that doesn't overhang. Locate a face with a blocky overhang close to the ground with a jam crack. Now walk right to a spruce tree.

1. Follow holds and grooves up good rock to a birch tree. 150', 5.4
FA: Dave Cilley, free-solo April 16, 1973

MOUNT WASHINGTON

Named Agiocochook, "Place of the Storm Spirit" or "Home of the Great Spirit" by the Native Americans who lived around New England's tallest peak, the mountain was apparently first ascended by the adventurous Darby Field from Exeter, New Hampshire in 1642, accompanied by two Native Americans who may have stopped short of the summit in respect of their religious beliefs. In 1784, after the conclusion of the American Revolution, but before General George Washington was elected President, Agiocochook was renamed Mt. Washington (6,288') by Dr. Jeremy Belknap, leader of the 1784 White Mountain scientific expedition. The remaining Presidential Range peaks were "named" in 1820 by a distinguished group of local politicians and scientists from Lancaster, New Hampshire led by the indefatigable mountain guide Ethan Allen Crawford. Many people, however, including the well known author, the Reverend Starr King, detested these "new" names, writing in 1871: "What a pity the mountains could not have kept the names the Indians gave to them. What a wretched jumble (we now have) in exchange for Agiocochook, the baptismal title of Mt. Washington."

Mt. Washington has two, large glacial cirques on its eastern flank. Rounded-edged, snow-filled Tuckerman Ravine, named for Dr. Edward Tuckerman, Professor of Botany at Amherst College from 1858 to 1886, and the earliest expert in White Mountain botany, is justly famous with New England skiers who flock to its slopes each spring. Just to its north, of more interest to rock climbers, is the impressive, craggy cirque of Huntington Ravine, named in honor of Professor J. H. Huntington. The first scientist to study winter climate and weather conditions atop Mt. Washington, Professor. Huntington lived in the summit buildings of the Cog Railway during the winter of 1870–1871.

Huntington Ravine was quickly recognized for its climbing potential by the pioneers of New Hampshire rock climbing. Given their seasons in the Alps in Chamonix and Wyoming's Tetons, it's easy to see why Robert L. M. Underhill and Kenneth A. Henderson, amongst others, were so attracted to the obvious challenge of the Pinnacle Buttress. Of their successful ascent of the Pinnacle Rock Climb in 1928, Henderson wrote, "For a continuous course, this ridge of the Pinnacle offers the best yet found in Huntington Ravine." He could just have easily said the best yet found in the eastern United States, for modern climbers unanimously agree that the NE RIDGE OF THE PINNACLE is one of the East Coast's premiere alpine rock routes, and an important yardstick for ambitious, young New England mountaineers.

Unexpected postscripts to the history of rock climbing in Huntington Ravine regard four "new" climbs that have come to light. Most astonishing is Guy & Laura Waterman's confirmation that the true first ascent of the Pinnacle was made in 1910 by a climb (THE OLD ROUTE) to the left of the traditional 1928 ascent. Equally fascinating was the roped ascent of the Huntington Headwall by an AMC party—Dr. Ralph C. Larrabee, Dr. Frederic J. Cotton, Davis, and an unknown companion—in 1912 (see photograph!) Yet another AMC party, Kenneth Henderson, Miriam O'Brien, John Hurd, Jr., & Marjorie Hurd ascended HENDERSON RIDGE in 1927, while Willard Helburn & Stephen Helburn made the first recorded rock ascent of CENTRAL GULLY in 1929. These nearly forgotten ascents should give modern climbers better insight into the long, colorful history of rock climbing in Huntington Ravine.

WEATHER & WIND

In her 1846 masterpiece *History of The White Mountains*, Lucy Crawford observed the great weather changes the mountain is often subject to. "While seated on the summit of Mount Washington, all may be still and silent, a clear atmosphere, and the eye suffered to feast upon the country for miles around, while tomorrow how great the change—the valleys a dense sheet of fog—no object to be seen save the dense ocean, which to appearance, is spread before you, with here and there a mountain top peering above it in imitation of small islands."

Weather conditions on Mt. Washington can indeed rapidly become some of the worst in America—if not the world. The reason: three major weather systems have a nasty (and all too frequent) habit of converging on Mt. Washington's rocky, wind-blown summit. On April 12, 1934, the highest wind speed on Earth was clocked here—an astounding 231 mph before the meter blew away! Wind gusts exceeding 100 mph have been recorded on the peak in each month of the year. (By way of comparison, hurricane strength is only 75 mph, a wind speed topped yearly on Mt. Washington on over 100 days.) July is the mountain's warmest month, where the average daily temperature reaches a balmy 49 degrees F. Remember, all the climbs on the Pinnacle and the Central Buttress in Huntington Ravine face due north, and receive almost no sunshine—so don't forget to bring along some extra clothing! The chances are extremely good you'll be glad you brought it.

THE AMC PINKHAM NOTCH CAMP

The approach to Huntington Ravine is from the Appalachian Mountain Club's (AMC) Pinkham Notch Camp on Route 16, north of Glen. The base lodge, dining room, and other facilities are open year round. The daily weather report posted in the base lodge should always be checked before any climb on Mt. Washington. For more information or lodging reservations, telephone:

- **THE AMC PINKHAM NOTCH CAMP:** (603) 466-2727.
- **WEATHER & TRAIL INFORMATION:** (603) 466-2725.

Ed Webster leading Pitch one (5.10a R) of Roof Of The World (5.11d / 5.10a R) in Huntington Ravine during the first ascent in 1987. This was the first 5.11 free climb to be done on Mount Washington. Photograph by Kurt Winkler.

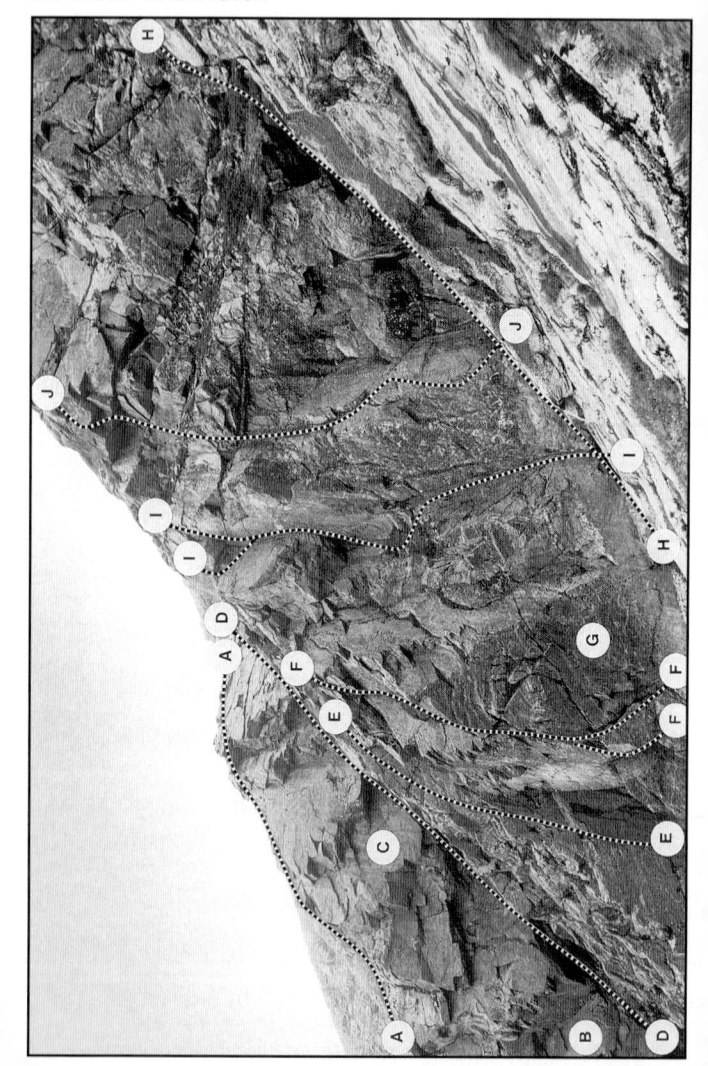

550 MOUNT WASHINGTON

MT. WASHINGTON - HUNTINGTON RAVINE

A.	***	**THE NORTHEAST RIDGE OF THE PINNACLE** III 5.7 (THE PINNACLE ROCK CLIMB)	Page	554 & 558
B.		**The Pinnacle Buttress**	Page	552
C.	***	**PRIMAL SCREAM** III 5.10d (5.10a R)	Page	559
D.		**Pinnacle Gully**		
E.	*	**CLOUD WALKERS** II 5.7 (or 5.8)	Page	561
F.	*	**MISTY** II 5.8	Page	561
G.		**The Central Buttress**	Page	561
H.	*	**CENTRAL GULLY** II 5.4	Page	565
I.	***	**MECHANIC'S ROUTE** III 5.10b (5.7 R)	Page	562
J.	**	**ROOF OF THE WORLD** III 5.11d (5.10a R)	Page	564

HUNTINGTON RAVINE

To hike up to Huntington, start from Pinkham Notch, and head up the Tuckerman Ravine Trail for 1.3 miles to the Huntington Ravine Trail on your right. Branch right here, hike past the venerable Harvard Cabin, and continue up to the rescue cache at the ravine's base. Central Gully is Huntington's most obvious feature, while the Central Buttress and Pinnacle Buttress lie just to the left. The distance from Pinkham to the bottom of the Pinnacle is roughly three miles—for most people, a two to three hour hike. The lazy man's way to approach Huntington Ravine rock climbs is to drive up the Mt. Washington auto road ($$$) for 6.4 miles to the Alpine Gardens, park on the left at the Huntington Ravine trailhead, and hike down the Huntington Ravine trail into the cirque. Do your climb, hike back up, stroll over to your car, and drive back down! The rock routes in Huntington Ravine are now described from left to right.

THE PINNACLE BUTTRESS

There are essentially four separate climbs on the Pinnacle Buttress, although at just about any point it's possible to merge with one of the other routes. Included for historical value is Robert L. M. Underhill's original 1928 route description for the Pinnacle Rock Climb, followed by a modern, pitch by pitch description. The Pinnacle was the earliest roped climb accomplished in the White Mountains of New Hampshire—and one of the very first in New England.

THE OLD ROUTE II 5.5 (*)

The first technical climb in the White Mountains was made up the left-hand flank of the Pinnacle in 1910, an astounding achievement for that early era. Begin the same as THE NORTHEAST RIDGE at the prominent, left-slanting crack that starts 75 feet down and to the left of PINNACLE GULLY.

1 & 2. Climb the first two leads of THE NORTHEAST RIDGE up the short, left-diagonalling crack to easy ground and a long, bushy ledge system. 250', 5.4
3. Off the left end of the ledge, climb a short, steep section (5.5), then traverse left around the corner onto the easier southeast-facing slopes.
4–6. As to the actual route taken on the first ascent, the upper part of the climb is pure conjecture. The easiest line stays on the more broken terrain to the left of the actual ridge, gaining the easier angled upper portion of THE NORTHEAST RIDGE near the top.

HISTORY: The historic first ascent was made by George A. Flagg, Mayo Tollman, Paul Bradley, & a Mr. Dennis on August 20, 1910. Confirmation of their ascent is in the form of a series of sketches which accurately portray several sections of the route and surroundings. Some of the route was done unroped, other parts were climbed with the help of a clothesline or a horse rope—but the climbers had virtually no knowledge of "correct" belaying technique, as the drawing of Mr. Dennis clearly shows!

HUNTINGTON RAVINE - PINNACLE BUTTRESS (THE OLD ROUTE) 553

MR. DENNIS COMES OVER THE FIRST BAD PLACE

This historic sketch of the first technical, roped rock climb in the White Mountains—The Old Route (5.5) on the Pinnacle Buttress in Huntington—was one of several made by George Flagg, a newspaper cartoonist and a member of the first ascent party. In this memorable scene, "Mr. Dennis comes over the first bad place." Drawing by George A. Flagg, courtesy of Shirley Foynes Hargraves, and Guy and Laura Waterman, *Yankee Rock & Ice*, Stackpole Books, 1993.

554 MOUNT WASHINGTON

THE NORTHEAST RIDGE OF THE PINNACLE III 5.7 (***)

The following is Robert Underhill's original route description for the Pinnacle Rock Climb from Appalachia, 1928: "The Pinnacle is easily ascended over the scrub and scattered rocks of its southeast back (The line of THE OLD ROUTE.) However, directly east of the deep cleft which separates it from the wall to the south of the main gully a ridge of pure rock, except near its base, descends steeply in a series of pitches. The parties made it their objective to adhere as closely as possible to this ridge. Its various difficulties can, it is true, always be avoided by passing for a longer or shorter distance over to the left (east), and this undoubtedly detracts somewhat from the interest of the climb in comparison with that (route) up the cliff on Cannon Mountain.

"Some 40 feet down (east) from the cleft or side gully separating the Pinnacle from the south wall of the main gully, and in the middle of its sheer north wall, a crack containing three trees rises some 40 feet, slanting left, to scrub slopes. Up this crack and then sharply right, over steep scrub, parallel with the ridge and about 12 feet from it, for 30 feet to the foot of an open chimney. Diagonal right over a slab to the ridge, and up it 75 feet to an abrupt and unclimbable rise. Left up in an angle of rock 20 feet to a shoulder, and down the other side 15 feet over a smooth slab (hand holds only in the crack between it and the main wall).

"An open chimney, its left wall, of some four feet in width, slanting somewhat backward, here presents itself. The leader, given a shoulder, was able to reach good holds on the right and ultimately to complete the pitch by moving around left up to a good stance. Just above, a ledge two feet wide and covered at the beginning by an overhang, slants right at an angle of 25 degrees up the face. With difficulty, step up into balance upon this ledge (an ice axe—on the second occasion, a wooden stake—was fixed in a crack at the beginning of the ledge for the leader's belay), and then along it, crawling, about five feet to a point beyond the overhang where it was possible to stand up. Having faced about towards the edge of the overhang, up this latter (exposed, but good holds) to a platform with an excellent rock belay.

"The wall above is unclimbable, (Today's 5.8 DIRECT VARIATION) and the party of May, 1927, who had so brilliantly developed the route up to this point, believed themselves forced to traverse left around upon the easier east slope. They brought back the problem of how the more direct advance could be continued. The party of October, 1928, eventually found a solution in a passage which gave the most exacting climbing on the whole ascent.

"The traverse to the left was begun, down a short slab to a grassy shelf. Now immediately above, a narrowing, square, and deeply cut chimney rises for

HUNTINGTON RAVINE (THE NORTHEAST RIDGE OF THE PINNACLE) 555

William P. Allis (wearing the black beret) & Kenneth A. Henderson (dressed in his customary suit, tie, and hat) belaying an unknown partner on the Pinnacle Rock Climb (5.7) in June of 1930. "Will always wore that beret climbing because he was the son of a French count," Ken explained. "And you should have seen that suit of mine. I climbed in it all the time. It was really worn out." This very unusual picture is a vertical composite of two separate photographs taken by Bradford Giddings.

From the Underhill family collection. Photograph courtesy of Brian Underhill.

Bill Chase belaying Roger Walcott on Pitch three of the Northeast Ridge of the Pinnacle (5.7) in 1936. Photograph by Walter H. Howe.

some 50 feet, its base cut off from the shelf by a wall crowned by a slanting slab. The leader (here William P. Allis for the whole party) given a shoulder and with his foot held upon the slab was able to reach the foot of the chimney, and accomplish its ascent, which proved very difficult (total absence of pull holds) (Today's 5.7 crux), up to a chockstone at its head. Here, he unroped and passed his rope around the chockstone for security. An excellent hold over the top of the chockstone could be reached and an exit made from the chimney, delicately, to the right. For the following members of the party a rope was fixed and they gained the foot of the chimney by a pendulum starting from the slab used in the descent from the grassy shelf.

"To the right 30 feet, at first over easy rocks, then around a bad corner (good belay for the first man only), and finally along a narrow ledge (no hand holds), back to the ridge. To the right, and then around left up a semi-circular ramp to the spacious top of the next step. Left 10 feet along a ticklish traverse (grass and some loose rock; the upper of two levels was preferable, allowing a hand hold above), and right up a short slanting crack to the broad slabs of the ridge, along which it was then possible to walk for 25 yards to another steep rise, in the shape of a 15 foot wall. There is an opening in this some yards to the left, but the party climbed it by a series of ledges close to its right corner at the ridge. The next, overhanging, step is also easily turned by a chimney to the left, but the party surmounted it by a short exposed traverse out upon the right wall of the ridge followed by an arm pull to the left. Fifteen yards of walking over slabs; up a 12 foot wall on good holds; and over easy rocks 15 more yards to the summit. Time, somewhat over three hours."

HISTORY: The first partial ascent of the Pinnacle's NORTHEAST RIDGE was made by Lincoln O'Brien, D. K. Howard, & Marjorie Hurd; and a second rope of Chester C. Dodge, O. Cameron Biewend, & Helen A. Smith on May 29, 1927. The first complete ascent, described above, was accomplished by William P. Allis & Robert L. M. Underhill, alternating leads, plus Dana Durand, Kenneth A. Henderson, & Jessie M. Whitehead on October 14, 1928. Recalling his superb lead of the crux 5.7 chimney, Will Allis later remembered, "As a boy I knew how to get up between trees not too far apart, and I tried the same thing, and it worked. Underhill told me to alternate feet, and it worked even better. He was rather solicitous, and asked if it felt safe, but I was quite comfortable." Ken Henderson remembered the crux somewhat differently: "After much struggling and a certain amount of buoyant language, (Allis) reached a chockstone near the top (of the chimney) and breathed a quite audible sigh of relief." Repeating the climb during the Summer of 1933, Fritz Wiessner & Robert Underhill established one or more variations to the original route, but their exact line is not known.

558 MOUNT WASHINGTON

THE NORTHEAST RIDGE OF THE PINNACLE III 5.7 (***)
This classic route of the Pinnacle Rock Climb, as the climb is also known, offers a memorable combination of airy alpine situations at an intermediate standard, great rock and protection, and a unique and colorful history. Many variations are possible. In general, you can make the route harder by heading right, and a bit easier by staying left. Below is a modern route description, slightly condensed! Begin 75 feet down and left from the base of PINNACLE GULLY.

1. Climb up an easy, left-slanting crack or ramp past small trees for 40 feet to a terrace. Angle right on easy ground to a shallow, right-facing corner (piton; 5.5). Climb this, then trend right across a slab to a belay on the arete. 150', 5.5
2. Up easy ground to a good ledge below a steep wall. 150', 4th class.
3. Layback up a tricky, right-facing corner (peg; 5.7) to good holds, followed by another awkward move up and right to an excellent belay ledge. 60', 5.7
4. The Allis Chimney (5.7) is the crux. Down climb a short ramp to the left towards a shallow, inverted V chimney on the left. (You may also reach this same place from the left.) Step up left (tricky 5.7) onto a slab at the base of the Allis Chimney, and stem up it (more 5.7; old piton) past a chockstone, exiting right onto another good ledge. 100', 5.7
5. Easy, up and across a terrace. Belay at the base of the next step. 120', 5.2
6. Climb the step via left-slanting cracks (5.6), move right past an awkward traverse, & "saunter up to a magnificent ledge you could park a bus on." 100', 5.6
7. Finish over one last step, just left of the void, up the dramatic, final ridge to the summit of the Pinnacle. 100', 5.4 You can also spice up the top section by heading right onto the exposed North Wall above PINNACLE GULLY. 5.5
HISTORY: This is how the Pinnacle Rock Climb is usually done today.

VARIATION: THE 5.8 DIRECT VARIATION I 5.8 (**)
A clump of rappel slings usually identifies this harder, more direct variation.
3a. Climb the right-facing corner on the normal third pitch, but continue straight up a smooth 25 foot wall to pitons (and retreat slings) below an overhang. Make a hard layback move (5.8) past the overhang, then climb out left, very exposed, onto easier ground. Continue over blocks to ledges above. 120', 5.8
FA: Unknown.

PINNACLE DIRECT III 5.9+ (***)
An excellent, exposed, and more taxing free climb than the original route. Many variations are possible, and at nearly any point you can escape back left.
1–5. Stay as close to the arete as possible throughout the length of the climb, following your nose and the many fixed pitons en route, mostly 5.7 and 5.8, with a couple of sections of 5.9 thrown in. Near the top, a spectacular variation traverses right from the arete across a steep wall, then on up to the top.
FA: Unknown.

HUNTINGTON RAVINE (PINNACLE ROCK CLIMB & PRIMAL SCREAM) 559

PRIMAL SCREAM III 5.10d (5.10a R) **(***)**

A long and impressive route ascending the blocky, often overhanging wall around the corner to the right of PINNACLE DIRECT and directly above PINNACLE GULLY. Bring a very modern rack—and plenty of nerve! Start below and to the left of PINNACLE GULLY at the lowest point of a large, rectangular face with a curving overhang 30 feet up.

1. Climb up moderate rock to a 15 foot overhanging wall. Layback a thin crack through a bulge (5.10d) on good holds onto the upper face, then face climb straight up the 70 degree, green wall above (5.8) to a big ledge. 150', 5.10d

Tom Dickey on the Pitch one overhang of Primal Scream (now 5.10d / 5.10a R) during the first ascent in 1980. Photograph by Ralph Munn.

2. Diagonal right across a broken area to twin, 20 foot hand cracks. Jam the cracks (5.8) to a stance before an obvious finger traverse. 70', 5.8

3. Finger traverse right along a horizontal edge (exposed; 5.10c) just above an overhanging wall onto another beautiful green face. Then jam up a thin, vertical crack (5.9), then angle right to a left-facing corner. Climb up the corner and the ramp above past loose blocks to a large belay ledge. 110', 5.10c (There is a possible escape to the left from here.)

4. Make an unprotected traverse right (5.6 R) along a narrowing ledge out onto a sharp, exposed arete. Move up the arete (nut placement), then face climb straight right (psychological crux; 5.10a R), with plenty of empty space below your feet, into a flaring chimney. Groan up this crack (5.8) to a small belay stance underneath a large roof. 60', 5.10a R

5. Move right, up and over a short wall (5.9) to an obvious handtraverse crack. Traverse right along this crack (5.6) for 50 feet to a good belay stance. 65', 5.9

6. Face climb down and right for 40 feet (5.8; top-rope the second down this section) to a stance above the lip of an overlap. Belay on the right at the base of an obvious finger crack. 50', 5.8

7. Climb the finger crack (5.9) which leads up and right onto the next face. Follow the crack to the right, then climb up and left up a series of sloping holds and discontinuous vertical cracks (5.8) immediately left of a dirty, V groove or corner. Continue past a bulge at a prominent, curving flake (piton) up to a left-facing corner capped by a roof. Belay on a ledge at the corner's base. 120', 5.9

8. Step right, climb a right-facing dihedral (5.9) to a roof, turn it on the right (5.10b), then diagonal right up the final exposed face to vertical cracks and finally the easier, upper ridge. 100', 5.10b

8a. An easier finish finger traverses left (5.8; piton) around the corner to join with the top of THE NORTHEAST RIDGE. 50', 5.8

9. Follow Pinnacle's NORTHEAST RIDGE to the summit.

HISTORY: Tom Dickey & Ralph Munn made the first ascent of this very adventurous climb on May 24 & 25, 1980. Dickey later said: "It was one of those climbs where at the start of each pitch we thought, 'No way, it'll never go!'—but it did." Pitch one was first free climbed in July, 1985, by Ray Omerza & Peter Lewis. On their initial attempt, Brad White & Ian Cruickshank made the first free ascent of the route (except for the last pitch, which was wet) on August 25, 1991—finishing via Pitch 8a. Then, in July, 1993, Steve Larson & Paul Boissonneault free climbed the top pitch.

VARIATION: **THE DIRECT FINISH** I 5.10b (*)

5a. Most of the way across the 5.6 handtraverse, pull through a roof and jam up a nice hand crack (5.10b), joining THE NORTHEAST RIDGE. 110', 5.10b

FA: Jerry Handren & Terry Young Summer, 1990

THE CENTRAL BUTTRESS

Next to the Pinnacle Buttress, the best rock climbs in Huntington are found on the somber, north-facing bulk of the Central Buttress—the steep, shaded wall between PINNACLE GULLY and CENTRAL GULLY. There are several, fine full length routes up the buttress: the easiest route, CLOUD WALKERS, the superb MECHANIC'S ROUTE, the committing ROOF OF THE WORLD, the varied INDEPENDENCE LINE, plus two old climbs, STEP LADDER and EYE OF THE NEEDLE, which ascend only the shorter, final section above the upper, right-hand traverse ledge. To descend back into Huntington from on top of the Central Buttress, first scramble and bushwhack up to the Alpine Gardens, then descend the Huntington Ravine Trail just to the north of CENTRAL GULLY. You can also hike south across the Alpine Garden, following the cairns, and descend the Lions Head Trail to the Tuckerman Ravine Trail, and back down to Pinkham Notch. If you drove up the Mt. Washington auto road (for 6.4 miles) and parked at the Huntington Ravine trailhead above the Alpine Gardens, from the top of the Central Buttress, just hike back up the Huntington Ravine Trail (past the massive stone cairn marking the top of CENTRAL GULLY) to your car.

CLOUD WALKERS II 5.7 (or 5.8) (*)
Ascends the thin, vertical crack system up the left wall of the brown, grassy, right-facing dihedral on the left side of the Central Buttress, starting 50 feet to the left of MISTY. Well protected with a normal rack.

1. From the corner's base, move up and left to a horizontal, grassy ledge at the start of a vertical finger crack. Use some pockets to gain the crack, which is jammed (5.7) straight up to a good belay ledge level with, and to the left of the top of the grassy dihedral. 125', 5.7

2. Diagonal up and left onto the skyline ridge, move around the arete to the left towards Pinnacle Gully, and up to the bushes. 120', 5.4

2a. A harder and better finish continues easily up face (5.4) to a right-leaning finger crack (5.8) splitting the left-hand wall of the upper, lower angled corner. Climb this crack to the top of the face. 60', 5.8 Rappel off, or thrash through the bushes up to the Alpine Garden.

HISTORY: Bill Boyle, Al Stebbins, & Pat Stebbins made the route's first ascent on August 23, 1987. Paul Cormier & Mike Pelchat climbed the more direct alternate 5.8 finish on August 25, 1995.

MISTY II 5.8 (*)
Start this unlikely, but surprisingly climbable route at the center of an imposing, vertical headwall 40 feet to the left of the base of the CENTRAL GULLY watercourse. Look for a striking, vertical finger crack in the center

of the vertical face to the left of MECHANIC'S ROUTE. Bring a modern rack including some Tri-cams. Sustained climbing.

1. Climb up a left-slanting groove to a small stance at the start of the main finger crack—or from the bottom of the crack, step left moving up the face to an old piton, and continue up a short, right-facing corner (hidden holds on the right wall) past two ring pitons to reach the same stance. Next, traverse 10 feet right on flakes, and jam up the vertical crack system (5.8) up the steep headwall past one good ledge to a higher belay ledge (piton). 120', 5.8

2. Face climb up flakes slightly right until you can step left into a hand crack that splits the overlaps or bulge overhead (5.8) to a belay stance just above. Belay anchor in blocks in the bushes. 80', 5.8 Thrash up through the bushes to the Alpine Garden, or rappel off with two ropes.

FA: Unknown.

MECHANIC'S ROUTE III 5.10b (5.7 R) (***)

Probably the best hard free route on Mount Washington. Excellent, and in general, very well protected climbing leads up the center of three, obvious, right-facing dihedrals in the middle of the Central Buttress. The stupendous, eye-catching corner/hand crack on Pitch three is impossible to miss. From the bottom of CENTRAL GULLY, scramble up easy slabs to a small belay ledge (bolt) at the base of the first inside corner. Carry a normal rack.

1. Step over the small stream flowing down the back of CENTRAL GULLY (keeping your feet dry!) and move up (5.7 R) to the first protection. Above, stem and finger jam up a beautiful, left-facing corner (5.9) to a bushy ledge on the left. Walk 20 feet left, then move up 15 feet to a better belay ledge with a fixed piton anchor. 140', 5.9 (5.7 R)

2. Jam up a steep, fingery, right-facing dihedral past a strenuous layback move (5.10b) into the upper corner system. Belay 30 feet higher on a small stance on the left with a fixed piton & bolt anchor. 80', 5.10b

3. Make 5.9 moves up the wide crack directly above the belay, then jam and layback a hand crack around a bulge in the top dihedral (5.10a) to an easy escape left, or finish up an overhanging hand crack on the right around a block (5.9+) to the bushes and the top. 100', 5.10a Scramble over small rock outcrops and through thick bushes and *krummholz* (leg-eating, stunted trees) heading generally up and right to reach the Alpine Gardens.

HISTORY: Ed Webster made the first complete and free ascent of the route, rope-solo, on August 2, 1987—and named the climb in honor of his unknown, hammer-wielding predecessors. Evidence of an unsuccessful aid attempt was found on the first two pitches, including an old ring piton at the belay ledge at the top of Pitch one, and an enigmatic, bleached rappel sling around a block below the final, crux dihedral at the start of Pitch three.

HUNTINGTON RAVINE - CENTRAL BUTTRESS (MECHANIC'S ROUTE) 563

Jason Laflamme on the crux layback corner on Pitch two of Mechanic's Route (5.10b / 5.7 R) in 1995. Photograph by Ed Webster.

Ed Webster on the first 5.11 roof on Pitch three of Roof Of The World during the first ascent in 1987. Photograph by Kurt Winkler.

ROOF OF THE WORLD III 5.11d (5.10a R) (**)

This spectacular, high altitude route ascends the striking roof/hand crack looming over the right-hand part of the Central Buttress. Proper acclimatization, bold climbing, and Harmonic Convergence all will be found helpful! The upper roofs are well protected, but the first pitch arete is definitely not, at least at the start. Carry a modern rack, plus many Friends including a #3.5 and a #4. The first two pitches ascend the right-hand of the three, right-facing corners on the Central Buttress. From the base of CENTRAL GULLY, scramble up slabs for another 80 feet above the belay ledge and bolt at the start of MECHANIC'S ROUTE.

1. Step across the stream (keep your shoes dry!), then face climb up and left (scary; 5.10a R) to a small stance on the exposed arete on the left side of the prominent, right-facing dihedral. Continue up the arete (peg; 5.10a), before eventually climbing a finger crack on the right, and belay at a ledge higher on the arete. 130', 5.10a R

2. Climb a left-facing corner (5.9) to a terrace below the final roofs. 75', 5.9

3. Move up to a smaller ledge, then climb the left side of a sharp flake to the first roof, split in the middle by an awkward finger crack (5.11d). Climb this to a stance beneath the even more imposing upper roof, which is split by a body length hand/fist crack. Very strenuous moves underclinging and jamming (5.11c) leads out the top roof to a short face and the bushes. 90', 5.11d

HISTORY: Ed Webster & Kurt Winkler did the first ascent on the mystical day of the astrological Harmonic Convergence—August 15, 1987.

HUNTINGTON RAVINE (ROOF OF THE WORLD & CENTRAL GULLY) 565

CENTRAL GULLY II 5.4 (*)
A very obvious weakness, this was yet another of the first technical climbs accomplished in Huntington Ravine.

1. Climb (quoted from Appalachia), "dry shod up the big friction slab on the right side of CENTRAL GULLY, making delicate and exposed moves from 50 to 100 feet above the first platforms"—the belay stances at the base of MECHANIC'S ROUTE and ROOF OF THE WORLD. Continue higher "to a crack that leads over the arete formed by the edge of the slab." The rest of the gully is an easy scramble to the top of the ravine.

HISTORY: Willard Helburn & Stephen Helburn made the first recorded ascent on September 1, 1929. A full ten years earlier, Willard Helburn and his wife Margaret made the probable first ascent, roped, of Katahdin's Chimney in northern Maine. Robert Underhill described Helburn as "the man who got things started" organizing the AMC climbers in Boston.

LARRABEE'S ROUTE I 5.2
Although by modern standards this is an easy climb, historically this previously unknown route represents yet another of the earliest uses of a climbing rope in Huntington Ravine and in the White Mountains of New Hampshire. From the photographic evidence found at the AMC Library in Boston—Dr. Larrabee took additional pictures of Central Buttress that day from a vantage point farther right near today's present Huntington Headwall Trail—the first ascent party probably traversed off right from the top of their first pitch. Begin at the base of the large, friction slab halfway between the bottom of CENTRAL GULLY and the Huntington Headwall Trail below a shallow, round, vertical groove.

1. Climb easily up the low-angled groove (5.2) to a good ledge. 60', 5.2 Traverse off right across ledges and slabs onto easier terrain until you can connect with the Huntington Ravine Headwall Trail.

HISTORY: This was the second technical climb accomplished in Huntington Ravine after THE OLD ROUTE which was climbed two years previously, in 1910. Dr. Frederic J. Cotton, Davis, an unknown climber, and Dr. Ralph C. Larrabee made the climb's first ascent on September 10, 1912. The distinguished Dr. Larrabee was an avid and accomplished photographer, trail-builder, conservationist, as well as President of the Appalachian Mountain Club (AMC) in 1912 and 1913. Back in 1906, Dr. Larrabee was a member (and later the Chairman) of the original AMC White Mountain Guidebook committee that researched the trail information and authored the first hiking guidebook to the region—currently in its 25th edition!

> The next three climbs ascend the upper, right-hand portion of the Central Buttress.

INDEPENDENCE LINE III 5.8
More variety than THE NORTHEAST RIDGE OF THE PINNACLE. Begin at the base of the smooth slabs immediately right of CENTRAL GULLY.
1. Climb up the slab to a belay just to the right of the watercourse. 100'
2. Angle right, then climb the slab's right side to a vegetated area where the slabs become lower angled. 150'
3. Cross left over CENTRAL GULLY, walk left along the traverse ledge and terrace, and scramble up to a large dihedral. In the corner's left wall, climb a left-angling crack to a good belay at its top on the left side of the face. 5.7
4. Climb an arete formed by the left edge of the face until forced right across a small foot ledge leading right. Join the large dihedral for the last few moves. 5.8 Fourth class up to the Alpine Gardens.
FA: George Hurley, John Mulgrew, & Vic Benes July 4, 1985

STEP LADDER II Grade Unknown.
Named for a once commonly used climbing technique, the *courte echelle* or shoulderstand was also known as "combined tactics." Near CENTRAL GULLY's top is a large recess. A rubble-strewn ledge leads from here to the left across the north-facing wall on the upper, right side of the Central Buttress.
1. From the recess, walk left 100 feet following the wide ledge almost to its end. Make a delicate traverse to the right under an overhang using a mossy fingertip crack. Higher, make an awkward *courte echelle* (or shoulderstand). After moving to the right around a rocky shoulder, "climb left through an interesting tunnel taken back and knee fashion to the final face, which although rather devoid of holds, permits good balance climbing."
HISTORY: Payson T. Newton, Leland W. Pollock, & Robert L. M. Underhill made the first ascent of this route in June, 1931.

EYE OF THE NEEDLE II Grade Unknown.
Fifty feet to the right of the CENTRAL GULLY recess, and diagonally up above it, is a prominent crack system—as Underhill described the route:
1. "Climb left up a wide crack behind a slender, needle-like flake. From its top, make an exposed traverse back right into the main crack. Climb straight up to a high shelf, then move right with difficulty around the corner to the steep head of the crack. This route, although the shorter of the two, is more interesting."
HISTORY: Robert L. M. Underhill, Payson T. Newton, & Leland W. Pollock climbed the first ascent in June, 1931.

DAMNED UP NORTH II 5.4
This worthwhile two pitch, alpine rock route ascends the buttress between DAMNATION GULLY and NORTH GULLY. You can start up either of two lower toes of rock at the base of the buttress.
FA: Unknown.

HUNTINGTON RAVINE (LARRABEE'S ROUTE & INDEPENDENCE LINE) 567

Dr. Frederic J. Cotton, Davis, and an unknown climber on the first ascent of Larrabee's Route (5.2) in 1912. Photograph by Dr. Ralph C. Larrabee. This is the first known rock climbing picture taken in the White Mountains of New Hampshire—and probably one of the oldest climbing photographs in America. Photograph courtesy of the Appalachian Mountain Club Library in Boston.

HENDERSON RIDGE II 5.4 (*)

This 600 foot climb ascends the ridge of the buttress immediately to the right of NORTH GULLY, the right-hand most gully in Huntington Ravine. This was the third technical climb accomplished on Mount Washington. Many variations are possible, in addition to an easy, but bushy, escape on the right the entire way up. The fastest descent is to traverse the Alpine Gardens left (south) to the Lions Head Trail. Other choices include a long and strenuous hike down the Nelson Crag Trail to the Old Jackson Road which eventually leads to Pinkham, or to simply rappel off back down the route. Make three, double rope rappels back down the ridge (carry pitons), or the same number of rappels (with down climbing) down NORTH GULLY, a poorer option because of the large amounts of loose rock in the gully.

1 & 2. Start at the base of the ridge, and climb up an aesthetic, low-angled slab for two pitches. 5.4

3. The ridge ends briefly at a broken wall. Climb through this wall via a left-leaning corner (5.4), and work up to another 15 foot step. Exit right up an open, 5.3 corner, and belay at a crack. 5.4

4. Climb left over to the "diving board", an unusual feature. Scramble past this to another 15 foot open corner (5.4) leading out right onto the top of the ridge and the end of the 5th class climbing. 5.4 Finish by scrambling up NORTH GULLY (be very careful of loose rock), or up the broken, bushy terrain on the right (also difficult) to reach the top of Nelson Crag.

HISTORY: Kenneth Henderson, Miriam O'Brien, John Hurd, Jr., & Marjorie Hurd made the first ascent of this historic climb on May 30, 1927. Amazingly, Henderson even made a movie documenting their adventure, which was accomplished on the first AMC-sponsored rock climbing weekend trip to the White Mountains—a successful venture that helped initiate other subsequent explorations of the region's major cliffs. On December 7, 1985, the two teams of climbers, Kurt Winkler & Alain Comeau, and Jim Surette & Randy Rackliff, rediscovered the route, and climbed several more difficult variations along the way.

SQUARE LEDGE

Pinkham Notch's local crag is located directly across Route 16. In fact, you can see the cliff from the AMC Pinkham parking lot, just to the east. To approach, park at Pinkham, carefully cross over Route 16, walk south about 100 yards, and hike up the Lost Pond Trail. Go over a wooden bridge, turn left on the Square Ledge Trail at a signpost, head directly across a cross country ski trail, and continue up to the base of the cliff, all in roughly 15 to 20 minutes from Pinkham. The trail continues up and around the cliff's right-hand side to the open, rocky summit which offers superb views of nearby Mt. Washington. Unlike other White Mountain cliffs, Square Ledge is composed of a unique, horizontally-banded schist/gneiss which offers excellent, sharp holds. Routes are now described from left to right, beginning with the Face.

THE FACE

When you first reach the cliff, you'll be standing at the base of an attractive, relatively low-angled 130 foot face. There are three fairly obvious, thin cracks running up this face. The left-hand two routes are well protected, and numerous variations are possible as the holds are so plentiful and positive that you can climb almost anywhere at will. From left to right, the routes are:

THE PRIZE I 5.5 (**)

In the middle of the lowest part of the Face is a left-slanting series of finger cracks, starting 25 feet left of STANDARD ROUTE, which is the central, finger crack system. Wonderful climbing for the grade.

1. Climb the first finger crack for 20 feet, move 10 feet right, then continue up the next finger crack, which also slants slightly to the left. When the crack ends, face climb on good holds up and right to the top crack, finishing just to the left of STANDARD ROUTE. 130', 5.5

HISTORY: Brooks Dodge & Mary Backus first top-roped the route in 1944, and Brooks later returned to lead it.

STANDARD ROUTE I 5.4 (***)

This easy, classic line ascends the middle and most prominent of the three finger cracks that split the Face. Well protected climbing on absolutely great holds! The most popular climb on the cliff. Start 25 feet to the right of THE PRIZE at the left-hand, stepped edge of a 10 foot high, right-facing corner beside two white birch trees.

1. Climb the left edge of the corner (5.4), then continue up a short face to reach the start of the central finger crack. Jam and face climb straight up the crack (5.3) to the summit. 130', 5.4

HISTORY: Bill Putnam & Brooks Dodge made the first ascent of the route in 1943, first on a top-rope, and then returned to lead it.

JOE'S PLACE I 5.6 (*)

The right-hand of the three crack systems is harder to see from the cliff base, and protection is also a little trickier than on the previous two routes. Begin 15 feet right of STANDARD ROUTE at a short, jutting overhang.

1. Climb past the overhang on big holds (5.6), then continue past two small overlaps into the farthest right-hand finger crack, which is about 15 feet to the left of a sharp, outside corner (THRILLER ARETE) which forms the right edge of the Face. Climb up the top finger crack (5.5) and the face above to a small birch and the summit. 130', 5.6

HISTORY: Bill Putnam & Brooks Dodge made the first ascent in 1944. The route is named in honor of Brooks' father, Joe Dodge, who ran the AMC Pinkham Notch Camp from 1922 to 1927, and was the AMC Huts Manager from 1928 to 1959.

THRILLER ARETE I 5.10a or 5.10c (***)

This is the stupendous, sharp, overhanging arete running up the right-hand side of the Face. An unmistakable line, strenuous and daunting. It is well protected—if you can hang on—with wired nuts and small cams. If you escape left from the top bucket, the route is 5.10a. Begin 50 feet to the right of STANDARD ROUTE.

1. Cruise up 15 feet to a ledge on the left. Rest, then power up the arete to a bucket. Escape left onto a slab (5.10a), or crank up and right onto the right-hand face before moving back left (5.10c) onto the exposed, upper arete. Moderate climbing (5.6) gains the top. 100', 5.10a or 5.10b

FA: Bob Parrott & Rob Adair June, 1990

BLOCKHEADS I 5.12b (*)

Masters the blank, overhanging face between THRILLER ARETE and THE CHIMNEY. Look for three bolts on an impeccably smooth wall on the cliff's right-hand side. Razor sharp crimping! Start 15 feet to the right of THRILLER ARETE, and bring several medium sized Friends.

1. Face climb past a bolt to horizontal edges, and crank past two more bolts (5.12b crux at the second bolt) to THRILLER ARETE. 35', 5.12b

HISTORY: After placing the protection bolts on rappel, Bob Parrott & Rob Adair made the first ascent in June, 1990.

THE CHIMNEY I 5.5 (**)

An unmistakable line, the chimney crack on the cliff's right-hand side. Excellent holds and great protection. Start at the crack's base, on the left.

1. Climb up the crack on good face holds into the upper chimney, which gradually narrows in width, providing the 5.5 crux at the top. 80', 5.5

FA: Brooks Dodge & friends 1943

SQUARE LEDGE (THRILLER ARETE & BLOCKHEADS) 571

Brooks Dodge on Standard Route (5.4) in 1995. Photo by Ed Webster.

Mike Jewell on Thriller Arete (5.10a or 5.10c) in 1995. Photo by Ed Webster.

THE TUMOR I 5.11a (*)
Thirty feet to the right of THE CHIMNEY is a rounded, overhanging nose topped by a V groove. Bring a modern rack and double ropes.
1. Start up a short, left-facing corner capped by a roof. Pull past the roof to good holds, protect, then traverse left to the base of a V groove on the left side of the nose. Struggle up the flare (5.11a) to the top. 40', 5.11a
HISTORY: The route had been previously top-roped. Ed Webster & Jason Laflamme made the first recorded ascent on the lead on August 2, 1995.

THE NOSE I 5.9 (Tope-rope) (**)
Very popular—but only on a top-rope.
1. Start up the first dihedral on THE TUMOR, then face climb up and right, very steeply, but on good holds, to the top. 40', 5.9
HISTORY: In a determined effort, Brooks Dodge first top-roped the climb way back in 1945—in sneakers!

THE BRAIN I 5.8 (Top-rope) (**)
Look for a blob of white crystalline rock, nicknamed the Brain, about 15 feet to the right of THE NOSE. The climb is usually top-roped.
1. Face climb up past the Brain to the top of the ledge. 35', 5.8
FA: Unknown.

PRACTICE SESSION I 5.6
The obvious crack/corner 20 feet to the right of THE BRAIN.
1. Climb up a finger/hand crack in a right-facing corner. 30', 5.6
FA: Brooks Dodge & friends 1944

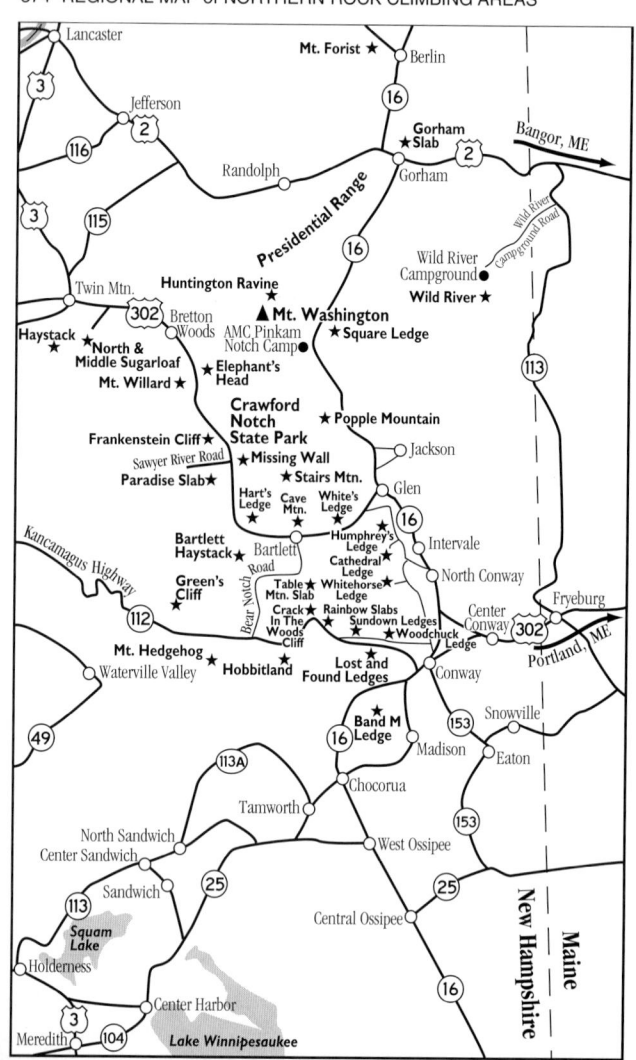

574 REGIONAL MAP of NORTHERN ROCK CLIMBING AREAS

THE NORTHERN AREAS

This section contains descriptions to three unpublished cliffs: the Gorham Slab just north of Gorham, Mt. Forist near Berlin, and Wild River, a fantastic crag offering unbelievably spectacular sport and traditional routes in a true wilderness setting near Evan's Notch and the Maine Border.

THE GORHAM SLAB

From Gorham, heading north on Route 16, one sees a prominent, smooth face on the Androscoggin River's north side. Approach in either of two ways:

- Drive down the Hogan Road from Shelburne until you are across from Gorham, then park where the power lines cross the river, or:
- Walk along the road from the Mascot Mine trailhead on the west end of town to reach the power lines. From them, hike straight up to the cliff base in 10 minutes. The routes are described from left to right.

IVY LEAGUE I 5.7 Ascends the cliff's far, left-hand wall.
1. Climb several obvious flakes and an inside corner (5.7) to the top. 80', 5.7
FA: Paul Cormier & Jon Eagleson May, 1995

SPRING ISSUE I 5.10b or 5.11b
Takes a line straight up the center of the face.
1. The direct start ascends a crack at the lowest part of the cliff. Climb to a bolt, then cross a blank spot (5.11b) to a vegetated crack, finishing up the face to the top. Or, start to the left, climb up hand cracks until level with the bolt, and traverse right into the vegetated crack. 130', 5.10b or 5.11b
FA: Paul Cormier & Greg Cloutier May, 1995

CHANGING SEASONS I 5.9 (*)
Fifty yards up and right of SPRING ISSUE is another large and steep wall. Begin in the center of the wall at a diamond-shaped hole.
1. Climb up through the hole, then step left to cracks that lead up to a roof. Jug haul through the roofs past a bolt (5.9) and a piton to the top. 130', 5.9
FA: Paul Cormier & Mike Pelchat September 13, 1995

WISHFUL THINKING I 5.11a (*)
Begin 25 feet to the right of CHANGING SEASONS.
1. Climb cracks past a bolt to an unlikely-looking roof. Undercling out the roof past a second bolt (5.11a), then head up the face to the finish. 140', 5.11a
FA: Paul Cormier & Greg Cloutier September 20, 1995

LESS THAN I A4 (*)
Carry all sizes of skyhooks, plus bashies and thin pins—the usual A4 rack.
1. Ten feet right of WISHFUL THINKING, hook flakes to a bolt 30 feet up. Bat hook moves and steep, fun A4 lead to the final, left-slanting A1 crack. 160', A4
FA: Paul Cormier & Abby Morrison October 13, 1996

MT. FORIST

This three pitch friction slab is located in Berlin in the northeastern section of the White Mountains. Most of the slab is similar in nature and inclination to Whitehorse, but with more bushes. The steepest climbing is found on the upper, right-hand side, which also has several cracks. In years past, the Green Berets practiced climbing here as evidenced by the many army pitons and handful of bolts which dot the cliff. Climbing at Mt. Forist (also known as Elephant Mountain) would be better except for two unpleasant facts: Crown Vantage Paper Mill's rotten egg smell on an east wind, and the years of soot from the mill on the slab, which blackens hands and clothes, and makes the rock slick. To reach the cliff from Berlin: start on Third Street, then take Madigan Avenue, drive to its end, park, and hike directly up to the base. To descend from the summit (which offers fine views of the North Country and the Presidential Range), a trail leads steeply back down the cliff's north side.

MADIGAN ROUTE I 5.7
A nice direct line up the slab's left side.
1. Climb slabs past small vegetated ledges and cracks to an old bolt belay. 5.7
2 & 3. Zig zag up the slabs past the occasional bush and cracks which offer both protection and belay anchors. 5.7
FA: Unknown.

SURVEYOR'S ROUTE II 5.7 R
A three pitch steep slab. Begin about 50 feet left of the preceding climb, but before the tree line starts to rise steeply uphill.
1. Climb straight up reasonably protected slabs, then over a harder bulge (5.7 R) to an overlap. 165', 5.7 R
2. Head directly up to a belay at a small, left-facing arch. 165', 5.5 R
3. Climb straight up to trees, past blueberries and some trash. 120', 5.5
HISTORY: Rob Adair & Ed Bergeron made the first recorded ascent on April 29, 1993.

BUSINESS TRIP II 5.8+ R
From the area near the hiking trail, walk left until the slab steepens. Look for a bulge with an old piton in it, 20 to 30 feet above the base.
1. Climb to the old fixed pin through trash and brush all the way up (5.8+ R) to a belay at a flake (needs a better anchor) 200 feet up. The second must simul-climb up to the piton so the leader can reach the belay. 200', 5.8+ R
2. Climb up to the trees, and exit right. Descend the hiking trail.
FA: Rob Adair & Ed Bergeron April 29, 1993

WILD RIVER

Although only 140 feet tall, Wild River is without a doubt one of the most out of this world crags in the eastern United States. Almost every inch of the cliff overhangs, creating mind-bending, adrenaline-producing sport routes. There are also several outrageously steep cracks and dihedrals. Place these routes in the forested wilderness of Wild River, and you have a truly incredible cliff. From the south, drive north on Route 113 through Evans Notch, turn left onto the Wild River Campground Road (one tenth of a mile north of Hastings Campground), then drive 5.6 miles southwest along this dirt road to a trailhead parking lot on the left. If you're coming from the north, turn off Route 2 heading south on Route 113 to the Wild River Campground Road. From the parking lot, hike up the Basin Trail, a beautiful, wooded hike of roughly 30 to 40 minutes until you will suddenly see the cliff on your right looming above the surrounding forest—an absolutely, unmistakable sight. Jump across the small stream, Blue Brook, then stroll up a short trail to reach the cliff base. Just to your left is the striking, overhanging crack/corner line of BIG RED. Just about every climb here has a double bolt belay/rappel anchor on top. Rappel the routes with two 50 meter ropes to descend. The wildly overhanging routes of Wild River are now described from left to right:

BLUE BY YOU I 5.11a

The first route on the cliff. From the base of WILD LIFE, scramble 40 feet easily up and left up a rounded slab onto a good ledge with amazing views of the surrounding routes. This ledge is also at the base of a large flake with a wide crack running up its right side. Carry a normal rack with several Friends.
1. Step right into the base of the flake, and stem/offwidth up the flake/crack past three bolts (5.11a by the first bolt). Just below the top of the flake, step right (bolt; also 5.11a) onto a ledge (bolt), then traverse right to the belay ledge and the double bolt anchor halfway up WILD LIFE. 75', 5.11a
2. Continue up the top, left-facing dihedral (5.10b) past a bolt at the start, up a slab, and finish up the corner (5.10c). 50', 5.10c
FA: Bob Parrott, Rob Adair, & Harry Tucker   October, 1993

VARIATION: **NAUGHTY BY NATURE** I 5.12a (**)
If you like mischievously steep bucket-hauling, this is your route! Five bolts. The short, bolt-protected wall just left of BLUE BY YOU's upper dihedral.
1. Make "really fun" face moves on surprisingly good holds (long reach on the crux after the third bolt) past five bolts to a two bolt anchor on top. 40', 5.12a
FA: Bob Parrott & Barry Rugo   July, 1996

WILD CHILD I 5.11c (**)

The wild sister to the WILD LIFE arete! This continuation above BLUE BY YOU ascends the steep wall and arete directly above that route's initial

578 THE NORTHERN AREAS

WILD RIVER

A.		WILD CHILD I 5.11c	Page	577
B.	**	BLUE BY YOU I 5.11a	Page	577
C.	*	THE SUPERIOR B SIDE I 5.12c	Page	580
D.	***	WILD LIFE I 5.12a	Page	580
E.	***	WILD THING I 5.13a	Page	582
F.	***	BIG RED I 5.11d	Page	582
G.	***	GET A LIFE I 5.12c or 5.12d	Page	582
H.	***	GRAND LARSONY I 5.11b	Page	584
I.		STICK-MAN I 5.12b (Top-rope)	Page	584
J.	**	FOSSIL CLUB I 5.10c	Page	587
K.	*	FATMAN LAMENT I 5.12b	Page	587
L.		The Bonney Cave	Page	587

crack/flake. Including the start up BLUE BY YOU, bring 12 quick draws.
1. Climb BLUE BY YOU up the flake/crack (5.11a), then step out right on the traverse, moving up to the sixth bolt. Next face climb straight up a steep wall (5.11a) to a ledge, and finish strenuously up an exposed arete (5.11c) on sharp in-cuts past several more bolts to a double ring bolt anchor on top. 100', 5.11c
FA: Bob Parrott & Maury McKinney   October, 1995

THE ACME TRAVERSE I 5.12a (**)
The Nightflyer of the '90s! This "sport girdle" takes an incredibly pumpy traverse line horizontally right, starting at BLUE BY YOU and ending at a two bolt lower-off just right of GET A LIFE. Although extremely sustained, technically none of the moves are 5.12a. Bring at least a dozen quick draws.
1. Starting on BLUE BY YOU, head horizontally right past many bolts across a consistently overhanging wall, crossing over several routes, to a chained, two bolt anchor 20 feet right of the overhanging arete on GET A LIFE. 90', 5.12a
FA: Bob Parrott & Barry Rugo   August, 1996

> The following three routes all share a common start up WILD LIFE which is 35 feet uphill to the left of BIG RED, at the next higher scoop at the base of a steep, white, crystalline face creased by three thin, vertical crack/seams. The three seams (from left to right) are: THE SUPERIOR B SIDE, WILD LIFE, and WILD THING. The latter two sport climbs are the real gems at Wild River—along with BIG RED, which is half sport and half traditional.

THE SUPERIOR B SIDE I 5.12c (*)
So named because although it is one of WILD LIFE's companion routes, and has good climbing and even a harder crux—it is nowhere near as memorable.
1. Start up WILD LIFE (5.11a) to the horizontal break, then face climb over a small bulge (5.12c) and up the left-hand of the three vertical seams on this part of the face. Climb to a small, flat ledge, then continue up and slightly right to reach the double bolt anchor at the top of Pitch one of WILD LIFE. Be aware of a large, semi-detached flake at mid height on this pitch. 70', 5.12c
FA: Barry Rugo & Mark Richey   September, 1994

VARIATION: **THE DIRECT START** I 5.11d (Top-rope) (*)
Begin 10 feet to the left of the regular start below an obvious arete.
1a. Up the arete to the break, move right, & up SUPERIOR B SIDE. 40', 5.11a
FA: Barry Rugo & Bob Parrott, top-rope   August, 1994

WILD LIFE I 5.12a (***)
Along with its neighbor, WILD THING, this is a real heart-stopper guaranteed to give your arms, fingers (and brain!) the ultimate pump. This was the first of the three sport climbs done on the cliff's left-hand side. The route may be done in one pitch (120', 5.12b) if desired—but bring a rack of 18 quick draws!

Jim Ewing on Pitch two of Wild Life (5.12a) in 1995. Photo by Ed Webster.

1. Face climb past four bolts (5.11a) to a horizontal break, then go straight up a thin, vertical seam/finger crack (5.12a) past more bolts to a ledge & a double ring bolt anchor below a spectacular, clean-cut, overhanging arete. 70', 5.12a
2. Face climb up and right onto the arete past several bolts (with the 5.12a crux after the fifth bolt), making outrageous moves up the very exposed edge, with oceans of air below you. Finish left up to a double bolt belay/rappel anchor on top of the cliff. 70', 5.12a Use two ropes to descend.
FA: Bob Parrott & Ken Reville June, 1994

WILD THING I 5.13a (***)

Just how long can you hold on, that's the question on this route! The wildly overhanging, upper dihedral just to the right of WILD LIFE is one of the longest and hardest sport routes in New Hampshire. Bring a wadge of quick draws (18 to be specific) plus a #1.5 Friend for the top of the corner. Otherwise, the entire route is bolt protected. Start at the base of WILD LIFE.

1. Face climb up the start of WILD LIFE on crystalline, white rock (5.11a) to the horizontal break. Traverse several feet right along the break, then climb up the thin, vertical crack on the right. Follow the crack over a bulge, then straight up the wall into the base of the radically overhanging, top, left-facing dihedral (5.13a) just to the right of the WILD LIFE arete. Hang on! There is a double bolt belay/rappel anchor on top. 130', 5.13a

FA: Bob Parrott & Ken Reville October, 1994

BIG RED I 5.11d (***)

Another of the best routes on the cliff—and in New England. Powerful moves lead up a continuously overhanging inside corner on great jams with real spine-tingling exposure. A must-do route! Start on slanting ledges just left of the long, narrow, left-facing dihedral system which is 30 feet to your left when you first hike up to the cliff base. You can use one point of aid on the 5.11d crux, and do the rest of the route at 5.10d. Carry a normal, but very well supplied rack.

1. Face climb up a white streak past three bolts (5.10b) into a layback flake, and make an iron cross move to the left (5.11d) to reach an orange scoop. Rest, then step right past two bolts into the overhanging base of the corner, jamming and stemming up the dihedral (5.10d) with incredible positions and exposure to a ledge. Face climb past two more bolts to gain the final, right-facing corner (5.10d) and a two bolt belay/rappel anchor on top. 140', 5.11d

HISTORY: On the earliest attempt to climb a route at Wild River, Alain Comeau & Chris Noonan tried the route in November, 1977, and aid climbed the first 30 feet before being defeated by cold and snow. Bob Parrott & Chris Misavage made the first ascent of this extraordinary climb on July 4, 1994, and named the route for Bob's father.

DIRECT START: GET A LIFE I 5.12c or 5.12d (***)

Probably good advice. More wild moves and completely overhanging!

1a. Start up BIG RED until just below the crux, head right, then face climb and stem up the orange, overhanging dihedral 10 feet right of the regular route past five bolts (5.12c) to a horizontal break. Rejoin the BIG RED dihedral on the left (5.12c), or avoid using the corner completely, and climb straight up the arete on the right (5.12d) for even more of a pump. 50', 5.12c or 5.12d

HISTORY: Bob Parrott, Alex Drummond, & Rich Baker made the first ascent on July 3, 1995, taking the harder 5.12d version.

Rob Adair leading Big Red (5.11d) in 1995. Photograph by Ed Webster.

584 THE NORTHERN AREAS

HAIRY MONSTER I 5.12b
Walk right across the slanting ledge at the base of BIG RED to a two bolt anchor. You can use this anchor to top-rope the following fun problem:
1. Face climb on pockets up a bulging, orange wall. 20', 5.12b
FA: Andy Hannon & A. J. Jones September, 1994

THE BAT I 5.12b (*)
Begin just right of BIG RED, at the lowest point of the cliff. Normal rack.
1. Climb either a 5.7 layback flake, or boulder up the 5.9 pocketed wall just to the right of the flake to a ledge 30 feet up. Now handtraverse up and right along a slightly rising horizontal break (sustained 5.11) past six bolts, staying just above a pair of orange scoops. The 5.12b crux is at the end of the traverse, getting to and mantling onto a stance with a double bolt anchor. 70', 5.12b
HISTORY: Bob Parrott & Matt Gillette did the first ascent in August, 1996. A bat was disturbed in the crack on the crux traverse—but it didn't bite!

GRAND LARSONY I 5.11b (***)
This is the right-hand of the two most prominent, vertical cracks systems on the cliff, BIG RED being the left-hand of the two. The TURNKORNER of New Hampshire—a continuously and challenging crack climb of exceptional beauty—especially if you like to undercling out bomb bay offwidth cracks. The climb is surprisingly well protected, but you've got to really hang on to place the nuts. Normal rack. Start 75 feet to the right of BIG RED below an obvious, vertical crack with an offwidth chimney halfway up. A 15 foot finger crack rises above the middle of a rectangular flake sitting on the ground at the cliff base.
1. Climb the finger crack to a short face (bolt) leading to the next finger crack (5.9) to your right. Above a rest ledge, struggle up a short, steep headwall split by another, harder finger crack (5.11b) to a good ledge at the base of the psychological crux—the offwidth chimney. Place your protection, undercling left out the bomb bay nose (5.11a), and swing into the chimney which yields more easily to a good ledge. A real hand eating crack in a right-facing corner leads to a large ledge with a double bolt belay/rappel anchor. 140', 5.11b
HISTORY: The climb, not surprisingly, was initially top-roped, by the team of Ken Reville, Bob Parrott, Maury McKinney, & A. J. Jones in the Autumn of 1993. After Jones made an earlier attempt to lead the route, Steve Larson, Rob Adair, & Ed Webster made the first ascent on July 30, 1995.

STICK-MAN I 5.12b (Top-rope)
The thin, vertical finger crack 60 feet to the right of GRAND LARSONY.
1. Climb a surprisingly difficult finger crack, up a shallow, right-facing corner (5.12b) past a bulge to a ledge with a pine tree & a two bolt anchor. 50', 5.12b
FA: Bob Parrott, top-rope May, 1994

Steve Larson leading the first ascent of Grand Larsony (5.11b) in 1995.
Photograph by Ed Webster.

Rob Adair on the first ascent of Fossil Club (5.10c) in 1995. Photo by Ed Webster.

WILD RIVER (FOSSIL CLUB & FATMAN LAMENT)

FOSSIL CLUB I 5.10c (**)
To the right of GRAND LARSONY and above STICK-MAN are three parallel dihedrals. The left-hand of these three corners, FOSSIL CLUB, is the easiest of the trio. Walk around the cliff's right-hand side up onto a large, sloping ledge. Traverse left across the ledge, then down climb (5.2; rope advisable) to a small ledge with a pine tree and a double bolt anchor.
1. Climb up flakes into a shallow, right-facing corner with a small birch tree. Jam a hand crack up the right side of an obvious, but securely-wedged block to gain entry into the upper, left-facing dihedral (5.10c), which is laybacked to the right end of a tree ledge. Protect your second, then walk left 30 feet to a pine tree belay. 100', 5.10c Rappel with two ropes off the two bolt anchor to your left, down GRAND LARSONY, back to the ground.
FA: Rob Adair, Steve Larson, & Ed Webster July 30, 1995

FATMAN LAMENT I 5.12b (*)
Fifty feet to the right of FOSSIL CLUB, above the right end of the sloping access ledge, is the imposing start of the right-hand of the three dihedrals.
1. Make powerful layback moves (5.12b) up an overhanging, left-slanting seam past three bolts to an awkward stance below a right-facing, black corner. Continue up the dihedral past four bolts (5.10c) to a ledge, then step out left (5.11a), face climbing up the corner's left-hand wall, past a small overlap, onto the exposed arete (5.9) on the left. Finish up a finger crack. 100', 5.12b
HISTORY: After top-roping the route and placing the bolts on rappel, Mark Richey, Bob Parrot, & Barry Rugo made the first ascent in September, 1994.

> To the right of the main cliff at Wild River is a relatively well known cave, the Bonney Cave, which was named for John H. Bonney and his son Norman who discovered it. An article and photograph about this cave published in Appalachia led Rob Adair, Bob Parrott, & Dave Lattimer to re-explore the cliff in May, 1993. Hike up the worn, steep trail around the Wild River's right-hand side to reach the cave's entrance which lies just to the left of several massive, jammed boulders. Down and to the right of the Bonney Cave is another smaller cliff which, as yet, has only one route.

TRIPLE PLAY I 5.9
At the right-hand end of this small cliff is an alcove with a flat floor and a left-curving roof. A classic of its kind! Short, but sweet. Normal rack.
1. Stem up a left-facing corner, undercling left out the roof, and jam up a short finger and hand width crack to the trees. 35', 5.9 Sustained.
FA: Ed Webster, Steve Larson, & Rob Adair July 30, 1995

Bill Lutkus climbing the first ascent of Bad Dogs (5.12d) on Cathedral Ledge in 1991. Photograph by S. Peter Lewis.

ROUTE INDEX

	007 (*) II 5.9+	
	1-800-CLIMB-IT I 5.12b	
	18 HOLES I 5.5	
	3 CYLINDERS (***) 5.9+	
	(Complete Route: (**) IV 5.11c / 5.8 R)	
	5.10 COMBINATION, THE (*) II 5.10b	70
	5.7 FLAKE, THE I 5.7	242
	5.8 COMBINATION, THE (**) II 5.8+	84
	5TH AVENUE I 5.9	532
	5TH AVE BYPASS I 5.8	532
	5TH AVE DIRECT I 5.9, A1 (2 Points of Aid)	537
	A BOLT TOO FAR I 5.9	357
	A DAY AT THE RACES I 5.10b	197
	A FISTFUL OF DOLLARS I 5.11d	344
	À LA MODE I 5.10b	411
	A LITTLE SLABBA DO YA (*) I 5.8+	355
	A NAP ASIDE ELSIE I 5.7+	343
	A PIECE OF CAKE I 5.7+ (5.6 R)	477
	A SCHOLARLY PURSUIT I 5.8	328
	A STITCH IN TIME (**) I 5.8	477
	A TALE OF THREE CITIES I 5.8+	86
	A. P. TREAT (*) I 5.9	399
	AARP CHALLENGE (*) I 5.9+ R	183
	ABRAKADABRA (*) III 5.11b	386
	ACE OF SPADES I 5.9+	411
	ACE'S PLACE I 5.7	329
	ACME TRAVERSE, THE (**) 5.12a	580
	ADAGIO I 5.8	469
	ADVENTURES IN 3D (*) II 5.10b (5.10a R)	360
	AFRICAN QUEEN I 5.9	427
	AFTER THE FOX (OPEN PROJECT) I 5.13	539
	AFTERMATH, THE II 5.10b	48
	AGENT ORANGE (*) I 5.11b	545
	AIRATION (***) I 5.11b	48
	AIRY AERIE II 5.9 R	546
	AIWASS (***) I 5.11d or 5.12a	485
	AKU AKU (**) I 5.6	365
	ALBERT'S SHUFFLE I 5.10d	250
	ALLERGIC REACTION I 5.10b R	515
	ALL BANGED UP I 5.11d	541
	ALPHA AREA I 5.9 R	187
	ALPHA ARETE I 5.8	346
	ALPHA CORNER I 5.9+	357
	ALPHA ROUTE I 5.4	264
	ALPINE DIVERSIONS II 5.8	407
	ALTERED STATES I 5.12a	272
	ANCIENT JOURNEYS (*) I 5.11a+	182
	AND THEN THERE WERE TWELVE I 5.6	149
	ANGEL HEART (***) I 5.13a	480
	ANGEL'S HIGHWAY III 5.8, A2	465
	ANGELS WITH DIRTY FACES I 5.8	65
	ANIMAL CRACKERS (*) I 5.9	427
	ANSWERED PRAYERS (**) I 5.12c	438
	ANTE I 5.10b	338
	ANTICHRIST, THE (*) III 5.12a (5.9 R)	149
	ANTLINE III 5.10b	
	APOCALYPSE (**) III 5.11d	
	ARCH, THE I 5.8 R	
	ARE YOU EXPERIENCED? I 5.9, A3	
	ARETE, THE (**) I 5.11b R	
	ARETE-Z-VOUS I 5.10a	
	ARGONAUT, THE I 5.13a	
	ARIES (**) II 5.10b	
	ARMAGEDDON (*) III 5.12b R	

122	ARNO'S CORNER (*) I 5.10b	285
261	ASPIRING (*) II 5.11b	386
513	ASSAULT & BATTERY I 5.10b	447
281	ASYLUM I 5.11a	59
	ATLANTIS (***) II 5.10b (or 5.9)	309
70	ATROSSITY (*) I 5.13a	428
242	AURORA III 5.6 X	498
84	AUTOBOT (**) I 5.10a	399
399	AUTOCLAVE (*) I 5.12c R	133
532	AVATAR (**) I 5.8+	514
532	AVENGER I 5.9 R	260
537	AWAY THE WEE MAN (*) I 5.11a (Top-rope)	112
357	BABY FACE (*) I 5.10c	322
197	BACK STAIRS DIRECT II 5.9+	520
344	BACKDRAFT (**) I 5.11c (5.8 R)	313
411	BAD DOGS (**) I 5.12d	70
355	BAD TO THE BONE (*) I 5.11b	463
343	BALLHOG, THE II A3	169
477	BANANA HEAD (**) I 5.13b	432
328	BANDIT (*) I 5.9	360
477	BARBER DIRECT (*) I 5.10c R	76
86	BE SHARP OR BE FLAT I 5.10a X	201
399	BEAST 666, THE (***) III 5.12a	94
183	BEAT THE CLOCK (*) I 5.6+, A0	349
386	BEAT THE DEVIL I 5.10d	347
329	BEATING A DEAD HORSE (**) I 5.11c	471
580	BECAUSE THEY CAN I 5.11d	358
469	BEDO BEDO I 5.11c	362
360	BEELZEBUB CORNER, THE (**) I 5.4	271
427	BEELZEBUB III 5.11b	273
333	BEELZEBUB I 5.10c	433
265	BEER CAN BYPASS I 5.7	111
433	BEGINNER'S BLESSING (*) I 5.4	284
142	BEGINNER'S EASY VARIATION (*) II 5.3	214
300	BEGINNER'S ROUTE II 5.5 (5.4 R) (Whitehorse)	215
265	BEGINNER'S ROUTE: BEGINNER'S DIRECT II 5.7 R	218
546	BEGINNER'S ROUTE: RIGHT-HAND FINISH II 5.4 R	218
360	BEHIND ENEMY LINES I 5.5 R	115
427	BELFRY I 5.8	474
539	BETA WAY I 5.9	52
48	BETE NOIR (*) I 5.11b	431
545	BICYCLE ROUTE, THE (***) III 5.11b (5.10b R)	180
48	BIFOCAL UKULELE I 5.8	323
546	BIG BANANA (*) I 5.12a	56
485	BIG DEAL ROCK CLIMB (*) I 5.12a	398
365	BIG DOGS DON'T CRY I 5.10d	112
250	BIG FLUSH, THE I 5.6 (Not Recommended)	533
515	BIG LICKS I 5.8	430
541	BIG PICKLE, THE I 5.13a	207
187	BIG PLUM, THE (**) V 5.10d, A0	582
346	BIG RED (***) I 5.11d	413
357	BIG WHOOP, THE (*) I 5.12b	423
264	BIGGER THAN A BREAD BOX I 5.11c	79
407	BIRCH HOUSE I 5.8 R	352
272	BIRCH TREE CORNER (*) I 5.6	394
182	BIRCHFIELD BOOK I 5.5	202
149	BIRD'S NEST (***) I 5.9	368
480	BITING BULLETS (**) I 5.12b	271
427	BITS & PIECES (**) I 5.11b R	423
465	BLACK CORNER, THE (*) I 5.6	463
65	BLACK CRACK I 5.10b R	66
427	BLACK FLIES CONSUME JIM DUNN (**) I 5.12d	511
438	BLACK JADE (**) II 5.10b (or 5.10a R)	228
338	BLACK LUNG (***) I 5.8	67
149	BLACK MAGIC II 5.11c	199

590 ROUTE INDEX

Route	Page
BLACK PLAGUE I 5.10c	370
BLACK SUNDAY I 5.7 R	432
BLACK WALL, THE I 5.7+ R	462
BLACK WOLF I 5.10c	446
BLANK IN THE HEAD I 5.10b	461
BLANK ON THE MAP (*) II 5.10a	461
BLD (BONFIRE LEDGE DIRECT) II 5.6, A4	176
BLOCKHEADS (*) I 5.12b	570
BLOODSPORT (**) I 5.12c	352
BLOODY SUNDAY I 5.9	433
BLUE BY YOU I 5.11a	577
BLUE SKY DIKE I 5.4	394
BLUEPOINT I 5.8 R	360
BODY ENGLISH II 5.9+	467
BODY SURFING II 5.11a R or X	227
BOGEY I 5.9	348
BOIL MY BONES (*) I 5.12c	172
BOLT LADDER, THE (*) I 5.9	226
BOMBARDMENT (***) I 5.8 (5.6 R)	75
BON TEMPS ROULER I 5.9-	446
BON VIVANT'S WALL (*) I 5.6	446
BONDI BEACH I 5.10b	340
BONGO FLAKE VARIATION IV 5.9 (or 5.11d), A3	157
BONSAI I 5.9 R	497
BOOK 'EM DANO I 5.7	147
BOOK OF SOLEMNITY, THE (***) II 5.9+	68
BOOKLET, THE (*) I 5.9	239
BORBETOMAGIC ELUSION I 5.8	447
BOSWELL'S BIG BREAK I 5.11 (Top-rope)	202
BOY'S BRIGADE I 5.9	273
BRAIN POLICE, THE I 5.11c	110
BRAIN, THE (**) I 5.8 (Top-rope)	573
BRAINDEAD I 5.11b	320
BRAT TRACK I 5.11c R	292
BREEZE, THE (*) II 5.12a R	346
BRIDGE OF KHAZAD-DUM, THE (***) IV 5.11d	163
BRIMSTONE I 5.5	319
BRITISH ARE COMING, THE (*) III 5.9, A3	189
BRITISH ARE HERE, THE (*) I 5.7	226
BROKEN ARROWS I 5.8	480
BROKEN BONES (*) I 5.10c (5.9+ R)	86
BROKEN ENGLISH (*) I 5.9 (or 5.10b)	467
BROWN STAR I 5.10b R	317
BROWN'S FIST (*) I 5.9+	86
BRUIN I 5.4 X	493
BRUSHMASTER I 5.6	398
BUBBLE OF ENLIGHTENMENT I 5.5 R	237
BUCKET LOADER (*) I 5.11d	480
BUDAPEST (***) I 5.11d	194
BUGS EAT FROGS (*) I 5.8	504
BULLET THE BLUE SKY I 5.11c	317
BULLETPROOF I 5.9	262
BULLY, THE (*) I 5.9 (or 5.10b)	383
BUMBLE'S BOUNCE I 5.5	384
BURNING BRIDGE III 5.11d (5.9 R)	189
BURNING DOWN THE HOUSE (*) II 5.11a R (5.10a X)	316
BUSINESS TRIP II 5.8+ R	576
BUTCHER BLOCK I 5.12c	371
BY BOSCH, BY GOLLY! (**) I 5.11c	536
CAGE, THE I 5.7	328
CAKEWALK II 5.6+	343
CALIFORNIA DETOUR I 5.9	402
CALIFORNIA GIRLS I 5.11d R	75
CALIMARI (*) I 5.10c	507
CALL OF THE WILD I 5.8	455
CAMBER (***) II 5.11b	137
CAN IT CHALLENGE I 5.9+ R	357
CANNIBAL CRACK I 5.10b	457
CANNON FIRE I 5.12a (5.10b R)	281
CANNON FODDER (*) I 5.11b	475
CAPITOL GAINS I 5.11d X	127
CAPRICORN CORNER I 5.4	373
CAPTAIN, THE I 5.10a	428
CAROLINA DREAM'IN (*) I 5.11c (5.10 R)	261
CARPET SLABBER I 5.3	414
CARRION (**) I 5.9+	436
CASABLANCA I 5.9 R	347
CASEY'S VARIATION I 5.4	514
CASH FLOW I 5.10b R or X	253
CASTAWAYS (**) I 5.11a	338
CATCH-22 I 5.7 (5.6 R)	514
CATHEDRAL DIRECT III 5.7 (or 5.12a), A2	173
CAUSE FOR CONCERN I 5.12a	282
CEILING I 5.6	262
CEMETERY GATES (*) I 5.10d	304
CENTAUR, THE (**) I 5.11b	290
CENTER ROUTE, THE I 5.7	362
CENTRAL EPIC I 5.8	480
CENTRAL GULLY (*) II 5.4	565
CENTURION I 5.9+	399
CERBERUS, THE (***) I 5.12d	94
CHANGING SEASONS (*) I 5.9	575
CHARLATAN I 5.12c	427
CHICKEN DELIGHT (**) I 5.9	56
CHICKEN LITTLE I 5.10b	71
CHILD'S PLAY (***) I 5.6	204
CHILDREN'S CRUSADE (***) II 5.9	276
CHILDREN'S CRUSADE DIRECT FINISH (***) III 5.11a	276
CHILLY WILLY I 5.8	388
CHIMNEY ROUTE I 5.7	546
CHIMNEY, THE (*) I 5.6	570
CHINA I 5.10d R	388
CHOCKLINE II 5.10d	64
CHRONOLOID CONTINUUM I 5.5	543
CINDERELLA THEORY, THE (*) I 5.12c	508
CINNEREA I 5.11a	273
CIRCADIAN CRACK I 5.8	465
CIRCADIAN RHYTHM I 5.7	465
CIRCLE OF LIFE I 5.9	261
CIRCUS I 5.9	475
CIRCUS TIME I 5.10b	386
Citadel Boulder (Whitehorse): STANDARD RTE I 5.3	324
Citadel Boulder: NORTH FACE II 5.10d	324
Citadel Boulder: THE NE RIDGE I 5.9+	324
Citadel Boulder: THE SOUTH FACE I 5.5	324
CITY OF LOST CHILDREN, THE I 5.8	504
CLAMBAKE I 5.12b	451
CLEAN SWEEP (**) I 5.11b	133
CLIENTS ARE PEOPLE TOO! I 5.7	328
CLING FREE I 5.9	538
CLING-ON I 5.9	329
CLOUD WALKERS (*) I 5.7 (or 5.8)	561
COFFIN NAIL (*) I 5.9	309
COLOR MY WORLD I 5.8+	320
COLORING BOOK (*) I 5.7	493
COMEAU FINISH, THE (*) I 5.6	102
COMMANDO RUN I 5.8	101
CONFEDERACY OF DUNCES (***) I 5.12c	442
CONNECTICUT YANKEE I 5.9+	348
CORBETT'S CRACK I 5.8	249

ROUTE INDEX 591

Route	Page
CORIANDER I 5.8	476
COSMIC AMAZEMENT (**) I 5.9	323
COSMIC BOOKS I 5.7	323
COTE'S CHIMNEY I 5.8	409
COUNTER CULTURE (**) I 5.10d	469
COUNTRY ROAD I Class 3 or 4	392
COVER GIRL (*) I 5.5	415
CRACK BETWEEN WORLDS (*) I 5.11d R	157
CRACK COLLECTION I 5.7	322
CRACK DETECTIVES I 5.8+	322
CRACK IN THE WOODS (***) I 5.10d	501
CRANK CASE I 5.11a	433
CRANKSHAFT (*) I 5.9	383
CRAZY HORSE I 5.9 R	252
CRAZY WISDOM (*) III 5.11b, A1 (12 Points of Aid)	110
CRAZY WOMAN DRIVER (*) I 5.9 X	497
CREATION, THE (*) II 5.12b (5.10 R)	140
CREOLE LOVE CALL (*) III 5.10b R	304
CRISS CROSS I 5.7+	319
CROSSWALK I 5.7	319
CRUISE CONTROL (***) I 5.7+	496
CRUSADE OF THE LIGHT BRIGADE (*) I 5.11b	279
CRY FOR YESTERDAY (*) I 5.11d	530
CRYSTALLINE DIKE, THE I 5.8 R	242
CUFF LINK (*) I 5.11d R	76
CULPRITS, THE (*) I 5.9+	88
CULTURE SPONGE (**) (*) I 5.10d R	469
CURE FOR THE BLUES (*) I 5.10d	284
CURIOUS GEORGE LEAVES TOWN I 5.11c	350
CURLY I 5.11a (Top-rope)	165
DARCY-CROWTHER VAR (*) II 5.6	245
DARCY ROUTE, THE II 5.6 X	118
DARCY'S TRAVERSE (*) II 5.6	120
DAG-NABIT I 5.8	513
DAMNED UP NORTH II 5.4	566
DARK FORCE, THE I 5.10b	485
DARK HORSE I 5.8 R	250
DARKENING OF THE LIGHT (*) I 5.11b	393
DARKNESS AT THE EDGE OF TOWN (*) I 5.8	348
DAVY JONE'S LOCKER (*) II 5.10b	432
DAWN PATROL I 5.8 R	79
DAY FOR NIGHT I 5.9 R	115
DAY OF THE MAILMAN I 5.13a	427
DEAD BIRCHES (*) I 5.12c (Top-rope)	169
DEAD EASY I 5.1	79
DEADLINE I 5.9	493
DEATH OF A SALESMAN I 5.10b R	393
DEBASER I 5.11d	375
DECEPTICON (*) I 5.10c	544
DEDICATION (**) II 5.7+	404
DEDICATION DIRECT I 5.4	340
DELIGHTMAKER (*) II 5.11d	341
DEPTHS OF DOOM I 5.4	195
DEVIATION I 5.10d	472
DEVIL MADE ME DOG IT, THE (*) I 5.12a	389
DEVIL'S ADVOCATE I 5.10b	172
DEVIL'S DISCIPLE I 5.9	113
DHARMA BUMS I 5.8	112
DIAGONAL (*) II 5.9+ R	360
DIAMOND EDGE (**) I 5.10d	150
DICK TO THE RESCUE (*) I 5.10c	391
DIEDRE (***) II 5.9+	505
DIEDRE DIRECT II 5.9+	191
DIKE ROUTE (*) II 5.6	194
DIKENSTEIN (**) I 5.11c	248
DIVISION OF LABOR (**) II 5.10d	162
DMZ (*) I 5.9	115
DOGGIE-STYLE I 5.11a	371
DON'T FIRE UNTIL YOU SEE THE WHITES OF THEIR EYES (*) III 5.11c R	190
DON'T FLY OVER RUSSIA (*) I 5.11 R	102
DONDONGO I 5.8	329
DOORS, THE I 5.9	397
DOUBLE VEE (*) I 5.9+	56
DOW JONES AVERAGE I 5.10a (5.7 R)	375
DR. LEAKEY, I PRESUME? (*) I 5.9+ R	341
DRAGGIN I 5.8+	462
DRAGON CURVE (*) I 5.9+	403
DRAGON FLY I 5.6	502
DREAM TIME I 5.9+	364
DRESDEN (*) I 5.10d (5.7 R)	53
DRESDEN DIRECT 5.11a R or X	53
DRESS RIGHT (*) I 5.11b	280
DROID WHERE PROHIBITED I 5.10d	320
DRY ROASTED (**) I 5.13a	112
DUNN'S DECEPTION I 5.10d (Top-rope)	411
DUNN'S DIVERSION I 5.11b X	266
DUNN'S OFFWIDTH (***) I 5.11c	95
DUTY CALLS I 5.8	327
DYKES TO WATCH OUT FOR (*) I 5.11d (5.9 R)	506
EAGLES' DARE I 5.10d (Top-rope)	407
EASIER ISLAND REUNION (*) I 5.10b	545
EASY DOES IT (**) I 5.10a R (5.2 R)	226
EASY ENOUGH I 5.6	518
EASY STREET I 5.4	383
ECHO (*) I 5.5	262
ECLIPSE II 5.7	342
ECONOMY OF FORCE (*) I 5.12a	320
EDGE OF NIGHT I 5.8	447
EDGE OF THE WORLD (***) I 5.13c	106
EFFECTS OF WOODEN TOYS I 5.6	405
EGO TRIP (**) I 5.11c (or 5.11b)	77
EIGENVECTOR I 5.10c	390
EL CAMINO NON REAL I 5.8+	530
EL JORRO I 5.12c (Top-rope)	544
EL ROSCO (*) I 5.12a	544
ELIMINATE DIRECT (*) I 5.10d	281
ELIMINATE, THE (***) IV 5.11c (5.8 R)	280
ELSA, DWARF DOG OF GOR I 5.6	347
END OF STORY I 5.11c	67
END OF THE TETHER (***) I 5.12a (or 5.11d, A0)	443
ENDEAVOR (**) III 5.7+	528
ENDLESS SUMMER (*) II 5.12b (5.9 R)	137
ENERGY CRISIS (*) I 5.11b (5.11a R)	84
ERADICATE III 5.7 R, A3	278
ERASER HEAD I 5.12a	147
EREMITE I 5.7	358
EROSION GROOVE I 5.6	416
ESPECIALLY WHEN THE OCTOBER WIND I 5.8	530
ETHEREAL CRACK (***) I 5.10d (or 5.11a)	266
EVEN CAVEGIRLS GET THE BLUES I 5.10a R	341
EVERYTHING THAT GLITTERS (**) II 5.11b R	361
EVOLUTIONARY THROWBACK I 5.9 R	341
EXASPERATION (*) I 5.11d	176
EXILES IN BABYLON I 5.9+	206
EXODUS (**) I 5.12c	439
EYE OF THE NEEDLE II Grade Unknown	566
EYELESS IN GAZA (***) I 5.12b	439
FACE DANCES (**) I 5.6+	492
FAILSAFE I 5.11d R	202

592 ROUTE INDEX

Route	Page
FALL CLEANING I 5.8+	470
FALL LINE I 5.9+	318
FAMILY MATTERS I 5.8	485
FAT GIRLS WITH ACNE (*) I 5.11c	445
FATMAN LAMENT (*) I 5.12b	587
FAULT LINE I 5.11b	48
FAUX PAS ARETE, THE (**) I 5.11c	102
FEAR FACTOR I 5.9	329
FEAR OF EJECTION (*) I 5.11b	509
FIFTY CENTER I 5.4	492
FINAL FRONTIER (*) II 5.11d	518
FINAL GESTURE (*) I 5.7+	67
FINALLY DUNN (*) I 5.10d	371
FINGER FOOD FROM THE FUTURE (*) I 5.9+	423
FINGERTIP TRIP (*) I 5.10a	240
FIREBIRD I 5.7+	384
FIRING ALL EIGHT (***) I 5.10d (Complete Route: (***) IV 5.11c / 5.8 R)	280
FIVE MINUTES LATER III 5.7, A3+	519
FLAKE LEFT I 5.6	204
FLAKE OF FEAR I 5.9 R	348
FLAKE OUT I 5.9	351
FLARE, THE (**) I 5.10d (5.7 R)	509
FLESH FOR FANTASY I 5.13a	369
FLEXIBLE FLAKE I 5.10a R	357
FLIGHT OF THE FALCON (*) I 5.10d	436
FLIRTING WITH DIKES (*) I 5.10c R	439
FLYING DUTCHMAN I 5.8	327
FLYING ENGLISHMAN (*) I 5.11d R	358
FOLLOW YOUR OWN ROAD I 5.10d (5.8+ R)	328
FOLLOW YOURSELF I 5.9+ R	354
FOOL'S GOLD (*) I 5.10d	68
FOOLS FOR A DAY (***) I 5.10b	374
FOOTSY-QUENCE (*) II 5.9+ R	318
FOR CHICKENS ONLY I 5.9	56
FOR DEAR LIFE I 5.9+	354
FORCES OF GRAVITY I 5.9+	379
FORCHRISAKE I 5.10c	536
FORE PAWS (*) I 5.7	422
FOREST OF DOOM I 5.7	407
FOREST OF FANGORN IV 5.7, A3	168
FORTITUDE III 5.12b X	175
FOSSIL CLUB (**) I 5.10c	587
FOUR HOLES I 5.5	414
FRAGALROCK I 5.7+	508
FREE FALL I 5.9+	318
FREE FINALE (***) III 5.12a (5.11c R)	151
FREEDOM (***) I 5.10a	127
FRENCH CONNECTION, THE I A3	157
FRIENDLY ADVICE I 5.8, A2	539
FRIGID RELATIONS (*) I 5.12b	430
FRODO I 5.7+	508
FROG HAIRS I 5.10d R	271
FROSTY FINGERS (*) I 5.9	371
FUNHOUSE (***) I 5.7	
FUNHOUSE: LEFT-HAND CORNER, THE (*) I 5.8	80
FUTURE SHOCK (**) I 5.11c, A1 (3 Points of Aid)	81
GALE FORCE I 5.10c X	263
GARDEN STATE THRUWAY I 5.5	365
GASH, THE I 5.10b	70
GATE CRASHER II 5.9	460
GEMINI (*) I 5.6	123
GEMINI DREAM'IN (*) I 5.10b	383
GENERAL HOSPITAL II 5.7, A3	373
GENERATION GAP I 5.5	358
	319

Route	Page
GENERATION WHY (**) I 5.13b	172
GENERATION X (*) I 5.10b (Top-rope)	205
GENEVIEVE I 5.8 R (5.6 X)	504
GENTLEMEN OF LEISURE (*) I 5.10a	351
GERIATRIC CHALLENGE I 5.10b R	64
GET A LIFE (***) I 5.12c or 5.12d	582
GILL'S CRACK I 5.11b (Top-rope)	132
GILL'S GROOVE (**) I 5.12b	456
GIMP CRACK I 5.9 (5.8 X)	531
GIRDLE OF THE EAST LEDGES II 5.6+	514
GIRDLE TRAVERSE OF WHITEHORSE (***) III 5.8 (5.7 R), A0 (3 Points of Aid) or 5.10b (5.7 R)	324
GIUOCO PIANO II 5.8 (5.7 R)	333
GOLDEN BOOK OF BAD DOGS, THE (*) I 5.10d	70
GOLDEN ILLUSION I 5.8	190
GOLDEN SLIPPERS (*) I 5.8	537
GOOFER'S DELIGHT II 5.9+	133
GRAND FINALE	154
(***) IV 5.12b (5.11c R), Clean A2 or 5.8, Clean A3	
GRAND FINALE, THE I 5.4	392
GRAND ILLUSION I 5.8 5.10 (5.9 R)	318
GRAND LARSONY (***) I 5.11b	584
GRANDMOTHER'S CHALLENGE (*) I 5.12b	172
GRANITE STATE (*) I 5.9	410
GRAVE DIGGER I 5.8	430
GRAVEROBBER (***) I 5.11d	58
GRAVITATIONAL MASS (*) I 5.10d	322
GREAT ESCAPE, THE (**) II 5.11d	332
GREEN DIHEDRAL BYPASS I 5.6	457
GREEN DIHEDRAL I 5.5	457
GRENDAL'S LAIR (**) I 5.10a	530
GRIM REAPER, THE (*) I 5.10d R	58
GROOV'IN I 5.4	416
GROOVEDOGS I 5.10d	533
GUIDE'S ROUTE, THE (*) II 5.9	344
GUILLOTINE I 5.8+	466
GUNSLINGER, THE (*) II 5.12a	284
GYMCRACK (*) I 5.8	466
GYPSY III 5.9+	99
HADES I 5.6 R	311
HAIRLINE I 5.9 R	535
HAIRY MONSTER I 5.12b	584
HALLOWED EVE (**) III 5.9+ R	301
HALLOWEEN II 5.9-	340
HALLOWEEN III 5.10b	340
HANGERLANE (*) I 5.12b	413
HAPPILY EVER AFTER I 5.6	66
HAPPY FACE I 5.5 R	327
HAPPY TRAILS I 5.8 R	71
HARMONIC CONVERGENCE (*) II 5.8, A1 (3 Points of Aid) or 5.11b, A0	401
HART ATTACK (**) I 5.10d	542
HART TO HART I 5.7	542
HARTRICH'S HORROR I 5.11c	539
HARVEST II 5.9 R	296
HAT TRICK I 5.9+	471
HATFUL OF HOLLOW (*) I 5.12a	62
HAVANNUTHA DRINK (**) I 5.11b	451
HAWK, THE I 5.7	465
HEAD CEMENT (*) I 5.10d R	282
HEART OF GOLD I 5.9+ R	543
HEART OF THE NIGHT (***) I 5.12c	541
HEAT PAIN I 5.10b	532

ROUTE INDEX 593

Route	Page
HEAT WAVE (*) I 5.12a	163
HEATHER (*) I 5.12b	145
HEAVEN CAN WAIT I 5.9	355
HEAVENLY LIGHT I 5.10c	518
HEAVY WEATHER SAILING (***) II 5.12a	365
HELPING HANDS I 5.8	353
HEMLOCK ARETE I 5.8 R	352
HENDERSON RIDGE (*) II 5.4	568
HERCULES I 5.11b	322
HERE COME THE JUGS (*) I 5.7	332
HERE COMES THE SUN II 5.9	518
HERE'S STAIRING AT YOU (*) I 5.7	466
HERMAPHRODITE FLAKE I 5.4	438
HIDDEN CHIMNEY I 5.0	413
HIGH & DRY (*) I 5.9, A3	136
HIP-HOP-BE-BOP, DON'T STOP (**) I 5.12a	508
HIPPODROME (*) I 5.10c	183
HOBBITLAND (*) I 5.8	414
HOCUS POCUS (*) I 5.11d	285
HOLE TRAVERSE, THE I 5.5	503
HOLLOW MEN (*) I 5.11c	503
HOLY GRAIL, THE I 5.7	59
HOLY SMOKE (*) I 5.5	402
HOMICIDAL MANIAC (**) I 5.11d	402
HONEMASTER DIRECT I 5.9+	329
HONEMASTER I 5.7	321
HORIZONTAL BOP, THE II 5.9	505
HORIZONTAL CHIMNEY I 5.7+	321
HORNET, THE II 5.7 R	367
HORSE OF A DIFFERENT COLOR (*) I 5.10b	402
HOSS COCK (*) I 5.12a	313
HOTEL CALIFORNIA (*) II 5.11a	537
HOTTER THAN HELL (***) I 5.9	404
HOW GREEN WAS MY VALLEY I 5.8	197
HUFF I 5.10d	196
HUMAN RACE, THE I 5.12b	332
HUMPHREY'S HERBITUDE I 5.7	464
HUNTING HUMANS (*) II 5.11b	472
HURLEY WARNING WALL, THE (*) I 5.10 R	76
HURRY UP SUNDOWN I 5.5	358
HYPERSPACE (***) II 5.10b	514
HYPERVENTILATOR I 5.11d (5.10d R)	355
IF DOGS RUN FREE (***) II 5.11b	96
IMAGINATION I 5.8+	310
IMMORTALITY I 5.9	81
IN THE BELLY OF THE BEAST I 5.10d	566
IN YOUR FACE (*) II 5.10d	312
INCIPIENT ARETE I 5.10b R	453
INDEPENDENCE LINE III 5.8	310
INDIAN SUMMER (**) II 5.12b	413
INDIAN SUNBURN (**) I 5.12a	531
INFERNO (***) II 5.8	488
INQUISITION, THE (*) I 5.11d	230
INSIDE STRAIGHT (**) I 5.10a	232
INSPECTRUM I 5.6 R	232
INTERLOPER (***) II 5.10b (5.8 R)	230
INTERLOPER: CATLIN-INGLE FINISH I 5.10b R	232
INTERLOPER: TOP SECRET I 5.8+	232
INTERNATIONAL MOUNTAIN CRACK (**) I 5.10b	533
INTERROGATOR I 5.9	369
INTERZONE (***) I 5.11a	413
INTIMIDATION (**) III 5.10b	531
IRON LUNG I 5.10d	488
IT'S TIME (*) I 5.10a	537
IVY LEAGUE I 5.7	575
JACK THE RIPPER (*) II 5.12a or (**) II 5.11c	197
JAGEN DIE SIEBEN II 5.9+	333
JAWS OF DOOM, THE I 5.7	280
JAZZ SLIPPERS I 5.12b	413
JESSIE I 5.10d	145
JING & TONIC (***) II 5.10b	451
JOE'S PLACE (*) I 5.6	570
JOKE BOOK, THE I 5.12a	68
JOKER'S WILD (*) I 5.10c R	531
JOLT (*) I 5.12a	54
JOPLIN-HENDRIX ROUTE, THE I 5.9- R	515
JUDGEMENT DAY I 5.11a (**)	391
JUNGLE WORK I 5.11d	364
JUNGLE WORK: THE DIRECT START I 5.10b	364
JURASSIC CRACK (*) I 5.9	382
K-NINE (*) I 5.9	535
KAMPALA I 5.5	394
KAREN'S VARIATION II 5.8 (5.9 finish up DIEDRE)	196
KENNEBUNK BOGGLE I 5.8	406
KEY LARGO II 5.10c	341
KIDDY CRACK (***) I 5.7	205
KILL YOUR TELEVISION I 5.11 R	142
KILT FLAPPER I 5.12b	439
KIMBERLLY'S FOLLY I 5.8	329
KINESIS (**) I 5.11d	194
KING CRAB V 5.9+, A0	209
KING TUT'S TREASURE I 5.9	427
KNIGHT IN WHITE SATIN (*) I 5.10d	206
KNIGHTS IN WHITE SATIN I 5.7	503
L'ANNIVERSAIRE I 5.8	493
LACERATION GULLY I 5.7	545
LADIES & GENTLEMEN II 5.9	262
LADY LARA (*) II 5.11d R	197
LADYSLIPPER II 5.9+ (5.7 R)	296
LADYSLIPPER to WONDER WALL (**) I 5.9+	296
LANCELOT LINK / SECRET CHIMP (*) I 5.10b	129
LARRABEE'S ROUTE I 5.2	565
LARRY I 5.10a R	164
LAST DANCE I 5.11d (Top-rope)	263
LAST EXIT I 5.9	322
LAST GASP I 5.10d R	67
LAST LAUGH (***) I 5.12c	401
LAST RUNG ON THE LADDER I 5.9	348
LAST STRAND, THE I 5.11c	285
LAST TANGO, THE (*) I 5.11c	263
LAST TEMPTATION, THE (*) II 5.10d	191
LAST UNICORN, THE (**) III 5.10b	290
LAST WAVE, THE I 5.8 or 5.9+	232
LAUNCH THE KITTY (*) I 5.11b	328
LAWN DARTS I 5.11c (5.9 X)	54
LAYTON'S ASCENT (*) I 5.9	56
LE GRANDE ÉCART I 5.8	425
LEATHER & LYCRA (*) I 5.12a	370
LEATHERFACE I 5.12c	453
LEAVES OF GRASS (*) I 5.8	539
LEFT-OUT I 5.7 R	226
LEGIONS OF POWER (**) I 5.11d	400
LESS THAN (*) I A4	575
LET THEM EAT CAKE (*) II 5.7	343
LICHEN DELIGHT (***) I 5.11a	59
LICHEN DELIGHT: THE DIRECT FINISH I 5.10b	62
LICHEN IT A LOT (*) I 5.10d	59
LICHEN RUNS THROUGH IT I 5.10a	538
LIGHTS IN THE FOREST (***) IV 5.11c	163
LIQUID SKY (***) III 5.13b (5.11a R)	106

594 ROUTE INDEX

Route	Page
LISA I 5.7 R	205
LITTLE BIG MAN I 5.7+ R	338
LITTLE BRUCE I 5.11d X	101
LITTLE FEAT (*) I 5.9-	411
LITTLE RAGE I 5.12a (Top-rope)	460
LITTLE ROCK LINE I 5.10a	101
LITTLE STALKING I 5.11d R	283
LONDON CALLING (**) I 5.12b	534
LOOK MA, NO HANDS I 5.9	410
LOOKING FOR GOLDILOCKS (**) I 5.11b	101
LOOKOUT CRACK, THE (*) I 5.8+	271
LOOSE LIPS (***) I 5.10a	502
LOST & FOUND I 5.10a	415
LOST ARCH (*) I 5.8	515
LOST DUTCHMAN I 5.10b	302
LOST SOULS (***) III 5.10a	475
LOVE CRACK (***) I 5.12b	169
LUCIFER IN CHAINS I 5.13a	489
LUCKY CHARMS I 5.7 R	413
LUMBERJACK CRACK (*) I 5.11c	342
MACADAMIA II 5.10b	513
MacDOUGAL'S VARIATION (*) I 5.7	362
MACHINA EX DEUS (**) I 5.10d	132
MADARA'S CRACK I 5.10b	379
MADARA-DAMP ROUTE, THE I 5.10	576
MADIGAN ROUTE I 5.7	508
MAGIC EARTH I 5.5	364
MALT THERAPY (*) I 5.11a	337
MAN FRIDAY (**) I 5.9+ X	261
MAN'S BEST FRIEND (**) I 5.8	253
MAN-O-WAR (*) I 5.9+ (5.7 R)	406
MANTLE BLOCK, THE I 5.5 R	205
MANTLESHELF PROBLEM, THE (*) I 5.7+	379
MASS EXTINCTION I 5.10b	476
MATA HARI I 5.9-	390
MATHEMATICA (***) II 5.10c	534
MEAN LINE (**) I 5.10b or 5.9	285
MEATLOAF IN MOTION I 5.12a (5.9 R)	562
MECHANIC'S ROUTE (***) III 5.10b (5.7 R)	62
MEDUSA I 5.12b	538
MENETHESIS I 5.8 or 5.9	172
MERCY, THE (**) I 5.13d	503
MERLIN (*) I 5.8	523
MERLIN'S WAY II 5.10b (5.9 R)	201
MERRILL'S VARIATION I 5.9+	522
MICHAEL'S WAY II 5.9	534
MIDLIFE CRISIS (**) I 5.10c	436
MIDNIGHT GROOVE I 5.8	405
MIGHTY ROCK I 5.5	405
MINER-JOSEPH-KING ROUTE, THE II 5.6 R	157
MINES OF MORIA, THE (**) IV 5.6 (or 5.11d), A2	158
MINES OF MORIA: THE DIRECT START I A4	118
MISS SAIGON I 5.8	457
MISS SCARLET WITH THE ROPE I 5.6	128
MISSING LINK, THE (**) III 5.10a (5.7 R)	129
MISSING LINK, THE: DIRECT START I 5.8 R	387
MISSION, THE (***) I 5.13b	492
MISSISSIPPI RAMBLE (*) I 5.4	253
MISTAKEN IDENTITY II 5.6	561
MISTY (*) II 5.8	442
MITHRAS (**) I 5.12d	400
MODERN MATURITY (*) I 5.9+	164
MOE I 5.10c	533
MOHEGAN I 5.9 R	173
MOLSON'S MADNESS (***) I 5.12a	
MONARCH BUTTERFLY (*) I 5.9	353
MORDOR ROOF, THE (***) IV 5.11d	162
MORDOR WALL (***) IV 5.7 (or 5.12c), A3	155
MOTHER OF INVENTION (**) III 5.11d, A3	365
MOUNTAINEER'S ROUTE, THE I 5.6	533
MU II 5.9+	239
MUSCLE BEACH (*) I 5.12b	353
MYSTERY ACHIEVEMENT (*) I 5.11d	361
MYSTERY MAN I 5.12a	88
NANDOR VARIATION, THE II 5.8+	252
NATURAL ORDER (*) I 5.8	518
NATURAL SELECTION I 5.9	382
NAUGAHYDE (*) I 5.13a	453
NAUGHTY BY NATURE (**) I 5.12a	577
NEBULOUS (*) II 5.6	525
NEEDFUL THINGS (*) I 5.11b (5.8 R)	240
NEUROMANCER (*) I 5.12a	389
NEW WAVE TRAVERSE, THE III 5.9 (5.7 R)	325
NEW YORK TIMES (**) I 5.7+	532
NIGHTFLYER (**) II 5.13a	368
NINTH WAVE, THE (**) II 5.9+ R	219
NO GRIPPAGE I 5.0	411
NO MAN'S LAND (*) II 5.6 R	119
NO SELF CONTROL (*) I 5.11d	533
NO TICKET TO GLORY I 5.7+	207
NOBLE GESTURE I 5.9- R	504
NOBLE INTENTIONS I 5.10b R or X	276
NOMAD CRACK (**) I 5.10b	56
NORTHEAST RIDGE OF THE PINNACLE (***) II 5.7	554 & 558
NORTHEAST RIDGE OF THE PINNACLE: 5.8 DIRECT VARIATION, THE (*) I 5.8	558
NORTHWEST PASSAGE I 5.7	479
NOSE, THE (**) I 5.9 (Tope-rope)	573
NOSTRIL (*) I 5.9+	207
NUTCRACKER (**) I 5.9+	53
O'BRIEN'S ROUTE I Grade Unknown	511
OBJECT OF GREAT DESIRE, THE I 5.9	476
OBJECTS ARE CLOSER (*) I 5.12b	279
OFF THE HOOK (*) I 5.11c	56
OGBP I 5.10c	425
OH XANA II 5.8+	449
OKTOBERFEST (*) I 5.6	394
OLD NASHUA ROAD I 5.5	416
OLD ROUTE, THE I 5.5 (Mt. Washington)	552
OLD ROUTE, THE I 5.2 (Humphrey's Ledge)	346
OLD TIMES (*) II 5.8 R	246
OLD VARIATION, THE I 5.6	225
OMINOUS CRACK I 5.7	457
ONCE UPON A CLIMB (*) I 5.11c	78
ONE HIT TO THE BODY (*) II 5.12b (or 5.11d) (5.10d R/5.9+ X)	80
ONE STEP BEYOND I 5.12a (5.11a R or X)	54
ONE WAY STREET I 5.6	71
ONION HEAD (***) I 5.11c	122
ONTOGENY II 5.9+	485
OOH MOW MAO (**) I 5.10a	398
OPTION 9A III 5.11a	168
ORANGE PEEL I 5.8	460
ORC II 5.8	81
OREGANO I 5.8	476
ORION III 5.7 X	498
OUTCAST I 5.10b (Top-rope)	88
OUTSHINED I 5.13b	452
OVER DONE (**) I 5.10a	371

ROUTE INDEX 595

Route	Page
OVERTIME CRACK (**) I 5.11b	353
OZONE BYPASS (*) I 5.11c	126
PACE MAKER I 59+	542
PALE MARY I 5.8 R	472
PANORAMA I 5.9	457
PAPILLON I 5.7+	71
PARADISE LOST II 5.10d R	309
PARALLEL WORLDS I 5.11b	470
PASSING THOUGHTS (*) III 5.11c	184
PASTRYWORKS (***) I 5.13b	428
PATHFINDER (**) II 5.9	248
PB & J I 5.5	513
PEANUT GALLERY FLAKE, THE I 5.11b	111
PEER PRESSURE I 5.11a R	163
PENCILNECK GEEK (*) I 5.7	494
PENDULUM ROUTE (***) IV 5.11b	159
PENTATONIC SCALE I 5.8	465
PEREZ DIHEDRAL (*) I 5.4	466
PERFECT WAVE, THE (***) I 5.7	495
PERSONA (*) I 5.9+	271
PETRIFIED FOREST I 5.9+	348
PETROGLYPH, THE I 5.8+ X	497
PETTY LARSONY I 5.12a (Top-rope)	142
PETUNIA I 5.7	407
PHANTOM OF THE WOODS (**) I 5.8 or 5.9	469
PHYLOGENY II 5.9	484
PICK OF THE LITTER (**) I 5.8+	536
PICKING WINNERS (*) I 5.11b	206
PICNIC TABLE I 5.6	505
PIERCED BOYS I 5.10c	506
PINE TREE ELIMINATE (***) I 5.8+	146
PINNACLE DIRECT (***) III 5.9+	558
PINNACLE ROCK CLIMB, THE (***) III 5.7	558
PINNACLE ROCK CLIMB: 5.8 DIRECT VAR (**) I 5.8	558
PINS & NEEDLES I 5.9	468
PINSNATCHER I A4	169
PISS EASY II 5.10c	194
PISTOLERO I 5.8	360
PLAY MISTY I 5.11d	147
PLAYMATE I 5.11b (Top-rope)	147
PLEASANT STREET (*) I 5.7 (5.6 R)	71
PLEISTOCENE (**) I 5.10c	393
POINT, THE (*) I 5.10d R	76
POKEMAN CRACK I 5.11a	411
POLICE & THIEVES (**) I 5.12c	436
PONDEROSA I 5.7	515
POOH (**) I 5.7	81
PORTALEDGE ROUTE, THE I 5.9	471
PORTLAND CEMENT (*) I 5.10d	282
PORTUGUESE APPLE (*) I 5.6	407
POSSESSED, THE (***) II 5.11d	198
POT OF GOLD I 5.6	488
POTATO CHIP, THE I 5.5	472
POWDERFINGER (*) I 5.10d	321
POWER CHILD (*) I 5.13c	515
PRACTICE CHIMNEY, THE I 5.7	147
PRACTICE MAKES PERFECT I 5.8	147
PRACTICE SESSION I 5.6	573
PRESSURE DROP (*) I 5.11b	461
PRIMAL SCREAM (***) III 5.10d (5.10a R)	559
PRIMAL SCREAM: DIRECT FINISH (*) I 5.10b	560
PRIMATES R US I 5.9	382
PRIME MERIDIAN II 5.8, A2	409
PRIMROSE PATH, THE F 5.8	528
PRIZE, THE (**) I 5.5	569

Route	Page
PRO CHOICE (*) I 5.10c	129
PROBLEM CHILD (*) II 5.10d R	279
PROCESSION (***) I 5.12b (5.12c Both pitches)	344
PROMISED LAND, THE (*) I 5.12c	439
PROW, THE (***) III 5.11d (or 5.7, Clean A2)	103
PROW, THE: THE 5.7 START (***) I 5.7	104
PROW, THE: THE 5.9 SLAB (***) I 5.9	104
PROW, THE: ANOTHER PRETTY FACE (**) I 5.10a	104
PROW, THE: THE BLANK BULGE I 5.11c	106
PROW, THE: THE MARCH OF IDES (*) I 5.8	104
PROW, THE: THE 5.10 FINISH (*) I 5.10a	104
PRUDENCE I 5.9	382
PRUFROCK I 5.7	348
PSYCHOHOLIC SLAG I 5.9	354
PSYCHOKINETIC PRAXIS I 5.8 R	347
PUB CRAWL, THE (*) I 5.10c	468
PUFF (*) I 5.9	404
PUMPING ADRENALINE I 5.11b R	337
PUMPING POCKETS (*) I 5.10b	536
PUMPING STATION (*) II 5.11b	501
PURGATORY II 5.8	309
PYRAMID I 5.8	327
QUARTZ POCKET, THE (***) I 5.3	225
QUEEN OF HEARTS (*) I 5.9+	384
QUESTION OF ETHICS I 5.10d	59
QUITS COMPLETELY I 5.8	449
RAIN DANCE I 5.9	296
RAPID TRANSIT (***) II 5.10a or 5.10b	120
RAPTOR I 5.9	476
RAPTOR ROOF, THE (*) I 5.11d	477
RAPTURE OF THE STEEP (**) I 5.10b	384
RASTER SCAN I 5.11c	404
RAT'S EYE I 5.12b	368
RAVEN'S WAY I 5.7	464
RAZOR CRACK (*) II A1 (Possible 5.11 Finish)	444
REACH THE SKY (**) I 5.11c	142
REALITY CHECK (**) III 5.8, A4+	186
REBELLIOUS YOUTH (*) I 5.10b or 5.10c	462
RECLUSE (***) I 5.10d	203
RECOMBEAST (***) III 5.9	98
RECOMPENSE (***) III 5.9	96
RECONCILIATION (*) II 5.11d (5.11a R)	62
RECONSIDER (*) I 5.9	99
RED BETWEEN THE LINES I 5.8	405
RED FLASH I 5.7	406
REELING IN THE FEARS (*) I 5.10a X (5.9 R)	374
REFUSAL I 5.11c	66
REFUSE (**) I 5.9	87
REFUSE FINISHES I 5.3 - 5.4	101
REGGAE PARTY I 5.11b, A2	460
REGRESSION (*) II 5.9 (5.8 R)	336
REMIRRETH II 5.11c	196
REMISSION (*) I 5.8 R	187
REPEAT PERFORMANCE (*) I 5.10b	471
REPENTENCE (*) II 5.10a R	184
REPO-MAN (*) I 5.11d	77
REPTILIAN RESPONSE I 5.8	474
REPULSION II 5.8 or 5.9	129
RETALIATION (***) II 5.9	62
REVERSE CAMBER (***) I 5.10b	138
REVERSE CAMBER/ROOM W/A VIEW LINK (*) I 5.12a	140
REVOLT OF THE DIKE BRIGADE (**) II 5.11a (5.9+ R)	273
RHINO SKIN I 5.6 R	493
RHODE ISLAND MEMORANDUM I 5.7	464
RHUMB LINE I 5.8	415

596 ROUTE INDEX

Route	Page
RHYME OF THE ANCIENT MARINER III 5.9, A3	480
RICE CRISPIES I 5.8	409
RIGHT DIKE, THE I 5.6 R	232
RIGHTEOUS SLAB (*) I 5.9	403
RINGWRAITH I 5.4	513
RISKY BUSINESS I 5.9	403
ROAD TO LHASA (*) I 5.7	489
ROAD TO SHAMBALA II 5.10d, A2 (Five Points of Aid)	522
ROADSIDE ATTRACTION (*) I 5.9+	351
ROBINSON CRUSOE (***) II 5.10b R	337
ROBINSON CRUSOE: CENTER I 5.9+ (Top-rope)	337
ROBINSON CRUSOE: LEFT ARETE 5.10b (Top-rope)	337
ROBINSON CRUSOE: MAN FRIDAY I 5.9+ X	337
ROBINSON CRUSOE: PUMPING ADRENAL I 5.11b R	337
ROBOT HEART I 5.13c	350
ROBUSTUS II 5.9+ (5.9 R)	342
ROCK GARDEN (**) I 5.4	422
ROCKFISH I 5.8+ R or X	237
ROGER'S SPIRE I 5.5	387
ROLLIN' & TUMBLIN' II 5.10b (5.9 R)	81
ROMPER ROOM (***) I 5.12a	430
ROOF OF THE WORLD (**) III 5.11d (5.10a R)	564
ROOF, THE I 5.9	199
ROOFER MADNESS (*) I 5.11d	538
ROOM WITH A VIEW (*) I 5.12a (5.10d R)	140
ROPE DRAG III 5.12b (5.7 R), A0 (3 Points of Aid)	115
ROSE MADDER I 5.9	115
ROSEBUD I 5.9 R	99
ROTATION, THE (**) I 5.12c	534
ROTTEN LOG, THE I 5.9- R	241
ROUGH BOYS (***) I 5.10a	446
ROUGH TRADE I 5.11d	207
ROUTE OF ALL EVIL, THE I 5.7	393
ROYAL ARCHES REMINISCENCE I 5.10b (5.9 R)	111
RUBBERNECK I 5.6	425
RUNNING HANDS I 5.9+	352
SACO CRACKER (**) I 5.12a	351
SACO POTATOES I 5.10d	367
SACRED SPACE (***) II 5.12a	132
SAFETY IN NUMBERS I 5.9 R	403
SAINT GEORGE (*) I 5.9 R	170
SANCTUARY (***) I 5.13b	382
SASHA I 5.8	506
SAY MR. CONGRESSMAN II 5.8	389
SCALAR I 5.10c	67
SCENIC ROUTE, THE I 5.8 (5.7 R)	292
SCIENCE FRICTION WALL (**) III 5.12b or 5.11a (5.8 R)	292
SCIENCE FRICTION WALL: BRAT TRACK I 5.11c R	292
SCIENCE FRICTION WALL: SKY STREAK (**) I 5.10b	294
SCIENCE FRICTION WALL: ORIGINAL (**) I 5.12b	292
SCIENCE FRICTION WALL: WEBSTER'S (**) I 5.10b	292
SCIMITAR I 5.8	84
SCORPION ARETE (**) I 5.11a	456
SCREAMING YELLOW ZONKERS CRACK (***) I 5.11c	386
SCYTHE, THE (*) I 5.11b	354
SEA OF HOLES (***) II 5.7	242
SEA OF HOLES with THE DIRECT FINISH (***) II 5.8	244
SEPTEMBER MORN I 5.10a R	302
SEVEN YEAR ITCH, THE I 5.8- X	425
SEVENTH SEAL (*) I 5.10a	266
SEVENTH SOJOURN (***) III 5.12b (5.9 R)	167
SHADOW AT NIGHT (**) I 5.9-	352
SHADOWLINE (***) I 5.11d	447
SHAKE'N BAKE I 5.6	474
SHAMBLE ROAD I 5.10b	522
SHE'S CRAFTY (*) I 5.12c	438
SHE-RA (***) I 5.10d	400
SHOCK THERAPY I 5.12d (Top-rope)	264
SHORT BUT SWEET (*) I 5.10d	409
SHORT ORDER (***) I 5.9	257
SIDEREAL MOTION I 5.11b	323
SIDEWINDER I 5.10d	278
SILENT LUCIDITY I 5.7 R	507
SILVER SURFER I 5.8 X	495
SINISTER GROOVE I 5.5	406
SIR BOR'S DREAM I 5.7 R	503
SKELETONS IN THE CLOSET II 5.9	206
SKY STREAK (**) I 5.10b	294
SLAB OF THE WOODS I 5.3 X	489
SLABS DIRECT, THE (**) II 5.7 R (5.4 X)	221
SLAM DANCE I 5.8	539
SLAP HAPPY I 5.10b	205
SLASH, THE III 5.9+, A2	519
SLEDGEHAMMER (**) I 5.10d	392
SLEEPING BEAUTY (**) I 5.10d	260
SLEEPING SWAN I 5.10d	180
SLIDING BOARD (***) II 5.7 (5.4 R)	229
SLIGHTLY LESS THAN ZERO I 5.9-	353
SLIMOR I 5.6	405
SLINGS & ARROWS I 5.9+ R	84
SLIP'N SLIME (*) I 5.9	474
SLIPPING INTO DARKNESS (*) I 5.11d	449
SLIPSHOD II 5.6 R	241
SLIPSHOD: THE 5.7 FLAKE I 5.7	242
SLIPSHOD: THE CRYSTALLINE DIKE I 5.8 R	242
SLOT, THE (**) I 5.10b	201
SLOT, THE: THE DIRECT FINISH I 5.10b	201
SMALL CHANGE I 5.8, A0 (One rappel)	349
SO WHAT! I 5.12d	353
SOFT IRON ROUTE (**) II A3+	158
SOL I 5.9	488
SOLITUDE CRACK II 5.10b, A1 (3 Points of Aid)	176
SOLSTICE II 5.12d (5.11a R)	86
SOMETHING FOOLISH I 5.9	449
SON OF A BIRCH I 5.11d (5.10d R)	79
SOUL SURVIVOR II 5.11a	336
SOUTH BUTTRESS DIRECT	286
(***) III 5.11b R, A1 (5 Points of Aid)	287
SOUTH BUTTRESS DIRECT: ORIGINAL FREE VARIANT I 5.9 R	287
SOUTH BUTTRESS OF WANKERS WALL I 5.8+ R	220
SOUTHERN BELLE II 5.7+ X	302
SPACE WALK (*) II 5.9+ R	122
SPANKING, THE (*) I 5.11c	147
SPIDERLINE (*) I 5.10a	398
SPIDERS ON HOLIDAY I 5.7+	464
SPINEY NORMAN I 5.2	514
SPLIT DECISION I 5.10b	323
SPRING ISSUE I 5.10b or 5.11b	575
SQUEEZE PLAY I 5.3	384
SQUIRM, THE I 5.9	477
STADTMÜLLER-GRIFFIN ROUTE II 5.6	244
STAGE FRIGHT (***) I 5.12c X	142
STANDARD & POOR (**) I 5.9	374
STANDARD ROUTE (*) I 5.11d (Alcohol Wall)	452
STANDARD ROUTE I 5.5 (Band M Ledge)	364
STANDARD ROUTE (**) II 5.6 R (Cathedral)	130
Cathedral STANDARD: THE TOE	132
CRACK DIRECT START (*) I 5.8	132

ROUTE INDEX 597

Route	Page
Cathedral STANDARD: THE TOE CRACK (***) I 5.7	131
Cathedral STANDARD: THE DIRECT START (*) I 5.7+	131
Cathedral STANDARD: SAFETY IN NUMBERS I 5.9 R	132
Cathedral STANDARD: THE DIRECT FINISH I 5.7+	132
Cathedral STANDARD: GILL'S CRACK I 5.11b (TR)	132
Cathedral STANDARD: MADARA'S CRACK I 5.10b	132
STANDARD ROUTE (***) I 5.4 (Square Ledge)	569
STANDARD ROUTE (***) II 5.5 (5.2 R) (Whitehorse)	221
Whitehorse STANDARD: THE DIRECT START TO THE ARCH I 5.3 R	225
Whitehorse STANDARD: QUARTZ POCKET (***) I 5.3	225
Whitehorse STANDARD: THE OLD VARIATION I 5.6	225
Whitehorse STANDARD: LEFT-OUT I 5.7 R	225
Whitehorse STANDARD: DIRECT FINISH (***) I 5.7	226
Whitehorse STANDARD: BOLT LADDER (*) I 5.9	226
STARFIRE (*) I 5.11b	78
STARRY, STAIRY NIGHT (*) I 5.9+	518
START ME UP I 5.7 R	123
STARVING FOR STARS I 5.10d	411
STEAK SAUCE (*) I 5.12c	321
STEAMROLLER (**) I 5.12a	387
STEP FUNCTION II 5.10b	390
STEP LADDER II Grade Unknown	566
STEPS, THE II 5.10c	369
STEWART'S CRACK (*) I 5.9	511
STICK-MAN I 5.12b (Top-rope)	584
STICKS & STONES I 5.11b R (5.10a X)	85
STICKY WICKET (*) I 5.8	338
STILETTO (**) I 5.12a	446
STILL IN SAIGON (***) I 5.8	118
STING, THE I 5.7	383
STONE COLD (*) I 5.10d	355
STONE FREE (**) II 5.11b	392
STONE'S THROW I 5.5	513
STONED FOR FREE (*) I 5.10d	392
STOP & STARE I 5.10d	422
STOP IF YOU DARE I 5.8 X	220
STORMY MONDAY (*) I 5.7	485
STRAIGHT UP I 5.9+ R	333
STRAITS OF MAGELLAN, THE III 5.9+ R	481
STRAY CATS I 5.11b	423
STUDENT DAZE I 5.7+ R	237
SULTANS OF SWILL I 5.13a	350
SUMMER BREEZE I 5.2	489
SUMMER OF '82, THE I 5.9	470
SUNDOG DELIGHT I 5.12d	442
SUNNY DAYS (*) I 5.11b	369
SUPER SLAB I 5.7 R	497
SUPERBA (**) I 5.5	466
SUPERFRIENDS I 5.10a R	406
SUPERIOR B SIDE, THE (*) I 5.12c	580
SUPERIOR B SIDE: DIRECT START (*) I 5.11d R	580
SURF PSYCHO (**) I 5.13a	452
SURFING PRIMITIVES I 5.8 R	237
SURREAL II 5.10c (5.9 R)	317
SURVEYOR'S ROUTE II 5.7 R	576
SUSPENDED ANIMATION I 5.8	205
SUSPENDED SENTENCE (**) I 5.11d	470
SWEATHOG I 5.12b	352
SWINGING HIPS (**) I 5.10d	272
SWORD OF OMENS (**) I 5.11d	401
TABLE SCRAPS (**) I 5.9	504
TABLE TALK I 5.10b	505
TABU (***) I 5.9 R	137
TAINT, THE (*) I 5.11d	317

Route	Page
TAKE A GIANT STEP (***) I 5.8+	494
TAKE MY TUNA I 5.8	407
TALCUM POWER I 5.10b X	96
TAO OF DOW, THE (*) I 5.9	374
TAO OF POOH, THE (*) I 5.6	405
TAPE WORM I 5.8	539
TAR & FEATHER (*) I 5.11d	433
TARNSMAN OF GOR I 5.9-	347
TEN YEARS AFTER (*) II 5.9	528
TERMINATOR (*) I 5.11d	391
TERROR AT SEA (*) I 5.10a Tricky Protection	351
TERROR INFIRMA I 5.6	477
THEY DIED LAUGHING (***) I 5.9	202
THIN AIR (***) II 5.6	125
THIN AIR: THE 5.8 CORNER I 5.8	126
THINK FAST, MR. MOTO I 5.9 R	342
THINNER I 5.8 R	126
THINNER STILL I 5.5a (Top-rope)	126
THIRTY SECONDS OVER TOKYO (*) II 5.10b	545
THIS MORTAL COIL I 5.9	350
THREE BIRCHES (**) I 5.8+	79
THREE BIRCHES: THE EASY FINISH I 5.6	79
THREE GEMS I 5.9	537
THREE SAINTS (*) I 5.9	285
THREE STARS I 5.7	477
THREE WAGS I 5.10b	365
THREE WOGS (**) I 5.9	361
THRESHER, THE (*) I 5.10b R	206
THRILLER ARETE (***) I 5.10a or 5.10c	570
THROMBOSIS I 5.8	542
THUMB, THE I 5.7	508
THWARTHOG (*) II 5.9	461
TICKET TO RIDE I 5.9 R	295
TIDAL WAVE II 5.10b (5.8 R)	229
TO THE TERRITORY I 5.9	520
TODD FOOLERY (*) I 5.8	447
TOE CRACK DIRECT START, THE (*) I 5.8	132
TOE CRACK, THE (***) I 5.7	131
TOLKIEN HIGHWAY I 5.7 R	507
TOMB, THE I 5.9	427
TONIGHT I 5.11a	397
TOO THIN TO BE FUN I 5.11c (Top-rope)	533
TOOTHLESS GRIN (***) I 5.12a	444
TOOTHLESS GRIN: THE DIRECT START I A4	444
TOP DOG (*) I 5.11a (or 5.10c)	535
TOPLESS TELLERS (**) I A4	158
TOTAL RECALL (***) II 5.11b	278
TOTALLY SAVAGE I 5.12d	438
TOURIST TREAT (***) II 5.12c	137
TOUTE SUITE (*) I 5.11b (or straight up; 5.12a)	257
TRAINING WHEELS (*) I 5.11b R	182
TRANQUILITY (**) II 5.10b R	312
TRAPEZE I 5.10a	430
TRAPEZIUS (**) I 5.10d	400
TRAVESTY II 5.8, A2	86
TREACH CRACK I 5.10b	284
TREASURE HUNT I 5.11d	488
TREEBEARD I 5.6	514
TREETOTALERS I 5.9+	346
TREMORS I 5.11d or 5.12b	52
TRIASSIC CRACK I 5.8	379
TRICYCLE I 5.8	353
TRIPLE PLAY I 5.9	587
TRIPTYCH I 5.9	466
TROUBLED WORLD II 5.9	362

598 ROUTE INDEX

Route	Page
TRUE COLORS I 5.7 X	493
TRUE LIES I 5.12b	110
TRUE STORIES (**) I 5.11c (5.11a R / 5.10a X)	313
TRUE TEMPER I 5.11d (5.10d R)	78
TRUMP CARD (*) I 5.10a	531
TSUNAMI (**) I 5.6	495
TUMOR, THE I 5.11a	573
TURNER'S FLAKE (***) I 5.8	128
TWO PINTS OF LAGER & CRISPS (**) I 5.12a	352
UNCERTAINTY PRINCIPLE, THE (*) I 5.10d	323
UNDERCOVER AGENT I 5.8	476
UNDERSTATEMENT, THE I 5.8	371
UNDERWORLD I 5.6 X	319
UNFINISHED SYMPHONY (*) I 5.12c	442
UNFORGETTABLE FIRE (**) II 5.11b (5.9 R)	316
UNINVITED, THE I 5.8	506
UNWANTED GUESTS (**) I 5.12b	264
UP FRONT I 5.8	469
UP ON THE ROOF I 5.9	425
UP ROPE (*) I 5.11d	266
UPPER REFUSE (***) I 5.5	66
V GROOVE, THE (**) I 5.8	353
V I 5.9	397
V-8 I 5.8	338
VALLEY GIRL I 5.6+	94
VECTOR I 5.8	415
VEEDAUWOO EAST II 5.10b	522
VEMBER I 5.6	360
VENI-VIDI-WIMPI I 5.11a R	295
VENTILATOR (***) I 5.10b	75
VENUS VERMICULATE I 5.8	502
VERTICAL VENTURE I 5.10b	346
VETERAN'S DAY I 5.10b	475
VETERANS OF FOREIGN WALLS (**) II 5.10b	523
VIA COGNOSCENTI II 5.9+	484
VIA COGNOSCENTI: DIRECT FINISH II 5.10d	484
VIGILANTE I 5.10b R or X	260
VIRGIN, THE (**) I 5.11c	367
VIRGO RISING I 5.9	323
VISITORS, THE I 5.9	327
VLADD THE IMPALER (**) I 5.12b	502
VOODOO CHILE I 5.11d	544
VULTURES (***) I 5.10d	467
WAITING FOR COMEAU (*) I 5.9	436
WAITING FOR WEBSTER I 5.9 X	253
WAKE UP CALL (*) I 5.9+	285
WALKABOUT (**) I 5.12b	312
WALKABOUT I 5.9	412
WALKING MAN I 5.9 (Top-rope)	470
WANDERER I 5.8	546
WANDERLUST II 5.8 R	58
WARLOCK III 5.12c (5.10b R)	342
WATERMELON, THE I 5.8	187
WAVE BYE-BYE I 5.9+ R	488
WAVELENGTH (***) II 5.8	220
WAVELENGTH: THE DIRECT START (*) II 5.7+	228
WAVY GRAVY I 5.7 R	228
WAY IN THE WILDERNESS II 5.9	232
WAY RADICAL (*) II 5.9+ R	484
WAYWARD SON (**) I 5.11b	370
WEAK NUTS I 5.6	463
WEBSTER'S FINISH (**) I 5.10b	415
WEBSTER'S UNABRIDGED (*) I 5.11a	292
WEBSTER'S WORKOUT I 5.11b (Top-rope)	68
WEBSTER-ROSS ROUTE I 5.10b (Unfinished)	266
WEDGE (**) II 5.6 (5.5 R)	237
WEDGE: THE DIRECT FINISH I 5.9	239
WEDGE: THE RIGHT-HAND VARIATION I 5.6 R	238
WESTERN LADY (**) I 5.11b	75
WET DIHEDRAL (*) I 5.8	405
WEZ, THE (*) II 5.12b	191
WHAT WAS, WAS OVER (**) I 5.13c	171
WHAT'S UP YANKEE? I 5.5	489
WHERE EAGLES DARE (**) II 5.11a	546
WHERE GERBILS DARE I 5.9-	207
WHERE SPIDERS HANG I 5.11c	355
WHIP FINISH (**) I 5.11b	282
WHIPPING POST (**) I 5.11c	460
WHITE EYE (*) III 5.12b, A0	175
WHITE EYE: THE DIRECT START I 5.11a	175
WHITE SNAKE (*) II 5.11c R	399
WHITE STREAK, THE (*) II 5.8	529
WHITE WILDERNESS I 5.7 X	219
WHITE WILDERNESS: THE DIRECT FINISH I 5.9	219
WHITE ZONE, THE (**) II 5.12a	250
WIESSNER ROUTE (**) II 5.8 R	331
WILD (*) I 5.11b	94
WILD AT HEART (*) I 5.11a	463
WILD CALLING I 5.10b	456
WILD CHILD (**) I 5.11c	577
WILD EYED & THE INNOCENT, THE (**) I 5.10b	348
WILD JOURNEY I 5.10b	456
WILD KINGDOM (**) III 5.11c or 5.11d	102
WILD KINGDOM: FAUX PAS ARETE (***) I 5.11c	102
WILD KINGDOM: PROW FINISH (**) I 5.11d	102
WILD LIFE (***) I 5.12a	580
WILD THING (***) I 5.13a	582
WILD WOMEN (***) III 5.12a (5.10b R)	94
WILDEBEAST (*) I 5.8	94
WILKINSON SWORD I 5.10a	320
WINDFALL (***) I 5.10a (5.8 R)	127
WINDJAMMER (***) I 5.11b	481
WINGED EEL FINGERLING (***) I 5.12d (Top-rope)	387
WISHFUL THINKING (**) I 5.11a	575
WIT'S END (*) I 5.6 R	488
WITCHCRAFT (**) I 5.10a	383
WIZARD OF OZ (**) I 5.12c	260
WOMBAT (*) I 5.12a	446
WOMEN IN LOVE (***) III 5.12a (or Clean A2)	90
WOMEN IN LOVE / THE BOOK LINK-UP (***) II 5.11d	90
WONDER WALL (***) III 5.12a (5.8 X)	294
WONDERS NEVER CEASE (**) II 5.10c (5.9 R)	301
WOODCHUCK EDGE I 5.8 R	389
WOODCHUCK LODGE I 5.10a	389
WOODEN NICHOLS I 5.11a	321
WORKOUT CRACKS, THE I 5.9 & 5.10	147
WORKSHOP ORGY I 5.12a	310
WORM DRIVE I 5.10c	110
YAK BETWEEN WORLDS I 5.8	110
YELLOW BRICK ROAD (*) III 5.13b (5.11a R), A3	109
YELLOW MATTER CUSTARD (***) I 5.13a	430
YOU CAN TAKE IT WITH YOU I 5.8	532
YOUTH CHALLENGE (*) I 5.10d	64
ZANZIBAR (*) I 5.5	394
ZEN & NOW (*) I 5.10c	374
ZERO GULLY I 5.6	388
ZIG ZAG I 5.7+	383
ZIGGURAUT (*) I 5.9	327
ZONKED OUT (**) I 5.12b	386

STAR INDEX

Free Climbs (Aid Routes at end of Index.)

5.3 (*)
BEGINNER'S EASY VARIATION II 5.3	214
STANDARD ROUTE: THE DIRECT START TO THE ARCH I 5.3 R (Whitehorse Ledge)	225

5.3 (***)
STANDARD ROUTE: THE QUART POCKET I 5.3 (Whitehorse Ledge)	225

5.4 (*)
BEGINNER'S BLESSING I 5.4	284
CENTRAL GULLY II 5.4	565
HENDERSON RIDGE II 5.4	568
MISSISSIPPI RAMBLE I 5.4	492
PEREZ DIHEDRAL I 5.4	466

5.4 (**)
BEELZEBUB CORNER, THE I 5.4	271
EASY DOES IT II 5.4 (5.2 R)	226
ROCK GARDEN I 5.4	422

5.4 (***)
STANDARD ROUTE I 5.4 (Square Ledge)	569

5.5 (*)
COVER GIRL I 5.5	415
ECHO II 5.5	262
HOLY SMOKE I 5.5	503
OLD ROUTE, THE II 5.5	552
SLIP'N SLIME I 5.5	474
ZANZIBAR I 5.5	394

5.5 (**)
CHIMNEY, THE I 5.5	570
PRIZE, THE I 5.5	569
SUPERBA I 5.5	466

5.5 (***)
BEGINNER'S ROUTE II 5.5 (5.4 R) (Whitehorse Ledge)	215
STANDARD ROUTE II 5.5 (5.2 R) (Whitehorse Ledge)	221
UPPER REFUSE I 5.5	66

5.6 (*)
BEAT THE CLOCK II 5.6+, A0	349
BIRCH TREE CORNER I 5.6	352
BLACK CORNER, THE I 5.6	463
BON VIVANT'S WALL I 5.6	464
CAKEWALK II 5.6+	343
COMEAU FINISH, THE I 5.6	102
DARCY-CROWTHER VARIATION, THE II 5.6	245
DARCY'S TRAVERSE I 5.6	120
DIKE ROUTE II 5.6	248
GEMINI I 5.6	383
JOE'S PLACE I 5.6	570
NEBULOUS II 5.6	525
NO MAN'S LAND II 5.6 R	119
OKTOBERFEST I 5.6	394
PORTUGUESE APPLE I 5.6	407
TAO OF POOH, THE I 5.6	405
WIT'S END I 5.6 R	488

5.6 (**)
AKU AKU I 5.6	546
FACE DANCES I 5.6+	492
STANDARD ROUTE II 5.6 R (Cathedral Ledge)	130
STILETTO I 5.6	446
TSUNAMI I 5.6	495

5.6 (***)
CHILD'S PLAY I 5.6	204
THIN AIR II 5.6	125
WEDGE I 5.6 (5.5 R)	237

5.7 (*)
BRITISH ARE HERE, THE I 5.7	447
COLORING BOOK I 5.7	493
CLOUD WALKERS II 5.7	561
DEDICATION II 5.7+	340
FINAL GESTURE I 5.7+	67
FORE PAWS I 5.7	422
HERE COMES THE JUGS I 5.7	322
HERE'S STAIRING AT YOU I 5.7	518
LET THEM EAT CAKE II 5.7	343
MacDOUGAL'S VARIATION I 5.7	513
MANTLESHELF PROBLEM, THE I 5.7+	205
PENCILNECK GEEK I 5.7	494
PLEASANT STREET I 5.7 (5.6 R)	71
ROAD TO LHASA I 5.7	489
STANDARD ROUTE: THE DIRECT START I 5.7+ (Cathedral Ledge)	131
STORMY MONDAY I 5.7	485
WAVELENGTH: DIRECT START II 5.7+	228

5.7 (**)
ENDEAVOR III 5.7+	528
NEW YORK TIMES I 5.7+	532
POOH I 5.7	81
SLABS DIRECT, THE II 5.7 R (5.4 X)	221

5.7 (***)
CRUISE CONTROL I 5.7+	496
FUNHOUSE I 5.7	80
KIDDY CRACK I 5.7	205
NORTHEAST RIDGE OF THE PINNACLE III 5.7	554 & 558
PERFECT WAVE, THE I 5.7	494
PINNACLE ROCK CLIMB, THE III 5.7	558
PROW, THE: THE 5.7 START I 5.7	104
SEA OF HOLES II 5.7	242
SLIDING BOARD II 5.7 (5.4 R)	229
STANDARD ROUTE: THE DIRECT FINISH I 5.7 (Whitehorse Ledge)	226
STANDARD ROUTE: THE TOE CRACK I 5.7 (Cathedral Ledge)	131

5.8 (*)
A LITTLE SLABBA DO YA I 5.8+	411
A. P. TREAT I 5.8	86
BUGS EAT FROGS I 5.8	504
CIRCADIAN CRACK I 5.8	465
CLOUD WALKERS I 5.8	561
COMMANDO RUN I 5.8	101
DARK HORSE I 5.8	250
DARKNESS AT THE EDGE OF TOWN I 5.8	348
FUNHOUSE: THE LEFT-HAND CORNER I 5.8	81
GOLDEN SLIPPERS I 5.8	537
GYMCRACK I 5.8	466
HARMONIC CONVERGENCE II 5.8, A1 (3 Points of Aid)	401
LAST WAVE, THE I 5.8	232
LEAVES OF GRASS I 5.8	539
LOOKOUT CRACK, THE I 5.8+	101
LOST ARCH I 5.8	415
MERLIN I 5.8	503
MISTY I 5.8	561
NATURAL ORDER I 5.8	518
OLD TIMES II 5.8 R	246
PHANTOM OF THE WOODS I 5.8	469
REMISSION II 5.8 R	187
STICKY WICKET II 5.8	338

600 STAR INDEX

TAO OF DOW, THE I 5.8	374
TODD FOOLERY I 5.8	447
TOE CRACK DIRECT START, THE I 5.8	132
THINNER I 5.8 R	126
WHITE STREAK, THE II 5.8	529

5.8 (**)

5.8 COMBINATION, THE II 5.8+	84
AVATAR I 5.8+	514
BRAIN, THE I 5.8 (Top-rope)	573
MAN'S BEST FRIEND I 5.8	261
PICK OF THE LITTER I 5.8+	536
PINNACLE ROCK CLIMB: THE 5.8 DIRECT VARIATION I 5.8	558
THREE BIRCHES II 5.8+	79
V GROOVE, THE I 5.8	353
WIESSNER ROUTE II 5.8 R	331

5.8 (***)

BLACK LUNG I 5.8	67
BOMBARDMENT I 5.8 (5.6 R)	75
GIRDLE TRAVERSE OF WHITEHORSE III 5.8 (5.7 R), A1 (3 Points of Aid)	324
INFERNO II 5.8	310
PINE TREE ELIMINATE I 5.8+	146
SEA OF HOLES with THE DIRECT FINISH II 5.8	242
STILL IN SAIGON I 5.8	118
TAKE A GIANT STEP I 5.8+	494
TURNER'S FLAKE I 5.8	128
WAVELENGTH II 5.8	228

5.9 (*)

ANIMAL CRACKERS I 5.9	357
BOOKLET, THE I 5.9	239
BROKEN ENGLISH I 5.9	467
BULLY, THE I 5.9	383
CHANGING SEASONS I 5.9	575
CRANKSHAFT I 5.9	383
CRAZY WOMAN DRIVER I 5.9 X	497
DEADLINE I 5.9	393
DMZ I 5.9	115
FOOTSY-QUENCE II 5.9 R	318
GRANITE STATE I 5.9	410
GUIDE'S ROUTE, THE II 5.9	344
HOBBITLAND I 5.9	508
JURASSIC CRACK I 5.9	382
K-NINE I 5.9	535
LAST RUNG ON THE LADDER I 5.9	348
LAYTON'S ASCENT I 5.9	56
LITTLE FEAT I 5.9-	101
MONARCH BUTTERFLY I 5.9	353
PHANTOM OF THE WOODS I 5.9	469
PINS & NEEDLES I 5.9	468
PUFF I 5.9	404
REGRESSION II 5.9 (5.8 R)	336
RIGHTEOUS SLAB I 5.9	403
ROSEBUD I 5.9 R	518
SAINT GEORGE I 5.9 R	403
STANDARD ROUTE: THE BOLT LADDER I 5.9 (Whitehorse Ledge)	226
STEWART'S CRACK II 5.9	511
TEN YEARS AFTER II 5.9	528
THINK FAST, MR. MOTO II 5.9 R	342
THREE SAINTS I 5.9	285
WAITING FOR COMEAU I 5.9	253
ZIGGURAUT I 5.9	327

5.9 (**)

A STITCH IN TIME I 5.9	328
CHICKEN DELIGHT I 5.9	56
COSMIC AMAZEMENT I 5.9	323
MEAN LINE I 5.9 or 5.10b	534
NOSE, THE I 5.9 (Tope-rope)	573
PATHFINDER II 5.9	248
REFUSE I 5.9	87
SHADOW AT NIGHT I 5.9-	352
STANDARD & POOR I 5.9	374
TABLE SCRAPS I 5.9	504
THWARTHOG I 5.9	461

5.9 (***)

ATLANTIS II 5.9	309
BANDIT I 5.9	360
BIRD'S NEST I 5.9-	202
CHILDREN'S CRUSADE II 5.9	276
HOTTER THAN HELL I 5.9	313
PROW, THE: THE 5.9 SLAB I 5.9	104
RECOMBEAST III 5.9	98
RECOMPENSE III 5.9	96
RETALIATION II 5.9	62
SHORT ORDER I 5.9	257
TABU I 5.9	137
THEY DIED LAUGHING I 5.9	202

5.9+ (*)

007 II 5.9+	122
AARP CHALLENGE I 5.9+ R	399
BROWN'S FIST I 5.9+	86
CENTURION I 5.9+	399
COFFIN NAIL I 5.9+	309
CULPRITS, THE I 5.9+	88
DIAGONAL II 5.9+ R	150
DOUBLE VEE I 5.9+	56
DRAGON CURVE I 5.9+	403
DR. LEAKEY, I PRESUME? I 5.9+ R	341
FINGER FOOD FROM THE FUTURE I 5.9+	423
LAST WAVE, THE I 5.9+	232
MAN-O-WAR I 5.9+ (5.7 R)	253
MODERN MATURITY I 5.9+	400
NOSTRIL I 5.9+	207
PERSONA I 5.9+	271
QUEEN OF HEARTS I 5.9+	384
ROADSIDE ATTRACTION I 5.9+	351
SPACE WALK II 5.9+ R	122
STARRY, STAIRY NIGHT I 5.9+	518
WAKE UP CALL I 5.9+	312
WAY RADICAL II 5.9+ R	370

5.9+ (**)

3 CYLINDERS I 5.9+	281
HALLOWED EVE III 5.9+ R	301
LADYSLIPPER to WONDER WALL I 5.9+	296
NINTH WAVE, THE II 5.9+ R	219

5.9+ (***)

BOOK OF SOLEMNITY, THE II 5.9+	68
DIEDRE II 5.9+	191
LADYSLIPPER II 5.9+ (5.7 R)	296
NUTCRACKER I 5.9+	53
PINNACLE DIRECT III 5.9+	558

5.10a (*)

BLANK ON THE MAP II 5.10a	461
FINGERTIP TRIP I 5.10a	240
GENTLEMEN OF LEISURE I 5.10a	351
IT'S TIME I 5.10a	537
PROW, THE: THE 5.10 FINISH I 5.10a	104
REELING IN THE FEARS I 5.10a X (5.9 R)	374
REPENTENCE I 5.10a R	184
SEPTEMBER MORN I 5.10a R	302
SPIDERLINE I 5.10a	398
TERROR AT SEA I 5.10a Tricky Protection	351
TRUMP CARD I 5.10a	531

STAR INDEX 601

5.10a (**)
ANOTHER PRETTY FACE I 5.10a	104
AUTOBOT I 5.10a	399
BLACK JADE II 5.10a R	228
GRENDAL'S LAIR I 5.10a	530
INSIDE STRAIGHT I 5.10a	531
MISSING LINK, THE III 5.10a (5.7 R)	128
OOH MOW MAO I 5.10a	398
OVER DONE I 5.10a	371
THREE WOGS I 5.10a	361
WITCHCRAFT I 5.10a	383

5.10a (***)
FREEDOM I 5.10a	127
LOOSE LIPS I 5.10a	271
LOST SOULS III 5.10a	302
RAPID TRANSIT II 5.10a	120
ROUGH BOYS I 5.10a	446
SEVENTH SEAL I 5.10a	266
THRILLER ARETE I 5.10a	570
WINDFALL I 5.10a (5.8 R)	127

5.10b (*)
5.10 COMBINATION, THE II 5.10b	70
ADVENTURES IN 3D II 5.10b (5.10a R)	123
ARNO'S CORNER I 5.10b	285
ASPIRING II 5.10b	386
BROKEN ENGLISH II 5.10b	467
BULLY, THE I 5.10b	383
DAVY JONE'S LOCKER II 5.10b	432
EASTER ISLAND REUNION I 5.10b	545
GEMINI DREAM'IN I 5.10b	203
GENERATION X I 5.10b (Top-rope)	205
HORSE OF A DIFFERENT COLOR I 5.10b	321
LANCELOT LINK / SECRET CHIMP I 5.10b	129
PRIMAL SCREAM: THE DIRECT FINISH I 5.10b	560
PUMPING POCKETS I 5.10b	536
REBELLIOUS YOUTH I 5.10b	462
REPEAT PERFORMANCE I 5.10b	471
THIRTY SECONDS OVER TOKYO II 5.10b	545
THRESHER, THE I 5.10b R	206

5.10b (**)
ARIES I 5.10b	338
BLACK JADE II 5.10b	228
CREOLE LOVE CALL III 5.10b R	304
INTERNATIONAL MTN. CRACK I 5.10b	533
MEAN LINE I 5.10b or 5.9	534
NOMAD CRACK I 5.10b	56
RAPTURE OF THE STEEP I 5.10b	384
SCIENCE FRICTION: WEBSTER'S FINISH I 5.10b	292
SKY STREAK I 5.10b	294
SLOT, THE I 5.10b	201
TRANQUILITY II 5.10b	312
VETERANS OF FOREIGN WALLS II 5.10b	523
WEBSTER'S FINISH I 5.10b	292
WILD EYED AND THE INNOCENT I 5.10b	348

5.10b (***)
ATLANTIS II 5.10b	309
FOOLS FOR A DAY I 5.10b	374
GIRDLE TRAVERSE OF WHITEHORSE, THE III 5.10b (5.7 R)	324
HYPERSPACE II 5.10b	472
INTERLOPER II 5.10b (5.8 R)	230
INTIMIDATION III 5.10b	180
JING & TONIC I 5.10b	451
LAST UNICORN, THE III 5.10b	290
MECHANIC'S ROUTE III 5.10b (5.7 R)	562
RAPID TRANSIT I 5.10b	120
REVERSE CAMBER I 5.10b	138

ROBINSON CRUSOE II 5.10b R	337
VENTILATOR I 5.10b	75

5.10c (*)
BABY FACE I 5.10c	322
BARBER DIRECT I 5.10c R	76
BROKEN BONES I 5.10c (5.9+ R)	86
CALIMARI I 5.10c	507
DECEPTICON I 5.10c	404
DICK TO THE RESCUE I 5.10c	505
EIGENVECTOR II 5.10c	390
FLIRTING WITH DIKES I 5.10c R	439
GALE FORCE I 5.10c X	365
HIPPODROME I 5.10c	136
JOKER'S WILD I 5.10c R	531
MOE I 5.10c	164
PRO CHOICE I 5.10c	129
REBELLIOUS YOUTH I 5.10c	462
TOP DOG I 5.10c	535
ZEN & NOW I 5.10c	374

5.10c (**)
FOSSIL CLUB I 5.10c	587
MATHEMATICA II 5.10c	390
MIDLIFE CRISIS I 5.10c	534
PLEISTOCENE II 5.10c	393
WONDERS NEVER CEASE II 5.10c (5.9 R)	301

5.10c (***)
THRILLER ARETE I 5.10c	570

5.10d (*)
CEMETERY GATES I 5.10d	304
CURE FOR THE BLUES I 5.10d	284
DRESDEN I 5.10d (5.7 R)	53
ELIMINATE DIRECT I 5.10d	281
FINALLY DUNN I 5.10d	371
FLIGHT OF THE FALCON I 5.10d	436
FOOL'S GOLD I 5.10d	68
GOLDEN BOOK OF BAD DOGS, THE I 5.10d	70
GRAVITATIONAL MASS I 5.10d	322
GRIM REAPER, THE I 5.10d R	58
HEAD CEMENT I 5.10d R	282
HURLEY WARNING WALL II 5.10d R	332
IN YOUR FACE I 5.10d	310
IRON LUNG I 5.10d	475
KNIGHT IN WHITE SATIN I 5.10d	206
LAST TEMPTATION, THE II 5.10d	191
POINT, THE I 5.10d R	76
PORTLAND CEMENT I 5.10d	282
POWDERFINGER I 5.10d	321
PROBLEM CHILD II 5.10d R	279
PUB CRAWL, THE I 5.10d	468
RECONSIDER I 5.10d	99
SHORT BUT SWEET I 5.10d	409
STONE COLD I 5.10d	355
STONED FOR FREE I 5.10d	392
UNCERTAINTY PRINCIPLE, THE I 5.10d	323
YOUTH CHALLENGE II 5.10d	64

5.10d (**)
BIG PLUM, THE V 5.10d, A0	207
COUNTER CULTURE I 5.10d	469
CULTURE SPONGE I 5.10d R	469
DIAMOND EDGE I 5.10d	391
DIVISION OF LABOR II 5.10d	162
FLARE, THE I 5.10d (5.7 R)	509
HART ATTACK I 5.10d	542
LICHEN IT A LOT I 5.10d	59
MACHINA EX DEUS I 5.10d	362
SLEDGEHAMMER I 5.10d	392
SLEEPING BEAUTY I 5.10d	260

602 STAR INDEX

SWINGING HIPS I 5.10d	272
TRAPEZIUS I 5.10d	400

5.10d (***)

CRACK IN THE WOODS, THE I 5.10d	501
ETHEREAL CRACK I 5.10d	266
FIRING ALL EIGHT I 5.10d	280
PRIMAL SCREAM III 5.10d (5.10a R)	559
RECLUSE I 5.10d	203
SHE-RA I 5.10d	400
VULTURES I 5.10d	436

5.11a (*)

ANCIENT JOURNEYS I 5.11a+	250
AWAY THE WEE MAN I 5.11a (Top-rope)	112
BURNING DOWN THE HOUSE II 5.11a R (5.10a X)	316
CINNEREA II 5.11a	273
DON'T FLY OVER RUSSIA I 5.11a R	102
HOTEL CALIFORNIA II 5.11a	402
MALT THERAPY I 5.11a	364
TOP DOG I 5.11a	535
TUMOR, THE I 5.11a	573
WEBSTER'S FINISH I 5.11a	292
WEBSTER'S UNABRIDGED I 5.11a	68
WILD AT HEART I 5.11a	463
WISHFUL THINKING I 5.11a	575

5.11a (**)

CASTAWAYS I 5.11a	338
CENTAUR, THE I 5.11a	290
JUDGEMENT DAY I 5.11a	391
REVOLT OF THE DIKE BRIGADE II 5.11a (5.9+ R)	292
SCIENCE FRICTION WALL III 5.11a (5.8 R)	456
SCORPION ARETE I 5.11a	
WHERE EAGLES DARE II 5.11a	546

5.11a (***)

CHILDREN'S CRUSADE DIRECT FINISH III 5.11a	276
ETHEREAL CRACK I 5.11a	266
LICHEN DELIGHT I 5.11a	59

5.11b (*)

ABRAKADABRA III 5.11b	183
AGENT ORANGE I 5.11b	433
BAD TO THE BONE I 5.11b	463
CANNON FODDER I 5.11b	475
CRAZY WISDOM III 5.11b, A1 (12 Points of Aid)	110
CRUSADE OF THE LIGHT BRIGADE I 5.11b	279
DARKENING OF THE LIGHT I 5.11b	393
DRESS RIGHT I 5.11b	280
ENERGY CRISIS II 5.11b (5.11a R)	84
FEAR OF EJECTION I 5.11b	509
HARMONIC CONVERGENCE II 5.11b, A0	401
HERCULES I 5.11b	371
HUNTING HUMANS II 5.11b	196
LAUNCH THE KITTY I 5.11b	328
NEEDFUL THINGS I 5.11b (5.8 R)	240
PICKING WINNERS I 5.11b	206
PRESSURE DROP I 5.11b	461
PUMPING STATION II 5.11b	501
SCYTHE, THE I 5.11b	354
STARFIRE I 5.11b	78
STRAY CATS I 5.11b	423
TOUTE SUITE I 5.11b	257
TRAINING WHEELS I 5.11b R	182
WILD I 5.11b	94

5.11b (**)

ARETE, THE I 5.11b R	65
BETE NOIR I 5.11b	431
BICYCLE ROUTE, THE III 5.11b (5.10b R)	180
BITS & PIECES I 5.11b R	271
CLEAN SWEEP I 5.11b	133
EGO TRIP I 5.11b	77
HAVANNUTHA DRINK I 5.11b	451
LOOKING FOR GOLDILOCKS I 5.11b	410
OVERTIME CRACK I 5.11b	353
STONE FREE II 5.11b	392
UNFORGETTABLE FIRE II 5.11b (5.9 R)	316
WAYWARD SON I 5.11b	463
WESTERN LADY I 5.11b	75
WHIP FINISH I 5.11b	282

5.11b (***)

AIRATION I 5.11b	142
CAMBER II 5.11b	137
GRAND LARSONY I 5.11b	584
IF DOGS RUN FREE II 5.11b	358
SOUTH BUTTRESS DIRECT	286
III 5.11b R, A1 (5 Points of Aid)	
TOTAL RECALL III 5.11b	278
WINDJAMMER III 5.11b	481

5.11c (*)

CAROLINA DREAM'IN I 5.11c (5.10 R)	261
DON'T FIRE UNTIL YOU SEE THE	190
WHITES OF THEIR EYES III 5.11c R	
FAT GIRLS WITH ACNE I 5.11c	445
HOLLOW MEN I 5.11c	285
LAST STRAND, THE I 5.11c	285
LAST TANGO, THE I 5.11c	263
LUMBERJACK CRACK I 5.11c	413
OFF THE HOOK I 5.11c	56
ONCE UPON A CLIMB I 5.11c	78
OZONE BYPASS I 5.11c	126
SPANKING, THE I 5.11c	147

5.11c (**)

3 CYLINDERS IV 5.11c (5.8 R)	281
BACKDRAFT I 5.11c (5.8 R)	313
BEATING A DEAD HORSE I 5.11c	471
BY BOSCH, BY GOLLY! I 5.11c	536
DIKENSTEIN I 5.11c	428
EGO TRIP I 5.11c	77
FUTURE SHOCK II 5.11c, A1 (3 Points of Aid)	263
JACK THE RIPPER II 5.11c	197
PASSING THOUGHTS III 5.11c	184
REACH THE SKY I 5.11c	142
TRUE STORIES I 5.11c (5.11a R / 5.10a X)	313
VIRGIN, THE II 5.11c	367
WHIPPING POST I 5.11c	460
WHITE SNAKE I 5.11c R	399
WILD CHILD I 5.11c	577
WILD KINGDOM III 5.11c	102

5.11c (***)

DUNN'S OFFWIDTH I 5.11c	95
ELIMINATE, THE IV 5.11c (5.8 R)	280
FAUX PAS ARETE, THE I 5.11c	102
LIGHTS IN THE FOREST IV 5.11c	163
ONION HEAD II 5.11c	122
SCREAMING YELLOW ZONKERS CRACK I 5.11c	386

5.11d (*)

AIWASS III 5.11d	265
BUCKET LOADER I 5.11d	388
CALIFORNIA GIRLS I 5.11d R	75
CRACK BETWEEN WORLDS II 5.11d R	157
CUFF LINK I 5.11d R	76
DELIGHTMAKER II 5.11d	195
DYKES TO WATCH OUT FOR I 5.11d (5.9 R)	506
EVERYTHING THAT GLITTERS IS NOT	361
GOLD II 5.11d R	
EXASPERATION I 5.11d	176

STAR INDEX 603

HOCUS POCUS II 5.11d	183
INQUISITION, THE I 5.11d	413
LADY LARA II 5.11d R	197
MYSTERY ACHIEVEMENT I 5.11d	361
NO SELF CONTROL I 5.11d	533
ONE HIT TO THE BODY II 5.11d (5.10d R/5.9+ X)	80
RAPTOR ROOF, THE I 5.11d	477
RECONCILIATION II 5.11d (5.11a R)	62
REPO-MAN I 5.11d	77
ROOFER MADNESS I 5.11d	538
SLIPPING INTO DARKNESS I 5.11d	449
SON OF A BIRCH I 5.11d (5.10d R)	79
STANDARD ROUTE I 5.11d (Alcohol Wall)	452
SUNNY DAYS II 5.11d	369
SUPERIOR B SIDE: DIRECT START I 5.11d (Top-rope)	580
TAINT, THE I 5.11d	317
TAR & FEATHER I 5.11d	433
TERMINATOR I 5.11d	391
TREMORS I 5.11d	52
UP ROPE I 5.11d	266
WILDEBEAST I 5.11d	94

5.11d (**)

APOCALYPSE III 5.11d	149
CARRION I 5.11d	436
CRY FOR YESTERDAY I 5.11d	530
GREAT ESCAPE, THE II 5.11d	332
HOMICIDAL MANIAC I 5.11d	59
KINESIS II 5.11d	194
LEGIONS OF POWER I 5.11d	400
MINES OF MORIA IV 5.6 (or 5.11d), A2	157
MOTHER OF INVENTION III 5.11d, A3	365
ROOF OF THE WORLD III 5.11d (5.10a R)	564
SUSPENDED SENTENCE I 5.11d	470
SWORD OF OMENS I 5.11d	401
WILD KINGDOM III 5.11d	102
WILD KINGDOM: THE PROW FINISH II 5.11d	102

5.11d (***)

BIG RED I 5.11d	582
BRIDGE OF KHAZAD-DUM, THE IV 5.11d	163
BUDAPEST I 5.11d	194
END OF THE TETHER I 5.11d, A0 (One shoulderstand)	443
FINAL FRONTIER II 5.11d	518
GRAVEROBBER I 5.11d	58
MORDOR ROOF, THE IV 5.11d	162
PENDULUM ROUTE IV 5.11d	159
POSSESSED, THE II 5.11d	198
PROW, THE III 5.11d	103
SHADOWLINE I 5.11d	447
WOMEN IN LOVE / BOOK OF SOLEMNITY LINK-UP II 5.11d	90

5.12a (*)

AIWASS III 5.12a	265
ANTICHRIST, THE III 5.12a (5.9 R)	272
BIG DEAL ROCK CLIMB I 5.12a	56
BREEZE, THE II 5.12a R	346
DEVIL MADE ME DOG IT, THE I 5.12a	172
ECONOMY OF FORCE I 5.12a	320
EL ROSCO I 5.12a	544
GUNSLINGER, THE II 5.12a	284
HATFUL OF HOLLOW I 5.12a	62
HEAT WAVE I 5.12a	163
HOSS COCK I 5.12a	367
JACK THE RIPPER II 5.12a	197
JOLT I 5.12a	54
LEATHER & LYCRA I 5.12a	370
NEUROMANCER I 5.12a	389
REVERSE CAMBER / ROOM WITH A VIEW LINK-UP I 5.12a	140
ROOM WITH A VIEW I 5.12a (5.10d R)	140
TOUTE SUITE I 5.12a	257
WOMBAT I 5.12a	446

5.12a (**)

ACME TRAVERSE, THE I 5.12a	580
ECONOMY OF FORCE I 5.12a	320
HIP-HOP-BE-BOP, DON'T STOP I 5.12a	413
INDIAN SUNBURN I 5.12a	453
NAUGHTY BY NATURE I 5.12a	577
NIGHTFLYER II 5.12a	368
SACO CRACKER I 5.12a	352
STEAMROLLER I 5.12a	387
TWO PINTS OF LAGER & A PACKET OF CRISPS I 5.12a	352
WHITE ZONE, THE II 5.12a	250

5.12a (***)

DUNN'S OFFWIDTH I 5.12a	95
BEAST 666, THE III 5.12a	94
END OF THE TETHER I 5.12a	443
FREE FINALE III 5.12a (5.11c R)	151
HEAVY WEATHER SAILING II 5.12a	365
MOLSON'S MADNESS I 5.12a	173
ROMPER ROOM I 5.12a	430
SACRED SPACE I 5.12a	367
TOOTHLESS GRIN I 5.12a	444
WILD LIFE I 5.12a	580
WILD WOMEN III 5.12a (5.10b R)	94
WOMEN IN LOVE II 5.12a	90
WONDER WALL III 5.12a (5.8 X)	294

5.12b (*)

ARMAGEDDON III 5.12b R	149
BAT, THE I 5.12b	584
BIG WHOOP, THE I 5.12b	413
BITING BULLETS I 5.12b	368
BLOCKHEADS I 5.12b	570
CREATION, THE II 5.12b (5.10 R)	140
ENDLESS SUMMER II 5.12b (5.9 R)	137
FATMAN LAMENT I 5.12b	587
FRIGID RELATIONS I 5.12b	430
GRANDMOTHER'S CHALLENGE I 5.12b	172
MUSCLE BEACH I 5.12b	353
OBJECTS ARE CLOSER (THAN THEY APPEAR) I 5.12b	279
ONE HIT TO THE BODY II 5.12b (5.10d R/5.9+ X)	80
TREMORS I 5.12b	52
WEZ, THE II 5.12b	191
WHITE EYE II 5.12b, A0	175

5.12b (**)

GILL'S GROOVE I 5.12b	456
HANGERLANE I 5.12b	413
INDIAN SUMMER II 5.12b	312
LONDON CALLING I 5.12b	283
RAT'S EYE I 5.12b	368
SCIENCE FRICTION WALL III 5.12b (5.8 R)	292
UNWANTED GUESTS I 5.12b	264
VLADD THE IMPALER I 5.12b	544
WALKABOUT I 5.12b	412
ZONKED OUT I 5.12b	386

5.12b (***)

EYELESS IN GAZA I 5.12b	439
GRAND FINALE IV 5.12b (5.11c R), Clean A2	154
HEATHER I 5.12b	145
LOVE CRACK I 5.12b	475
PROCESSION I 5.12b	344
SEVENTH SOJOURN III 5.12b (5.9 R)	167

604 STAR INDEX

5.12c (*)
AUTOCLAVE I 5.12c R	133
BOIL MY BONES I 5.12c	172
BUTCHER BLOCK I 5.12c	371
CHARLATAN I 5.12c	427
DEAD BIRCHES I 5.12c (Top-rope)	79
PROMISED LAND, THE I 5.12c	439
SHE'S CRAFTY I 5.12c	438
SUPERIOR B SIDE, THE I 5.12c	580
UNFINISHED SYMPHONY I 5.12c	442

5.12c (**)
ANSWERED PRAYERS I 5.12c	264
BLOODSPORT I 5.12c	352
CINDERELLA THEORY, THE I 5.12c	508
EXODUS I 5.12c	439
POLICE & THIEVES I 5.12c	436
ROTATION, THE I 5.12c	99
STEAK SAUCE I 5.12c	321
WIZARD OF OZ I 5.12c	260

5.12c (***)
CONFEDERACY OF DUNCES I 5.12c	442
GET A LIFE I 5.12c	582
HEART OF THE NIGHT I 5.12c	541
INTERZONE I 5.12c	471
LAST LAUGH II 5.12c	401
MORDOR WALL Pitch one, I 5.12c	155
PROCESSION I 5.12c (Both pitches combined)	344
STAGE FRIGHT II 5.12c X	142
TOURIST TREAT II 5.12c	137

5.12d
SUNDOG DELIGHT I 5.12d	442

5.12d (**)
BAD DOGS I 5.12d	70
BLACK FLIES CONSUME JIM DUNN II 5.12d	511
MITHRAS I 5.12d	442

5.12d (***)
CERBERUS, THE I 5.12d	94
GET A LIFE I 5.12d	582
WINGED EEL FINGERLING I 5.12d (Top-rope)	387

5.13a (*)
ATROSSITY I 5.13a	428
BIG PICKLE, THE I 5.13a	430
FLESH FOR FANTASY I 5.13a	369
THIS MORTAL COIL I 5.13a	350

5.13a (**)
DRY ROASTED I 5.13a	112
SURF PSYCHO I 5.13a	452

5.13a (***)
ANGEL HEART I 5.13a	541
NAUGAHYDE I 5.13a	453
WILD THING I 5.13a	582
YELLOW MATTER CUSTARD I 5.13a	430

5.13b (*)
OUTSHINED I 5.13b	452
YELLOW BRICK ROAD III 5.13b (5.11a R), A3	109

5.13b (**)
BANANA HEAD I 5.13b	432
GENERATION WHY I 5.13b	172

5.13b (***)
LIQUID SKY III 5.13b (5.11a R)	106
MISSION, THE I 5.13b	387
PASTRYWORKS I 5.13b	428
SANCTUARY I 5.13b	170

5.13c (*)
BIG BANANA I 5.13c	432
POWER CHILD I 5.13c	169

5.13c (**)
WHAT WAS, WAS OVER I 5.13c	171

5.13c (***)
EDGE OF THE WORLD I 5.13c	106

5.13d (**)
THE MERCY I 5.13d	172

AID ROUTES

A0
BEAT THE CLOCK (*) II 5.6+, A0 (One rappel)	349
BIG PLUM, THE (**) V 5.10d, A0 (Several rappels & pendulums)	207
END OF THE TETHER (***) I 5.11d, A0 (One shoulderstand)	443

A1
PRACTICE SLAB cracks (***) aided on nuts (Cathedral Ledge)	202
CRAZY WISDOM (*) III 5.11b, A1	110
RAZOR CRACK (*) II A1	444

A2
ANGEL'S HIGHWAY III 5.8, A2	187
CATHEDRAL DIRECT III 5.7, Clean A2	173
MINES OF MORIA III 5.7, A2	157
PROW, THE (***) III 5.7, Clean A2)	103
THE SLASH III 5.9+, A2	519
TRAVESTY II 5.8, Clean A2	86
WOMEN IN LOVE (***) III Clean A2	90

A3
BALLHOG, THE II A3	169
BONGO FLAKE VARIATION IV 5.9, A3	157
BRITISH ARE COMING, THE (*) III 5.9, A3	189
ERADICATE III 5.7 R, A3	278
FIVE MINUTES LATER III 5.7, A3+	519
FOREST OF FANGORN IV 5.7, A3	168
GENERAL HOSPITAL II 5.7, A3	358
GRAND FINALE (**) III 5.9, Clean A3	154
HIGH & DRY (*) II 5.9, A3	438
MORDOR WALL IV 5.7, A3	155
MOTHER OF INVENTION (**) III 5.11d, A3	365
RHYME OF THE ANCIENT MARINER III 5.9, A3	480
SOFT IRON ROUTE (**) II A3+	158
YELLOW BRICK ROAD III 5.13b (5.11a R), A3	109

A4
BLD (BONFIRE LEDGE DIRECT) II 5.6, A4	176
LESS THAN (*) I A4	575
MINES OF MORIA: THE DIRECT START I A4	158
PINSNATCHER I A4	169
TOOTHLESS GRIN: THE DIRECT START I A4	444
TOPLESS TELLERS (**) I A4	158

A4+
REALITY CHECK (**) III 5.8, A4+	186

BIBLIOGRAPHY

A guidebook author is eternally indebted to those guidebook authors whose original research forms the foundation of our collective climbing history. This illustrious group of authors and climbers whom I wish to thank are: Robert L. M. Underhill, Kenneth A. Henderson, Earle Whipple, Robert B. Hall, Joseph Cote & Karen Cote, Henry Barber, Howard Peterson, Paul Ross, Chris Ellms, and Jerry Handren. I also wish to give my sincere thanks to climbing historians Guy Waterman and Laura Waterman for permission to use selected quotations from their excellent treatise on Northeastern rock climbing, plus John T. B. Mudge for additional quotes from his superb history of places names and legends of the White Mountains.

1. *Lucy Crawford's History of the White Mountains (1846)*, by Lucy Crawford. Edited by Stearns Morse. Dartmouth Publications, Hanover, NH, 1966.
2. *Sixty Years Of Art and Artists*, by Benjamin Champney, 1899.
3. *Rock Climbing Notes*, Robert L. M. Underhill, assorted issues of Appalachia, between 1928 and 1933.
4. *Some Rock Climbs in the White Mountains*, by Kenneth A. Henderson, Appalachia, December, 1929. Pages 343-350.
5. *Climbing Routes on Cannon Cliff*, by Earle Whipple. Appalachia, June, 1965. Pages 518-538.
6. *Rock Climbs on Cannon Cliff, Part 1*, by Robert B. Hall, Appalachia, June, 1971. Pages 145-165.
7. *Rock Climbs on Cannon Cliff, Part 2*, by Robert R. Hall, Appalachia, June, 1972. Pages 103-113.
8. *A Climber's Guide to Cathedral & White Horse Ledges*, by Joseph Cote & Karen Cote, 1969.
9. *A Climber's Guide to Mt. Washington Valley*, by Joseph Cote, 1972.
10. *A Climber's Guide to Mt. Washington Valley, 1973 Supplement*, by Henry Barber.
11. *Cannon, A Climber's Guide*, by Howard Peterson, 1975.
12. *Cannon, Cathedral, Humphrey's & Whitehorse, A Rock Climber's Guide*, by Paul Ross & Chris Ellms, 1978.
13. *Cannon, Cathedral, Humphrey's, & Whitehorse, A Rock Climber's Guide, Second Edition*, by Paul Ross & Chris Ellms, 1982.
14. *Rock Climbs In The White Mountains Of New Hampshire*, by Ed Webster. Mountain Imagery, Conway, New Hampshire, 1982.
15. *Rock Climbs In The White Mountains Of New Hampshire, Second Edition*, by Ed Webster. Mountain Imagery, Eldorado Springs, Colorado, 1987.
16. *The White Mountains Names, Places, & Legends*, by John T. B. Mudge. The Durand Press, Etna, NH, 1992.
17. *Yankee Rock & Ice, A History of Climbing in the Northeastern United States*, by Laura & Guy Waterman, and S. Peter Lewis—Photography. Stackpole Books, Harrisburg, Pennsylvania, 1993.
18. *Cathedral and Whitehorse Ledges*, by Jerry Handren. Vertical Brain Publications, Bishop, California, 1996.

This Guidebook was made possible with support from:

- Climb High
- American Mtn. Guides Association
- Rock & Ice Magazine
- Black Diamond
- Eastern Mountain Sports
- Climbing Magazine
- International Mountain Equipment
- Scarpa Boots & Fabiano Boot Co.
- Ragged Mountain Equipment
- Mountain Guides Alliance
- Wired Bliss
- Nereledge Inn
- Adventurous Traveler Bookstore
- A5 Adventures
- The Farm By The River
- North Country Outfitters
- Profile Mountaineering
- Lowe Alpine Systems
- Top Of The World Books
- All Outdoors
- Boston Rock Gym
- Wilderness House

SALTICS

In a pair of Shivas, a little edge goes a long way.

Undersized nubbins, ripples and dime edges look a lot bigger in a pair of Shivas.

See Saltic's entire line at a Climb High dealer near you.

▲ClimbHigh

Shelburne, VT 05482
802/985-5056
FAX 1-802-985-9141

The store for all your climbing, backpacking, mountaineering, and B/C skiing needs.

INTERNATIONAL MOUNTAIN EQUIPMENT INC.

Main St., No. Conway, NH (603) 356-7013

Nereledge Inn

where climbers have been accommodated for generations.

On the road to the ledges & a short walk from the village, Nereledge Inn is a small bed & breakfast where climbers are welcomed year round to comfortable, relaxed surroundings. Reasonable rates include hearty breakfast. Packed lunches available. Drying room for gear.

For brochure and reservations:

P.O. Box 547, River Road, North Conway, NH 03860
Tel: 603-356-2831 Fax: 603-356-7085

BLACK
DIAMOND
EQUIPMENT

READY
WHEN
YOU ARE

2084 EAST 3900 SOUTH, SALT LAKE CITY, UTAH 84124 (801) 278-5533
FROM A PHOTO BY CATHY BELOEIL

**Mail orders welcome!
Camming units reslung**

ragged mountain
equipment

- **Hardware**
- **Ropes**
- **Harnesses**
- **Ironmongery**
- **Rock Shoes**
- **Ice Gear**
- **Hiking Gear**
- **Camping Gear**
- **Clothing**

**Featuring our own
Harnesses, Web Gear,
& Technical Clothing**

Made in our
Mt. Washington Valley Shop

Ragged Mountain Equip. 3 Miles north of North Conway
Open seven days, Rt. 16-302, Intervale N.H. 603-356-3042

REPRESENTING INDEPENDENT GUIDES
ALAIN COMEAU · MIKE JEWELL
IAN TURNBULL · KURT WINKLER

Mountain Guides
A L I A N C E

**BOX 266 · NORTH CONWAY, NH 03860
603-356-5310 · At Ragged Mt. Equipment**

Eastern Mountain Sports

We've been outfitting rock and ice climbers since 1967. Stop by one of our more than 70 EMS stores or try a rock or ice course at the AMGA-accredited EMS Climbing School. For information on EMS Climbing School classes, call (603) 356-5433.

EMS North Conway, NH
Main St. at The Eastern Slope Inn
Phone: (603) 356-5433

THE FARM "By The River" B & B (1785)

2555 West Side Road North Conway, NH 03860
(603) 356-2694

Relax with fellow climbers and enjoy the picturesque setting of "The Farm" by the Saco River—on 65 acres.

Our 10 guest rooms radiate country charm and hospitality.

Enjoy views to the Ledges and our garden while having a full breakfast on the patio.

A fireside breakfast is offered in the cooler months.

On site: swimming w/sandy beach, fishing, snowshoeing.

Climbing Schools are only 2 miles away.

Climbing

News   Equipment Reviews
Profiles   Destinations
Training   Technique

Eight issues a year plus the Climbing Gear Guide/$28

CONTACT

Telephone: 970-963-9449
Fax: 970-963-9442
Email: circ@climbing.com

Climbing Magazine, 1101 Village Rd. LL1B
Carbondale, CO 81623 U.S.A.
Prepayment in U.S. funds required.
Add $10 per year postage to Canada;
$15 per year surface postage to other foreign countries.

Lowe alpine

**Backpacks
Outdoor Clothing
and
Climbing Hardware**

Lowe Alpine Systems
P.O. box 1449 - Broomfield CO 80038

A5 Adventures

1109 S. Plaza Way #296
Flagstaff, AZ 86001
A5Info@aol.com
520-779-5084

*The Finest in
Big Wall Gear!*

NORTH COUNTRY OUTFITTERS

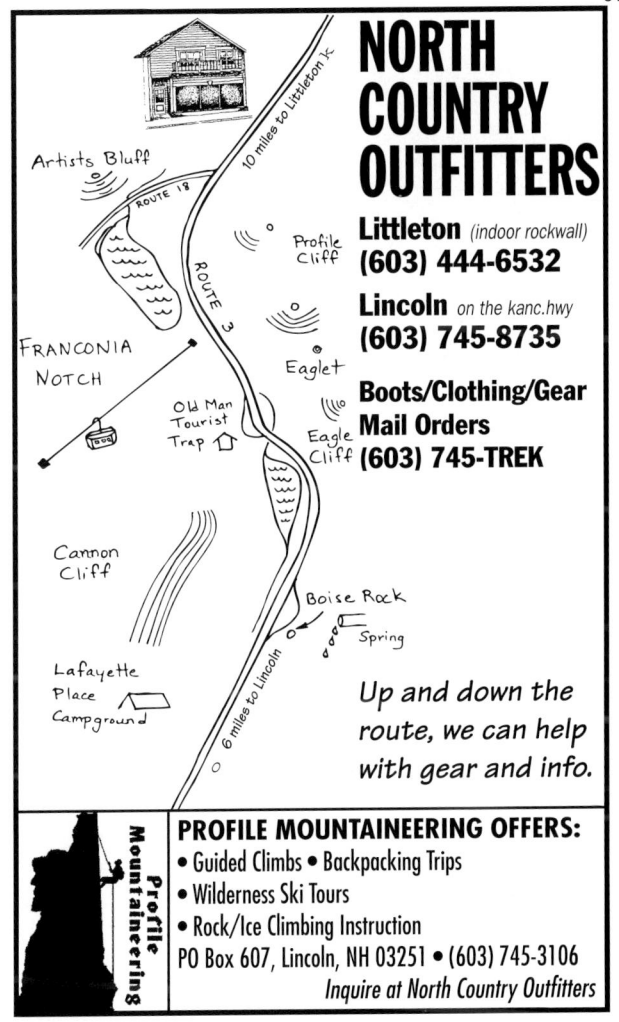

Littleton (indoor rockwall)
(603) 444-6532

Lincoln on the kanc.hwy
(603) 745-8735

**Boots/Clothing/Gear
Mail Orders
(603) 745-TREK**

Up and down the route, we can help with gear and info.

Map labels: Artists Bluff, Route 18, 10 miles to Littleton, Profile Cliff, Route 3, Franconia Notch, Eaglet, Old Man Tourist Trap, Eagle Cliff, Cannon Cliff, Boise Rock, Spring, Lafayette Place Campground, 6 miles to Lincoln

PROFILE MOUNTAINEERING OFFERS:
- Guided Climbs • Backpacking Trips
- Wilderness Ski Tours
- Rock/Ice Climbing Instruction

PO Box 607, Lincoln, NH 03251 • (603) 745-3106
Inquire at North Country Outfitters

WILDERNESS HOUSE
...A climbing partner you can count on

Boston's finest selection of climbing gear, expert customer sevice, and a climbing wall to test your new equipment.

Wilderness HOUSE

1048 Comm. Ave. Boston Mass. 617-277-5858. Free parking

MOUNTAINEERING & POLAR BOOKS

Call, fax, or write for our free catalogue of new & used books!

Top Of The World Books
20 Westview Circle, Williston, VT 05495
Phone / Fax: (802) 878-8737
E-mail: glade@topworld.com   www.topworld.com/books

WIRED BLISS
CAMMING DEVICES

*"It was all possible because our protection was great. The **Wired Bliss** cams were excellent!"*

Eric Brand & Team
First ascent of the North Face of the Nameless Tower, Pakistan

Toll Free 1-800-752-5477
Post Office Box 579 • 1000 East Butler Avenue • Flagstaff, Arizona 86002
(520) 774-2359   FAX (520) 779-5662

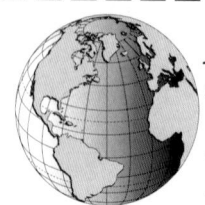

Adventurous Traveler Bookstore

The world's most complete source of outdoor adventure books and maps.

Free catalog! **1-800-282-3963**

or see us on the internet at:
http://www.gorp.com/atbook.htm

PO Box 1468, Williston VT 05495 email: books@atbook.com

BOSTON ROCK GYM

THE BEST INDOOR CLIMBING FUN IN NEW ENGLAND

Beginner classes through to extreme training. We provide the expertise, the equipment and the best indoor climbing structures so that you can test your limits and be ready to explore the wild rock faces and cliffs of America and the World.

1-617-935-PEAK

Climbing Instruction, Climbing Equipment, Climbing Fun

BOSTON ROCK GYM, 78G Olympia Avenue, Woburn, MA 01801.

If you're not wearing Scarpa boots...

Assault

Cinque Terre

SL

...Stay inside

Our boots have been engineered over decades and experienced outdoor enthusiasts and magazine field testers agree that Scarpa boots are the best boots made for the serious trekker.

We use only the highest quality components. Our superior attention to construction and generations of experience mean boots exactly suited to the environment, your needs and your feet.

Give us a try. And get outside again.

**For a complete brochure, call or write Fabiano Shoe Company at
850 Summer St. South Boston, MA 02127-1575
617-268-5625
http://World.std.com/~Fabiano/info.Html**

**321 ELM ST.
MANCHESTER
N.H. 03101
603-624-1468**

*CLIMBING
MOUNTAINEERING
HIKING - MTN. BIKING
KAYAKING
CANOEING
TELEMARK SKIING*

OPEN 7 DAYS A WEEK
Mail Order Welcome
Fax & Mail 603-641-5329

All Outdoors *Mountain Gear*

- Keeping climbing areas open
- Representing climbers' interests
- Working to preserve all types of climbing opportunities
- Promoting conservation and minimum-impact climbing
- Financing land acquisitions, educational brochures, toilets, signs, etc.

the ACCESS FUND

Membership makes it happen—
Join the Access Fund today!

**The Access Fund • P.O. Box 17010
Boulder, CO 80308 • 303.545.6772**

AMERICAN MOUNTAIN·GUIDES ASSOCIATION

"DEDICATED TO RAISING THE TECHNICAL AND PROFESSIONAL STANDARDS OF AMERICAN MOUNTAIN GUIDING THROUGH TRAINING AND EVALUATION PROGRAMS. SERVING THE PUBLIC INTEREST BY WORKING TO IMPROVE CLIMBER SAFETY AND RESPONSIBLE LAND USE."

American Mountain Guides Association
710 10th Street, Suite 101
Golden, CO 80401
303-271-0984

624 CLIMBING NOTES

ABOUT THE AUTHOR

Ed Webster began rock climbing at age 11 on the cliffs around Boston. After getting rescued off Beginner's Route (5.5) on Whitehorse Ledge in 1971, he went on to climb over 100 first and first free ascents in New Hampshire's White Mountains, and to author three popular editions of *Rock Climbs In The White Mountains Of New Hampshire*. His most significant new routes and first free ascents in the area include Women In Love (5.12a), Pendulum Route (5.11d), The Last Unicorn (5.10b), and Sea Of Holes (5.7). Ed also pioneered many new climbs in Colorado and the Desert of Utah. His significant firsts out West include Bright Star (V 5.9, A3), a solo new route on the Diamond on Long's Peak, plus The Scenic Cruise (IV 5.10d) in the Black Canyon, and the world famous climbs, Super Crack (5.10b), and The Primrose Dihedrals (5.11d) on Moses, both in Canyonlands. Ed climbed the 7th ascent of The Pacific Ocean Wall on El Capitan in Yosemite, The North Face Direct on Mt. Robson in Canada, plus numerous classic rock routes in England, Wales, Scotland, France, Italy, Spain, Norway, and Sweden. In 1994, he wrote the only English language rock climbing guidebook to Norway, *Climbing In The Magic Islands*, to the majestic Lofoten Islands north of the Arctic Circle.

Ed Webster climbing on Sea Of Holes (5.7) on Whitehorse in 1995. Photo: John Climaco.

In the Himalayas and Asia, Ed has participated on numerous trips, including the 1985 American Everest West Ridge Expedition, the 1986 Everest Solo Expedition when he soloed a new route up Changtse (24,780'), Everest's North Peak, and the 1988 International Everest Expedition where Ed and three partners climbed a new route up Everest's dangerous Kangshung Face without oxygen, Sherpa assistance, or radios. Ed's high point was 28,750', just 300 feet short of the top. Although seriously frostbitten on Everest, Ed recovered to lead rock routes of up to 5.11 difficulty again. He also returned to Asia, becoming the first American to climb in Mongolia in 1992, and the following year, attempted a 24,500' peak, Masagang, in Bhutan, and summited on the West Rib of Cholatse (21,140') near Everest in Nepal. On his most recent expeditions, both in 1994, Ed attempted several Himalayan new routes: in the Karakoram on Ultar (24,500') in Hunza in Pakistan, and on Ama Dablam (23,500') in Nepal.

Ed has received three awards: the 1988 Seventh Grade Award for Outstanding Achievements in Mountaineering from The American Mountain Foundation, the 1990 Literary Award from the American Alpine Club, and the 1994 David A. Soules Award, for saving the life of a fellow climber, also from the American Alpine Club. He currently lives in Boulder, Colorado—and every once in a while, when he's back East—in Brownfield, Maine, near the White Mountains.